LAW AND POLICY IN MODERN FAMILY FINANCE

This book has been made possible with the support
of the New Zealand Law Foundation

LAW AND POLICY IN MODERN FAMILY FINANCE

Property Division in the 21st Century

Edited by
Jessica PALMER
Nicola PEART
Margaret BRIGGS
Mark HENAGHAN

intersentia
Cambridge – Antwerp – Portland

Intersentia Ltd
Sheraton House | Castle Park
Cambridge | CB3 0AX | United Kingdom
Tel.: +44 1223 370 170 | Fax: +44 1223 370 169
Email: mail@intersentia.co.uk
www.intersentia.com | www.intersentia.co.uk

Distribution for the UK and Ireland:
NBN International
Airport Business Centre, 10 Thornbury Road
Plymouth, PL6 7PP
United Kingdom
Tel.: +44 1752 202 301 | Fax: +44 1752 202 331
Email: orders@nbninternational.com

Distribution for Europe and all other countries:
Intersentia Publishing nv
Groenstraat 31
2640 Mortsel
Belgium
Tel.: +32 3 680 15 50 | Fax: +32 3 658 71 21
Email: mail@intersentia.be

Distribution for the USA and Canada:
International Specialized Book Services
920 NE 58th Ave. Suite 300
Portland, OR 97213
USA
Tel.: +1 800 944 6190 (toll free) | Fax: +1 503 280 8832
Email: info@isbs.com

ISBN 978-1-78068-464-2
D/2017/7849/105
NUR 822

British Library Cataloguing in Publication Data. A catalogue record for this book is available from the British Library.

FOREWORD

If there ever was a period of maturity in my professional life it was largely devoted to family finances either in silk, as a trial judge, or in the Court of Appeal. So when Mark Henaghan asked me to write a foreword for this book of collected papers I did not hesitate to agree, partly from my familiarity with the territory and partly from my regard for Mark and his ability to conceal his scholarship in waves of warmth and irreverence.

The Introduction explains the context in which the papers were written:

> November 2015: the New Zealand Minister of Justice refers to the Law Commission a comprehensive review of the Property (Relationships) Act 1976 and requests recommendations for reform.
>
> December 2016: the four editors convene the International Colloquium at which the papers were presented.

Ahead, as I write, lies the publication of the papers and the Law Commission's report and recommendations. I am in no doubt that this is how family law reform should be managed: Law Reform Commission expertise supplemented by international and comparative expertise to guide the legislators.

New Zealand seems to have a healthy readiness to legislate in this dangerous territory: dangerous because many politicians have had personal experience and leaders fear that public reaction to legislation will depress their prospects of re-election. New Zealand seems to follow the precept instilled in children here: if at first you don't succeed, try, try, try again. Would that the Westminster parliament would embrace the same spirit of adventure. For the UK, excepting Scotland, we have been 45 years without major reform and it has had to be the judges who have re-interpreted the 1970 statute to reflect social and other change.

As the editors write in their Introduction, the relevance of the themes analysed in the 15 papers is unrestricted:

> '[T]he wider discussion to which this book contributes is an important one that must be ongoing. While the context in which these chapters were written was the reform of New Zealand's rather unique approach to the sharing of property in intimate relationships, we are confident that the ideas and debates discussed in this book will be of value beyond the shores of Aotearoa New Zealand. The way in which the law regulates the property consequences of family relationships is a significant issue in any

> civilised society and the questions posed in this book must be thoughtfully considered and answered in any jurisdiction seeking to have a coherent and justifiable property sharing regime.'

The scholars were selected for the Colloquium for the expertise that each could bring to a relevant theme within the whole or to a jurisdiction relevant for comparative study. Their contributions are uniformly excellent, some refreshingly brief, none a struggle to comprehend.

Now that I am well past my doubtful maturity I am perhaps permitted to express my reservations as to the complexity of concepts developed by scholars and judges as they have perforce had to in order to modernise the law. At least in the pre-*White* days of reasonable requirements it was easy enough to explain to parties whose affluence took them high above the bare plain of needs what was the law and how to prepare for its application. That era that lasted some 20 years is now long gone and necessarily so. But now distinguished academics have abundant material in judicial pronouncements to analyse, to explain, and to condemn. In my post-judicial career as expert and mediator I see the huge benefits of Alternative Dispute Resolution (ADR). The litigation experience in this jurisdiction is outrageously expensive and often inflicts long-term damage on those who pay the bills.

ADR is affordable, since its costs can more readily be made commensurate to the means of the family, easier to explain and to be understood, and far less damaging to the parties.

The Rt Hon Sir Mathew Thorpe

ACKNOWLEDGEMENTS

The editors acknowledge with gratitude the generous financial support from the New Zealand Law Foundation and the University of Otago. Without their support this book and the Colloquium that preceded it would not have been possible. Our special thanks go to Ms Kyla Mullen IMOT LLB (Hons) and Jonathan Yeldon BFA LLB for their meticulous editorial work, and to Andrew Snoddy JD for his editorial assistance in the latter stages of the project. We are also very grateful to Ruth Ballantyne BA (Hons) LLB, professional practice fellow in the Faculty of Law, University of Otago, for her oversight and guidance of the editorial work on the manuscript and her support of the project as a whole.

Thank you to Intersentia for its willingness to publish the work, in particular to Ann-Christin Maak-Scherpe for collaborating with us on the project and to Rebecca Moffat for her role as Intersentia's editor in charge of the project.

We are very grateful to Sir Mathew Thorpe for readily agreeing to write the Foreword to this book.

Finally, we thank most sincerely the contributing authors for their insightful responses to the difficult questions that arise about sharing property at the end of a marriage or similar relationship, and to the participants at the New Zealand Property (Relationships) Act 1976 Colloquium in December 2016 for engaging in those questions and commenting on the authors' ideas.

Dunedin
August 2017

CONTENTS

TABLE OF CASES

LIST OF CONTRIBUTORS

Bill Atkin
Professor of Law, Victoria University of Wellington, Wellington, New Zealand

Margaret Briggs
Professor of Law, University of Otago, Dunedin, New Zealand

John Caldwell
Associate Professor of Law, University of Canterbury, Christchurch, New Zealand

Rosalind Croucher AM
Emeritus Professor, Macquarie University, and President, Australian Human Rights Commission, Sydney, Australia

The Hon Robert Fisher QC
Bankside Chambers, Auckland, New Zealand

Mark Henaghan
Professor of Law, University of Otago, Dunedin, New Zealand

Simon Jefferson QC
Trinity Chambers, Auckland, New Zealand

Joanna Miles
Reader in Family Law & Policy, University of Cambridge, England

Paul Moriarty
Principal, Moriarty Associates Limited, Auckland, New Zealand

Jessica Palmer
Associate Professor of Law, University of Otago, Dunedin, New Zealand

Patrick Parkinson AM
Professor of Law, University of Sydney, Australia

Nicola Peart
Professor of Law, University of Otago, Dunedin, New Zealand

Jacinta Ruru (Raukawa, Ngāti Ranginui)
Professor of Law, University of Otago, and Co-Director, Ngā Pae o te Māramatanga, Dunedin, New Zealand

Jens M Scherpe
Reader in Comparative Law, University of Cambridge, and Director of Cambridge Family Law, England

The Rt Hon Sir Mathew Thorpe
Formerly Lord Justice of Appeal, England, and Head of International Family Justice

Leo Watson
Barrister and Solicitor, Napier, New Zealand

CHAPTER 1
INTRODUCTION

Nicola PEART, Jessica PALMER and Margaret BRIGGS

Marriage traditionally gives rise to property consequences, sometimes during the marriage, but nowadays more often when the marriage ends either during the lifetime of the parties or because one of them has died. In the European civil law jurisdictions, the property consequences take the form of an entitlement to an equal share of property classed as matrimonial property.[1] These regimes, commonly referred to as community property systems, apply in default of agreement between the parties on divorce as well as on death.[2]

The common law approach to the property consequences of marriage differs significantly from the civilian approach. Following the abolition of the unitary principle of marriage by the Married Women's Property statutes in the late nineteenth century, a separate property system applied in the common law jurisdictions.[3] Each spouse was entitled to retain assets he or she had brought in to, or acquired during, the marriage. Marriage did not give rise to a property interest in any of the assets of the other spouse, not even the family home. However, by the mid-twentieth century, concerns about the adverse effects of the separate property system, particularly for women and dependent children, persuaded the legislatures in Australia, New Zealand, and England and Wales to pass legislation giving the courts discretion to adjust title to property between former spouses on separation and divorce.[4] Australia and England and Wales still

---

1 See JM SCHERPE, 'Contracting Out of the Default Relationship Property Regime – Comparative Observations', ch 14.

2 N PEART, 'Family Finances on Death of a Spouse or Partner', ch 5.

3 Married Women's Property statutes were adopted in England in 1874 and 1882, in the Australian jurisdictions between 1879 (NSW) and 1892 (WA), and in New Zealand in 1884. See further N PEART, above n 2. For a New Zealand historical perspective on the property consequences of marriage, see J PRIESTLEY, 'Whence and Whither? Reflections on the Property (Relationships) Act 1976 by a Retired Judge' (2017) 15 *Otago Law Review* (forthcoming).

4 Marriage Act 1958 (Vic), s 161, as amended by the Marriage (Property) Act 1962 (Vic), s 3, was the first statutory change, followed by the Matrimonial Property Act 1963 (NZ), s 5; the Matrimonial Causes Act 1973 (Eng&W), s 24; and the Family Law Act 1975 (Cth), s 79.

operate this individualised system of property adjustment, based on principles developed by the courts.

England's Matrimonial Causes Act 1973 lists a number of matters to which the court must have regard when making property adjustment orders on divorce, of which the welfare of any minor child of the family is the 'first consideration'.[5] The Act does not state what the aim of the court's exercise of discretion should be. The courts have inferred that the implicit objective of their power is 'to achieve a fair outcome' for the parties involved.[6] In *Miller v Miller; McFarlane v McFarlane*, the House of Lords held that 'fairness' encompassed three strands: the financial needs of the parties; compensation for prospective economic disparity resulting from the division of functions during the marriage; and equal sharing.[7] This last strand derives from the modern concept of marriage as a partnership of equals. However, '[t]he yardstick of equality is to be applied as an aid, not a rule'.[8] The Matrimonial Causes Act now applies to marriage, including same-sex marriage, and to civil partnerships, but not to de facto relationships or to relationships ending on death of a spouse or partner.[9]

In Australia, the Family Law Act 1975 (Cth) empowers the court to make an order altering the parties' property rights if it is 'satisfied that, in all the circumstances, it is just and equitable to make the order'.[10] If this jurisdictional threshold is met, the court 'may make such order as it considers appropriate',[11] taking into account a range of factors listed in the Act, including the parties' financial and non-financial contributions to the property, family welfare, children of the family, and the effect of any proposed order on the parties' earning capacity.[12] As in England and Wales, equality is not a rule and orders commonly favour the party whose earning capacity has suffered because of the division of functions during the relationship.[13] The Australian Act applies to marriage and to de facto relationships.[14] It does not apply on death. In both Australia and England and Wales the ending of a marriage or equivalent relationship on the death of a party is a matter for succession law and family provision legislation.[15]

---

5 Matrimonial Causes Act 1973 (Eng&W), s 25(1).
6 *White v White* [2001] 1 AC 596 (HL) at [23].
7 *Miller v Miller; McFarlane v McFarlane* [2006] UKHL 24, [2006] 2 AC 618 at [9]–[20].
8 Ibid, at [16].
9 See N Peart, above n 2.
10 Family Law Act 1975 (Cth), s 79(2).
11 Family Law Act 1975 (Cth), s 79(1).
12 Family Law Act 1975 (Cth), s 79(4).
13 N Peart and M Henaghan, 'Children's Interests in Division of Property on Relationship Breakdown', ch 4.
14 Family Law Act 1975 (Cth), Long Title. See further P Parkinson, 'Reconsidering Family Property Law in the Post-Marital Age', ch 2; M Briggs, 'Which Relationships Should be Included in a Property Sharing Scheme?', ch 3; N Peart, above n 2.
15 N Peart, above n 2.

The advantage of a discretionary system of property adjustment on separation or divorce is that it provides an outcome that is tailored to the particular needs and circumstances of the parties and allows the courts to respond to changing social circumstances and current expectations. The disadvantage is that it is unpredictable and uncertain.[16]

New Zealand's discretionary system operated for about 12 years. Its Matrimonial Property Act 1963 (NZ) allowed the courts to make orders adjusting property as between the parties based on their respective contributions to the property in dispute.[17] Although both financial and non-financial contributions were relevant, the courts were reluctant to treat domestic contributions as relevant to the division of non-domestic assets.[18] Wives, in particular, tended to receive less than half of the assets acquired during the marriage. Dissatisfaction with the courts' failure to appreciate the value of domestic contributions and its relevance to the acquisition of the family wealth, as well as the unpredictability of outcomes, led to legislative rejection of the discretionary approach in 1976 in favour of a strong presumption of equal sharing.[19]

The Matrimonial Property Act 1976 (NZ) characterised marriage as a partnership to which both spouses were presumed to contribute equally, albeit in different ways, entitling them to an equal share of their 'matrimonial property'.[20] Matrimonial property included the family home and family chattels, even if they were acquired prior to the marriage, and any property acquired during the marriage other than property acquired by gift, succession, or as a beneficiary of a trust.[21] The parties shared their matrimonial property equally, subject to limited exceptions.[22] Property that was not matrimonial property was retained by the owning spouse as their separate property. The parties could opt out of the statutory regime by entering into a written contract with independent advice prior to or during the marriage, or on separation. The New Zealand system was a deferred property sharing system, akin to some of the European matrimonial property systems. During the marriage each spouse was free to acquire and deal with his or her assets, but on separation the assets then owned by each spouse were classified, valued, and divided.[23]

By treating marriage as a partnership and having a strong presumption of equality, New Zealand's Matrimonial Property Act 1976 was seen as ahead of

16 See J Miles, 'Should the Regime be Discretionary or Rules-Based?', ch 11.
17 Matrimonial Property Act 1963, ss 5–6.
18 See N Peart, above n 2.
19 Ibid.
20 Matrimonial Property Act 1976, s 11. See further N Peart, above n 2.
21 Matrimonial Property Act 1976, ss 8–10.
22 Matrimonial Property Act 1976, ss 13–15. See further M Henaghan, 'Sharing Family Finances at the End of a Relationship', ch 12.
23 On the issue of valuation, see S Jefferson and P Moriarty, 'Valuation of Relationship Property: An Evaluation of Practice and Procedure', ch 10.

its time in the common law world. Yet, it soon revealed shortcomings. The Act dealt with capital, not income. There was no equality in outcome if one spouse (usually the husband) had enhanced his earning capacity while the other spouse (usually the wife) had primarily looked after the home and the children. There was no scope within the Matrimonial Property Act 1976 (NZ) to divide earning capacity. The Act was a code of rules with limited discretion to take account of consequences beyond the confines of conventional property concepts. The advantage of the Act was the certainty it provided about matrimonial property entitlements, but it lacked the flexibility that the English and Australian courts had to respond to changing social expectations. There were other problems with the Matrimonial Property Act 1976 (NZ). The Act's scope was seen as too narrow on a number of different fronts: it did not apply to marriages ending on death, whereas the 1963 Matrimonial Property Act did; it did not apply to de facto relationships, which were becoming increasingly common and socially acceptable; and it was ineffectual in dealing with trusts, which had become popular as a means of avoiding the reach of the Act. Further reform was therefore required, which came in 2001 when the Act was amended and renamed the Property (Relationships) Act 1976 (NZ).

The 2001 amendments sought to remedy many of the shortcomings in the Matrimonial Property Act 1976 (NZ), whilst retaining the strong presumption of equal sharing as the default system. It is debatable whether the amendments have achieved their purpose, as many of the chapters in this book indicate. John Priestley QC, a retired High Court Judge and former family law practitioner, is of the view that the amendments made what was otherwise a well-delineated highway somewhat slippery.[24]

The compensation provision for economic disparity has been problematic from the start. The Property (Relationships) Act 1976 (NZ) gives the court discretion to depart from equal sharing of relationship property to compensate for economic disparity resulting from the division of functions during the marriage. In the context of a well-established rule of equal division, the courts have been reluctant to embrace this power.[25]

When a relationship ends on death, the surviving spouse or partner has the right to elect between claiming his or her relationship property entitlement under the Act and taking the provision available under the deceased's will or the intestacy rules.[26] This election is both practically and conceptually problematic. It seems that few testators know about the election when they are making their will and their surviving spouse faces a stark choice, the effect of which can generally be ameliorated only through family provision legislation.

---

24 J Priestley, above n 3.

25 See M Henaghan, above n 22.

26 See N Peart, above n 2.

The inclusion of de facto relationships has resulted in lengthy court battles after the relationship has ended to determine whether it qualified as a de facto relationship for the purposes of the Act and, if so, whether it endured for the statutorily required minimum period of three years to be entitled to equal division of relationship property.[27] These questions of fact sit uncomfortably alongside a code of legal rules that operates as an opt-out system.

With regard to trusts, the strict jurisdictional requirements and the inability to make orders against trust capital have rendered the statutory power to compensate for dispositions of relationship property to trusts largely ineffectual.[28] In a country with a very high number of trusts, as compared to other common law countries, the statute's inadequate remedies to prevent loss of relationship property entitlement has led to a range of judicially inspired arguments to bring trust assets or their value within the scope of the equal sharing regime. But none of these arguments provides a comprehensive response to the problem.

In November 2015, the Minister of Justice referred the Property (Relationships) Act 1976 to the New Zealand Law Commission for a comprehensive review of the current sharing regime and recommendations for reform. In December 2016, while the review was still ongoing, the editors of this book convened a colloquium to consider options for reform. The intention of the colloquium was to debate the underlying conceptual questions to which all property sharing regimes must provide answers, whether such answers are present by design or merely by effect. To ensure a broad spectrum of views, several overseas academics were invited to provide an international perspective and contribute to the ideas proffered. The papers presented at that colloquium were then revised for publication in this book.

The book has a strong emphasis on New Zealand law, but the issues considered in each of the chapters are equally relevant to other jurisdictions, and the law of other jurisdictions is frequently referred to throughout this work. In our view, three main questions lie at the core of any property sharing regime and they provide the framework around which the chapters in this book are organised:

I. Who should be covered by a property sharing regime?
II. What property should be covered by a property sharing regime?
III. How should property be shared at the end of a relationship?

Part I takes the first question as its focus and includes chapters that consider the extent to which non-traditional forms of intimate relationships, relationships ending by death, and the interests of children should be accounted for in property sharing regimes. Modern conceptions of what are accepted familial

27 See P Parkinson, above n 14; M Briggs, above n 14.
28 J Palmer, 'What to Do about Trusts?', ch 8.

relationships have changed significantly in the past 50 years, as has the voice that is now afforded to children in the law. These issues raise important questions for the application of property sharing regimes.

In considering what property should be covered by a property sharing regime, Part II includes chapters reflecting on whether and how particular types of property should be incorporated into property sharing regimes and the vexed process of valuation. It also features a more general and very important discussion on how seriously the notion of partnership ought to be taken when setting the parameters of what property is captured by a regime.

Part III addresses the question of how property should be shared. It considers difficult issues such as the extent to which property sharing regimes should balance discretion with rules, and finality with fairness, and whether and how exceptions to the regime should operate.

There are common themes, or perhaps underlying debates, that emerge in all three parts of this book. The first theme is the specialness of family. Why should an intimate family relationship have consequences for property and income in a way that other common relationships do not? Should property be conceived of differently because of the special nature of a marriage or equivalent relationship? Should any particular property be given a special status because of its association with the family? A variety of views are expressed on this debate throughout the book, with some authors committed to a strong conception of partnership[29] while others are somewhat more sceptical.[30]

A second evident theme is the need to identify the underlying objective of a property sharing regime. Some view the division of property at the end of a relationship as premised on an entitlement to the property of the relationship based on both the financial and non-financial contributions made to the relationship.[31] In that sense, a division of property in effect recognises that the property-owning party owes a *debt* to the other party to compensate for contributions made.[32] Others view property sharing regimes as a means of ensuring that the wealthier party meets his or her moral *duty* to provide for the needs of the other party where the other party is economically more vulnerable.[33] A third conception rests on neither debt nor duty, but on a more explicit emphasis on the value of partnership and the principle of equality.[34]

---

29 See P Parkinson, above n 14; B Atkin, 'Classifying Relationship Property: A Radical Re-Shaping?', ch 7; R Fisher, 'Should a Property Sharing Regime be Mandatory or Optional?', ch 13.

30 See M Briggs, above n 14; JM Scherpe, above n 1.

31 See JM Scherpe, above n 1; N Peart, above n 2.

32 Valuation of the debt then becomes a critical issue: see S Jefferson and P Moriarty, above n 23.

33 See R Croucher, 'A Lament for "Testator's Family Maintenance" – A Good Idea Gone Wrong? Australian Reflections', ch 6.

34 See M Henaghan, above n 22.

A third theme concerns the role of the state. There is a clear competition in this area between values of autonomy and self-determination on the one hand, and protection and paternalism on the other. To what extent should the state regulate the proprietary consequences of relationship dissolutions? Should parties be allowed to depart from a statutory scheme? Are there any core aspects of such a regime that should not be excludable to ensure that the objective of the regime is achieved? Should the regime be rules-based or subject to judicial discretion? New Zealand is well known as a relatively young state with a willingness to experiment and an inclination to favour 'fairer' outcomes for society as a whole. This has encouraged significant regulation in several areas, including relationship property.[35] The use of legislation in this way has important consequences, not just for the underlying philosophy of the chosen regime, but also because it can have very practical effects on litigation strategies, costs, and delays.

The fourth theme worth noting relates to the role of regulation. In New Zealand, the financial consequences of a relationship ending, on separation as well as on death, are fragmented across several statutes.[36] A property sharing regime can obviously affect other related laws, such as those pertaining to spousal maintenance, child support, and family provision. Treating each of these areas of law as being discrete can lead to inconsistencies both of approach and of underlying objectives. To what extent is it desirable to pursue a holistic approach to legal regulation affecting these wider topics?

Finally, there is the important question of Indigenous and multicultural perspectives. Should they be accommodated and, if so, how? Indigenous populations may have concepts of property, ownership, equality, and sharing that differ markedly from those held by European-based cultures.[37] In New Zealand, for example, land and chattels of particular cultural significance to Māori people are not shared between parties to a marriage or equivalent relationship. They remain with the person who has the ancestral relationship to the property in accordance with Māori law and custom. Alternative arrangements may have to be made that appropriately acknowledge the cultural differences.

All of these themes are related to each other and require the input of many voices across society. They are not, and cannot be, the sole domain of legal experts.

---

35 Notable New Zealand examples are the 'no fault' state-funded accident compensation scheme in the Accident Compensation Act 2001 (NZ); the Contractual Remedies Act 1979 (NZ), the Contracts Privity Act 1982 (NZ), and the Contractual Mistakes Act 1977 (NZ), now incorporated in the Contract and Commercial Law Act 2017 (NZ); the Family Protection Act 1955 (NZ) and the Law Reform (Testamentary Promises) Act 1949 (NZ); the Crimes Act 1961 (NZ); the New Zealand Bill of Rights Act 1990 (NZ); and the Personal Property Securities Act 1999 (NZ).

36 JM Scherpe, above n 1; N Peart, above n 2; J Caldwell, 'Maintenance – Time for a Clean Break?', ch 15.

37 See J Ruru and L Watson, 'Should Indigenous Property be Relationship Property?', ch 9.

It is also true that societal positions on these debates will change over time and across countries and cultures. It is, of course, acknowledged that enacting legislation is a complicated, political process that is affected by many factors that can compete with the goal of having a regime with a consistent philosophical underpinning. Margaret Wilson, the Government Minister responsible for the introduction of the 2001 amendments to the Property (Relationships) Act 1976 (NZ) and now a Professor of Law, makes this point:[38]

> 'While I agree good legislation relies on good policy that in turn relies on good theory that produces a coherent principled approach, in my experience this process is not always found in reality.'

This, we think, shows that the wider discussion to which this book contributes is an important one that must be ongoing. While the context in which these chapters were written was the reform of New Zealand's rather unique approach to the sharing of property in intimate relationships, we are confident that the ideas and debates discussed in this book will be of value beyond the shores of Aotearoa[39] New Zealand. The way in which the law regulates the property consequences of family relationships is a significant issue in any civilised society and the questions posed in this book must be thoughtfully considered and answered in any jurisdiction seeking to have a coherent and justifiable property sharing regime.

It only remains, in this introductory chapter, to mention terminology briefly. As in other areas of law where jurisdictional approaches are compared, there is potential for misunderstanding when different technical terminology is employed. To avoid such confusion, we clarify here some terms that are used regularly throughout this book.

In this book, the term 'regime' is used in a broader sense than in the civilian tradition, which is familiar with true 'regimes' such as the French *régime primaire et secondaire*. Rather, we use the term 'regime' more generically to include not just the civilian codes, but also common law statutes that pertain to the division of property between parties in an intimate relationship – in other words, 'systems' or 'methods' of property sharing. Readers may also note that the expressions 'property sharing' and 'property division' are used interchangeably throughout the book. Again, these are terms of art rather than science and they are used broadly to denote methods of 'splitting up' the property at the end of the relationship.

New Zealand's Property (Relationships) Act 1976 includes some terms that may not be immediately recognisable to readers from other jurisdictions.

---

38 M Wilson, 'The New Zealand Context – Setting the Legal and Social Scene of the PRA 1976' (2017) 15 *Otago Law Review* (forthcoming).

39 Aotearoa is the Indigenous name of New Zealand.

The term 'relationship' acknowledges that the Property (Relationships) Act covers not just married couples, but also registered civil union partners and de facto partners in informal qualifying relationships. The expression 'relationship property' is the property of spouses, civil union partners, and de facto partners that is classified as the property of the 'relationship' and shared by the parties, as opposed to the 'separate property' which belongs to individual partners and is not shared. Lastly, the term 'de facto partners' will be more familiar to many readers as 'cohabitants'.

PART I

WHO SHOULD BE COVERED BY A PROPERTY SHARING REGIME?*

Questions are frequently raised in family law jurisprudence about the meaning of 'family'. Why, and for what reasons, does the state recognise some relationships but not others? Should 'family' be an inclusive or an exclusive club? The responses to these questions are not immutable, since the notion of 'family' is a fluid concept influenced in large part by social attitudes. In recent decades many Western jurisdictions have experienced major social changes that have directly impacted on what we take to mean by the term 'family'. Factors including the increasing incidence of unmarried cohabitation, more single parent families, and more blended families have all contributed to weaken the status of the traditional family unit (that is, a family consisting of two married parents and their children) as the predominant family form.

Part I of the book considers a discrete aspect of the wider 'family' issue – namely, in these changing times, which 'family' relationships should be regarded as subject to the rights and obligations attendant on a property sharing regime? In the context of property division this inquiry is of no small importance, since deciding exactly *who* should be recognised is an important antecedent to determining what types of property should be included in a sharing regime and even the shape of the regime itself.

There are significant differences in the way that individual countries apply inclusion and exclusion criteria to the types of family relationships that are subject to family property laws. Some jurisdictions regulate the property affairs of married couples only, others include couples in registered civil partnerships, and some go so far as to include unregistered cohabitants whose informal relationships function in a 'marriage-like' way. On another level, some jurisdictions put the interests of the children of the family at the forefront of any property division between the parents, whereas others treat children's interests as a largely separate issue from that of the division of the relationship property between the parents. On yet another level, different countries treat relationships that end on separation and relationships that end on death in different ways.

---

* Part I Introduction by Margaret Briggs.

The chapters in Part I of the book explore the three general but connected themes outlined in the preceding paragraph: (i) what sorts of domestic relationships should be included in a property sharing regime; (ii) what role children should play in such a scheme; and (iii) whether relationships that end on the death of one of the partners should be treated in the same way as relationships that end on separation during the life of the partners. As in Parts II and III of the book, the focus in this Part is largely on common law jurisdictions, with emphasis on New Zealand's regime. When compared with other jurisdictions, New Zealand's Property (Relationships) Act 1976 as amended in 2001 might best be described as adopting an idiosyncratic approach to these three issues. In the first place, the legislation is very inclusive in its equal treatment of different adult relationships. Unlike many countries, in New Zealand unmarried cohabitants (referred to in the Act as 'de facto' partners) are treated in much the same way as spouses and civil union partners when it comes to sharing the relationship property. However, unlike other countries, including England and Wales, and Australia, in New Zealand the needs of the children of the relationship are seen as peripheral to the central question of the property rights vis-à-vis the spouses or partners. In New Zealand the needs of children are addressed as a separate matter and are compartmentalised into separate legislation. Lastly, the Property (Relationships) Act 1976 (NZ) also takes an unorthodox approach to the treatment of relationships that end on death by merging property entitlement and family duty.

In Chapter 2 Patrick Parkinson examines family property law in what he refers to as a 'post-marital age' and questions the assumption that living with someone in an intimate partnership entitles a person to share in the other person's property. Parkinson explores this problem via the technique of storytelling. Through the lens of three vignettes he argues that where legislation providing for property sharing is based on community property assumptions, there are problems with assimilating unmarried cohabiting relationships with marriage. Parkinson suggests that the marriage analogy should not be applied to couples who do not have children together, but that a system of separation of assets may be more appropriate in such cases. The author concludes by raising the question whether it should in fact be parenthood that provides the main justification for asset sharing. Nicola Peart and Mark Henaghan revisit the relevance of children in Chapter 4 (below).

In Chapter 3 Margaret Briggs considers two different methods of identifying the types of relationships that should be subject to property sharing. The 'formal' approach posits that relationship registration is a precondition to property sharing, whereas the 'functional' approach is based on how the couple's relationship works in practical terms irrespective of the formalities of registration. With reference to the English, Australian, and New Zealand systems, Briggs argues that neither approach is ideal. Whereas the formal approach excludes unmarried cohabitants and often disadvantages the financially weaker party, the functional approach is open to criticism on grounds of inherent uncertainty. The discussion then proceeds to a more detailed examination of the New Zealand scheme and considers some possible alternatives to the way that it currently operates, before ultimately concluding that its advantages outweigh the disadvantages.

In Chapter 4 Nicola Peart and Mark Henaghan question whether the interests of children should be taken into account in the division of property between their parents and, if so, how those interests should be accommodated. Following an examination of the family-centric approaches to property division taken in England and Wales, and Australia, Peart and Henaghan provide a detailed analysis of the New Zealand system which identifies and discusses the conceptual and practical barriers to a family-centred approach. The authors conclude that while all of the jurisdictions discussed in the chapter recognise that property division on the breakdown of a marriage affects children of the relationship and have sought to protect their interests, the measures taken in New Zealand have been less effective than those adopted in England and Wales, and Australia. The authors conclude by considering some options for reform that would put more emphasis on the needs of children than currently exists in the legislation.

The final two chapters in Part I discuss how relationships that end on death should be treated. In Chapter 5 Nicola Peart considers whether surviving spouses should have the same property rights on death as on divorce or whether the death of a spouse is sufficiently different from divorce that succession law should determine the rights of the survivor. Peart explains that New Zealand is the only common law jurisdiction to entitle surviving spouses and partners to make a contribution-based claim in addition to a family provision claim and, in so doing, it has created confusion and uncertainty by blurring the distinction between property entitlement and any succession right the survivor may have to the assets of the deceased. The author concludes with the suggestion that a spouse's relationship property entitlement should be treated as distinct from succession law in order that the survivor can achieve an outcome that differentiates between his or her property entitlement and the deceased's obligations of support.

Lastly, in Chapter 6 there is a change of focus away from property sharing regimes. Instead, Rosalind Croucher provides insights into legislative restrictions on testamentary freedom – generically referred to as 'family provision' or 'family protection' laws – with emphasis on developments in Australian law. Beginning with an analysis of the historical foundations of family protection laws, Croucher reflects that modern family protection laws have strayed far from their roots, to the point that the current law pays scant heed to the concept of testamentary freedom. The author identifies the two major issues in modern family protection laws as being the approach to spouses and partners, and the problem of adult children claimants. She argues that the law should clearly distinguish the position of spouses/partners from that of children because marriage/partnership is based on a different logic than simply being a child of someone. Croucher concludes that rather than continuing to tinker with existing family provision legislation, a fresh eye should be cast over the role that property does, and should, play in families.

CHAPTER 2

RECONSIDERING FAMILY PROPERTY LAW IN THE POST-MARITAL AGE

Patrick Parkinson

1. INTRODUCTION

The last 40 years or so have seen massive changes in family life in many post-Christian countries. Marriage is no longer the only accepted basis for family formation and, indeed, in many countries more children are born outside of marriage than within it. Ours is, to some extent, a post-marital age. What kinds of relationships, then, should be covered in default rules for property division if the relationship breaks down? These issues are explored through three vignettes:

- Cameron and Sandra are in their mid-20s and are contemplating if and how to formalise their relationship.
- Amir, a refugee from Afghanistan, is married to Sanaubar. They have three children together. He takes a second (de facto) wife, Basira, and they also have a child together. The relationship with Basira does not last.
- Melissa has had a succession of relationships, including a failed marriage. She gains sole ownership of the former matrimonial home in the divorce. Then she lives with Jim for over five years in an intimate domestic relationship; but neither want to marry. Finances are kept separate.

In the light of these vignettes, consideration is given to whether dyadic Judaeo-Christian marriage can remain the paradigm for a default law of property division on separation.

2. THE EMERGENCE OF THE POST-MARITAL AGE

The last 40 years have seen very rapid social change, especially in terms of family life and moral values about sexual behaviour in Western countries. New Zealand, it seems, is no exception to the patterns of change in post-Christian societies.

The idea that many of these societies could actually be post-marital societies, as well as post-Christian societies, may at first be confronting. Marriage still remains reasonably popular as a basis for a long-term commitment amongst university-educated people in Western countries. It remains obligatory as the basis for family life in deeply religious communities. For many in the lesbian, bisexual, gay and transgender (LBGT) communities, achieving legal recognition of their relationships as marriages has been a fervently sought goal.

However, as university-educated people moving in professional circles, we need to resist the temptation to see the world around us through the coloured glasses of those with whom we associate. For a large proportion of the population in Western societies, marriage is no longer seen as the conventional norm for founding a family.[1] Marriage still remains the most common form of couple relationship within Western Europe, but the gap between marriage and cohabitation as a family form is narrowing. For example, figures from 2013 show that in Sweden, 24 per cent of people aged 18–49 were cohabiting and 27 per cent were married.[2] The gap is not as close in other European countries, but France is not too far behind Sweden. In 2006, 26 per cent in that age group were cohabiting and 39 per cent were married.[3] Fewer people in other European countries are in any form of cohabiting relationship at all. More than 45 per cent in this age group are single in some European countries.[4]

---

1 In the United States, see the analysis by C Murray, *Coming Apart: The State of White America, 1960–2010*, Crown, New York 2012, which compares the situation for university-educated and non-university-educated people respectively, and shows great disparities in terms of marriage rates. See also JD Vance, *Hillbilly Elegy: A Memoir of a Family and Culture in Crisis*, Harper Collins, New York 2016.

2 Child Trends, *World Family Map 2015: Mapping Family Change and Child Well-Being Outcomes*, Washington DC 2015, 15 <www.childtrends.org/wp-content/uploads/2015/09/2015-39WorldFamilyMap2015.pdf> accessed 30.04.2017.

3 Ibid.

4 Ibid. For example, in Germany in 2013, 42% were married and 11% in de facto relationships, a total of only 53% living in intimate domestic partnerships. In Ireland the figures were 38% and 14% respectively in 2011, that is, only 52% in any form of intimate domestic partnership.

If the growth in cohabitation as a form of family formation was confined to childless couples it would not represent a major transformation in family life. Cohabitation could be seen then as a form of trial marriage or precursor to marriage. However, increasingly, cohabitation is a context for childrearing, and a significant percentage of women give birth to children without cohabiting with the father.

In Britain, for example, 47.4 per cent of all births occurred outside of marriage in 2013.[5] Half or more of all births are ex-nuptial in Belgium, Bulgaria, Estonia, France, Iceland, Slovenia, Norway, and Sweden. The highest rate is in Iceland at 65 per cent of all births.[6] In New Zealand, nearly half of all births are now outside of marriage.[7]

While many ex-nuptial births across Europe are in cohabiting unions, there are significant variations between countries. In the USA, between 2006 and 2010, 24 per cent of first births were to women who were neither married nor cohabiting.[8] In Australia in 2005, about 13 per cent of all births were to single mothers without the father living in the home, double the rate in the first half of the 1980s.[9]

Rates of ex-nuptial births are particularly high in certain South American countries. According to one comparative study, 84 per cent of births in Colombia occur outside marriage. In Peru it is 76 per cent, Nicaragua 72 per cent, Chile 71 per cent, and in Brazil 66 per cent.[10] Some cohabiting couples who have children will go on to marry (as the capstone to their committed relationship rather than the foundation stone); but many see no need to do so.

It follows that in many countries of Europe, North and South America, and in the Antipodes, we live increasingly in a post-marital age. While de jure marriage may be a common form of family structure, it is no longer the only conventional context for conceiving and raising children. Indeed, in many countries of Europe and South America, a substantial majority of children are

---

5 Office of National Statistics (UK), *Births in England and Wales: 2013*, 16 July 2014, 6 <www.ons.gov.uk/peoplepopulationandcommunity/birthsdeathsandmarriages/livebirths/bulletins/birthsummarytablesenglandandwales/2014-07-16> accessed 30.04.2017.

6 C Haub, *Rising Trend of Births Outside Marriage*, Population Reference Bureau, April 2013 <www.prb.org/Publications/Articles/2013/nonmarital-births.aspx> accessed 30.04.2017.

7 See Organisation for Economic Co-operation and Development (OECD), *OECD Family Database – SF2.2: Share of Births Outside of Marriage* <www.oecd.org/social/family/SF_2_4_Share_births_outside_marriage.pdf> accessed 30.04.2017.

8 G Martinez, K Daniels and A Chandra, *Fertility of Men and Women Aged 15–44 Years in the United States: National Survey of Family Growth, 2006–2010*, National Health Statistics Reports, no 51, National Center for Health Statistics (USA), 12 April 2012, 9 <www.cdc.gov/nchs/data/nhsr/nhsr051.pdf> accessed 30.04.2017.

9 P Laws et al, *Australia's Mothers and Babies 2005*, National Perinatal Statistics no 20, Australian Institute of Health and Welfare, Canberra 2007 <www.aihw.gov.au/WorkArea/DownloadAsset.aspx?id=6442458959> accessed 30.04.2017.

10 Child Trends, above n 2 at 20.

not born within marriage, and many may well go throughout their childhoods without living in a home in which two adults, including at least one of their parents, are married to one another.[11]

3. FAMILY LAW – RETHINKING FOUNDATIONAL CONCEPTS

These demographic changes create challenges for many jurisdictions because marriage has traditionally provided the structural framework for the family law system. Property sharing and spousal maintenance rights have historically been premised upon marriage. Remedies became available upon separation and divorce. Spousal maintenance, while it has more than one rationale, has traditionally been conceived as a remedy available to an innocent party in the event of a divorce for fault. Typically, and if he had disposable income, the guilty husband was held to his promise of lifelong support for his wife, a promise which was sometimes given effect through indefinite maintenance. Cohabiting couples make no such public promises of lifelong support to each other.

Broadly speaking, jurisdictions have responded in three ways to the conundrum of how to treat non-marital relationships. The first is to adopt an assimilationist approach in which informal heterosexual and same-sex relationships are treated as equivalent to marriage after a certain time. This is the position, for example, in Australia and New Zealand. In Australia, once the parties (whether heterosexual or same-sex) have lived together for more than two years or have a child, the property and maintenance consequences of marriage apply to them.

The second approach is to allow people to register their partnerships without getting married. In the Netherlands, for example, registered partnerships are open to both heterosexual and homosexual couples, and have almost the same effects as marriages.[12] The consequence of choosing neither to marry nor to register one's partnership is that the relationship does not attract marriage-like consequences.

The third approach is to recognise cohabiting relationships for some purposes but to leave property rights on the breakdown of the relationship

---

11 For American data, see L Bumpass and H-H Lu, 'Trends in Cohabitation and Implications for Children's Family Contexts in the United States' (2000) 54 *Population Studies* 29.

12 W Schrama, 'Reforms in Dutch Family Law During the Course of 2001: Increased Pluriformity and Complexity' in A Bainham (ed), *International Survey of Family Law 2002*, Jordan Publishing, Bristol 2002, 277; I Sumner and H Warendorf (trans), *Family Law Legislation of the Netherlands: A Translation including Book 1 of the Dutch Civil Code, Procedural and Transitional Provisions and Private International Law Legislation*, Intersentia, Antwerp 2003.

to the general law. Recognition of cohabiting relationships has long been a feature of social security law in many jurisdictions, for example. Governments have taken the view, understandably, that a person should not be able to claim unemployment or sickness benefits without taking account of the income of a cohabiting partner, just as would be the case if the couple were married. To do otherwise is to impose a marriage penalty. Such jurisdictions have ad hoc recognition for cohabiting relationships across a range of other areas of law, but stop well short of full assimilation.

4. EXPLORING THE ISSUES THROUGH STORIES

The issues confronting any law reform body seeking to evaluate options for reform are explored, in this chapter, through three vignettes, three stories. All of them are fictional, but all of them reflect real issues for people whose circumstances, if they break up at least, are governed by a single default regime of property law, subject to their capacity to contract out of it. Their stories illustrate the square pegs seeking to fit into the round holes of the existing law. Storytelling is perhaps not a conventional technique for legal writing, but it has its uses.[13] In this chapter, the stories may help to expose the fictions on which the law itself is founded – for example that de facto relationships are 'just like' Judaeo-Christian marriages.

4.1. CAMERON, SANDRA, AND THE MEANING OF 'MARRIAGE'

Cameron and Sandra are a young couple in their mid-20s. Cameron graduated from Monash University. He has been working in a hospital as a radiologist. Sandra is a nurse. They met just over two-and-a-half years ago at a social event in the hospital. One thing led to another. Before too long, their relationship became sexual.

In the first few months that they were a couple, they had a conventional dating relationship involving occasional overnight stays at one place or the other. Sandra lived at that time in nurses' quarters, close to the hospital. She had her own room, but it was not all that large, and she only had a single bed. Cameron felt a little awkward sleeping over there, so they tended to have sex at Cameron's place, and Sandra would stay the night there unless she was on the early shift. Initially, she stayed over about two nights per week, but after a while,

13 L Sarmas, 'Storytelling and the Law: A Case Study of *Louth v Diprose*' (1994) 19 *Melbourne University Law Review* 701.

that increased to about four nights per week. Of course, it varied from one week to another, and no one kept records. Why would it matter?

Cameron's apartment is a one bedroom place in the inner city. Cameron had managed to purchase it with a $100,000 loan from his parents and a huge, but manageable, mortgage.

About 20 months ago, Cameron suggested to Sandra that she might like to move into his place. There was no point in her paying rent for the room in the nurses' quarters if she wasn't living there all that often. She agreed and, about three weeks later, she moved in.

Mostly, they kept their finances separate. Cameron paid all the mortgage and outgoings on the apartment. They put money into a joint account for groceries. When they went out to a restaurant or to the cinema, Sandra usually paid because Cameron really couldn't afford it while paying the mortgage and electricity bills. Sandra didn't mind. It was the price of going out and having a good time together.

Over the last few weeks, they have been talking about their future. Sandra would quite like to get married – or at least she thinks so. There is a part of her that is very traditional. Sandra, in that frame of mind, wants the white dress and the large party. She wants that special day. However, another part of her recognises that the special day can be extraordinarily expensive and changes little, because after that special day – and perhaps the honeymoon in an exotic location – their lives will be exactly the same as they were before. Sandra is not religious, so marriage is not important to her from that perspective; but it is what her parents did, and while they probably wouldn't say it so bluntly to her, it is what they would like for her too.

Cameron is very hesitant about marriage. He loves Sandra; but he is also not sure whether this relationship is a long-term prospect. One reason is the arguments they have had recently; he knows these are mostly his fault. He buries his feelings and they build up until he explodes. Then he finds it really difficult to get over the fight for days on end. He sulks and broods. Apologies are eventually offered and received, but each of these arguments have left their relationship just a little more unsteady. Another reason for being uncertain about marriage is that he is really attracted to a female colleague in his office. Cameron is just not too sure about the whole fidelity thing.

Perhaps the main reason why he is hesitant is that his long-term plan has been to work overseas for a few years – perhaps in the UK, maybe in Germany. He has a UK passport, and can quite easily find work as a radiologist. Sandra has made it clear that she doesn't want to move overseas, and in particular has no interest in living in Europe. She is very close to her parents and her older sister who has two young children. Sandra's sister loves having her around to help out.

Cameron and Sandra have yet to have a serious conversation about children. Sandra still feels too young, and is content to enjoy her sister's children while being able to hand them back.

Cameron has a friend, Tim, who recently graduated in law and now works for a family law firm in Melbourne. They invited him over to dinner one night and openly talked about their thoughts about getting married. Tim went through the different options. They may choose a religious wedding, as long as they can find a minister of religion prepared to marry them. There are some nice old Anglican churches with a medieval stone look, if that is the kind of setting that they want for their wedding.

Alternatively, if they just want something secular, they could get married in a registry office. Tim showed them the website for the Victorian Marriage Registry which promises 'elegant civil marriage ceremonies on weekdays and weekends for couples seeking an intimate and simple wedding' in an old heritage-listed building in the city.[14] Another option, he explained, is to purchase the services of a private marriage celebrant who may be able to conduct the wedding in some other special location.[15] 'If you don't want to marry', Tim explained, 'you could just register your relationship.' In Victoria,[16] as in many other parts of the country, for example Queensland,[17] couples can enter into a 'registered relationship'. A registered relationship has the same effects as marriage for the purposes of the law of that jurisdiction.[18] In federal law, the relationship will be treated as a 'de facto relationship'.[19]

'How is a registered relationship different from a marriage at a registry office?' Sandra asked.

'I don't know really,' said Tim. 'I suppose you just skip the "elegant ceremony" bit.'

'Much cheaper,' said Cameron.

Tim explained that while these are all options for Sandra and Cameron to formalise their relationship, actually they have no need to do so, for they will be treated as married just by living together for at least two years.

'There is now almost no difference at all between being married and living in a "de facto relationship" in any area of state or federal law,' he told them.

He went on to explain (in a little more detail than Cameron and Sandra wanted to hear) that the trajectory of law reform at both state and federal levels

14 Births, Deaths, Marriages, *Victorian Marriage Registry* <www.bdm.vic.gov.au/home/marriages/victorian+marriage+registry/> accessed 30.04.2017.

15 By authorising marriage celebrants, Australia has partially privatised the solemnisation of marriages. It need not be a state official who pronounces the couple duly married. It is sufficient that it is someone who has been authorised by the government to take weddings. For secular celebrants it is a professional occupation, or a business.

16 Relationships Act 2008 (Vic).

17 Registered Relationships Act 2011 (Qld).

18 For example, the Civil Unions Act 2012 (ACT), s 6(2) provides: 'A civil union is different to a marriage but is to be treated for all purposes under territory law in the same way as a marriage.'

19 Family Law Act 1975 (Cth), s 4AA.

over the last 20 years had been to insert the words 'or de facto' wherever the word 'marriage' or 'spouse' appears in legislation. Initially this was to address the issues for heterosexual couples who do not marry, and later the term 'de facto' was extended to include same-sex couples.

'So you mean that it doesn't matter whether you marry, register your relationship without marrying, or don't formalise your relationship at all – you just end up being married anyway?' said Sandra, astonished.

'Oh no,' Tim replied, 'if you are married and the relationship ends you need to get divorced.'

Then he thought for a moment, and went on: 'Well, you need to get divorced if you want to marry again; but I suppose if you just want to live with someone else you don't really need to get divorced at all. Anyway, a divorce is just a formality. It takes less than five minutes for the Registrar to pronounce the divorce, and if there are issues about property, maintenance, or the children, they are dealt with entirely separately.'

'So all roads lead to Rome?' said Cameron.

'Exactly,' Tim replied.

A few days later, Cameron rang Tim and asked him what counts as a de facto relationship. Tim explained that it is very complicated. You don't actually have to be living together full-time to be treated as a de facto couple. Cameron said that he and Sandra had now been living together for about 20 months, but for some time before that Sandra had been sleeping over quite regularly.

'How regularly?' asked Tim.

'Well, it varied,' Cameron replied. 'Sometimes two nights a week; often it was four nights per week. To be honest, I can't remember all that clearly. Why does it matter?'

'It matters,' Tim replied, 'because the court may say you were living together long before Sandra actually moved in full-time; but there is no rule about it. Two nights per week might not be enough. Four nights per week probably would be. It all depends on the judge.'[20]

'Do you mean that already, we could have been living together for over two years when I thought we had only been living together for 20 months?'

---

[20] Mushin J observed in *Moby v Schulter* [2010] FamCA 748 at [140]: 'In my view, if a couple do not live together at any time, they cannot be seen as being in a de facto relationship. However, the concept of "living together" does not import any concept of proportion of time. In particular, it does not require that a couple live together on a full-time basis. On the basis that one or both members of the couple may also be legally married or in another de facto relationship at the same time as they are in the subject relationship, it must follow that it is feasible that the subject relationship might involve the parties living together for no more than half of the time of that relationship. Further, there is nothing to suggest that it must be even as much as half of the time.'

'Yes, and that has just the same legal effect as being married,' said Tim. At least, Tim consoled him, he and Sandra are not living together in New Zealand. There, if they split up after three years,[21] Sandra could be entitled to half the apartment.[22]

***

Cameron and Sandra illustrate the situation of many young people who live in a post-marital age. Forty years ago, their story would have had little resonance. Few couples in the 1970s lived together before marriage and even fewer lived together without necessarily intending to marry at all. Forty years ago, Cameron and Sandra would probably have been married by the time they were 24 and the assumption on which that marriage was predicated was that it would be for life. Implicit also in the idea of marriage was that they would become a single socio-economic unit in which the major items of property were not his or hers, but theirs – whatever the state of the legal title.

Marriage was also a necessary precursor to having children together. Ex-nuptial births were then quite uncommon. Australian data indicates that in 1976, only 10 per cent of births were ex-nuptial.[23] Less than half of the ex-nuptial births in 1977 were acknowledged by the father,[24] and it is likely that in the cases where the father was not on the birth certificate he was not living with the mother.

There were not even any statistics available for de facto relationships in Australia before 1982. In that year, a survey by the Australian Bureau of Statistics indicated that about 5 per cent of all couples living together were unmarried. They were concentrated in the under-30 age group.[25] All that has changed now.

Cameron and Sandra are not a married couple. They moved from living apart to living together for practical reasons to some extent – there was no point in paying rent on an additional place if they were comfortable living together.[26] Are they 'like' a married couple? Perhaps the closest analogy to the Camerons and Sandras of 40 years ago is that they are a couple who are in a committed dating relationship, thinking about engagement, perhaps already engaged. Of course, that is a distant analogy, for the stages of relationship-building of old – involving

---

21 Property (Relationships) Act 1976 (NZ) ('PRA'), s 4(5).

22 PRA, s 11(a).

23 S Khoo and P McDonald, 'Ex-Nuptial Births and Unmarried Cohabitation in Australia' (1988) 5 *Journal of the Australian Population Association* 164.

24 Ibid, Table 2, at 167.

25 Ibid, at 168.

26 Research by Carmichael and Whittaker found that for many people they interviewed in their study, the move from living apart to living together occurred for pragmatic reasons. The most important of these was to avoid the cost of maintaining two residences: GA Carmichael and A Whittaker, 'Living Together in Australia: Qualitative Insights into a Complex Phenomenon' (2007) 13 *Journal of Family Studies* 202.

acquaintance, dating, engagement, marriage, commencement of cohabitation, and then childbirth – are no longer the most conventional pathways for people to start living together as a couple. Most couples in Australia who get married live together beforehand these days, and many will not marry at all. That pattern is common to post-Christian societies.

Cameron and Sandra's relationship has lasted two-and-a-half years, and they are contemplating means of formalising it; but whatever analogy one draws to the formation of relationships 40 years ago misses an important aspect of their relationship – that Cameron and Sandra live in the present. Except when they have arguments, they enjoy the present together. There is a possible future to be sure, but commitment is at best in the category of 'maybe, but not yet'. Cameron is seriously contemplating another future – work in Europe – of which Sandra will not be a part.

The Camerons and Sandras of 40 years ago thought of marriage as being both about the present and the future. Marriage was the precondition to living together for all but a very few; for many it was also the precondition for beginning a sexual relationship. The wedding night was the consummation of the marital covenant and the culmination of a (usually) long process of courtship, involving consideration about whether this man or this woman was someone to whom they could commit till death do them part.

That is simply not the world of many of the modern Camerons and Sandras. Sandra hears in her head the cultural echo of that idea of marriage – a cultural echo from her parents and the older generation of which they are a part; but she is understandably confused about what exactly marriage is, when it may involve simply paying a commercial celebrant whom they have never met before and who means nothing in particular to them, to pronounce them husband and wife. Sandra will certainly hope for longevity, as may Cameron if he commits, but for decades now, marriage has been terminable by the decision of one partner without the other one having any right to prevent it. It is as freely terminable, in Australia at least, as a de facto relationship, but for the need to pay the government a substantial fee in order for a court official to pronounce the divorce.

Furthermore, Sandra is not the dependent woman of 40 years ago, and she does not intend to be in the future. Theirs is not, at this stage anyway, a union of hearts, minds, and finances. Their finances are separate but interconnected. Yes, in some ways she helps him out with a few extra expenses, and indirectly that helps him pay the mortgage; but if she were still paying rent on her nurses' quarters, she would have been able to save far less than she has done now.

Cameron is troubled by the idea that the law might treat him as if he were married. The very choice that he is weighing up – whether to commit to Sandra in the long-term – is the choice that the law presumes to have already made for him by conferring, or perhaps imposing, upon him marital rights and obligations.

Furthermore, no Australian lawyer could confidently advise Cameron whether he has already been in a de facto relationship for more than two years and whether Sandra will have a claim for property settlement if they break up because he moves to England or Germany. So much depends on the broad discretion that judges have, both in determining when the de facto relationship began and what significance it has for their property rights.

4.2. AMIR, BASIRA, AND DE FACTO POLYGAMY

Amir and Sanaubar were married 15 years ago. They are both first-generation migrants to New Zealand. Their families came from Afghanistan as refugees. Amir works as a security guard in downtown Wellington. Theirs is a traditional Afghan marriage. Sanaubar stays at home and covers up if she goes out in public. They have three children.

Just over four years ago, Amir told Sanaubar that he wanted to take another wife. Basira is nine years younger than Sanaubar. Sanaubar was not all that happy about it, but she acceded to it as this is an accepted norm within her cultural and religious tradition. Amir approached a visiting imam from Pakistan to conduct the ceremony. He and Basira were married in accordance with Afghan Islamic customs a few weeks later. Basira fell pregnant quite soon thereafter and now has a son who has just turned three years old.

Sanaubar and Basira have been in constant conflict ever since Basira joined the household. Sanaubar did not like the way that Basira cooked and cleaned up in the kitchen and there were a thousand other conflicts, great and small, that disturbed the harmony of the family. Amir would come home frequently from a tiring day (or nightshift) to find that he was caught in a battle between his two wives, as well as having to deal with squabbling children.

He loved both his wives and all his children, but the situation was becoming intolerable. He thought about divorcing Sanaubar, but that was difficult. She came from an influential family within the Afghan community in New Zealand, and he feared repercussions if he were to divorce her. Besides, she was the mother to his three oldest children and she ran the household well. He decided instead that Basira had to go. So he pronounced the talaq divorce in accordance with his tradition, and Basira went back to live with her parents.

Basira was distraught. It is shameful to be divorced in her culture. She left school when she was 17 and before her marriage to Amir was working as a checkout assistant in a supermarket. She has no particular skills or qualifications to fall back on.

Basira, in the presence of her mother, spoke with a cousin Khaled, who was a law graduate. 'What can I do?' Basira asked, tears welling up in her eyes. 'Amir says my rights are in accordance with our marriage contract – nothing more'. Khaled explained that under New Zealand law, Basira wasn't actually married at all. Was she in a de facto relationship? He explained that this is defined in section 2D of the Property (Relationships) Act 1976 (NZ) ('PRA') as 'a relationship between 2 persons … who live together as a couple'. 'We weren't a couple!' said Basira. 'There were three of us all living together with our children!' Khaled looked troubled. Could Amir and Sanaubar be a couple and Amir and Basira be a couple?[27] Surely Amir and Sanaubar did not cease to be a 'couple' at the time that Basira joined the household?

Eventually he asked a friend, Bill, who is a family lawyer. He told Khaled to look at sections 52A and 52B of the PRA. According to these sections, you can have a marriage and a de facto relationship at the same time, and two de facto relationships at the same time. 'These relationships can be contemporaneous,' said Bill. That means Amir could be in a de facto relationship with someone while still living with his wife.[28] The problem, Bill explained, is that the sections only apply to cases where the court is faced with competing property orders, that is, an application made by the wife and another one by the de facto partner.

'That's not the situation,' said Khaled. 'Amir continues to live with, and be married to, Sanaubar. They live in the family home owned by Amir. He won't divorce Sanaubar ever, because he likes her, she is the mother of three of his children, and he is terrified of her uncle. So what will the court do if there is an application by Basira as a former de facto partner to get half the house and furniture?'

Bill had no idea.

***

Amir and Basira are, of course, fictional. There is very little information about the extent of de facto polygamy amongst members of the Islamic community in Western countries; but anecdotally at least, the given scenario is not unrealistic in Australia.[29] Such polygamous relationships may exist in New Zealand also. Assuming this is so, how should the law deal with the issue?

---

27 Similar issues of interpretation arise in Australian law. Judicial interpretation of the idea of a de facto relationship remains dyadic (see *Jonah v White* [2011] FamCA 221; affirmed on appeal in *Jonah v White* [2012] FamCAFC 200) but it is explicitly recognised that two de facto relationships can exist at the same time: Family Law Act 1975 (Cth), s 4AA(5). It remains unclear whether de facto polygamy within the one household can be recognised, or whether it is necessary that the one who is party to two different de facto relationships simultaneously should live across two different households with each of the partners during parts of each week or month: J Richards and H Esmaeili, 'The Position of Australian Muslim Women in Polygamous Relationships under the Family Law Act 1975 (Cth): Still "Taking Multiculturalism Seriously"?' (2012) 26 *Australian Journal of Family Law* 142.

28 Section 52A(3) of the PRA provides: 'For the purposes of this section, a marriage and a de facto relationship are successive if the de facto relationship begins during the marriage, but after the spouses cease to live together as a married couple.' If the relationships are not 'successive' (PRA, s 52A(2)(a)) in this sense then they may be 'at some time contemporaneous' (PRA, s 52A(2)(b)). That is, one can be in a de facto relationship while still living together with one's wife.

29 See J Richards and H Esmaeili, above n 27. See also *Mohammed Salah v Gastana* [2011] FamCA 440.

Amir and Basira were married in accordance with the norms and traditions of their culture, and it is probably quite irrelevant to them that they were not married in the eyes of the law in New Zealand. Their marriage was recognised by their families and the extended Afghan community of which they are a part; and that is probably all that mattered to them; but it was a very different form of marriage to that in Western countries. Purists may object to the description of their relationship as a 'marriage' because the law prohibits bigamy. However, it does not prohibit a wife and a de facto partner living together with the man in the same household.

While, according to their culture and faith, Amir and Basira were married, the analogy to marriage breaks down if the paradigmatic relationship of marriage, with which this is being compared, is dyadic. Judaeo-Christian marriage provides the normative substratum for legislation like the PRA. The notion, in Christian teaching, that a man should be joined to his wife and the two should become one flesh,[30] was translated into the common law by seeing the husband and wife dyad as involving one socio-economic unit. The traditional position was that married women had no legal existence apart from their husbands. This was expressed most famously by Sir William Blackstone in his *Commentaries on the Laws of England*:[31]

> 'By marriage, the husband and wife are one person in law: that is, the very being or legal existence of the woman is suspended during the marriage, or at least incorporated and consolidated into that of the husband: under whose wing, protection, and *cover* she performs every thing.'

In the civil law, the idea of community property was the norm, but management of the community property was typically undertaken by the husband.

Marriage, in the Christian tradition at least, was indissoluble; if a marriage broke down, separation from bed and board was permissible. Eventually, and with some reluctance at first, countries of the Western legal tradition permitted divorce. However, the lifelong nature of the marriage covenant was reflected in the ancillary relief. Spousal maintenance was the means by which an erring husband could be held to his promise to support his wife till death do them part.

The equal division of the marital property on divorce still reflects the idea that in the intact family the husband and wife have everything in common, justifying the equal sharing if they separate. That doesn't work for Amir, Sanaubar, and Basira's situation where one out of three adults in this domestic

30 Bible, North American Standard Version, Genesis 2:24.

31 W Blackstone, *Commentaries on the Laws of England*, vol 1, Clarendon Press, Oxford 1765–69, ch 15, [442] (footnote omitted).

triad is leaving the family home, together with her young child, while the other two adults remain.

One imagines that a New Zealand judge would rely on the exception to the rule of equal sharing of the family home and other marital property to avoid the absurdity of forcing the sale of the home in which Sanaubar lives with Amir and their children.[32] Basira's claim must be satisfied in some other way, and no doubt it will be; but on what principles? Certainly, Australian law has no answer to this problem. The entire jurisprudence of family property law, such as it is, rests upon assumptions about what is just and equitable when dyadic relationships break down.[33]

Another question that this scenario raises is the extent to which New Zealand law should recognise and respect the religious and cultural substratum of Amir and Basira's relationship. As Afghans living in a foreign land, Amir and Basira maintain their cultural identity and traditions, together with the migrant Afghan community, and their divorce is likely to be governed by Islamic norms mediated through the imams.[34] New Zealand has welcomed them as refugees. Their polygamous relationship is entirely lawful (as long as no one tries to register the second marriage as a de jure marriage). Their relationship is also recognised to some extent in sections 52A and 52B of the PRA. Should New Zealand law respect their cultural traditions when it comes to property division?

These issues do not only arise for new migrants from countries where polygamy is accepted. They will also arise if the courts have to adjudicate on the breakdown of a relationship that is polyamorous. Polyamorous relationships are sexually intimate relationships between three or more consenting adults. Sexual relations may occur between any of the participants in the group, rather than involving concurrent dyadic heterosexual relationships with one man.[35] Furthermore, polyamorous relationships may be primary and secondary – that is, there may be a primary couple with openly acknowledged secondary or tertiary relationships involving some level of commitment outside of the household.[36] According to Aviram and Leachman, the polyamorous community distinguishes itself from the religious variant of multiparty relationships, polygamy, in its members' commitment to non-monogamy and acceptance of

---

32 PRA, s 13.

33 See Family Law Act 1975 (Cth), s 79(2).

34 In Australia, see G Krayem, *Islamic Family Law in Australia: To Recognise or Not to Recognise*, Melbourne University Press, Melbourne 2014.

35 H Aviram and GM Leachman, 'The Future of Polyamorous Marriage: Lessons from the Marriage Equality Struggle' (2015) 38 *Harvard Journal of Law and Gender* 269, 273.

36 Ibid, at 298.

queer sexualities.[37] These relationships may not be common in Western societies but they are not numerically insignificant.[38]

4.3. MELISSA, JIM, AND INTIMATE HOUSE-SHARING

Melissa, who lives in Christchurch, New Zealand, has had a succession of intimate domestic partnerships. In her 20s she had two de facto relationships lasting about 18 months each. The first one ended when her boyfriend got a job in Auckland, New Zealand. She had good reasons for not wanting to move from Christchurch and they decided to part ways. They remain friends. The second de facto relationship ended with her boyfriend being charged with assault following an argument in which he lost control, pinned her to a wall, and held her arms so strongly that he caused bruising.

After that, Melissa was wary of intimate relationships with men; but she wanted children and saw marriage as the necessary precondition for bringing a child into the world. She married Barry when she was 29. At first, the marriage was a happy one. They had two children. Life was busy, but relatively content. However, Barry began to drink more and more. Eleven-and-a-half years after they were married, Melissa told Barry that the marriage was over. This was eight years ago.

The divorce was messy. Eventually, they reached a property settlement. Melissa, who works as a nurse, was able to buy Barry out and to take over ownership of the family home with a mortgage of $130,000. She had primary care of the children who, at the time of separation, were eight and nine years old.

Not long afterwards, she met Jim. He had recently divorced his wife and was living in a small rented one bedroom apartment. They got on really well; Melissa invited Jim to come to live in her house. They agreed that they would keep their finances separate. They preferred to have separate bedrooms, but typically they had sexual intercourse about twice per week, and they represented themselves to others as a couple. Melissa introduced Jim as her 'partner'. Neither of them were interested in marriage.

Melissa paid the mortgage and all the outgoings. Jim gave her $400 per week as his contribution to the food, electricity bills, and the general expenses of the

---

37 Ibid. See also M Schippers, *Beyond Monogamy: Polyamory and the Future of Polyqueer Sexualities*, New York University Press, New York 2016; L Brunning, 'The Distinctiveness of Polyamory' (2016) *Journal of Applied Philosophy* <http://onlinelibrary.wiley.com/doi/10.1111/japp.12240/full> accessed 30.04.2017.

38 Reliable estimates of prevalence are difficult to obtain and highly dependent upon definition. In the United States, polyamorists form an identifiable group and movement with their own conferences, magazines, and websites. See for example, *Loving More* <www.lovemore.com> accessed 30.04.2017.

home. A couple of years later he increased that contribution to $425 per week. Melissa worked full-time. Jim was a tradesman, and the amount of work he obtained varied from one week to the next. Jim helped out with the children, but they did not look upon him as a 'stepdad'. Barry saw the children quite regularly and paid child support. Melissa did most of the cooking, but Jim sometimes cooked as well.

About a year ago, Melissa's mother died. She inherited $71,000 which she used to pay out the mortgage.

Last week, after over five years of living together, Jim told Melissa that he had decided to move out. Melissa was very surprised. They had had sexual relations only a few days earlier, although sex had not been as frequent in the last three to four months as it had been previously. They got on well. There had been conflicts, but typically they had resolved them more easily than she and Barry had done.

She asked Jim why he wanted to split up. Sheepishly, he explained that he had been seeing another woman, Angela, for a few weeks now. They had had sexual relations on many occasions. She had invited him to live with her, and he felt that his future would be happier if he accepted her invitation. He liked Melissa, but they hadn't made any commitment to each other, after all. He thanked her for the years they had spent together. Her response is not printable.

***

Melissa's story raises the issue of how the law should treat relationships in which the parties have rather explicitly rejected the option of marriage and kept their finances separate. Jim's relationship with Melissa was, from a financial point of view, scarcely distinguishable from that of a housemate. He put in money for the food and other household expenses. They had a sexual relationship, and held themselves out as being partners. However, describing someone as your 'partner' these days is a deliberately ambiguous term which could cover any relationship from husband and wife to new boyfriend or girlfriend. In Australia at least, it is likely that they would be treated as being in a de facto relationship notwithstanding that they kept their finances separate and had separate bedrooms.

What is it about sharing a house, having sex regularly, and presenting to the world as a 'couple' that should entitle Jim to a share of Melissa's property?[39] Is it unconscionable for Melissa to retain sole legal title to her home? Perhaps it could be argued on Jim's part that he conferred a financial benefit on her by his contributions to the household expenses which included the mortgage; but he would have had to pay all of that money and much more if he were living on his

---

39 I have discussed the 'proprietary consequences of love' in P Parkinson, 'Quantifying the Homemaker Contribution in Family Property Law' (2003) 31 *Federal Law Review* 1, 8–20.

own. Melissa provided him with a place to live. In cohabiting relationships, there is usually a situation of mutual benefit conferral which makes arguments about unjust enrichment problematic.[40]

If Jim and Melissa lived a few doors away from each other, maintaining a relationship of 'living apart together',[41] but had the same frequency of sexual intercourse and held each other out to be 'partners', how would that be so different from living together? Why does living together make the difference – in terms of proprietary remedies – on the demise of the relationship? The conventional justification for property sharing for childless couples is that when people live together, they intermingle finances and contribute to the acquisition, maintenance, and improvement of property in ways which may not be reflected in legal title. Of course that is true, but it is not inevitable. Melissa and Jim both understood this, and kept their finances separate.

In contributing $400 or more per week to the household budget, Jim did not think of himself as acquiring an interest in her property nor in being in a socio-economic partnership of lives that was similar to a marriage. There are no doubt those who would say that living together in a home, having a sexual relationship, and holding themselves out to be a couple makes their relationship 'like marriage'; but that is to ignore their intentions and all the differences between their relationship and marriage. The relationship between Melissa and Jim ended, but it did not break down, at least not in the conventional sense of the term. Theirs was not a story of fiery conflict, betrayal, or even gradual estrangement leading to irreconcilable differences. Nor did Jim perceive himself as having had an 'affair' with Angela. He had never promised Melissa sexual exclusivity. Jim left Melissa because he was perfectly free to do so and preferred now to pursue a relationship with another woman. It is not that living with Melissa was intolerable – it was not. The relationship had just come to its natural end.

Melissa's relationship with Jim was her fourth cohabiting relationship and she is not yet 50. Only one of them she viewed as a marriage, and that is because it was a marriage. She had gone into that one seeking and expecting permanency, and had been bitterly disappointed by the failure of the relationship. The marriage analogy assumes that people like Melissa and Jim who enter into a de facto relationship intend it to be as permanent as marriage is – or at least hope that it will be. For some, that may be so; but it cannot be assumed to be so across the population.

The consequences for Melissa would be particularly severe if Jim decided to pursue a property claim and the outcome was that she had to give Jim a share

---

40 P Parkinson, 'Beyond *Pettkus v Becker*: Quantifying Relief for Unjust Enrichment' (1993) 43 *University of Toronto Law Journal* 217.

41 See S Duncan et al, 'Why do People Live Apart Together?' (2013) 2 *Families, Relationships and Societies* 323.

of the family home or pay him out a monetary equivalent.[42] She gained that house after difficult negotiations with her former husband. She has paid out the mortgage with the help of an inheritance. If the genders were reversed and it was Jim who owned the house, perhaps we would perceive less of an injustice. Equitable distribution laws have been greatly influenced by the need to protect women, who are often more vulnerable financially when the relationship breaks down,[43] and that has often required ordering men to transfer money or property to their former spouse. Melissa benefitted from that when she went through her divorce from Barry; but now she is wanting to protect her nest egg from the claims of another male. Family property law has to be gender-neutral. It must cut both ways.

5. REVISITING THE MARRIAGE ANALOGY

It is important in any discussion of the future of family property law that we are grounded in the lived reality of people's daily lives, rather than approaching the subject using the typical discourses of family lawyers. In recent years, when family property laws have been revised to include de facto relationships, all too little attention has been paid to the actual intentions and circumstances of the population to whom the law applies, and for whom it has such profound impacts.

De facto relationships are heterogeneous.[44] Some people live together with the intention of getting married.[45] Others may enter a cohabiting relationship

---

42 It is unclear what property, if any, Jim would get under Australian law. In Australia, the problem is the uncertainty of the law making it extremely difficult to negotiate a settlement against a shared backdrop of understanding between one lawyer and another, about 'what the court will do'. See P Parkinson, 'Why Are Decisions on Family Property So Inconsistent?' (2016) 90 *Australian Law Journal* 498.

43 For international evidence, see H-J Andreß et al, 'The Economic Consequences of Partnership Dissolution – A Comparative Analysis of Panel Studies from Belgium, Germany, Great Britain, Italy, and Sweden' (2006) 22 *European Sociological Review* 533. See also L Weitzman and M Maclean (eds), *The Economic Consequences of Divorce: The International Perspective*, OUP, New York 1992. There is evidence from the USA that the economic consequences of the breakdown of cohabiting relationships are very similar to those of marriage breakdown. See S Avellar and PJ Smock, 'The Economic Consequences of the Dissolution of Cohabiting Unions' (2005) 67 *Journal of Marriage and Family* 315.

44 See S Buchler et al, 'The Social and Demographic Characteristics of Cohabiters in Australia: Towards a Typology of Cohabiting Couples' [2009] 82 *Family Matters* 22. See also JM Lindsay, 'An Ambiguous Commitment: Moving into a Cohabiting Relationship' (2000) 6 *Journal of Family Studies* 120.

45 The Australian Bureau of Statistics reported that 42% of those in a de facto marriage in 2006–07, stated that they expected to enter into a registered marriage with their current partner: Australian Bureau of Statistics, *Family Characteristics and Transitions, Australia, 2006–07*, 26 May 2011 <www.abs.gov.au/AUSSTATS/abs@.nsf/Lookup/4442.0Main+Features12006-07?OpenDocument> accessed 30.04.2017.

with a hope or intention, on the part of at least one of them,[46] that they will marry, but the relationship does not survive long enough for this to occur. Others reject the idea of formal marriage entirely, but see themselves as being in a committed and ongoing relationship.[47] Many de facto relationships are not socio-economic partnerships of a kind that is typical for married couples.[48] Furthermore, as Scott Stanley et al observe: 'Cohabiting partners often do not even share the same understanding of the path they are on together.'[49]

This is problematic for the assimilation approach. To a large extent, the law has expanded by analogy, and has drawn upon a Judaeo-Christian marriage paradigm which no longer reflects the way in which many couples view their relationships. Professor Bill Atkin neatly summarises the issues in New Zealand as they are conventionally discussed in the legal literature:[50]

> 'There are good reasons for distinguishing marriage (plus civil unions, civil partnerships or similar institutions) from non-marriage: freedom of choice and association; "one size does not fit all"; the wide variety of relationships makes it inappropriate to equate them to marriage; priority should be given to marriage either for ideological and cultural reasons or because of a sense that the public commitment in marriage makes it a better bet for secure family life.
>
> However, there are also good reasons why the law should treat unmarried partners much the same as married couples: their relationships are usually functionally very similar to marriages with similar needs and problems requiring resolution; there are advantages in drawing upon the same body of jurisprudence instead of re-inventing the wheel each time an issue arises; ... many countries have laws that militate against discrimination on the basis of marital or other status; and definitions of the relevant relationships and a duration requirement as a condition of jurisdiction (in New Zealand three years) can weed out the fringe associations that should be outside a marriage-based regime.'

46 PM Huang et al, 'He Says, She Says: Gender and Cohabitation' (2011) 32 *Journal of Family Issues* 876; SL Brown, 'Union Transitions among Cohabiters: The Significance of Relationship Assessment and Expectations' (2000) 62 *Journal of Marriage and Family* 833.

47 On the different meanings of commitment, see JE Pryor and J Roberts, 'What is Commitment? How Married and Cohabiting Parents Talk About Their Relationships' [2005] 71 *Family Matters* 24.

48 S Singh and C Morley, 'Gender and Financial Accounts in Marriage' (2011) 47 *Journal of Sociology* 3.

49 See SM Stanley, GK Rhoades and HJ Markman, 'Sliding versus Deciding: Inertia and the Pre-Marital Cohabitation Effect' (2006) 55 *Family Relations* 499, 503. See also WD Manning and PJ Smock, 'Measuring and Modelling Cohabitation: New Perspectives from Qualitative Data' (2005) 67 *Journal of Marriage and Family* 989.

50 B Atkin, 'The Legal World of Unmarried Couples: Reflections on "De Facto Relationships" in Recent New Zealand Legislation' (2008) 39 *Victoria University of Wellington Law Review* 793, 794.

Cameron and Sandra are, for now, a 'fringe association that should be outside a marriage-based regime' in New Zealand;[51] it is very difficult to say whether they are outside the marriage-based regime in Australia. That depends on when the relationship is deemed to have commenced. That question cannot really be answered by any objective criteria, making it impossible for lawyers to advise with confidence. Greater certainty would be achieved if the law were changed to require the parties to have set up a single home which each of them recognises as their ordinary place of residence, notwithstanding the exigencies of work that may require them to sleep occasionally elsewhere.

Amir and Basira have a marriage, albeit not one recognised as such in New Zealand law. Their case raises issues of how the courts should deal with non-dyadic intimate domestic relationships, and what fairness to Basira is likely to mean for the wife, Sanaubar, and her three children who remain with Amir in the family home.

The case of Melissa and Jim raises issues of how some women may be disadvantaged by laws which were designed to assist them and which apply too broadly the idea that all de facto relationships which last a sufficient time should be treated as if they were marriages.

The extension of the marriage analogy to de facto relationships is particularly driven by a concern for women who sacrifice their earning capacity in order to give a primary focus to child-rearing. The generation of women who went through divorce in the 1970s and 1980s were quite likely to have withdrawn from workforce participation entirely either after marriage or at least with the arrival of the first child.[52] These women devoted themselves to the care of the home and family. Women and men had discrete roles, one doing most of the homemaking and parenting while the other brought in the income for the household.

Pure role-divided marriages still exist, but the patterns of life for the majority of mothers now is one in which the care of home and children is combined with workforce participation, with women moving in and out of part-time or full-time work at different stages of their lives.[53] Nonetheless, the common pattern remains for women and men as parents to make differential life-course investments, with fathers' primary investment being in the marketplace of career or self-employed business, while women's life investments are more diversified, and include a major orientation towards the care of children.[54]

---

51 PRA, s 4(5).

52 See for example, SF Berk, *The Gender Factory: The Apportionment of Work in American Households*, Plenum Press, New York 1985.

53 C Hakim, *Work-Lifestyle Choices in the 21st Century: Preference Theory*, OUP, Oxford 2000.

54 See for example, J Baxter, B Hewett and M Haynes, 'Life Course Transitions and Housework: Marriage, Parenthood, and Time on Housework' (2008) 70 *Journal of Marriage and Family* 259.

There is still a need for family property laws which assist and protect the mother whose specialisation in caring for the daily needs of the family represents an indirect investment in the earning capacity of the primary wage-earner. Once the children reach an age at which they are more independent, the mother can, and usually does, alter the pattern of her investments and take a greater role in paid work. But if the relationship breaks down, then she loses out on her investment in her partner's earning capacity if her role is not compensated in some way through a property settlement and/or maintenance.

The case for treating non-marital relationships as marriages when there are no children of the relationship, and when legal title may properly reflect the intentions of the parties to that relationship, is now a very weak one – however much it may have seemed justified many years ago. If family laws across the Western world follow the lead of social security laws, then the organising basis for legal rights and obligations will not be the adult–adult dyad, but the relationship of those adults as parents of dependent children.

The most important reason for equitable distribution laws is to address the financial impacts of parenthood. It therefore makes sense to allow the possibility of maintenance of mothers beyond the provision of child support, irrespective of whether the parents ever lived together. This is a very sensible aspect of New Zealand law which has few parallels in other jurisdictions.[55]

6. CONCLUSION

The question of what relationships should be covered by legislation such as the PRA cannot be answered without considering the rights and obligations that flow therefrom. If the legislation is tightly drawn to provide limited remedies to alter legal title on equitable or restitutionary grounds, as well as making future provision for primary caregivers of children of the relationship, then its reach could be quite extensive. If the legislation provides for property sharing which is based, to a greater or lesser extent, upon community property assumptions, then assimilating de facto relationships with marriages is highly problematic.

Family lawyers have long operated on an assumption that living with someone in an intimate partnership entitles a person to share in the other person's property. There is a 'Robin Hood' element in all of this. It is an assumption that ought to be challenged in the law reform process.

Two years before the enactment of the PRA in New Zealand, Mary Ann Glendon, one of the greatest thinkers about family law in her generation, published an article entitled 'Is There a Future for Separate Property?'[56] Looking

55 Family Proceedings Act 1980 (NZ), s 79.

56 MA Glendon, 'Is There a Future for Separate Property?' (1974) 8 *Family Law Quarterly* 315.

then to a future in which many more married women would be economically independent, she observed:[57]

> 'when the widespread expectation that marriage will last only so long as it performs its function of providing personal fulfillment is put together with the reality of unilateral divorce, a diminished sense of economic responsibility after divorce, the increasing economic independence of married women, and the expansion of social welfare, the resulting state of affairs does not lead inevitably to the sharing of worldly goods …
>
> Seen in this light, the system of separation of assets with the possibility it has always offered for purely voluntary co-ownership may come to have the most appeal for the greatest number of people.'

More than 40 years later, surely this must now be right, at least as far as couples who do not have children together are concerned. Limited remedial provision could be made by statute, if need be, to address situations where retention of legal title would be unjust without some relief based upon equitable or unjust enrichment grounds. However, the marriage analogy ought not to be applied to couples who do not have children together. There is an argument that property sharing ought not to be compulsory even in the marital relationship. Grown-ups can make these decisions for themselves, and they will often choose to place assets in joint names. When there are children, different equities arise – for the parent who has prioritised home and family over career, and for the children who need housing; but to recognise that is to recognise that it is parenthood that is the major justification for asset sharing, not the marriage itself. That involves a major re-conceptualisation of family property law.

57 Ibid, at 327.

CHAPTER 3

WHICH RELATIONSHIPS SHOULD BE INCLUDED IN A PROPERTY SHARING SCHEME?

Margaret Briggs*

* I am grateful to the Otago Faculty of Law Research Assistants, Kyla Mullen IMOT LLB (Hons) and Jonathon Yeldon BFA LLB, for their editorial assistance with this chapter, and to my colleagues Professors Nicola Peart and Mark Henaghan and for their helpful comments on earlier drafts.

1. INTRODUCTION

It is common knowledge that many Western jurisdictions have undergone rapid social change since the 1970s, not least in the context of domestic relationships. Declining marriage rates, high divorce rates, more people living together outside marriage, more single parent families, more childless couples, and more blended families are just some of the influences that have weakened the dominance of the traditional nuclear family.

States have responded in a variety of ways to the shifting demographic trends in their populations, applying different inclusion and exclusion criteria to the types of domestic relationships that are subject to their family property laws. Some jurisdictions continue to regulate the property affairs only of those couples that formally marry, although an increasing number now extend the notion of the 'formal relationship' to registered civil partnership as well as marriage. Other jurisdictions take a more interventionist approach by recognising unregistered cohabitants whose informal relationships function in a 'marriage-like' way, and a few jurisdictions have moved beyond the paradigm of the intimate dyadic relationship by recognising certain platonic domestic relationships such as those between family members, companions, or home sharers.

There are also key jurisdictional differences regarding the types of property arrangements that should apply, involving important questions about the sorts of property that should be subject to sharing between partners and how that property should be shared. These matters are, of necessity, connected to the question of what types of domestic relationships should be recognised, resulting in a complex three-dimensional pattern of variables across different legal systems.

This chapter considers two different methods used to identify the relationships that qualify for relationship property sharing – the 'formal' approach premised on relationship registration, and the 'functional' approach based on how the couple's relationship operates in practical terms. Drawing on the laws in countries including England, Australia, and New Zealand, this chapter suggests that neither approach is ideal – the formal approach no longer accurately reflects modern social trends, excludes too many couples from property sharing, and routinely disadvantages the more financially vulnerable party; the more inclusive functional approach is also open to criticism on grounds of uncertainty because it is not always clear whether a couple is in the sort of informal relationship that justifies property sharing.

As its central focus, the chapter highlights aspects of the writer's home jurisdiction of New Zealand which presents an internationally atypical combination of variables – a broadminded attitude to the types of domestic relationships that should be regulated, coupled with a single rules-based equal sharing regime that applies irrespective of relationship type. Significantly, the New Zealand Law Commission is currently reviewing the jurisdiction's relationship property laws, including the question of what relationships should be covered.[1] The discussion finishes with an examination of the relative merits of New Zealand's one-size-fits-all scheme, considers some potential alternatives to the way that it operates at the present time, but ultimately concludes that, while not perfect, the advantages of the scheme outweigh the disadvantages.

On a final note, the scope of this chapter is limited to a consideration of adult domestic relationships that end during the joint lives of the parties. Other chapters in Part I of this book examine different facets of the 'family' question, including the tensions that arise between succession law and family property law on the death of a spouse or partner,[2] and the importance of children in the context of relationship property schemes.[3] Questions of what sort of property should be subject to sharing and what type of scheme should apply are analysed in Part II and Part III respectively.

2. RELATIONSHIP FORMALISATION AS THE MARKER OF FINANCIAL ENTITLEMENT

2.1. GENERAL

Marriage 'has been at the epicentre of family law' for centuries.[4] In the days when marriage was essential to becoming part of a family, the boundaries of 'family' were unambiguous. 'Family' denoted the traditional nuclear family consisting of two people of opposite gender married to each other and their children. The policy issues were similarly uncomplicated:[5]

> '[T]he status of marriage, predicated on religious teaching, was the defining factor in carrying a cluster of familial rights and responsibilities. Not only were all other forms of partnership or living arrangements "external" to the law, but "why" the status of marriage should be the defining factor was unquestionable.'

1 Law Commission (NZ), *Review of the Property (Relationships) Act 1976* <www.lawcom.govt.nz/our-projects/review-property-relationships-act-1976> accessed 19.04.2017.

2 See N Peart, 'Family Finances on Death of a Spouse or Partner', ch 5, and R Croucher, 'A Lament for "Testator's Family Maintenance" – A Good Idea Gone Wrong? Australian Reflections', ch 6.

3 See N Peart and M Henaghan, 'Children's Interests in Division of Property on Relationship Breakdown', ch 4, and P Parkinson, 'Reconsidering Family Property Law in the Post-Marital Age', ch 2.

4 A Barlow et al, *Cohabitation, Marriage and the Law: Social Change and Legal Reform in the 21st Century*, Hart Publishing, Portland 2005, 91.

5 A Bottomley and S Wong, 'Introduction: Changing Contours of Domestic Life, Family and Law: Caring and Sharing' in A Bottomley and S Wong (eds), *Changing Contours of Domestic Life, Family and Law: Caring and Sharing*, Hart Publishing, Portland 2009, 1.

That marriage was a religious institution was emphasised in the landmark case of *Hyde v Hyde* where Lord Penzance defined marriage 'as understood in Christendom … as the voluntary union for life of one man and one woman'.[6] However, the passage of time has seen the gradual erosion of the ideals espoused in *Hyde* to the point that little of that definition of marriage remains relevant today.[7] Although marriage is still highly valued as an ideal,[8] religion is no longer the only basis for marriage in modern secular society. Nor is marriage regarded by many as a lifelong institution terminated only by the death of one of the spouses. Moreover, in a significant number of countries, marriage is no longer the exclusive preserve of heterosexual couples.[9] Accordingly, 'the decision to marry or cohabit has become more of a personal choice in which the legal significance of the couple's actions does not figure highly, if at all'.[10] A further trend that has challenged the traditional marriage model has been the need for family law to extend its boundaries to recognise all children, whether born in wedlock or not.[11]

Notwithstanding the declining relevance of traditional marriage to many people in the community at large, legislation in most countries continues to favour marriage over less formal relationships such as unmarried cohabitation. Marriage registration is thus a crude but highly effective way to regulate intimate adult relationships, not least in the context of property sharing rights and obligations and, as Anne Barlow et al have observed, there are administrative benefits to be derived from regulating relationships:[12]

> '[A] national system of marriage registration, which clearly and publicly records the ostensibly lifelong commitment made by two married partners to their intimate relationship in a tri-partite contract to which the state itself is the third party, is uniquely able to control the contractual terms in an administratively convenient way.'

In more recent times many Western countries have extended the marriage model to include registered partnerships (same sex and/or opposite sex) and, although in some respects this represents a loosening of traditional values, the same element of state control nonetheless exists. That is, in order to participate in the state-endorsed relationship property scheme, the relationship must first

---

6 *Hyde v Hyde* (1866) LR 1 P&D 130 (HL) at 133.

7 See R Deech, 'Civil Partnership' [2010] *Family Law* 468.

8 A Barlow et al, above n 4 at 85.

9 At the time of writing, same-sex marriage is legally recognised in Argentina, Belgium, Brazil, Canada, Colombia, Denmark, France, Iceland, Ireland, Luxembourg, Mexico, the Netherlands, New Zealand, Norway, Portugal, South Africa, Spain, Sweden, the United Kingdom, the United States, and Uruguay.

10 A Barlow et al, above n 4 at 85.

11 A Bottomley and S Wong, above n 5 at 1.

12 A Barlow et al, above n 4 at 91–92.

comply with the state's relationship registration requirements. Unmarried cohabitants, who for whatever reason fail to register their relationship, continue to fall outside the qualifying criteria. Registered partnership is now recognised in 18 of the 28 European Union countries[13] as well as New Zealand,[14] most states in Australia,[15] and some provinces in Canada.[16]

2.2. ENGLAND

In England and Wales, same-sex couples may formalise their relationship by entering into a registered civil partnership pursuant to the Civil Partnership Act 2004 (UK) and the legal consequences, including ancillary relief,[17] are virtually identical to those available to married couples under the Matrimonial Causes Act 1973 (Eng&W).[18]

England and Wales do not yet provide a property scheme for unregistered cohabitants, notwithstanding public surveys indicating that a substantial majority of people think that cohabitants should have access to financial relief at the end of their relationship.[19] In 2005 the Government tasked the Law Commission (Eng&W) with reviewing the financial consequences for cohabiting couples on relationship breakdown. In its Report published in 2007 the Commission rejected arguments that cohabitants should have access to exactly the same remedies as married couples and civil partners. It highlighted the problem that whereas some cohabitants have relationships very similar to those of spouses, others do not. Rather, 'there is a broad range of cohabiting

13 Austria, Belgium, Croatia, the Czech Republic, Denmark, Germany, Finland, France, Greece, Hungary, Ireland, Luxembourg, Malta, Netherlands, Slovenia, some regions of Spain, Sweden, and the United Kingdom. In 17 of those countries same-sex couples may register their partnerships, and five countries permit both opposite and same-sex couples to register: European Commission, *Property Effects of Marriage and Registered Partnership* <http://ec.europa.eu/justice/civil/family-matters/marriage/index_en.htm> accessed 19.04.2017. In Sweden, marriage for same-sex partners has been recognised since 2009 when registered partnerships were abolished; though they continue to exist if concluded before May 2009: OECD, *OECD Family Database* <www.oecd.org/els/family/database.htm> accessed 19.04.2017.

14 Civil Union Act 2004 (NZ).

15 Civil Unions Act 2012 (ACT), Relationships Register Act 2010 (NSW), Civil Partnerships Act 2011 (Qld), Relationships Act 2003 (Tas), Relationships Act 2008 (Vic), Statutes Amendment (Registered Relationships) Act 2017 (SA).

16 Vital Statistics Act 1989 (Nova Scotia); Civil Code of Quebec, Book Two, Title I.1, Arts 5.21.1–5.21.19; Common-Law Partners' Property and Related Amendments Act 2002 (Manitoba); Adult Interdependent Relationships Act 2002 (Alberta).

17 Civil Partnership Act 2004 (UK), s 72.

18 Following the enactment of the Marriage (Same Sex Couples) Act 2013 (Eng&W) any couple registered in a civil partnership can convert their partnership into a marriage: s 9.

19 See the discussion in Law Commission (Eng&W), *Cohabitation: The Financial Consequences of Relationship Breakdown*, Law Com No. 307, 2007, [1.4].

relationships, exhibiting different degrees of commitment and interdependence. And cohabitants have not made the distinctive legal and public commitment that marriage entails.'[20] The scheme proposed by the Commission was therefore to be different from that which applies between spouses on divorce. The Commission recommended an opt-out scheme[21] based on qualifying contributions to the parties' relationship which had given rise to certain enduring consequences at the point of separation.[22] Nor would the mere fact of cohabitation activate a presumption of entitlement to share in any pool of property. Rather, the scheme would be limited to cohabitants who had had a child together or who had lived together for a certain length of time. The Report did not make a specific recommendation as to what the minimum duration requirement should be, but suggested that a period of between two and five years would be appropriate.[23]

The Government deferred making a decision on the Commission's recommendations until after the completion of a future review of the impact of the Scottish legislation on cohabitation,[24] but later announced that the research findings did not provide a sufficient basis for changing the law and that the Government would not progress the Commission's recommendations in the then current Parliamentary term. Unless and until that position alters, the steadily rising numbers of unmarried cohabitants living together outside marriage or civil partnership[25] must continue to rely on the general law, especially that of constructive trust, to resolve their property disputes.[26]

---

20 Law Commission (Eng&W), *Cohabitation: The Financial Consequences of Relationship Breakdown: Executive Summary*, Law Com No. 307, 2007, [1.10]. See also Law Commission (Eng&W), *Cohabitation: The Financial Consequences of Relationship Breakdown – A Consultation Paper*, Law Com CP 179, 2006. For a critical analysis of the Law Commission Report see FR Burton, 'Formalised Cohabitation: A Critical and Comparative Study of an Element of English Law in a Normative Regime', PhD thesis, Liverpool John Moores University, 2015 <http://researchonline.ljmu.ac.uk/4446/1/158301_burtonphd.pdf> accessed 19.04.2017.

21 Law Commission (Eng&W), *Executive Summary*, above n 20 at [1.16].

22 Ibid, at [1.17].

23 Ibid, at [1.14].

24 Unlike England and Wales, the Family Law (Scotland) Act 2006 provides a scheme for unmarried cohabitants that enables a cohabitant to apply to the court for financial provision at the end of the relationship to remedy any injustice caused by contributions made or disadvantages suffered during the relationship.

25 Cohabiting couple families were the fastest growing family type in the UK between 1996 and 2016, more than doubling from 1.5 million families to 3.3 million families: Office for National Statistics, *Families and Households in the UK: 2016*, 4 November 2016 <www.ons.gov.uk/peoplepopulationandcommunity/birthsdeathsandmarriages/families/bulletins/familiesandhouseholds/2016> accessed 19.04.2017.

26 See *Stack v Dowden* [2007] UKHL 17, [2007] 2 AC 432; *Jones v Kernott* [2011] UKSC 53, [2012] 1 AC 776.

3. RELATIONSHIP FUNCTIONALITY AS THE MARKER OF FINANCIAL ENTITLEMENT

3.1. GENERAL

A cogent reason for including unmarried cohabitants in a relationship property scheme is functional equivalence – that is, many unmarried couple relationships *function* in much the same way as marriage or civil partnership despite lacking their *formal* attributes, and so should be subject to the same property rights and obligations. A number of family law theorists argue that inflexible distinctions between relationships no longer provide a rational basis for legal policy, but that what is required is a more inclusive method of determining when and how adult personal relationships are recognised in the law.[27]

The functional approach argues that relationship status turns on the performance of relationship functions, not the fulfilment of formalised legal status. It identifies the essential characteristics of, or functions performed by, the paradigmatic relationship (the nuclear marital family) and determines whether an alternative relationship shares those characteristics.[28] If it does, it follows that the alternative relationship should be subject to the same rights and responsibilities as those 'accorded to the conventionally recognised relationship'.[29] 'The primary goal of this approach is to gain inclusion of non-conventional family forms in the definition of "family" so that they may receive benefits enjoyed by modern marital families.'[30]

This is also linked to arguments that state intervention can be justified on grounds of protecting the weaker party.[31] Extending relationship property rights for unmarried cohabitants therefore has the practical advantage of helping to protect the more vulnerable party to the relationship. Bill Atkin and Wendy Parker explain that this tends to be a gradual process. The authors note that although the legal responses to the new societal matrix have varied in different jurisdictions, they have often followed a pattern that begins with de facto and/or same-sex relationships being illegal, which is then followed by a period

27 See, for example, B Cossman and B Ryder, 'What is Marriage-Like Like? The Relevance of Conjugality' (2001) 18 *Canadian Journal of Family Law* 269. Some theorists continue to take a 'pro-marriage' stance: see for example, LD Wardle, 'Deconstructing Family: A Critique of the American Law Institute's "Domestic Partners" Proposal' [2001] *Brigham Young University Law Review* 1189.

28 V Hamilton, 'Mistaking Marriage for Social Policy' (2004) 11 *Virginia Journal of Social Policy and the Law* 307, 319–20.

29 Ibid, at 320.

30 Ibid, at 320 (footnote omitted).

31 See A Barlow et al, above n 4 at 114 ff.

of more neutral tolerance and acceptance, which later shifts to the introduction of protective measures and, occasionally:[32]

> 'moves on to a complete equating of these relationships with marriage. Common threads in the different regimes are that the parties are not married and that the law sets out to protect the more vulnerable party.'

Anne Barlow et al argue that in modern society the labels attached to different relationships may mean less than they once did. Rather, current social trends reveal a 'functional convergence' of married and unmarried cohabitation whereby:[33]

> 'Unmarried cohabitation has taken on many of the functions of marriage, displacing shotgun weddings and formal engagements as well as providing companionship, emotional support, sexual intimacy, financial interdependence and a site for homemaking and parenting.'

Correspondingly, marriage is becoming more like cohabitation in that 'it is increasingly a negotiated partnership, not necessarily involving financial dependency, which may be terminated almost at will'.[34]

The rising incidence of cohabitation outside marriage is a trend experienced in many Western countries.[35] A number of jurisdictions including Australia,[36] Scotland,[37] and New Zealand[38] now extend property rights to unmarried couples in informal unregistered relationships on relationship breakdown,[39] although there are marked differences in how individual jurisdictions have gone about implementing property sharing laws for cohabitants. The following discussion briefly examines the system in place in Australia, before focusing on New Zealand's experience.

---

32 B Atkin and W Parker, *Relationship Property in New Zealand*, 2nd ed, LexisNexis, Wellington 2009, 24 (footnote omitted).

33 A Barlow et al, above n 4 at 86.

34 Ibid.

35 See the discussion in K Kiernan, 'The Rise of Cohabitation and Childbearing Outside Marriage in Western Europe' (2001) 15 *International Journal of Law, Policy and the Family* 1. See also P Parkinson, above n 3 at 16–18, for a discussion of trends across a number of jurisdictions. For further information on international family trends see also OECD, above n 13.

36 See 3.2 below.

37 Family Law (Scotland) Act 2006. See F McCarthy, 'Cohabitation: Lessons from North of the Border?' (2011) 23 *Child and Family Law Quarterly* 277. For further discussion of overseas trends see B Atkin and W Parker, above n 32 at 24–27; G Lind, *Common Law Marriage: A Legal Institution for Cohabitation*, OUP, New York 2008, ch 12.

38 See 3.3 below.

39 For a comprehensive discussion see G Lind, above n 37.

3.2. AUSTRALIA

Australia was in the vanguard of countries to recognise relationship property protections for unmarried cohabitants. Prior to 2009 each of the states and territories applied their own laws to deal with the financial consequences of the breakdown of de facto relationships. New South Wales was the first state to recognise property protections for unmarried cohabitants ('de facto' partners) when it enacted the De Facto Relationships Act 1984 (NSW). The Family Law Act 1975 (Cth) has applied to de facto partners since 1 March 2009[40] when the individual states and territories (with the exception of Western Australia)[41] referred their powers regarding de facto relationships to the federal jurisdiction. The Family Law Act (Cth) now allows opposite-sex and same-sex de facto couples 'living together on a genuine domestic basis'[42] access to the same property rights as married couples.

As in England, a discretionary system of property sharing applies at the end of the relationship. On separation, each spouse or partner retains ownership of the property to which they have legal title, but the court has the discretion to alter a couple's property interests on relationship breakdown if it is satisfied that, in all the circumstances, it is just and equitable to make the order.[43] For a de facto partner to seek an order for property settlement, the court must be satisfied that the de facto relationship lasted for at least two years, or there is a child of the de facto relationship, or that failure to make an order would result in serious injustice due to the substantial contributions made by one party, or the relationship is or was registered under a prescribed law of a state or territory.[44]

In addition to de facto relationships, a majority of jurisdictions in Australia now also provide property rights for people in close domestic relationships other than marriage or a de facto relationship, whether or not related by family.[45] Thus, platonic relationships such as those between parents and children, siblings, people who share a residence, and close companions can also be treated as the functional equivalent of married spouses and de facto couples. Each state and territory operates a discretionary system of property sharing although, unlike de facto relationships, state powers in relation to close domestic relationships have not been referred to the federal jurisdiction. Although the legislation in each

---

40 In South Australia, since 01.07.2010.

41 Family Court Act 1997 (WA), pt 5A.

42 Family Law Act 1975 (Cth), s 4AA(1)(c).

43 Family Law Act 1975 (Cth), ss 79(2) and 90SM(3). See R Croucher, above n 2, for a discussion of the Australian system.

44 Family Law Act 1975 (Cth), s 90SB.

45 Domestic Relationships Act 1994 (ACT), Property (Relationships) Act 1984 (NSW), Relationships Act 2003 (Tas), Domestic Partners Property Act 1996 (SA), Relationships Act 2008 (Vic). Alberta (Canada), Belgium, and Norway also recognise domestic relationships.

jurisdiction is worded differently, each shares in common the requirement that the relationship is one where the parties provide care and support to each other, and each jurisdiction recognises that domestic relationships can exist between family members or between unrelated parties. All of the jurisdictions exclude relationships where the care and support is provided for a fee or payment, such as under an employment relationship between the persons or on behalf of an organisation such as a government agency. The minimum period that the parties must be in a domestic relationship ranges between two[46] and three years.[47] In some jurisdictions there is no requirement that the parties must live together under the same roof,[48] and some also provide the option of relationship registration schemes.[49]

3.3. A NEW ZEALAND CASE STUDY

3.3.1. Historical Context

Until 2001 New Zealand followed a conventionally formalistic approach to qualifying relationships with effect that the only relationship that gave rise to property sharing rights and obligations was marriage.[50] However, significant shifts in the composition of the traditional family unit in the last decades of the twentieth century, including rapidly increasing numbers of unmarried couples living in de facto relationships, led the policymakers and legislators to question whether the existing law, the Matrimonial Property Act 1976 (NZ), supported the sorts of informal living arrangements that were becoming widespread in the community, and whether it was fair to continue to exclude those couples who, for whatever reason, had not formalised their relationships.[51]

A brief snapshot of New Zealand's demographic data reveals a rapidly changing social landscape in the last four decades. In 2015 the marriage rate (including civil union) was 11.1 per 1,000 head of population aged 16 years and over. That figure is less than one quarter of the 1971 peak when the rate reached

---

46 ACT, New South Wales, Tasmania, and Victoria.

47 South Australia.

48 ACT, Tasmania, and Victoria. The Relationships Act 2008 (Vic), s 5, goes so far as to expressly state that a relationship may exist whether or not the parties 'are living under the same roof'.

49 Relationships Act 2003 (Tas), s 5(4), Relationships Act 2008 (Vic), s 10(3)(ab).

50 Self-evidently, the Matrimonial Property Act 1963 (NZ) and the Matrimonial Property Act 1976 (NZ) only applied to married couples.

51 For an excellent account of the pathway to legislative recognition of de facto relationships see B Atkin, 'Family Property' in M Henaghan and B Atkin (eds), *Family Law Policy in New Zealand*, 4th ed, LexisNexis, Wellington 2013, 209 at 213–18.

45.5 per 1,000 head of adult population.[52] In 2015 the divorce rate (including civil union) was 9.3 divorces for every 1,000 couples.[53] The rates of unmarried partners living together have risen very sharply since the 1980s. In 1981 just 3.8 per cent of people lived with a partner to whom they were not married. By 1996 the number had climbed to 8.5 per cent, and by 2006 the figure had reached 20 per cent.[54] The most recent New Zealand Census conducted in 2013 records another modest rise to approximately 21.5 per cent.[55] Ex-nuptial birth rates have also risen. In 2015, 46.7 per cent of births were to parents who were not married or in a civil union at the time of the birth.[56] In 1971 only 13.9 per cent of births were ex-nuptial.

The Property (Relationships) Amendment Act 2001, which substantially amended the Matrimonial Property Act 1976, marked a turning point in New Zealand family property legislation. One of the most fundamental changes was the extension of the legislation's equal property sharing regime to heterosexual and same-sex unmarried cohabitants ('de facto' couples) in qualifying relationships of three years or longer.[57] While the inclusion of de facto partners was a response to the demographic shifts in the population outlined

---

52 Statistics New Zealand, *Marriages, Civil Unions, and Divorces: Year ended December 2015 – Commentary* <www.stats.govt.nz/browse_for_stats/people_and_communities/marriages-civil-unions-and-divorces/MarriagesCivilUnionsandDivorces_HOTPYeDec15/Commentary.aspx> accessed 19.04.2017.

53 Divorce rates rose sharply following the introduction of the Family Proceedings Act 1980 (NZ), which allowed for the dissolution of marriage on the grounds of irreconcilable differences. Analysis of divorce statistics by year of marriage shows that 36% of New Zealanders who married in 1990 had divorced before their silver wedding anniversary (25 years), compared with 34% for those who married in 1980, and 28% for those who married in 1970: Statistics New Zealand, above n 52.

54 M Henaghan, 'Legally Defining the Family' in M Henaghan and B Atkin (eds), *Family Law Policy in New Zealand*, 4th ed, LexisNexis, Wellington 2013, 11. For a discussion of international trends see B Atkin and W Parker, *Relationship Property in New Zealand*, 2nd ed, LexisNexis, Wellington 2009, 24–27.

55 Statistics New Zealand, *2013 Census Totals by Topic* <www.stats.govt.nz/Census/2013-census/data-tables/total-by-topic.aspx> accessed 19.04.2017.

56 Statistics New Zealand, *Infoshare* <www.stats.govt.nz/infoshare/> accessed 19.04.2017. There were 28,527 ex-nuptial births in 2015 from a total of 61,038 births. These statistics were gathered by selecting the 'Population' folder, the 'Births – VSB' subfolder, and the page titled 'Live births by nuptiality (Maori and total population) (Annual-Dec)'. Note that this data was last updated on 16.08.2016 and has been randomly rounded to three.

57 The Property (Relationships) Amendment Act 2001 (NZ) came into force on 01.02.2002. De facto relationships that ended before that date are not covered by the Act: s 4C. De facto relationships of less than 3 years are not covered (s 4(5)) unless the Court is satisfied that there is a child of the de facto relationship or that the applicant has made a substantial contribution to the de facto relationship, and the Court is further satisfied that failure to make the order would result in serious injustice (s 14A(2)). If so, the share of each de facto partner in the relationship property is to be determined in accordance with his or her contribution to the de facto relationship (s 14A(3)).

above, it was nonetheless a significant change to the law, and one that was arguably ahead of the expectations and desires of some parts of the community at that time. The amendments were initially contained in two separate bills, the Matrimonial Property Amendment Bill 1998 (54) and the De Facto Relationships (Property) Bill 1998 (108-1). There were significant differences between the rights of married couples and de facto partners under the two bills and there was no provision at all for claims by same-sex partners. However in 2000, a newly elected Labour–Alliance coalition government altered the Matrimonial Property Amendment Bill[58] to include heterosexual and same-sex de facto couples, giving them the same rules for the division of property. This indicated a critical new policy direction that reflected the view that there was little to distinguish the nature of these relationships and the property issues they faced.[59] The legislation was re-named the Property (Relationships) Act 1976 (NZ) ('PRA') to recognise the wider range of relationships covered.[60] Parliament bowed to public pressure over terminology, however, accepting that the special status of marriage ought to continue to be respected notwithstanding the inclusion of opposite and same-sex de facto relationships within the Act. The neutral expressions 'relationship' and 'partner' were abandoned in favour of the terms 'marriage' and 'de facto relationship', and 'spouse' and 'de facto partner'.

Following the enactment of the Civil Union Act 2004 (NZ), the PRA was further amended to include registered heterosexual and same-sex civil unions.[61] Much like the inclusion of de facto couples a few years before, the Civil Union Bill proved controversial.[62] Some opponents argued that the next legislative step would be 'gay marriage'. In 2013 New Zealand did eventually amend the

---

58 Matrimonial Property Amendment Bill 2000 and Supplementary Order Paper no 25 (109-3).

59 See N Peart, M Briggs and M Henaghan, *Relationship Property on Death*, Thomson Brookers, Wellington 2004, 15–16. The proposal to give de facto couples equal property rights to married couples met with strong opposition. The Select Committee received hundreds of submissions opposing the inclusion of de facto and same-sex couples in the same Act as married couples.

60 Property (Relationships) Amendment Act 2001 (NZ), s 5(1). A proposal in the Matrimonial Property Bill 1975 to extend the new Act to de facto relationships met with vocal opposition on the grounds that the recognition of these relationships would devalue marriage, and it was dropped before the Bill was passed into law: see N Peart, 'Towards a Concept of Family Property in New Zealand' (1996) 10 *International Journal of Law, Policy and the Family* 105, 113.

61 Civil Union Act 2004 (NZ), s 4.

62 The Justice and Electoral Select Committee received over 3,000 public submissions on the Bill, more than 80% of which were opposed to the law being passed: Civil Union Bill 2004 (149-2) (Commentary), 3. A common concern was that the Bill would negatively impact on the number of people choosing to marry and that marriage was being systematically eroded: Civil Union Bill 2004 (149-2) (Commentary), 11.

Marriage Act 1955 (NZ) to provide for marriage equality, and 'marriage' is now defined as 'the union of 2 people, regardless of their sex, sexual orientation, or gender identity'.[63]

Despite the enactment of the Civil Union Act (NZ), marriage continues to be by far the most widely preferred mode of formalising a relationship in New Zealand. In the years between 2005 and 2016, there were 276,129 marriages registered in New Zealand. By comparison, only 3,402 civil unions had been registered in the same time period.[64] With the passing of the marriage equality laws in 2013, a small number of all marriages now include same-sex marriages. The availability of same-sex marriage has also had a dramatic effect on the numbers entering into civil unions. In 2014 (the first full year in which data has been collected since the introduction of same-sex marriage in 2013), just 63 couples entered a civil union in New Zealand, compared to the peak of 429 registered civil unions in 2006. Similarly, in 2015 and 2016 respectively, just 66 and 60 couples entered a civil union in New Zealand.[65]

3.3.2. *De Facto Relationships*

Of the triumvirate of relationships included in the PRA, it is the informal de facto relationship that sits apart from the other two. The PRA defines a de facto relationship as a relationship between two persons over the age of 18, who live together as a couple and who are not married to, or in a civil union with, one another.[66] The 'central plank'[67] – the marker of functionality – is that the parties

---

63 Marriage Act 1955 (NZ), s 2(1), as amended by the Marriage (Definition of Marriage) Amendment Act 2013 (NZ), s 5. Same-sex marriage has impacted on the numbers entering into civil unions. In 2014 the number of couples entering a civil union dropped to 63: <www.stats.govt.nz/browse_for_stats/people_and_communities/marriages-civil-unions-and-divorces/CivilUnionsAndMarriages_HOTPDec14qtr.aspx> accessed 19.04.2017.

64 Of the civil unions registered, 2,619 were to same-sex partners and 783 to opposite-sex partners. Of those, 2,796 were registered to New Zealand residents (2,100 to same-sex partners and 669 to opposite-sex partners), and the remaining 600 to overseas residents (531 to same-sex partners and 78 to opposite-sex partners): Statistics New Zealand, *Infoshare* <www.stats.govt.nz/infoshare/> accessed 12.05.2017. These statistics were gathered by selecting the 'Population' folder, the 'Marriages Civil Unions and Divorces – VSM' subfolder, and the page titled 'Marriages and civil unions by relationship type, NZ and overseas residents (Annual-Dec)'. Note that this data was last updated on 03.05.2017 and has been randomly rounded to three. Further note that while these statistics do not include separate information for female same-sex couples and male same-sex couples, earlier statistics did: <www.stats.govt.nz/browse_for_stats/people_and_communities/marriages-civil-unions-and-divorces/CivilUnionsAndMarriages_HOTPDec14qtr.aspx> accessed 17.05.2017.

65 Ibid.

66 Property (Relationships) Act 1976 (NZ) ('PRA'), s 2D(1).

67 *L v P* [2008] NZFLR 401 (HC) at [44] per Asher J: '[T]he central plank of a de facto relationship is the parties living together'. Note also that the effect of the requirement that both partners must be 18 years is that the PRA does not recognise the relationship until the younger of the two partners turns 18. If a relationship ends before the younger partner turns 18, the Act does

live together as a 'couple'. In determining whether two persons live together as a 'couple', the PRA provides that all the circumstances of the relationship are to be taken into account, including (as is relevant in a particular case): the duration of the relationship; the nature and extent of common residence; whether or not a sexual relationship exists; the degree of financial dependence or interdependence, and any arrangements for financial support, between the parties; the ownership, use, and acquisition of property; the degree of mutual commitment to a shared life; the care and support of children; the performance of household duties; and the reputation and public aspects of the relationship.[68] No finding in respect of any of these matters is regarded as necessary, and a court is entitled to have regard to such matters, and to attach such weight to any matter, as may seem appropriate to the court in the circumstances of the case.[69]

New Zealand copied the phrase 'live together as a couple', and the criteria referred to above from the New South Wales Property (Relationships) Legislation Amendment Act 1999.[70] But, in one important respect, New Zealand has transplanted the Australian definition into a very different legislative environment. In contrast to Australia, which operates a discretionary system where the courts may alter a couple's property interests based on principles of justice and equity, the PRA is a rule-based scheme akin to a deferred community of acquests. New Zealand first introduced the rules-based regime in the Matrimonial Property Act 1976 (NZ). The 1976 Act replaced the earlier Matrimonial Property Act 1963 (NZ), which was a discretionary scheme whereby the courts redistributed the property of spouses according to their contributions to the property.[71] The changes made in 1976 were designed to avoid very unequal property divisions that almost invariably disadvantaged wives under the old 1963 legislation. In contrast, the PRA treats marriage, civil union, and de facto relationships as partnerships to which both parties are presumed to have made equal contributions, and the parties should therefore share equally in the fruits or assets of the partnership unless they have contracted out of the Act or one of the narrow exceptions applies.[72]

The extension of the property sharing rights available under the PRA to de facto partners has given rise to certain problems. First, it is not always easy to determine whether a couple is in a qualifying relationship given that de facto

---

not apply. While most very young partners are unlikely to have much property to dispute unless they are the recipients of inheritances or the like, it seems unsound in both principle and policy to exclude a section of the population from the Act for no good reason.

68 PRA, s 2D(2).

69 PRA, s 2D(3).

70 The Family Law Act 1975 (Cth) now also applies the same New South Wales criteria in '[w]orking out if persons have a relationship as a couple': s 4AA(2)–(5).

71 For a discussion see *Brookers Family Law – Family Property* (looseleaf ed, Brookers) at PRIntro.01.

72 N Peart, above n 60.

relationships come in all shapes and sizes, with varying degrees of commitment, interdependency, and so forth. Secondly, determining whether the couple was 'living together as a couple' inevitably involves the courts in retrospective decision-making about the relationship.

3.3.2.1. Judicial Discretion

While there may be good grounds in functional theory for according de facto partners the same property rights as married couples and civil union partners, the practical reality of importing de facto relationships into the PRA – rules-based legislation originally designed in the 1970s to resolve property disputes between married couples – reveals a number of difficulties. There is no doubt that the PRA has made the legal position for many de facto couples less precarious and more predictable on relationship breakdown than under the previous law, where parties with a property grievance had to resort to other measures such as asserting a constructive trust.[73] But in some of the less conventional de facto case scenarios,[74] determining the existence and/or duration of the relationship is a complex task and can frustrate one of the avowed principles of the PRA: 'that questions … about relationship property should be resolved as inexpensively, simply, and speedily as is consistent with justice.'[75]

Marriage and civil union are registered legal states, have a definite starting point, and are entered into through conscious choice, whereas de facto relationships are informal, tend to develop gradually, and more often than not have no identifiable start date. The waters are often muddied, however, where a marriage or a civil union is immediately preceded by a de facto relationship between the parties, in which case the de facto relationship must be treated as if it were part of the marriage or civil union. In this context, the start date for the marriage or the civil union is the start date of the de facto relationship.[76]

It is a question of fact and degree for the court to decide if a couple was in a qualifying de facto relationship and if so, when it began and when it ended.[77]

---

73 See *Lankow v Rose* [1995] 1 NZLR 277 (CA).

74 While the writer is not aware of any studies on the proportion of cases where a problem arises in relation to the existence of the relationship, anecdotally, they appear to be in the minority.

75 PRA, s 1N(d).

76 PRA, ss 2B and 2BAA.

77 Note that the same definition of de facto relationship is not currently applied in all legislation. Section 29A(1)(a) of the Interpretation Act 1999 (NZ) provides that a de facto relationship is a relationship between two people who 'live together as a couple in a relationship in the nature of marriage or civil union'. The definition was inserted by the Interpretation Amendment Act 2005 (NZ), and applies to statutes that do not contain a definition of de facto relationship (s 4). The result of the two different definitions is that a couple might be in a de facto relationship in certain facets of their lives (eg a property dispute

A substantial body of case law has developed around what it means to 'live together as a couple', with the courts consistently emphasising that a general and not overly technical methodology is required. In one leading case the Court noted that the approach must be broad, with various factors to be weighed up in an evaluative task, similar to those the courts are frequently called upon to undertake when drawing conclusions from circumstantial evidence.[78] The task requires the application of common sense and '[i]t is the cumulative weight of all factors whether specified in the Act or not … which is decisive.'[79]

Crucially, the case law discloses conspicuous variations in de facto couples' personal circumstances and living arrangements. One judge recognised as much, commenting:[80]

> 'By their very nature, disputes … will often arise out of the unconventional living arrangements of particular individuals. To some extent, there will always be the problem of trying to fit a square peg (representing the parties' choices about their own living arrangements) into a round hole (representing the concept of a *de facto* relationship, for the purposes of the Act). Nevertheless, even in an unusual relationship, the law requires a Court to evaluate the evidence to determine whether the legal threshold is met.'

The courts have had to make difficult decisions in different factual contexts, and in borderline cases outcomes can be somewhat unpredictable. Examples of the 'unconventional living arrangements' referred to above include cases where an applicant has asserted the existence of a de facto relationship where the couple has maintained a high level of independence such as living apart in separate dwellings for at least part of the relationship,[81] where there is no sexual relationship,[82] or where the relationship is more in the nature

---

involving the PRA) but not in a de facto relationship in other aspects of their lives (eg for welfare benefit purposes under the Social Security Act 1964 (NZ)).

78 *Scragg v Scott* [2006] NZFLR 1076 (HC) at [64].

79 Ibid, at [64]. In *B v F* [2010] NZFLR 67 (HC) at [51], Heath J warned judges against reaching final judgments 'by an overly-mechanical application of non-exhaustive statutory criteria'. In *L v P*, above n 67 at [36], Asher J cautioned that '[t]he factors in s 2D(2) … should not be allowed to assume primacy on their own as qualifiers for a de facto relationship.' See also *S v M* HC Wellington CIV-2006-485-1940, 24 May 2007; *Benseman v Foster* (2006) 25 FRNZ 803 (HC), also reported as *Benseman v Ball* [2007] NZFLR 127 (HC).

80 *B v F*, above n 79 at [54] per Heath J.

81 See *Scragg v Scott*, above n 78; *G v B* [2006] NZFLR 1047 (HC); *B v F*, above n 79 at [61].

82 See *Horsfield v Giltrap* (2001) 20 FRNZ 404 (CA), where the partners maintained separate homes and abstained from a sexual relationship because of their religious beliefs, but spent most of their non-working waking hours together, were emotionally dependent on each other, ran a joint investment portfolio, and had a relationship lasting 22 years. Although decided just prior to the enactment of the PRA, the High Court in *Scragg v Scott*, above n 78, commented that the relationship in *Horsfield v Giltrap* would have qualified as a de facto relationship under the PRA.

of lovers,[83] or companions.[84] Arguments that some married couples and registered civil partners may in fact conduct their relationships in an equally unconventional manner are beside the point because evidence of functionality is unimportant when there is objectively identifiable proof of the registered relationship. Hence, the functionality of the supposed stereotypical marital relationship against which an informal cohabiting relationship is to be tested may, at least in some cases, be more of an ideal than a reality. Frankie McCarthy aptly observes:[85]

> 'Couples in formalised adult relationships do not conduct themselves in a uniform manner. Whilst some spouses and civil partners may own property together, have a sexual relationship and co-parent children, none of these factors is essential to the existence of the marriage or partnership. A husband and wife who choose to live apart and speak rarely are just as married as spouses who spend each day together. This notion is reinforced by our modern law of marriage and civil partnership, which has stripped away most of the historical obligations owed by spouses to one another, leaving only a minimal obligation to aliment and title to claim financial provision should the relationship end. The only characteristic which all spouses and civil partners necessarily have in common is that they have formally registered their relationship. In other words, the one characteristic shared by all spouses and partners is the very characteristic that cohabitants by definition do not share.'

As noted earlier, the Law Commission (Eng&W) expressed similar concerns when it rejected arguments that unmarried couples should have exactly the same remedies as married couples and civil partners. It noted that the range of cohabiting relationships is very broad and exhibits 'different degrees of

---

83 Numerous examples exist: *DEBW v EFP* FC New Plymouth FAM-2010-043-928, 18 May 2011 at [86], where the Court held that the relationship was 'one of close friends who have cared for each other'; *PH v GH* [2013] NZHC 443, [2013] NZFLR 387 at [46], where 'the overall tenor of the relationship [during the relevant period] was of a mature "dating" or "boyfriend/girlfriend" type relationship'; *Coll v West* FC Morrinsville FAM-2009-039-160, 26 April 2010, where the Court rejected the respondent's claim that the applicant was no more than a boarder whom she took in out of financial need. Even a very lengthy relationship may fall short of what is required for a de facto relationship. In *Greig v Hutchison* [2016] NZCA 479, [2016] NZFLR 905 at [81], the Court of Appeal concluded there was no qualifying de facto relationship contemporaneous with the 47-year marriage of the respondent and his wife, notwithstanding that the alleged de facto relationship had endured for 37 years. Even after all that time the Court found that there was an insufficient degree of mutual commitment to a shared life to support the existence of a de facto relationship. See also *Chapman v P* [2010] NZFLR 855 (HC); *C v S* FC Dunedin FAM-2005-012-157, 28 September 2006.

84 The notion of de facto partnership is also potentially open to opportunism, not the least in cases where the elderly or physically disabled take another person into their home on terms that may begin on a business footing but subsequently develop into a closer relationship. The elderly and disabled may be at particular risk in this context, having neither the health nor the energy to resist the claim, leading to them cut their losses and opt for a settlement rather than go through the stress and uncertainty of court proceedings.

85 F McCarthy, 'Defining Cohabitation' (2014) 31 *Scots Law Times* 143, 143.

commitment and interdependence'.[86] The Law Commission was also aware that 'cohabitants have not made the distinctive legal and public commitment' that marriage and civil partnership entail.[87]

3.3.2.2. Retrospectivity

In addition to the judicial discretion aspect of de facto relationships, the court must also engage in a process of retrospective decision-making:[88]

> 'Marriage and civil unions are opt-in relationships in which the commencement date is known, but the law may impose the legal status of a de facto relationship retrospectively upon parties whose relationship gradually and without conscious election assumed that character.'

The concern is that if an individual does not know that he or she is in a de facto relationship and subject to the PRA until the court decides that is the case, the individual cannot take pre-emptive measures to protect his or her property by, for example, contracting out of the Act. The prospective quality of marriage and civil union mean that they do not suffer from the same 'element of surprise'. Marriage has always carried some proprietary consequences, even if only to impose maintenance obligations on separation, and spouses can reasonably be held to expect consequences will flow from the change of status. Similarly, a civil union is a registered relationship and the parties will normally have put their minds to the property consequences of entering the union, or at least be aware that the change in status will have proprietary consequences.

Whereas people formally opt in to marriages and civil unions, they generally only drift[89] into de facto relationships, and this aspect may make all the difference to a person's awareness of their property rights and obligations. To apply an opt-out sharing regime such as the PRA to de facto relationships arguably creates unfairness if one does not know there is a law from which one may opt out. Such an uncertain pathway into a rules-based equal property sharing regime therefore creates an awkward mix of discretion and inflexibility.

3.3.2.3. Postscript – Relationships not Covered in New Zealand

While it is correct that New Zealand 'stands out on the international stage for its statutory equating of different types of relationship',[90] New Zealand has thus

[86] Law Commission (Eng&W), *Executive Summary*, above n 20 at [1.10].
[87] Ibid, at [1.10].
[88] *DM v MP* [2012] NZHC 503, [2012] NZFLR 385 at [23] per Miller J.
[89] B Atkin, 'Family Property' in M Henaghan and B Atkin (eds), *Family Law Policy in New Zealand*, 4th ed, LexisNexis, Wellington, 2013, 216.
[90] B Atkin and W Parker, above n 32 at 52.

far restricted relationship recognition to people living together in 'marriage-like' or 'intimate couple' relationships. Unlike Australia, people in close domestic relationships such as a parent and an adult child, siblings,[91] or platonic housemates, are excluded from the rights and obligations imposed by the PRA. If the inclusion of de facto relationships in the Act is taken as state acknowledgement that they are functionally indistinguishable from marriage despite lacking the formal attributes of a marriage then, by extension, the functional approach could also allow the case to be made that close domestic relationships are, in many ways, the normative equivalent to marriage and marriage-like relationships. As one writer has fittingly observed: 'Sex is expendable, but other aspects of domesticity are required.'[92] A sexual relationship is a relevant consideration under the PRA – an important one, even[93] – but it is not a precondition for a de facto relationship. This arguably supports recognition of domestic relationships in New Zealand, since all the other criteria listed in the legislation support a functional approach and can be carried out by non-conjugal domestic partners just as they can by de facto partners.[94] Bill Atkin has argued that it is somewhat anomalous that other domestic relationships such as family ones have not been brought within the scope of the PRA:[95]

> 'given that the focus is now firmly on the law of property, rather than the nature of the relationship, and is illustrated by the change of name from the *Matrimonial Property Act* to the *Property (Relationships) Act*.'

There would, admittedly, be practical objections to extending the PRA to non-intimate domestic partners. One concern would be that their inclusion would add more complications to the already difficult decision-making the courts engage in regarding de facto relationships. Moreover, whether the current gap in the law should be regarded as a matter of concern depends, at

---

91 See *Re Cotton (deceased)* HC Dunedin CP18/00, 5 April 2001; *Burden v United Kingdom* (2008) 47 EHRR 38 (Grand Chamber, ECHR).

92 LA Rosenbury, 'Friends with Benefits?' (2007) 106 *Michigan Law Review* 189, 222.

93 B Atkin and W Parker, above n 32 at 42.

94 There has been some limited support in New Zealand for the recognition of non-intimate domestic relationships within the property sharing regime. For a discussion see M Briggs, 'Rethinking Relationships' (2015) 46 *Victoria University of Wellington Law Review* 649. Some New Zealand legislation already recognises non-sexual domestic relationships for certain purposes: eg the Domestic Violence Act 1995 (NZ), s 4, provides that a person is in a 'domestic relationship' with another person if the person is a spouse or partner, family member, ordinarily shares a household, or has a 'close personal relationship' with the other person.

95 B Atkin and W Parker, 'De Facto Property Developments in New Zealand: Pressures Impeded Progress' in J Dewar and S Parker (eds), *Family Law Processes, Practices and Pressures: Proceedings of the Tenth World Conference of the International Society of Family Law*, Hart Publishing, Oxford 2003, 555 at 562.

least in part, on one's view of the extent to which the state should assume an interventionist role in dealings between private individuals. That said, statistics reveal that significant numbers of New Zealanders currently live together in ways that could potentially qualify as non-intimate domestic relationships. In the most recent Census in 2013, there were 1,549,890 households in New Zealand,[96] of which more than 71 per cent were defined as 'families'.[97] Of those 'families', around 9 per cent were defined as 'extended families'.[98] Many families included adult children living at home,[99] and there was also a significant number of 'other' multi-person households, defined as 'households not forming a family', comprising either related people (for example, siblings), or related and unrelated people, or unrelated people (for example, flatmates).[100] If even only a small percentage of the atypical living arrangements identified above could be said to qualify as non-intimate domestic relationships, a significant number would still be excluded from the property rights and protections accorded to those people in marriages, civil unions, or de facto relationships.

Cases such as the oft-cited *Burden v United Kingdom* highlight the difficulty for people in non-intimate domestic relationships who are excluded from the legal rights and protections accorded to people in marriage and marriage-like relationships.[101] In that case, the European Court of Human Rights rejected the elderly sisters' claim of discrimination[102] that when the first of them died, the survivor would be required to pay inheritance tax on the dead sister's share of

96 Statistics New Zealand, *2013 Census QuickStats about Families and Households* (PDF version), 2014, 21 <www.stats.govt.nz/Census/2013-census/profile-and-summary-reports/qstats-families-households.aspx> accessed 19.04.2017: 'The census definition of a household is either one person who usually lives alone, or two or more people who usually live together and share facilities (such as for eating or cooking) in a private dwelling. A household may contain one or more families, other people in addition to a family, or no families at all, such as unrelated people living together.'

97 Ibid, at 6. There were 1,136,397 'families', defined as 'two or more people living in the same household, who are either a couple with or without children, or one parent and their children.'

98 Ibid, at 19. There were 100,605 'extended families', defined as 'a group of related people usually living together either as a family with one or more other related people, or as two or more related families, with or without other related people', ranging between one generation and three or more generations living in the same dwelling. By composition, 58.2% of extended families consisted of three or more generations, 36.4% consisted of two generations, and the remaining 5.4% were one-generation families (such as couples living with siblings or cousins).

99 Statistics New Zealand, *2013 Census QuickStats about Families and Households* (Excel version), 2014, Table 7. 110,559 families included adult children aged 20 years or older, 42,894 of which included a child aged 30 years or over. Also see PDF version at 13: 'In 11.9% of one-parent families, the youngest child was aged 30 years or over.'

100 Statistics New Zealand, *2013 Census QuickStats about Families and Households* (Excel version), 2014, Table 24. There were 72,384 'other multi-person' households identified.

101 *Burden v United Kingdom*, above n 91.

102 They complained under Art 14 (prohibition of discrimination) of the European Convention on Human Rights taken in conjunction with Art 1 of Protocol No 1 (protection of property).

the family home, whereas the survivor of a married couple or a registered civil partnership would be exempt from paying inheritance tax in the circumstances.

The New Zealand case of *Re Cotton (deceased)*[103] further reveals that relationship functionality can exist outside the borders of marriage, civil union, or de facto relationship. In that case the plaintiff was the long-term 'housekeeper, personal assistant and hostess'[104] for her physically disabled brother on the understanding that 'she would be reimbursed financially by her retirement being taken care of by [her brother]'.[105] Unfortunately, on his death she discovered he had left the bulk of his estate to his two nephews. The Court observed that to the outside world they appeared as a couple, the plaintiff's services going much further than the natural incidents and consequences of family life, thereby enabling the brother to accumulate his estate. Finding for the plaintiff under the Law Reform (Testamentary Promises) Act 1949 (NZ), the judge acknowledged: 'It is hard to conceive of a case where the support was as great as this particular one.'[106]

It was fortunate that the existence of the testamentary promises could be established in that case. Some individuals in domestic relationships may also have recourse to remedies under the Family Protection Act 1955 (NZ),[107] or the ordinary principles of contract, property, and trust law provided that they satisfy the qualification criteria. But even if they do, the outcomes under these laws are less predictable than under the rules-based equal sharing regime of the PRA. Moreover, if these other avenues of redress are unavailable, a claimant could be left entirely without provision. This may be especially problematic if the claimant had assumed a domestic caring role in the relationship, and is left without current work skills, or is at an age where re-entry into the workforce would be difficult. Spouses, civil partners, and de facto partners left in such circumstances would instead have recourse to the PRA as well as claims for maintenance.[108]

4. LOOKING FORWARD

The consequences of recognising or not recognising certain relationships for family property sharing purposes are important at both the individual

103 *Re Cotton (deceased)*, above n 91.

104 Ibid, at [35]. See also [41], where the plaintiff 'characterised her life with [her brother] as an excellent one ... [T]hey were committed companions for life; they lived together, travelled together, and had a good life ... [S]he cooked a three course meal every night for [her brother], got his breakfast ready, and had lunch waiting for him when he came home in the afternoon. She washed and ironed his clothes.'

105 Ibid, at [13].

106 Ibid, at [103].

107 Family Protection Act 1955 (NZ), s 3. The plaintiff in *Re Cotton (deceased)*, above n 91, as the sister of the deceased, would not have been able to make a claim.

108 Family Proceedings Act 1980 (NZ).

and state level because, when a relationship is accorded legal recognition, the responsibilities attendant on that relationship result in a corresponding reduction in the parties' freedom to conduct their affairs, including their property affairs, in the ways they might otherwise choose. It is therefore important to strike the right balance between individual autonomy and protection of the more vulnerable party to the relationship. Has New Zealand skewed that balance? One of the achievements of New Zealand's one-size-fits-all paternalistic treatment of relationships has been to level the playing field for all couples (barring non-intimate domestic couples) at the end of the relationship. Statutory approaches based solely on relationship registration do not achieve the same degree of equality, and nor do they reflect the diversity of human relationships in the modern world. At another level, however, placing de facto relationships into a system originally designed for married couples is awkward because it introduces uncertainty into legislation designed for optimum clarity. The scheme may therefore work to the disadvantage of certain individuals in ways that were not initially foreseen, with the practical effect of 'overprotecting' in some cases. The following discussion considers the case for change and the case for maintaining the status quo.

4.1. OPTIONS FOR CHANGE

4.1.1. Two Schemes

One means of addressing the concern that the PRA is 'overly protective' in some instances would be to bifurcate formal and informal relationships and operate two separate schemes. De facto relationships could be removed from the PRA, which would be limited to marriage and civil union. A separate scheme could then be created for informal relationships, possibly also including non-intimate domestic relationships (with an appropriate definition of the qualifying criteria). While it is outside the remit of this chapter to inquire into alternatives for property *division* for informal relationships, one option would be to forgo the current equal sharing regime of the PRA, perhaps justified on the basis that since informal relationships are found at the discretion of the court, a more discretionary basis for property sharing is likewise warranted. An attenuated version of a discretionary scheme would be to regard equal sharing as no more than a presumptive starting point, but with greater room to depart from equal sharing in those cases where the relationship presents as 'unconventional'.

A similar proposal was originally made in the De Facto Relationships (Property) Bill 1998 (108-1), before it and the Matrimonial Property Amendment Bill 1998 (54) were subsumed into the Property (Relationships) Amendment Act 2001 (NZ). Under the original Bill, the presumption of equal sharing was to apply only to the family home and chattels, although if the court considered that equal sharing would cause serious injustice it would have a discretion to depart from the equal sharing presumption and divide the family home and chattels on the basis of the contributions of the partners. Relationship property other than the family home and chattels would have been divided according to the contributions of the partners.[109]

The Family Law (Scotland) Act 2006 provides a set of basic rights and responsibilities to protect cohabitants on separation or death which are less far-reaching than those available to spouses and civil partners. While the Scottish Parliament wanted to protect adults and children on relationship breakdown, it also wanted to protect, as far as possible, the rights of adults to live free of any obligations towards partners if they so chose.[110] In its Report published in 2007, the Commission (Eng&W) did not think that cohabitants should have access to exactly the same remedies as married couples and civil partners. The reasons given for that conclusion were that the Commission considered the range of cohabiting relationships to be very broad, exhibiting different degrees of commitment and interdependence, and that cohabitants have not made the legal and public commitment that marriage entails.[111]

The disadvantages of such a proposal should not be dismissed lightly, however. Greater discretion would inevitably fuel the incentive to engage in litigation, resulting in less certainty and more time and expense for the parties involved – problems frequently lamented in those jurisdictions with discretionary schemes. Also, the mere fact that de facto partners were treated differently from married spouses may mean that the courts would exercise their discretion to ensure a less favourable outcome to the applicant partner, much like the New Zealand courts did with de facto partners prior to the PRA.[112] They avoided equal sharing to maintain the distinction.

In terms of policy, moreover, to reduce the level of protection currently enjoyed under the PRA would also be seen by many as a retrograde step, a rejection of relationship equivalence, and a value judgement that informal relationships are less worthy of equal sharing rights than married couples and civil union partners.

---

109 De Facto Relationships (Property) Bill 1998 (108-1), cl 42.

110 Scottish Executive, *Family Matters: Living Together in Scotland* <www.gov.scot/Resource/Doc/113318/0027450.pdf> accessed 17.05.2017.

111 Law Commission (Eng&W), above n 19.

112 See *Pasi v Kamana* [1986] 1 NZLR 603 (CA) at 605, where Cooke P noted that, unlike married couples, de facto couples had no statutory property rights: 'The New Zealand Courts are not here concerned with statutory rights, such as those existing in a marriage partnership between husband and wife under the Matrimonial Property Act 1976. We have no such statute as has been enacted in New South Wales, the *De Facto Relationship Act 1984*. Whether New Zealand needs one is debatable; it is a field in which perhaps justice may be better achieved in the end by proceeding cautiously on a case by case basis.'

4.1.2. *Opt-in versus Opt-out Schemes*

Göran Lind observes that an ideological argument against cohabitation legislation is that it:[113]

> 'can be forced upon the parties without their choice ... The state can be said to infringe upon the parties' individual freedom to determine whether they are to be subjected to the systems of regulation or not.'

As explained earlier, the PRA can have the effect of imposing the default equal sharing regime on de facto couples who, for whatever reason, are not proactive in considering the legal consequences of their relationship. A possible way to counteract that concern would be to treat the PRA as an opt-in scheme for informal relationships, allowing de facto couples (and perhaps also non-intimate domestic partners) to sign up for the property sharing regime. That would ensure that only those couples who had jointly considered their property choices would be bound by the regime.

The disadvantage of an opt-in scheme is that it militates against the core protective function of including de facto couples under the PRA in the first place. The problems would be amplified in the case of non-intimate domestic relationships. For example, it is unlikely that many people in close family relationships (such as the sister in *Re Cotton*) would think that they would need to opt in to the PRA to protect their property interests. They would assume (as the sister in *Re Cotton* did) that the other family member would not fail to make adequate testamentary provision for them or otherwise not defeat their accrued property entitlements. An opt-in scheme could also be susceptible to claims of unequal treatment for informal partners.[114] In addition, a very real practical drawback is that only a minority of couples presently contract out of the PRA, so it is unrealistic to assume that large numbers of de facto partners and domestic partners would actively contract into the Act. The practical result for the vast majority of people in informal relationships would be a return to the pre-PRA era, when de facto couples had to rely on the general law, including constructive trust, to resolve their property disputes.

4.1.3. *The Case for the Status Quo*

Cogent arguments exist for maintaining the current scheme of treating married couples, civil union partners, and de facto partners as functional equivalents.

---

113 G Lind, above n 37 at 1065.

114 For example, the Human Rights Act 1993 (NZ), s 21(1)(b) prohibits discrimination on the grounds of marital status.

For the most part the inclusion of de facto couples in the PRA has been a positive addition and it is arguable that to make wholesale changes to rectify problems in the unconventional de facto couple cases would disrupt settled patterns of law that work well for the majority. Laws, after all, are better drafted for the norm rather than the exception.

A practical advantage in treating de facto partners the same as married couples is that 'the same body of jurisprudence' may be drawn upon 'instead of re-inventing the wheel each time an issue arises'.[115] To establish a separate statutory system tailored for de facto couples would arguably create unnecessary duplication, incur the expense of setting up and operating a separate system, and could lead to claims of unfairness if an individualised scheme for de facto couples were to implement different rules for sharing. Therefore, it may be as well to retain the current system in much the same form and concede that, as with any law, there will inevitably be the occasional 'difficult case'. While it may be possible to add to, or alter, the existing list of indicia[116] used to help determine whether the parties are 'living together as a couple', it is debatable whether this would make any tangible difference to the decision-making task already faced by the courts.

Various mechanisms already exist in the PRA that provide the courts some leeway in both determining the length of the relationship and sharing the relationship property. These safeguards help to address some, though not all, of the difficult or marginal de facto couple cases. Firstly, if the relationship is one of short duration (generally, less than three years) orders cannot be made under the PRA unless there is a child of that relationship or the court finds that the applicant has made a substantial contribution to the de facto relationship and that in either of those circumstances a failure to make an order would result in serious injustice.[117] If those grounds are made out, the ordinary presumption of equal sharing is displaced and the share of each de facto partner in the relationship property is to be determined in accordance with the contributions of each partner. Second, the court may make a finding that a de facto relationship is of short duration notwithstanding that it lasted for more than three years 'if the court, having regard to all the circumstances of the de facto relationship, considers it just to treat the de facto relationship as a relationship of short duration.'[118] As a further backstop, the court may depart from equal sharing where 'the court considers that there are extraordinary circumstances that make

115 B Atkin, 'The Legal World of Unmarried Couples: Reflections on "De Facto Relationships" in Recent New Zealand Legislation' (2008) 39 *Victoria University of Wellington Law Review* 793, 794.

116 PRA, s 2D(2).

117 PRA, s 14A.

118 PRA, s 2E(1)(b)(ii). See for example, *Aschenbrenner v Williams* [2015] NZFC 3602; *F v B* FC Auckland FAM-2004-004-1787, 27 May 2005.

equal sharing of property … repugnant to justice',[119] although this test sets a very high threshold.[120]

Finally, a possible way to reduce the number of problematic de facto couple claims would be to review the three-year requirement for qualifying relationships. It is often in those cases where the relationship has not endured for a particularly long period that problems arise. There is no special significance attached to the current three-year requirement. Australia, for example, imposes a two-year threshold (together with a discretionary sharing model) and, as noted earlier, the Report of the Law Commission (Eng&W) suggested a period of between two and five years.[121] An argument for increasing the current New Zealand threshold would be that it would help to secure evidence of a more settled and committed relationship. An argument against raising the current three-year requirement, however, would be that it could expose some vulnerable parties in relationships of less than the new qualifying period to financial hardship.[122] Extending the 'probation period' for de facto relationships would not necessarily require an equivalent change for short duration marriages and civil unions because the formal entry requirements already put couples on alert to the property implications of their change in relationship status.

5. CONCLUSION

Any attempt to locate a universally workable formula for determining what relationships should be included in a relationship property scheme is destined for failure because laws are inexorably shaped by the distinct historic developments, social influences, and religious attitudes that prevail in individual jurisdictions. The aims of this chapter have been more modest. Drawing on New Zealand's unusual (some might say 'unique') system, the discussion has highlighted the advantages and disadvantages of the PRA in its current form and considered some ways these concerns might be addressed. Although not without its faults, the PRA's method of identifying relationship equivalence premised on principles of functionality is preferable to a system based on formal relationship

---

119 PRA, s 13. Where ss 14–14AA potentially apply, 'an alternative argument can be mounted that the brevity of the relationship and a gross disproportionate contribution by one party should be addressed by application of section 13. This also could be particularly useful if the length of the relationship exceeds the limits of ss 14–14AA and the court is not minded to treat the relationship as one of short duration': *Brookers Family Law – Family Property*, above n 71 at PR13.05(3).

120 See, for example, *Martin v Martin* [1979] 1 NZLR 97 (CA).

121 Law Commission (Eng&W), *Executive Summary*, above n 20 at [1.14].

122 Against that argument, shorter duration relationships with extenuating circumstances could continue to fall under the protection of s 14A.

registration. While changes could perhaps be made to enhance the identification of qualifying relationships, the practical effect of these may achieve little more than replacing existing problems with new ones, thereby generating additional litigation, expense, time, and anxiety for affected parties.

The question of who counts as 'family' for property sharing purposes is fraught with difficulties, and not merely those of a legal nature. In 1977 Kevin Gray observed:[123]

> 'Family law uniquely represents a conjunction of law, sociology, ethics, religion and economics. This statement is particularly true of that part of family law which touches upon the property relations of husband and wife. There is a sense in which the law of matrimonial property is concerned, not with property at all, but with human relations and ideologies in respect of property.'

Little has changed in the four decades that have followed. Family property law continues to be a mixed bag of disciplines that must be balanced against one another. Any alterations to existing laws, particularly those that determine who should be included, and who should be excluded, from the regime require careful consideration for fear of upsetting the delicate ecosystem already in place, which reflects the particular values of the particular society. In the New Zealand context, there have been no significant protests against the current approach of including de facto relationships, and the courts have interpreted the legislation to a point where it is reasonably predictable.

123 KJ Gray, *Reallocation of Property on Divorce*, Professional Books, Abingdon 1977, 1.

CHAPTER 4

CHILDREN'S INTERESTS IN DIVISION OF PROPERTY ON RELATIONSHIP BREAKDOWN

Nicola PEART and Mark HENAGHAN*

1. INTRODUCTION

The breakdown of a marriage, civil union, or de facto relationship inevitably affects children of the relationship, particularly minor and dependent children.[1] It disrupts their home and family life. How their parents divide their

* We are indebted to Ruth Ballantyne BA (Hons) LLB, Kyla Mullen IMOT LLB (Hons), Jonathon Yeldon BFA LLB, and Lucy Henderson B Com LLB (Hons) for their valuable research assistance.

1 R KASPIEW and L QU, 'Property Division after Separation: Recent Research Evidence' (2016) 30 *Australian Journal of Family Law* 1, where the authors discuss the empirical evidence on separated parents and child support. See also B FEHLBERG, B SMYTH and L TRINDER, 'Parenting Issues after Separation: Developments in Common Law Countries' in J EEKELAAR and R GEORGE (eds), *Routledge Handbook of Family Law and Policy*, Routledge, Abingdon 2014, 215. For a New Zealand perspective, see NJ TAYLOR and M GOLLOP, 'Children's

relationship property is likely to have a direct impact on their lives. They may have to move house, leave their neighbourhood and friends, change schools, and they may experience a financial setback. The question this chapter addresses is whether the interests of children should be taken into account in the division of property between their parents and, if so, how those interests should be accommodated. This chapter is concerned only with relationships ending during the joint lives of the parties. The property consequences of relationships ending on death of a spouse or partner are dealt with elsewhere.[2]

In England and Wales, the welfare of any minor children of the marriage is the first consideration when courts exercise their discretion under the Matrimonial Causes Act 1973 (Eng&W) to adjust property between former spouses on divorce.[3] Australia's Family Law Act 1975 (Cth) also has a discretionary regime in which the interests of children are a mandatory consideration.[4] When exercising their discretion under these Acts, the courts in both jurisdictions consider the needs of the family as a whole, with the aim of achieving a fair or just outcome for the parties.[5] Furthermore, these Acts deal not only with property division, but also with spousal maintenance and child support, as well as care of the children after divorce. Covering all these issues in one statute facilitates a holistic approach to the consequences of marital breakdown.[6]

New Zealand differs from England and Wales, and Australia by having separate statutes for property division, spousal maintenance, child support, and care of the children.[7] The Property (Relationships) Act 1976 (NZ) deals only with property division. The regime that this Act establishes is similar to a system known in the civil law jurisdictions as a deferred community of acquests.[8]

Views and Participation in Family Dispute Resolution in New Zealand' in AB Smith (ed), *Enhancing Children's Rights: Connecting Research, Policy and Practice*, Palgrave MacMillan, London 2015, 242. See also the comments of the New Zealand Commissioner for Children: R McClay, *Submissions of the Commissioner for Children to the Government Administration Committee on the Matrimonial Property Amendment Bill 1998*, Wellington, July 1998, 3.

2 N Peart, 'Family Finances on Death of a Spouse or Partner', ch 5; R Croucher, 'A Lament for "Testator's Family Maintenance" – A Good Idea Gone Wrong? Australian Reflections', ch 6.

3 Matrimonial Causes Act 1973 (Eng&W), ss 24 and 25(1); *White v White* [2001] 1 AC 596 (HL); *Miller v Miller; McFarlane v McFarlane* [2006] UKHL 24, [2006] 2 AC 618.

4 Family Law Act 1975 (Cth), ss 79(4) and 75(2); *Stanford v Stanford* [2012] HCA 52, (2012) 247 CLR 108.

5 *Miller v Miller; McFarlane v McFarlane*, above n 3; *Stanford v Stanford*, above n 4. See further 3.1 and 3.2 below.

6 Matrimonial Causes Act 1973 (Eng&W), pt II deals with financial relief for the parties to the marriage and children of the family and pt III deals with protection and custody of the children. Australia's Family Law Act 1975 (Cth) deals with care and parenting orders of children in pt VII, including child maintenance, and with property division and spousal maintenance in pt VIII.

7 Property (Relationships) Act 1976 (NZ) ('PRA'); Family Proceedings Act 1980 (NZ), pt 6; Child Support Act 1991 (NZ); and Care of Children Act 2004 (NZ).

8 The New Zealand system differs from a community of acquests by including the family home and family chattels even if they were acquired by one of the parties before the relationship

It gives limited discretion to depart from equal division between the parties to the relationship.[9] While taking account of the interests of children is mentioned in the Act's purpose section, and one of the sections mandates the courts to have regard to the interests of minor or dependent children when making orders under the Act, the courts have made little use of these provisions.[10] The focus is on the property entitlements that the parties have acquired during their relationship, rather than the future needs of the family, and in that context the emphasis has been on achieving equality between the parties and a clean break to enable each party to move on with their lives.[11] Such powers as this Act gives to make orders for the benefit of minor or dependant children have been narrowly construed.[12] Children's needs are normally addressed separately through child support orders under the Child Support Act 1991 (NZ), variations to nuptial settlements under the Family Proceedings Act 1980 (NZ), and care arrangements under the Care of Children Act 2004 (NZ).[13]

This chapter will begin with a brief historical overview of property consequences on divorce and how children's interests were accommodated in that context. It will then outline the family-centred approach to property division in the current law of England and Wales, and Australia, followed by a more detailed analysis of the current law in New Zealand in which conceptual and practical barriers to a family-centred approach will be addressed. The chapter will conclude by suggesting options for reform.

2. HISTORICAL OVERVIEW

The adoption of the Married Women's Property Acts in the common law jurisdictions in the late 1800s liberated married women from the constraints of their husband's coverture by removing most of their legal disabilities and giving them the freedom to acquire, hold, and dispose of property in

began: PRA, s 8. See further AH Angelo and WR Atkin, 'A Conceptual and Structural Overview of the Matrimonial Property Act 1976' (1977) 7 *New Zealand Universities Law Review* 237 and JM Scherpe, 'Contracting Out of the Default Relationship Property Regime – Comparative Observations', ch 14.

9 Note, however, that since 2001 the exceptions to equal division have expanded to include, as part of the relationship property regime, a discretion to compensate for economic disparity: PRA, ss 15 and 15A. See M Henaghan, 'Sharing Family Finances at the End of a Relationship', ch 12. JM Scherpe explains that in civil law jurisdictions compensation for economic disparity is addressed separately from matrimonial property division: above n 8.

10 PRA 1976, ss 1M(c) and 26.

11 See 4 below.

12 PRA 1976, ss 26–28D. See further 4.4 below.

13 There are also provisions in the Domestic Violence Act 1995 (NZ) to make occupation and tenancy orders of the family home.

their own right.[14] The Acts established a system of separate property. Each spouse retained such property as he or she brought into or acquired during the marriage. While these Acts were seen as a triumph for women's emancipation, the freedom that thousands of women had yearned for came at a price.[15] The new system treated husband and wife virtually as strangers in relation to property.[16] Questions between the spouses about ownership or possession of property were determined by the ordinary rules of common law and equity.[17] A wife had no entitlement to any property legally owned by her husband, not even the home, unless she could show she had made financial contributions to its acquisition, in which case a resulting trust could arise.[18] The wife's contributions in the home, to the care of the children, and any non-financial support she had given her husband or his career did not translate into a property entitlement. Unless a former wife had property of her own,[19] she remained dependent on her ex-husband for financial support.[20] Both the husband and the wife were

---

14 The Married Women's Property Act 1870 (UK) removed some of the wife's legal disabilities, while the Married Women's Property Act 1882 (UK) removed virtually all legal disabilities and effectively established the separate property system for married couples. The Married Women's Property Act 1884 (NZ) was similar to the English 1882 Act. So, too, the Married Women's Property Acts adopted in the Australian jurisdictions between 1879 (NSW) and 1892 (WA).

15 B Bradbury, 'From Civil Death to Separate Property: Changes in the Legal Rights of Married Women in Nineteenth-Century New Zealand' (1995) 29(1) *New Zealand Journal of History* 40, 66, where the author quotes Mary Ann Müller's comment to Kate Sheppard that the Married Women's Property Act was an even greater triumph for women than getting the vote.

16 JR Hanan, 'The Future of Family Law' in BD Inglis and AG Mercer (eds), *Family Law Centenary Essays*, Sweet & Maxwell, Wellington 1967, 12. For a more detailed history of the property rights of wives and widows, see Peart and Croucher, above n 2.

17 Married Women's Property Act 1884 (NZ), s 20, retained in Married Women's Property Act 1908 (NZ), s 23 and Married Women's Property Act 1952 (NZ), s 19; Married Women's Property Act 1882 (UK), s 17; Married Women's Property Act 1890 (Vic), s 20; Married Women's Property Act 1893 (NSW), s 21; Married Women's Property Act 1883–4 (SA), s 17.

18 *Hill v Hill* [1916] WN 59 (Ch), where after separation the wife and children continued living in the home owned by the husband. She had no property interest in the home and was ordered to vacate when her husband wanted to sell it to discharge his debts. The husband was required to provide alternative accommodation for his wife and children as part of his support obligations. See also *Kain v Kain* [1943] NZLR 342 (CA), where the wife was ordered to vacate the home owned by her husband, because she had no legal or equitable title in it. See also *Masters v Masters* [1954] NZLR 82 (SC), where the wife was unable to establish an equitable interest in the home legally owned by her husband, and *Hendry v Hendry* [1960] NZLR 48 (SC), where the wife successfully argued that her husband held the home on a resulting trust, because she had contributed financially to its acquisition.

19 As, for example, in *Richards v Richards* [1930] GLR 126 (SC), where the wife was granted possession of her property against her husband.

20 Alimony could be ordered in periodic payments or as a lump sum. As conduct was a relevant factor, a wife could be denied alimony if she was responsible for the marital breakdown: Divorce and Matrimonial Causes Act 1857 (Eng&W), s 32; Divorce and Matrimonial Causes Act 1867 (NZ), s 27; Divorce and Matrimonial Causes Act 1928 (NZ), s 33; Matrimonial Causes Act 1873 (NSW), s 29; Matrimonial Causes Act 1899 (NSW), s 39; The Marriage and Matrimonial Causes Statute 1864 (Vic), s 71; Marriage Act 1890 (Vic) s 87. Furthermore,

responsible for maintaining their children, but the husband might be the only parent with financial means to provide such support.[21] If there was a nuptial settlement for the benefit of the couple and their children, the court had the power to vary the settlement on divorce for the benefit of the children of the marriage and/or their parents.[22] Without such a settlement or a property entitlement, wives were very vulnerable on the breakdown of their marriage and, as they generally had custody of the children, their children were also vulnerable.

World War II brought about significant social change in the United Kingdom, Australia, and New Zealand.[23] Wives were more likely to be in paid employment or self-employed.[24] A wife's work in the home and care of the couple's children was gaining recognition as economically valuable.[25] It freed the husband to concentrate on building the family's financial assets. Another factor was the housing shortage in England as well as New Zealand and Australia.[26] This made rights to the matrimonial home critical. The English courts responded to

---

if the divorce was granted on the basis of the wife's adultery, the court had the power to order a settlement of her property in favour of her husband, if he was innocent of wrongdoing, and the children: Divorce and Matrimonial Causes Act 1857 (Eng&W), s 45; Divorce and Matrimonial Causes Act 1867 (NZ), s 38; Divorce and Matrimonial Causes Act 1928 (NZ), s 36; Matrimonial Causes Act 1873 (NSW), s 39; Matrimonial Causes Act 1899 (NSW), s 55; The Marriage and Matrimonial Causes Statute 1864 (Vic), s 82; Marriage Act 1890 (Vic), s 99. While that power still appeared in the Marriage Act 1958 (Vic), s 105, it was not included when the Commonwealth of Australia adopted its Matrimonial Causes Act 1959 (Cth).

21 Divorce and Matrimonial Causes Act 1857 (Eng&W), s 35; Divorce and Matrimonial Causes Act 1867 (NZ), s 36; Divorce and Matrimonial Causes Act 1928 (NZ), s 38; Matrimonial Causes Act 1873 (NSW), s 33; The Marriage and Matrimonial Causes Statute 1864 (Vic), s 79; Marriage Act 1890 (Vic), s 96; Matrimonial Causes Act 1899 (NSW), s 60. See, for example, *Thomson v Thomson* [1944] NZLR 469 (SC), where the husband and wife had been separated for 20 years and the wife remained dependent on her husband for support in the form of maintenance and occupation of the home.

22 Divorce and Matrimonial Causes Act 1857 (Eng&W), s 5; Divorce and Matrimonial Causes Act 1867 and 1928 (NZ), s 37; Matrimonial Proceedings Act 1963 (NZ), s 79; Matrimonial Causes Act 1873 (NSW), s 40; Matrimonial Causes Act 1899 (NSW), s 56; Marriage and Matrimonial Causes Statute 1864 (Vic), s 81; Marriage Act 1890 (Vic), s 98.

23 H Sargisson, 'Matrimonial Property Legislation – "Its History, and a Critique of the Present New Zealand Law"' (1976) 3(1) *Auckland University Law Review* 82, 87 and 104.

24 A Milner, 'Policy-Orientation in Matrimonial Property Law' (1959) 22(2) *Modern Law Review* 207, 209–10.

25 For example, in *Fibrance v Fibrance (No 2)* [1957] 1 All ER 357 (CA) the English Court of Appeal followed earlier rulings in *Rimmer v Rimmer* [1952] 2 All ER 863 (CA) and *Cobb v Cobb* [1955] 2 All ER 696 (CA), making orders with respect to property by referring to the joint efforts of the spouses, which included non-domestic efforts, such as looking after the home.

26 *Thomson v Thomson*, above n 21 at 474, where the Court refers to the housing shortage as a reason for declining the husband's application for possession of his house. Although the parties had been separated for 20 years and the wife had occupied the house ever since, initially with the couple's children, the husband had somewhere to live, whereas the wife would not have the means to find alternative accommodation. See also H Sargisson, above n 23 at 93.

these changes by construing their powers under the Married Women's Property Act 1882 (UK) more liberally, in the interests of justice and fairness. They were of the view that strict rules of property should not apply to family assets, such as the matrimonial home, particularly not when there were children involved. They were willing to vest title in the non-owning spouse.[27]

The New Zealand and Australian courts were less adventurous. They did not believe the wording of their Married Women's Property statutes gave them the power to make orders affecting title to property in the interests of justice and fairness.[28] Their only concession to the marital relationship being different from a relationship between strangers was to presume that the beneficial interest would be shared equally if a resulting trust arose, because it was often too difficult to determine how much each spouse had directly or indirectly contributed financially to the property's acquisition.[29] If no such equitable interest could be established, the courts would, at most, grant possession to the non-owning spouse, usually the wife, especially if she had the care of the couple's minor children.[30] Widespread criticism of the Married Women's Property legislation's failure to address the special problems arising on marital breakdown was the impetus for legislative change in the 1960s.[31]

The state of Victoria in Australia led the way. It adopted the Marriage (Property) Act 1962 (Vic) to empower the courts to make orders adjusting title as between spouses, but not so as to defeat any common intention expressed by the spouses.[32] It also inserted a presumption that the matrimonial home

---

27 *Rimmer v Rimmer*, above n 25; *Hine v Hine* [1962] 3 All ER 345 (CA). That view of the jurisdiction to make orders under the Married Women's Property Act 1882 (UK) was subsequently rejected by the House of Lords in *Pettit v Pettit* [1970] AC 777 (HL): the Court had jurisdiction only to determine who the property belonged to; the Act gave the Court no power to take property from one spouse and allocate it to the other spouse.

28 *Barrow v Barrow* [1946] NZLR 438 (CA); *Masters v Masters*, above n 18; *Taylor v Taylor* [1956] NZLR 99 (SC); *Wirth v Wirth* (1956) 98 CLR 228; *Martin v Martin* (1959) 110 CLR 297; *Hepworth v Hepworth* (1963) 110 CLR 309.

29 *Hendry v Hendry*, above n 18, where the Court ordered that the husband held the home on trust for himself and his wife in equal shares. In doing so, the Court followed English Court of Appeal precedent in *Rimmer v Rimmer*, above n 25. See also *Peychers v Peychers* [1955] NZLR 564 (SC).

30 In *Masters v Masters*, above n 18, for example, the Court granted the wife possession of the home until further order of the court. In *Dillon v Dillon* [1956] NZLR 162 (SC) the husband was granted possession of the land he occupied after he had improved the land in reliance on his wife's promise that she would gift it to him. As she had revoked the gift, no order could be made vesting title in him.

31 For example, *Hofman v Hofman* [1965] NZLR 795 (SC) at 798 cite the following reports: *Report of the Royal Commission on Marriage and Divorce in the United Kingdom*, Cmd 9678, HMSO, London 1956; *Report on Proceedings of the Second Commonwealth Law Conference* (1960) 303, (1953) 16 MLR 34, 148, [1959] Can Bar Rev 473, (1959) 22 MLR 241.

32 Marriage (Property) Act 1962 (Vic), s 3, amending the Marriage Act 1958 (Vic), s 161. *Haskin v Haskin* [1964] VR 37; *Hogben v Hogben* [1964] VR 468; *Moore v Moore* [1965] VR 61.

acquired by either spouse during, or in contemplation of, marriage was held as a joint tenancy.[33] These changes indirectly broadened the court's existing powers to make orders with respect to maintenance, custody, and education of minor children of the marriage.[34]

New Zealand modelled its Matrimonial Property Act 1963 (NZ) on the Victorian statute, giving the court similar powers to make orders affecting title, but stopping short of creating a presumption of joint tenancy in respect of the matrimonial home.[35] The courts could make such orders as appeared just in the circumstances, having regard to the applicant's financial and non-financial contributions to the property in dispute.[36] The courts were required to have regard to those contributions in relation to the family home and were empowered to do so in relation to other property.[37]

The purpose of the Victorian and New Zealand statutes was to give the courts a broad discretion to depart from conventional property law and acknowledge the important contributions that a skilful housewife could make to general family welfare by assuming domestic responsibility and freeing her husband to earn the income they both needed for the furtherance of their joint enterprise.[38] Unlike the Victorian legislation,[39] which covered all consequences of a marital breakdown including custody and maintenance of the children, the focus of New Zealand's Matrimonial Property Act 1963 was on property division as between the parties to the marriage. The Act made no mention of children. However, its companion statute, the Matrimonial Proceedings Act 1963 (NZ), adopted on the same day as the Matrimonial Property Act 1963 (NZ), did make provision for the custody, maintenance, and welfare of minor children of the marriage. In addition to maintenance, the courts were empowered to order that property of the husband or wife be settled for the benefit of the children of the marriage and to make orders in relation to the matrimonial home for the children's benefit.[40]

In *Hofman v Hofman*, for example, the New Zealand Supreme Court[41] ordered that £750 be set aside from the proceeds of sale of the family home for the benefit of the couple's children and that the balance be divided equally between

---

33 Marriage (Property) Act 1962 (Vic), s 3(4)(b), amending the Marriage Act 1958 (Vic), s 161.

34 Marriage Act 1958 (Vic), ss 102 and 103 and Matrimonial Causes Act 1959 (Cth), ss 84 and 86.

35 Matrimonial Property Act 1963 (NZ), ss 5 and 6. *Matrimonial Property: Report of a Special Committee*, Wellington, June 1972, [13].

36 Matrimonial Property Act 1963 (NZ), s 6(1A), inserted by Matrimonial Property Amendment Act 1968 (NZ), s 6(1).

37 Matrimonial Property Act 1963 (NZ), s 6(1).

38 *Hofman v Hofman*, above n 31 at 800–01.

39 Marriage Act 1958 (Vic), as amended by the Marriage (Property) Act 1962 (Vic).

40 Matrimonial Proceedings Act 1963 (NZ), ss 52, 53, and 57–59. The provisions in relation to the matrimonial home applied to orders under the Matrimonial Property Act 1963 (NZ), s 7(4).

41 Now the High Court of New Zealand.

the former spouses.[42] In *Pay v Pay* the Court assessed the wife's contribution to the home at an amount that the husband could afford to pay without having to sell the home.[43] The wife had left the home for another man and her husband had been awarded custody of their four young children. The interests of the children played a prominent role in the Court's decision. Such orders were rare, however. Generally speaking, matrimonial property orders did not take account of the interests of children. The needs of children were addressed through their parents' support obligations.

3. CURRENT LAW IN ENGLAND AND AUSTRALIA

Both England and Australia have retained a separate property system, but with a broad discretion to make orders affecting title for the benefit of spouses and children.

3.1. ENGLAND

In 1970 England adopted the Matrimonial Proceedings and Property Act (Eng&W). It greatly extended the court's powers to make orders in respect of title and financial provision for the benefit of spouses and children of the family.[44] Those provisions were re-enacted without substantial amendment in the Matrimonial Causes Act 1973 (Eng&W). That Act is still in force today, though some of its provisions have since been amended. It applies to civil partnerships as well, but not to cohabitants.[45]

Section 23 of the Matrimonial Causes Act 1973 (Eng&W) empowers the court, on the granting of divorce or judicial separation, to order one spouse to make financial provision in the form of periodic or lump sum payments to the other spouse, or to a person for the benefit of a child of the family, or to the child directly. A 'child of the family' includes not only a child of both parties to the marriage, whether born in or out of wedlock or adopted, but also a child treated by both parties as a child of the family other than a child fostered with the family by a local authority or voluntary organisation.[46]

Section 24 provides for property adjustment orders. The court can order one spouse to transfer property to the other spouse, to a child of the family, or to

42 *Hofman v Hofman*, above n 31 at 802. The decision was affirmed on appeal: *Hofman v Hofman* [1967] NZLR 9 (CA).
43 *Pay v Pay* [1968] NZLR 140 (CA).
44 Matrimonial Proceedings and Property Act 1970 (Eng&W), ss 2–5.
45 Civil Partnership Act 2004 (Eng&W), s 72.
46 Matrimonial Causes Act 1973 (Eng&W), s 52.

a specified person for the benefit of a child. It may also order a settlement of property for the benefit of a spouse or one or more children of the family.

In deciding whether to exercise its powers under sections 23 and 24, the court is under a duty:[47]

> 'to have regard to all the circumstances of the case, first consideration being given to the welfare while a minor of any child of the family who has not attained the age of eighteen.'

Section 25 then lists a number of other matters to which the court must have particular regard when making an order. They include:[48]

> 'income, earning capacity, property and other financial resources, [as well as the] financial needs, obligations and responsibilities [that each party] has or is likely to have in the foreseeable future; [the] standard of living enjoyed by the family before the breakdown of the marriage; [and the] contributions [that each] party has made, or is likely … to make, to the welfare of the family including any contribution by looking after the home or caring for the family.'

When exercising discretion in relation to a child, the court is mandated to have particular regard to:[49]

> '[the child's] financial needs, … the income, earning capacity (if any), property and other financial resources of the child, … any physical or mental disability of the child, … the manner in which [the child was expected] to be educated, [as well as the] income, earning capacity, property and financial resources [available to] the parties to the marriage, [their] financial needs, [and] standard of living.'

The Matrimonial Causes Act 1973 (Eng&W) thus mandates a family-centred approach to the division of assets at the end of a marriage in which the interests of children feature prominently. However, the Act does not articulate the purpose of the exercise of discretion when dividing such assets. The courts have deduced that the objective must be to achieve a 'fair outcome'.[50] In *Miller v Miller; McFarlane v McFarlane* the House of Lords conceded that fairness is an 'elusive concept … grounded in social and moral values … that change from one generation to the next'.[51] Fairness has three strands. The first is the parties' financial needs, which includes their respective responsibilities for any minor children, their

---

47 Matrimonial Causes Act 1973 (Eng&W), s 25(1).

48 Matrimonial Causes Act 1973 (Eng&W), s 25(2).

49 Matrimonial Causes Act 1973 (Eng&W), s 25(3).

50 *White v White*, above n 3 at 604, where Lord Nicholls describes the history of the legislation and criticises the courts' longstanding limited approach to their powers.

51 *Miller v Miller; McFarlane v McFarlane*, above n 3 at [4].

earning capacity, age, health, and living standard.[52] The second strand is compensation to redress 'any significant prospective economic disparity between the parties arising from the way they conducted their marriage'.[53] The third strand is equal sharing. This strand acknowledges that marriage is a 'partnership of equals', but equality is a 'yardstick', to be applied as an aid, not a rule'.[54] The Court accepted that in most cases the search for fairness will not move beyond the first stage, because the assets will be insufficient to provide for the needs of two homes, in which case the 'courts seek to stretch modest finite resources so far as possible to meet the parties' needs'. Where children are involved, a fair outcome may include periodic payments from future earnings.[55] The duration of the marriage is not determinative and no property is excluded from consideration, though its source might be taken into account if the parties' financial resources exceed the parties' financial needs.[56]

There were no children in *Miller v Miller*. But in *McFarlane v McFarlane* there were three school-aged children and their needs were central to the Court's decision. The parties had agreed that the wife should retain the family home and live there with the children. There was insufficient capital for a clean break between the parties, but the husband was earning a very high income that far exceeded the needs of both the husband and the wife. The contentious issue was the periodic payments required to provide for the wife and children. In addition to £60,000 annual maintenance for the children, the Court ordered Mr McFarlane to make an annual payment to his ex-wife of £250,000 for their joint lives, of which £180,000 was for her needs and the balance was compensation for her loss of earning capacity. As the youngest child was only six years old at the time, the wife could not be expected to acquire or improve her earning capacity until that child reached secondary school age.

The interests of children were also a primary consideration in *Tattersall v Tattersall*.[57] The husband and wife were in their mid-30s when their 10-year marriage ended. They had a three-year-old child who lived with the wife after the divorce. Mrs Tattersall was a researcher at Oxford University, while her ex-husband was a clinical lecturer in obstetrics and gynaecology at Liverpool

---

52 Ibid, at [10].

53 Ibid, at [13].

54 Ibid, at [16].

55 Ibid, at [12]. For a discussion of property division in cases where there is less wealth, see E Hitchings, 'The Impact of Recent Ancillary Relief Jurisprudence in the "Everyday" Ancillary Relief Case' (2010) 22 *Child and Family Law Quarterly* 93.

56 As in *White v White*, above n 3, where the husband's father made a capital sum available to the couple early on in their marriage.

57 *Tattersall v Tattersall* [2013] EWCA Civ 774. See also *WF v HF* [2012] EWHC 438 (Fam) at [77], where the High Court varied a nuptial settlement to vest two thirds of the proceeds of sale of the family home in the wife. Unequal division was appropriate as she had primary responsibility for the couple's children.

University. The Court awarded the wife 70 per cent of the parties' capital, because she had greater needs than her husband. She had the day-to-day care of their child and her income and earning capacity was lower than her husband. The Court held that the needs of the wife and daughter could not be satisfied unless the wife had access to more than half the family resources.[58] The decision thus gave effect to the court's duty to give first consideration to the welfare of the couple's minor child.

In *Radmacher v Granatino* children were also central to the court's orders.[59] Mr Granatino, a Frenchman, and Ms Radmacher, a German national, made an ante-nuptial contract in Germany in which each of them renounced any interest in, or benefit from, the other's property. The parties entered into the agreement at the insistence of Ms Radmacher's father. He was concerned to protect his family's considerable wealth and business interests. The couple married in 1998 in London and lived there for most of their marriage. They had two children, born in 1999 and 2002. Mr Radmacher transferred substantial capital assets to his daughter during the marriage, believing they were safe from any matrimonial property claim. Mr Granatino was a successful investment banker, but a few years into the marriage he lost interest and resigned to do a doctorate full-time at Oxford University. Following the parties' separation in 2006, the husband applied for orders under the Matrimonial Causes Act 1973 (Eng&W).

The Supreme Court of the United Kingdom concluded that its jurisdiction under the Matrimonial Causes Act 1973 (Eng&W) to make orders after the breakdown of a marriage could not be ousted by an ante-nuptial contract. While it would be a relevant factor in the court's exercise of discretion, and could be decisive if it was freely entered into with full information and was not unfair, a nuptial agreement could not be 'allowed to prejudice the reasonable requirements of any children of the family' who were under the age of 18.[60] At first instance the Court gave little weight to the agreement, finding that it fell foul of the requirements an English court would expect, even though it was valid under German law. The judge awarded the husband £700,000 to help clear his debts, £25,000 to buy a car, £2.5m to buy himself a home in London, and £2.335m capital to provide him with an annual income for life of £100,000. The Court also ordered that €630,000 be used to buy a home in Germany, to be owned by the wife, where the husband could care for his children when they were residing with him in Germany.

On the wife's appeal, the Court of Appeal set aside the lower Court's orders and the Supreme Court upheld the Court of Appeal ruling.[61] The ante-nuptial

---

58 Ibid, at [49].

59 *Radmacher v Granatino* [2010] UKSC 42, [2011] 1 AC 534.

60 Ibid, at [77].

61 *Radmacher v Granatino* [2009] EWCA Civ 649; *Radmacher v Granatino*, above n 59.

agreement was not tainted. Mr Granatino had entered the agreement freely and understood he would forego any entitlement to his wife's wealth. It was fair to hold him to that agreement and it would be unfair to depart from it. The agreement was therefore binding to the extent that it provided for the husband's own needs, but it was not decisive in regard to his care of the children. The sum of £2.5m for housing in London was not to become the husband's property absolutely, but only for the years of parenting, and the income fund was to be capitalised at a rate to cover his needs only until the younger child's 22nd birthday. Mr Granatino was 'extremely able and ha[d] added to his qualifications by [gaining a doctorate] in biotechnology'. He was able to provide for his own needs and would benefit indirectly from 'the generous relief given to cater for the needs' of his children.[62] This was a creative way of dealing with the children's needs. It shows that even where there is no reason to make property orders for the benefit of a party to the marriage, the court may nonetheless do so to ensure that each party has the necessary means to care for the children in an appropriate manner.

3.2. AUSTRALIA

Australia's Family Law Act 1975 (Cth) has similarly wide powers to make property and maintenance orders, but its terms and structure are somewhat different from those in England's Matrimonial Causes Act. The Family Law Act 1975 (Cth) applies to marriage and civil partnerships, and to de facto relationships of at least two years' duration.[63] Unlike the English Act, the Australian Act states the purpose of the exercise of discretion. The court may not make an order altering the parties' property rights 'unless it is satisfied that, in all the circumstances, it is just and equitable to make the order'.[64] Section 79 establishes a two-stage inquiry. The first stage is to determine whether it is just and equitable to alter the parties' existing property rights.[65] If so, then the court may alter those rights by taking into account a range of factors listed in section 79(4).

The first stage requires a determination of what property each of the parties legally or beneficially owns.[66] The Act defines 'property' as 'property to which [each of the parties to the marriage is, or may be,] entitled, whether in possession or reversion'.[67] This definition has been construed broadly to give effect to the purpose of the legislation. How or when the property was acquired

62 *Radmacher v Granatino*, above n 59 at [119].
63 Family Law Act 1975 (Cth), s 90SB.
64 Family Law Act 1975 (Cth), s 79(2).
65 *Stanford v Stanford*, above n 4.
66 Ibid, at [37].
67 Family Law Act 1975 (Cth), s 4(1).

is not material and property may include interests that would not be property according to conventional rules of common law and equity, such as interests that a spouse may have in a discretionary trust.[68] Having established the parties' existing property interests, the question is whether they should be altered. The court must have a principled reason for doing so. Where the parties have voluntarily separated, it will generally be just and equitable to alter the parties' property interests, because the assumption of common use of property will no longer apply.[69]

If the court is satisfied that it is just and equitable to alter the parties' property interests, it may make 'such order as it considers appropriate'.[70] In considering what order (if any) is appropriate, the court is mandated by section 79(4) to have regard to the parties' direct and indirect financial and non-financial contributions to any of the property of the parties, the contribution made to the welfare of the family and any children of the marriage, the effect of any proposed order on the earning capacity of either party to the marriage, as well as child support or other orders made to a party or child of the marriage. The court is also required to take into account the matters listed in section 75(2), which include:

> 'the age and state of health of each [party,] the income, property and financial resources of each [party,] ... whether either party has the care or control of a child of the marriage who has not yet attained the age of 18 years, ... the commitments of each [party] that are necessary to support him or herself and a child or another person that the party has a duty to maintain, and the responsibilities of either party to support any other person.'

While the welfare of children is not a 'first consideration' their interests are a mandatory consideration when deciding whether to make a property adjustment order and, if so, what sort of order to make. It is common for the party with primary responsibility for minor children of the relationship to receive between 5 and 20 per cent more of the parties' capital assets.[71] Nonetheless, as Skellern found in her research, the Australian Act does appear to be more adult focused than the English Act.[72]

---

68 *Kennon v Spry* [2008] HCA 56, (2008) 238 CLR 366.

69 *Stanford v Stanford*, above n 4 at [42].

70 Family Law Act 1975 (Cth), s 79(1).

71 For example, *Telfer v Telfer* [2016] FCWA 2; *Marlowe-Dawson v Dawson (No 2)* [2014] FamCA 599, (2014) 53 Fam LR 568; *Harrison v Harrison* [2007] FamCA 115.

72 AM Skellern, *Children and the Property (Relationships) Act 1976*, LLM dissertation, Faculty of Law, Victoria University of Wellington, 2012, ch VB.

4. CURRENT LAW IN NEW ZEALAND

4.1. THE PUSH FOR EQUALITY

New Zealand's Matrimonial Property Act 1963 was liberal in intent, but failed to achieve its objective of fully recognising the economic value of contributions to the home and the family.[73] The Act was, in essence, an extension of the Married Women's Property Act 1884 (NZ). The New Zealand Court of Appeal required proof of contributions to each asset to which a claim was made.[74] As a result, wives seldom received an equal share of the fruits of the marriage, even after many years of marriage. A discretionary system also created uncertainty and unpredictability.[75] The interplay between the Matrimonial Property Act 1963 (NZ) and the Matrimonial Proceedings Act 1963 (NZ) in relation to the matrimonial home was confusing because the court's powers differed depending on the Act under which the claim was made.[76]

In 1972 a Special Committee of representatives from the New Zealand Law Society and the Department of Justice recommended the adoption of a coherent and rational code to regulate property relations between spouses.[77] In the Committee's view, marriage should be seen as a partnership to which both spouses contribute equally, albeit in different ways, and that should be the central concept of matrimonial property legislation.[78] The Committee made a series of recommendations aimed at removing the inequitable treatment for wives. None of the recommendations specifically addressed the interests of children.

In 1975 the Select Committee on Women's Rights, specially appointed to examine the role of women in New Zealand society and recommend policies to further the attainment of gender equality, endorsed the Special Committee's recommendations as an important step towards recognising the economic value of married women.[79] The Women's Rights Committee recommended that the law should presume that contributions of both husband and wife were of equal value, thus entitling them to share equally in the assets produced by the marriage

---

73 Select Committee on Women's Rights, *The Role of Women in New Zealand Society*, Government Printer, Wellington, June 1975, I.13 at 75.

74 *E v E* [1971] NZLR 859 (CA). It was not until the Privy Council decision in *Haldane v Haldane* [1976] 2 NZLR 715, [1977] AC 673 (PC) that domestic contributions were seen as indirectly referable to non-domestic assets, but by then Parliament had decided to introduce an equal sharing regime for married couples.

75 AM Finlay, 'Matrimonial Property – Comparable Sharing: An Explanation of the Matrimonial Property Bill 1975' [1975] *Appendix to the Journals of the House of Representatives* E6, 5.

76 Ibid, at 5.

77 *Matrimonial Property: Report of a Special Committee*, above n 35.

78 Ibid, at [19].

79 Select Committee on Women's Rights, above n 73.

partnership.[80] It was concerned about the effect that equal sharing might have on the interests of children, but was reassured by the Department of Justice that children could be better off because their mother, who was likely to have custody, would be in a better position to benefit her children if she received a more generous share of the matrimonial property.[81] The Department went on to say:[82]

> 'The interests of children in their parents' property should not be allowed to stand in the way of doing justice to wives if the present law denies wives a share in the family property to which their total contribution to the family entitles them.'

The needs of children were addressed separately through other legislation, including the Matrimonial Proceedings Act 1963 (NZ). But therein lies the problem, which still exists in New Zealand today. By dealing with children's needs in separate legislation, there is no opportunity for a holistic family-centred approach to all the property and financial consequences of marital breakdown. The needs and interests of children are subsidiary to the principle of equal division of matrimonial property between the former spouses.

The Matrimonial Property Act 1976 (NZ) ('MPA 1976') adopted the central concept of marriage as a partnership of equals with a strong presumption of equal sharing of matrimonial property, subject to limited exceptions.[83] Matrimonial property was defined to include the matrimonial home and family chattels, whenever they were acquired, and any assets produced by the partnership.[84] Gifts, inheritances, and distributions from trusts were generally retained by the recipient as separate property as they were not produced by the partnership.[85] The interests of children were mentioned in the long title to the Act, but they were not made a primary consideration in the division of property as in England's Matrimonial Causes Act 1973. The policy of the MPA 1976 was to provide a clean break as between the parties by dividing the matrimonial property equally, enabling them both to move on independently of each other.

When the MPA 1976 was adopted, section 26 was the only section that specifically referred to the interests of children of the marriage. It mandated

---

80 Ibid, at 75.

81 Ibid, at 75–76.

82 Ibid, at 76. See further M Wilson, 'The New Zealand Context – Setting the Legal and Social Scene' (2017) *Otago Law Review* (forthcoming).

83 Matrimonial Property Act 1976 (NZ) ('MPA 1976'), ss 11–15. See M Henaghan, above n 9.

84 MPA 1976, s 8. Increases in the value of separate property attributable to the application of matrimonial property or the actions of the non-owning spouse were also matrimonial property: s 9.

85 MPA 1976, s 10. These assets could become matrimonial property through intermingling: s 10(2).

the court to have regard to the interests of any minor or dependent children of the marriage and gave the court discretion to make an order settling any part of the matrimonial property for the benefit of the children. If there were special circumstances that made it necessary or expedient for children to be represented in the proceedings, the court could appoint counsel for the children.[86] The courts were conscious of the potential impact of section 26. It could totally displace the property rights and statutory interests or claims of the spouses. It was therefore not a 'power to be exercised lightly'.[87] Nor could it be used simply to reduce the property entitlement of one spouse and increase that of the other.[88]

With such a broad discretion in the context of a strong presumption of equal sharing, and little guidance on how it should be used, it was hardly surprising that the courts were reluctant to make orders settling property for the benefit of children.[89] It was in the nature of an 'expropriation' from a spouse's entitlement.[90] The courts insisted on evidence of exceptional or extraordinary circumstances, such as criminal offending or severe parental neglect.[91]

In *R v R* Judge Adams presented 10 propositions of relevance to section 26 applications:[92]

> '1) Prima facie the matrimonial property is to be regarded as the property of the parties.
> 2) In every case where there are minor or dependent children the Court is obliged to have regard to the respective interests of each such child.
> 3) The context of the consideration of the welfare and interests of the children is "*In the light of the property division between husband and wife, to ensure their financial protection during minority or dependency*" (per Casey J in *Rhodes* (supra) – I note also the discussion of s 26 by His Honour Judge Inglis QC in *Wheeler v Wheeler* (1984) 2 NZFLR 385).
> 4) The Court is not precluded from considering the interests of adult children and may have jurisdiction under s 26 to settle property for the benefit of an adult child (*Voorburgh* [(1979) 2 MPC 197)]; *Roberts* [[1993] NZFLR 731]: *Lockie v Lockie* (1993) 11 FRNZ 81).
> 5) It will be the exceptional case where the consideration leads to an actual award for a child.
> 6) It would be a wrong principle to use s 26 to anticipate succession.

86 MPA 1976, s 26(2).
87 *Walker v Walker* [1983] NZLR 560 (CA) at 565.
88 *Coxhead v Coxhead* [1993] 2 NZLR 397 (CA) at 408.
89 AM Skellern, above n 72.
90 *S v C* [1998] NZFLR 734 (FC) at 739.
91 In *RN v RN* (1985) 3 NZFLR 694 (FC) the husband killed his wife and his share of the home was vested in her estate for the benefit of their children. In *R v R* [1998] NZFLR 611 (FC) a sum of money was vested in the adopted daughter to enable her to obtain help for the mental health problems she suffered as a result of her father indecently assaulting her as a child.
92 *R v R*, above n 91 at 622.

7) Default or inability of a parent to provide appropriate maintenance, upbringing, shelter or nurture for a child are relevant factors, whether or not the default is wilful.
8) In the general run of cases a s 26 order should not be used to substitute or supplement child support arrangements. Nonetheless the Court's discretion is unfettered by statute.
9) Section 26 is not a backhanded means of providing damages to a child for ordinary parenting shortcomings.
10) An award under s 26 must be reasonable in all the circumstances.'

These propositions indicate that the courts had to be persuaded that there was a real need to depart from the equal sharing regime to provide for children of the relationship, despite the long title of the Act explicitly referring to the interests of children of the marriage. The courts were of the view that the main purpose of the Act was to divide the property of the spouses or partners between them. The parties could then be entrusted to care and provide for their children as best they could. Only where that trust was not justified, whether for reasons within or beyond the parties' control, was the court willing to intervene to protect the interests of children. Even then, orders less draconian than removing property from a spouse were preferred, such as an occupation order of the home for the duration of the children's dependency.[93]

Section 27 of the MPA 1976 gave the court the power to grant exclusive possession of the matrimonial home to one of the spouses. This was a restatement of an existing power. In addition, section 28 gave the court a similar power to make tenancy orders of a dwelling house that one or both spouses held as a sole or joint tenancy. In 1981, in *Doak v Turner*, the Court of Appeal commented that the power to grant occupation orders was 'wide'.[94] Its availability indicated that the 'clean break principle'[95] was relevant, but not determinative. A flexible approach was required to do what was 'just and fair in the particular circumstances of the case'.[96]

In 1983 Parliament inserted section 28A to mandate the court to have 'particular regard to the need to provide a home for any minor or dependent child of the marriage' and authorised the court to 'also have regard to all other

93 For example, *S v W* HC Auckland CIV-2008-404-4494, 27 February 2009.

94 *Doak v Turner* [1981] 1 NZLR 18 (CA) at 22. The wife's application for an occupation order of the home was declined. Although she was 55 years old and in poor health, she had occupied the home for five years post-separation and it would be unfair to deprive the husband any longer of his share of the home.

95 A 'clean break' describes the principle that spouses should settle their financial matters promptly so that each of them can get on with building a new life: Department of Justice, *Report of the Working Group on Matrimonial Property and Family Protection*, Wellington 1988, 7.

96 *Doak v Turner*, above n 94 at 23.

relevant circumstances'. This provision was inserted because the courts were reluctant to grant occupation orders to custodial parents, preferring instead to order sale of the home.[97] But the provision created uncertainty as to the status of the children's interests relative to other considerations. Some judges were of the view that section 28A made the children's interests 'the first and most important' consideration in applications for occupation or tenancy orders.[98] Others cautioned against giving children's interests such a prominent status, arguing that the provision did not fetter the court's discretion.[99] While children's needs were to be accorded greater weight than other considerations, where children would not be significantly prejudiced, competing considerations were not to be overlooked.[100] Applications for occupation orders were often declined and when they were granted they were usually limited to a relatively short period of time.[101] The importance of a clean break and giving each spouse their share of the matrimonial property remained a dominant factor.

4.2. EQUALITY IS NOT EQUITY

In 1988 a Ministerial Working Group on Matrimonial Property and Family Protection ('Working Group') found that the MPA 1976 had failed to secure an equitable division of the fruits of the marriage.[102] The clean break principle adversely affected women and children. Women's living standards tended to drop off after dissolution, particularly if they had custody of the children, while those of their former husbands tended to rise, even though they had shared their matrimonial property equally. The family home was often the principal asset and, despite section 28A, the courts commonly ordered its sale and division to avoid denying one party – usually the husband – access to their share of the matrimonial property. Responsibility for the children post-separation had a negative impact on the wife's earning capacity. It made her dependent on her ex-husband or the state for financial support and lowered her standard of living significantly.[103] This conclusion echoed comments made by the

---

97 D Webb et al (eds), *Family Law in New Zealand*, 10th ed, vol 2, Butterworths, Wellington 2001, 1463.

98 *Wheeler v Wheeler* (1984) 2 NZFLR 385 (FC) at 390, endorsed in *Sweeney v Sweeney* [1985] 2 NZLR 673 (HC).

99 *Gordon v Gordon* (1988) 4 NZFLR 721 (HC); *W v W* [1997] NZFLR 543 (HC).

100 *W v W*, above n 99.

101 D Webb et al, above n 97. N Peart, 'Occupation Orders under the PRA' [2011] *New Zealand Law Journal* 356.

102 Department of Justice, above n 95 at 4.

103 Ibid, at 6.

Royal Commission on Social Policy in its 1988 Report.[104] The Working Group made a number of recommendations aimed at increasing the property entitlement of wives. But it could not see what more could be done to protect the interests of children while preserving a fair and reasonable balance between their interests and the property entitlement of the non-custodial spouse.[105]

4.3. INTERNATIONAL OBLIGATIONS

A year after the Working Group released its Report, the United Nations adopted the Convention of the Rights of the Child. New Zealand was a signatory to the Convention and ratified it on 6 April 1993, thus endorsing the rights in the Convention. Articles 3, 12, and 27 are particularly relevant to matrimonial property proceedings. They deal with the child's best interests being the primary consideration in all actions by private and public institutions, the child's right to be heard, and the child's living conditions. While Article 27 places the primary responsibility for living standards on parents, including the provision of housing, there is also a state responsibility to assist when parents are unable to carry out that responsibility. Article 4 requires states to take all appropriate measures, including legislative measures, to implement the rights set out in the Convention. While the Convention has not been adopted into New Zealand's domestic law as a whole, some of its Articles have been incorporated into domestic legislation, notably in the Care of Children Act 2004 (NZ).[106] The principles of the Convention have also been held to be relevant to other domestic legislation.[107] In matrimonial property proceedings, however, the Convention was not mentioned. It seems that its relevance to property division was not appreciated.[108]

---

104 I Richardson, 'Social Perspectives' in *Report of the Royal Commission on Social Policy: Future Directions*, vol 4, Government Printer, Wellington 1988, 18.

105 Department of Justice, above n 95 at 38.

106 Care of Children Act 2004 (NZ), s 6. The principles on that Act draw on other Articles of the Convention: *Kacem v Bashir* [2010] NZSC 112, [2011] 2 NZLR 1.

107 *Tavita v Minister of Immigration* [1994] 2 NZLR 257 (CA), where the Court of Appeal accepted that the Convention was relevant to a review of the order to remove Mr Tavita from New Zealand, as he had a young child who was a New Zealand citizen; *Chief Executive of the Ministry of Social Development v Black* [2016] NZHC 1274, [2016] 3 NZLR 341, where the Court considered the application of the Convention to decisions about social welfare benefits. See also *K v P* [2004] 2 NZLR 421 (HC) at [40], where the Court held that domestic laws should be interpreted in such a way as to accord with the Convention wherever possible.

108 For an analysis of the Convention in relationship to property proceedings, see further AM Skellern, above n 72 at ch 2.

4.4. PROPERTY (RELATIONSHIPS) AMENDMENT ACT 2001 (NZ)

In 2001, after a lengthy legislative process, Parliament eventually amended the MPA 1976, adopting many of the recommendations of the 1988 Working Group Report. The Act was renamed the Property (Relationships) Act 1976 ('PRA') to take account of the wider range of relationships to which it was to apply.[109] It made significant changes to give better effect to the equal sharing principle, but it did little to advance the interests of children.

Several Members of Parliament were aware of the adverse effects on children of the clean break and equal sharing principles.[110] They referred to Australia's model of property division and the need for a family-centred approach was suggested.[111] The Commissioner for Children voiced similar criticisms in his submissions to the Government Administration Committee considering the proposed amendments.[112] He identified the importance for children of continued occupancy of the family home, along with continued access to schools, friends, and other community networks. It helped to maintain security and certainty in children's lives, especially when family relationships were undergoing dramatic changes.[113] He was concerned that the clean break principle frequently overrode the duty to have particular regard to the needs of dependent children when making orders in relation to the home.[114]

> 'When compared with the English law, New Zealand law showed a lack of legislative concern for the economic interests of children. UK Courts can make total financial provision for children both in property and maintenance terms. Housing provision for children is a legislative priority – a "first consideration". Satisfaction of legitimate property interests are [*sic*] superseded by the need to maintain the home for the children. New Zealand has greater regard for ownership of property and satisfaction of property rights. Reallocation after marriage breakdown must be part of a financial package designed to minimise hardship, maintain children in their home, and enable the homemaker to re-establish herself.'

---

109 The Act also applies to de facto relationships of three or more years' duration: PRA, s 4C. In 2005 the Act was amended again to include civil unions: Property (Relationships) Amendment Act 2005 (NZ).

110 J Fitzsimons, *New Zealand Parliamentary Debates*, 6 May 1998, vol 567, 8281, made the same observations, blaming the clean break principle for condemning women and children to poverty. See also S Kedgley, *New Zealand Parliamentary Debates*, 29 February 2000, vol 582, 840.

111 D Yates, *New Zealand Parliamentary Debates*, 29 February 2000, vol 582, 842.

112 R McClay, above n 1.

113 Ibid, at 2.

114 Ibid, at 2–3.

The Children's Commissioner reminded the Committee of New Zealand's social and political commitment to the United Nations Convention on the Rights of the Child and his obligations to report on whether the proposed legislative reforms complied fully with the principles of the Convention.[115] To ensure compliance with the Convention, he recommended: the development of new statutory principles to guide the use of judicial discretion when children's interests were relevant, including acting in the best interests of children; the creation of a separate category of children's property, distinct from family chattels; and a new provision deferring the sale of the matrimonial home until the youngest child was 16 years old, unless the party seeking to sell could prove that deferring the sale would cause undue hardship to that party.[116]

However, there was no political will to depart from the clean break principle or the equal sharing model other than to include a compensation provision for economic disparity resulting from the division of functions within the marriage.[117] That provision is primarily concerned with the effect that the division of functions had on the spouse or partner's earning capacity. The needs of any minor or dependent children are relevant to compensation only to the extent that they delay a spouse or partner from regaining their full earning capacity. While compensation may improve the living standards of the children, the purpose of the provision is to acknowledge the impact of the relationship on the earning capacity of the spouse or partner. Its primary aim is not to protect the needs and interests of the children.

The same point can be made in relation to the new compensation provision in section 44C for dispositions of relationship property into trust that have the effect of defeating the rights of one of the parties to the relationship. Its purpose is to compensate a spouse or partner for the unequal benefit resulting from the disposition. An award of compensation might well improve the living standards of children, but the purpose of the provision is to prevent the undermining of the equal sharing principle.[118]

As section 1C of the PRA explains:

> 'This Act is mainly about how the property of married couples and civil union couples and couples who have lived in a de facto relationship is to be divided up when they separate or one of them dies.'

---

115 Ibid, at 5–6.

116 Ibid, at 6–7.

117 See further on this compensation, M Henaghan, above n 9.

118 N Peart, 'Protecting Children's Interests in Relationship Property Proceedings' (2013) 13(1) *Otago Law Review* 27, 35–39. The abolition of gift duty in 2011 has made it easier for owners to divest themselves quickly of all assets, leaving no property outside the trust from

In regard to children, the 2001 reforms made very few amendments. The new purpose section in the PRA gives children no greater prominence than the long title in the MPA 1976 did. The reference to children is tucked in at the end of section 1M(c), where one of the purposes of the Act is:

> 'to provide for a just division of the relationship property between the spouses or partners when their relationship ends by separation or death, and in certain other circumstances, *while taking account of the interests of any children of the marriage or children of the civil union or children of the de facto relationship*' (emphasis added).

The inclusion of civil unions and de facto relationships of three or more years' duration on the same basis as married couples means that the powers and duties of the court in relation to children apply to a wider pool of children. As before, the purpose section is not confined to minor or dependent children and a 'child of a marriage' or other relationship is defined to include a child of both parties to the relationship as well as a child who is a member of the family when the relationship ended but may not be a child of either spouse or partner.[119]

The mandate in section 26 to have regard to the interests of minor or dependent children of the relationship in proceedings under the PRA has been retained without substantive amendment. The mandate applies not only to the ongoing use of the home. It requires the court to consider the interests of minor or dependent children against all claims, rights, and entitlements of the parties to the relationship. Children's interests may be relevant to ownership, classification, valuation, and division of property. For example, property legally or ostensibly owned by either or both parties to the relationship may in fact be beneficially owned by a child.[120] The presumption that property will be valued at the date of hearing could conceivably be rebutted to take account of children's interests. However, in *JAM v GFM*, the Court of Appeal agreed with the High Court that the Family Court was wrong to value the home at separation date because the

---

which compensation can be ordered: Taxation (Tax Administration and Remedial Matters) Act 2011 (NZ), s 245. See further J Palmer, 'What to Do about Trusts?', ch 8.

119 MPA 1976, s 2; PRA, s 2.

120 *Sydney v Sydney* [2012] NZFC 2685, where a valuable painting hanging in the family home was found to be held on trust by Mr Sydney for the benefit of his children of his first marriage, and thus not included in the relationship property pool of the second marriage. In *L v P* HC Auckland CIV-2010-404-6103, 17 August 2011, the couple's young daughter's inheritance from her aunt had been used to repay the mortgage on the family home without according her any interest in the home. See also *Canavan v Cullen* [2016] NZFC 3269, where some of the property ostensibly owned by the children's parents was found to be owned by the children.

children wanted to remain in the home and the husband hoped his wife could buy him out.[121] In the High Court Woodhouse J held:[122]

> 'it was not open to the Judge to meet the needs of the children by altering the presumed valuation date designed to achieve equality between the husband and wife.'

The interests of children may also be relevant to the division of property and compensation for post-separation actions.[123] The Family Court decision in *WMM v SJM* is a rare example of a child's needs being submitted as a reason for departing from equal division.[124] Although the case for unequal division in the interests of a dependent child was particularly strong, it still failed. The applicant and respondent commenced a de facto relationship in 1994. The respondent had an 18-month-old daughter, D, from another relationship. Shortly after the relationship with Mr M began, D was diagnosed with Angelman syndrome as a result of which she was severely disabled and in need of care. The couple's own child, H, was born in August 1995 and shortly thereafter the couple married. Mrs M had significant physical and mental health problems of her own throughout the marriage. The couple purchased a house early in their relationship, but it was not ideal for the children, especially D. In 2004 they bought a new house for $265,000. They were able to do so because Mrs M contributed $100,000 from an inheritance she had received earlier that year which she had deposited into their joint account. When the parties separated 18 months later in June 2006, some $70,000 was still owing on the mortgage. Mrs M continued living in the home with both children. Their daughter H moved out in 2010, leaving only Mrs M and D in the home. Mrs M was receiving a state benefit to enable her to care for D. Mr M filed proceedings in 2007, but due to Mrs M's health issues the case was not heard until June 2012, six years after the couple had separated. D was by then 19 years old and H was 17. The home was the principal relationship property asset and Mrs M had lived there since separation.

Mrs M mounted a series of arguments aimed at retaining the home for herself and D. The first was that her injection of inheritance money only 18 months before separation and the difficulty of re-housing D were

---

121 *JAM v GFM* FC Auckland FAM 2006-004-002610, 4 November 2010; *JAM v GFM* [2012] NZHC 290, [2012] NZFLR 469; *GFM v JAM* [2013] NZCA 660, [2014] NZFLR 418. The Supreme Court declined to grant leave to appeal because it was not persuaded that the Court of Appeal was wrong to uphold the High Court that there were no reasons to depart from the presumption that the property should be valued at hearing date: *GFM v JAM* [2014] NZSC 32, [2014] NZFLR 599.

122 *JAM v GFM* [2012] NZHC 290, [2012] NZFLR 469 at [133].

123 For example, *Roocker v Delgado* [2015] NZFC 9450, [2016] NZFLR 37, where the wife successfully relied on s 26 to argue against her husband's claim for compensation for his post-separation contributions.

124 *WMM v SJM* [2012] NZFC 5019.

extraordinary circumstances that made equal sharing repugnant to justice.[125] This exception to equal division sets a notoriously high threshold. So, it is perhaps unsurprising that Mrs M did not meet the threshold. The Court acknowledged that D's needs were high and complex, but it could not see why Mr M should receive less than an equal share of the relationship property by giving more weight to D's interests, taking into account all the circumstances, including Mr M's ongoing financial support of D.[126]

Mrs M's application for an order under section 26 settling a capital sum for the benefit of D was also unsuccessful.[127] The relationship property pool was too modest to set aside a fund for D. Mrs M made no such claim for her younger daughter, who had been living independently since 2010. Mrs M's claim under the newly inserted section 26A seeking deferral of division was also dismissed. A deferral for D's lifetime would cause serious inequity for Mr M. It was already close to six years since the couple separated, during which time Mrs M continued to occupy the home without paying rent.

Section 26A imposes stringent conditions. An order postponing the vesting of any share of relationship property until a future date or specified future event may be granted only:[128]

> 'if the Court is satisfied that immediate vesting would cause undue hardship for a spouse or partner who is the principal provider of ongoing daily care for 1 or more minor or dependent children of the marriage, civil union, or de facto relationship'.

Furthermore, such orders may be made 'only for as long as necessary, and only to the extent necessary, to alleviate the undue hardship'.[129] These stringent conditions may explain the small number of cases where orders under section 26A have been made.[130] Although the Court did not refer to these conditions in *WMM v SJM*, it is clear from the Court's reasoning that it was not persuaded that whatever hardship Mrs M might suffer by having to move house outweighed Mr M's property entitlement. There was no suggestion that D was at risk of imminent death. She could outlive her stepfather, so an order postponing vesting might deprive Mr M from ever receiving his share of the relationship property.

If Mrs M had applied for an occupation order under section 27, it would not have been granted either. Although section 28A was amended as part of the

---

125 PRA, s 13.

126 *WMM v SJM*, above n 124 at [48].

127 The 10 propositions of relevance to s 26 applications identified in *R v R*, above n 91 at 622 continue to be relevant under the amended Act: *BJR v VMR [Economic Disparity]* [2007] NZFLR 177 (FC).

128 PRA, s 26A(1).

129 PRA, s 26A(2).

130 N Peart, above n 118 at 52–53.

2001 reforms to refer to the need to provide a home for 'minor or dependent' children, rather than 'minor dependent' children, thus broadening the scope of the Court's duty to have particular regard also to minor children who are not dependent and to adult children who are dependent, Mrs M had occupied the home to the exclusion of Mr M for nearly six years. Despite section 28A according with New Zealand's obligation under the United Nations Convention on the Rights of the Child, the clean break principle continues to militate against long-term occupation orders.[131] So does the move away from sole custody to shared parenting of children. There is now less likelihood of one parent being the primary caregiver.[132]

Where a spouse or partner has had the exclusive possession of the home, the other spouse or partner may apply for occupation rent as compensation for his or her post-separation contribution to the relationship.[133] Mr M made such an application for the six years that he had not had access to his half share of the home, seeking payment of half the market rent for the home. Given the unusual and complex circumstances of Mrs M and the modest pool of relationship property, occupation rent was ordered only from December 2010, when the couple's daughter H left home to live independently. As Mrs M had paid for all the outgoings on the house and been primarily responsible for the care of D since separation and for H for four years post-separation, the occupation rent Mrs M owed to Mr M was fully offset against her own post-separation contributions.[134]

Mrs M lodged an appeal against the Family Court decision rejecting her claims for unequal division and orders based on the needs of D. In an application by Mr M for security for costs, the High Court indicated that success on the appeal might be an 'uphill struggle' and an uplift for security for costs was accordingly ordered.[135] It seems the appeal did not proceed, presumably because legal aid was declined.

While *WMM v SJM* is only one example, its rulings on each of the claims were consistent with earlier cases.[136] It confirms the dominance of equal sharing of relationship property and the clean break principle, despite the amendments in 2001 seeking to place greater emphasis on the interests of children. The relevance of the United Nations Convention on the Rights of the Child is rarely mentioned and has not had a significant impact on property division on the breakdown of a relationship.[137]

---

131 *S v W*, above n 93; Peart, above n 101.

132 B Atkin and W Parker, *Relationship Property in New Zealand*, 2nd ed, LexisNexis, Wellington 2009, 254.

133 PRA, s 18B.

134 *WMM v SJM*, above n 124 at [77]–[78].

135 *SJM v WMM* [2012] NZHC 2659 at [4].

136 N Peart, above n 101 and n 118.

137 *Hislop v Hislop* (2004) 23 FRNZ 710 (FC) and *DPC v PMB [Relationship Property]* [2013] NZFC 1105, [2014] NZFLR 277, are rare examples of a court referring to the Convention in

4.5. PROBLEMS WITH THE CURRENT LAW

Since 1963, New Zealand has steadily moved away from formal equality towards substantive equality between spouses and partners in regard to property sharing. The aim of the 2001 amendments to the relationship property regime was to enhance substantive equality, most obviously by including a compensation provision for economic disparity, thereby seeking to include earning capacity as human capital to be shared. These changes were thought also to benefit children of the relationship. But when the assets are limited, equal sharing of property is likely to impact adversely on the minor or dependent children of the relationship.[138] The home is likely to be sold, treasured possessions may be divided, education may be disrupted, and friendships will be lost, all of which is likely to undermine a child's sense of security and well-being with adverse consequences to their welfare and personal development.

New Zealand's current system of relationship property division makes it both conceptually and practically difficult to accommodate the needs and interests of children. On the breakdown of a marriage, civil union, or de facto relationship, there is an inevitable tension between family obligations and property entitlements. The PRA tips the balance firmly towards property. It provides limited scope to depart from the fundamental principle of equal sharing. The focus is on the parties to the relationship and their property entitlements, rather than the needs of the family as a whole.

This imbalance is exacerbated by the fragmented approach to the consequences of a relationship breakdown.[139] The property rights of the parties to the relationship are governed by the PRA. Spousal maintenance is regulated separately by the Family Proceedings Act 1980 (NZ). Its relationship with the economic disparity provisions in the PRA is unclear and has caused confusion in the courts.[140] Parenting orders and guardianship of children are regulated by the Care of Children Act 2004 (NZ), while financial support of children is governed by the Child Support Act 1991 (NZ) and the Family Proceedings Act 1980 (NZ). Each statute has its own principles. There is no coherent and consistent set of

relationship property proceedings. In *Hislop* the Court awarded the wife exclusive occupation of the family home to give the children stability in their lives. In *DPC v PMB* the Court declined to order the sale of the family home to enable the wife to continue living there with the children, for whose care she had been almost exclusively responsible since separation.

138 R Kaspiew and L Qu, above n 1.

139 This fragmented approach was criticised during the parliamentary debates on the Matrimonial Property Bill 1975: P Wilkinson, *New Zealand Parliamentary Debates*, 3 October 1975, vol 406, 5118, who refers to Australia's Family Law Act 1975 (Cth) as a better model for dealing comprehensively with all matters arising on marital breakdown. See also the comments by P Schnauer on the Matrimonial Property Amendment Bill 1998: P Schnauer, *New Zealand Parliamentary Debates*, 6 May 1998, vol 568, 8272.

140 See M Henaghan, above n 9.

principles to govern the consequences of a relationship breakdown. The status of children's interests varies depending on the statute.

While section 26 of the PRA does mandate the courts to have regard to the interests of minor or dependent children, and includes some provisions aimed at addressing those interests, there is no incentive on the parties to put their children's interests ahead of their own. The children's interests are rarely pleaded. Parties will do so only if it serves their own interests. The courts are therefore seldom made aware of issues relating to the children. The court does have the power to appoint a lawyer to represent minor or dependent children in relationship property proceedings, but it may do so only if it believes 'special circumstances make the appointment necessary or desirable'.[141] The fee must be paid by one or both of the parties. Unsurprisingly, the power is rarely used.[142] Without independent representation, the interests of children are easily overlooked or sidelined. The obligation in Article 12(2) of the United Nations Convention on the Rights of the Child to give the child the opportunity to be heard in proceedings affecting them is rarely seen as relevant in relationship property proceedings.

The New Zealand system is in sharp contrast to the English approach where the Matrimonial Causes Act 1973 (Eng&W) deals with property division, maintenance, custody, and child support in one comprehensive statute. Children's interests are given primary consideration throughout. Division of property is firmly tipped in favour of the family's needs. Equal sharing is a subsidiary consideration. Australia's Family Law Act 1975 (Cth), while less obviously focused on the interests of children, nonetheless results in unequal division of property to ensure the welfare of children is adequately addressed. A discretionary system allows for orders that are tailored to the particular circumstances of the case. The downside is the uncertainty inherent in any system that gives wide discretion to the courts. As explained below, we would not advocate that New Zealand move to a fully discretionary system.

5. OPTIONS FOR REFORM

The breakdown of a marriage or equivalent relationship can have devastating consequences for children of the relationship, especially when the assets of the

141 PRA, s 37A. *H v R* [2017] NZFC 761 is a rare example where children of the marriage were joined as parties in their capacity as final beneficiaries of the family trust that held the home where they lived.

142 *L v P*, above n 120, is a rare example of the court appointing counsel for the young child of the couple. It did so when it discovered that the child's inheritance had been used to repay the mortgage on the family home that the parties were seeking to divide between them without regard to the child's investment in the home.

former spouses or partners are limited. Domestic and international law impose on states a duty to protect minor and dependent children. All the jurisdictions discussed in this chapter have recognised that property and financial division on the breakdown of a marriage affects children of the relationship and have sought to protect their interests. The courts in New Zealand have been less attuned to the interests of children in the division of property than the courts in England and Wales, and Australia. While the best interests of children are paramount in proceedings relating to their care, when it comes to their material well-being the New Zealand courts have not taken their interests as seriously as the interests of their parents in securing financial equality and a clean break. This contrasts with England and Wales, and Australia, where the interests of children are at the forefront in all decision-making following a marital breakdown.

In 2016 the Minister of Justice asked the New Zealand Law Commission to undertake a review of the PRA.[143] The Commission is expected to report its findings and recommendations by November 2018. Its terms of reference are very broad and touch on all aspects of the current law. There is therefore potential for quite radical reform. If New Zealand decides to retain a strong presumption of equal sharing, then inevitably the emphasis will remain on the property entitlements of the parties to the relationship. But that does not preclude children's interests having a more prominent influence in the division of property. The Child Support Act 1991 (NZ) could be amended to give the courts greater powers to make orders in respect of the resources available to each of the former spouses or partners. The risk is that the division of property might already have taken place under the PRA, thus removing the option of making property orders under the Child Support Act 1991 (NZ) for the benefit of the children, such as retaining the family home until the youngest child completes school.

The MPA 1976 was retrospective in outlook. It sought to divide the assets that the parties had accumulated during the marriage and left forward-looking matters, such as spousal maintenance and child support, to other statutes. The 2001 reforms introduced a forward-looking element into the Act by providing for compensation for economic disparity. Parliament has therefore already moved some way towards a future assessment by allowing for unequal division where the future income and living standards of one party to the relationship are likely to be significantly lower than those of the other party, as a result of the division of functions within the relationship.

A similar forward-looking assessment could be undertaken in relation to minor or dependent children of the relationship. The court could be mandated not to make an order dividing the parties' relationship property unless it is

143 Law Commission (NZ), *Review of the Property (Relationships) Act 1976*, Media Release, 25 May 2016.

satisfied that the children's needs are adequately met.[144] Those needs should include the children's financial needs, their housing, the standard of living enjoyed by the family during the relationship, the manner in which the children were being educated and the parties' expectations as to their children's education, any special needs arising from a child's physical or mental disability, the financial resources available to each party and the children, and the parties' own financial needs. This duty would arise only if there were minor or dependent children and only after the parties' relationship property entitlement had been provisionally determined, including any provision for economic disparity.

A similar provision currently exists in the Family Proceedings Act 1980 (NZ) in relation to the granting of an order dissolving a marriage or civil union.[145] The court must normally be:[146]

> 'satisfied that arrangements have been made for the day-to-day care, maintenance, and other aspects of the welfare of [any] child of the marriage or civil union who is under the age of 16 years, [or, in special circumstances over the age of 16,] and [that] those arrangements are satisfactory or are the best that can be devised in the circumstances.'

The problem about that provision is that a dissolution can only be sought after the parties have ceased living together for two years, whereas relationship property division is triggered on separation.[147] It also does not apply to de facto relationships. The duty would have to be included in the PRA, where it would apply following separation to all relationships where division of property is sought. By including such a provision as a condition of relationship property division, the welfare of children would be better protected. It would provide for a family-centred approach in decisions affecting property division and improve New Zealand's compliance with its obligations under the United Nations Convention of the Rights of the Child.

---

144 M Hobbs made a similar suggestion during the debates on the Matrimonial Property Amendment Bill in 1998: M Hobbs, *New Zealand Parliamentary Debates*, 6 May 1998, vol 567, 8285.

145 Family Proceedings Act 1980 (NZ), s 45. *Meyers v Meyers* [2016] NZFC 6078 is a recent example of the application of this section.

146 PRA, s 45(1)(a). Under PRA, ss 45(1)(b) and (c), the court need not be so satisfied if 'it is impracticable for the party or parties appearing before the court to make such arrangements; or there are special circumstances justifying the making of an order dissolving the marriage or civil union, [even though] the court is not satisfied that any such arrangements have been made'.

147 Family Proceedings Act 1980 (NZ), s 39.

CHAPTER 5

FAMILY FINANCES ON DEATH OF A SPOUSE OR PARTNER

Nicola PEART*

1. INTRODUCTION

On death there is an inevitable tension in succession law between property and family, between testamentary freedom and the deceased's duty to provide for family members. Balancing these two potentially conflicting interests is an ongoing challenge, affected by changing social values and expectations. If the

* I am greatly indebted to Kyla Mullen IMOT LLB (Hons), for her invaluable research assistance and to my colleagues Professors Mark Henaghan and Margaret Briggs for their helpful comments on earlier drafts.

deceased leaves a spouse (or a civil union partner, or de facto partner)[1] a further tension may exist between succession law and a spouse's contribution-based property entitlement, referred to in this chapter as a relationship property entitlement. Should surviving spouses have the same relationship property rights on death as on divorce, or is death of a spouse sufficiently different from divorce that succession law should determine the rights of a surviving spouse? The common law and civil law jurisdictions have responded differently to this question, while New Zealand draws on both civil law and common law principles. It thus offers a unique perspective on the rights of a surviving spouse or partner.

In common law jurisdictions, such as England and Australia, a separate property system applies to married couples on death and on divorce.[2] Neither jurisdiction has a 'matrimonial property regime' with a code of rules governing property division at the end of a marriage.[3] If the marriage ends during the joint lifetime of the spouses the courts have discretion to adjust their property rights in the interests of fairness or justice for the family as a whole.[4] That power is not available if the marriage ends because one of the spouses has died. A deceased spouse may freely dispose of his or her property by will. To the extent that the surviving spouse lacks financial provision, the courts have the power to override the terms of the will or the intestacy rules by ordering provision from the estate for the surviving spouse.[5] Property distribution on both death and divorce is therefore premised on the duty of one spouse to provide for the other spouse, rather than on any property entitlement or notion of community property. It is a matter of family duty rather than property entitlement, and on death the duty is governed by succession law rather than the law governing property division on divorce.[6]

Most civil law jurisdictions in continental Europe have matrimonial property regimes that prescribe rules for the division of property with little or no discretion.[7] On divorce and on death the matrimonial property regime

---

1 Hereafter referred to as 'spouse' unless the context requires otherwise. See J Palmer, N Peart and M Briggs, 'Introduction', ch 1 for an explanation of terminology.

2 Matrimonial Causes Act 1973 (Eng&W); Family Law Act 1975 (Cth).

3 JM Scherpe, 'The Financial Consequences of Divorce in a European Perspective' in JM Scherpe (ed), *European Family Law Volume III: Family Law in a European Perspective*, Edward Elgar Publishing, Cheltenham 2016, 146 at 147.

4 Matrimonial Causes Act 1973 (Eng&W), s 24; Family Law Act 1975 (Cth), s 79.

5 Inheritance (Provision for Family and Dependants) Act 1975 (Eng&W), s 1; Succession Act 2006 (NSW), s 59; Succession Act 1981 (Qld), s 41; Administration and Probate Act 1958 (Vic), s 91; Inheritance (Family Provision) Act 1972 (SA), s 7; Testator's Family Maintenance Act 1912 (Tas), s 3; Family Provision Act 1972 (WA), s 6; Family Provision Act 1969 (ACT), s 8; Family Provision Act 1970 (NT), s 8.

6 R Croucher, 'A Lament for "Testator's Family Maintenance" – A Good Idea Gone Wrong? Australian Reflections', ch 6.

7 JM Scherpe, above n 3 at 149–62. Austria is the exception. Its system is discretionary and applicable only on divorce, not on death: JM Scherpe, above n 3 at 162–65.

dissolves by operation of law, with each party taking their property entitlement.[8] Succession law applies to the assets comprising the deceased spouse's estate. Historically, the estate passed to the deceased's descendants to the exclusion of the surviving spouse.[9] While most jurisdictions have amended their laws to provide for the surviving spouse as well, the distinction between property entitlement and support obligations remains. Property and family are thus kept separate, both on death and on divorce.

New Zealand straddles the common law and civil law systems. It has a relationship property regime akin to some civil law systems, which applies to married and unmarried couples on death and on separation.[10] Unlike the civil law regimes, however, when a relationship ends on death New Zealand blurs the distinction between relationship property law and succession law by giving the surviving spouse the option of taking his or her share of the relationship property or inheriting from the deceased.[11] The survivor is not normally entitled to both.[12] Whichever option is chosen, surviving spouses may apply for further provision from the estate if the deceased has failed to make adequate provision for their proper maintenance and support.[13] New Zealand thus merges property entitlement and family duty.

This chapter considers the rights of a surviving spouse (or partner) in common law jurisdictions. It compares England and Australia with New Zealand. It makes reference to civil law jurisdictions, but only as a backdrop against which to assess the relative merits of the common law systems.[14] While the focus is on surviving spouses, their rights cannot be considered in isolation of the deceased's intergenerational relationships and associated obligations. On death, the interests of the deceased's children and other family members come into play more prominently than on separation or divorce. All three common law jurisdictions adhere to the principle of testamentary freedom, but testators are expected to exercise this freedom with due regard to their moral responsibilities to family members and dependents.[15] These jurisdictions all accord primacy to the surviving spouse, but do not balance the rights of the surviving spouse and

---

8 K Boele-Woelki et al, *Principles of European Family Law Regarding Property Relations Between Spouses*, Intersentia, Cambridge 2013, 173 and 305.

9 KGC Reid, MJ De Waal and R Zimmermann, 'Intestate Succession in Historical and Comparative Perspective' in KGC Reid, MJ De Waal and R Zimmermann (eds), *Comparative Succession Law: Volume II – Intestate Succession*, OUP, Oxford 2015, 442.

10 Property (Relationships) Act 1976 (NZ).

11 Property (Relationships) Act 1976 (NZ), s 61.

12 Property (Relationships) Act 1976 (NZ), s 76.

13 Property (Relationships) Act 1976 (NZ), s 57; Family Protection Act 1955 (NZ), ss 3 and 4.

14 See K Boele-Woelki et al, above n 8 for details of the property rights of spouses in the European civil law jurisdictions.

15 *Banks v Goodfellow* (1870) LR 5 QB 549 (QB).

the interests of others in the same way. Nor do they protect the interests of the surviving spouse to the same extent.

This chapter concludes that surviving spouses are still in a state of dependency and vulnerable to the claims and interests of others, particularly in Australia and New Zealand. To reduce their dependence, this chapter recommends that spouses should be given a relationship property entitlement on death to acknowledge their respective contributions to the creation of their combined wealth. Determining the property entitlements of the surviving spouse and the estate of the deceased spouse should take priority over any succession rights or claims that either the surviving spouse or others may have in respect of the assets truly belonging to the estate. The current liberal approach to family provision claims by adult children in New Zealand and Australia and its impact on testamentary freedom is questioned in this chapter, while in the next chapter Croucher addresses this imbalance in the Australian context and argues for a reversal to dependency as an eligibility requirement for adult children.

2. RIGHTS OF SURVIVING SPOUSES TO THE PRESENT DAY

2.1. HISTORICAL INTRODUCTION

Until the common law jurisdictions adopted Married Women's Property legislation in the late nineteenth century, the principle of matrimonial unity applied. On marriage husband and wife became one person in the eyes of the law.[16] The husband had legal control over the family and its property, while his wife lived under his protection or coverture with no independent capacity to enter legal relations. The husband became the owner of all personalty that his wife brought into or acquired during the marriage, including any money, and controlled and managed his wife's realty, retaining any income derived from her realty. If the wife predeceased her husband the right of curtesy entitled him to a life interest in her realty, provided there was issue of the marriage capable of succeeding to the land. The right of dower entitled the widow to a life interest in a third of her husband's land, which survived any dispositions her husband made

---

16 W Blackstone, *Commentaries on the Laws of England*, vol 1, London 1809, 441; AR Buck, '"A Blot on the Certificate": Dower and Women's Property Rights in Colonial New South Wales' (1987) 4 *Australian Journal of Law and Society* 87; B Bradbury, 'From Civil Death to Separate Property: Changes in the Legal Rights of Married Women in Nineteenth-Century New Zealand' (1995) 29(1) *New Zealand Journal of History* 40.

during his lifetime or by will.[17] The adverse effect of dower on conveyancing and testamentary freedom led to its abolition by the late nineteenth century.[18]

The Married Women's Property statutes, adopted in the 1880s, introduced a system of separate property in England, Australia, and New Zealand. Each spouse retained the property he or she brought into or acquired during the marriage and neither spouse acquired by virtue of their marriage any legal entitlement to the property of the other spouse.[19] Section 17 of the Married Women's Property Act 1882 (UK) gave the court jurisdiction to make orders in regard to questions as to title and possession of property on granting a decree of divorce. Until the 1950s those questions were determined by applying the ordinary rules of common law and equity, though the courts did sometimes grant possession of the matrimonial home to the non-owning spouse, usually the wife.[20] After World War II, when there was an extreme shortage of housing, the family home became more important and the English courts started using the power in section 17 to make orders affecting title to property.[21] The power was subsequently formalised and can now be found in the Matrimonial Causes Act 1973 (Eng&W).

The Australian and New Zealand courts had powers equivalent to section 17, but did not believe they could use them to override legal or beneficial title.[22]

17 R Atherton, 'Expectation Without Right: Testamentary Freedom and the Position of Women in 19th Century NSW' (1988) 11(1) *University of New South Wales Law Journal* 133; M Briggs, 'Historical Analysis' in N Peart, M Briggs and M Henaghan (eds), *Relationship Property on Death*, Thomson Brookers, Wellington 2004, 1 at 3–5.

18 Deceased Persons Estates Act 1874 (Tas); Intestacy Act 1877 (Qld), s 28; Dower Abolition Act 1880 (Vic); Probate Act 1890 (NSW, including ACT), s 33, confirmed by the Dower Abolition Act 1906 (NSW); Administration and Probate Act 1891 (SA, including NT), s 64; Administration Act 1903 (WA), s 15. In New Zealand the Real Estate Descent Act 1874 (NZ) rendered dower practically obsolete and the Property Law Act 1905 (NZ), s 21 formally abolished it. Curtesy was abolished at about the same time: for example, Married Women's Property Act 1884 (Vic), s 25; Intestacy Act 1877 (Qld), s 28; Wills, Probate and Administration Act 1898 (NSW), s 52; Married Women's Property Act 1884 (NZ), s 4. In England dower and curtesy were abolished by the Administration of Estates Act 1925 (Eng&W), s 45.

19 Married Women's Property Acts were adopted in England in 1874 and 1882, in the Australian jurisdictions between 1879 (NSW) and 1892 (WA), and in New Zealand in 1884. See further O Kahn-Freund, 'Matrimonial Property: Some Recent Developments' (1959) 22(3) *Modern Law Review* 241.

20 For example, *Hutchison v Hutchison* [1947] 2 All ER 792 (CA), where the Court declined the husband's application for a possession order of the home he left on entering an adulterous relationship. He was still married to his wife and had no right to turn her out. She had behaved properly and it was unjust to order her to vacate their home.

21 *Rimmer v Rimmer* [1952] 2 All ER 863 (CA); *Fribance v Fribance (No 2)* [1957] 1 All ER 357 (CA). The House of Lords curtailed this approach in *Pettit v Pettit* [1970] AC 777 (HL) and *Gissing v Gissing* [1971] AC 886 (HL).

22 For example, Law of Property Act 1936–1956 (SA), s 105, and Married Women's Property Act 1952 (NZ), s 19. *Wirth v Wirth* (1956) 98 CLR 228; *Martin v Martin* (1959) 110 CLR 297; *Hepworth v Hepworth* (1963) 110 CLR 309; *Barrow v Barrow* [1946] NZLR 438 (CA);

It was not until the law was changed in the 1960s that the courts started to adjust title as between spouses.[23] In Australia that power is now in the Family Law Act 1975 (Cth) and in New Zealand in the Property (Relationships) Act 1976.[24] In England and Australia the power to adjust title to property is available only when a marriage, civil partnership or de facto relationship ends during the joint lifetime of the parties, whereas in New Zealand it can also be invoked if death terminates such a relationship.

When dower was abolished testamentary freedom became absolute in the common law jurisdictions. Concerns about the vulnerability of widows and minor children to testamentary abuse persuaded New Zealand in 1900 to give the courts the power to override the terms of a will if the deceased had failed to make adequate provision for the proper maintenance and support of his or her spouse or children.[25] By 1920 the Australian jurisdictions had followed New Zealand's lead, and in 1938 England and Wales did so too.[26]

2.2. ENGLAND AND AUSTRALIA

2.2.1. *Property Adjustment*

The Matrimonial Causes Act 1973 (Eng&W) applies in England and Wales when a marriage or civil partnership ends during the lifetime of the spouses.[27] It gives

---

Watson v Watson [1952] NZLR 892 (SC); *Masters v Masters* [1954] NZLR 82 (SC); *Peychers v Peychers* [1955] NZLR 564 (SC).

23 Marriage (Property) Act 1962 (Vic), s 3 amended the Marriage Act 1958 (Vic), s 161, the eventual successor to the Married Women's Property Act 1870 (Vic), s 12, to give the courts the power to make orders adjusting title as between spouses, but not so as to defeat any common intention expressed by the spouses: *Haskin v Haskin* [1964] VR 37; *Hogben v Hogben* [1964] VR 468; *Moore v Moore* [1965] VR 61. Marriage (Property) Act 1962 (Vic), s 3(4)(b), also inserted a presumption that the matrimonial home acquired by either spouse during or in contemplation of the marriage was held by the parties as joint tenants.

24 Matrimonial Causes Act 1973 (Eng&W), s 24; Family Law Act 1975 (Cth), s 79; Property (Relationships) Act 1976 (NZ), s 11.

25 Testator's Family Maintenance Act 1900 (NZ). The current statute is the Family Protection Act 1955 (NZ). The social and legislative history of this statute is described by R Atherton, 'New Zealand's Testator's Family Maintenance Act of 1900: The Stouts, the Women's Movement and Political Compromise' (1990) 7(2) *Otago Law Review* 202.

26 Widows and Young Children's Maintenance Act 1906 (Vic); Testator's Family Maintenance Act 1912 (Tas); Testator's Family Maintenance Act 1914 (Qld); Testator's Family Maintenance and Guardianship of Infants Act 1916 (NSW); Testator's Family Maintenance Act 1918 (SA); Guardianship of Infants Act 1920 (WA). Australian Capital Territory and Northern Territory were governed by the laws of New South Wales and South Australia respectively. They adopted their own family provision statutes in 1929: Testator's Family Maintenance Ordinance 1929 (NT); Administration and Probate Ordinance 1929 (ACT). The statute adopted in England and Wales was the Inheritance (Family Provision) Act 1938 (Eng&W).

27 Civil Partnership Act 2004 (UK), s 72. There is no statutory property division regime for cohabitants in England and Wales.

the court the power to make property adjustment and financial provision orders to provide for the future needs of each spouse and their children.[28] The welfare of minor children of the marriage is the first consideration.[29] Fairness is the touchstone for making property adjustment orders.[30] It has three strands: the financial needs of the parties, compensation for economic disparity, and equal sharing.[31] Equality is a yardstick to be used as an aid, not a rule.[32] In most cases, there are insufficient assets to consider anything other than the needs of the parties and their children.[33] Property adjustment orders can be supplemented by financial provision orders in the form of lump sums or periodic payments.[34]

Australia's Family Law Act 1975 gives its courts a similarly broad discretion to make property settlement and spousal maintenance orders on the breakdown of a marriage, civil partnership, or de facto relationship.[35] Property settlement orders empower the court to alter the parties' property interests to achieve a 'just and equitable' outcome, having regard to the parties' contributions to property and the welfare of the family as well as their respective needs.[36] As in England, the starting point is the parties' existing legal and beneficial interests. There must be a principled reason to alter those interests, for example because there will no longer be common use of property after a relationship breakdown.[37]

The power to alter spouses' property interests in England and Australia does not apply if their relationship ends on death. Separate property applies and any property arrangements, such as joint tenancies and trusts, settled during the lifetime of the couple and continuing after the death of a spouse without forming part of his or her estate, may provide for the surviving spouse.[38] Succession law governs the distribution of the deceased spouse's estate. The deceased's will or

28 Matrimonial Causes Act 1973 (Eng&W), ss 21–25.

29 Matrimonial Causes Act 1973 (Eng&W), s 25(1).

30 *White v White* [2001] 1 AC 596 (HL); *Miller v Miller; McFarlane v McFarlane* [2006] UKHL 24, [2006] 2 AC 618.

31 *Miller v Miller; McFarlane v McFarlane*, above n 30 at [10]–[16].

32 Ibid, at [16].

33 E Hitchings, 'The Impact of Recent Ancillary Relief Jurisprudence in the "Everyday" Ancillary Relief Case' (2010) 22 *Child and Family Law Quarterly* 93.

34 For a discussion of the weaknesses of a discretionary system generally and of the system in England and Wales in particular, see J Miles, 'Should the Regime be Discretionary or Rules-Based?', ch 11.

35 Family Law Act 1975 (Cth), ss 75 and 79. Proceedings commenced during the lifetime of the parties can be continued after death by the personal representative of the deceased: s 79(8). See *Stanford v Stanford* [2012] HCA 52, (2012) 247 CLR 108.

36 Family Law Act 1975 (Cth), s 79(2). See *Stanford v Stanford*, above n 35.

37 *Stanford v Stanford*, above n 35 at [35]–[42].

38 A Braun, 'Will-Substitutes in England and Wales' and N Peart and P Vines, 'Will-Substitutes in New Zealand and Australia' in A Braun and A Röthel (eds), *Passing Wealth on Death: Will-Substitutes in Comparative Perspective*, Hart Publishing, Oxford 2016, 51 and 107.

the intestacy rules determine whether and to what extent the surviving spouse shares in the assets of the deceased spouse, subject to any orders for family provision.[39]

2.2.2. *Family Provision in England and Wales*

If the deceased has failed to make adequate provision for his or her surviving spouse or civil partner, family provision jurisdiction can be invoked to claim further provision from the estate.[40] In England and Wales the surviving spouse or civil partner has to show that the deceased has failed to make reasonable financial provision for him or her, but does not have to establish a need for maintenance, whereas other eligible claimants do, including a surviving de facto partner.[41] The aim in making reasonable financial provision for a surviving spouse or civil partner is to ensure that he or she is at least as well provided for as a divorcee.[42] Such provision as a spouse might have received on divorce is a relevant matter for the court to consider as a cross-check. It includes the financial resources and likely needs of the surviving spouse, his or her age and likely earning capacity, the duration of the marriage or civil partnership, the contribution the spouse made to the welfare of the deceased's family, and the living standards of the couple immediately before death.[43] Other matters relevant to family provision are the size and nature of the estate, the competing interests and claims of others, and the spouse's conduct.[44] While the surviving spouse or civil partner has a paramount claim on the deceased, it still leaves him, or more usually her, in a position of being dependent on the deceased for appropriate provision for her during their joint lifetime or on death. She has no property entitlement by virtue of marriage or the civil partnership.

Children have to prove that they are in need of maintenance. While maintenance is not limited to bare necessities of life, it is confined to provision to

---

39 The intestacy rules in both England and Australia give priority to the surviving spouse over the deceased's children: Administration of Estates Act 1925 (Eng&W), s 46; Succession Act 2006 (NSW), ch 4.

40 R Croucher, above n 6; Inheritance (Provision for Family and Dependants) Act 1975 (Eng&W).

41 Inheritance (Provision for Family and Dependants) Act 1975 (Eng&W), s 1(2). In *Ilott v The Blue Cross* [2017] UKSC 17, [2017] 2 WLR 979 at [13], the Supreme Court commented that the statutory limitation to maintenance for claimants other than surviving spouses or civil partners was a deliberate legislative choice and demonstrated the significance of testamentary freedom in England.

42 Inheritance (Provision for Family and Dependants) Act 1975 (Eng&W), s 3(2). There are anti-avoidance provisions in s 10 of the Act.

43 *Cunliffe v Fielden* [2005] EWCA Civ 1508, [2006] Ch 361 (CA) at [20]; *Lilleyman v Lilleyman* [2012] EWHC 821 (Ch), [2013] Ch 225.

44 Inheritance (Provision for Family and Dependants) Act 1975 (Eng&W), s 3. In *Ilott v The Blue Cross*, above n 41 from [49] onwards Lady Hale criticises the lack of guidance on how to evaluate and balance the various factors that the court is expected to take into account.

meet everyday living expenses.[45] Adult children who are financially independent are unlikely to succeed unless there is some special circumstance or moral obligation.[46] The blood relationship alone is not enough to warrant intervention in the testate or intestate distribution of the estate, not even if the applicant is in modest financial circumstances and the estate is large enough to provide for all with an interest in the estate.[47] Testamentary freedom thus enjoys considerable respect in England and Wales.[48]

2.2.3. *Family Provision in Australia*

The Australian family provision statutes do not differentiate between the surviving spouse, civil partner, or de facto partner and other eligible claimants in the way the English Act does, but the courts do prioritise the surviving spouse or partner over other eligible claimants and beneficiaries of the estate.[49] Nonetheless, as Croucher explains in the next chapter, the courts have adopted a fairly liberal approach to adult children's claims. While children are expected to establish some degree of financial need, the statutes refer to 'proper' maintenance, which the courts have construed as more than 'adequate' maintenance. It goes beyond provision of basic financial needs and takes account of the size of the estate, the family's station in life, the relationship between the applicant and the deceased, the current and likely future financial position of the applicant, and the relative urgency of competing claims on the deceased's bounty.[50] Whereas an adult child in modest financial circumstances might not succeed in England, he or she might well do so in Australia. In New South Wales family provision is considered so important that certain lifetime property transactions, such as dispositions to trusts and joint tenancies, can be designated as notional estate of the deceased for family provision purposes.[51]

The Australian courts' expansive view of their power to order family provision interferes with testamentary freedom to a significant extent, creating uncertainty about estate distribution and increasing the risk of litigation at

45 *Ilott v The Blue Cross*, above n 41 at [14].

46 In *Ilott v The Blue Cross*, above n 41, the applicant daughter received only a small award. Although she was dependent on state benefits for income, she had no moral claim on her mother because she had been estranged from her mother for all of her adult life.

47 *Coventry v Coventry* [1980] 1 Ch 461 (CA).

48 *Ilott v The Blue Cross*, above n 41 at [13].

49 *Magill v Magill* [2006] HCA 51, (2006) 226 CLR 551.

50 *Bosch v Perpetual Trustee* [1938] AC 463 (PC); *Dark v Dark* [2016] NSWSC 1223.

51 Succession Act 2006 (NSW), ss 74–89. *Hitchcock v Pratt* [2010] NSWSC 1508, (2010) 79 NSWLR 687. None of the other Australian jurisdictions have notional estate provisions. See further R Croucher and P Vines, *Succession, Families, Property and Death*, LexisNexis, Chatswood 2013, 654–64.

considerable financial and emotional expense to all parties involved.[52] In an era of serial relationships and complex family structures, family provision claims are more likely, especially from children of a prior relationship of the deceased.[53] Without a secure property entitlement that is immune to the rights and claims of others, surviving spouses and partners in Australia are more vulnerable than they are in England and Wales.

2.3. CIVIL LAW JURISDICTIONS

Most of the European civil law jurisdictions differ from England and Australia by having a matrimonial property regime that entitles spouses to an equal share of their matrimonial property on death and divorce, unless they have contracted out of the default system.[54] There is considerable variation in the default systems in the different jurisdictions. Several countries have some form of community property system that applies immediately upon marriage.[55] Others have a separate property system during marriage and at the end of the marriage a deferred community property system applies or a system of participation in the acquests or accrued gains of the marriage.[56] All of the matrimonial property

52 B White et al, 'Estate Contestation in Australia: An Empirical Study of a Year of Case Law' (2015) 38(3) *University of New South Wales Law Journal* 880.

53 R Croucher, above n 6.

54 JM Scherpe, above n 3 and K Boele-Woelki et al, above n 8. If a matrimonial property agreement is unjust it can generally be set aside, in which case the default system applies: JM Scherpe, above n 3 at 194 and 202–05. Austria differs from the other civil law jurisdictions in having a discretionary system of property division, which applies on divorce but not on death: §83 *Gesetz zur Vereinheitlichung des Rechts der Eheschließung und der Ehescheidung im Lande Österreich und im übrigen Reichsgebiet (EheG)*, dRGBl no 106/1938. See further JM Scherpe, above n 3 at 162–65.

55 JM Scherpe, above n 3 and K Boele-Woelki et al, above n 8. The Netherlands is the only country to retain universal community property as its default system. All property brought into and acquired during the marriage are part of the community, including gifts and inheritances from third parties if the third party has not excluded them from the recipient's community property regime: Burgerlijk Wetboek, Book 1, Art 93. However, on 28 March 2017 Parliament passed an amendment to replace the universal community with a more limited form of community, which is likely to come into effect on 1 January 2018. In most of the other community property systems a community of acquests or acquisitions applies, in which only the assets generated by the marriage are part of the community. Pre-marital property and gifts and inheritances received from third parties remain the separate property of the owning spouse: JM Scherpe, above n 3 at 149–55.

56 The Nordic countries have a deferred community property system as their default regime. All the assets owned by the spouses at the end of their marriage become community property except for gifts and inheritances that were excluded by the donor from the recipient's community property regime: JM Scherpe, above n 3 at 155–57. Germany has a system of accrued gains, in which each spouse has a claim to his or her share of the gains accrued during the marriage JM Scherpe, above n 3 at 158–60.

regimes dissolve by operation of law on divorce and on death.[57] There is little scope for discretion in the default regimes.[58] On divorce, harsh results are ameliorated through maintenance and compensation for economic disparity.[59]

On death, succession law governs distribution of the estate, after the matrimonial property regime has been dissolved. Children of the deceased have a statutory right to a share of the estate of the deceased, regardless of need or contribution.[60] These succession rights have their origin in Roman law and remain a central feature of modern succession law in the European civil law jurisdictions.[61] Surviving spouses had no statutory entitlement to provision from the estate of their deceased spouse until quite recently, but their entitlement is often limited, for example, to a life interest in the home and other assets.[62] Consistent with the civilian preference for clearly defined rules regulating legal relations, the succession rules provide clarity and certainty, thereby reducing the risk of litigation. The interests of the surviving spouse are protected by a combination of property entitlement and family obligation. Unlike the common law jurisdictions, the civilian jurisdictions regard these interests as distinct and they deal with them separately. Matrimonial property law does not stray into support obligations.

2.4. NEW ZEALAND

Prior to 1963, New Zealand had a strict separate property system similar to England and Australia. The effect of the Married Women's Property Act 1884 (NZ) was to treat husband and wife virtually as strangers for property purposes.[63]

---

57 K Boele-Woelki et al, above n 8.

58 For example, the Nordic countries give the courts discretion to depart from equal division in marriages of less than five years' duration or if one spouse brought significantly more assets into the marriage or acquired a major gift or inheritance during the marriage: JM Scherpe, above n 3 at 156–57.

59 JM Scherpe, above n 3.

60 A Röthel 'Will-Substitutes and the Family: A Continental Perspective' in A Braun and A Röthel (eds), *Passing Wealth on Death: Will-Substitutes in Comparative Perspective*, Hart Publishing, Oxford 2016 at 303. For example, in France up to three quarters of the estate is reserved for the deceased's children depending on the number of children: Code Civil, Art 913-1. In the absence of children the surviving spouse is entitled to a reserved portion of one quarter of the estate: Code Civil, Art 914-1. In Germany the descendants are entitled to a compulsory portion of one-half of their intestate share, and it takes the form of a monetary claim against the heir: Bürgerliches Gesetzbuch (BGB), §2303(1).

61 B Nicholas, *An Introduction to Roman Law*, Clarendon Press, Oxford 1962 at 261–64.

62 For example, the Dutch Civil Code entitles the surviving spouse to a usufruct of the home, household effects, and other assets unless they have no need for such support: Burgerlijk Wetboek 2003, Arts 4:29 and 4:30. The children are entitled to a monetary claim, normally payable only on the death of the surviving spouse.

63 JR Hanan, 'The Future of Family Law' in BD Inglis and AG Mercer (eds), *Family Law Centenary Essays*, Sweet & Maxwell, Wellington 1967, 12.

As in Australia, the New Zealand courts did not use their powers under the Act to make orders affecting title.[64] Joint ownership was also uncommon, because gift duty imposed a substantial penalty on such settlements.[65] Unless a widow had assets of her own, she was dependent on her husband for support. If he failed to provide adequately for her proper maintenance and support, she could apply for provision from his estate under the Family Protection Act (NZ).[66] Although husbands had a paramount obligation to provide for their widows, awards took the form of annuities for the duration of the applicant's widowhood.[67] Capital awards were rare because they might be used to support the deceased husband's successor or to provide for strangers on the widow's death, thus depriving the deceased's children of their patrimony.[68]

A significant change in social policy occurred in 1950 when the Joint Family Homes Act (NZ) was introduced. Its aim was to strengthen the family bond and recognise the common interest of husband and wife in the family home.[69] The formal settlement of the family home as a 'joint family home' provided some relief from gift and estate duty, some protection against unsecured creditors, and allowed the home to pass by survivorship to the surviving spouse.[70] While this option was apparently popular,[71] it depended on the willingness of the legal owner, usually the husband, to agree to the settlement. The vast majority of homes were not settled.[72] Widows could therefore be left without a home or capital and remain dependent on their late husband for ongoing financial support.

2.4.1. *The Matrimonial Property Act 1963 (NZ)*

The courts' unwillingness to make orders affecting title under the Married Women's Property Act 1884 (NZ), particularly in relation to the home, led to the adoption of the Matrimonial Property Act 1963 (NZ) ('MPA 1963'). It empowered the courts to make orders adjusting title as between spouses based on their financial and non-financial contributions to the property in question,

---

64 See cases above n 22.

65 *Matrimonial Property: Report of a Special Committee*, Wellington, June 1972 ('Special Committee Report'), [7], n 1.

66 Family Protection Act 1908 and 1955 (NZ), ss 3 and 4.

67 *Re Rush* (1901) 20 NZLR 249 (SC); *Re McInnes* [1942] NZLR 547 (SC); *Re Crewe* [1956] NZLR 315 (CA); *Re Edkins* [1965] NZLR 916 (SC).

68 *Re Williamson* [1954] NZLR 288 (CA) at 299; *Re Wilson (deceased)* [1973] 2 NZLR 359 (CA) at 362.

69 Special Committee Report, above n 65 at [9].

70 See, for example, *Milne v Commissioner of Inland Revenue* [1959] NZLR 566 (HC).

71 Special Committee Report, above n 65 at [10].

72 AM Finlay, 'Matrimonial Property – Comparable Sharing: An Explanation of the Matrimonial Property Bill 1975' [1975] *Appendix to the Journals of the House of Representatives* E6, 4.

but not so as to defeat any common intention expressed by the parties.[73] In contrast to the Australian and English statutes, the New Zealand courts could exercise their power on death as well as on divorce on the application of the surviving spouse or the personal representative of the deceased spouse.[74] Surviving spouses usually applied for an order to improve their own asset position.[75] Applications by the estate were commonly made to recover assets for beneficiaries of the estate,[76] or to enable the estate to satisfy family provision claims under the Family Protection Act 1955 (NZ) ('FPA').[77]

The MPA 1963 empowered the court to make such orders with respect to the property in dispute as appeared just,[78] having regard to the parties' respective contributions to the property in question, 'whether in the form of money payments, services, prudent management, or otherwise howsoever'.[79] The Court was mandated to take the parties' respective contributions into account in relation to the matrimonial home and had a discretion to do so in relation to any other property, thus acknowledging the importance of the home in a marriage. While contributions were a jurisdictional requirement, orders were at the discretion of the court and not necessarily co-extensive with contributions.[80]

The MPA 1963 was amended in 1968 to clarify that financial as well as non-financial contributions were relevant.[81] That amendment was intended to recognise that a wife's contributions in the home and to the care of children freed her husband to perform his economic activities.[82] Yet, financial contributions still carried more weight than domestic contributions, especially in relation to non-domestic property. In reality, wives and widows were seeking an award out of their (late) husband's assets, rather than a share of 'their' assets.[83] Even after a long marriage, wives and widows rarely received a half share of the pool of assets accumulated during the marriage.[84] It was not until the 1980s that the

---

73 Matrimonial Property Act 1963 (NZ) ('MPA 1963'), ss 5 and 6. This section was modelled on Victoria's Marriage (Property) Act 1962 (Vic), s 3: Special Committee Report, above n 65 at [13].

74 MPA 1963, s 5A.

75 *Robinson v Public Trustee* [1966] NZLR 748 (SC).

76 *Morris v Miles* [1967] NZLR 650 (SC); *Poppe v Grose* [1982] 1 NZLR 491 (CA); *Re Welch* [1989] 2 NZLR 1 (HC).

77 *Irvine v Public Trustee* [1989] 1 NZLR 67 (CA).

78 MPA 1963, s 5.

79 MPA 1963, s 6(1).

80 *Haldane v Haldane* [1976] 2 NZLR 715, [1977] AC 673 (PC).

81 MPA 1963, s 6(1A), inserted by Matrimonial Property Amendment Act 1968 (NZ), s 6(1).

82 AM Finlay, above n 72 at 4–5.

83 Ibid, at 5.

84 The typical amount allocated to a former wife was 1% of the husband's property for each year of marriage: B Atkin and W Parker, *Relationship Property in New Zealand*, 2nd ed, LexisNexis, Wellington 2009, 2–3. See also M Henaghan and N Peart, 'Relationship Property Appeals in the New Zealand Court of Appeal 1958–2008: The Elusiveness of Equality' in R Bigwood (ed), *The Permanent New Zealand Court of Appeal: Essays on the First 50 Years*, Hart Publishing, Oxford 2009, 99.

socio-economic value of non-financial contributions gained greater recognition, and awards under this Act became more generous.[85]

The MPA 1963 was primarily designed as a measure to resolve property disputes between spouses on divorce.[86] It did not address the relationship between matrimonial property orders and the applicant's rights to provision from the estate of the deceased spouse.[87] There was no power under the MPA 1963 to vary the deceased's will or the intestacy rules in the light of a matrimonial property award. The question therefore was whether an award under the MPA 1963 should be reduced or declined on account of the provision available to the surviving spouse from the estate. In some cases the inheritance was disregarded, for example where the surviving spouse was merely left an annuity or life interest, or where all interested parties consented to the matrimonial property award being made.[88] In other cases the inheritance either reduced or eliminated the matrimonial property award.[89]

In 1985, in *Re Mora*, the High Court declined to make an order under the MPA 1963, because the award was less than the widow would receive under the intestacy rules.[90] The Court of Appeal overruled that decision, allowing Mrs Mora to retain her intestate entitlement in addition to her matrimonial property award.[91] It held that a husband owed obligations to his widow going well beyond the recognition of her contributions to matrimonial property. Absent any competing interests to the estate, Mrs Mora's inheritance fulfilled Mr Mora's duty to provide for her proper maintenance and support and acknowledged her loyalty and affection over a long and happy marriage.[92] If there were competing interests to the estate, succession law could reduce a spouse's matrimonial property award.[93]

It was also unclear whether orders under the MPA 1963 should take precedence over claims under the FPA. In *Re McNaughton* the Court declined the widow's matrimonial property claim, instead awarding her additional provision from the estate under the FPA, because it would be wrong to erode the principles of the FPA by allowing an application under the MPA 1963.[94]

---

[85] See 2.4.2 below for discussion of the MPA 1963's continued application to marriages ending on death after the adoption of the Matrimonial Property Act 1976 (NZ) ('MPA 1976').

[86] *Re Snow* [1975] Current Law (NZ) 1192 (SC) as cited in *Re McNaughton (deceased)* [1976] 2 NZLR 538 (SC) at 542–43.

[87] This omission may be attributable to the fact that the Act was in essence an extension of the powers under s 19 of the Married Women's Property Act 1952 (NZ), which the courts construed narrowly, avoiding questions about the relationship between applications about title and succession law.

[88] *Mora v Mora* (1988) 4 NZFLR 609 (CA) at 614.

[89] *West v West* (1985) 2 FRNZ 1 (HC); *Re Mora* HC Christchurch M160/84, 11 July 1985.

[90] *Re Mora*, above n 89.

[91] *Mora v Mora*, above n 88.

[92] Ibid, at 614 and 616.

[93] For example, *Clifford v Clifford* (1988) 4 FRNZ 297 (HC).

[94] *Re McNaughton (deceased)*, above n 86.

The relevance of competing interests prompted the Court to question whether the MPA 1963 should be invoked to deal with what was essentially a succession question.[95] In *Re Barna*, on the other hand, the Court saw the claims as serving different purposes. An order under the MPA 1963 'enable[d] each spouse to obtain proper recognition of what is truly his or hers', whereas an order under the FPA enforced a moral duty that the deceased owed to his or her surviving spouse to make provision out of what was truly his or her estate.[96] Hence, it was appropriate to deal with the matrimonial property claim first. Any order made under the MPA 1963 would then be taken into account when determining the surviving spouse's family protection claim.[97]

Central to the uncertainty about the relationship between matrimonial property claims and succession rights was the ambiguous status of the matrimonial property award. It was not an equitable interest, because it crystallised both as to interest and quantum only when the Court exercised its discretion in favour of the applicant.[98] Yet, in effect the MPA 1963 was a fetter on, or qualification of, the property rights of spouses.[99] Orders under the MPA 1963 were not initially exempt from estate duty, even though the effect of the order was to reduce the size of the estate.[100] But in 1983 the Estate and Gift Duties Act 1968 (NZ) was amended to remove the subject matter of an order under the MPA 1963 from the estate of the deceased spouse for estate duty purposes.[101] Clearly, Parliament did not consider such property really belonged to the deceased. However, the discretionary nature of the award still prevented it from becoming property of the applicant until the order was made.[102] After the 1983 amendment to the Estate and Gift Duties Act 1968 (NZ) matrimonial property claims were commonly brought to reduce or eliminate the estate's liability for estate duty, as in *Re Mora*.[103]

2.4.2. The Matrimonial Property Act 1976 (NZ)

Dissatisfaction with the courts' ungenerous approach to claims under the MPA 1963 and the uncertainty generated by a discretionary regime persuaded

---

95 Ibid, at 543.

96 *Re Barna* (1985) 1 FRNZ 521 (HC) at 523. See also *Re Anderson* CA116/94, 10 November 1995.

97 *Re Baigent (deceased)* (1988) 4 FRNZ 170 (HC).

98 *Byfield v Public Trustee* [1976] 2 NZLR 442 (SC) at 447.

99 *Re Snow*, above n 86, as cited in *Re McNaughton (deceased)*, above n 86 at 543.

100 *Thompson and Preest v CIR* (1982) 5 MPC 157 (CA).

101 Estate and Gift Duties Act 1968 (NZ), s 31A, inserted by Estate and Gift Duties Amendment Act 1983 (NZ), s 4.

102 H Sargisson, 'Matrimonial Property Legislation: Its History, and a Critique of the Present New Zealand Law' (1976) 3(1) *Auckland University Law Review* 82, 96–97.

103 *Mora v Mora*, above n 88.

Parliament to introduce an equal sharing regime similar to a deferred community of acquests.[104] The new Matrimonial Property Act 1976 (NZ) ('MPA 1976') applied instead of the rules of common law and equity.[105] During the marriage a separate property system applied.[106] Each spouse was free to acquire and deal with their own assets as if the Act had not been passed.[107] But on separation the matrimonial property regime crystallised.[108] The parties' assets were then classified as either matrimonial property or separate property.[109] Provided the marriage had lasted for three or more years,[110] and the parties had not formally contracted out of the MPA 1976,[111] domestic assets were shared equally unless there were extraordinary circumstances that made equal sharing repugnant to justice, a notoriously high threshold.[112] A more liberal exception applied to the division of the balance of matrimonial property.[113] Separate property was retained by the owning spouse.

The MPA 1976 was a radical change from the past and a major piece of social reform. It viewed marriage as a partnership of equals to which each spouse was presumed to contribute equally and hence there was a strong presumption that matrimonial property would be equally shared. In contrast to orders under the MPA 1963, orders under the 1976 Act were declaratory of a pre-existing

---

104 It differed from the civil law system of community of acquests by including the family home and family chattels even if they were acquired prior to marriage: MPA 1976, s 8.

105 MPA 1976, s 4.

106 MPA 1976, s 20(2) protected a spouse's interest in the family home in the event that the other spouse went bankrupt during the marriage. Section 42 allowed a spouse to lodge a notice of claim against land to protect his or her claim or right to that land under the Act, thus preventing dealings with the land. See further AH Angelo and WR Atkin, 'A Conceptual and Structural Overview of the Matrimonial Property Act 1976' (1977) 7 *New Zealand Universities Law Review* 237. These exceptions to the deferred property system were retained when the Act was amended in 2001: Property (Relationships) Act 1976 (NZ) ('PRA'), ss 20B and 42.

107 MPA 1976, s 19. Secured and unsecured creditors of a spouse had the same rights against that spouse and any property owned by that spouse as if the Act had not been passed: s 20.

108 MPA 1976, s 25(2)(a). The court was also empowered to make orders on dissolution of marriage, bankruptcy of a spouse, or gross mismanagement or wilful dissipation of property: s 25(2).

109 Matrimonial property was exhaustively defined in the MPA 1976, ss 8–10. It included the family home and family chattels, whenever they were acquired, and property acquired in contemplation of marriage or during the marriage other than property acquired from a third party by gift, inheritance, survivorship, or as a beneficiary of a trust. Property that was not matrimonial property was separate property of the owning spouse and not subject to division. Any separate property that was intermingled with matrimonial property and any increase in value of separate property that was attributable to the application of matrimonial property or the actions of the non-owning spouse became matrimonial property.

110 MPA 1976, s 13.

111 MPA 1976, s 21.

112 MPA 1976, s 14. See *Martin v Martin* [1979] 1 NZLR 97 (CA); *Joseph v Johansen* (1993) 10 FRNZ 302 (CA).

113 Non-domestic matrimonial property could be unequally divided if the contributions of one spouse were clearly greater than the contributions of the other spouse: MPA 1976, s 15.

property interest.[114] However, the 1976 Act applied only during the joint lifetime of the spouses.[115]

The 1963 Act continued to apply to marriages ending on death, with all the disadvantages of a discretionary system and the burden of proving contributions to property. The 1976 Act did reflect a change in society's perception of the economic value of a wife's work, which the courts eventually recognised when assessing awards under the 1963 Act.[116] But the focus was still on contributions to property, rather than the relationship, and hence the court could not be influenced by awards obtainable under the 1976 Act.[117] Unequal division remained the norm on death, even in long marriages where the applicant spouse had made substantial contributions.[118] Marriages ending on death were therefore treated less favourably than marriages ending on separation.[119]

The White Paper accompanying the Matrimonial Property Bill 1975 acknowledged this unsatisfactory situation, but the effect of a matrimonial property entitlement on succession law and estate duty raised delicate and complex questions.[120] As the demand for reform of the law on separation was more urgent, the Government decided not to delay the introduction of the Bill pending resolution of the problems relating to death, promising to introduce a comprehensive measure as soon as possible.[121] It would take another 25 years for Parliament to reform matrimonial property law for marriages ending on death.[122]

2.4.3. The Property (Relationships) Act 1976, as Amended in 2001

In 2001 Parliament radically amended the MPA 1976, incorporating recommendations made in 1988 by a Ministerial Working Group established to advise on Matrimonial Property and Family Protection as part of a wider social reform programme.[123] The 2001 amendments extended the matrimonial

114 *Report of the Working Group on Matrimonial Property and Family Protection*, Wellington, October 1988 ('Working Group Report'), 40.

115 MPA 1976, s 5.

116 *Mora v Mora*, above n 88.

117 *Re Mora*, above n 89 and on appeal *Mora v Mora*, above n 88.

118 In *Mora v Mora*, above n 88, the Court of Appeal awarded the widow 40% of the farm, in spite of her exceptional contributions around the farm, because her husband was more directly involved in the farm and had acquired it on favourable terms from his parents.

119 Working Group Report, above n 114 at 3.

120 AM Finlay, above n 72 at 13. See 2.4.1 above. Also, the 1983 amendment to the Estate and Gift Duty Act 1968 (NZ) had not yet been passed.

121 AM Finlay, above n 72 at 14.

122 Reform of the MPA 1976 was recommended to ensure a surviving spouse was no worse off than a spouse whose marriage had broken down during the joint lives of the spouses: Working Group Report, above n 114 at 40.

123 Working Group Report, above n 114. For a description of the reform process, see B Atkin and W Parker, above n 84 at ch 1.

property regime to de facto relationships of three or more years' duration[124] and to relationships ending on death.[125] To take account of the wider range of relationships to which the amended Act was to apply, the MPA was renamed the Property (Relationships) Act 1976 (NZ) ('PRA').[126] The 2001 amendments reformed the equal sharing regime in other significant ways as well, making it 'the second substantive statutory code of major importance within twenty-five years in the New Zealand law of matrimonial and relationship property', the first being the MPA 1976.[127]

Equality between the parties to the relationship remains the core principle of the statutory regime. However, the scope of the regime has been expanded to give better effect to this principle. A wider range of property is included in the relationship property pool.[128] The more liberal exception to equal division of non-domestic assets is no longer available.[129] All relationship property, including non-domestic property, is now subject to equal division,[130] unless the relationship was of less than three years' duration,[131] or extraordinary circumstances make equal sharing repugnant to justice.[132] The latter exception still sets a very high threshold.[133] Equal division of relationship property is therefore the norm in relationships of more than three years' duration, unless the parties have formally contracted out of the PRA.[134] As many couples see such contracts as questioning their commitment to the relationship, the default system applies to the great majority of couples. New provisions were adopted to address economic disparity resulting from the division of functions during

---

124 PRA, s 2D defines a 'de facto relationship' in these terms. Whether a de facto relationship exists is a question of fact, which is determined by taking all the circumstances of the relationship into account: *Scragg v Scott* [2006] NZFLR 1076 (HC); *Benseman v Foster* (2006) 25 FRNZ 803 (HC). The PRA applies to de facto relationships that existed when the Act came into force on 1 February 2002 or came into existence thereafter: s 4C. See further M Briggs, 'Which Relationships Should be Included in a Property Sharing Scheme?', ch 3.

125 PRA, Part 8.

126 Property (Relationships) Amendment Act 2001 (NZ), s 5(2). In 2005 civil unions were included as well, on the same basis as marriage: Property (Relationships) Amendment Act 2005 (NZ).

127 BD Inglis, *New Zealand Family Law in the 21st Century*, Thomson Brookers, Wellington 2007 at 1050.

128 See B Atkin, 'Classifying Relationship Property: A Radical Re-Shaping?', ch 7.

129 The exception to equal division of non-domestic assets in s 15 of the MPA 1976, referred to above in n 113, was repealed by the Property (Relationships) Amendment Act 2001 (NZ).

130 PRA, s 11.

131 PRA, ss 14–14AA.

132 PRA, s 13.

133 *De Malmanche v De Malmanche* [2002] 2 NZLR 838 (HC), where the Court observed at [140] that the unchanged wording of the section meant that '[t]he lodestar of s 13 remains, but the ocean on which it provides a navigational aid is of greater breadth.'

134 PRA, ss 21 and 21A.

the relationship[135] and the widespread use of discretionary trusts that put relationship assets beyond the reach of the court.[136]

For relationships ending on death of a spouse (or partner), a new part was inserted into the PRA in 2001. It gives the surviving spouse a choice of two options.[137] Under option A the surviving spouse elects to apply for a division of relationship property under the PRA.[138] The consequence of electing this option is that the surviving spouse loses his or her entitlement under the deceased's will or the intestacy rules. The estate is distributed as if the surviving spouse had pre-deceased the deceased, unless the deceased expressed a contrary intention in the will or the Court permits the surviving spouse to take some or all of the inheritance to avoid injustice.[139] Under option B the surviving spouse elects not to proceed under the PRA.[140] In that case the survivor retains the assets he or she owns, takes whatever property he or she is entitled to by survivorship, and inherits such provision as is available under the deceased's will or the intestacy rules. Option B is the default option if option A is not elected in the prescribed manner and within the stipulated time limit.[141] Regardless of which option is elected, the surviving spouse or partner may apply under the FPA for further provision from the estate.[142]

If the deceased is survived by multiple partners, for example a surviving spouse from whom the deceased was separated but not divorced and a de facto partner, each one has the right to make the election.[143] If more than one elects option A, special provisions govern the classification and division of the parties' relationship property.[144]

The relationship property entitlement of the surviving spouse has priority over any beneficial interest a person may have under the deceased's will or the intestacy rules, as well as any claim to the estate under the FPA or the Law Reform

---

135 PRA, ss 15 and 15A. See further M Henaghan, 'Sharing Family Finances at the End of a Relationship', ch 12.

136 PRA, ss 44A–44C. See further J Palmer, 'What to Do about Trusts?', ch 8.

137 PRA, s 61.

138 PRA, s 61(2).

139 PRA, ss 76–77.

140 PRA, s 61(3).

141 PRA, s 68. Section 62 sets the time limit and s 65 prescribes the election formalities.

142 PRA, s 57.

143 Divorce requires a minimum of two years' separation: Family Proceedings Act 1980 (NZ), s 39.

144 PRA, ss 52A and 52B. There have been no cases as yet where these sections have been applied. In *Chapman v P* [2010] NZFLR 855 (HC), the deceased was survived by his wife and a de facto partner. The widow elected option A, while the surviving de facto partner elected option B. As the deceased died intestate, the surviving de facto partner was deemed to be the sole surviving partner for succession purposes. For guidance on the application of ss 52A and 52B on death, see M Henaghan, 'Multiple Relationships on Death' in N Peart, M Briggs and M Henaghan (eds), *Relationship Property on Death*, Thomson Brookers, Wellington 2004, 347.

(Testamentary Promises) Act 1949 (NZ), and any duties or fees payable in respect of the deceased estate under any Act imposing duties or fees.[145] Prioritising the relationship property claim acknowledges that the surviving spouse is claiming what is rightfully his or her property, so that succession law is applied only to assets that legitimately belong to the estate. But the loss of succession rights consequent upon claiming the relationship property entitlement undermines testamentary freedom and prevents the deceased from providing for his or her surviving spouse in the manner anticipated by the deceased.

In *EM v SL*, for example, the deceased left his widow a life interest in his half share of the family home and the residue of his estate to his two adult children from his first marriage.[146] His widow elected option A, which provided a modest increase in her asset position. As a result of her election, her life interest in her husband's share of the home was automatically revoked and his children's residuary gift was accelerated. Rather than claim under the PRA for reinstatement of the life interest, the widow applied under the FPA for the home to be fully vested in her. The Court declined her application, reinstating the life interest in the estate's share of the home plus a $30,000 legacy. The Court held that the deceased owed a moral duty to his widow as well as his children, even though the children were adult and financially independent. As the widow had children from her first marriage, vesting the entire home in the widow would most probably deprive the deceased's children of most of their inheritance. The deceased's testamentary wishes were thus largely respected in this case. But that cannot be guaranteed, because family provision is at the discretion of the court.

In contrast to the MPA 1963, the personal representative of the deceased is not entitled to apply as of right for a division of relationship property. The estate requires leave from the Court, which may be granted only if serious injustice would otherwise result.[147] The Working Group on Matrimonial Property and Family Protection recommended that the estate should have no right to bring proceedings against the survivor:[148]

> 'The broad object of the reform is to ensure that the survivor is no worse off than a spouse whose marriage has come to an end during the joint lives. It does not follow that the estate should be able to sue the survivor to ensure that the survivor is left with no more than his or her share of matrimonial property. Where one spouse has died

---

145 No estate duty has been payable in New Zealand in respect of estates of persons dying on or after 17 December 1992: Estate Duty Abolition Act 1993 (NZ), s 3. Estate duty was repealed by the Estate Duty Repeal Act 1999 (NZ), s 5. Prior to the abolition of estate duty, orders under the MPA 1963 on death of a spouse had priority over estate duty owed in respect of the estate and could be made to reduce the deceased's estate to below the dutiable level: *Mora v Mora*, above n 88.

146 *EM v SL* [2005] NZFLR 281 (FC).

147 PRA, s 88(2).

148 Working Group Report, above n 114 at 46.

> the contest is no longer between two partners who take their share and then go their different ways. It is between the survivor of a marriage and the beneficiaries under a will or on an intestacy, or potential family protection claimants.'

The original Bill reforming the MPA 1976 adopted that recommendation, but it was amended during the legislative process to allow for a restricted claim by the estate. No explanation was given for the change, but submissions were made identifying the potential injustice if an estate had insufficient assets to meet support obligations to persons other than the surviving spouse or partner. Not long after the PRA came into force in 2002 an obvious example of injustice arose in *Public Trust v Whyman*.[149] The matter came before the Court as competing applications by the deceased's surviving de facto partner, Ms Whyman, and the Public Trust for the grant to administer the deceased's intestate estate. The estate had minimal assets, which passed to Ms Whyman under the intestacy rules, leaving nothing for the deceased's two minor children from his former marriage.[150] The deceased had deliberately registered his properties as joint tenancies with Ms Whyman to avoid his children taking anything from his estate. The Court appointed the Public Trust, because it was highly likely that leave would be granted to apply for a division of relationship property. The deceased's children were minors and dependent on their father for child support until his death. The Court held that leave should be granted to facilitate meritorious claims against an estate.[151] Nonetheless, there are instances where leave has not been granted and the estate has been left with insufficient assets to satisfy family provision claims.[152]

2.4.4. Family Provision

New Zealand's approach to claims for provision under the FPA has developed differently from Australia and England and Wales. While the surviving spouse or partner has a paramount claim for provision from the deceased,[153]

---

149 *Public Trust v Whyman* [2005] 2 NZLR 696 (CA).

150 As the surviving de facto partner of the deceased, Ms Whyman was entitled to the deceased's personal chattels, a capital sum of $121,500, and one third of the residue, while the deceased's children were entitled to the remaining two thirds of the residue: Administration Act 1969 (NZ), s 77. However, the estate had substantially less than $90,000 in assets.

151 For example, *Morgan v Public Trust* HC Auckland CIV-2006-404-3636, 20 November 2006 (daughter's Family Protection claim); *Public Trust v Relph* [2009] 2 NZLR 819 (HC) (Family Protection claim by adult children in modest circumstances).

152 In *Ruocco v Wright* HC Christchurch CIV-2008-409-311, 16 December 2008, for example, the deceased's minor children from an earlier relationship were denied the opportunity to make a family protection claim because their father's primary duty was to his second wife and the very young children from that relationship.

153 B Patterson, *Law of Family Protection and Testamentary Promises*, 4th ed, LexisNexis, Wellington 2013, 8.1.

the parent–child relationship has assumed greater prominence in New Zealand than in either Australia or England and Wales.[154] Parents owe a moral duty to provide for their children, regardless of age or financial need, to recognise the importance of the family bond.[155] In *Williams v Aucutt* the Court of Appeal held in response to a claim by an affluent adult daughter:[156]

> 'The test is whether adequate provision has been made for the proper maintenance and support of the claimant. "Support" is an additional and wider term than "maintenance". In using the composite expression, and requiring "proper" maintenance and support, the legislation recognises that a broader approach is required and the authorities referred to establish that moral and ethical considerations are to be taken into account in determining the scope of the duty. "Support" is used in its wider dictionary sense of "sustaining, providing comfort". A child's path through life is supported not simply by financial provision to meet economic needs and contingencies but also by recognition of belonging to the family and of having been an important part of the overall life of the deceased. Just what provision will constitute proper support in this latter respect is a matter of judgment in all the circumstances of the particular case. It may take the form of lifetime gifts or a bequest of family possessions precious to its members and often part of the family history. And where there is no economic need it may also be met by a legacy of a moderate amount. On the other hand, where the estate comprises the accumulation of the family assets and is more than sufficient to meet other needs, provision so small as to leave a justifiable sense of exclusion from participation in the family estate might not amount to proper support for a family member.'

This dictum, which is now the leading statement on family protection claims,[157] came not long after the New Zealand Law Commission had criticised the liberal treatment of adult children's claims and recommended that adult children should be confined to provision for financial need.[158] The Court of Appeal acknowledged in *Williams v Aucutt* that some awards had been 'out of line with current social attitudes',[159] but the dictum above represents a judicial rejection of the Law Commission recommendation. The practical reality is that New Zealand has moved towards a form of forced heirship where only the

---

154 In *Flathaug v Weaver* [2003] NZFLR 730 (CA), the Court of Appeal observed at [32]: 'The relationship of parent and child has primacy in our society.'

155 N Peart, 'The Direction of the Family Protection Act 1955' [1994] *NZ Recent Law Review* 193; J Caldwell, 'Family Protection Claims by Adult Children: What Is Going On?' (2008) 1 *New Zealand Family Law Journal* 4.

156 *Williams v Aucutt* [2000] 2 NZLR 479 (CA) at [52].

157 *Auckland City Mission v Brown* [2002] 2 NZLR 650 (CA); *Henry v Henry* [2007] NZCA 42, [2007] NZFLR 640; *Fisher v Kirby* [2012] NZCA 310, [2013] NZFLR 463.

158 Law Commission (NZ), *Succession Law: A Succession (Adjustment) Act – Modernising the Law on Sharing Property on Death*, R 39, NZLC, Wellington 1997, 11–15.

159 *Williams v Aucutt*, above n 156 at [45].

quantum is at large.[160] Unless the estate is too small to do justice to all moral claims, the courts will seek to balance provision for a surviving spouse and children of the deceased, because the parent–child relationship has primacy in New Zealand society.[161] That is a far cry from the position in England and Wales.

2.4.5. *Conceptual Confusion*

There is conceptual confusion in New Zealand's PRA. The PRA's death provisions are based on an unstated policy objective that is inconsistent with the PRA's objective on separation. On separation the legislative aim is equality between the parties to the relationship, whereas on death the policy objective is that 'the surviving spouse should be no worse off than one whose marriage has broken down during the joint lives of the spouses'.[162] That policy objective was formulated by the Working Group on Matrimonial Property and Family Protection in 1988 and underpins the death provisions enacted in 2001. It is most obviously implemented by the election that the surviving spouse or partner has to make and by restricting the estate's right to apply for a division of relationship property.

The survivor's election was a key recommendation of the Working Group on Matrimonial Property and Family Protection.[163] The majority of the Group's members favoured the election for pragmatic reasons. They had evidence, from some years earlier, that about two thirds of all husbands and about half of all wives left their entire estate to their spouse.[164] The Working Group formed the view that compulsory division would complicate estate administration unnecessarily and force survivors to take half of the matrimonial property where they may not wish to do so. A division could also put them in a worse financial position or defeat the deceased's intention that the estate pass directly to their children.[165] The Working Group saw no point in forcing spouses into a legislative straitjacket to implement a principle when the objective of reform could be achieved by a more flexible and pragmatic approach. There was no need to treat death and separation alike.

When the New Zealand Law Commission undertook its review of succession law eight years later, it adopted the Working Group's recommendation of giving the surviving spouse a choice, clarifying that electing to apply for division of

---

160 N Peart, 'Awards for Children under the Family Protection Act' (1995) 1 *Butterworths Family Law Journal* 224; N Peart, 'Forced Heirship in New Zealand?' (1996) 2 *Butterworths Family Law Journal* 97; N Peart, 'New Zealand's Succession Law: Subverting Reasonable Expectations' (2008) 37(8) *Common Law World Review* 356.

161 *Flathaug v Weaver*, above n 154 at [32]; *Wylie v Wylie* (2003) 23 FRNZ 156 (CA).

162 Working Group Report, above n 114 at 40.

163 Ibid, at 44.

164 Ibid, at 44.

165 New Zealand still had estate duty at the time of the Working Group Report in 1988.

relationship property would result in the survivor not taking under the will or the intestacy rules.[166] The survivor could, in addition, make a support claim against the estate if the survivor had insufficient resources to maintain a reasonable, independent, standard of living.[167] Those recommendations ensured consistency with the law on marital breakdown, which was the Law Commission's policy objective.[168] Its aim was to treat death and separation alike. Any differences between the two endings of a marriage could be addressed through the support obligations.

There is a conceptual dissonance in forcing surviving spouses or partners to choose between their relationship property entitlement and their inheritance. As the Working Group acknowledged in its Report, when spouses apply for their share of the relationship property they are claiming what is rightfully their own property.[169] When they inherit, they are receiving the deceased's property. By denying survivors who take what is rightfully their property the right to inherit from their deceased spouse or partner, the PRA strays beyond the boundaries of relationship property law into succession law.[170] The deceased can avoid this outcome by stating in the will that testamentary provision for the surviving spouse or partner should not be treated as revoked if the survivor elects to take his or her relationship property entitlement.[171] That ignores the conceptual confusion about the survivor's relationship entitlement. Furthermore, it appears to have little practical relevance. Anecdotal evidence suggests that a contrary intention clause is seldom included in wills, out of ignorance about the relationship property entitlements on death.

In regard to the estate's right to apply for a division, the Law Commission disagreed with the Working Group that the estate should have no right to sue the survivor. In keeping with its objective of consistency with the law on separation, the Law Commission proposed that the personal representative of the deceased be entitled to apply for a division of matrimonial property as

---

166 New Zealand Law Commission, *Succession Law: Testamentary Claims – A Discussion Paper*, PP24, NZLC, Wellington 1996, 25; Law Commission (NZ) *Succession Law: A Succession (Adjustment) Act*, above n 158 at 58, draft s 11.

167 Law Commission (NZ), *Succession Law: A Succession (Adjustment) Act*, above n 158 at 81–82, draft ss 24 and 25.

168 Law Commission (NZ), *Succession Law: Testamentary Claims*, above n 166 at 25 and 29–30.

169 Working Group Report, above n 114 at 40.

170 If the parties had separated and divided their relationship property before one of them died, the survivor could still inherit. A will is not revoked by separation and a surviving spouse or civil union partner retains the right to succeed on intestacy until the legal bond is severed by a court order. A de facto partner loses the intestate entitlement on separation because there is no legal bond: Administration Act 1969 (NZ), s 2 where 'surviving de facto partner' is defined as the partner living with the deceased in a de facto relationship when the deceased died. See *Re Estate of Te Rore* HC Whangarei CIV-2004-488-658, 20 July 2006.

171 PRA, s 76(1).

of right.[172] The Working Group's rationale, that the deceased no longer had a need for property and the only persons who would benefit from enlarging the estate by a relationship property claim were volunteers, is flawed in several respects.[173] First, it again blurs the distinction between the relationship property entitlement and inheritance. The surviving spouse or partner retains not only his or her share of the relationship property pool, but also takes some or all of the deceased's share, as in *Public Trust v Whyman* where Ms Whyman took the couple's jointly owned properties by survivorship.[174] Secondly, it ignores the obligations that the deceased may have to others, which may not be met without recovering the deceased's relationship property entitlement. In view of the increase in serial relationships and blended families, a deceased's obligations are likely to differ from the obligations that their surviving spouse or partner may have, for example where they each have children from prior relationships. Furthermore, it is nearly 30 years since the Working Group Report. Its rationale for opposing claims by the estate no longer withstands scrutiny and the evidence on which it was based is bound to be outdated.

In November 2015 the Minister of Justice referred the PRA to the New Zealand Law Commission for review and reform. The death provisions are included in the terms of reference. Reform of these provisions may resolve the current conceptual confusion.

3. THE WAY FORWARD

None of the common law jurisdictions treats death and divorce (or separation) alike. There is good reason not to do so.[175] Divorce is a conscious decision to end a relationship, whereas death is normally not. Following divorce both parties have ongoing needs and responsibilities, whereas on death only the surviving party has ongoing needs and responsibilities. On divorce, the aim is to adjust the parties' property between them to enable them to move on independently of each other and achieve a clean break. On death, the clean break principle is not relevant unless there is hostility between the deceased's surviving spouse and the deceased's children. The equality principle, which plays an important role on divorce, is less important on death.[176] The deceased is no longer alive to benefit from equal sharing of assets. A deceased is expected to make sufficient provision for his or her spouse to enable him or her to live out their life in the style they

---

172 Law Commission (NZ), *Succession Law: A Succession (Adjustment) Act*, above n 158 at 58, draft s 10(2).

173 Working Group Report, above n 114 at 46.

174 *Public Trust v Whyman*, above n 149.

175 *Cunliffe v Fielden*, above n 43 at [30].

176 Ibid, at [21].

enjoyed during the relationship.[177] That may be achieved by making appropriate arrangements during the parties' lifetime or by making suitable provision on death.

In a separate property system, such as applies in Australia and in England and Wales, the ordinary rules of common law and equity determine what each spouse beneficially owns. When a spouse dies, distribution of the estate is left to the deceased's unfettered discretion on the assumption that:[178]

> 'the instincts, affections, and common sentiments of mankind may be safely trusted to secure, on the whole, a better disposition of the property of the dead ... than could be obtained through a distribution prescribed by the stereotyped and inflexible rules of a general law.'

To the extent that the assets retained by the surviving spouse or provided by the deceased are inadequate, the surviving spouse may seek further provision from the estate of the deceased under family provision legislation. While this combination of rights and claims may secure sufficient, even generous, provision for surviving spouses, without property of their own they are dependent on others to make provision for them. They do not have the security of a property entitlement that acknowledges their contributions to the creation of the deceased's wealth. They have at most a hope or expectation that the deceased will provide adequately for them, either during their lifetime or on death. If no such provision has been made, they are in the unenviable position of having to ask for financial support with the associated emotional and financial costs of a potentially unpleasant contest against others with an interest in the estate, such as children from a former relationship of the deceased.

In most civil law jurisdictions the surviving spouse has a matrimonial property entitlement, which is immune to anyone with an interest in the estate. It acknowledges that assets forming part of the community are the product of the couple's joint efforts and it provides the surviving spouse with some level of financial security independent of any succession rights or claims he or she may have against the estate of the deceased spouse. The estate is distributed in accordance with succession law to the deceased's descendants, generally subject to additional protection for the surviving spouse in the form of either capital or income provision or a maintenance claim. Relationship property law and succession law are thus treated as distinct jurisdictions.

New Zealand blurs that distinction, thereby creating confusion and uncertainty for everyone concerned. Having adopted a regime that gives spouses

---

177 *Re Rush*, above n 67; *Re Wilson (deceased)*, above n 68; *Re Z* [1979] 2 NZLR 495 (CA); *Re Hilton* [1997] 2 NZLR 734 (HC); *EM v SL*, above n 146.

178 *Banks v Goodfellow*, above n 15 at 564.

and partners a relationship property entitlement, that entitlement should endure on death without loss of inheritance rights. According priority to the relationship property entitlement provides certainty and predictability for all parties with an interest in the estate and reduces dependency of the surviving spouse or partner. It also avoids interference with testamentary freedom by not revoking provision made for the surviving spouse and accelerating gifts to others. If other family members are adversely affected by the property received by the surviving spouse, they may bring a family protection claim.

The deceased's paramount duty to support his or her surviving spouse is well established in the common law jurisdictions. It has its roots in the commitment that spouses make on marriage to support each other. That sort of commitment is now acknowledged to exist in other relationships as well, including de facto relationships in Australia and New Zealand where a surviving de facto partner has the same claim on the deceased partner as a surviving spouse. The extent to which the surviving spouse (or partner) is accorded priority over beneficiaries or claimants against the estate differs in each of the common law jurisdictions. While testamentary freedom is the starting point in the common law jurisdictions, the approach to family provision has diverged over time.

In England and Wales the surviving spouse and civil partner is favoured over other eligible claimants. By requiring all other eligible claimants, including de facto partners and children, to establish a need for maintenance, competing claims on the deceased's bounty are minimised to the advantage of the surviving spouse. The risk of interference with testamentary freedom and the associated uncertainty is thereby reduced and the use of will-substitutes to avoid family provision claims is likely to be minimised. The absence of any relationship property entitlement is less of a concern in this context than it is in jurisdictions with an expansive view of family provision, such as New Zealand and Australia. The Australian and New Zealand courts are more likely to override the terms of a will than are the courts in England and Wales. The surviving spouse or partner in Australia and New Zealand is therefore more vulnerable to the claims of children, including financially independent adult children. The ability of adult children to make a successful claim for family provision encourages the use of trusts and other will-substitutes to put assets beyond the reach of the courts. Only in New South Wales can those assets be brought into account through the notional estate provisions.

The scope of family provision is influenced by the values and expectations of a particular society. Whereas in England the deceased is considered to know best how to provide for his or her family, subject to limited oversight by the courts, in New Zealand and Australia it is society as a whole, expressed through the medium of the courts, that determines how a particular individual should provide for his or her family on death. The approach to family provision in those countries has significantly curtailed testamentary freedom and altered the way property owners deal with their assets. Despite criticism of the judicially expanded approach to family provision in Australia and New Zealand, the legislatures have done nothing to curb this development, which suggests that the legislatures are satisfied with the status quo.

In New Zealand a plausible explanation for Parliament's inaction on family provision, despite the New Zealand Law Commission recommending radical curtailment in 1997, is its 2001 reform of matrimonial property law to extend the equal sharing regime to relationships ending on death. By according priority to that entitlement over succession law and family provision, at the election of the surviving spouse or partner, Parliament may have thought it was achieving an appropriate balance between the rights of the surviving spouse and others with an interest in the estate, in particular children of the deceased. The same inference may be drawn from Parliament's decision to give the estate only a qualified right to apply for division of relationship property. It favours the surviving spouse over anyone with an interest in the estate. However, both the surviving spouse and deserving family provision claimants face the significant disadvantage of having to make a claim to secure provision, and are thus dependent on others to ensure that the deceased meets his or her obligations. If both the surviving spouse and the estate had an unqualified right to their respective relationship property entitlements and those entitlements did not affect succession rights, the principles underpinning relationship property division on separation could also apply on death and be dealt with in the same Act. There would be no reason to distinguish between the two endings of the relationship. Succession law would then apply only to the assets that truly belonged to the deceased, with testamentary freedom as the starting point, modified where necessary by family provision obligations. The relationship property entitlement would be secure, but relevant to any family provision claim that the surviving spouse or partner made.

4. CONCLUSION

Throughout the twentieth century, succession law in the common law jurisdictions has been dominated by testamentary freedom modified by family provision legislation. The challenge has been to balance property and family. Surviving spouses have been dependent on the generosity of the deceased or the court. While the surviving spouse, especially the widow, has been treated more favourably than other family members in family provision litigation, her claim is founded on support for future needs, rather than on recognition of her contribution to the creation of her late husband's wealth. Even in England, the provision that the applicant spouse might have received on divorce is merely a cross-check for family provision purposes and of uncertain value. It does not give her a predictable secure entitlement to property. New Zealand is the only common law jurisdiction to entitle surviving spouses and partners to make a contribution-based claim in addition to a family provision claim. But it has blurred the distinction between the property entitlement and any succession right the surviving spouse may have to the assets of the deceased spouse. Only when a spouse's relationship property entitlement is treated as distinct from, and unaffected by, succession law, will surviving spouses achieve an outcome that appropriately differentiates between their property entitlement and the deceased's support obligation. Furthermore, only reform of family provision to restrict provision for adult children will give better effect to testamentary freedom and provide greater certainty and predictability for surviving spouses and partners.

CHAPTER 6

A LAMENT FOR 'TESTATOR'S FAMILY MAINTENANCE' – A GOOD IDEA GONE WRONG?

Australian Reflections

Rosalind CROUCHER

'The English law leaves everything to the unfettered discretion of the testator, on the assumption that, though in some instances, caprice, or passion, or the power of new ties, or artful contrivance, or sinister influence, may lead to the neglect of claims that ought to be attended to, yet, the instincts, affections, and common sentiments of mankind may be safely trusted to secure, on the whole, a better disposition of the property of the dead, and one more accurately adjusted to the requirements of each particular case, than could be obtained through a distribution prescribed by the stereotyped and inflexible rules of a general law.'[1]

1. THE POST-MORTEM QUESTION

The Property (Relationships) Act 1976 (NZ) ('PRA') is principally concerned with property resolution between couples during their lifetimes. But there is

---

1 *Banks v Goodfellow* (1870) LR 5 QB 549 (QB) at 564 per Cockburn CJ.

also an aspect that is post-mortem: on the premise that a person, especially a woman, should be no worse off on death than on divorce. It is here that my work comes in. A large part of my research and writing has concerned what was first called 'Testator's Family Maintenance', after the New Zealand statute of 1900 that brought this legislative genre into being. Such legislation was to be a counterweight to the freedom allowed to testators who could, in theory, leave their property to whomever they liked and, in practice, exclude widows and children. The Testator's Family Maintenance Act 1900 (NZ) enabled a court to override a will, in limited circumstances, in favour of the applicant. In this respect it represented a significant shift in the nineteenth-century laws of inheritance. This legislation is now variously known as 'family provision' or 'family protection' laws. The latest New Zealand iteration is the Family Protection Act 1955 (NZ).

This chapter complements the other chapters, which have focused on the lifetime dynamics and operation of the PRA, in providing insights into legislative interventions on death in favour of certain family members.[2] It also provides some reflections from experiences in Australia.

Combining lifetime *and* post-mortem property resolution is not possible in Australia in the manner of the PRA. The Australian Constitution limits the matters on which the federal parliament may make laws. While laws concerning marriage and divorce were included, thus providing the constitutional foundation for the Family Law Act 1975 (Cth) and the Marriage Act 1961 (Cth), laws concerning inheritance and property distribution on death were not. The ability of the federal parliament to make laws can be expanded, but only by referral from the states, pursuant to section 51(xxxvii) of the Constitution.[3] Referrals of power included, for example, the ability to make laws with respect to 'guardianship, custody, maintenance and access' of ex-nuptial children, and the resolution of property matters between unmarried couples.[4] The effect of these referrals is that the federal parliament has jurisdiction over marriage, divorce, parenting, and family property on separation. But without such a referral, there cannot be an Act in Australia with the embracing jurisdiction of New Zealand's PRA. All matters concerning wills, estates, and family provision remain squarely within the jurisdiction of the states and territories.

In each case, lifetime and post-mortem, the abiding questions are: why should relationships have property consequences – and which relationships

---

2 Please see N Peart, 'Family Finances on Death of a Spouse or Partner', ch 5.

3 A referral of power to the Commonwealth is not required from the Australian Capital Territory, the Northern Territory, and Norfolk Island because s 122 of the Australian Constitution assigns to the Commonwealth plenary power to 'make laws for the government' of the territories.

4 For a summary, see B Fehlberg and J Behrens, *Australian Family Law: The Contemporary Context*, OUP, Melbourne 2008, 34–35.

should do so;[5] and what conduct, if any, should have property consequences? There are several 'lenses' that may be applied to such questions. The first may be described as a 'practitioner lens', of the person who is working intimately with the law on a practical day-to-day basis. The second is a 'law reform lens', through which the operation and trends in law are identified and located within a conceptual context to propel review and revision of the law. The third lens I would describe as that of the legal historian, where big trends in law are seen and conceptualised in their historical context. This chapter is essentially a combination of the second and the third such lenses.

My doctoral study was of testamentary freedom: a story of conflicted and necessarily balanced ideas – between the idea of *family* and that of *property*.[6] One critical chapter was the story of the introduction of New Zealand's pioneering Testator's Family Maintenance Act of 1900 (NZ).[7] I have framed my contribution with the title of a 'lament', because I consider that something has gone strangely wrong with family provision law as it currently operates – certainly in Australia. The family provision of today is nothing like it was imagined to be at the outset. This may mean that family provision today is a different idea altogether. But, if that *is* the case, it is better to acknowledge that squarely, rather than still using the trappings of old. In particular, what is the place of testamentary freedom, the importance of which is embodied in the opening quote? Family provision today pays very little heed to testamentary freedom, apart from largely lip service, although it was very much anchored within the context of testamentary freedom. The litigation that has overtaken wills has made testamentary wishes but a bit of kindling in a costs bonfire.

2. THE CONTEXT OF TESTAMENTARY FREEDOM

While today we may take it as a 'given' that testamentary freedom is the norm, the freest form of will-making power had only a fairly brief window of ascendancy: after the abolition of the widow's dower right in the nineteenth century.[8] Although the abolition of dower was a necessary part of achieving the

5 Please see M Briggs, 'Which Relationships Should be Included in a Property Sharing Scheme?', ch 3.

6 R Atherton, '"Family" and "Property": A History of Testamentary Freedom in New South Wales with Particular Reference to Widows and Children', PhD thesis, Faculty of Law, University of New South Wales, 1994. Note that since 2004, I have published under the surname of 'Croucher'.

7 I published this as an article: R Atherton, 'New Zealand's Testator's Family Maintenance Act of 1900: The Stouts, the Women's Movement and Political Compromise' (1990) 7(2) *Otago Law Review* 202.

8 The detail of dower is described in RE Megarry and HWR Wade, *The Law of Real Property*, 5th ed, Sweet & Maxwell, London 1984, 544–46. The story of the abolition of dower in New South Wales is told in R Atherton, 'Expectation Without Right: Testamentary Freedom

security of the purchaser's interest in conveyancing – particularly in bringing land under Torrens title in Australia – it was at the cost of the interest of married women. But a desire to abolish dower did not amount to an overt attack on the position of wives. There was a tacit acknowledgment of a duty to provide for her. 'A man's wife is his first creditor,' is how one person put it.[9] Dower, however, was no longer the means for settling that debt. It may have been *expected* that he would 'give her preference over all others',[10] but it was an expectation without right. If that expectation were unfulfilled, a widow's only 'right' was defined by the difficult, costly, and totally unpredictable prospect of a challenge to her husband's testamentary capacity.[11] The women's movement of the late nineteenth century shifted the focus on testamentary freedom, however, from a power of men to *provide* for their wives, to a power to *disinherit* them. This characterisation was to have a powerful impact in the introduction of Testator's Family Maintenance legislation.

The first form of the Bill in 1896 was based on fixed shares, the 'Limitation of the Power of Disposition by Will Bill'.[12] Its proponent was the Scottish migrant, Robert (later Sir Robert) Stout.[13] But the idea of reintroducing a fixed shares approach, based on the 'widow and bairns' parts' of old,[14] was out of step with the liberal mood of the times. Some other form had to be found. Robert McNab, who took over the campaign after Stout left politics to become Chief Justice, found a handy precedent for his 'Testator's Family Provision Out of Estate Bill' in 1898. The new title and its discretionary model had appeal, reflecting the mood of the times. The model was a clever, and strategic, political compromise;[15] and it became the principal feature of such legislation as we have come to know it since: in Australia, the UK, and in parts of Canada.

Where the pattern of preceding centuries had been to increase the domain of testamentary freedom, this legislation sent a different message, but it was a

---

and the Position of Women in 19th Century New South Wales' (1988) 11(1) *University of New South Wales Law Journal* 133 and AR Buck, '"A Blot on the Certificate": Dower and Women's Property Rights in Colonial New South Wales' (1987) 4 *Australian Journal of Law and Society* 87. See also M Briggs, 'Historical Analysis' in N Peart et al, *Relationship Property on Death*, Brookers, Wellington 2004, 1 at [1.2].

9 E Burton, Examiner of Titles, in evidence given to the Royal Commission appointed to inquire into the working of the Real Property Act in New South Wales in 1879: *Votes & Proceedings*, Legislative Assembly (NSW), 1879–80, vol 5, no 973, 1021, 1074.

10 Ibid, at 1074.

11 R Atherton, above n 8.

12 *New Zealand Parliamentary Debates*, 26 June 1896, vol 92, 386.

13 Robert Stout was married to Anna Stout, a leader in the NZ Women's movement. This provides an interesting side-story all of its own. See my article: R Atherton, above n 7.

14 See, for example, G Gross, 'The Medieval Law of Intestacy' (1904) 18(2) *Harvard Law Review* 120; Sir W Holdsworth, *History of English Law*, 5th ed reprint, vol III, Methuen and Sweet & Maxwell, London 1966, 550–63.

15 The story behind it is a good illustration of the often idiosyncratic – and quirky – nature of law reform: see R Atherton, above n 7.

limited one, intended as a modest inroad into the testamentary arena.[16] The Court did not have power to re-write the will of the testator,[17] nor to provide simply for equal division amongst children.[18] It was to provide only for proper maintenance, education and advancement in life. But the emphasis was, principally, upon 'maintenance' and its very language reflected the intellectual tradition from which it grew – one in which 'testamentary freedom' meant different things depending on the lens of the observer: 'property', or 'family'.

2.1. THE PROPERTY LENS

The concept of 'testamentary freedom', or 'liberty of testation', was the intellectual cousin of freedom of contract and laissez-faire economics. Each expressed the idea of freedom *from* state control in favour of the power and choice of the individual.[19] It was a philosophy of individual rights, especially in relation to property, informed in large measure by the work of those like John Locke, who advocated the protection of citizens in their 'lives, liberties and estates'.[20] 'The end of Law', Locke stated, was 'not to abolish or restrain, but *to preserve and enlarge Freedom*'.[21] But the idea of enlarging freedom or liberty was not, however, an unlimited concept, it sat within 'the allowance of laws'.[22]

When viewed through a *property* lens, the power of testation was seen as a natural extension of the lifetime rights of disposition of property. John Stuart Mill, for example, considered that testamentary powers formed 'one of the *attributes* of property'; and 'the ownership of a thing cannot be looked upon as complete without the power of bestowing it, at death or during life, at the owner's

16 See R Atherton, 'The Concept of Moral Duty in the Law of Family Provision: A Gloss or Critical Understanding?' (1999) 5(1) *Australian Journal of Legal History* 5.

17 See, for example, *Pontifical Society for the Propagation of the Faith v Scales* (1962) 107 CLR 9 at 19 per Dixon CJ.

18 See, for example, *Cooper v Dungan* (1976) 50 ALJR 539 (HCA) at 540 per Gibbs J.

19 The doctrine of economic freedom is seen best in the writings of the English Classical economists, such as Adam Smith (1723–1790) and David Ricardo (1772–1823): see, for example, the excellent discussion in PS Atiyah, *The Rise and Fall of Freedom of Contract*, OUP, Oxford 1979. This period in the development of liberal ideas is considered, eg, by R Bellamy, 'TH Green and the Morality of Victorian Liberalism' in R Bellamy (ed), *Victorian Liberalism: Nineteenth Century Political Thought and Practice*, Routledge, London 1990, 131.

20 WH Hamilton, 'Property: According to Locke' (1932) 41(6) *Yale Law Journal* 864. See 868 n 6 for the various forms in which this phrase appeared in Locke's work. CB Macpherson analyses Locke's debt to the work of Thomas Hobbes (1588–1679): CB Macpherson, *The Political Theory of Possessive Individualism: Hobbes to Locke*, Clarendon Press, Oxford 1962.

21 J Locke, *Two Treatises of Government* (1690), P Laslett (ed), Cambridge University Press, Cambridge 1960, Second Treatise, ch VI 'Of Paternal Power', [57].

22 See my article on this conceptualisation: R Croucher, 'How Free is Free? Testamentary Freedom and the Battle Between "Family" and "Property"' (2012) 37 *Australian Journal of Legal Philosophy* 9.

pleasure'.[23] It was an incentive to industry and the accumulation of wealth,[24] but it was also preferable to a system of fixed inheritance rights, which held no incentive to heirs to work.[25] Subject only to rules that governed the validity of trusts (and various qualifications developed ostensibly on 'public policy' grounds), the owner's post-mortem powers could reach down generations through the power of the 'dead hand'.[26]

2.2. THE FAMILY LENS

When viewed through a *family* lens, however, testamentary freedom reflected other ideas. Locke, for example, located the power of testation as 'a part of *Paternal Jurisdiction*'.[27] This was not a new idea. Even in the Statute of Wills 1540 (UK) the power of devise was described as a power for a testator to make provision 'to and for the advauncement of his wife, preferment of his children, and payment of his debtes, or otherwise at his will and pleasure'.[28] 'Preferring', or choosing, among his children provided, as Locke later argued, 'a tye on [their] Obedience', a power men had 'to *bestow their Estates* on those, who please them best'.[29] Even though the father's estate was considered to be 'the *Expectation* and Inheritance of the Children ordinarily in certain proportions' (like the approach in civil law systems), it was the father's power 'to bestow it with a more sparing or liberal hand according as the Behaviour of this or that child hath comported with his Will and Humour'.[30] Through the 'hopes of an Estate', the father secured their obedience to his will.[31]

In the late eighteenth and early nineteenth century, Jeremy Bentham, like Locke, saw the father's testamentary power as providing an incentive to children. Bentham described it as a power to reward 'dutiful and meritorious conduct';[32] and as 'an instrument of authority, confided to individuals, for the

---

23 JS Mill, *Principles of Political Economy*, John W Parker, London 1848, bk II, ch 2, [4].

24 H Sidgwick, *The Elements of Politics*, 2nd ed, Macmillan, London 1897, ch VII 'Inheritance'; J Wedgwood, *The Economics of Inheritance*, Penguin, Harmondsworth 1939 (first published 1929), 200–01.

25 J Wedgwood, above n 24 at 194; HJ Laski, *A Grammar of Politics*, Allen & Unwin, London 1925, 528; H Dalton, *Some Aspects of the Inequality of Incomes in Modern Communities*, Routledge, London 1929, ch VII 'Effects of the Non-Fiscal Law', esp s 4 at 301.

26 See, for example, LM Simes, *Public Policy and the Dead Hand: Five Lectures Delivered at the University of Michigan, February 7, 8, 9, 14, and 15, 1955*, University of Michigan Law School, Ann Arbor 1955.

27 J Locke, above n 21 at Second Treatise, ch VI 'Of Paternal Power', [72].

28 Statute of Wills 1540 (32 H VIII c 1), s 4.

29 J Locke, above n 21 at ch VI 'Of Paternal Power', [72].

30 Ibid, at [72] (emphasis added).

31 Ibid, at [72].

32 J Bentham, 'Principles of the Civil Code' in *The Works of Jeremy Bentham: Published under the Supervision of His Executor John Bowring*, vol 1, Tait, Edinburgh 1843, 337.

encouragement of virtue and the repression of vice in the bosom of families'.[33] In other words, it was a power to *reward* or *punish*. In this way the power of testation was conceptualised both as an aspect of individual fulfilment (*to* the property owner) – 'for the good of those who command';[34] and an instrument of social control (*by* the property owner) – 'the preferment of his children'.[35] So, as William Blackstone had written in the century before Bentham, testamentary freedom was valued as a 'principle of liberty' and as a power of 'peculiar propriety',[36] won by the gradual stripping away of the medieval restraints on a man's testamentary powers. After the French Revolution of 1789 these views, if anything, hardened in defence of the common law's freedom over the civilian system of 'forced' shares.[37] As JJ Park, the author of a major treatise on the *Law of Dower*, wrote in 1819:[38]

> 'Independence of mind, as well as the finer sensibilities, revolt from the idea of a stated compulsory appropriation of property in a case where moral duty, and the domestic affections, afford a surer pledge among the virtuous than positive institutions.'

The freedom of testation thus established was confirmed as the rule in succession law by section 3 of the Wills Act 1837 (UK), which formed the basis of the Wills Acts throughout Australia and remains the foundation of the modern law in former British colonies. Behind this expansion of liberty was a belief that it would achieve a better balance among family members and others than could be achieved through fixed rules of law. But it was not without responsibility.

2.3. A POWER WITH A MORAL RESPONSIBILITY

The value of testamentary freedom is seen in one of the classic statements on testamentary capacity – that defining prerequisite for the exercise of testamentary powers – in the 1870 judgment of Cockburn CJ in *Banks v Goodfellow*, which

---

33 Ibid, at 337.

34 Ibid, at 337. Although Bentham expressed some concern that 'in making the father a magistrate, it is proper to guard against making him a tyrant', he considered that fathers needed such a power not only for their own good, but for the good of him who commands'.

35 Statute of Wills 1540 (32 H VIII c 1), s 4.

36 See, for example, W Blackstone, *Commentaries on the Laws of England*, vol 1, Clarendon Press, Oxford 1765–1769, 437–438.

37 See, for example, B Willenbacher, 'Individualism and Traditionalism in Inheritance Law in Germany, France, England, and the United States' (2003) 28(1) *Journal of Family History* 208.

38 JJ Park, *A Treatise on the Law of Dower: Particularly with a View to the Modern Practice of Conveyancing*, W Clarke and Sons, London 1819, 3.

is extracted in the opening quote. To that power, he said, 'a moral responsibility of no ordinary importance attaches', because of the faith placed in the testator's judgment to achieve 'a better disposition' of his property, 'more accurately adjusted to the requirements of each particular case, than could be obtained through a distribution prescribed by the stereotyped and inflexible rules of the general law'.[39] It provided, in Park's words, 'a surer pledge'.[40]

A power to give by will was allowed, but it was circumscribed by the 'moral responsibility' to provide for the maintenance, education, and advancement in life of children; and to adjudicate among family members according to their virtue, or vice. Freedom, in this context, was not to exist in the abstract. It was located, philosophically, in a framework of moral duty and obligation – 'for the advauncement of his wife' and 'the preferment of his children' in Statute of Wills terms.[41] But the judgement of the 'worthiness' of the individual's claim was entrusted to the testator, on the basis that his judgement was more reliable overall, and more finely calibrated, than fixed shares of the civilian model. It was, in essence, an endorsement of the father's power to give, or to withhold, judging those around him worthy or unworthy, as the case may be. In this way, Cockburn CJ's statement is a natural summary of the liberal intellectual tradition of over two hundred years previously.

Children may have *expected* something from their father's estate, but they were only *entitled*, in Mill's view, to expect maintenance and education to the extent of making them independent and self-reliant, to 'enable them to start with a fair chance of achieving by their own exertions a successful life',[42] but no more. This was the extent of the 'moral claim' of a child to any provision from a parent; and, conversely, the 'moral duty' of the parent to satisfy it. However, if parents *wanted* to leave their children more than this, Mill considered that 'the means are afforded by the liberty of bequest': 'that they should have the power of showing marks of affection, of requiting services and sacrifices, and of bestowing their wealth according to their own preferences, or their own judgment of fitness'.[43]

There is something profoundly sensible about this approach. We can also see in Mill's limitation of entitlement to 'maintenance and education', the seeds of the legislative formula of family provision laws. So, what is the relevance of these ideas in contemporary family provision law in Australia?

---

39 *Banks v Goodfellow*, above n 1 at 563–65.
40 JJ Park, above n 38 at 3.
41 Statute of Wills 1540 (32 H VIII c 1) (UK), s 4.
42 JS Mill, above n 23 at ch 2, [3].
43 Ibid, at [3].

3. AUSTRALIAN FAMILY PROVISION LAWS

Family provision legislation in Australia retains the main architecture of the New Zealand original: a list of eligible applicants, now much wider than the original set of widow and children; an assessment of what has been left under the will against a standard of 'adequate provision for proper maintenance' or variants – the 'jurisdictional question';[44] and a discretionary evaluation of what, if anything, should be provided. Other matters go to the time within which an application should be made, the criteria to be considered, and the property that might be 'caught' under an order. The legislation is broadly similar; and patterns of amendment are also broadly in parallel. There are two significant exceptions: the inclusion of 'notional estate' in the New South Wales statute in 1982;[45] and, for a time, the definition of eligibility in Victoria, which, after a period of trying a more broadly cast, circumstances-based form of eligibility, returned to more of a categories-based approach in 2014.[46]

The Uniform Succession Laws Project sought to align inheritance legislation in Australia. Initiated by the Standing Committee of Attorneys-General in 1991, the brief of the National Committee on Uniform Succession Laws was to achieve consistency through uniform legislation, or at least to achieve up-to-date legislation in all areas of succession law, so that it would be easier, and therefore cheaper, to administer the estates of people across Australia, wherever their assets were held.[47]

With respect to family provision,[48] the two main areas to which changes were recommended concerned eligibility to apply for family provision and the property out of which provision may be ordered. With respect to eligibility, the National Committee recommended that three categories of persons should be able to apply for provision: the husband or wife of the deceased person;

---

44 A handy summary of the wording of the jurisdictional formula as of 2009 is included in M McGregor-Lowndes and F Hannah, 'Reforming Australian Inheritance Law: Tyrannical Testators vs Greying Heirs?' (2009) 17 *Australian Property Law Journal* 62, 66.

45 Family Provision Act 1982 (NSW).

46 Justice Legislation Amendment (Succession and Surrogacy) Act 2014 (Vic).

47 Succession law was divided into workable chunks and undertaken as separate discrete areas by participating law reform bodies: the law of wills; family provision; intestacy; and the administration of estates. The last piece, completed in 2009, was the massive four-volume report on Administration of Estates: Queensland Law Reform Commission, *Administration of Estates of Deceased Persons: Report of the National Committee for Uniform Succession Laws to the Standing Committee of Attorneys General*, Report no 65, vols 1–4, QLRC, Brisbane, April 2009.

48 Comprising: Queensland Law Reform Commission, *Uniform Succession Law for Australian States and Territories: Family Provision*, WP no 47, 1995 (Issues Paper 11 in New South Wales); National Committee for Uniform Succession Laws, *Report to the Standing Committee of Attorneys General on Family Provision*, MP no 28, QLRC, December 1997; National Committee for Uniform Succession Laws, *Family Provision: Supplementary Report to the Standing Committee of Attorneys General*, Report no 58, QLRC, July 2004.

a non-adult child of the deceased person (meaning under 18 years); and a person for whom the deceased person had a responsibility to make provision for the person's maintenance, education, or advancement in life. The last of these categories was based on the eligibility provision of the Administration and Probate Act 1958 (Vic) (introduced in 1997 by section 55 of the Wills Act 1997 (Vic), now significantly amended), where this was then the sole basis on which a person's eligibility could be established. The approach of the National Committee was therefore to combine the then Victorian approach of a criteria-based category as well as a category based on status.

De facto spouses were a notable omission in the category list, in the first iteration of this work in 1997.[49] They would have to be considered under the general category. By the time of the report in 2004,[50] the matter was considered less 'sensitive' and de factos were added to the status list. The Model Bill therefore included wife or husband; de facto partner; and non-adult child. As to who was a de facto partner, this was left to each jurisdiction to determine. This left the issue of whether de facto partners included same-sex couples to be negotiated jurisdiction by jurisdiction.[51] Since then, same-sex partners have been included in all jurisdictions.[52]

The National Committee also recommended the introduction of provisions, based on the Family Provision Act 1982 (NSW), to enable the court to designate certain property as part of the 'notional estate' of the deceased and to order that provision be made out of it. However, there was no interrogation of why this model was appropriate. The New South Wales provisions were used because they were *there* and had been in force for a while, with apparently little bother. But the model has always bothered me.[53] For a start, it was based on the old 'death duty' provisions – state inheritance tax provisions. There the formula was a complex one, the end result of which was to determine, precisely, the assessable value of assets on death for tax purposes. It was not about attaching property in any way. It served a different purpose. In the family provision context, the question is to give an expanded definition of property that might be available in making provision for family members. A precisely formulated scheme like that of death duties places the emphasis in the wrong place: on whether property should be 'in' or 'out', rather than whether the court *should* make an order in relation to it and how much that should be. A second problematic aspect of the definition of

49 National Committee for Uniform Succession Laws, *Report to the Standing Committee*, above n 48.

50 National Committee for Uniform Succession Laws, *Family Provision: Supplementary Report*, above n 48.

51 Ibid, at [2.9]–[2.10].

52 See R Croucher and P Vines, *Succession: Families, Property and Death – Text and Cases*, 4th ed, LexisNexis Butterworths, Chatswood 2013, [2.31] and Table 2.1.

53 See, for example, R Atherton, 'Notional Estate and the Family Provision Act 1982: Consideration of a Prerequisite' (1987) 25 *Law Society Journal* 37.

notional estate was the mixing up of subjective and objective elements, again placing extra hurdles in the way of getting to the *real* issue under the legislation. Understanding that the property situation in the particular family is more than what was just left in the estate is a fair enough thing to recognise, but the practicality of calculation and the various hurdles involved in 'notional estate' are not really necessary to achieve that goal.

Although the National Committee recommended the introduction of the notional estate provisions, no other jurisdiction has followed suit. Eligibility is still a mixed bag, reflecting a mixture of status-based and circumstances-based categories. The reality has been that the wider the range of eligibility, the greater the canvas for fights; and the wider the idea of 'proper provision' and 'advancement' are cast, the greater the claims of children that seem to be made to fill it.

4. REFLECTIONS AND REFORM

The two major issues in my 'reflections' are the approach to spouses (and spouse-like relationships) and the problem of adult children. It is an opportunity to consider the appropriate balance of family on the one hand, and property on the other. The later twentieth and now twenty-first century have seen similar rhetoric displayed whenever shifts in the balance are considered. The definition of eligible persons and the property reach of the Act were intense points of engagement in the reform discussions in New South Wales in the 1970s.[54] The New South Wales Law Reform Commission framed its inquiry then in terms of: 'What, in 1974, is the best way for the law to assure to the family of a deceased person adequate provision out of his estate?'[55] While it put the question squarely in the spotlight, it did not remain there. In the 1977 Report it was dropped altogether, because, as the Commission said: 'We think that the time for proposing fundamental changes in [the laws of succession] has not yet come'.[56] Putting the question in that way, of course, was not a question about testamentary freedom, but cast as a 'family' question.

Let us bring it forward to today and ask: 'What, in *2016*, is the best way for the law to assure to the family of a deceased person adequate provision out of their estate?' New Zealand has certainly found one distinct pathway for couples in

---

54 For a study on this work see R Croucher, 'Law Reform as Personalities, Politics and Pragmatics: *The Family Provision Act* 1982 (NSW): A Case Study' (2007) 11(1) *Legal History* 1.

55 Law Reform Commission (NSW), *Testator's Family Maintenance and Guardianship of Infants Act, 1916*, WP 12, October 1974, 19 [2.1]; and see 22–23 [3.1]–[3.23].

56 Law Reform Commission (NSW), *Testator's Family Maintenance and Guardianship of Infants Act, 1916*, Report no 28, LRC 1977, [1.6].

the PRA, particularly in its inclusion of post-mortem aspects. A complementary question that we could – indeed *should* – ask, is 'what is the place of testamentary freedom in 2016?'

4.1. THE RIGHT APPROACH TO SPOUSES

What role does family provision play in relation to spouses in Australia? Given the constitutional constraints, it needs to be considered at state and territory level. But it is worth noting that, in the 1970s, at the same time as New South Wales was looking at its family provision law, there was also a serious attempt to review federal family law concerning property division on divorce. The Joint Select Committee on Family Law considered replacing the discretionary system of allocating matrimonial property established under the Family Law Act 1975 (Cth) with a scheme of community of property.[57] But, for a variety of reasons, this chapter in the history of family law in Australia stalled in the 1980s. The Committee recommended that, before proceeding with such proposals, several steps should be undertaken: a comprehensive survey of attitudes; a detailed law reform commission study of the implications of such a scheme; and a comparative assessment of community property regimes in other countries.[58] The Australian Law Reform Commission's work that followed,[59] and the heated debate it provoked,[60] recommended change, but the method of determining 'equality' produced no general agreement. The central point of contention was whether a system of *equal* rights to marital assets or a system which produced *equality of result* should be supported.

Looking at such issues through a lens of family property, if the review of family law begun in the 1970s is to continue with the object of producing some system of sharing, either on the basis of community of property during marriage or of a deferred sharing, the question of property distribution on death would need to be fundamentally re-considered, preferably at the same time as has been

57 Parliament of the Commonwealth of Australia, *Family Law in Australia: A Report of the Joint Select Committee on the Family Law Act*, Australian Government Publishing Service, Canberra, July 1980.

58 Ibid, at [5.158].

59 Law Reform Commission (Australia), *Matrimonial Property Law*, Summary of DP 22, Australian Government Publishing Service, June 1985; Law Reform Commission (Australia), *Matrimonial Property*, Report no 39, Australian Government Publishing Service, Canberra, 1987.

60 R Graycar, 'Feminism and Law Reform: Matrimonial Property Law and Models of Equality' in S Watson (ed), *Playing the State: Australian Feminist Interventions*, Allen & Unwin, Sydney 1990, 156; JA Scutt, *Women and the Law: Commentary and Materials*, Law Book, North Ryde (NSW) 1990.

done in England and in several of the Canadian reviews.[61] Indeed this seems to be the very premise of the amendments in New Zealand in 2001[62] and the earlier change effected by the Matrimonial Property Act 1976 (NZ), which introduced a system of deferred sharing of matrimonial property.[63]

When it comes to family provision, the way that the jurisdiction operates and the way that eligible applicants are defined should reflect the *function* of the legislation:[64]

> 'In the case of children there may be far more justification for supporting freer testation: that the control factor that property may bring *is* functional, both within the family and within society, and viewed from the perspective of father *or* mother as parent and testator. But to justify freer testation by limiting the role of the legislation to the provision of *maintenance* for spouses cannot be justified in the same light: this is patriarchal in form and substance, anachronistic, and misplaced in contemporary families and contemporary society in Australia.'

This is where the reflections about property division on divorce become most relevant.

Where a discretionary framework for family provision is retained, then unless the legislation achieves at least 'reasonable' provision for spouses, spouses would continue to be located within a framework of relationships of *dependence*. While flexibility in the application of the 'maintenance, education, and advancement' formula has permitted some recognition of contribution – and the court is specifically directed to consider it now at the discretionary stage in the New South Wales legislation[65] and the model bill[66] – the recognition of such contributions through a formula which permits only 'proper maintenance' arguably strains what are really family *maintenance* statutes at the seams. This may be seen to be the biggest weakness of the Australian legislation. As the courts have strained to recognise more fully the claim of a spouse, surely the legislation should also do so.[67] Spouses should not be worse off on death than on divorce.

---

61 For example, Law Reform Commission of British Columbia, *Report on Statutory Succession Rights*, Report no 70, December 1983, 104 ff; Law Commission (Eng&W), *Family Law: Family Property Law*, WP 42, 26 October 1971, 162.

62 Property (Relationships) Amendment Act 2001 (NZ), s 3.

63 M Briggs, above n 8 at 11–13.

64 R Atherton, *Victorian Attorney-General's Law Reform Advisory Council: Expert Report 1 – Family Provision*, Victorian Attorney-General's Law Reform Advisory Council, Melbourne 1997, [4.38] (emphasis of 'maintenance' added).

65 Succession Act 2006 (NSW), s 60(2)(h).

66 Model Bill, cl 9(3), set out in National Committee for Uniform Succession Laws, *Report to the Standing Committee*, above n 48 at 162, Appendix 2.

67 R Atherton, above n 64 at [4.63].

One way of striking the balance would be to give the spouse of a small estate an elective share linked to the share under the scheme of distribution on intestacy. This would involve a policy decision as between the rights of the spouse and children in relation to the property of the deceased spouse and parent. It would be a decision to favour the claim of the spouse and leave the children to such claims as they may have under the principles of the general law.[68] But this may be over-simplistic. One of the difficulties facing any attempt to make the law clearer and more equitable is the fact that family relationships and property relationships in families are becoming increasingly more complex. Simple solutions suit simple families – and simple arrangements in property ownership. On the property level, any solution of this kind would need to involve, at least, a concept of 'augmented estate', as under the Uniform Probate Code 1969 in the United States, to take into account the greater variety of property forms in families that in law amount to lifetime dispositions of property and not within the estate. Even a 'small estate' may be expanded to include a matrimonial home held on joint tenancy and a life insurance policy or superannuation benefit to which the spouse is entitled to succeed. Some estates may comprise virtually *only* such assets. Indeed, with the 'superannuation guarantee' of compulsory superannuation in Australia since 1993, and the increase in property values, especially in the principal capital cities, this may well become the norm. In addition, the question of qualification *as* spouse has become increasingly layered.

If a pre-emptive share were introduced, who would be entitled to seek it? One 'spouse' only, or should the South Australian solution on intestacy be used as a model, whereby the lawful spouse and putative spouse share the spouse's share?[69] Such difficulties counsel caution in considering the option of an elective share, but it is one that certainly could alleviate some of the difficulties in relation to smaller estates. A recurring theme in the cases concerning small estates is that so much of the estate will vanish, through the fact of the litigation itself, in costs.[70]

A further possibility could be an accruing elective or forced share, as proposed by Professors John Langbein and Lawrence Waggoner in the United States.[71] Under this proposal the rights of the spouse would *accrue*, and therefore the problem of the 'windfall' created by the forced share approach in the context of marriages of short duration could be overcome.

---

68 Ibid, at [4.36].

69 Administration and Probate Act 1919 (SA), s 72H(2).

70 For an empirical study, see P Vines, *Bleak House Revisited? Disproportionality in Family Provision Estate Litigation in New South Wales and Victoria*, Australasian Institute of Judicial Administration, Melbourne 2011.

71 JH Langbein and LW Waggoner, 'Redesigning the Spouse's Forced Share' (1987) 22(2) *Real Property, Probate and Trust Journal* 303.

4.2. BALANCING THE CLAIMS OF SPOUSES AND CHILDREN

Of course, family provision claims are not just about spouses. They are about balancing the claims of spouses and children, a problem aggravated by the phenomenon of 'serial monogamy' in an age of increasing longevity. Many family provision claims concern the very difficult problem of balancing the claims of adult children of an earlier marriage and the surviving spouse (particularly a widow). The jealousies in such cases are not surprising. The question is, however, as to what role the court should play in adjusting the balance between the testator's choice (or distribution on intestacy) and the sense of unfairness perceived by various family members. How does the legislation deal with the 'gut instincts' of the children, that they *deserve* a share of the property? More fundamentally, *should* it do so at all?

While family provision legislation began as a modest intrusion upon testamentary freedom, it has been subject to great pressure for expansion, both through the interpretation of the legislation in Australia, particularly in relation to adult children, and through specific legislative amendment. The biggest issue from my point of view in a 'back to basics' reform reflection concerns adult children, particularly adult able-bodied children, and the related issues of dutifulness and unworthiness. What happened to rewarding virtue and punishing vice in the bosom of the testator's family? The Australian courts, in an earlier era, were much tougher on adult sons.[72]

In its 1970s review, the Law Commission for England and Wales approached children differently from spouses. While spouses had to be considered in a new light, children's claims were solely to be considered on the basis of parental maintenance responsibilities. The Commission was supported in its view by a survey it commissioned, which demonstrated that this was the view of the majority of English and Welsh couples surveyed.[73]

The National Committee on Uniform Succession Laws in Australia took its role seriously and recommended a *reversal* of the pattern in relation to the eligibility of adult children, by moving them out of the status list and into the circumstances list: just being a child was no longer enough to bring a claim against the deceased parent. I have also argued that the legislation in relation to children ought to be restricted principally to the case of dependency during minority or to the completion of education. Indeed, the National Committee

---

72 *Re Sinnott* [1948] VLR 279; *Hughes v National Trustees, Executors & Agency Co of Australasia Ltd* (1979) 143 CLR 134.

73 JE Todd and LM Jones, *Matrimonial Property: A Survey Carried out on Behalf of the Law Commission, among Married Couples and Formerly Married People in England and Wales, Establishing the Current Pattern of Ownership of Matrimonial Property and the Opinions of Those Interviewed on Some of the Fundamental Issues of Matrimonial Property*, HMSO, London 1972; 1,877 married couples were surveyed.

referred to my work and also to that of the New Zealand Law Commission in coming to this conclusion.[74]

Limiting children's applications under family provision legislation could be justified in several ways. It might be considered that the limit of a parent's obligations to their children is controlled by relationships of dependency, reflected, for example, in the parental obligations spelled out in the Family Law Act 1975 (Cth). Beyond this, it might be argued that the parent's testamentary freedom is *necessary* within a family context. Some would argue, for instance, that a power to include or exclude children by such freedom is essential in order to take into account the proper claim of a spouse.[75] The parent's testamentary power, limited only by claims of dependency, could also be justified on the principle that it can be asserted as a control mechanism within the family, as advocated by Bentham. If the role of family provision legislation were defined by such concerns, it would then have a limited role in relation to a person's children or other adults. The jurisdictional basis in relation to adult children would then be confined solely to the provision of maintenance. If this were the favoured approach, it would mean a reduction in the operation of the legislation as it presently applies in Australia. Others have raised similar concerns;[76] and in its review of the relevant law in a 1997 report,[77] the New Zealand Law Commission recommended a much more restrained approach to adult children:[78]

> 'Powers to provide for adult children that are as extensive and indeterminate as those in the present law would, if applied to the living, be judged rightly as unacceptable. No reason has been advanced why they should apply after a will-maker's death.'

The New Zealand Law Commission favoured both a 'reward' role and a support one, in terms of maintenance, where needed, for adult children. First, the Law Commission recommended that: '*Adult, independent children* should have a claim only in respect of valuable benefits they have conferred on a parent during

---

74 National Committee for Uniform Succession Laws, *Report to the Standing Committee*, above n 48 at ch 2.

75 Professor Lawrence Friedman argued in 1966, for example, that in such circumstances 'disinheritance of children is both common and natural': LM Friedman, 'The Law of the Living, the Law of the Dead: Property, Succession and Society' [1966] (2) *Wisconsin Law Review* 340, 362–63.

76 For example, in 2009, Professor Myles McGregor-Lowndes and Frances Hannah suggested that reform with respect to children could be to limit claims to dependent or disabled children; or even to go down the road of a system of fixed shares for spouses and dependent or disabled children, with testamentary freedom over the rest: M McGregor-Lowndes and F Hannah, above n 44 at 84.

77 Law Commission (NZ), *Succession Law: A Succession (Adjustment) Act*, Report 39, Wellington, August 1997.

78 Ibid, at [75]. See also 2014 amendments in Victoria, above n 46.

the parent's lifetime.'[79] In other respects the Law Commission recommended cutting back eligibility. Recognising the conferral of a benefit *on the parent* is essentially about using family provision legislation to reward a particular kind of dutifulness expressly. The philosophical problem, however, is the extent to which such matters can, or should, be addressed in the context of family provision statutes, rather than the general law. The Manitoba Law Reform Commission, for example, was plainly of the view that such concerns should not be the province of family provision legislation.[80] But if the jurisdiction were limited to maintenance, there may be a gap: between 'maintenance' and the unrewarded services or the disappointed expectation of inheritance. If the law of family provision is not to be the general vehicle for overriding wills that do not reward children or others to whom the deceased may be said to be morally obliged, how else will such persons seek recompense? Sometimes the reward can be based on some other forms of obligation, such as contract; estoppel; constructive trust; quantum meruit. In the family context, however, the application of such doctrines may be obscured by questions of proving such things as intention to enter legal relations and relevance of particular activities to alleged contracts, as well as problems of proving consideration (rather than simply love and affection), and by what is unstated rather than what is stated.[81] The problem of the illusive 'testamentary promise', and the failure of classical contract doctrine to adequately deal with it, was accorded specific recognition in New Zealand's Law Reform (Testamentary Promises) Act 1949. Should family provision legislation be made the place for this? Rewarding the virtuous was certainly in the mind of the New Zealand Law Commission in its 1997 report. A new chapter in the dutiful child story is, and will continue to be, the role of children, or one among siblings, in caring for aging parents.

In other respects, however, the claims that adult children could make in New Zealand were to be greatly circumscribed. The Law Commission was quite firm in saying that there was no basis for a consideration of equal shares for adult children:[82]

> 'As far as the Commission can determine from the sociological advice and the submissions it has received, there is no clear and uniform expectation that all New Zealanders must leave their property to their adult children either equally or at all. There would be little or no public support for a legal rule that would compel all or part of a parent's estate to be shared (in the absence of a partner) equally among adult

---

79 Ibid, at [72].

80 Manitoba Law Reform Commission, *Report on 'the Testator's Family Maintenance Act'*, Report no 63, 16 December 1985, 70–71.

81 R Atherton, above n 64 at [4.32].

82 Law Commission (NZ), above n 77 at [73]–[74].

> children at the option of any adult child. We have referred already … to the absence of any agreement about what precisely the content of a will-making parent's "moral duty" to an adult child might be. In the absence of agreement of this kind, judicial rewriting of wills is in the Commission's view not supportable. The view has been advanced that even so there is a point where the terms of a will are so patently capricious as to justify interference. But this argument employs an extreme case to support a logically untenable proposition.'

The only circumstances in which 'logic must yield to compassion' were these:[83]

> 'Adult, independent children should also be entitled to make claims:
>
> - where they are genuinely in need and it is possible, without unfairness to those otherwise entitled to the estate of the deceased, to provide periodic payments sufficient to alleviate their need (the child would make a needs claim for a needs award); and
> - where what is sought by the child is no more than a memento or keepsake of modest value (these memento claims would be disposed of swiftly and simply by a Disputes Tribunal).'

Clearly the Law Commission and I were on the same page. In 2007 I included a consideration of some cases under the heading, 'Bludging as a career move?', expressing some frustration on my part with what I saw as an overly generous approach – particularly where adult children were concerned.[84] To translate such gut reactions into a momentum for reform on a sound evidence base, however, needs something more.

4.3. BUILDING THE EVIDENCE BASE

There has been some foundational work undertaken here, both in terms of canvassing attitudes to inheritance and surveying patterns of estate contests. Professor Prue Vines undertook a significant empirical study about estate litigation, published in 2011: *Bleak House Revisited? Disproportionality in Family Provision Estate Litigation in New South Wales and Victoria*.[85] Vines points to studies about inheritance expectations and the principal finding in those that 'members of the traditional nuclear family continue to be dominant in people's

---

[83] Ibid, at [77].

[84] See similarly, M McGregor-Lowndes and F Hannah, above n 44 at 71: 'the pendulum has swung too far in favour of family provision applicants'.

[85] P Vines, above n 70.

minds as the obvious objects of inheritance'.[86] She referred, for example, to the 2009 British study of inheritance attitudes, which showed that:[87]

> 'there was strong support for the original nuclear family over later spouses and for spouses over children to inherit; the further the relationship moved from traditional marriage and family relationships the less support for inheritance rights there was. It was also clear that "a substantial proportion of respondents favoured the children receiving *something* from the estate", a departure from favouring complete testamentary freedom. The respondents "viewed entitlement to inherit as based on objective criteria such as kinship or length of relationship and subjective criteria such as commitment or emotional closeness". There was a strong emphasis on retaining property within bloodlines and maintaining family stability and less emphasis on the individual choice of the testator.'

Vines then refers to the study undertaken by the New South Wales Law Reform Commission in 2006 on attitudes to inheritance, reporting similar findings.[88] She concluded:[89]

> 'Although there is recognition and acceptance of wider created relationships the view of family is still very much centred on blood-related families based on partnership and the raising of children. Over the twentieth century the notion that some expectation of inheritance could exist for all of these continued to grow, and the idea that the testator could do whatever he or she wished diminished accordingly. In response to this expectation legislatures expanded the range of possible applicants for family provision.'

Vines's work has been built upon by a major empirical project on estate contestation in Australia, conducted by a team of University of Queensland academics, some of the findings of which were published in an article in 2015.[90] Vines's focus had been on the issue of legal costs and the question of their proportionality with respect to the size of the estate in issue. The University of Queensland study was of a year of estate litigation, 2009, comprising over half of those in that litigation year. While only providing a slice of empirical data, what we learn is intriguing. New South Wales, while the most populous state,

---

86 Ibid, at [2.5]. She refers at n 13 to: A HUMPHREY ET AL, *Inheritance and the Family: Attitudes to Will-Making and Intestacy*, National Centre for Social Research, August 2010; JE DEKKER and MVA HOWARD, *I Give, Devise and Bequeath: An Empirical Study of Testators' Choice of Beneficiaries*, RR 13, New South Law Reform Commission, February 2006; J FINCH ET AL, *Wills, Inheritance and Families*, Clarendon Press, Oxford 1996.

87 P VINES, above n 70 at [2.5], citing A HUMPHREY ET AL, above n 86 at 9 and 8 respectively.

88 JE DEKKER and MVA HOWARD, above n 86.

89 P VINES, above n 70 at [2.6].

90 B WHITE ET AL, 'Estate Contestation in Australia: An Empirical Study of a Year of Case Law' (2015) 38(3) *University of New South Wales Law Journal* 880.

was disproportionately represented when it came to family provision matters – but in New South Wales, with notional estate possibilities, the potential 'pie' is bigger.

Vines's study included speaking to mediators, who are the first port of call in the litigation process in New South Wales and Victoria. Mediation became mandatory in all family provision cases in New South Wales from June 2009;[91] and has become the practice in Victoria.[92] The aim of mediation was to reduce litigation – and especially costs. In both New South Wales and Victoria, mediation can be provided by the court or by private practitioners; in the former case it is cost-free.

So, what *do* people fight about? The 'fiercest litigation', anecdotal conversations with mediators reported, occurred in two situations: 'where siblings are in contest about the disposition of the estate; and where the children of a former marriage contest the rights of the later widow/er to the estate':[93]

> 'Emotions run high in such situations and there is a risk that litigation may be used as a weapon for vendetta. Several lawyers spoke of clients who said they didn't care if the entire estate was used up in litigation, as long as the other claimant didn't get anything.'

Increasing longevity has meant that the fights among siblings involve a much older cohort – and the possibility of several marriages (and consequently complex families) and financial arrangements extending over much longer periods. Professor Myles McGregor-Lowndes and Frances Hannah observed that:[94]

> 'Older generations are, and will be, living longer, with consequent pressure on savings which might largely be spent in maintaining health and accommodation in old age. Therefore wealth transmission at death takes place much later than it did at the time that family provision laws were first developed in 1900 meaning that surviving spouses and children are older. Secondly, wealth is now increasingly expended on education and housing (or housing assistance) for younger generations, so that wealth is transferred from parents to children at an earlier point in the life-cycle than at death. Wealth transmission of the latter type is often unrecognised as such at the point of transfer, resulting in family provision claims being made by adult children on the death of their parents, which could be seen as a form of "double-dipping".'

---

91 Succession Act 2006 (NSW), s 98. See, for example, PA Bergin, speech by Hon Chief Judge in Equity, 'Executors/Trustees and Mandatory Mediations', 25 November 2009 <http://www.supremecourt.justice.nsw.gov.au/Documents/Publications/Speeches/Pre-2015%20Speeches/Bergin/bergin251109.pdf> accessed 17.05.2017.

92 P Vines, above n 70 at [3.19].

93 Ibid, at [3.18].

94 M McGregor-Lowndes and F Hannah, above n 44 at 70–71.

Tough issues involve estrangement; and this touches on the raw nerve of 'reward and punish', in Benthamite terms. Courts in Australia and New Zealand may be toughening up, however.[95] I note the study made of New Zealand cases by Nicola Peart and Bill Patterson, reported in 2007, where the authors observed that 'the tide has turned', the courts adopting a more conservative approach to family provision claims, with a 'consequential enhancement of testamentary freedom'.[96]

4.4. CONFUSED LOGIC

In 2005, the *Sydney Law Review* published a piece I wrote, prompted in part by the High Court's 2003 decision in *Barns v Barns*.[97] This decision led me to look at family provision law, at lifetime transactions and their intersection with family provision legislation, and, basically, to reflect upon the wider question of the foundational ideas in contemporary succession law in Australia. It also led me to comment that family provision today 'is in a muddle': 'It jumbles up its original logic and dilutes the logic of testamentary freedom. Succession law as a whole, moreover, is straining under conflicting pressures'.[98] The motivation for saying this was what I saw as the pull of different forces.[99] On the one hand, testamentary freedom is being *extended* through the introduction of 'dispensing powers' in all jurisdictions in Australia to overcome deficiencies in compliance with wills formalities;[100] and by powers of rectification of wills to get closer to what the testator really wants to happen with his or her property on death.

Here we are giving greater scope for the operation of the traditional notion of 'testamentary freedom'. We are giving to the individual a broader power to express his or her views through wills, or things that are near enough to be good enough, through an expansion of the operation of testamentary instruments into what was formerly an impenetrable domain of highly technical rules as to validity – the 'foot or end of the will' itself filled chapters of textbooks. And, if the testator's intention is not wonderfully clear, there is an increasing role for powers of rectification to correct, or fathom, the testator's real intention.[101] All of this

95 See, for example, *Revell v Revell* [2016] NSWSC 947; *Penfold v Predny* [2016] NSWSC 472; *Burke v Burke* [2015] NSWCA 195.

96 N Peart and B Patterson, 'Charities and the FPA: A Turning Tide' [2007] (2) *New Zealand Law Journal* 53, 53.

97 R Croucher, 'Contracts to Leave Property by Will and Family Provision after *Barns v Barns* (2003) 196 ALR 65: Orthodoxy or Aberration?' (2005) 27(2) *Sydney Law Review* 263.

98 Ibid, at 287.

99 This theme was developed in R Croucher, above n 22.

100 For a consideration of the varying provisions see R Croucher and P Vines, above n 52 at 323–53.

101 For a consideration of the varying provisions see R Croucher and P Vines, above n 52 at 401–26.

allows *more* freedom to the testator. But then, at the same time, and in a totally different direction, we are steadily, and at times dramatically, expanding family provision legislation. We are being pushed to recognise more claimants; to grab, or claw back, more property; to override a testator's wish to limit provision for, or exclude, particular family members in favour of others, or for other reasons – all of which represents an overriding of the individual testator's judgement with respect to the property in his or her particular family.

My pondering upon such things has led me to conclude that there is a real clash between 'individual' and 'family' in the directions of succession law: it is expressed *philosophically* through conflicting narratives on the purpose of, for instance, family provision legislation; it is expressed *practically* through legislation which expands powers to intrude upon testamentary territory for entirely opposite reasons.

There are other issues at play. There is a balancing between the 'state' and the 'estate'.[102] There is a balancing between intestacy law, the law of wills, and family provision. If you are pushed out of one, you may be pushed into another. The Law Commission for England and Wales recognised, for example, that it would be undesirable if the intestate schemes did the work of family provision. There is also an important balancing between autonomy and dynasty; and this is played out most clearly in the family provision arena. The National Committee for Uniform Succession Laws in Australia, and the New Zealand Law Commission, signalled pegging back the claims of adult able-bodied children; and I think this is a good move. There is room for looking after those who need it, who might otherwise 'become a burden on the state' – Mill himself supported this,[103] but self-reliance is a laudable principle. It is often lost sight of in family provision cases. While the principles may be those of 'past times and do not express the values of the present age', according to Bryson JA in *Lloyd-Williams v Mayfield*,[104] they still have a place in the overall philosophical rationale of property and the decision-making that is allowed to those who 'own' it.

Dynastic expectations are one thing; increasing longevity is another. The esteemed American academic, Professor John Langbein, has spoken of the fact that children now 'get their inheritance early': largely through an investment by parents in their education.[105] Parents do not die now in a way that produces an orderly fulfilment of dynastic expectations of children. Wills, after all, are the one last great act of control over one's children, the right to be respected and honoured in one's dotage through the power that testamentary freedom gives us.

---

102 I explored this issue in the context of the first of the NZ Bills in R Atherton, above n 7 at 216–18.

103 JS Mill, above n 23 at bk V, ch 9, s 1.

104 *Lloyd-Williams v Mayfield* [2005] NSWCA 189, (2005) 63 NSWLR 1 at [29].

105 JH Langbein, 'The Twentieth-Century Revolution in Family Wealth Transmission' (1988) 86(4) *Michigan Law Review* 722.

This sounds harsh, but it is the reality of the lives of many seniors. Such feelings are as alive and living and well in contemporary probate practice as they were at the time people like Locke, Bentham, and Mill wrote. The children usually do not see it that way – hence family provision practice. From their side of the family equation there is a gut sense of 'entitlement', an almost dynastic assertion of right.

Succession law is one of the slower-moving waterways of jurisprudence – but also one of the most fundamental and most significant philosophically in relation to property in families. The key issue is, ultimately, the balance – between the widow (spouse) and the bairns' parts of old. The challenge, in contemporary terms, is not only this, but also to accommodate the increasing move of family property into non-estate areas. The goal of simplicity may founder upon – or at least have to navigate through – these challenges. The dispensing power cases and the family provision cases show the tensions that are evident in succession law today. They are not getting better. Family provision is, in my view, on a slippery slope where adults are concerned. I would clearly distinguish the position of partners/spouses from that of children. Marriages, or marriage-like relationships, are based on a different logic than simply being a child (or analogous relationship) of someone. A good look at family provision legislation in its real context is needed: namely what role does, and should, property play in families. Unless we seriously look at such questions, we will continue to tinker with family provision legislation, a bit this way, a bit that, and end up writing a blueprint for bludging.

PART II

WHAT PROPERTY SHOULD BE COVERED BY A PROPERTY SHARING REGIME?*

In addition to identifying to whom a property sharing regime should apply, as discussed in Part I, a key question that must be answered is over what property should such a regime apply? What might seem the obvious answer – property owned by either or both of the parties to the relationship – is too simplistic. The chapters in Part II of the book consider the wider question of property identification through analysis of three more specific enquiries. While the chapters here place significant emphasis on New Zealand's regime, as do many of the chapters throughout this book, the questions posed and the responses suggested provide helpful reflections for thinking about the scope of property sharing regimes more generally.

Property is acquired for all sorts of reasons and for many different uses. A link between the property and the relationship that would justify sharing of the property between the partners on dissolution of the relationship may not be altogether clear. Some property may be used by both partners in their day-to-day living within the relationship, while some is used or enjoyed only by one of the partners. Some assets are acquired using income earned during the relationship, but some may have been received by way of gift or inheritance or acquired before the relationship commenced. The first enquiry, then, is should all property owned by the parties to the relationship be captured by a property sharing regime?

Bill Atkin addresses this question in Chapter 7. He identifies a spectrum of approaches available for the exercise of classifying property either as separately owned and outside the scope of the regime, or subject to division between the parties. The spectrum ranges, at the one extreme, from a presumption that all assets owned by either of the parties are to be shared, to, at the other extreme, the exclusion of all separately owned assets from the pool of property to be shared. Atkin advocates a position toward the 'all assets' end of the spectrum in order that the concept of partnership is taken seriously. The important point is

* Part II Introduction by Jessica Palmer.

that the underlying philosophy of the particular regime must be reflected in the classification of property used in the regime. Related issues of onus of proof and appropriate definitions of property are also canvassed.

The second enquiry concerns the relevance of property not owned by either partner. It is not uncommon for partners to benefit from property they do not formally own, as beneficiaries or other related parties to a trust. In other instances, property owned by one of the partners may be significantly fettered by statutory or other limitations so that the partners are not free to deal with it as their own and yet one or both of the partners benefits from the property. Should such property be captured by a property sharing regime and, if so, how?

Two chapters relate to this problem but concern quite different types of property. In Chapter 8, Jessica Palmer examines whether property sharing regimes can and should cover property held on trust where neither partner has a fixed or vested beneficial property interest in the trust property. She describes common trust practices that are thought to frustrate property sharing regimes and evaluates the various judicial and statutory responses that have been proffered. Palmer argues that the barriers these trusts are creating to the effective implementation of property sharing regimes can only appropriately be removed by resort to legislative mechanisms. Reliance on general principles of trust and property law has only led to confusion and incoherence in the New Zealand jurisdiction where statutory recourse is significantly restricted.

In Chapter 9, Jacinta Ruru and Leo Watson examine issues relating to Indigenous views of property which differ from European views. The current New Zealand legislative framework excludes Māori land and specific Māori chattels (such as traditional feather cloaks worn on special ceremonial occasions) from the relationship property regime. The exclusion reflects the very different cultural understanding relating to ownership of property among Māori people that is carefully explained by Ruru and Watson. Ownership of Māori property is based on ancestral or blood ties with each owner having obligations of guardianship that require care and preservation of the property for future generations. For these reasons, Māori land and special chattels cannot be divided between partners upon dissolution of the relationship, making their exclusion from the relationship property regime justifiable. This does, however, give rise to potential injustice for partners of Māori owners who contribute to the building of non-removable homes on Māori land and are then left with no entitlement to share in that property. While the authors consider the current exclusion appropriate, they suggest ways in which this problem could be minimised, including by the recognition of equitable interests and the availability of compensation orders.

A third very practical, but no less challenging, enquiry concerns how property, once identified, is to be valued for the purpose of a property sharing regime. The authors of Chapter 10, Simon Jefferson and Paul Moriarty, have significant experience in valuation disputes. They ask whether property sharing regimes should provide rules for valuation. They consider methods of, and the factors appropriate to, the process of valuing property. Close attention is paid to the role of expert witnesses and how courts should use expert testimony. Ultimately, the authors advocate judicial flexibility in order to enable courts to deal appropriately with the diversity of factual circumstances inherent in relationship property disputes.

CHAPTER 7

CLASSIFYING RELATIONSHIP PROPERTY – A RADICAL RE-SHAPING?

Bill Atkin*

* Special thanks to Jo Miles and Jens Scherpe, and my study time in Cambridge that they facilitated. I owe a great debt of gratitude to my very fine research assistant, Sean Brennan.

1. INTRODUCTION

The New Zealand Property (Relationships) Act 1976 ('PRA') is sometimes described as one of deferred community. It usually operates when couples separate or one of them dies, and thus its impact is 'deferred' or delayed until a crystallising event.[1] A critical step is determining what constitutes the 'community' property, that is, what property is available for division. This is the 'classification' issue. Under the PRA, the distinction is drawn between 'relationship property' and 'separate property', the equal division rule applying to the former and not the latter. This is simplistic because the court has power in some situations to make orders affecting separate property,[2] but we put that to one side for present purposes.

The key classification rules are found in sections 8–10 with the definitions provided in section 2. In many respects these provisions are opaque and confusing. They are possibly the most complex in the world. The underlying philosophy behind them is not spelt out, though it is possible to discern what it might be. While amendments made by the Property (Relationships) Amendment Act 2001 (NZ) in general extended the relationship property pool, they did so modestly and were largely tacked into the pre-existing structure. Can New Zealand not do a lot better?

The rules for classification should be based on appropriate principles. This chapter explores what these principles might be. Even so, the principles do not lead inexorably to just one model of classification. There is, I suggest, a spectrum of approaches to classification. The choices are stark at the edges but with a wide range of variations in-between. The implications of these options are many and varied but help us understand what is at stake. In this chapter, I recommend that New Zealand move to what is the left of the spectrum, as discussed later in Part III. It could be said that this involves taking the concept of partnership in the family law sense seriously.

Two sub-issues relating to the spectrum are discussed: the basic meaning of 'property' for the purposes of the PRA, and the question of onus of proof, a matter that is suppressed in the current PRA but potentially of intense importance. It is also important, for the purposes of this topic, to tackle the detail of the current regime and ask very specific questions about how property is classified and why, and whether changes are justified. Even if the radical option that I propose

---

1 At certain points, the Property (Relationships) Act 1976 (NZ) ('PRA') can operate while the parties are still together, which means that 'deferred community' is not entirely accurate: A Angelo and W Atkin, 'A Conceptual and Structural Overview of the Matrimonial Property Act 1976' (1977) 7 *New Zealand Universities Law Review* 237.

2 For example, in relation to post-separation events, ss 18B and 18C, debts, s 20E, and economic disparity if it comes under s 15A, but, perhaps unwisely, not if it comes under the main disparity section, s 15. See also s 33(3)(n).

were to be accepted, some detailed matters still need careful examination. For instance, what should be considered the 'family home'? What should be regarded as 'family chattels'? Why do we treat inheritances as sometimes relationship property and sometimes separate?

In considering classification in a system such as that of New Zealand, a few assumptions are made in the course of writing this chapter. First, I assume that New Zealand will retain a distinct statutory regime of some kind and will not simply revert to the rules of common law and equity. To put the point another way, the basic rules of the scheme should be determined by Parliament and not left to the courts, as has in effect happened in England.[3]

Another assumption is that the regime will apply to the three main ways of legal coupling: marriage, civil unions, and de facto relationships. The place of de facto relationships was controversial when the PRA was extended to them in 2001, but arguably too much water has gone under the bridge for them now to be excluded. Such a move would sit awkwardly with the non-discrimination laws in the Human Rights Act 1993 (NZ) and would belie the considerable jurisprudence that has grown in the interim. That said, I acknowledge that the inclusion of de facto relationships may have its problems at the edges, especially with an unnecessarily loose definition of the concept of 'de facto relationship'.[4] My proposal on classification may compound those problems rather than ease them but in a 2015 judgment, Gendall J stated that:[5]

> 'the threshold required to establish a de facto relationship is a high one. A certain degree of rigour and some caution is required in carrying out an analysis of whether or not a de facto relationship exists.'

If this approach is adopted more widely, there is less reason to be worried.[6]

---

3 See for example, the discussion of fairness and who should determine it in J Miles and JM Scherpe, 'The Legal Consequences of Dissolution: Property and Financial Support between Spouses' in J Eekelaar and R George (eds), *Routledge Handbook of Family Law and Policy*, Routledge, Oxford 2014, 138–52. At 143, they describe the decision of the House of Lords in *White v White* [2001] 1 AC 596 (HL) as 'revolutionary' in moving away from need as the basis of awards. The English Law Commission has also discussed the development of the concept of 'non-matrimonial property' in English law, which had no place in the law prior to *White* and was 'entirely developed by the judiciary': Law Commission (Eng&W), *Matrimonial Property, Needs and Agreements*, Law Com 343, TSO, London 2014, [8.2].

4 The case law on the phrase 'de facto relationship' has been somewhat erratic but a tendency against a finding of such a relationship is apparent in cases involving more than one coupling, eg where a person is both married and in some other kind of association. See for instance *Greig v Hutchison* [2015] NZHC 1309, [2015] NZFLR 587.

5 Ibid, at [52].

6 Briggs has discussed the possibility of extending the law to other domestic relationships such as family ones; see M Briggs, 'Rethinking Relationships' (2015) 46 *Victoria University of Wellington Law Review* 649; and 'Which Relationships Should be Included in a Property Sharing Scheme?', ch 3.

Thirdly, I am assuming that the default rule for division will be equality. The discussion of classification does not depend on this, but a substantially different division regime may raise questions about classification.

Fourthly, I am assuming that New Zealand will not develop a bifurcated scheme, for instance as proposed by Goubau for de facto couples.[7] Under this model, division rules would apply when there are children, but not otherwise. This approach has a policy justification in that it places a premium on children, but it raises questions about how long the impact of children should last, how to reflect contributions other than child care, and so forth, and in any event still relies on a classification system.

2. PRINCIPLES

A useful starting point for considering the policy drivers in determining classification is the current legislative statement of purpose and principles. These are found in sections 1M and 1N.

First, section 1M refers to the parties' equal contribution to the marriage or de facto partnership or the civil union. Section 1N expands on this by referring to the parties' equal status and the need to maintain equality between them. Further, all forms of contribution are to be treated equally. Several points emerge from this:

- No substantial distinction is made between the three forms of relating (marriage, civil union, and de facto relationship).
- The concept of 'partnership', although not mentioned in relation to civil unions perhaps because it is contained in the word 'union', implies a philosophical stance based on the common life or community of the couple, rather than one based on individualism. The two parties are not strangers in law or in reality, but are or were partners in a common enterprise.
- The reference to contributions is designed to avoid what Woodhouse J referred to as 'the hypnotic influence of money' determining outcomes.[8] A partnership is not solely about finance but about life and family in all its various manifestations. Thus, non-financial contributions are given as much weight as financial ones. This approach gives real substance and meat to the concept of partnership.
- The use of the concept of equality provides the backdrop to the concept of economic justice and fairness in the PRA: fair and just redistribution is, in general, secured through equal division of the relationship property.

---

7 D Goubau, 'Division of Family Assets and De Facto Conjugality: The Limits of a Free Choice Approach' in B Verschraegen (ed), *Family Finances*, Jan Sramek Verlag, Vienna 2009, 271.

8 *Reid v Reid* [1979] 1 NZLR 572 (CA) at 581. See also *Reid v Reid* [1982] 1 NZLR 147 (PC).

Neither need nor vulnerability is mentioned. The PRA is not based on a finding of needs and the somewhat paternalistic satisfaction of them. A person does not have to be vulnerable or needy to gain a share of property, an approach that in part arises under the English Matrimonial Causes Act 1973.[9] The share of property is a right based on the notion of partnership, not the provision of a private form of welfare.

Likewise, a share of property does not depend on any particular contribution or action for which compensation should be paid (which is how section 15 and its economic disparity compensation in part operates). A share is a right flowing from the concept of partnership. Further, autonomy is absent as a concept, although it can be said to govern Part 6 with its rules for contracting out of the PRA.[10] Another concept not mentioned is fault. Most jurisdictions now relegate it to a minor element and usually require some form of financial fault for it to be relevant.[11]

The approach just outlined is not beyond challenge. It could be argued, for instance, that, once the parties have separated, it is disingenuous to rely on the partnership concept for property division. Others may object more fundamentally to this concept and argue that the starting point should be two individuals whose own property interests should prevail unless a case is made out to the contrary. As we shall see, these different philosophies may well affect the issue of classification.

A second principle was added in 2001 and is found in section 1N(c):

> 'the principle that a just division of relationship property has regard to the economic advantages or disadvantages to the spouses or partners arising from their marriage, civil union, or de facto relationship or from the ending of their marriage, civil union, or de facto relationship.'

This is redolent of the Scottish principle:[12]

> 'fair account should be taken of any economic advantage derived by either party from contributions by the other, and of any economic disadvantage suffered by either party in the interests of the other party or of the family.'

---

9 See, for instance, *Miller v Miller; McFarlane v McFarlane* [2006] UKHL 24, [2006] 2 AC 618, with its three heads of need, compensation, and sharing. See also J Miles and R Probert, 'Sharing Lives, Dividing Assets: Legal Principles and Real Life' in J Miles and R Probert (eds), *Sharing Lives, Dividing Assets*, Hart Publishing, Oxford 2009, 7.

10 Note W Pintens, 'Matrimonial Property Law in Europe' in K Boele-Woelki, J Miles and JM Scherpe (eds), *The Future of Family Property in Europe*, Intersentia, Cambridge 2011, 19 at 42 refers to the way in which various systems in Europe emphasise spousal autonomy but 'also attach great importance to the solidarity of spouses towards each other'.

11 Under the PRA, see ss 18A and 18C.

12 Family Law (Scotland) Act 1985, s 9(1)(b). See also s 9(2): '"economic advantage" means advantage gained whether before or during the marriage and includes gains in capital, in income and in earning capacity, and "economic disadvantage" shall be construed accordingly.'

The reference in particular to disadvantage could be seen as relating to hardship but this is to misunderstand the concept introduced in 2001. Behind the principle is the notion that technical equality may not necessarily produce equality in reality as it does not take into account the effect of cohabitation on earning capacity. Obviously, under the PRA sections 15 and 15A represent the primary vehicle for the fulfilment of this principle. However, a classification system that leads to a small pool of relationship property will militate against an equitable sharing of property, because the disadvantaged party will receive a lesser share under the basic division of property. On the other hand, a system that classifies more property as divisible will assist the disadvantaged party.

A third but subdued theme in sections 1M and 1N is the position of the children. Section 1M(c) refers to a just division of the property 'while taking account of the interests of any children'. This is not limited to minor children, although section 26, which empowers the court to settle property on children, states that regard must be had to the interests of minor or dependent children. Few would deny that the well-being of children is an important policy goal but how it is to be achieved leads to quite different responses around the world. In terms of classification, a wide pool of relationship property is ultimately more likely to benefit children than a narrow one. This is because the primary caring parent is likely to end up being in a better financial position than otherwise.

A final point about principles and policies is found in section 1N(d): 'the principle that questions arising under this Act about relationship property should be resolved as inexpensively, simply, and speedily as is consistent with justice'. This is in the interests of the parties but also of the children. Speedy and predictable outcomes also assist negotiations and the resolution of disputes without formal litigation. Having straightforward rules for classification, as opposed to murky ones, is consistent with this principle.

Let us pause for a moment and check some other approaches to the articulation of principles. Kórös refers to four guidelines in relation to Hungarian law:[13]

'– the protection of the family relationships;
– the protection of child interests;
– the principle of equality of the spouses; and
– the principle of equity and the protection of the weaker party.'

We might hesitate to use the language of 'protection', which sounds paternalistic, and we might prefer to say 'disadvantaged' instead of 'weaker'. Those points aside, a moment's reflection suggests that the New Zealand law is not too far removed from these guidelines.

---

13 A Kórös, 'New Features of Hungarian Matrimonial Property Law in the Draft of a New Civil Code' in B Verschraegen (ed), *Family Finances*, Jan Sramek Verlag, Vienna 2009, 675 at 677.

A different perspective is brought by Miles and Scherpe.[14] They explore a wide range of jurisdictions and discern four 'key ingredients of fairness internationally':

- sharing based on partnership;
- alleviation of need based on matrimonial obligation;
- compensation of relationship-generated losses; and
- respect for couple autonomy.

These points have all been touched upon. Various jurisdictions tend to emphasise one of the ingredients ahead of others. In New Zealand, the first predominates but the others also have their place, more particularly when we include the needs-based rules of maintenance found in Part 6 of the Family Proceedings Act 1980 (NZ).[15] When it comes to classification, Miles and Scherpe conclude that there are considerable differences between jurisdictions but the trend is towards treating the 'fruits of joint labour' as being divisible.[16] This is consistent with the most common approach in Europe and South America, the community of 'acquests'. As in Germany, for example, accrued gains, that is, the difference between initial assets and accrued assets, lead to a monetary claim.[17] This looks relatively simple at first sight, but determining what are acquests or community assets is 'often easier said than done'.[18] Wise counsel may be to keep detailed records of who owns what property when people start living together, but the practicality of this is surely doubtful (even more so for de facto partners). It is also worth noting that in some jurisdictions a system based on acquests is secondary. For example, in South Africa the default regime is community of property, with parties having the ability to contract 'out of community' in favour of alternatives such as division based on accruals or separate property.[19]

---

14 J Miles and JM Scherpe, above n 3 at 142.

15 See J Caldwell, 'Maintenance – Time for a Clean Break?', ch 15.

16 J Miles and JM Scherpe, above n 3 at 142 and 152.

17 See H Lücke, 'Dividing the Assets on Family Breakdown: The German Civil Code' in R Bailey-Harris (ed), *Dividing the Assets on Family Breakdown*, Family Law, Bristol 1998, 29 ff. See also W Pintens, above n 10 at 19 ff.

18 JM Scherpe, 'The Financial Consequences of Divorce in a European Perspective' in JM Scherpe (ed), *European Family Law Vol III: Family Law in a European Perspective*, Edward Elgar, Cheltenham 2016, ch 5, 146 and JM Scherpe, 'Contracting Out of the Default Relationship Property Regime – Comparative Observations', ch 14.

19 J Heaton (ed), *The Law of Divorce and Dissolution of Life Partnerships in South Africa*, Juta, Cape Town 2014, [2.1]–[2.3]. 'Out of community' is language found in the South African Matrimonial Property Act 88 of 1984. The law in the Netherlands is similar in having a full community property system.

The principles that we choose to guide us are the DNA of law reform. So, with this discussion of principles in mind, what is the range of options for classification of property?

3 THE CLASSIFICATION SPECTRUM

3.1. THE SPECTRUM

The discussion of principles indicates that the question of classification can be tackled in different ways. It is useful to consider this with the help of a spectrum. This spectrum is inevitably simplistic and many variations are possible. However, it may put the choices into sharp contrast. At one end of the spectrum, all assets owned by the parties will be 'relationship property'; at the other end none will be. Here is the spectrum containing four steps:

all assets – all core assets and gains – gains – no assets

3.1.1. *'All Assets'*

The 'all assets' approach means that it is not necessary to have a sophisticated set of rules about classification, as 'all' property is assumed to be relationship property. This is simplicity writ large. It could nevertheless be accompanied by a power to exclude certain categories of assets if a case was made out to do so. These could include such things as inheritances that have nothing at all to do with family life. An 'all assets' approach could apply to property legally and beneficially owned by the parties or, depending on the particular legislation, also include property controlled by one of the parties such as a trust. Policy choices are involved in determining how far the assets extend.

This model is based on a high view of the family and cohabitation, and allows less scope for autonomy. 'Contracting out', however, might be permitted.[20] In some jurisdictions that use this model, division of the property may be on a more discretionary basis and may be combined with maintenance – this is not an accurate picture of the English and Australian systems[21] but they could be

[20] See JM Scherpe (ed), *Marital Agreements and Private Autonomy in Comparative Perspective*, Hart Publishing, Oxford 2012.

[21] It may be a misnomer to refer to the English and Australian laws as 'systems'. Fehlberg, commenting on the Australian law, refers to 'lack of conceptual clarity and coherence that continues to exist in this area, reflective of a broader lack of social consensus on these issues': B Fehlberg et al, *Australian Family Law the Contemporary Context*, 2nd ed, OUP, Melbourne 2014, 492. See also JM Scherpe, 'Contracting Out of the Default Relationship Property Regime' above n 18 at [4.3], on the English legislation.

seen loosely fitting in here. However, a discretionary system is not the inevitable corollary. In Ontario, for example, the system is one of equalisation of the value of all assets, but with a number of exclusions and deductions.[22]

3.1.2. Core Assets and Gains

The idea is not novel that certain assets are so central to family life that, irrespective of their source, they should be part of the common property available for division. In New Zealand and Scotland,[23] this applies to the home and furniture. Other property is divisible if it can be shown to be related in some way to the period of cohabitation. This system therefore resembles 'acquests plus'. However, what about taking this concept to another level? Family life is not solely dependent on the home. It is also dependent on the financial wherewithal for daily life. So, this model could be seen as going much further than those currently in place in New Zealand and Scotland: it would, for instance, include the family farm and the family business, irrespective of their source. If a family trust provided funds for the family's existence, it would be included in the divisible pool.

As with the first model, this one has a strong view of the family and of relationships. Because of the basis in family life, the interests of children are at least indirectly taken into account. However, it does not rely on the existence of dependent children or indeed of any children. Where the children have grown up and left home, the notion of family life still makes sense over the course of a period of cohabitation, because of its ongoing effects. Where there have never been children, it is disingenuous to say that the parties did not share a family life. 'Family' is a wide term, ranging from a couple to whānau[24] (and possibly beyond). The presence of children alters the dynamics but not, it is suggested, the basic nature of family.

---

22 Family Law Act 1990 (Ont). See JD Payne and MA Payne, *Canadian Family Law*, 4th ed, Irwin Law, Toronto 2011, ch 12. The 1978 Act distinguished between family and non-family assets but this distinction was removed in 1990 in favour of equalisation of the value of all assets. Other Canadian provinces have similar models, for example, Family Law Act 2011 (BC), pt 5.

23 Family Law (Scotland) Act 1985. See K Norrie, 'Marital Agreements and Private Autonomy in Scotland' in JM Scherpe (ed), *Marital Agreements and Private Autonomy in Comparative Perspective*, Hart Publishing, Oxford 2012, 289 ff. See also Law Commission (Eng&W), above n 3 at [8.32], where it is stated that treating the home as non-matrimonial property undermines the purpose of the home as being for the parties and their children. It was also thought to be discriminatory against women and a contradiction in terms.

24 A Māori term, used in common parlance in New Zealand, meaning the extended family or relatives who usually live in the same geographical area.

3.1.3. *Gains – 'Fruit of Joint Labour'*

The third model is the system of gains or acquests. The theory behind this is that cohabitation involves 'joint labour', which produces wealth for both parties. Labour is, of course, not limited to paid employment – the precise actions of each of the parties are not, as such, to be examined but it is assumed that the differing efforts of both parties have helped to create the gains of the partnership. Because of the emphasis on the causal effect of cohabitation, gifts and inheritances are usually excluded as they are not the result of joint labour but are a windfall.

This model takes relationships seriously but with more of an emphasis on the adults than the first two models. It raises issues about proof of what is a gain, and ancillary issues may be how to factor in contributions to non-acquests. These points can apply to the 'core assets and gains' category, but to a lesser extent depending on how widely the core assets are defined. The 'fruit of joint labour' model sets a high premium on individual rights to pre-relationship property. In this sense, it is a mixture of autonomy and common life.

3.1.4. *No Assets*

The fourth model starts with the assumption that assets should normally be held according to legal and beneficial interests. In other words, no property is classified as 'relationship' because it is not necessary. Like the first model, this simplifies the law considerably but for very different reasons. Arguments could abound over beneficial interests, in particular about the constructive trusts that at one stage were endemic in de facto relationship cases prior to the 2001 amendments that brought such relationships under the PRA umbrella.[25] This model is arguably consistent with legislative provision that permits departure from ordinary title on specified grounds, for instance based on contributions that do not give rise to a beneficial interest.[26] Contracting into a scheme similar to the PRA could be provided for, the opposite of the contracting out that would apply to other models.

This model has a low view of families and relationships, but a high view of the individual and autonomy. Arguably it is in this sense consistent with neo-liberal thinking. It would leave interests in companies and trusts to be determined according to the relevant common law and statutory rules. It has the virtue, therefore, of minimally upsetting the operation of businesses and, in particular in the New Zealand environment, farms.

---

25 See *Lankow v Rose* [1995] 1 NZLR 277 (CA).

26 The repealed Matrimonial Property Act 1963 (NZ) could be seen as an example of this.

3.2. ONUS

Two subsidiary issues relate to the spectrum, but they are not unimportant. First, the operation of a classification system may turn to a certain extent on who has the burden of proof. The PRA does not, in general, expressly state who bears the onus, and the New Zealand courts have sometimes counselled against any onus of proof in family law cases.[27] Compare this, for example, with section 4(3) of the Ontario Family Law Act 1990, which expressly lays the onus on the person arguing for a deduction or exclusion from the equalisation regime.[28] Contrariwise, in Norway the onus is on the party claiming that pre-marital property, inheritances, or gifts should not be exempt from division, while in Germany the onus is on the spouse endeavouring to prove that assets are 'initial'; that is, owned by that spouse at the date of marriage.[29]

It is surely wise, as a matter of policy, for a statute to spell out who has to prove what. The terms of the onus may depend on where on the spectrum a system sits and policy choices about the balance between autonomy and collectivity. At the universal end of the spectrum, the claimant for a departure from the statutory rules should have to prove the case. At the traditional property end of the spectrum, the onus would rest on the person seeking a departure from legal and beneficial title. Elsewhere on the spectrum, the decision about onus could vary but most likely the presumption would lie in favour of having a tolerably large pool of assets to divide, with the onus therefore being on the party attempting to reduce this pool. The reason for this is that most schemes aim to redistribute assets to reflect policy goals and this aim would be prejudiced if the pool of property to be divided were depleted.

Who has the onus of proof can significantly affect the outcome of any scheme. The party with the onus is on the back foot. We therefore need to be clear about our principles and policy stances before determining this issue.

3.3. THE MEANING OF 'PROPERTY'

Undergirding any system of classification is the concept of property itself, the second subsidiary issue. Typically, only 'property' can be classified, although

---

27 *M v B* [2006] 3 NZLR 660 (CA) at [45] and [50]: 'onus seldom a relevant consideration'; *Hyde v Hyde* [2009] NZCA 125, [2010] 1 NZLR 224 at [45]: 'The Court does not necessarily sit back as if this was a pure forensic joust in the traditional common law style'; and *X v X [Economic Disparity]* [2009] NZCA 399, [2010] 1 NZLR 601 at [95] ff.

28 For another example, see s 85(2) of the Family Law Act 2011 (BC): 'A spouse claiming that property is excluded property is responsible for demonstrating that the property is excluded property.'

29 JM Scherpe, 'The Financial Consequences of Divorce in a European Perspective', above n 18 at 157–58.

the more discretionary approaches may follow a different path. For example, in Australia, the court can take account of 'the income, property and financial resources of each of the parties', and so the outcome of proceedings does not turn entirely on the existence of 'property'.[30] Nevertheless, for most regimes a definition of 'property' is necessary. How broad or narrow it is may be crucial. The left hand end of the spectrum would prefer a broad definition in order to meet its policy goals, while the right-hand end of the spectrum would prefer the opposite, again for policy reasons though of a rather different kind.

The PRA defines 'property' widely and in a rather open-ended way:

> '**property** includes—
>
> (a) real property:
> (b) personal property:
> (c) any estate or interest in any real property or personal property:
> (d) any debt or any thing in action:
> (e) any other right or interest.'

The New Zealand Supreme Court in *Clayton v Clayton [Vaughan Road Property Trust]* held that this should be interpreted in the light of the legislative aims and the Court thus reinforced the apparent width of the definition by including powers of appointment within its scope.[31]

In Ontario, we find an even broader and more extensive definition:[32]

> '"property" means any interest, present or future, vested or contingent, in real or personal property and includes,
>
> (a) property over which a spouse has, alone or in conjunction with another person, a power of appointment exercisable in favour of himself or herself,
> (b) property disposed of by a spouse but over which the spouse has, alone or in conjunction with another person, a power to revoke the disposition or a power to consume or dispose of the property, and
> (c) in the case of a spouse's rights under a pension plan, the imputed value, for family law purposes, of the spouse's interest in the plan, as determined in accordance with section 10.1, for the period beginning with the date of the marriage and ending on the valuation date; ("bien").'

---

30 See Family Law Act 1975 (Cth), ss 79(4)(e) and 75(2)(b). Financial resources cannot themselves be divided but can be taken into account in the exercise of the discretion: B Fehlberg et al, above n 21 at 510. The definition of 'property' in s 4(1) is potentially narrow: '[property] means property to which those parties are, or that party is, as the case may be, entitled, whether in possession or reversion', although a case such as *Kennon v Spry* [2008] HCA 56, (2008) 238 CLR 366 has taken a broad view of interests in trusts.

31 *Clayton v Clayton [Vaughan Road Property Trust]* [2016] NZSC 29, [2016] 1 NZLR 551. See also B Atkin, 'What Kind of Property is Relationship Property?' (2016) 47 *Victoria University of Wellington Law Review* 345.

32 Family Law Act 1990 (Ont), s 4(1).

The references to powers of appointment and revocation are of special interest in New Zealand in the light of *Clayton*.

Whatever approach to classification is taken, it would be helpful to have a reasonably comprehensive definition of 'property', possibly either including or excluding some of the issues that have arisen in relation to trusts.[33]

4. WHICH MODEL?

4.1. TAKING THE PRINCIPLES SERIOUSLY – A RADICAL SOLUTION

The position taken in this paper is that New Zealand should embrace the family law goals of the current PRA and enshrine them more deeply into the rules about classification. This means that the starting point would be that all property owned by the parties is relationship property. Exemptions should be narrowly crafted, with the onus on the party seeking such an exemption. This approach recognises the partnership nature of relationships, the interests of children (though indirectly), and economic disadvantage by bolstering the share of the disadvantaged party. It provides for greater predictability. It is assumed that the primary rule of equal division will remain but the approach is not incompatible with other sharing rules so long as they do not end up whittling away the share that a non-owner (in some situations the main child carer) would otherwise get, thus negating the effects of the wide reach of the new classification rule. It is also compatible with a narrow exception from equal sharing where equalisation would otherwise lead to serious injustice. As the relevant exception to the equal sharing provision in the New Zealand legislation[34] has been interpreted very strictly from the earliest days of the PRA, the objective behind using the 'all property' model would not be prejudiced. The continuation of economic disparity provisions (maybe amended to give more clarity) is not inconsistent with the model, although a larger pool of relationship property may ameliorate the need for compensation in some cases.

Without limiting the universal nature of the central rule, the statutory framework could nevertheless spell out in detail what is included. The British Columbia Family Law Act 2011 does this in section 83 and explicitly includes an interest in a corporation, partnership, association, organisation, business, or venture, and various superannuation entitlements. Trusts are addressed, but it may be appropriate for jurisdictions to adopt varying approaches to trusts to

33 See J Palmer, 'What to Do about Trusts?', ch 8.

34 PRA, s 13.

reflect the particular practices relating to trusts that have developed in different places.

The 'all assets' model would allow a party to argue that certain property should be excluded from the pool. That party would have the onus of proof. This, of course, could be an invitation for challenges and litigation, and could eat away at the whole point of the 'all assets' approach. British Columbia has a list of exclusions including pre-relationship acquisitions, inheritances, gifts, personal injury compensation, life insurance pay-outs, certain trust holdings, and property derived from excluded property.[35] These exclusions are not so very different from the current law in the PRA, though the PRA makes no mention of personal injury compensation, doubtless because of New Zealand's accident compensation scheme. It could even be argued that, subject to the onus, British Columbia ends up much further towards the middle of the spectrum. Similarly, Ontario, which starts with an 'all assets' approach, has a deduction for pre-acquired property other than the home, and exclusions for gifts and inheritances other than the home. The rationale is, of course, that things like inheritances are not, as such, the product of cohabitation but are often a matter of luck and good fortune for the recipient. How do we make sure that the impact of the exclusion provisions does not undermine the goal of benefiting the partners and the family?

In order for the proposed classification system to work, it is suggested that the test for exclusions should be a negative one. For pre-cohabitation property, gifts, or inheritances to be excluded, it would be necessary to prove that the item had nothing to do with the life of the partnership or family. The home and chattels would, by definition, not be excluded. Commercial assets would generally be seen as helping to maintain the living standards of the family and so would typically not be excluded. On the other hand, 'a purely passive investment'[36] would likely be excluded. So, a bequest of shares in a company that has nothing to do with the life of the family – left to linger – would not form part of the relationship property pool. This does not rule out the possibility of a court order affecting, at least indirectly, such property – for example, an order for compensation to be paid pursuant to provisions concerned with economic disparity or post-separation events.[37] Such orders do not, however, depend on classification for their efficacy.

---

35 Family Law Act 2011 (BC), s 85(1).

36 Language used by the Supreme Court in *Rose v Rose* [2009] NZSC 46, [2009] 3 NZLR 1 at [44].

37 PRA s 15A, s 18B, or s 18C. There is an argument for extending the principal New Zealand economic disparity provision, s 15, to enable payments to be made out of separate property, not solely out of relationship property, but that is beyond the scope of this chapter.

My proposal is at the far left end of the spectrum. Is it unpalatable as representing too great an inroad into autonomy and ordinary title-holding? Will it be an incentive for people to find new ways of evading the system or contracting out? The latter is not inimical to the proposal: indeed, if both parties freely decide on an alternative approach that suits their circumstances, then that should be possible. Evasion, on the other hand, would defeat the policy objectives, and countering mechanisms may need to be crafted.

What about the family farm that has been in the owner's family for generations? A property order may upset family traditions (invoking here a different sense of family from that used elsewhere in this chapter). A party may be forced to sell the farm, especially if there is insufficient cash to 'buy out' the other party's share. This type of situation actually goes to the heart of the policy question: partnership/collectivity versus individuals. Do we accept that marriages, civil unions, and de facto relationships are genuinely about the coupling of people's lives and loves, or not? Or are they a little bit of this and a little bit of that? Can we talk about a marriage as a half-partnership, which is not as embracing as the policy suggests? 'One size does not fit all'? Our relationships are indeed many and varied, and this is part of their beauty (and their vice when they run into difficulties). We are not, however, talking about the psychology of relationships or how people can be counselled through difficult patches. We are asking what is a principled and fair basis for the division of property. As Carol Rogerson has said in the context of maintenance but applicable here, a formulaic legal model may offer systemic advantages over individualised justice and may be worth the sacrifice of a '"Rolls Royce" service offered by strong judicial discretion'.[38] More than that, are there not sufficient commonalities and sufficiently clear principles, with respect to relationship property, that a scheme with classification rules as proposed in this chapter can well be regarded as acceptable as a matter of policy? Principle may thus trump the tradition of the family farm, something that can happen, of course, even under the current PRA.

What about the proverbial gold digger who links up with a wealthy person only to leave shortly afterwards much enriched? This situation is in truth the antithesis of the principles outlined above. There is no real partnership because it is based on deception or abuse. Likewise, any family life was inherently false. It is possible to build into the classification rules an exclusion based on unconscionability. The more sensible approach, however, is to deal with this question in the context of the division of the property, ostensibly as an exception to equal division. Under the present PRA in New Zealand, as noted above, section 13 allows for a departure from equal sharing when extraordinary circumstances lead to the conclusion that such sharing would be repugnant to justice. A classic

[38] J Miles and JM Scherpe, above n 3 at 142, citing C Rogerson, *Developing Spousal Support Guidelines in Canada: Beginning the Discussion*, Department of Justice, Ottawa 2002.

case that illustrates this is *Banda v Hart*, where Judge Inglis QC denied a violent rogue, who took complete advantage of his wife, any share of the property.[39]

In relation to the gold digger, provisions which deal with marriages, civil unions, and de facto relationships of short duration are also effective.[40] The rules in the New Zealand regime awkwardly differ as between marriages and civil unions, on the one hand, and de facto relationships, on the other,[41] but, in brief, they enable the court to deal with couples whose association did not really get off the ground. There are policy questions about the relevant provisions – should they be retained at all and what form should they take? Is a section 13 equivalent enough to deal with short relationships? They do represent an acknowledgement that some situations fall so far outside the standard pattern envisaged by the principles that a different template is justified. The case of the gold digger does not mean that an 'all assets' model is doomed. Quite the contrary – the overall scheme can accommodate special exceptions.

4.2. A FALL-BACK POSITION?

This chapter argues for a radical revision of the classification rules. It has been suggested that, subject to narrow exceptions, all assets owned by the parties at the relevant date should be presumed to be relationship property and be divided accordingly. This is consistent with the key principles, at least of the New Zealand property sharing regime, and should simplify the statutory framework. A fall-back position is the 'core' assets model. It is not unlike the New Zealand legislation as presently drafted, but with an enhanced vision of what the core family assets are. The law in British Columbia at one stage distinguished between family and business assets, but later effectively removed this distinction, thus enhancing the core.[42] An alternative new model for New Zealand could retain, in part, its rules that treat pre-acquired property as separate property. However, the home, chattels, and family business would be relationship property no matter when or how acquired. What is meant by 'business' would have to be defined. This is not necessarily straightforward and is a downside of the model. What if there is more than one business? What if both parties have businesses?

---

39 *Banda v Hart* [1998] NZFLR 930 (FC). See also successful recent cases of brief but not 'short' relationships where one party contributed far more property than the other, eg *Venter v Trenberth* [2015] NZHC 545, [2015] NZFLR 571 per Woolford J and *Bowden v Bowden* [2016] NZHC 1201 per Mander J.

40 See T Panchal, 'Relationship Property and De Facto Relationships of Short Duration: How Can We Fix the Law?' (2016) 8 *New Zealand Family Law Journal* 206.

41 PRA, ss 14–14A.

42 See the repealed Family Relations Act 1996 (BC), replaced by the Family Law Act 2011 (BC). A similar movement occurred in Ontario when the former distinction between 'family assets' and 'non-family assets' was eliminated: see JD Payne and MA Payne, above n 22 at 589.

5. MICRO ISSUES

Despite the major debate above leading to the recommendation that New Zealand should adopt a radical 'all assets' approach to classification, several matters of detail remain. This section examines these in turn.

5.1. IMMOVABLE PROPERTY SITUATED OVERSEAS

The conflict of laws issues relating to relationship property deserve full-scale treatment in themselves. Here I can only touch on certain aspects. The current rules in the New Zealand regime are based on a conventional conflicts approach to property issues under which the distinction between immovable and movable property is crucial.[43] In short, a New Zealand court has jurisdiction over immovables that are situated in New Zealand – the lex situs. The implication usually drawn from this is that jurisdiction does not exist over immovables situated outside New Zealand.[44] In contrast, jurisdiction over movables turns not on location but on domicile, a technical legal term that is not necessarily the same as a person's actual place of residence.[45] In essence, one of the parties must have been domiciled in New Zealand at the time of an application or of death, in which case movables, no matter where they are situated, are within the jurisdiction of the court and the PRA can be applied.[46]

The PRA does not expressly address the choice of law issues – that is, which country's laws should apply – but it is usually assumed that the rules relate only to the operation of the PRA.[47] Nevertheless, section 7A affects jurisdiction and, arguably, choice of law as well, where there is an agreement. First, the New Zealand court has jurisdiction if the parties so agree, that is, they both submit to the jurisdiction of the New Zealand court. More importantly, the parties can agree that the law of some other country will apply to their situation but only if they do so at the time that their marriage, civil union, or de facto relationship began. This rule reflects the position in a number of European or European former colonies, whereby on marriage parties may opt for an alternative property regime.[48]

One case illustrates a modern-day problem with the New Zealand rule. In *Herbst v Herbst*, on their marriage in South Africa, the parties contracted

43 PRA, ss 7–7A.
44 See, for example, *Samarawickrema v Samarawickrema* [1994] NZFLR 913 (CA).
45 See inter alia the Domicile Act 1976 (NZ).
46 PRA, s 7(2).
47 In contrast, see, for example, the Family Law Act 2011 (BC), s 108 headed 'Choice of Law Rules'.
48 For example W Pintens, above n 10 at 37.

out of the standard regime applicable in that country.[49] However, they did not expressly state which country's laws were to apply and thus, under the terms of section 7A, their ante-nuptial agreement was ineffective in New Zealand. Besides this, their timing was wrong. They had lived together in a de facto relationship before getting married, common practice today, but section 7A requires them to have entered into their agreement when they first started cohabiting, not on marriage. This interpretation may, strictly speaking, be correct but it no longer makes sense in the light of contemporary living arrangements and needs to be amended.

A more fundamental question about the New Zealand rules arises. They treat relationship property as if it were ordinary property similar to that which is the subject of transactions between strangers. Given the principles and policy goals outlined above, is this still a sound basis or do we need to rethink? What if we consider relationship property questions more as personal family law matters rather than conventional property ones? In Ontario, marital property rights 'are governed by the internal law of the place where both spouses had their last habitual residence or, if there is no place where the spouses had a common habitual residence, by the law of Ontario'.[50] British Columbia has a much more detailed regime but the 'proper law of the relationship' is prima facie 'the internal law of the jurisdiction in which the spouses had their most recent common habitual residence'.[51] The concept of habitual residence, rather than domicile or lex situs, is used in a lot of Hague conventions[52] and proposals in Europe are to the effect that, in the absence of an agreement, the law of habitual residence will apply.[53]

The advantage of using habitual residence is that some potentially significant items of property do not slip out of the hands of the New Zealand court and thus evade the statute's policy goals. On the other hand, the usual justification for the lex situs approach is the inappropriateness of making orders with respect to

---

49 *Herbst v Herbst* [2013] NZHC 3535, [2014] NZFLR 460 per Brown J.

50 Family Law Act 1990 (Ont), s 15. In South Africa, the main rule is that the lex domicilii governs both movables and immovable in the absence of an ante-nuptial contract to the contrary: J Heaton (ed), *The Law of Divorce and Dissolution of Life Partnerships in South Africa*, Juta, Cape Town 2014, [4.3].

51 Family Law Act 2011 (BC), s 107(a).

52 Including one on matrimonial property of 1978, which only three states have ratified. See generally H Baker and M Groff, 'The Impact of the Hague Conventions on European Family Law' in JM Scherpe (ed), *European Family Law Vol I: The Impact of Institutions and Organisations on European Family Law*, Edward Elgar, Cheltenham 2016, ch 5 at 143 ff; D Martiny, 'The Impact of the EU Private International Law Instruments on European Family Law' in JM Scherpe (ed), *European Family Law Vol I: The Impact of Institutions and Organisations on European Family Law*, Edward Elgar, Cheltenham 2016, ch 7, 272 ff; and W Pintens, above n 10 at 45–46.

53 European Commission, *Proposal for a Council Regulation on Jurisdiction, Applicable Law and the Recognition and Enforcement of Decisions in Matters of Matrimonial Property Regimes*, COM (2011) 126/2, Brussels, 16 March 2011.

land in another country, with the issues of enforceability and comity of nations surfacing. There are two answers to this problem: first, the New Zealand court can take account of foreign immovables without actually making an order directly affecting them. British Columbia expressly covers this by stating that, instead of dividing extra-provincial property, the court can order the substitution of property in British Columba or the payment of compensation.[54] Secondly, the doctrine of forum non conveniens empowers the court to decline jurisdiction where it would be improper or against the public interest to exercise it. There is no reason why this doctrine could not continue to operate where it is more appropriate for the courts of another country to determine the dispute.

In summary, the law on immovables should be reconsidered with the thought of replacing lex situs with habitual residence.

5.2. HOME AND CHATTELS

Words such as 'family home', 'dwellinghouse', and 'homestead' are defined in section 2 of the PRA. One issue is the extent to which the home can be stretched to cover much more than the close surroundings when it is in effect a lifestyle block or smallholding. Given the resolution of this kind of issue in the *Hyde* litigation,[55] it is suggested that it may be unwise to tinker with the definitions.[56] One other issue, however, is why the classification rules limit the parties to just one home. Many people who work in the city have a base there but a getaway place for extended weekends. Under the PRA, a decision has to be made as to which one is the family home when in reality there are two of them. Why not change the rules to allow for this? If the 'all assets' approach is adopted, this may not be crucial, but it could be important for some form of 'core assets' approach.

'Family chattels' are also defined in section 2 of the PRA. Apart from the linguistic inappropriateness of treating things like pets as 'chattels', one issue is the exclusion of taonga[57] and heirlooms, which occurred with the 2001 reforms. The policy reason for excluding taonga is no doubt tied up with tikanga Māori[58] and the impropriety of dividing cultural treasures. Oddly, the main cases on taonga have involved pākehā,[59] and one wonders how useful the concept really

54 Family Law Act 2011 (BC), s 109(2)(a). Compare *Walker v Walker* [1983] NZLR 560 (CA).

55 *Hyde v Hyde*, above n 27.

56 For example, 'family home' includes land 'appurtenant to that dwellinghouse and used wholly or principally for the purposes of the household'; 'homestead' is where the home 'is situated on an unsubdivided part of land that is not used wholly or principally for the purposes of the household': PRA, s 2.

57 Māori cultural heirlooms and treasures.

58 That is, traditional Māori customs and understandings.

59 That is, people of non-Māori heritage and ethnicity, for example, *Perry v West* [2004] NZFLR 515 (HC) and *HES v GCS* [2012] NZFC 2685.

is. On an 'all assets' approach, taonga will ostensibly be relationship property whether or not they are chattels. The same would apply to heirlooms. Under other approaches, there may well be arguments for reversing the taonga exclusion.[60]

5.3. SUPERANNUATION AND INSURANCE

The current law on the classification of superannuation and insurance is found in section 8 of the PRA, with definitions in the interpretation section (section 2) and provisions on the kinds of orders that can be made in sections 30 and 31. Superannuation and other retirement schemes are the most critical as the future contingent benefits are taken into account. From the early Court of Appeal judgment in *Haldane v Haldane*, it has been clear that the true value of schemes, not their current sell up value, is relationship property.[61] The reason for this is that the period of cohabitation will have added to the ultimate value of the policy and this should be reflected in the classification. Appropriate discounts for contingencies and the early payment of a future sum take account of the non-cohabitation contributions to the scheme.

In 2001 the legislation was changed to exclude contributions made to the policy prior to cohabitation. Was this change justified? Under the acquests/gains model, the answer is yes – the value added before and after cohabitation should be excluded from what is classified as the relationship property gain. In many respects this makes sense. However, under the 'all assets' approach, a reversal of the 2001 changes may be merited. Retirement planning is a major contemporary exercise for families, with those in paid employment encouraged to 'plan'. It has now become an important part of 'family life' when that is assessed long-term – planning for retirement is an overall part of the present life of the partnership/family. Even the children benefit, because, while there may be less to spend on them in the present, the need to support parents in their older age is reduced (the issue of the intergenerational transfer of wealth).

5.4. JOINT PROPERTY AND PROPERTY ACQUIRED IN CONTEMPLATION

Section 8(1)(c) states that co-owned property is relationship property and this has given rise to little controversy. Arguably, all models on the spectrum would agree with the current law. Section 8(1)(d) treats property pre-acquired in contemplation of cohabitation and intended for common use or common

60 J Ruru and L Watson, 'Should Indigenous Property be Relationship Property?', ch 9.
61 *Haldane v Haldane* [1981] 1 NZLR 554 (CA).

benefit as relationship property. The 'all assets' approach is comfortable with this rule but it fits in far less easily to the other approaches. It is not a gain of the relationship as by definition it is a pre-acquired asset. Its inclusion may be justified on the basis that it was intended to be part of the core, along with the home and chattels. The 'use or benefit' language certainly implies that the PRA has this kind of subsidiary goal. What to do with section 8(1)(d) may depend on where we place our new scheme on the spectrum. If we move to the right, we may conclude that it should be deleted. If we are on the left of the spectrum, we are likely to want it kept.

5.5. GIFTS, INHERITANCES, AND TRUST DISTRIBUTIONS

The exclusion of gifts, inheritances, and trust distributions, provided for in section 10 of the PRA, ostensibly fits into the gains/acquests model because they are not 'gains' as such of cohabitation. This is consistent with the vast majority of jurisdictions worldwide. The different treatment of the home and chattels in the PRA flows from a model that combines gains and core assets and, as seen above, New Zealand is not unique in doing this.

Under the 'all assets' approach, these items are prima facie part of the property pool available for division. Apart from the general reasons already given for this model, we can ask why gifts and bequests are necessarily separate from family life (home and chattels aside). In some instances, thc reasons for, say, a bequest may be tied up with the personal connection of the beneficiary with the deceased. The will-maker is likely to have been well aware of the beneficiary's domestic situation and recognised that a legacy would assist the whole family while nevertheless identifying only one party as a beneficiary. Father is left a beach house – the will-maker will surely in most such situations expect that the mother and children will use the beach house, not solely the father. Thus, on examination, the explanation for the legacy may be more complex than at first appears.[62] In the light of this, it is argued that the section 10 items should be presumed to be relationship property. The party challenging this would then have the onus of proving that the bequest (and so forth) was purely personal and had no connection to the common life of the parties.

The remaining issue concerning section 10 is the test for determining whether separate property under this head has become relationship property by later events – the 'intermingling' test. This test has not been all that satisfactory – what do all the words, including 'unreasonable' and 'impracticable', really mean? Furthermore, why have a different test under section 10 from the one that applies to the classification of relationship and separate property more generally? It is

62 The point is made by the English Law Commission: LAW COMMISSION (Eng&W), above n 3 at [8.18].

suggested under the next heading that there should be a composite test for all these categories.

5.6. TRACING INTO SUBSEQUENT PURCHASES – USE OF PROCEEDS

The PRA law on subsequent acquisitions out of separate property is needlessly convoluted. Under section 8(1)(e), acquisitions during cohabitation are prima facie relationship property, but this is subject to section 9(2), which states that property acquired out of separate property remains separate property. This, in turn, is subject to section 8(1)(ee), which treats the acquisition as relationship property if it was for common use or common benefit of the parties.[63] Gifts, inheritances, and trust distributions are not part of this picture.

If the 'all assets' approach were adopted, all acquisitions would be relationship property. This is subject to exclusions if the party claiming one can satisfy the court that the acquisition had nothing to do with the common partnership or family life. This test is not unlike the 'common use or common benefit' one mentioned above from s 8(1)(ee), but potentially slightly broader, with the onus clearly stated. This approach removes the need for the awkward dance between sections 8–10.

If a different approach to classification is adopted, a revised basic rule should be stated that property acquired while the parties were living together is relationship property, subject to an exception where the property can be traced to pre-acquired, inherited, or gifted assets, or a trust payment, and can also be proved to have no connection with the common family life. This would obviate the need for the three different provisions that currently apply in New Zealand.[64]

An allied rule would have to cover the situation where separate property is retained but its use is changed. If the new use is connected to the common family life, then its classification should switch from separate to relationship property. The awkward intermingling test in section 10 is thereby abandoned.

5.7. INCREASES IN VALUE, GAINS, AND INCOME FROM SEPARATE PROPERTY

Section 9(3) of the PRA treats the income and gains from separate property and increases in value, as separate property. Section 9A, on the other hand, provides for exceptions to this default rule, so that increases, gains, and income attributable

---

63 Changes made in 1980 partly reversed *Reid v Reid* (CA), above n 8, which treated all acquisitions as 'matrimonial property' irrespective of source.

64 PRA, ss 8(1)(ee), 9(2), and 10.

to an application of relationship property or to the actions of the other party become relationship property. However, rather anomalously where the other party's actions are the causative factor, division is according to contributions to the increase rather than the usual equalisation rule. Amendments in 2001 widened the scope of section 9A and this was reinforced by the important Supreme Court judgment in *Rose v Rose*.[65] The latter, however, left passive or inflationary increases out of account, thus undercutting the policy objectives of the PRA.

Under an 'all assets' approach, a section 9A type of provision would be unnecessary. The items concerned – often something like the family farm – would be included in the pool anyway and it would be hard to argue for an exemption. Increases in value would therefore have already been dealt with. Under other approaches on the spectrum, the issue of increases in value would likely have to be addressed. Under the gains/acquests model, an increase in value could well be regarded as a product of living together but policy decisions would have to be made about the basis for clawing the increase back into the separate property category and who would bear the onus. Rather than the awkward distinctions currently found in section 9A, would it not be better to require the party claiming that the increase is separate, to satisfy the court that it has no connection to the common family life?

5.8. MISCELLANEOUS

Any revision of classification would need to deal with some miscellaneous provisions. For example, section 9(4) usefully enables the court to treat property acquired after the parties' separation as relationship property if, for example, it can be traced back to the proceeds of other relationship assets. Section 9(5) directs that acquisitions made after a court order are separate. This makes sense but whether a rule in the PRA is actually necessary is debatable. I do not go further into these kinds of provisions.

6. RADICAL RECLASSIFICATION

The current rules on classification under the PRA are an uneasy mélange of convoluted provisions. It is possible to discern a pattern: assets that can be described as the fruits of living together are categorised as relationship property

65 *Rose v Rose*, above n 36. See M Briggs and N Peart, 'Sharing the Increase in Value of Separate Property under the Property (Relationships) Act 1976: A Conceptual Conundrum' (2010) 24 *New Zealand Universities Law Review* 1.

and are thus divisible. In addition, and very significantly, the home and chattels are regarded as so central to the common life that they are relationship property regardless of whether they are the product of joint efforts. As we delve further into the provisions in sections 8–10, we find departures from this pattern, so that it is hard to do other than generalise about the current framework.

This chapter has examined the relevant principles and policy factors that may impact on a revised system of classification. In short, the current principle that treats couples as a partnership of equals should be maintained and reinforced. Other principles such as the importance of common family life and the interests of children (if any) are aspects of the partnership philosophy. Addressing economic disadvantage at the end of the common life fits comfortably with this philosophy.

If we are to take the principles seriously, how should we devise our classification rules? A spectrum of models is apparent but the conclusion drawn in this paper is that a radical revision, not tinkering, is needed. The best approach for New Zealand is to start with all assets being subject to division. Some narrow exceptions would focus on the connection, whether direct or indirect, with the partnership or family life. If no such connection exists, then the property would be separate but the onus of proof would be expressly on the party seeking the exception. Under this model, the pool of property available for division or equalisation would be expanded, thus undergirding the partnership concept of relationships. This, in turn, assists the economically disadvantaged party, often the woman and mother, and has a positive knock-on effect for children. The model is thus based on appropriate policies, which should find favour with the community and policy-makers.

CHAPTER 8
WHAT TO DO ABOUT TRUSTS?

Jessica PALMER

1. INTRODUCTION

There are two critical issues for any matrimonial or relationship property sharing regime: Which property of the parties to the relationship is to be captured by the regime? And how is that property to be shared?[1] These are fundamentally questions of policy that, once decided, give way to questions of implementation by law. In modern times, implementation is usually a matter of statutory law. The primary policy currently applicable in New Zealand[2] and commonly ascribed to elsewhere is that property owned by either party that was shared within the

[1] A more recent but important question arising for such schemes concerns which relationships the scheme ought to apply to: see P PARKINSON, 'Reconsidering Family Property Law in the Post-Marital Age', ch 2; M BRIGGS, 'Which Relationships Should be Included in a Property Sharing Scheme?', ch 3.

[2] Property (Relationships) Act 1976 (NZ) ('PRA'), ss 1M and 1N.

relationship or produced by the relationship ought to be divided equally between the parties upon dissolution of the relationship. Indeed, Professor Atkin suggests in his chapter that the goal should be complete sharing within the relationship and that the starting point ought to be that all property owned by the parties is relationship property.[3]

There are obviously many questions of detail that arise out of this approach but a basic presupposition is that the relevant property to which the regime can apply must be owned by either or both of the parties. Yet, one of the most controversial issues relating to property division regimes in recent times is whether such regimes can and should extend to property held on trust where neither partner has a fixed or vested beneficial property interest.

There are various ways to respond to the problem. One might say that the question of what a spouse or partner owns ought to be decided in accordance with orthodox rules of trust and property law and that a property sharing regime must apply consistently with those rules for reasons of certainty and sanctity of property rights. Alternatively, it can be argued that our notion of property may need to be broadened to recognise not only legal ownership but also real or practical control over assets so that a spouse who has such control or access ought to be considered the owner of the assets or at least the owner of something of value. This raises subsequent questions about the validity or otherwise of the trust and whether this approach is specific to the relationship dissolution context or extends to claims by other parties. Another response might be to leave the rules as they are but to provide the courts with an overriding discretion to vary property rights. This raises questions about the extent of such a power and the objectives that a variation ought to achieve.

This chapter seeks to analyse these methods both for their effectiveness in achieving the underlying policy of equal sharing in a property division regime and for their effect on the law more generally. Before this is done, it is necessary, however, to explain why the discretionary trust has become the 'supreme problem de jour' for relationship property regimes.[4]

2. THE NATURE OF THE DISCRETIONARY TRUST AND ITS MODERN USE

A trusts lawyer will say that the exercise of defining a trust is not an easy one and gives rise to difficult theoretical questions. But, for the purposes of this chapter,

---

3 See further, B Atkin, 'Classifying Relationship Property: A Radical Re-Shaping?', ch 7.

4 B Atkin, 'What Kind of Property is "Relationship Property"?' (2016) 47(3) *Victoria University of Wellington Law Review* 345, 359.

it is sufficient to say that the trust is an obligation on the legal owner of property, the trustee, to hold the property for the benefit of others, the beneficiaries. The trust is not an entity in itself.[5] The trustee may have declared themself trustee over assets that they had initially owned beneficially or the trustee may have had the property transferred to them on trust by the original owner, the settlor. Although the trustee has legal ownership of the property, their ownership is significantly fettered and the property cannot be used to meet any personal claims against the trustee.

The label 'discretionary trust' has no fixed meaning.[6] It is a description of a type of express trust in which certain dispositive discretions are conferred on the trustee: they may have the discretion to determine the type or extent of trust property to be distributed to each beneficiary and often which of the beneficiaries will receive trust property. A discretionary beneficiary thus has no proprietary interest in the trust property, only a right to compel the due administration of the trust and demand the trustee to *consider* exercising their discretion in his or her favour.[7] As a matter of property theory then, neither a trustee's interest nor a discretionary beneficiary's interest amounts to beneficial property capable of being the subject of a proprietary claim.

The discretionary trust has become a very popular mechanism for the holding of property within families in the past 50 years. These trusts have been used to avoid death duties, to take advantage of differential tax rates or governmental subsidies, and to safeguard significant assets from creditors where the income earners (the settlors) were professionals at risk of being sued for negligence.[8] While trusts no longer tend to offer the same fiscal and tax benefits as they once did, they are still used to protect more generally against claims of creditors and spouses. The common structure is for the husband and wife to declare themselves trustees, often along with an independent trustee or corporate trustee, of property held for the benefit of themselves and their children as discretionary beneficiaries.

There are two particular respects in which the discretionary trust can be seen to thwart the policy of relationship property sharing regimes. The first relates to one of the most notable features of modern discretionary trust practice: the range of broad powers that are often vested in the settlor or a third party called the protector. Such powers include, for example, powers to appoint and remove trustees and/or beneficiaries; powers to direct trustees to act; powers to veto

5 M Leeming, '"Chameleon-Hued Words": A Note on Discretionary Trusts' (2015) 89 *Australian Law Journal* 371.

6 *Fischer v Nemske Pty Ltd* [2016] HCA 11, (2016) 257 CLR 615 at [118] per Gordon J; *Chief Commissioner of Stamp Duties (NSW) v Buckle* [1998] HCA 4, (1998) 192 CLR 226 at 234 per curiam.

7 *Whaley v Whaley* [2011] EWCA Civ 617, [2012] 1 FLR 735 at [112] per Lewison LJ.

8 D Bryant AO, 'Heterodox is the New Orthodox – Discretionary Trusts and Family Law: A General Law Comparison' (2014) 20(7) *Trusts & Trustees* 654, 670.

trustees' decisions; and powers of revocation.[9] While these powers are usually non-dispositive, they are nevertheless significant because of the degree of control they confer on the holder to affect the affairs of the trust. These trusts have been met with a measure of popular suspicion. It has become increasingly common for creditors and spouses of both settlors and beneficiaries with significant control to seek ways to attribute trust property to them. The general gist of the claim is that the reality is quite different from the appearance: property apparently held in trust is really subject to the control or directions of one party (who is usually the settlor and also a beneficiary) who thus should be considered the real owner for the purpose of property division following relationship dissolution. I shall refer to these trusts as 'controlled trusts' for the remainder of this chapter.

The second respect in which discretionary trusts are a cause for concern in this context is what can be called 'dynastic trusts'. These are discretionary trusts used as a dynastic or multi-generational ownership structure common in family-run businesses with significant asset holdings, such as farms. The income-producing assets are held in trust for the benefit of parents, children, and grandchildren. As the children grow up and work in the business, alongside their spouses, they contribute significantly to the wealth accumulation of the family business but are not strictly legal owners of that wealth. Particularly problematic are those dynastic trusts where the assets include not solely business assets but also the parties' homes and other domestic assets. When the relationship dissolves, the assets are out of reach.

There are various ways in which the law has responded to these trusts. In some jurisdictions, various statutory means of access to the trust assets are employed.[10] But in the absence of such legislation, counsel and courts have turned to the common or judge-made law of trusts and property to find a justification for drawing in trust assets to the estate of either or both of the partners to the relationship. The following analysis of these methods begins with the common law methods because if these are effective, there may be no need for legislative intervention.

3. SOLUTIONS FROM WITHIN THE COMMON LAW[11]

In the absence of appropriate statutory intervention, the various attempts resorted to by the courts can be grouped into two categories. Some cases are

9 For an interesting empirical study of this practice see A Hofri-Winogradow, 'The Demand for Fiduciary Services: Evidence from the Market in Private Donative Trusts' (2017) 68 *Hastings Law Journal* (forthcoming).

10 These will be discussed further below in section 5.

11 By common law here, I mean judge-made law that may sound in either or both of the jurisdictions of equity and of the common law proper.

directed to the veracity of the trust itself. The trust may be held to be invalid as a sham; or pierced on the basis that it is the alter ego of the controlling party; or it may simply be that no trust is regarded as having been established because essential trust features are compromised or absent. Other cases instead recognise a property right distinct from the property of the discretionary trust itself. The controlling party's powers are deemed in combination to be themselves a property right; or a separate (constructive) trust in favour of the disadvantaged spouse is said to be imposed over part of the property on account of contributions made to the property by that spouse. These methods have been the subject of detailed academic scrutiny elsewhere[12] that shows that none of them measures up to orthodox principles of trust and property law, despite their varied success in the courts.

3.1. LOOKING THROUGH THE TRUST

Several different claims have been made on a similar theme that on account of the settlor's control of the trust, the trust property is in reality the property of the settlor and the trust should be disregarded.

First, the claim of sham has been regularly invoked in popular commentary and raised in several cases.[13] However, its application is in fact fairly limited. As a matter of principle, a trust is a sham because there was no true trust intention shared by the settlor and trustee, but rather an intention to create a façade or pretence.[14] A settlor's control of the trust is neither a necessary nor sufficient element in establishing a sham. It may serve as evidence of a sham intention but where a formal trust deed and other related documentation exist (even with the inclusion of significant retained powers), the presumption of trust intention is very difficult to rebut.[15] De facto or practical control of trust affairs whereby

12 See, for example, J Palmer, 'Controlling the Trust' (2011) 12(3) *Otago Law Review* 473; J Palmer, 'Dealing with the Emerging Popularity of Sham Trusts' [2007] (1) *New Zealand Law Review* 81; C Rickett, 'Instrumentalism in the Law of Trusts – The Disturbing Case of the Constructive Trust Upon an Express Trust' (2016) 47(3) *Victoria University of Wellington Law Review* 463.

13 *Shalson v Russo* [2003] EWHC 1637 (Ch), [2005] Ch 281; *Midland Bank plc v Wyatt* [1997] 1 BCLC 242 (Ch); *Re Esteem Settlement* [2004] WTLR 1 (Royal Court of Jersey); *MacKinnon v The Regent Trust Company Ltd* [2005] WTLR 1367 (Court of Appeal of Jersey); *Sharrment Pty Ltd v Official Trustee* (1988) 18 FCR 449; *Re Richstar Enterprises Pty Ltd v Carey (No 6)* (2006) 153 FCR 509; *Official Assignee v Wilson* [2008] NZCA 122, [2008] 3 NZLR 45; *Rosebud Corporate Trustee Ltd v Bublitz* [2014] NZHC 2018, (2014) 3 NZTR 24-025.

14 *Snook v London and West Riding Investments Ltd* [1967] 2 QB 786 (CA) at 802; *Official Assignee v Wilson*, above n 13; *A v A* [2007] EWHC 99 (Fam), [2009] WTLR 1; *Lewis v Condon* [2013] NSWCA 204; *Ben Nevis Forestry Ventures Ltd v Commissioner of Inland Revenue* [2008] NZSC 115, [2009] 2 NZLR 289 at [33] per Tipping, McGrath, and Gault JJ.

15 *Clayton v Clayton [Vaughan Road Property Trust]* [2016] NZSC 29, [2016] 1 NZLR 551.

a settlor continues to treat the property as his own and does not defer to the trustees on decisions in relation to the property might suggest a lack of trust intention but this, too, will usually fall short of establishing a sham.[16] Courts tend to require not just an absence of a positive trust intention, but a fraudulent intention to deceive.[17] The sham trust doctrine, then, is not responding directly to the problem of controlled trusts; it should not be, and usually is not, used to invalidate such trusts without more.

The nature of the settlor's intention plays no part in the second type of claim to be considered: the trust as the 'alter ego' of the settlor. The alter ego idea is well known in company law[18] and has been applied to trusts in several jurisdictions.[19] The settlor's control over trust affairs is said to render the trust the alter ego of the settlor, enabling parties claiming against the settlor to access trust property or at least to claim the value thereof. In evaluating the legitimacy of the alter ego claim, it is important to distinguish factual or unauthorised control from authorised control by virtue of powers conferred on the settlor by the trust deed. Acts of unauthorised control might include a failure to separate trust funds from a settlor's personal assets; a failure to pay rent for the use of trust property where no such benefit has been formally appointed by the trustee or where the settlor is not a beneficiary; or an understanding between settlor and trustee that the trustee will act in whatever way it is commanded to by the settlor, without exercising due consideration of the beneficiaries' interests. The alter ego notion effectively converts this conduct into actions of ownership.

But this is inconsistent with how property rights generally operate. Exercising factual, yet unauthorised, control over trust property cannot result in a proprietary interest in that property vesting in the controlling party.[20] Indeed, where someone exerts factual control over trust assets, equity will consider him or her to be a trustee de son tort for the beneficiaries, not an absolute owner.[21] In Australia, reliance on the alter ego idea is permissible because its matrimonial property regime extends beyond the parties' property to the parties' 'financial resources'.[22] The alter ego is not being used to subvert property rights because

16 *Vervoort v Spears* [2015] NZHC 808, [2015] NZFLR 525; *Official Assignee v Wilson*, above n 13.

17 *Official Assignee v Wilson*, above n 13 at [52]–[53] per Robertson and O'Regan JJ and [106] per Glazebrook J; *Lewis v Condon*, above n 14 at [63]; *Rosebud Corporate Trustee Ltd v Bublitz*, above n 13; cf *Midland Bank plc v Wyatt*, above n 13.

18 It was recently applied to companies in the context of matrimonial property litigation: *Prest v Petrodel Resources Ltd* [2013] UKSC 34, [2013] 2 AC 415.

19 *Ashton v Ashton* (1986) FLC 91-777 (FamCA); *Goodwin v Goodwin Alpe* (1991) FLC 92-192 (FamCA); *Stephens v Stephens* [2007] FamCA 680, (2007) FLC 93-336; *Senior v Senior* 1999 (4) SA 955 (W); *Land and Agricultural Development Bank of SA v Parker* [2004] ZASCA 56, [2004] 4 All SA 261; *Prime v Hardie* [2003] NZFLR 481 (HC); *Glass v Hughey* [2003] NZFLR 865 (HC).

20 *Sharrment Pty Ltd v Official Trustee*, above n 13 at 470–71.

21 *Lyell v Kennedy* [1889] 14 AC 437 (CA).

22 Family Law Act 1975 (Cth), ss 79(4) and 75(2)(b).

property rights are not required in order for property to be captured by the statutory framework there. But in jurisdictions where the regime is limited to property more traditionally formulated, such as in New Zealand and South Africa, '[a]ctual control alone does not provide justification for looking through/invalidating a trust'.[23]

An alter ego claim may look more promising in respect of authorised control because the settlor has chosen to retain some ownership-type powers by means of the very instrument that determines the ownership arrangement between the parties to the trust. However, powers of control should only substantiate an alter ego claim if those powers entitle the settlor to access the trust property and treat it as their own without such access being fettered by obligations owed to the beneficiaries. Of the powers commonly retained by settlors (powers to appoint and remove trustees and/or beneficiaries; powers to direct trustees to act; powers to veto trustees' decisions and powers of revocation), only the power of revocation would enable the settlor to take back the property without having to rely on the trustee also exercising a power to distribute the property to the settlor. The role of the trustee is crucial because, unlike the settlor, the trustee's powers are restrained by its fiduciary obligations to the beneficiaries to exercise the powers in what it believes to be in the best interests of the beneficiaries.[24] It is because it has this obligation that a trust exists and that the trustee cannot be said to be an absolute owner of the trust property.[25] And neither can it defer entirely to the demands of the settlor without exercising its own consideration. It would be entirely inconsistent with this trust relationship between trustee and beneficiary to say that a settlor's powers equate to ownership of the trust property when those powers do not in fact enable direct and unfettered access to the trust property. Of the powers that settlors do retain, only the power of revocation allows the settlor to bypass the trustee. Where such a power is reserved, it may therefore very well be open to a court to treat the trust as the alter ego of the settlor. Unsurprisingly, in the United States the Uniform Trust Code 2010 ('US UTC') provides that where these powers are present, the trust property is subject to claims by creditors of the settlor.[26] In New Zealand, trusts practitioners advise against retaining such a power in trust deeds.

Despite these conceptual difficulties, the alter ego notion has been embraced in several South African cases.[27] Its application there highlights a further

23 *Official Assignee v Wilson*, above n 13 at [70] per Robertson and O'Regan JJ; see also [126] per Glazebrook J.

24 L Smith, 'Fiduciary Relationships: Ensuring the Loyal Exercise of Judgement on Behalf of Another' (2014) 130 *Law Quarterly Review* 608.

25 J Palmer, 'Controlling the Trust', above n 12.

26 Uniform Trust Code 2010 (US), s 505(a)(1).

27 *Badenhorst v Badenhorst* [2005] ZASCA 116, [2006] 2 All SA 363; *BC v CC* 2012 (5) SA 562 (ECP); *Land and Agricultural Bank of SA v Parker*, above n 19; *RP v DP* 2014 (6) SA 243 (ECP).

difficulty. It is not clear whether the effect of an alter ego finding is to invalidate the trust altogether, or to permit the court to treat the trust property *as if* it belonged to the settlor, or only to attribute the value of the assets to the settlor.[28] It seems to me that logically it must be the first, but courts are extremely hesitant to deem the trust out of existence, especially when both trust intention and form are clearly present. The third explanation, which attributes to the controlling party only the value and not the property itself, does not sit well with a property division regime that is concerned with dividing property. How can value as separated from property really form part of a pool of property to be shared? The second explanation is a neat compromise between the two but it merely begs the question: does the trust property in specie or only its value now fall into the relationship property pool?

A further problem for the alter ego claim is that, unlike a company, the trust is not an entity or a legal person but a relationship of rights and obligations. It makes little sense to say, therefore, that the trust is an 'other self' of the settlor, just as a contract cannot be someone's alter ego. Hence, the claim must really be that the trust property is being controlled to such an extent that it should be treated as the property of the controlling settlor and the trust must be ignored. It is not that the trust is the settlor's alter ego, but that the trust is effectively little more than an illusion.

This leads nicely to the third type of claim that has been tried in an attempt to look through the trust but has met with little success: the 'illusory trust'. It is conceivable that despite a settlor's intention to create a trust, and despite the existence of a trust deed, trustees, and even regular trust administration, the substance of the arrangement created by the settlor does not in fact create the trust relationship that is crucial to the trust. If, by a combination of strong powers and reduced trustee duties, the settlor could effectively appoint trust assets to himself without having any accountability to the beneficiaries, it is surely arguable that the notions of alienation from the settlor and accountability fundamental to the trust[29] are absent and that a trust has not in fact been created. Such cases will likely be rare but they are not unheard of.

For example, in *BQ v DQ*, the settlor, who was also initially the sole trustee, had reserved to himself powers to revoke the trusts, to appoint and remove trustees, and to release the trustee from any liability.[30] The trustee had the power

---

28 F du Toit, 'South Africa – Trusts and the Patrimonial Consequences of Divorce: Recent Developments in South Africa' (2015) 8(2) *Journal of Civil Law Studies* 655, 683.

29 *Armitage v Nurse* [1998] Ch 241 (CA) at 253 per Millett LJ; *Spread Trustee Co Ltd v Hutcheson* [2011] UKPC 13, [2012] 2 AC 194; *Re Esteem Settlement*, above n 13 at [122].

30 *BQ v DQ* [2010] SC (Bda) 40 Civ.

to appoint income and capital to the settlor during his lifetime. Ground CJ, sitting in the Supreme Court of Bermuda, ruled that:[31]

> 'the concatenation of rights and powers in the settlor, when coupled with the fact that he was the sole trustee at the time of the constitution of the trusts, rendered this trust illusory during his lifetime.'

His Honour placed significant weight on the fact that as both settlor and trustee, 'he could not effectively be called to account'.[32]

Had there been an independent trustee, the indication was that the trust would have been valid. But surely the identity of the trustee mattered not. The substance of the 'trust' had the effect of enabling the settlor to vitiate any of the obligations owed by any trustee to the beneficiaries so that there was no absolute and enduring accountability. Trust law tells us that the trustee must act honestly and in good faith at all times, without exception. The relevant clause provided as follows:[33]

> 'The written approval by the [settlor] of any trust transaction during his lifetime shall be a complete release of the Trustee (including the [settlor]) of any liability or responsibility of the Trustee to any person with respect to this transaction.'

The effect of this clause was to render the beneficiary's right to hold the trustee to account meaningless or at least dependent on the whim of the settlor.[34] The trust was illusory not because of the identity of the trustee but because of the absence of a persistent accountability.

It could be argued that up until such time as the settlor chose to release the trustee from liability, the trustee was accountable to the beneficiaries. Likewise, although the trust was revocable, it was nevertheless effective until revocation. These claims must be evaluated by comparison with the essentials of a trust to determine whether the trust construct has been compromised by the provisions of the deed or not. Unfortunately, there is no accepted definitive statement beyond the core duty of the trustee being to act honestly and in good faith but that should have been sufficient to decide *BQ v DQ*: where a settlor purports to create a trust relationship but reserves to himself the ability to allow the trustee to escape liability for breach of the core duty, one of the essential features of a trust is thus missing.

The notion of the illusory trust was considered very recently by the New Zealand Supreme Court but the Court was unable to agree on a unanimous

---

31 Ibid, at [29].
32 Ibid, at [29].
33 Ibid, at [7], citing Art VIII H of the trust deed.
34 See further D Waters, 'Settlor Control – What Kind of Problem is it?' (2009) 15(1) *Trusts & Trustees* 12.

approach. In *Clayton v Clayton* ('*Clayton*'), the husband was both settlor and sole trustee.[35] In his personal capacity, he had powers to add and remove trustees and beneficiaries. The deed provided that as trustee, he had an absolute discretion to appoint any or all of the income and capital to any of the discretionary beneficiaries without considering the interests of all beneficiaries and could exercise dispositive powers contrary to the interests of any beneficiary. The trust deed included a clause expressly permitting trustees who were also beneficiaries to exercise any of the powers or discretions in their own favour.

If the question of whether an apparent trust is in substance not a trust, but illusory, is to be answered, the content of the essential or core features of the trust construct must be identified. A complete list of those features is not without controversy but I suggest it must include an alienation of the property from the settlor's own personal estate; an ultimate dispositive power that vests only in the trustee; and an enduring accountability of the trustee to the beneficiary. Without these, the trust is just a form of revocable agency or gift. In *Clayton*, the settlor had the ability to dispose of property to himself without having to consider or act in the interests of other beneficiaries. This effectively stripped the arrangement of any real accountability to the other beneficiaries. Indeed, the Court ruled that he could distribute property to himself 'unrestrained by fiduciary obligations'.[36]

While the Court accepted the theoretical possibility of an illusory trust,[37] it could not agree on whether the present case was one and so made no ruling, preferring to decide the case on an alternative basis that the combination of powers and entitlements held by the husband amounted to a general power of appointment (discussed further below). It noted two competing views on the illusory trust: either the settlor had failed to dispose completely of the property and the trustee was not sufficiently accountable to the beneficiaries such that there was no trust;[38] or the trust was 'effectively defeasible' on the exercise of particular powers but nevertheless still valid up until such exercise.[39] But if, as the Court had already found, he was not bound by any fiduciary obligation to the beneficiaries, how could there have been a trust?[40] The fate of the illusory trust notion remains unclear.

---

35 *Clayton v Clayton [Vaughan Road Property Trust]*, above n 15.

36 Ibid, at [58].

37 Ibid, at [123], although rejecting the label in preference for speaking more simply of there being 'no valid trust'.

38 Ibid, at [124].

39 Ibid, at [125].

40 N Peart, 'The Property (Relationships) Act 1976 and Trusts: Proposals for Reform' (2016) 47(3) *Victoria University of Wellington Law Review* 443, 449–50.

3.2. PROPERTY RIGHTS EXTERNAL TO THE TRUST

An alternative means of increasing the share of relationship property available for division to take account of the parties' connection to trust property is to recognise property rights external to the trust that do not compete with or attack the trust as such. In respect of controlled trusts, courts have in some cases recognised the particular powers themselves as amounting to a distinct property interest. Likewise, the courts have recognised a beneficial interest by means of a constructive trust in favour of parties who have made contributions to property that is held on an express trust and otherwise unavailable for division. This second technique could be particularly useful for those partners and spouses who have worked on property that is subject to a dynastic trust. Nevertheless, both approaches ought to be treated with suspicion, in my opinion.

3.2.1. *Powers as Property*

Courts have accepted that bundles of powers and entitlements as well as individual powers may amount to property where they enable the settlor or other power-holder to access trust property without any applicable obligations or restrictions on the exercise of those powers.[41] To that extent the claim is very similar to that underlying the alter ego claim already discussed, except that the outcome is not to treat the power-holder as the owner of the trust property, but rather as the owner of powers, albeit that the powers are usually said to carry the same value as that of the trust assets.

In *Tasarruf Mevduati Sigorta Fonu v Merrill Lynch Bank and Trust Co (Cayman) Ltd* ('*TMSF*'), the Privy Council described a power of revocation retained by the settlor as 'tantamount to ownership' and therefore subject to receivership.[42] As mentioned earlier, the US UTC provides that where such a power exists, the trust property is made subject to claims by the settlor's creditors despite the existence of the trust.[43]

In *Clayton*, the New Zealand Supreme Court ruled that the combination of powers and entitlements held by the settlor amounted to a general power of appointment that came within the statutory definition of property in the Property (Relationships) Act 1976 (NZ) ('PRA') as a 'right or interest'.[44] The value of the

41 *Clayton v Clayton [Vaughan Road Property Trust]*, above n 15; *Tasarruf Mevduati Sigorta Fonu v Merrill Lynch Bank and Trust Co (Cayman) Ltd* [2011] UKPC 17, [2012] 1 WLR 1721 ('*TMSF*'); *Walker v Walker* [2007] NZCA 30, [2007] 2 NZLR 261.

42 *TMSF*, above n 41 at [60]–[62], following *Re Triffitt's Settlement* [1958] Ch 852 at 861.

43 Uniform Trust Code 2010 (US), s 505(a)(1).

44 PRA, s 2; *Clayton v Clayton [Vaughan Road Property Trust]*, above n 15 at [98(a)]. See also [38]–[84].

interest equated to the value of the trust assets.[45] In reaching its conclusion, the Court drew support from *TMSF* and from several other cases from jurisdictions with a wider ambit of property caught by the relevant scheme that extends beyond orthodox ownership.[46] The Supreme Court's approach has been praised as being 'consistent with the PRA's goal to reflect the equal contributions of the parties and to address economic disadvantage'.[47] It certainly represents a less formalistic approach to the meaning of 'property'. The Court spoke of the need for 'worldly realism',[48] similar to that taken by the Privy Council in *TMSF*, where Lord Collins made clear that equity might at times consider the holder of a general power as owner 'for all practical purposes'.[49]

It is accepted that property can be a very broadly construed construct,[50] and that the general understanding that powers are not property is not a universal rule. Property subject to a general power of appointment exercised by will, for example, can be treated as property of the appointor for the purpose of satisfying his or her debts.[51] However, there is a significant difference between the powers recognised as property in each of *TMSF* and *Clayton*. While in *TMSF* the settlor was free to exercise the power of revocation as he liked unfettered by any duty to the beneficiaries,[52] that did not affect the trustee's fiduciary duty to carry out the trust in what it believed to be in the best interests of the beneficiaries. Hence a trust existed, despite the inclusion of the power of revocation. But in *Clayton*, the effect of the combination of powers and entitlements bestowed on the settlor/trustee meant that there was no effective accountability of the trustee to beneficiaries. The trustee's fiduciary duties had been so watered down as to be non-existent. There was no trust in the absence of this fundamental characteristic. The husband was entirely free, *as trustee*, to appoint trust assets to himself. That is an anathema to a trust. It was both unnecessary and unnecessarily complicated to hold that the powers amounted to property distinct from, but equal to the value of, the trust assets. The husband was already holding the assets beneficially despite the apparent form of a trust.

---

45 *Clayton v Clayton [Vaughan Road Property Trust]*, above n 15 at [104]–[107].

46 *Kennon v Spry* [2008] HCA 56, (2008) 238 CLR 366; *Charman v Charman* [2005] EWCA Civ 1606, [2006] 1 WLR 1053; *Charman v Charman (No 4)* [2007] EWCA Civ 503, [2007] 1 FLR 1246; *Whaley v Whaley*, above n 7 at [40]; *Kan Lai Kwan v Poon Lok To Otto* (2014) 17 HKCFAR 414 (CFA).

47 B Atkin, above n 4 at 360.

48 *Clayton v Clayton [Vaughan Road Property Trust]*, above n 15 at [77].

49 *TMSF*, above n 41 at [33].

50 *Jones v Skinner* (1835) 5 LJ (NS) Ch 87 at 90, XLII RR 274 at 276 per Sir Pepys MR.

51 *Beyfus v Lawley* [1903] AC 411 (HL) at 413; see also T Molloy QC, 'The Vulnerability of Asset Protection Trusts Revocable by the Settlor: "Equity's Tenderness for Creditors" and the Privy Council's Judgment in *Tasarruf Mevduati Sigorta Fonu*' (2011) 17(8) *Trusts & Trustees* 784. But it is understood to be an exception granted by equity, rather than a rule of property law: *O'Grady v Wilmot* [1916] 2 AC 231 (HL).

52 *TMSF*, above n 41 at [62].

If the response is that some sort of trust duty nevertheless applied to the trustee, then it cannot be said that the powers provided direct and unfettered access to the trust property. A power that comes with duties attached cannot be beneficial property. The two observations are inconsistent with each other.

A secondary problem that arises from the recognition of powers as property is the determination of the value of such powers. The powers are usually given a value equal to the net worth of the trust assets on the basis that a general power of appointment enables the holder to access the trust assets for his own benefit at any time.[53] All sorts of difficult questions arise here. Why is the full value of the trust assets to be ascribed to the powers when it is often not likely that the settlor will in fact distribute the property to himself? Why not have a discount for likelihood? When the Supreme Court referred to the sale price in *Clayton*,[54] to whom would such powers be sold? And would they really be willing to pay full price? And what difference does the identity of the trustee make to the value? What if the settlor is not also the trustee? Are the powers then worth less to acknowledge that the trust assets cannot be accessed without the trustee's accession?

3.2.2. Constructive Trusts on Express Trusts

In New Zealand relationship property litigation, there has been a growing trend to resort to a constructive trust in order to convert contributions made to property held on trust into property interests of the spouse or partner who is locked out of the express trust. Where qualifying contributions were made to the property *before* it was settled on trust, the claim is against the original owner and the resulting property right is traced through to the trustees now holding the property.[55] The claim in this instance is simply a vindication of property rights that arose prior to the settlement of the express trust and is not controversial.[56]

Courts have also shown a willingness to extend the constructive trust to claims directly against trustees for contributions made to property while it has been owned by the trustees.[57] If a spouse or partner can show that, in the circumstances, the trustees should reasonably expect to yield an interest in the trust property to the spouse, then a constructive trust will arise. While this might at first sight appear to be a logical development, it is in fact conceptually

---

53 *Clayton v Clayton [Vaughan Road Property Trust]*, above n 15 at [104]–[105].

54 Ibid, at [105].

55 *Marshall v Bourneville* [2013] NZCA 271, [2013] 3 NZLR 766; the claim being good against all but the bona fide purchaser for value.

56 *Foskett v McKeown* [2001] 1 AC 102 (HL).

57 *Murrell v Hamilton* [2014] NZCA 377, (2014) 3 NZTR 24-012; *Vervoort v Forrest* [2016] NZCA 375, [2016] 3 NZLR 807; *Hawke's Bay Trustee Co Ltd v Judd* [2016] NZCA 397, (2016) 4 NZTR 26-019.

inconsistent with the trust construct and risks subverting established trust principles.[58] Recalling that the trust is nothing more than a relationship between trustee and beneficiary, it is misleading to talk of a constructive trust against or over an express trust. The question is whether a constructive trust obligation can arise not on the express trust but on or against the trustee's title. Put another way, is it possible for the trustee to hold the benefit of his title on trust for the plaintiff?

Immediately, the problem becomes clear. What the spouse is seeking is the beneficial value of the property, but it is not something that the trustee has to give. The trustee does not have any right to benefit from the property which it could be obliged to hold for the spouse. The benefit already belongs to the beneficiaries of the express trust. Even if one considered it possible for the trustee to bind the property in equity to the spouse, the result would be a situation effectively of competing equities. The trustee is already obliged in equity to hold the property for the trust beneficiaries and cannot redistribute it, so to speak. The beneficiaries of the express trust have the earlier equitable right to that benefit and so would trump the spouse's later title.

This is not to say that the common law countenances no relief for a spouse in this situation. Claims against the trustee might potentially be mounted in estoppel[59] or unjust enrichment,[60] but the relief available will be a personal order against the trustee. As a matter of trust principle, a proprietary interest cannot arise. Yet, the New Zealand Court of Appeal has made it plain that, despite the logic of this argument, the modern context in which trusts are operating to defeat partnership claims demands a response:[61]

> 'It is acknowledging the reality of the New Zealand trust landscape as it has developed that has justified the recognition of the constructive trust beneficiary's claim. It is a further reality of that landscape that the trustees of family discretionary trusts are more often than not the beneficiaries of those trusts and in control of them. It is common in many trusts in New Zealand "for the settlor to retain some extent of control or to vest that control in someone other than the trustee". The effect is that the reality of a trustee's ability to give a third party expectations (in return for that third party's contributions) over trust property, which that trustee deals with as if their own, must be recognised. There is no misappropriation of property in that the beneficiaries of the express trust have no claim in conscience to the increases in value resulting from the contributions. Beneficiaries cannot expect trustees to retain for them an unearned benefit, extracted by expectations engendered by the trustees. The express trust beneficiaries should reasonably expect to yield the third parties an interest.'

58 For a detailed discussion, see C RICKETT, above n 12.
59 *Vervoort v Forrest*, above n 57 at [78]–[83].
60 Ibid, at [68].
61 Ibid, at [70], quoting J PALMER, 'Controlling the Trust', above n 12 at 477–78.

While their Honours' motivations are understandable, the mechanisms being employed are, with the greatest of respect, inappropriate and ultimately serve to undermine and confuse established principles of private property rights.

4. THE CASE FOR LEGISLATIVE INTERVENTION

The problems of controlled trusts and dynastic trusts are real for many partners on the dissolution of relationships and the efforts made by lawyers and courts to massage the common law in order to look past trust structures in the absence of express legislation are understandable. Nevertheless, those efforts are ultimately unconvincing. In respect of *controlled trusts*, control does not render the trust illusory or an alter ego so long as a trustee remains accountable to the beneficiaries. And recognising powers of control as separate property rights on the basis that they permit direct access to trust property undermines the trust indirectly. Either the powers are fettered by the trustee's fiduciary obligations or the powers are unfettered and there is therefore no trust in substance. In relation to the problem of *dynastic trusts*, such trusts commit no offence against general trust principles and recourse to the notion of a constructive trust over the express trust as a corrective measure is incoherent. It is therefore problematic to look to equity and the common law to provide justification for redistributing trust property to a spouse or partner. The result is an incoherent law of trusts.

Yet, the problems remain and a solution ought to be found. There is certainly an emerging judicial consensus that these types of trusts are being used inappropriately to enable parties to avoid the claims of their spouses, as is evident from the cases discussed above. In describing the Australian approach to this problem where an authorising statute exists to look through trusts, Bryant J, writing extra-judicially, says:[62]

> 'Family law rightly preferences reality over doctrinal purity when the two are in conflict. I do not believe that we are "outriders" or that our use of de facto control to look behind trust structures to treat assets as property in appropriate circumstances is heterodox, and I am not alone in that view. But if it be heterodoxy, let it be heterodoxy. To my mind, the law should be reflective of the realities of the way people order their lives, and in the context of the discretionary trust as it has developed in Australia, that has been as a vehicle to maximize parties' wealth and to receive favourable tax treatment. In fact, it seems heterodox to me to remove significant assets that have accumulated over the life of a marriage from the reach of one party, to the benefit of the other, simply because of the purported sanctity of trusts law and purity of principle.'

---

62 D Bryant AO, above n 8 at 669.

It must nevertheless be remembered that setting aside or looking through a trust because it is subjected to significant control by a non-trustee[63] or for any reason of perceived unfairness or practical reality amounts to judicial appropriation of property rights from the legal owner. It ought not to be done without authorising legislation. Trusts have always been a mechanism to ring-fence property from the claims or demands of others but it is open to Parliament to limit the reach of trusts where a conflicting policy is considered of greater value.

There would seem to be two obvious policies that justify Parliament acting to enable recourse to trust assets in the context of relationship dissolution. First, if the underlying policy of the applicable matrimonial property statute is indeed to effect equal sharing, this should extend to all property that was available to and used by both parties indiscriminately during the relationship *if* that property will otherwise continue to be used and enjoyed by one of the parties once the relationship has ended.[64] The parties' access to, rather than strict ownership of, the trust property may be the better criteria to determine its inclusion. Secondly, an economic argument can be made that in many situations, shutting one party off from property to which they would otherwise have continued to have access involves costs to society at large in effectively subsidising that party, usually by various allowances and benefits. As Schenkel has argued: 'Laws should reduce the social costs of trusts, not leverage their benefits to the few who can enjoy them.'[65]

It is for these reasons of policy that the 'doctrinal purity' of trusts law ought not to prevail in the context of relationship property. But such policy competes with the principles of autonomy and security of receipt that are so important to property doctrine. For this reason, any recourse to trust assets is more appropriately regulated and implemented by Parliament and not the courts. Legislation is required to correct or improve upon the common law. I turn now to consider in more detail the varying forms of legislative intervention that can be employed to deal with the problems of controlled trusts and dynastic trusts.

5. THE CONTENT OF LEGISLATIVE INTERVENTION

There are three types of statutory intervention commonly employed to claw back property from trusts for inclusion in the pool of property divisible upon relationship dissolution. The first concerns provisions that reverse fraudulent

---

63 This may include a settlor or other party who is also a trustee but who holds significant powers other than in their capacity as trustee and therefore without any fiduciary obligations attaching that would fetter their powers.

64 See further the arguments made by B Atkin in his chapter, above n 3.

65 KD Schenkel, 'Exposing the Hocus Pocus of Trusts' (2012) 45(1) *Akron Law Review* 63, 135.

dispositions, the second is a judicial discretion to vary a settlement that effectively frustrates the rights or expectations of the disadvantaged partner following the ending of the relationship, and the third is the adoption of a broader definition of property that extends beyond strictly legal (and equitable) property rights.

5.1. VOIDABLE DISPOSITIONS

Statutory provisions to reverse dispositions undertaken with the intent to defeat another party's property rights are common in many jurisdictions in both insolvency legislation and matrimonial property schemes. These types of provision have a wider application than the sham trust doctrine because they regulate a party's motivations for settling property on trust. A decision of the New South Wales Court of Appeal, *Lewis v Condon*, provides a good illustration.[66] There, the trustee of a bankrupt estate argued that a trust of which the bankrupt was a discretionary beneficiary was a sham, because it was alleged to have been set up to deceive the bankrupt's husband and the Family Court, and to avoid tax. But those dishonest motives did not mean that the trust was a sham. The uncontroverted evidence was that the bankrupt intended to create a trust on the terms set out in the trust deed so that she would not appear to own the property. The trust deed was not a false front. It was genuine. The courts in England and Wales have adopted a similar approach.[67] While these trusts are not shams, they could nevertheless still be caught by voidable transaction provisions where there is a clear intention to defeat the other party's interest by the settlement of the trust.

In respect of the relevant New Zealand provision in the PRA,[68] the courts initially required proof of a fraudulent motive[69] but that has recently been reinterpreted in line with the intention test used in the equivalent provision in insolvency legislation.[70] In that context, proof of intent has been held by the Supreme Court not to depend on evidence of a *fraudulent* motive or purpose.[71] The required intent can be established by showing that the debtor knew, or ought to have known at the time, that by disposing of the property there was a risk that creditors would not be able to recover payment of the debts owing to them. While this test of intention may ease the burden on creditors seeking to set aside a debtor's dispositions, the onus of proving the required knowledge at

66 *Lewis v Condon*, above n 14.
67 *A v A*, above n 14.
68 PRA, s 44.
69 *Coles v Coles* (1987) 4 NZFLR 621 (CA) at 624.
70 Property Law Act 2007 (NZ), ss 344–50; *Ryan v Unkovich* [2010] 1 NZLR 434 (HC) at [33].
71 *Regal Castings Ltd v Lightbody* [2008] NZSC 87, [2009] 2 NZLR 433 (in the context of a similar provision in the (now repealed) Property Law Act 1952 (NZ)).

the time of the disposition can still be a significant obstacle to creditors' recovery of payments. The test is less demanding but proving that the transferor knew that a consequence of the disposition was that it would defeat the rights of the particular spouse still sets a reasonable hurdle.[72] It is particularly difficult in relation to trusts settled before a relationship was entered into or where the trust is a dynastic one having been settled by someone other than either of the parties to the relationship.

It is possible to legislate for the reversal of dispositions where the *effect* of such dispositions is to defeat the interests of the other partner, even in the absence of any *intention* to defeat. A broader voidable transactions provision of this kind represents a significant limitation of the freedom of property owners to dispose of property as they so choose. Hence when section 44C of the PRA, the relevant voidable dispositions provision in the New Zealand statute, was introduced, it was deliberately restricted in its reach and in the relief available in order to balance the competing policy considerations.[73] So, while the disposition itself is not reversed, compensation can be ordered but only from the income of the trust property and only where the trust was settled over relationship property by either or both of the parties to the relationship. It is therefore ineffective against the problem of dynastic trusts and is of limited effect as a response to the problem of controlled trusts.

A more effective response to these problems might be a more flexible variation provision, exercised at the court's discretion. That is, in some sense, what section 44C is, albeit that it is too limited in scope and so amounts to an awkward interposition on the deferred community nature of the New Zealand scheme.

5.2. VARIATION OF NUPTIAL SETTLEMENTS

Statutory provisions permitting courts to vary trusts are reasonably common in relationship property regimes.[74] Variation powers are a very effective way to deal with the perceived injustice of the use of trusts to limit either or both parties' shares of relationship property in situations where, had the relationship continued, both parties would have benefitted. While they are, of course, a significant interference with the right of owners to deal with property as they so choose, it must be remembered that statutory property division schemes are generally, by their very nature, an interference in the property rights of owners,

---

72 See, for example, *K v V* [2012] NZHC 1129.

73 Ministerial Working Group, *Matrimonial Property Amendment Bill 1998 (109-1) (Select Committee Report)*, xii; see also N Peart, above n 40 at 450–51.

74 For example, Matrimonial Causes Act 1973 (Eng&W), s 24(1)(c); Matrimonial Proceedings and Property Ordinance (HK), s 6(1)(c); Family Proceedings Act 1980 (NZ), s 182.

albeit that they are accepted as an important feature of a just society. Variation powers should not be eschewed, but their scope and the criteria upon which they may be exercised ought to be carefully and clearly prescribed.

Several issues require careful thought. First, it is necessary to determine the trusts to which such a power can be applied. Often confined to 'nuptial settlements', courts have increasingly moved away from requiring that the trust was settled in contemplation of or resulting out of the particular marriage, requiring instead a more general connection or proximity between the settlement and the marriage.[75] This means it is entirely possible that trusts settled long before the marriage was formed or without a particular spouse in mind can be subject to variation. If, as has been discussed already, the property division regime is to give effect to the underlying policy that property owned or available to the parties as if it were owned by them must be shared upon dissolution of the relationship, it seems inevitable that 'nuptial settlement' should also be read to include settlements made by parties other than those of the particular relationship where such settlement was of property of which the relationship parties enjoy the benefit. This would mean that dynastic trusts would be included. So, the variation power should extend to settlements entered into by other parties where there is a sufficient connection between the relationship parties and the property.

In addition, the power should be applicable to all relationships to which the property division scheme applies, including – in New Zealand – de facto couples. There is no reasonable justification to so restrict it and thereby discriminate against one type of relationship that is otherwise treated alike for the purpose of property division.

Secondly, it is necessary to identify the criteria or objective that a variation ought to satisfy. Variations could be made in order to meet the needs of the party disadvantaged by the settlement following the relationship break down; or to give effect to the general intentions or expectations of the settlor and/or the trustees either at the time of the settlement or before the relationship ended; or simply to effect equal sharing. In exercising the discretion in *P v P*, the English Court of Appeal saw need as more important than the sharing principle,[76] in contrast to the view of the High Court.

In New Zealand, the variation power sits within a statute separate to the relationship property framework and was originally enacted in the time of fault-based divorce when the power was used to deny entitlements to the party at fault.[77] The Supreme Court in *Clayton (No 2)* has very recently considered the

---

75 *Kennon v Spry*, above n 46 at [228]–[230]; *Clayton v Clayton [Claymark Trust]* [2016] NZSC 30, [2016] 1 NZLR 590 at [34].

76 *P v P* [2015] EWCA Civ 447.

77 Family Proceedings Act 1980 (NZ), s 182.

New Zealand variation power in detail.[78] The Court described the purpose of the power this way: '[t]he purpose of s 182 … is to empower the courts to remedy the consequences of a failure of the premise (a continuing marriage) on which the settlement was made.'[79]

The Court rejected an approach based solely on the subjective expectations of the parties at the date of settlement of the trust. Instead, it said, the Court must make an objective assessment of what the applicant would have received of the trust property if the relationship had continued and compare that to the applicant's actual position following the dissolution of the relationship.[80] In this way, variation is being undertaken in response to a frustrating event and factors relevant to whether it will be ordered include[81] the terms of the settlement and how the trustees are likely to exercise their powers, including current and future benefit to the family unit; the type of assets; the relevant social context;[82] the interests of children in particular; and the parties' own expectations, which are relevant but not determinative.[83]

Variation of settlements is a significant judicial power that amounts to a very real challenge to owner autonomy. It represents a concession to the competing policy of the applicable relationship property regime that should only be granted in order to give necessary and sufficient effect to it. Where that policy is the equal sharing of property that would otherwise have been owned by or used for the benefit of the partnership, as it is in New Zealand, the settlement ought to be varied to achieve that objective. So the inquiry must not be directed to the parties' needs but rather to a consideration of what would likely have been done with the property. If it would likely have benefitted the partnership had it continued, then sharing of the extent of the benefit is required.

In respect of controlled trusts, if it is likely the controlling partner would have effected a distribution to either of the parties which would have benefitted both had the relationship continued, then it ought to be shared. In respect of dynastic trusts, if it is likely that the trustee would have done something similar, then the same result should apply.

This leads to the third issue: the likely form of variation that should be permitted and any limits. The form of relief should be a reflection of what would have been the case had the relationship not failed. For example, in respect of a

---

78 *Clayton v Clayton [Claymark Trust]*, above n 75. Although concerning the same parties and argued in the same hearing, the application for variation was in respect of a different trust than in the *Clayton* decision discussed earlier in this chapter and a separate judgment was issued.

79 Ibid, at [51], following *Ward v Ward* [2009] NZSC 125, [2010] 2 NZLR 31 at [15].

80 Ibid, at [48]–[49] and [53].

81 Ibid, at [57]–[68].

82 This was said to be that parties to a marriage contribute in different but equal ways.

83 Although no order was made because the parties settled their claim before judgment was issued, the Supreme Court said that it would have made orders to resettle property of the trust on two separate trusts.

dynastic trust, where the parties' home was a trust asset, it may be appropriate to settle half of the relevant assets of the trust on a separate trust. Alternatively, it may be appropriate to limit the order to the monetary equivalent of a life interest in the house if a life interest is what the party was effectively receiving or was likely to receive prior to the dissolution.[84] In other words, there should be no presumption that assets of the trust sought to be varied will be shared equally. Care must also be taken to identify the right parties against which variation can be sought, particularly if the relevant property is held in a dynastic family trust of which neither party to the relationship is a trustee. The presence of third party beneficiaries likely to be affected by variations means that proprietary orders should be subject to prior changes of position made in good faith.[85]

Finally, it must be asked whether parties may contract out of the variation power. In my opinion this is both inappropriate and difficult. It is inappropriate because the exercise of discretion involved in making a variation is itself a restriction on the use of trusts to prevent ring-fencing property from the pool of relationship property. It would be logically incoherent to enable parties to contract out of the court's discretion to vary settlements. Secondly, it would also be difficult for some parties to achieve in practice if the variation discretion is to cover settlements made prior to a relationship when the parties may not even have known each other or if it is extended beyond settlements made by the parties to the relationship to dynastic trusts.[86]

A judicial discretion to vary relationship settlements seems an appropriate means of limiting the nuisance of controlled trusts and dynastic trusts where they would otherwise prevent the policy of equal sharing from being achieved. However, clear statutory guidance on the criteria for variation would help to limit what could otherwise be arbitrary or inconsistent exercises of discretion. The approach taken by the Court in *Clayton (No 2)* would serve well as the basis for codification.

5.3. EXTENDED PROPERTY DEFINITION

A third means of statutory intervention to combat the problem of losing what would otherwise likely be relationship property to trusts is to extend the property

84 *P v P*, above n 76.

85 PRA, ss 44(4) and 44C(3); Family Proceedings Act 1980 (NZ), s 182(3).

86 An additional issue arises in relation to the variation by an onshore court of an offshore foreign-law trust, see further A Lynn, 'Applying the *Charman* Test to Trusts in Divorce: The Decision of the Hong Kong Court of Final Appeal in *Kan Lai Kwan v Poon Lok To Otto and HSBC International Trustee Limited*' (2015) 21(3) *Trusts & Trustees* 285, 299. This is certainly a significant matter but not one that can be resolved by the domestic law of the onshore court and not one that should prevent the appropriate development of the relationship property regime of each individual jurisdiction.

division regime beyond fairly orthodox conceptions of property in order to include the trust assets.

An extended definition could be fairly narrow and prescriptive, so as to respond only to the particular nuisance sought to be eliminated. Examples of this approach are taken in some Canadian provinces. In British Columbia and Ontario, property subject to division includes trust assets which a party has power to transfer to himself.[87] It excludes, however, trust property settled by someone else except to the extent of any increase in value to such property which must be shared. In Manitoba, trusts settled by others are also excluded unless they are intended to benefit the parties to the relationship.[88]

An even more prescriptive definition has been suggested by a South African commentator:[89]

> 'Property which is deemed to be property of the parties includes –
>
> (a) property of which any party was immediately prior to the divorce competent to dispose for his own benefit or for the benefit of his estate.
>
> (b) For purposes of paragraph (a) a person shall be deemed to have been competent to dispose of assets if (i) he had such power as would have enabled him, if he were sui generis, to appropriate or dispose of such property as he saw fit whether exercisable by will, power of appointment or in any other manner; or (ii) if under any deed of donation, settlement, trust or other disposition made by him he retained the power to revoke or vary the provisions thereof relating to such property.'

While these approaches can be commended for the added certainty they provide which limits the judicial discretion involved, their success depends upon how strictly trust deeds are read. Most trusts will not give an unrestrained power to a trustee or settlor to transfer or dispose of property. The trustee will usually have the power to distribute the property and that power will be moderated by fiduciary duties to act in the interests of the beneficiaries, not to profit and not to act in one's own interest. Where all of these are absent, there is no trust in the first place and the property already belongs beneficially to the controller. These narrower provisions do not properly capture the nuisance of parties who have de facto control and influence.

A broader definition can be employed that, although necessarily leaving greater discretion for the courts to determine whether in any given case a trust asset should be counted as that of one of the parties, enables the court to respond

---

87 Family Law Act 2011 (BC), ss 84 and 85; Family Law Act 1990 (Ont), s 4(1).

88 Family Property Act (CCSM c F25) (Manitoba), s 7(1).

89 A Van der Linde, 'Whether Trust Assets Form Part of the Joint Estate of Parties Married in Community of Property: Comments on "Piercing of the Veneer" of a Trust in Divorce Proceedings – *WT v KT* 2015 3 SA 573 (SCA)' 2016 (79) *Journal of Contemporary Roman-Dutch Law* 165, 173.

to the factual reality of the situation. Such approaches are taken in the United Kingdom,[90] Australia[91] and Hong Kong[92] where orders can be made in relation to the parties' 'financial resources'.

While this is certainly a departure from an approach based specifically on sharing only assets which the parties legally own, it is one that is clearly permitted by the relevant statutory frameworks. The emphasis is on access to resources, and not formal ownership of property.[93] It is said to better reflect the modern nature of wealth accumulation and takes an approach of substance over form to ownership:[94]

> '[The legislation] represents an acknowledgement by Parliament that if justice is to be achieved between spouses at divorce the court must be equipped, in a society where the forms of wealth-holding are diverse and often sophisticated, to penetrate outer forms and get to the heart of ownership.'

Legislation of this broader style exists in New Zealand in contexts other than relationship property division. For example, section 58 of the Criminal Proceeds (Recovery) Act 2009 (NZ) allows the court to treat a person as having an interest in property if they have 'effective control' over the property, notwithstanding that they may not have either a legal or equitable interest in it. Less explicit but still effective are provisions in the Child Support Act 1991 (NZ)[95] and the Legal Services Act 2011 (NZ)[96] that enable the court to take into account 'financial resources' and prior settlements into trust when assessing liability for child support and 'financial means' when assessing eligibility for legal aid. The approach of the Supreme Court in *Clayton* shows that it was very willing to take a broader view of what property includes when it ruled the particular mix of powers held and the lack of duties owed by the husband amounted to a general power of appointment capable of being regarded as property.[97]

Generally inherent in the broader approach is the need to identify an appropriate test to determine whether the particular assets will count as resources. The test that has been developed in England and Wales asks whether, if the party were to request the trustee to advance the whole (or part) of the

---

90 Matrimonial Causes Act 1973 (Eng&W), s 25(2)(a).

91 Family Law Act 1975 (Cth), ss 79(4) and 75(2)(b). See also *Kennon v Spry*, above n 46; *Public Trustee v Smith* [2008] NSWSC 397, [2010] ALMD 1670 at [125].

92 Matrimonial Proceedings and Property Ordinance (Cap 192) (HK), s 7. See also *Kan Lai Kwan v Poon Lok To Otto*, above n 46.

93 *Whaley v Whaley*, above n 7 at [113] per Lewison J.

94 *Thomas v Thomas* [1995] 2 FLR 668 (CA) at [3] per Waite LJ.

95 Child Support Act 1991 (NZ), s 105(2)(c)(i) and (ii).

96 Legal Services Act 2011 (NZ), s 14. See *Petricevic v Legal Services Agency* [2011] 2 NZLR 802 (HC), decided under the former Legal Services Act 2000 (NZ).

97 *Clayton v Clayton [Vaughan Road Property Trust]*, above n 15 at [84].

capital of the trust to him or her, the trustee acting in accordance with its duties would, on the balance of probabilities, be likely to accede to that request.[98] The Australian cases refer to property being in the de facto control of the party, of the party controlling the property as if they were the owner.[99] Although the underlying concern is indeed to capture assets over which one or other of the parties has control, using control alone as the criteria is not sufficiently nuanced nor informative. It provides little guidance as to how to assess which powers justify such a response. For example, does the power to appoint and remove trustees amount to control sufficient to give quasi-ownership of the assets? What of the power to add and remove beneficiaries? These powers could no doubt be used to influence a trustee to act in certain ways in relation to the trust property but are they enough to justify disregarding the beneficiaries' ownership in favour of the settlor?

I suggest that it is not the presence of such powers but how those powers are likely to be exercised that can determine whether the trust property should for practical purposes be considered property of the power-holder. The English test of likely accession is preferable because it looks to the effect of control. Focusing on whether it is more likely than not that if the party wanted the property, they would be given it provides greater explanation for why they should be considered the owner in practice. This test is also not limited to formal reserved powers. A beneficiary of a dynastic trust with no powers as such may nevertheless still have significant influence over trustees to have requests granted. Likewise, this approach also permits the possibility that powers of control may not be sufficient if a trustee can show that, in spite of the party's influence, the trustee is unlikely to make a distribution to the party. This might be because a distribution is, for example, detrimental to the interests of other beneficiaries or to the value of the trust property.[100]

There are, however, two qualifications that ought to be made to the likely accession test. First, an assumption or condition must hold that in (hypothetically) acceding to the party's request, the trustee would still be acting in compliance with its duties to the other beneficiaries. It is 'very common that trustees will have perfectly properly acceded to all the requests of a settlor without in any way abdicating their fiduciary duties and responsibilities'.[101] If not, the party's property right would really be no more than the result of coercion or of a breach

---

98 *Charman v Charman*, above n 46 at [12]; *Charman v Charman (No 4)*, above n 46 at [47]–[58]; *A v A*, above n 14 at [90]–[92].

99 *Public Trustee v Smith*, above n 91 at [125]; *Davidson v Davidson* (1991) FLC 92-197 (FamCA); *Ashton v Ashton*, above n 19.

100 *A v A*, above n 14 at [97]–[98] per Munby J.

101 *Re Esteem Settlement*, above n 13 at [167] per curium. See also [165]–[166]. Cited with approval in *Charman v Charman*, above n 46 at [70] and discussed in *Whaley v Whaley*, above n 7 at [54].

of the trustee's duty to exercise genuine consideration in making a distribution. The trust must be treated as having been validly performed.

The second qualification to the likely accession test is that it ought to be necessary not only that the trustee is likely to accede to a party's request to advance the property to him or her, but also that the party is likely to so request. It is possible that a settlor has reserved certain powers to himself, not to ensure he or she will benefit personally from the trust property, but to ensure that the trustees act in accordance with the purpose of the trust as the settlor expected it to be carried out. In other words, it is possible that the settlor has retained powers of control not to secure a personal benefit but to protect the beneficiaries' prospects of benefit. Likewise, it is possible that the influential beneficiary of the dynastic trust would not want to see the trust depleted and so would not request any advances.

A broader definition of property that includes resources likely to be made available to either of the parties is an effective way to enable trust assets to be drawn into the pool of relationship property. But not all trust assets should be caught. Only those of which the party to the relationship is likely to request a distribution and whose request is likely to be approved by the trustee should really be counted as property in fact of that party.[102] Such requirements operate to allow the court to anticipate the distribution of assets to one or other of the partners. This is surely a preferable approach to concluding that the relevant control or influence renders the trust the alter ego of the controller, drawing into question the validity of the trust. The approach here is effectively one of performance of the trust, rather than frustration of it.

6. THE BEST METHOD?

If, as this chapter has accepted, controlled trusts and dynastic trusts are indeed creating very real barriers to the effective implementation of the policy of equal sharing that is fundamental to a property sharing regime, it is necessary to find a means of including trust assets in the process of property division. I have argued that this cannot be done in the absence of authorising legislation. General principles of trusts and property law for the most part tolerate these trusts unless it can be shown that one party's control is so pervasive that there is in substance no real trust obligation. While the trust in *Clayton v Clayton* should have been seen in this light, it is a rare occurrence.

---

102 It must be remembered too that the property will not necessarily be subjected to equal sharing or any other division. That is a second order question. The concern here is simply with whether and how property in which a party has no beneficial interest can nevertheless be treated as their property.

Statutory mechanisms include voidability of fraudulent dispositions; judicial powers of variation; and a broader definition of property that extends beyond traditional property conceptions to identify which assets should be capable of being divided between the parties to the relationship. The first should always be available to reverse the effects of fraud but it is not sufficient to deal with the problems of controlled and dynastic trusts where there is no fraud present. I have suggested ways in which both the statutory variation power and the wider definition of relevant property can be appropriately controlled to enable the policy of equal sharing to be met without unreasonably trampling on either owner autonomy or the utility of trusts more generally.

The variation discretion should be capable of being applied not just to trusts settled by either of the parties to the relationship, but to trusts with other settlors as long as the settlement is in connection with the relationship. Dynastic trusts should be capable of variation to the extent they affect the interests of the parties to the relationship. The wide application of the power should be moderated somewhat by the inclusion of provisions that set out the purpose of the variation and the relevant factors to consider in deciding whether to exercise the discretion. The ultimate objective should not be to meet the needs of the disadvantaged party but to attempt to give effect to what would have been the likely application of the trust assets had the settlement not been effectively frustrated by the dissolution of the relationship.

A broadened definition of assets that can be caught by the property division regime is also an effective means to dealing with the perceived unfairness that arises from controlled trusts and dynastic trusts.

To some extent the inquiry under each method is similar: they are giving effect to anticipated distributions of trust property. In this author's view, the most appropriate mechanism is an expanded variation discretion that applies to settlements affecting de facto relationships as well as marriages and civil unions. The risk of differing objectives, inconsistent applications, and resulting uncertainty is greater with a broad definition of property than it is with a power of variation that can be accompanied more easily by statutory guidance as to the purpose of such variations and a list of valid factors to consider.

Ultimately, it must be borne in mind by courts and legislators that the powers to vary and expand property rights can have significant adverse effects on private ordering and security of receipt, crucial features of the harmonious and productive functioning of our society. As such, they must be carefully constrained with only as much discretion as is necessary and as much clarity of their purpose and limits as is possible without unduly limiting their application in the inevitable event of future innovations created by lawyers looking for alternative ways to enable their clients to retain control and benefit without the responsibility and burden of property ownership.

CHAPTER 9

SHOULD INDIGENOUS PROPERTY BE RELATIONSHIP PROPERTY?

Jacinta Ruru and Leo Watson*

1. INTRODUCTION

Once, not that long ago, significant tracts of land on earth were known only to the Indigenous peoples. The expansion of the European empire into the

* We are especially indebted to the unpublished work of Josie Te Rata, completed as part of her LLB (Hons) degree at the University of Otago in 2014 on the point about possible reform of the Property (Relationships) Act 1976 ('PRA'). With thanks also to Laura MacKay and Helen Baker, University of Otago, for assistance with research.

'new world' of the old homes of Indigenous peoples in lands now known as, for example, the United States of America, Canada, Australia, and New Zealand has brought about complex legal quandaries that remain mostly unresolved despite more than 200 years of contact. The European colonialists arrogantly assumed sovereignty of the Indigenous peoples and their lands.[1] While some of the English-styled domestic courts recognised Indigenous peoples' property tenure, they did so typically only on an occupancy use-rights scale, if at all. This was often justified on the premise that the local Indigenous peoples were 'savage' or 'barbarian' and certainly had no developed legal property tenure comprehensive to the Europeans.[2] While those early cases have now been overruled,[3] the present legal quandary remains about how best to reconcile with Indigenous peoples who mostly have had their sovereignty and property denied. Many contemporary domestic courts,[4] domestic legislatures,[5] and international instruments[6] are attempting to find palatable answers. Within this context, focus is predominantly on, for instance, lands, waters, forests, fish, and coastlines. Often not in the spotlight is relationship property. Still, the domicile question of whether the very little remaining Indigenous property should be capable of being deemed relationship property raises unique issues that deserve close attention. Where one or both of the persons in a relationship are Indigenous and hold Indigenous property, should that Indigenous property remain ring-fenced as separate property or fall into the relationship sharing pool? For example, if the family home has been built on the ancestral land of the Indigenous partner, upon divorce should the non-owning partner be able to make a claim to the home? This chapter focuses on these questions as an important component of modern family finances with particular emphasis on a once colonial country: New Zealand.[7]

---

1 For example, see F Hoehn, *Reconciling Sovereignties: Aboriginal Nations and Canada*, Native Law Centre, University of Saskatchewan, Saskatoon 2012; RJ Miller et al, *Discovering Indigenous Lands: The Doctrine of Discovery in the English Colonies*, OUP, Oxford 2010.

2 For example, see *Wi Parata v Bishop of Wellington* (1877) 3 NZ Jur NS 72 (SC); *St Catherine's Milling and Lumber v R* (1888) 14 AC 46 (PC on appeal from Canada); *Cooper v Stuart* (1889) 14 AC 286 (PC on appeal from Australia).

3 For example, see *Delgamuukw v British Columbia* [1997] 3 SCR 1010; *Mabo v Queensland (No 2)* (1992) 175 CLR 1 [*Mabo case*]; *A-G v Ngāti Apa* [2003] 3 NZLR 643 (CA).

4 For example, see *Tsilhqot'in Nation v British Columbia* 2014 SCC 44, [2014] SCR 257; *Proprietors of Wakatū v A-G* [2017] NZSC 17.

5 For example, Te Urewera Act 2014.

6 United Nations General Assembly, *Declaration on the Rights of Indigenous People*, GA Res 61/295 (2007).

7 The issues raised in this chapter are of relevance to other once colonial countries too. This issue has attracted much attention particularly in Canada. See Family Homes on Reserves and Matrimonial Interests or Rights Act 2013 (Canada). This Act gives the First Nations the ability to choose to enact their own matrimonial real property laws. For a collation of relevant material, see Indigenous and Northern Affairs, Government of Canada, *Matrimonial Real Property on Reserves* <www.aadnc-aandc.gc.ca/eng/1100100032553/1100

In New Zealand, the first peoples to call these islands home were Māori. The British arrived some hundreds of years later and declared their own sovereignty of New Zealand in 1840, pursuant in part to a signed treaty with many Māori chiefs: the Treaty of Waitangi.[8] Thereafter they sought to acquire ownership from Māori of most of the lands in the country. As is explained in this chapter, a unique system of land tenure was later introduced in 1862 that sought to transfer land from Māori customary ownership into a Māori freehold land tenure, regulated by the Crown for onward sale to the arriving Europeans. Today, less than 6 per cent of all land in New Zealand has this Māori freehold land status (and not enough to be quantifiable has remained with the original Māori customary land status). New Zealand's contemporary relationship property law excludes Māori land and specific Māori chattels (such as traditional feather cloaks to be worn on special occasions) from the division of property when a relationship in the nature of marriage, civil union, or de facto relationship ends through separation or death. This chapter considers why this is so and the issues that arise from such a rule. It is structured by first providing a background on the legal history of Māori land and treasured property, followed by a close examination of how the current law excludes Māori land and some Māori chattels, then a focused consideration of the family home issue, and concludes with some broader considerations for the way forward.

2. A LEGAL HISTORY OF MĀORI LAND AND TREASURED PROPERTY

2.1. TIKANGA PRINCIPLES RELATING TO MĀORI PROPERTY

There is a Māori proverb which says:

> Te toto o te tangata he kai; te oranga o te tangata he whenua
>
> Food is the blood of a person, but the well-being of a person lies in the land.

In the context of a discussion about familial relationships and the sharing of assets, the proverb serves as a reminder that for Māori the land (whenua) is at

---

100032557> accessed 22.04.2017. See also JT Flies-Away, C Garrow and M Jorgensen, 'Divorce and Real Property on American Indian Reservations: Lessons for First Nations and Canada' (2005) 29(2) *Atlantis: A Women's Studies Journal* 81; S Farran, 'What is the Matrimonial Property Regime in Vanuatu?' (2009) 5 *Journal of South Pacific Law* <www.paclii.org/journals/fJSPL/vol05/6.shtml> accessed 29.05.2017.

8 To see a copy of the Treaty, see Treaty of Waitangi Act 1975 (NZ). For discussion, see C Orange, *An Illustrated History of the Treaty of Waitangi*, Bridget Williams Books, Wellington 2004.

the centre of a person's welfare, well beyond its capacity as an asset to sustain humankind economically. The whenua represents a link to the spiritual, social, and mental well-being of the whole person, and his or her kin community. It is used as a noun to mean land, nation, ground, placenta, and afterbirth, reinforcing the Māori worldview that we are of the land: tangata whenua (people of the land).[9] The principles which relate to whenua Māori (Māori land) might be summarised as follows:

- The relationship to whenua derives from a connection to the Earth Mother (Pāpātuanuku) by way of genealogical ties (whakapapa).
- This connection cannot be severed regardless of the circumstances of ownership of the whenua, or the status of the whenua at law.
- The whakapapa connection is shared by the collective kin grouping who descend from those ancestors who held rights to the land. That collective kin grouping is primarily the wider family (whānau) and the broader collective of multiple families who descend from a common ancestor (hapū).
- The rights include the entitlement to exercise customary authority over the land (mana whenua). The application and extent of those rights is determined in accordance with cultural practices (tikanga).
- In addition to the rights which are granted to the descendants by virtue of genealogical ties, there are also obligations of guardianship (kaitiakitanga) which require the descendants to care for the land in a manner that preserves and sustains the whenua for future generations.

Many of these principles also apply to taonga Māori (treasured possessions of Māori), which have a collective and genealogical connection, and which imbue both rights and obligations on those who are entitled to the taonga. Traditional tangible family taonga include, for example, woven feathered and weaved flax garments, floor mats, baskets and panels; carved wood containers; carved pounamu (greenstone) ornaments; and carved whalebone, shell, and wood trolling lures and fishhooks.

Underpinning this Māori approach to property is tikanga Māori. Tikanga Māori are the first laws that applied in New Zealand. Sir Hirini Hoko Mead has explained:[10]

> 'Tikanga embodies a set of beliefs and practices associated with procedures to be followed in conducting the affairs of a group or individual. These procedures are

---

[9] See the online *Māori Dictionary* <http://maoridictionary.co.nz> accessed 29.05.2017 and HM Mead, *Tikanga Māori: Living By Māori Values*, revised ed, Huia, Wellington 2016.

[10] HM Mead, 'The Nature of Tikanga', paper presented to the Mai i te Ata Hāpara Conference, Te Wānanga o Raukawa, Ōtaki 2000, 3–4, cited in Law Commission (NZ), *Māori Custom and Values in New Zealand Law*, SP9, Wellington 2001, [72].

established by precedents through time, are held to be ritually correct, are validated by usually more than one generation and are always subject to what a group or individual is able to do …'

Justice Joseph Williams put it simply when he described tikanga as 'essentially the Māori way of doing things – from the very mundane to the most sacred or most important fields of human endeavour'.[11]

When the Europeans arrived in New Zealand, all land was already held in accordance with Māori customary title, underpinned by these complex rules. Māori jurist Moana Jackson has described this Māori Indigenous legal system in this way:[12]

> 'Tikanga is whakapapa based, and thus people lived *with the law* rather than under it, and necessarily as a consequence lived with the whenua rather than upon it. And because the whenua is part of our whakapapa it is axiomatic that making decisions in regard to it were as fundamental as making decisions in regard to say our mokopuna [grandchildren] – it was an authority jealously guarded and respectfully administered. The jurisprudence, institutions and practises of law were constructs which were uniquely developed by each Hapū and Iwi [tribe], but which shared a common philosophical and values base. Our tipuna [ancestors] lived in an ordered and organised society, our tipuna were never a law-less people.'

In accordance with tikanga Māori, the permanent transfer of property rights relating to whenua and taonga can only occur through a blood link. As stated by (now) Sir Eddie Durie, 'lands are associated with particular communities and, save for violence, do not pass outside the descent group.'[13] Therefore, aside from war or threats of war, rights to land are transferred within the line of descent.[14] A gift of a right typically only equated to a temporary right, as an absolute right required the establishment of a blood link. It was not unusual for different family groups to have multiple rights to access and use of whenua sometimes resulting in a 'crazy patchwork of rights' over one geographical area of land.[15] The permanent transfer of rights within a bloodline traditionally 'took

---

11 J Williams, 'He Aha Tikanga Māori', unpublished paper for the Law Commission, 1998, 2, cited in Law Commission (NZ), above n 10 at [71].

12 M Jackson, brief of evidence to the Waitangi Tribunal, October 2015 (doc A11) (copy held by the authors), [20]–[21], referenced in Waitangi Tribunal, *He Kura Whenua Ka Rokohanga – Report on Claims about Reform of Te Ture Whenua Māori Act 1993*, Wai 2478, Wellington 2016, 17.

13 ET Durie, 'Will the Settlers Settle? Cultural Conciliation and the Law' (1996) 8(4) *Otago Law Review* 449, 453.

14 A Eureti, 'Māori Customary Law and Land Tenure: An Analysis' in R Boast et al, *Māori Land Law*, 2nd ed, LexisNexis, Wellington 2004, 41 at 53.

15 Ibid, at 53.

place according to the custom of ōhākī (deathbed declaration).' Once spoken, the ōhākī, which can be 'likened to a formal oral will', was binding unless 'the person did not have the right to transfer the property.'[16]

In recent decades, state law and the courts have given increasing recognition to the continuing relevance of tikanga Māori for resolving issues relating to Māori. In 2001, New Zealand's Law Commission stated:[17]

> 'If society is truly to give effect to the promise of the Treaty of Waitangi to provide a secure place for Māori values within New Zealand society, then the commitment must be total. It must involve a real endeavour to understand what tikanga Māori is [Māori law], how it is practised and applied, and how integral it is to the social, economic, cultural and political development of Māori, still encapsulated within a dominant culture in New Zealand society.'

Today tikanga Māori is statutorily defined in certain Acts of Parliament as 'Māori customary values and practices'[18] and has remained relevant for understanding modern rights and interests in Indigenous property, including relationship property. But the European arrival to New Zealand and the subsequent creation of the colonial legal system has nonetheless done much to undermine the operation of tikanga Māori.

2.2. HISTORY OF COLONIAL MĀORI LAND LAW

New Zealand's colonial history following the Treaty of Waitangi in 1840 was characterised by a relentless stripping from Māori of their land, primarily to facilitate colonial settlement.[19] This included war,[20] land confiscations legitimated through the passing of legislation,[21] compulsory acquisition for public works, and the waiving of the Crown's right of pre-emption in favour of a new specialist court, the Native Land Court.[22] The Native Land Court's practice

---

16 J Ruru, 'Implications for Māori: Historical Overview' in M Briggs, N Peart and M Henaghan (eds), *Relationship Property on Death*, Brookers, Wellington 2004, 445 at 450.

17 Law Commission (NZ), above n 10 at [402]. See *Takamore v Clarke* [2012] NZSC 116, [2013] 2 NZLR 733 and *Leef v Bidois* [2017] NZHC 36.

18 See Te Ture Whenua Māori Act 1993 (NZ); Māori Land Act 1993 (NZ) ('Māori Land Act'), s 4; and Resource Management Act 1991 (NZ), s 2.

19 Following the signing of the Treaty, the Crown entered several land purchase agreements, especially in the South Island and upper North Island. See Waitangi Tribunal, *The Ngāi Tahu Report*, Wai 27, Wellington 1991; and Waitangi Tribunal, *Te Whanganui a Tara me ona Takiwa: Report on the Wellington District*, Wai 145, Wellington 2003.

20 See J Belich, *The New Zealand Wars and the Victorian Interpretation of Racial Conflict*, Penguin, Auckland 1988 and V O'Malley, *The Great War for New Zealand, Waikato 1800–2000*, Bridget Williams Books, Wellington 2016.

21 See New Zealand Settlements Act 1863 and Suppression of Rebellion Act 1863 (NZ).

22 Native Lands Act 1862 (NZ) and Native Lands Act 1865 (NZ).

of transforming Māori customary land into individualised titles derived from the Crown (named Māori freehold titles) proved a very effective method of dispossessing Māori from their land,[23] eventually leaving only approximately 6 per cent of New Zealand land as Māori freehold land.[24] Despite the extensive land loss, and the consequent effect on the well-being of Māori communities, the central concepts of whakapapa (genealogical connection) and mana whenua (authority to the land) remained.[25]

A suite of nineteenth-century legislative instruments, policies, regulations, and ordinances were enacted to deal with Māori land, culminating in the consolidated Native Land Act 1909 (NZ). That Act informed subsequent legislation through the twentieth century, including the Māori Affairs Act 1953 (NZ), and its amendments. From the 1970s, increased calls from within Māoridom for recognition of rights as affirmed and guaranteed under the Treaty of Waitangi resulted in the development of a new legislative scheme for Māori land in 1993.[26]

2.3. CURRENT MĀORI LAND LAW

The long gestation period of engagement with Māori landowners and stakeholders led to the passing of Te Ture Whenua Māori Act 1993 (NZ)/Māori Land Act 1993 (NZ) ('Māori Land Act'). The Māori Land Act centres on the new legal premise that Māori land ought to be retained by its Māori owners and their kin groups, and that the Māori Land Court should encourage the utilisation of Māori land for the benefit of its owners.[27]

The Māori Land Act defines Māori land as including Māori freehold land and Māori customary land.[28] The significant majority of Māori land is Māori freehold land,[29] usually held in multiple ownership (average number of owners: 85) whereby land interests are small and fragmented. Pockets of Māori land exist

---

23 To better appreciate the working of the Court, see R Boast, *The Native Land Court 1862–1887: A Historical Study, Cases and Commentary*, Thomson Reuters, Wellington 2013; and R Boast, *Buying the Land, Selling the Land: Governments and Māori Land on the North Island 1865–1921*, Victoria University Press, Wellington 2008; and Waitangi Tribunal, *The Kaipara Report*, Wai 674, Wellington 2006.

24 Office of the Controller and Auditor-General, New Zealand, *Māori Land – What is it and How is it Administered?* <www.oag.govt.nz/2004/maori-land-court/part2.htm> accessed 29.05.2017.

25 See HM Mead, above n 9.

26 For example, New Zealand Māori Council, *Kaupapa: Te Wahanga Tuatahi – Guidelines for Legislation on Māori Land*, Wellington 1983.

27 Māori Land Act, preamble and ss 2 and 17.

28 Māori Land Act, s 4.

29 Māori Land Act, s 129(2)(b).

throughout New Zealand, including along rural coastlines and in urban cities. The capacity of an owner to alienate his or her undivided share in the land is restricted by the rules set out in the Act, which limits alienation to those within the bloodline[30] (referred to in the Act as the 'preferred class of alienees').[31] A series of threshold rules exist if the owners pool together to seek alienation of their block of Māori land. For example, if sale is sought then more than 75 per cent of the owners must consent to the sale and they must first offer the right of refusal to purchase the land to those relatives within the preferred class of alienees.[32] Administration rules also reinforce that Māori land must remain with those who have a genealogical connection with the land, mostly prioritising children of the landowner as appropriate successors.

In summary, the Māori Land Act is unique in New Zealand's legislative context, expressing fundamental principles of the Treaty of Waitangi as they apply to Māori land and, in particular (as taken from the Preamble to the Act):

- the reaffirmation of the spirit of the exchange of governorship (kāwanatanga) for the protection of sovereignty (rangatiratanga) embodied in the Treaty of Waitangi;
- the principle of retention of Māori land as a generational treasure (taonga tuku iho);
- the protection of sacred land sites (wahi tapu);
- the facilitation of the occupation, development, and utilisation of Māori land for the benefit of Māori owners, their whānau, and their hapū; and
- the establishment of mechanisms, including the maintenance of the Māori Land Court, to achieve the implementation of these principles.

3. EXCLUSION OF MĀORI PROPERTY FROM RELATIONSHIP PROPERTY

3.1. EXCLUSION OF MĀORI LAND – HISTORICAL

In New Zealand, the Matrimonial Property Act 1963 (NZ) ('1963 Act') dictated a regime of judicial discretion based on contributions to property, whereas the Matrimonial Property Act 1976 (NZ) ('1976 Act') ordered a presumption of equal sharing of matrimonial property, but it applied only upon separation or

---

30 Māori Land Act, ss 108 and 109. For commentary see R Boast et al, *Māori Land Law*, 2nd ed, LexisNexis, Wellington 2004.

31 Māori Land Act, s 4.

32 Māori Land Act, s 147A.

divorce. The 1963 Act continued to govern matrimonial property claims on the death of a spouse. The Acts were inconsistent with regards to Māori land. The 1963 Act did not exempt Māori land, meaning that if the family home was built on Māori land, then it was matrimonial property. However, the 1976 Act took a different stance and explicitly stated that its regime did not apply to Māori land. That meant that if the family home had been built on Māori land and the couple then separated, the equal sharing rule would not apply to the home (it would remain in the ownership of whichever of the couple had ownership of the Māori land, be it the husband or wife).[33] In practice, the difference between these two Acts raised little concern. Little residential building had taken place on Māori land and, as John Chadwick, a prominent Māori lawyer, reflected:[34]

> 'Matrimonial Property is the only area of family law that I know of where whanaungatanga [family inter-relationships] prevails regardless of the law. This is because Māori, as a rule, do not have the same emotional attachment to property [family chattels] that the law guarantees. Since 1976 the Family Court, in its matrimonial property jurisdiction, has by and large been the exclusive preserve of the white middle class.'

The Property (Relationship) Amendment Act 2001 (NZ) radically recast matrimonial property law and re-named the Matrimonial Property Act 1976 (NZ) the Property (Relationships) Act 1976 (NZ) ('PRA'). The Amendment Act introduced new rules for the division of property upon separation and death for all New Zealanders, including Māori. Of most relevance to this chapter are the rules concerning Māori land and taonga.

3.2. EXCLUSION OF MĀORI LAND – CONTEMPORARY

The PRA now governs the legal division of property when a relationship in the nature of marriage, civil union, or a de facto relationship ends through separation or death. The PRA's primary principle is that (prima facie) those relationships should be acknowledged as equal partnerships by way of an equal division of property at the demise of a relationship.[35] This presumption of equal sharing applies to all New Zealanders, including Māori. Equal sharing applies to the family home and family chattels as well as assets acquired by either partner during the relationship.[36] The family home is defined as a 'dwellinghouse that … the spouses or partners use habitually'.[37] However, the PRA does not apply to

---

33 PRA, s 6.

34 J Chadwick, 'Whanaungatanga and the Family Court' (2002) 4 *Butterworths Family Law Journal* 91, 93.

35 PRA, ss 1C and 1M.

36 PRA, s 1N.

37 For the full definition see PRA, s 2, 'family home'.

Māori land. Section 6 of the PRA states that '[n]othing in this Act shall apply in respect of any Māori land'. At present, this is consistent with the codified approach to Māori land disposition under the Māori Land Act. Under section 146 of the Māori Land Act, owners have no ability to alienate land 'otherwise than in accordance with this Act.'

For Māori land, different considerations apply depending on the context of the relationship property division, be it because of the death of a partner and, if so, whether the deceased spouse/partner has died testate or intestate, and depending on the date of death,[38] or separation of the relationship.

3.2.1. Upon Death

Where a spouse or partner with Māori land interests dies, succession provisions under the Māori Land Act apply.[39] In the case of a deceased person leaving a will, no person can succeed to Māori land unless they fall within the specified classes of persons set out in section 108(2) of the Māori Land Act. These persons include children and grandchildren of the testator, siblings, other persons related by blood to the testator who are members of the subtribe associated with the land, and other owners of the land. These classes of persons affirm the statutory principle of retention of Māori land within the bloodline which is associated with the land block in question. A spouse/partner would not normally fall within any of these classes of persons. Section 108(5) provides that any provision of a will which purports to leave Māori land to anyone outside of the specified classes, such as a spouse, is 'void and of no effect', and the Māori land passes according to the intestacy provisions of the Māori Land Act. Section 109 sets out the rules for succession on intestacy, which again follow the bloodline principle although the class of persons is more limited than under section 108(2). The classes of persons who can succeed on intestacy are namely children and siblings.

A surviving spouse or partner could possibly fall into the classes of persons who are entitled to take an ownership interest under section 108(2), but only if they are already an owner in the land, or are related to their deceased spouse/partner by blood and are members of the subtribe associated with the land. But more often than not, section 108(2) operates to prevent a surviving spouse or partner from succeeding as an owner to Māori land. A surviving spouse or partner of a deceased who dies intestate will almost certainly never be eligible to inherit Māori land, because section 109(1) does not include the class of existing owners, or the broad 'related by blood' phrase.[40]

---

38 See Māori Land Act, s 100.

39 Note that under s 100, different legislative provisions will apply if the testator died before 01.07.1994, or where administration of an estate has been granted prior to 01.07.1993. Such instances are becoming increasingly rare.

40 Compare with Māori Land Act, s 108(2)(c).

Thus the main way in which a spouse or partner will benefit from Māori land on succession, is by way of an interest less than full ownership, namely a life interest. That is, it is permissible for a testator to devise his or her interest in Māori freehold land to his or her spouse, de facto, or civil union partner for life or a shorter period.[41] There is no requirement to relinquish that life interest if the surviving spouse/partner enters into a new relationship. If the deceased dies intestate, then different provisions apply. Section 109(2) provides that the surviving spouse or partner is 'entitled as of right to an interest … for life, or until he or she remarries or enters into a civil union or a de facto relationship.' Section 7 of the Relationships (Statutory References) Act 2005 (NZ) amended some legislative provisions to include de facto relationships, but unfortunately, there remains a serious omission in section 109(2) because it is only a 'surviving spouse or civil union partner' who is entitled, and this entitlement does not extend to a de facto partner. That is despite the fact that the entitlement ceases if he or she enters into a de facto relationship in the future. This drafting requires much clearer articulation to avoid being unjustifiably discriminatory.[42] Other subsections provide that the life interest can be surrendered by the surviving spouse or civil union partner[43] and that it is not permissible to provide a life interest to the spouse or civil union partner if there is a separation order or separation agreement in force at the date of death of the owner.[44]

The life interest in Māori land extends beyond an entitlement to income derived from the land. It grants to the holder of the life interest, an entitlement to be involved in management decisions relating to the block. In the context of multiply-owned land, this can include decisions as to long-term leasing or other alienations, occupation sites for other owners, title reconstructions, or changes to land status. The Māori Assembled Owner Regulations 1995 (NZ) also provide for the remaindermen interests to be included in voting on issues affecting the block. The details are complex and it is not necessary to explain them here, but, generally speaking, the life interest holder will account for 50 per cent of that share's vote, and the remaindermen will account for the other 50 per cent.[45] That said, the life interest cannot be alienated without the consent of all persons entitled in remainder; and section 150D of the Māori Land Act provides that the life interest holder is acting as a kaitiaki (defined in section 4 of the Act to mean 'guardian') in accordance with tikanga Māori.[46]

---

41 Māori Land Act, s 108(4).

42 J Ruru and M Stevens, 'Māori Land Owners and Their Spouses and Partners' [2007] (9) *New Zealand Law Journal* 325, 328.

43 Māori Land Act, s 109(3).

44 Māori Land Act, s 109(4).

45 See Māori Assembled Owner Regulations 1995.

46 Māori Land Act, s 150D, with definitions of 'kaitiaki' and 'tikanga Māori' in s 4.

Pursuant to section 116(1), a surviving spouse or partner who does not receive a life interest in the land can still apply to the Court to make an order conferring on him or her the income derived from the Māori land interest, or from the sale proceeds of that interest, for his or her life or for any shorter period. Subsection (3) explains why Parliament has enabled this:

> 'In enacting this provision, Parliament has in mind particularly the possibility of injustice arising in individual cases from the prohibitions enacted by this Act against the alienation of beneficial interests in Māori freehold land to persons outside defined classes, and is therefore desirous of conferring on the court some flexible, if limited, powers to ameliorate any such injustice.'

Section 116 has been used extensively by the Māori Land Court to provide a financial interest to a spouse/partner in relation to Māori land.[47]

Another possibility is the right to occupy. The Māori Land Act provides for those who hold beneficial interests in Māori land to have rights to occupy multiply-owned land, by way of occupation orders, granted by the Māori Land Court. These orders confer an exclusive right to occupy a specified area of the land block as a site for a house, and can be granted with a right of succession.[48] It is permissible for an occupation order to be granted to a surviving spouse or partner who has been vested a life interest (under sections 108(4) or 109(2)). This is because the life interest is a beneficial interest in Māori land. But this would require a fresh application by the surviving spouse or partner under section 328, given that occupation orders cannot themselves be succeeded to other than by way of the restricted class of persons within the deceased's bloodline.[49]

3.2.2. *Upon Relationship Breakdown*

The PRA does not apply to Māori land. The Māori Land Act does not address the implications for Māori land which may arise from a relationship breakdown, where spouses or partners separate. This has been referred to previously as a legislative gap that was overlooked by Parliament.[50] In the meantime, a possible

---

47 See, for example, the use of s 116 in favour of the surviving de facto partner in *Nicholas v Kameta – Te Puke 2A2A3B1 and 2A2A3B2* (2011) Māori Appellate Court MB 500 (2011 APPEAL 500) which was approved on appeal to the Court of Appeal, see *Kameta v Nicholas* [2012] NZCA 350, [2012] 3 NZLR 573.

48 Māori Land Act, s 328. See *Davis – Ahipara A8B* (2014) 88 Taitokerau MB 186 (88 TTK 186) where an owner of an interest in Māori freehold land successfully sought an occupation order for part of the site for her and her fiancée to build a family home.

49 Māori Land Act, ss 108(2A) and (2B).

50 J Ruru, 'Finding Solutions for the Legislative Gaps in Determining Rights to the Family Home on Colonially Defined Indigenous Lands' (2008) 41(2) *UBC Law Review* 315, 340–41 and 347.

remedy for a spouse or partner lies with the equitable jurisdiction of the Māori Land Court.

Section 237 of the Māori Land Act provides that, subject to the express provisions of Part 12, the Court:

> 'shall have and may exercise [in respect of trusts to which Part 12 applies] all the same powers and authorities as the High Court has (whether by statute or by any rule of law or by virtue of its inherent jurisdiction) in respect of trusts generally.'

These trusts include (under section 236) 'every … trust constituted in respect of any General land owned by Māori'. The effect of these provisions is that the Māori Land Court has been able to exercise its jurisdiction in relation to trusts which may arise in the context of relationship property. An early case was the 1994 Court of Appeal decision, *Grace v Grace*, in which a divorcing wife sought a beneficial interest in the matrimonial home that had been built on her husband's Māori freehold land pursuant to constructive trust principles.[51] However, during the court proceedings, she withdrew her claim and sought monetary compensation, relieving the Court from having to make a hard decision as to ownership of the land. The Court, though, left the possibility for a future court to accept a constructive trust.[52] The issue has arisen since and is discussed further in section 4 of this chapter, within the consideration of what happens when the family home has been built on Māori land.

An interesting case arose in 2016 concerning quite different facts. Here, Mr Nathan, the owner of land categorised as 'General land owned by Māori', had successfully sought to vest this land in a whānau trust.[53] A whānau trust is a specific trust enabled by the Māori Land Act that brings together Māori freehold land interests and other General land interests owned by Māori. Once the land is in a whānau trust, no persons are entitled to succeed to any interests or shares

---

51 *Grace v Grace* [1995] 1 NZLR 1 (CA).

52 There has been one interpretation that constructive trusts over Māori land do not sit comfortably within the scheme of the Māori Land Act, given that s 146 states that '[n]o person has the capacity to alienate any interest in Māori freehold land otherwise than in accordance with this Act' and s 4 states that an 'alienation' includes 'every form of disposition of Māori land or of any equitable interest in Māori land'. Nevertheless, to date the Māori Land Court has been comfortable in exercising an equitable jurisdiction to apply trust tools where appropriate. See J Te Rata, 'Papakāinga: Tool for Determining Rights to the Family Home in a Māori Land Context', unpublished paper, University of Otago, 2014, 8 (copy held by authors).

53 *Yates v Nathan - Neville David Nathan Whānau Trust* (2016) Chief Judge's MB 223. Note General land is land that has been alienated from the Crown for a subsisting estate in fee simple. General land owned by Māori is defined as land that has been alienated from the Crown for a subsisting estate in fee simple and is beneficially owned by a Māori or by a group of persons of whom a majority are Māori. See Māori Land Act, s 129.

in the trust.[54] Mr Nathan, when he sought to create the whānau trust, had omitted to advise the Court that there was the potential for a relationship property claim to the General land. Ms Yates, who was alleged to be in a de facto relationship with Mr Nathan, made an application under section 45 of the Māori Land Act for the Chief Judge to exercise jurisdiction to declare an error had been made in not seeking to establish whether there existed a potential claim under the PRA before transferring the land into a whānau trust. The Māori Land Court agreed that because there was the potential for a PRA claim (with the Family Court having the appropriate jurisdiction to determine whether there was a de facto relationship), an error by the Māori Land Court had been made. As part of Deputy Chief Judge Fox's decision, her Honour said:[55]

> 'I further note that the property is not Māori land. It is General land acquired by Mr Nathan when he purchased it in 1993. As such, it lacks the same characteristics associated with land to which Māori people are associated in accordance with tikanga. Therefore, the principles in the Preamble and the duties outlined in ss 2 and 17 of Te Ture Whenua Māori Act 1993 [the Māori Land Act] do not have the same application given the facts of this particular case. As a general rule, a property such as this is normally land that should be available for relationship property claims.'

This raises interesting issues between the intent of the Māori Land Act and the PRA, and the broader connection between the two distinct courts, the Māori Land Court and the Family Court, along with the complex issue of hiding property in trusts.

3.3. EXCLUSION OF SOME FAMILY CHATTELS – TAONGA

The PRA distinguishes between relationship property and separate property. Separate property is not subject to the equal sharing regime. Relationship property includes family chattels[56] but is defined to exclude chattels used for business purposes, money, heirlooms, and taonga.[57] These specific chattels are classified as separate property.[58] Taonga is not defined in the Act and interesting cases have arisen where non-Māori have sought to classify valuable artwork as a taonga. A report from the 1988 Working Group on Matrimonial Property Law argued there are valuable reasons why heirlooms and taonga should be excluded from relationship property and the equal sharing regime. Specifically, part of the value

---

54 Māori Land Act, s 214(6).
55 *Yates v Nathan*, above n 53 at [39].
56 PRA, ss 8(1)(b) and 10(4). Family chattels include items such as furniture, pets, and family vehicles.
57 PRA, s 2.
58 PRA, s 9(1).

of taonga stems from the objects being within the collective possession of the same family for generations where custom requires that the person in possession of it merely holds it as a guardian for the wider family and for future generations.[59]

However, the judiciary initially accepted the possibility of a more broad definition of taonga as 'anything highly prized' that extended to include non-Māori assets (assets not owned by Māori or having any connection to Māori or the Māori world).[60] For example, in 2003, in *Perry v West* where a divorced husband unsuccessfully sought sole ownership of a work from one of New Zealand's foremost painters by arguing it was his taonga, Judge Mather held that although taonga is a Māori word, 'it describes a relationship between a person or persons and property' and saw 'no reason why it cannot apply to a person of any ethnic or cultural background.'[61] Judge Mather held that because the husband wished to sell the painting, this meant it could not be taonga.[62] In the High Court, Laurenson J agreed with Judge Mather's definition of taonga, explaining that an object can attain the status of taonga in two ways: when it has special significance to that individual, or when others ascribe to it or bestow upon it a special significance.[63] However, Laurenson J disagreed that an intention to sell a taonga would be fatal to the object being regarded as a taonga.[64] Rather, Laurenson J considered that the husband had failed to consistently maintain a personal attachment to the painting and therefore this inaction meant it could not be a taonga.[65]

The courts have now restricted the interpretation of taonga. In *Sydney v Sydney*, Judge Coyle concluded that taonga could still be applied pan-culturally, but not in that case, which concerned artwork for reasons that brought the interpretation of taonga back to a more Māori-orientated realm. He accepted evidence from a Māori professor that:[66]

> 'for an item to become taonga it must be accompanied, through a marae [Māori meeting house] or marae like setting, with elements of whakapapa [genealogical ties], mana [authority], tapu [sacredness] and kōrero [oration and speeches]. For an item to become taonga it must therefore be presented, either by a group or an individual (but only on behalf of a kin group/tribal group) to another, in a marae like setting. It must

---

59 Department of Justice, *Report of the Working Group on Matrimonial Property and Family Protection*, Wellington, October 1988, 18.

60 See *Page v Page* (2001) 21 FRNZ 275 (HC) at [46]. Contrast *Kininmonth v Kininmonth* FC Auckland FAM-2004-004-509, 27 August 2008 at [26], where the Court held that a family holiday home could not be a taonga.

61 *Perry v West* DC Waitakere FP239-01, 16 May 2003 at [89].

62 Ibid, at [89].

63 *Perry v West* [2004] NZFLR 515 (HC) at [37(e)].

64 Ibid, at [37(f)].

65 Ibid, at [37(b)]. The husband only first made a claim to the painting nearly a decade after the divorce.

66 *Sydney v Sydney* [2012] NZFC 2685 at [57], referring to evidence presented by Professor Paul Tapsell.

> additionally have accompanying it a history or whakapapa, some particular significance or mana, and be presented in the context of an oration or kōrero.'

In that case, paintings created by Mr Sydney, a prominent New Zealand artist, could not be considered taonga as he did not acquire them in a marae-like setting, there was no particular speech or history associated with the paintings, and, most importantly, he never received the paintings on behalf of others who represented a wider group.[67] This case has provided a more Māori-aligned precedent for understanding taonga and thus has reduced any urgency for the legislature to clarify its intent to confine taonga to Māori generational treasures.[68]

Significantly, all the cases arising to date where one of the parties has sought to categorise valued property as his or her own separate property by relying on the taonga possibility have not involved separating Māori couples or traditionally treasured Māori items. This is probably because it is well accepted within the relationship that such items (such as the woven feathered garment or carved wood container) are cared for and not owned by an individual. This reinforces the continuing relevance of John Chadwick's 2002 reflection, noted earlier in this chapter, that tikanga Māori continues to govern Māori relationship property disputes concerning family chattels, especially taonga.[69] Those couples are not bringing these disputes to New Zealand's courts.

Turning to the primary question of this chapter – should Indigenous property be relationship property – New Zealand's legislation on the face of it tackles this head-on with a resounding no: Māori land and taonga are not relationship property. This makes sense and is good law. It recognises the importance of the blood connection that ties land and taonga to a collective rather than an individual responsibility. But a particularly perplexing issue is beginning to rise specifically for Māori land: what happens when the family home has been built on Māori land?

4. THE PARTICULARLY PERPLEXING ISSUE – THE FAMILY HOME

4.1. PRINCIPLES

Within the context of modern family finances, it is well known that the family home is at the heart of the relationship property pool. The family home is often

67 Ibid, at [59].

68 For a discussion of why it is problematic to interpret taonga as including chattels that do not have any Māori significance, see J Ruru, 'Taonga and Family Chattels' [2004] (7) *New Zealand Law Journal* 297.

69 J Chadwick, above n 34 at 94.

the major asset in any relationship. But what happens when the family home has been built on Māori freehold land? With the law excluding Māori land from relationship property,[70] the family home has also become exempt from the equal sharing regime when a relationship ends upon death or separation. This is because of the common law principle that ownership of fixtures runs with the land, specifically the principle of *quicquid plantatur solo, solo credit* (whatever is affixed to the soil, belongs to the soil). This principle is affirmed by section 99(2) of the Māori Land Act in the context of the administration of estates, where a beneficial interest in land is deemed to include the interest of the freehold owner in all buildings and other fixtures attached to the land, and all things growing on the land. Until recently, few family homes had been built on Māori freehold land compared to General land. But this is fast changing with central and local governments developing policies to better enable and encourage Māori owners and their families to build and live on their Māori land.[71]

4.2. DECLARING THE FAMILY HOME A CHATTEL

One judicial answer has been to declare the family home on Māori freehold land a chattel.[72] For example, one of the early cases on this issue arose in 2005 where the property-owning partner wished to build a house on his Māori freehold land for his family, but could only do so if his new wife contributed $200,000 towards its construction.[73] She would make this contribution only if she became the joint owner of the land. Without joint ownership, she would have no permanent rights to the property under a future relationship property division or an ability to devise her interest in the property to her son from a previous union (except perhaps via a constructive trust claim pursued in the High Court). The Māori Land Court accepted the reality of this dilemma. While the Court held that it had no jurisdiction to transfer half ownership of the land to her, and refused

70 PRA, s 6.

71 See Te Puni Kōkiri (Ministry of Māori Development), *Māori Housing Network* <www.tpk.govt.nz/en/whakamahia/maori-housing-network/> accessed 29.05.2017; Controller and Auditor-General, *Government Planning and Support for Housing on Māori Land: Ngā whakatakotoranga kaupapa me te tautoko a te Kāwanatanga ki te hanga whare i runga i te whenua Māori*, Performance audit report, Wellington, August 2011; Controller and Auditor-General, *Government Planning and Support for Housing on Māori land: Progress in Responding to the Auditor-General's Recommendations*, Wellington, December 2014; B Livesey, 'Housing Development on Māori Land – Two Case Studies in Developing and Retaining Māori Land' (2012) *Māori Law Review* 22; and V Kingi, 'Comment: Papakāinga Housing at Mangatawa' (2012) *Māori Law Review* 29.

72 See *Ngā Uri a Maata Ngapo Charitable Trust v McLeod – Harataunga West 2B2A1* (2012) 49 Waikato Maniapoto MB 223 (49 WMN 233).

73 *Epiha Hills – Kaiopoi MR 873 Blk XI Section 71B* (2005) MB 110 SI 85.

to allow the land to change its status to General land,[74] it declared that it could order the house to be a chattel solely owned by her. Therefore, if the house was built on the land, it would not be deemed 'part and parcel of the land.' It was to be built so it could be easily transported from the land in the case of a possible future separation.

Instances have also arisen where a house has been built on Māori freehold land but it is unclear who owns it. Applications are made to the Māori Land Court under section 18(1)(a) of the Māori Land Act:

> 'to hear and determine any claim, whether at law or in equity, to the ownership or possession of Māori freehold land, or to any right, title, estate, or interest in any such land or in the proceeds of the alienation of any such right, title, estate, or interest.'

The Court first determines if the house is fixed to the land. If it is not, then it is a chattel and the Māori Land Court has no jurisdiction to determine the ownership of chattels, even chattels on Māori land. For example, in one case the Māori Land Court determined that a bach (holiday home) and a shed could be removed without destruction and therefore they were chattels.[75] The jurisdiction concerning this issue within the context of relationship property is developing in an interesting manner that matters for property division, and therefore the finances of families whose family home is built on Māori land.

The reality of removable homes as a solution to the legislative gap in the PRA is feasible. Due to the growing threat of climate change and rising sea levels, the concept of removable or relocatable homes is becoming more and more common.[76] However, removable homes can be both logistically problematic and expensive. As noted in the 2003 Māori Land Court decision, *Matenga*, permitting the non-owning partner to remove a home allows them to recoup some of the money expended on the building; however, they will still suffer a loss due to the

74 The Māori Land Court does have jurisdiction to change the status of land, but only under specific circumstances, including where it is satisfied that 'the land can be managed or utilised more effectively as General land': Māori Land Act, s 136.

75 *Conner - Pataua 4B* (2016) 130 Taitokerau MB 17 (130 TTK 17). See also *Anderson - Te Raupo* (2015) 99 Taitokerau MB 206 (99 TTK 206) concerning a Housing Corporation of New Zealand mortgage agreement where the Court held the house was a fixture for the purposes of the Māori Land Act, s 18(1)(a) but could become a chattel if cl 21 of the mortgage deed were ever triggered.

76 In 2011, Victoria introduced new planning rules for a stretch of coast line particularly prone to flooding, shore erosion, and rising sea levels which meant all homes built in the area had to be relocatable: J Dowling, 'Is this the Solution to the Impact of Climate Change?' (2011) *The Age* <www.theage.com.au/victoria/is-this-the-solution-to-the-impact-of-climate-change-20110729-1i4cj.html> accessed 29.05.2017; see also AD Gordon, 'Disposable Infrastructure Including Relocatable Buildings: Adapting to Climate Change' (2013) 17(2) *Australasian Journal of Water Resources* 152.

costs involved in removing and relocating a house.[77] Furthermore, this solution adds yet another constraint to the effective utilisation of Māori freehold land. Finally, it is relevant to record that while each case would have to be determined on its merits, there is an aspect of tikanga that is common among whānau and hapū whereby the home is regarded as a taonga, or is imbued with a sense of tapu, or sacredness. Such tapu can arise from the activities within the house, or the status of the persons who resided in the house. In such circumstances, the solution of removal or relocation would be contrary to tikanga Māori and entirely unacceptable.

4.3. A SOLUTION IN EQUITY

A different response, purposively contrary to the 'fixture-to-chattel theory', was advanced by Judge Ambler in his 2012 decision *Stock v Morris – Wainui 2D2B*.[78] This case concerned a non-owner who had paid for the construction of a home on the owner's Māori freehold land. Judge Ambler considered prior relevant cases from the Māori Land Court and the Māori Appellate Court. He first considered whether the home was a fixture or a chattel. Judge Ambler adopted the test laid down in a 1997 House of Lords decision, *Elitestone Ltd v Morris*:[79]

> 'In the case of the house, the answer is as much a matter of common sense as precise analysis. A house which is constructed in such a way as to be removable, whether a unit or in sections, may well remain a chattel, even though it is connected temporarily to main services such as water and electricity. But a house which is constructed in such a way that it cannot be removed at all, save by destruction, cannot have been intended to remain as a chattel. It must have been intended to form part of the realty.'

Judge Ambler held that the Māori Land Court can declare existing ownership rights in law or at equity but cannot transfer or create rights.[80] He was clear that an order under section 18(1)(a) of the Māori Land Act cannot change the nature of a property such as a house.[81] In coming to this conclusion, Judge

---

77 *Matenga v Bryan – Parish of Tahawai Lot 18C-F and 18I* (2003) 73 Tauranga MB 150 (73 T 150).

78 *Stock v Morris – Wainui 2D2B* (2012) 41 Taitokerau MB 121 (41 TTK 121).

79 *Elitestone Ltd v Morris* [1997] 2 All ER 513 (HL) at 519 as cited in *Stock v Morris – Wainui 2D2B*, above n 78 at [20]. This test was also adopted in *Conner – Pataua 4B* (2016) 130 Taitokerau MB 17 (130 TTK 17) at [24].

80 *Stock v Morris – Wainui 2D2B*, above n 78 at [25]. See also *Clarke v Gray – Poukawa 9G Trust* (2016) 48 Takitimu MB 182 (48 TKT 182) at [43]; *Rautangata v Rautangata – Opuatia No 6D No 2D Block* (2013) 63 Waikato Maniapoto MB 132 (63 WMN 132) at [10].

81 *Stock v Morris – Wainui 2D2B*, above n 78 at [43]–[46].

Ambler preferred the approach taken in *Bidois*[82] where the Court 'separates' the ownership of a house under section 18(1)(a). If the house:[83]

> 'is a fixture, but the Court determines that someone other than the land owners own the fixture in equity, the nature of the property does not change. The Court is simply recognising equitable ownership of a fixture.'

Judge Ambler further considered that an order under section 18(1)(a) can be made in favour of a non-owner.[84] As the Court came to the conclusion that the house in this case was a fixture, it then faced the hurdle of recognising the non-owning partner's interest. The judge noted that although an order vesting land or an interest in the land in favour of a non-owner would offend the purpose of the Māori Land Act, the Court was unable to allow the actions of owners to cause injustice to non-owners.[85]

In thc 2016 case of *Owen v Hauiti – Kiwinui A*, Deputy Chief Judge Fox agreed with Judge Ambler's approach.[86] The case did not concern a relationship breakdown between spouses, but a surviving spouse. The Court acknowledged the remedial contributions of the surviving spouse to the house constructed on his deceased partner's Māori land.

When the Court concludes that a non-owner is entitled to equitable relief, it will first look to the possibility of awarding monetary compensation. If this is inappropriate or inadequate, the Court may award ownership of the house if it can be removed from the land.[87] This was the case in *Matenga*, where the Court allowed a non-owning partner to remove a house from the land, despite the fact it was a fixture.[88]

In the circumstances of *Stock v Morris*, Judge Ambler issued an order under section 18(1)(a) in favour of the owner; however, this was made conditional on a payment of compensation to the non-owner to the value of half of the home in question.[89] In order to enforce this compensation, Judge Ambler issued a

---

82 *Bidois and others – Te Puna 154D3B2B* (2008) 12 Waiariki Appellate MB 102 (12 APPEAL 102). For a different approach, see *Faulkner v Faulkner – Matapihi 3A2C1C2C* (2006) 86 Tauranga MB 141 (86 T 141); *Tohu – Te Horo 2B2B2B* (2007) 7 Whangarei Appellate MB 34 (7 APWH 34); *Insley v Insley – Awanui Haparapara 2B1B2* (2009) 108 Opotiki MB 255 (108 OPO 255).

83 *Stock v Morris – Wainui 2D2B*, above n 78 at [46]. Judge Armstrong agreed with this approach in the case of *Rata – Pakanae 2W1B* (2016) 125 Taitokerau MB 17 (125 TTK 17) at [29], stating: 'this approach is consistent with the overall objectives and kaupapa of the Act.'

84 *Stock v Morris – Wainui 2D2B*, above n 78 at [60].

85 Ibid, at [65]–[70].

86 *Owen v Hauiti – Kiwinui A* (2016) 57 Tairawhiti MB 73 at [70].

87 *Stock v Morris – Wainui 2D2B*, above n 78 at [70].

88 *Matenga v Bryan – Parish of Tahawai Lot 18C-F and 18I* (2003) 73 Tauranga MB 150 (73 T 150).

89 *Stock v Morris – Wainui 2D2B*, above n 78 at [73]–[74].

judgment debt against the property-owning partner. Furthermore, he also issued a charging debt under section 82 of the Māori Land Act, charging the property owner's interest in the home.[90] A similar order was issued in *Brokenshaw*, where the Māori Land Court made an order in favour of the children of the owner, conditional upon them paying within five years half the value of the building to the non-owning partner's estate.[91] Additionally, the Court made an interim order pursuant to sections 37(3) and 116 of the Māori Land Act, conferring the right to any income derived from the sale or rental of the building up to the amount owed to the non-owning partner's estate.

Therefore, as decided in *Stock v Morris*, recognition of a constructive trust over a house on Māori freehold land does not change the legal ownership of the home. However, it does acknowledge and protect a divorcing spouse or partner's equitable interest in the home by preventing the legal owner from exercising full beneficial ownership over the home. This can be enforced by imposing a charge on the land.

The focus on the case law in this context has been on the family home on Māori land. Research to date has not identified any case whereby a constructive trust claim has resulted in a vesting to a spouse or partner of an ownership interest in Māori land itself.

5. A WAY FORWARD

For New Zealand, the issue of whether Indigenous property should be relationship property is gaining judicial attention. Reform is on the horizon.

5.1. MĀORI LAND ACT REFORM

At the time of writing this chapter, New Zealand's Parliament is currently considering significant reform of the Māori Land Act. The Te Ture Whenua Māori Bill 2016 had its second reading in the House of Representatives in December 2016. If the National-led government is re-elected in the General Election in September 2017, it is expected that this Bill will be read a third time and enacted in early 2018.

---

90 Ibid, at [75]. In *Clarke v Gray – Poukawa 9G Trust* (2016) 48 Takitimu MB 182 (48 TKT 182) at [54], the Court acknowledged that the imposition of a charging order was not an uncommon way to enforce an equitable interest.

91 *Brokenshaw – Te Kaha 6X2* (2003) 81 Opotiki MB 18 (81 OPO 18).

The Te Ture Whenua Māori Bill 2016 is intended to be a deliberate overhaul of the existing law. It is designed to 'completely refresh and modernise' the current law by providing a:[92]

> 'new approach that aims to increase the ability of Māori land owners to use their land by empowering them to make decisions by and for themselves, supported by an owner-focussed Māori land service. At the same time, it aims to maintain, and even to strengthen, the protections that currently exist for the retention of Māori land for the benefit of future generations (a taonga tuku iho) by virtue of whakapapa.'

The Bill is controversial and not supported by all Māori landowners.[93]

The Bill states that the surviving spouse/partner has the right to occupy the principal family home if it is on Māori freehold land, and to receive any income or discretionary grants that the owner would have been entitled to receive (such as rent).[94] A survivor's rights are to end when any of the following events first occur: survivor remarries or enters a new civil union or de facto relationship, the survivor dies, or the survivor relinquishes the rights.[95] The Bill remains silent on the rights of the separating spouse to the family home built on Māori freehold land.

One issue is the appropriate judicial forum in which to determine constructive trust claims to family homes built on Māori land. While the Māori Land Court has specialised knowledge as to Māori land issues, the vast majority of relationship property claims will come before the Family Court. Judges of the Māori Land Court had proposed to the Crown, during the review of the Māori Land Act, that the issue of competing jurisdictions in the context of family law should be addressed, and had sought a wider jurisdiction, particularly in relation to Family Protection Act 1955 (NZ) claims.[96] The High Court has jurisdiction to consider constructive trust claims to property, which is not ousted if the subject matter is Māori land. That was established in the Court of Appeal case in *Grace v Grace*.[97] The Family Court is unlikely to have equitable jurisdiction of that nature (it does not have an equivalent to section 237 of Māori Land Act which imports that jurisdiction to the Māori Land Court).

---

92 Te Ture Whenua Māori Bill 2016 ('TTWM Bill'), 126-2, as reported from the Māori Affairs Committee, Commentary (English version), 1.

93 See Waitangi Tribunal, above n 12.

94 TTWM Bill, cl 253(2)(a) and (b).

95 TTWM Bill, cl 253(3).

96 See Māori Affairs Select Committee, *Te Ture Whenua Māori Bill 2016: Submission for the Judges of the Māori Land Court*, 11 August 2016, [189]–[191]. On 4 April 2017, the Committee of the whole House supported extending the jurisdiction of the Māori Land Court to Family Protection Act 1955 matters. See House of Representatives Supplementary Order Paper 4 April 2017 (2/SOP No. 279).

97 *Grace v Grace*, above n 51.

5.2. PROPERTY (RELATIONSHIPS) ACT REFORM

In May 2016, New Zealand's Law Commission commenced a review of the PRA. A principal issue being considered is '[w]hether the Act gives rise to matters of particular concern to Māori and how these should be addressed'.[98] One reform avenue for consideration could be enabling the Family Court to take into consideration Māori land interests when ordering compensation 'for the absence of an interest in the family home' as enabled by section 11B of the PRA. Section 11B(2) states that if there is 'no family home' under section 11B(1) then the court must award an equal share in other relationship property as it thinks just to compensate for the absence of a family home.

In cases involving General land where section 11B has been applied, one partner or spouse has usually been awarded a half-share in traceable proceeds of the sale of the family home which occurred after separation.[99] In *Brenssell v Brenssell*, the Court stated that the then section 11(3) of the Matrimonial Property Act 1976 (NZ) (which was replaced by section 11B of the PRA) required the Court to do its best to determine the value of the family home that it would expect the parties to have had, if they had owned one.[100] The Court of Appeal concluded that the sale price of the former family home was a fair indicator of appropriate compensation for the absence of a matrimonial home.

Section 11B has also been applied to family homes which are still owned by one partner, but for some reason do not come within the definition of 'relationship property'. For example in *Manuel v Manuel*, the wife was awarded a half interest in $30,000, being the value of the family home occupied by the parties prior to the separation but owned by a family trust of which her former husband was the trustee.[101] Therefore, it appears that a section 11B adjustment could be applied to award a non-owning spouse or partner a half share in the value of the home attached to Māori land.

But as it stands currently, section 6 of the PRA would exclude the court from taking Māori land interests into account when dividing relationship property under section 11B.[102] Therefore legislative change, allowing the court to consider

---

98 Law Commission (NZ), *Review of the Property (Relationships) Act 1976* <www.lawcom.govt.nz/our-projects/review-property-relationships-act-1976> accessed 16.04.2017.

99 For example, *Buckman v Buckman* (1979) 3 MPC 20 (SC), where the family home was sold after separation and a sum was awarded based on the value of the former family home; *Van Koeverden v Van Koeverden* (1981) 4 MPC 205 (HC), where the family home was sold by the husband and the wife was awarded an equal share of the traceable net proceeds; *Wilson v Wilson* (1981) 4 MPC 215 (HC) at 217, where the wife was also awarded a half-share of the proceeds following sale of the home by the husband, traced to a different property that had been purchased with the proceeds by the husband as a new family home with his second wife.

100 *Brenssell v Brenssell* [1998] NZFLR 28 (CA).

101 *Manuel v Manuel* (1978) 1 MPC 136 (SC).

102 PRA, s 6: 'Nothing in this act shall apply in respect of any Māori land within the meaning of Te Ture Whenua Māori Act 1993.'

family homes attached to Māori land when making a section 11B determination, would be necessary to give effect to this solution.[103]

A further option would be to introduce a new legislative provision permitting the court to take into account Māori land interests, broadly modelled on section 9A of the PRA which applies in respect of separate property.[104] Section 9A(2) provides that any increase in value of separate property that is attributable wholly or in part, directly or indirectly, to the actions of the non-owning partner becomes relationship property.[105] Each partner's share in that particular relationship property is then determined in accordance with their respective contributions to the increase in value of the separate property.[106] A similar mechanism could be provided for non-owning parties to be compensated for their actions in increasing the value of the family home, or other improvements, on Māori land. This would not categorise the Māori land itself as relationship property, but rather compensation would be effected by adjusting the division of other relationship property to recompense for the loss of the family home from the pool of relationship property.

Even with legislative involvement, adjustment of the division of relationship property is not without issues. Under a section 11B adjustment, the property-owning partner may not have adequate compensation available. If a provision based on section 9A was introduced, the pool of relationship property may still be too small to sufficiently compensate the non-owning partner for the absence of an interest in the family home, as the family home is usually the major asset. Issues of causation, degree of contribution, evidence, and inflation will undoubtedly arise.[107] However, in trying to strike a policy balance between retaining Māori land in the hands of its owners while compensating non-owning partner's for their contributions, it may provide direction on how to determine and give effect to a non-owning partner's rights.[108] There is arguably a need for legislative amendment, to avoid the effect of deterring non-owning partners from investing in Māori land, as was the issue in *Epiha Hills*.[109] Such a result is inconsistent with the utilisation tenet of the Māori Land Act.

With the Law Commission's current review, and the probable reform of the Māori Land Act on the near horizon, it is now timely to encourage further discussion on the issues raised in this chapter.

---

103 As emphasised by J Te Rata, above n 52.

104 As expressed by J Te Rata, above n 52 at 9.

105 PRA, s 9A(2).

106 PRA, s 9A(2)(b).

107 See *Nation v Nation* [2005] NZLR 46 (CA); *Palmer v Palmer* (1982) 5 MPC 116 (HC); *Ellis v Ellis* (2008) 27 FRNZ 266 (HC); *Smith v Smith* (1987) 4 NZFLR 569 (DC).

108 J Te Rata, above n 52 at 9.

109 *Epiha Hills – Kaiopoi MR 873 Blk XI Section 71B*, above n 73.

6. CONCLUSION

For New Zealand, the issue of whether Indigenous property should be relationship property has only started to gain judicial, legislative, and political traction. This is because, until recently, few lived-in residential family homes have been built on Māori land. Broad questions for New Zealand include: Why is the exclusion in our law? What are the characteristics of Māori land that justify it being an exception to the jurisdiction of the courts to determine a relationship property claim? Has the exclusion achieved the purpose for which it was intended? Are there improvements to the relationship between the PRA and Māori land which can be proposed? As New Zealand proceeds to focus on these questions, the debate is one that needs to connect with these issues internationally. These are complex issues for all countries with similar colonial histories to New Zealand to consider, and are an important component of modern family finances for many jurisdictions throughout the world.

CHAPTER 10

VALUATION OF RELATIONSHIP PROPERTY: AN EVALUATION OF PRACTICE AND PROCEDURE

Simon JEFFERSON and Paul MORIARTY

'Not everything that can be counted counts;
not everything that counts can be counted'[1]

1 WB CAMERON, *Informal Sociology: A Casual Introduction to Sociological Thinking*, Random House, New York 1963.

1. INTRODUCTION

This chapter addresses the topic of 'valuation' and considers how, when, and whether a property sharing regime should include 'rules on valuation'. The chapter will use the New Zealand Property (Relationships) Act 1976 ('PRA') to frame the discussion.

Rules are like clothes. They need to be adequate for the conditions. A straitjacket is of very limited utility. Relationship property litigation, no less than any other form of civil litigation, can be bedevilled by stultifying delay at considerable cost (both financial and personal) to litigants. Such delay is inimical to the delivery of justice and, in particular, to the inexpensive, simple, and speedy resolution of disputes, as is enjoined in the New Zealand statute.[2] In a real sense, that creates an impediment to access to justice.

Rules of civil procedure are designed to lubricate the litigation process. The question this chapter is designed to address is whether or not specific, or more precise, rules in relation to 'valuation' would enhance and improve the operation of property sharing regimes. This requires a consideration of the role valuation plays in the overall scheme of the PRA and a review of how issues of valuation have been addressed by the courts over the past 40 years (with particular reference to the role of the expert witness). It also requires an acknowledgment that so long as relationship property litigation continues to be conducted along orthodox, adversarial lines, the ability to make radical changes to the way in which valuation evidence is adduced and tested will be limited.

We conclude that, on balance, the introduction of 'rules on valuation' would not marry with the principles of property sharing regimes and the need for the court to maintain a considerable degree of flexibility in dealing with valuation issues.

2. THE RELEVANCE OF VALUE

2.1. THE SCHEME OF THE NEW ZEALAND STATUTE

The division of relationship property in New Zealand is determined by reference to the PRA. The principles governing such division are set out in Part 2 (Preliminary Provisions) of the PRA.[3]

---

2 Property (Relationships) Act 1976 (NZ) ('PRA'), s 1N(d).

3 See in particular, PRA ss 1M and 1N.

In the simplest representation of the process to be undertaken, division of relationship property may be seen in the following terms:

- IDENTIFY
- CLASSIFY
- VALUE
- DIVIDE
- ADJUST

Pursuant to section 20D of the PRA, the value of relationship property to be divided between the parties *must* be calculated by: (a) ascertaining the total *value* of the relationship property; and then (b) deducting from that total any secured or unsecured relationship debts. Plainly integral to the goal of achieving a just division of relationship property in accordance with the principles of the PRA, therefore, is the issue of valuation.

Yet valuation is not a science; nor does the PRA specify the principles to be applied in valuing relationship property.[4] It is, perhaps, hardly surprising that several important cases addressing valuation issues promptly (at least as that word is understood in juridical terms) found their way to the New Zealand Court of Appeal.[5]

In *Clark v Clark*, the Court was tasked with valuing superannuation rights.[6] Noting that a variety of approaches could be used, the Court set out its 'fundamental task' as being:[7]

> 'to select and apply an approach which, for the particular scheme and on the particular facts, most fairly reflects the contribution made to the marriage partnership by the other spouse.'

4 The Court of Appeal's frustration in this area was reflected 10 years after the PRA came into force in *Powell v Powell* [1987] 1 NZLR 192 (CA), which was characterised as a case concerned with 'general principles of valuation law' requiring a 'gentle reminder of basic valuation principles' (at 193). The Court was plainly mystified that its comments on a number of prior occasions had not sunk in: 'we may not have expressed ourselves forcefully enough' (also at 193). Its decision, whilst concerned with the valuation of the family home, did not (said the Court) turn on any point peculiar to the PRA.

5 *Haldane v Haldane* [1981] 1 NZLR 554 (CA); *Holt v Holt* [1987] 1 NZLR 85 (CA); *Callaghan v Callaghan* [1987] 2 NZLR 374 (CA); *Clark v Clark* [1987] 2 NZLR 385 (CA).

6 *Clark v Clark*, above n 5.

7 Ibid, at 386.

In so doing the Court of Appeal eschewed a template approach and emphasised the fact-specific nature of the enquiry in the context of 'contribution[s] made to the marriage partnership'.[8] Here, the Court sets down its marker:[9]

> 'relevant actuarial and accounting evidence can be useful in guiding the Court towards a figure intended to do justice between the parties, so long as such evidence is accepted as an aid rather than the answer.'

The relatively crude calculation undertaken by the Court, acknowledged as being 'obviously open to criticism',[10] might be chilling to a mathematician but in the context of relationship property division it is entirely consistent with the principles of the PRA. Indeed it might be argued that not all matters which might fall for consideration in assessing 'value' are, in fact, capable of 'valuation'. How, for example, does one value 'living standards' in terms of an analysis pursuant to section 15 of the PRA that is concerned with claims of economic disparity between the parties?[11] That is, ultimately, a judgement, a value judgement (to further confuse the semantics).

The real issue is whether, by utilising orthodox valuation methodology, a 'just division' is generally being achieved.[12] An allied concern is whether the means of addressing and testing valuation evidence is, of itself, inimical to an inexpensive, simple, and speedy resolution of questions arising under the PRA.

2.2. THE PURPOSE OF VALUATION IN THE RELATIONSHIP PROPERTY CONTEXT

In its standard paradigm, the division of relationship property involves a global division of all assets followed by appropriation of specific assets to one or other party with monetary adjustments being made between them to achieve the prescribed outcome. Where such monetary adjustments are required to be calculated (generally in circumstances where one or other party is retaining an asset on their side of the notional ledger or is being afforded the opportunity to acquire an asset as part of the division) the issue of valuation arises.

---

8 Ibid. A curious formulation given the entrenched equal division principles.

9 *Clark v Clark*, above n 5 at 391.

10 Ibid, at 389.

11 Amongst the interesting academic material available on this topic is J Jensen et al, 'The 2004 New Zealand Living Standards Survey: What Does it Signal about the Importance of Multiple Disadvantage?' (2007) 30 *Social Policy Journal of New Zealand* 110.

12 The suggestion that '"justice" in a matrimonial context is much more complex than is commonly appreciated' (*Carter v Carter* [2001] NZFLR 180 (HC) at [68]) opens up further, tantalising, possibilities for discussion beyond the scope of this chapter. Indeed, resort by the courts, when confronted by troublesome valuation issues, to comments about 'just division' and fairness do support that, at times, platitudes can trump principle.

Establishing the value of the relevant assets is, in such circumstances, an essential step in establishing just what monetary adjustments may need to be made. In the absence of statutory guidance, New Zealand courts have arrived at relevant values in a manner analogous to the valuation of assets for other purposes.

However, the overall purpose of having various assets valued is not necessarily to achieve, to a degree of scientific certainty, the value of a given asset (which might vary depending on the circumstances in which, and the purpose for which, the valuation is being sought) but:[13]

> 'to produce in a global sense a fair estimation of the worth of [the relationship] property so that its subsequent division will be achieved in a way which will be just as between the husband and the wife.'

This broad statement of principle reinforces the need to focus not so much on the valuation itself, but upon the justness of the division of property as between individuals whose relationship was not essentially commercial in nature and whose entitlements are not governed by economic models but by a statutory exhortation to achieve justice.[14]

3. VALUE DEFINED

Valuation allows the worth of an item to be expressed in monetary terms. Whilst the word 'value' is used throughout the PRA, there is no accompanying definition. The formulation long adopted, and applied, by the courts in New Zealand is that of the willing seller/willing buyer. This derives primarily from *Hatrick v Commissioner of Inland Revenue*[15] (not a matrimonial case) which was then applied in *Haldane v Haldane*[16] and is said to be rooted firmly in practicalities ('not to be overlaid by philosophical or legal niceties').[17] The exercise is a hypothetical one and may involve certain assumptions which do not accord with the particular facts of the case.[18]

The ultimate question in valuation is: what is the sum of money for which an asset or liability should exchange, on the valuation date, between a knowledgeable, willing, but not anxious buyer, and a knowledgeable, willing,

---

13 *Reid v Reid* [1980] 2 NZLR 270 (CA) at 272.

14 The provisions of ss 11 and 13 of the PRA, with their emphasis on *equal* sharing, plainly act as a restraint on the scope to develop the concept of 'a just division'. See *Garty v Garty* [1997] 3 NZLR 66 (HC) for an analysis of the approach to be adopted.

15 *Hatrick v Commissioner of Inland Revenue* [1963] NZLR 641 (CA).

16 *Haldane v Haldane*, above n 5.

17 *Hatrick v Commissioner of Inland Revenue*, above n 15 at 661.

18 *Holt v Holt*, above n 5.

but not anxious seller in an arm's length transaction, after proper marketing and where the parties had each acted in a wise and prudent fashion. Importantly, however, in the relationship property context, the parties must always be included as a 'hypothetical buyer'. That means that the value to be attributed is not limited to the sum of money which could be realised from a hypothetical unrelated buyer. The value of retention by one or other party must be considered. Non-commercial factors which might confound an orthodox valuation are introduced.

Relationship property valuations per se are based on the notion of 'fair value', which the Court of Appeal in 1996 endorsed as follows:[19]

> 'Fair value is based on the desire to be equitable to both parties. This recognises that as the transaction is not on the open market, the buyer has not been able to look around for the lowest price, nor has the seller been able to hold out for the highest price. Fair value recognises what the seller gives up in value and what the buyer acquires through the transaction.'

It is the last sentence which is crucial.[20] In many cases under the PRA, one party will retain an asset and the other will relinquish an interest in it. The fair value for such a transfer must thus be determined based on the parties' respective positions such that the valuation result is fair and just having regard to those positions, with no inequity arising to either party from the valuation of that asset, a stance which is consistent with the overarching requirements of the PRA.

Valuation can never simply be an exercise in mathematics. No two situations are the same. Overlaying a background of ever-changing economic and social conditions, the task of the valuer becomes one of fine judgement and assessment. The valuer is looking at just one part of the much wider collection of issues. Whatever value may be attributed to an item of property will be just one part of the mix of information which the court must consider in reaching a view as to the justness of the overall outcome.

3.1. WHAT IS BEING VALUED

Valuation issues arise in two contexts under the PRA – the valuation of 'property' (which can be as tangible as a piece of land or less tangible, such as

---

19 *Re James Davern Ltd; Davern v Davern* (1996) CA 47, 79/96, 24 April 1996 at 6.

20 An interesting comparative provision is s 339 of the New Zealand Property Law Act 2007, where the court is empowered, amongst other things, to require a co-owner of property to purchase the share of one or more other co-owners 'at a fair and reasonable price'. With no other statutory guidance provided, it has been held that this requires the court 'to adjust the rights of the co-owners in an equitable manner': *Long v Moore* (1989) 1 NZ ConvC 190,239 (HC) at [8], endorsed in *Bunyan v Parish* [2016] NZHC 2225 at [41].

business goodwill) and the calculation of compensatory adjustments by virtue of the provisions of the PRA.[21] The former is, generally, addressed by 'valuation evidence' adduced in the form of expert opinion testimony. The latter is the product of the exercise of the court's discretion informed by the evidence but subject to the broad dictates of justice.[22]

Debates, or disputes, as to the existence and/or characteristics of assets (the identification and classification issues) frequently obscure, or become confused with, issues of valuation. For example, in a business valuation the distinction between 'personal goodwill' (generally viewed as of no value in a relationship property sense) and 'business goodwill' (generally regarded as integral to the value of the business) is really a distinction which goes to the characteristics of the property to be valued rather than the value itself.[23] Only when the characteristics of the property in question have been clearly delineated is it possible to address the issue of valuation of that asset.

Valuation of many common assets is a relatively routine exercise if, at times, somewhat less than precise. Household chattels and family cars are seldom of great value in the overall context of the relationship property to be divided and resort to the appraisals of second-hand dealers or car dealers, coupled with a relatively robust analysis by the court, serves the statutory purpose (although, in a theoretical sense, there is no reason why these assets should be valued with any less rigour than any other asset).

The valuation of real estate (most usually the family home) poses its own difficulties in rapidly changing markets and where an option to acquire the property is being considered.[24] Moreover, the typical model of valuation of real estate relies on a combination of size (floor and land area) and market evidence (by definition historic with exact comparisons never easy to come by).

The valuation of a life interest, a reversionary interest, or an interest in a non-discretionary trust requires consideration of a complex range of factors but, essentially, is well within a suitably qualified valuer's scope.[25]

More complex are valuations of business enterprises (be they farms, partnerships, professional practices, or shareholdings in private companies). *M v B* is a salutary case in point.[26] The husband was an equity partner in a

---

21 Such as s 15 (economic disparity) or s 18B (compensation for contributions made post-separation).

22 For example, both ss 15 and 18B of the PRA enjoin the court to award compensation 'if it considers it just'. This, it is submitted, goes not only to the issue of whether there should be an award but also the quantum of that award.

23 See, for example, *Thompson v Thompson* [2015] NZSC 26, [2015] 1 NZLR 593.

24 See *GFM v JAM* [2013] NZCA 660, [2014] NZFLR 418; see also *Scott v Williams* [2016] NZCA 356, [2016] NZFLR 499.

25 See R Wise, 'What's It Worth' (2016) 14(1) *Trust Quarterly Review* 12 <www.step.org/journal/tqr-march-2016/what-s-it-worth> accessed 31.05.2017.

26 *M v B* [2006] 3 NZLR 660 (CA).

thriving Auckland law practice. It was accepted that his interest in that firm was relationship property and that it should be valued in terms of the model outlined in *Z v Z (No 2)*.[27] The fundamental dispute centred around the calculation derived from that approach. Two highly experienced and esteemed valuers were retained by the respective parties. For the husband it was contended that the correct answer was $182,000; for the wife a figure of $1.341 million was propounded.[28] The disparity between the parties caused the Court of Appeal to revisit, and reiterate the essence of, the model adopted by each party from *Z v Z (No 2)*. The guidance provided in that judgment had, it seemed, become adopted as a template, with a cautionary predicatory phrase – 'as is often the case in other fields, valuations may be made by more than one method to verify the outcome'[29] – having been apparently overlooked. As Robertson J noted in *M v B*, whatever approach is adopted 'must include clear and unambiguous reality checks. Justice between parties will not be achieved in circumstances in which formulaic approaches lead to outcomes which are manifestly unsustainable.'[30]

The difficulty with this statement of principle is determining what exactly it means: probably no more, and no less, than a reminder that the court needs to keep its eye focused not on issues of valuation as an empirical exercise but on the statutorily prescribed 'just' outcome. The emphasis on seeking to achieve *justice* can result in the unedifying spectacle of courts endeavouring to wrestle with the arithmetic.[31]

A recent Family Court case, *Tennison v Tennison*, left Judge Walsh struggling through competing share valuations of a once-thriving business, adversely affected by the Canterbury earthquake.[32] What had been valued at $1,310,000 prior to the earthquake (a figure adopted by the parties for the purpose of concluding an agreement pursuant to section 21A of the PRA)[33] was now valued at nil (for the husband) and $680,000 (for the wife). The evidence was heard over four days, most of which appears to have focused on the expert evidence. The experts had

---

27 *Z v Z (No 2)* [1997] 2 NZLR 258 (CA).

28 By the time this matter reached the Court of Appeal in *M v B* above n 26, the wife's lawyer was contending for a figure of $2.6 million which the Court of Appeal found a difficult calculation to accept if the simple but pragmatic question was asked: 'Is that the sum which the man and his wife would have paid in order to acquire the interest in the firm?' (at [71]). The exercise on which both parties engaged was described as 'undignified' (at [74]), leading to a conclusion (at least on the calculations promoted by the wife) lacking 'economic reality' (at [91]) and amounting to a loss of perspective ('the possibilities of *Z v Z (No 2)* became an end in themselves' [at 91]).

29 *Z v Z (No 2)*, above n 27 at 291.

30 *M v B*, above n 26 at [55].

31 *Clark v Clark*, above n 5; *Callaghan v Callaghan*, above n 5; *M v B*, above n 26.

32 *Tennison v Tennison* [2014] NZFC 5335, [2015] NZFLR 185.

33 And, incidentally, propounded by the valuer who ultimately advised the husband in the hearing.

conferred but could not resolve their differences. Two areas of dispute emerged: the methodologies of valuation employed by the competing experts; and the validity of the underlying assumptions each valuer had made. In the context of the case (seeking to set aside the agreement on the grounds of 'serious injustice')[34] it was sufficient for Judge Walsh to simply conclude that (on either analysis) there had been a substantial reduction in value of the shareholding. Beyond that, Judge Walsh would not (and felt he could not) go, commenting: 'I accept the valuation of the shares is essentially a speculative exercise.'[35] That speculation was thus reserved for another day. No one reading the decision, including the parties, will be any clearer as to what the answer may be.

A more prosaic example, exhibiting a robust approach to a potentially complex issue, is *Rivers v Rivers*.[36] At issue was valuation of the husband's interest in an employment-related superannuation scheme. The husband had joined the scheme many years prior to the marriage (17 years of his membership of 26 years pre-dated the marriage). Section 8(1)(i) of the PRA operated so that only the proportion of the scheme attributable to the marriage was relationship property. The husband sought a simple pro rata method of valuation; the wife favoured a more complex dual valuation method which would bring into account significant salary increases during the relevant period (and thus a higher level of contributions made by the husband during the marriage). A third possibility ('the price paid' method) was also noted. The two experts accepted that each of the possible methodologies 'had its difficulties' and that there was no necessarily 'right' answer.[37] The Court opted for the 'simplicity and transparency of the pro rata method'.[38] In doing so there is more than a hint that as a pure exercise in valuation, the outcome may have been different. However, the exercise was always to be overlaid by the need to achieve a fair outcome.

In *Clayton v Clayton*, the New Zealand Supreme Court held that the particular concatenation of powers held by the husband in relation to a trust amounted, in effect, to a general power of appointment in relation to the assets of the trust and were therefore 'tantamount to ownership'[39] and thus constituted 'property' in terms of section 2 of the PRA. What then is the value of such powers? In the earlier Court of Appeal decision, it was reasoned that 'the value of the right to the holder of the power … [was] the value of the property received in the event that the power were exercised'.[40] Grappling with this

---

34 PRA, s 21J.
35 *Tennison v Tennison*, above n 32 at [185].
36 *Rivers v Rivers* [2005] NZFLR 372 (FC).
37 Ibid, at [6].
38 Ibid, at [30].
39 *Clayton v Clayton [Vaughan Road Property Trust]* [2016] NZSC 29, [2016] 1 NZLR 551 at [104], following *Re Triffit's Settlement* [1958] Ch 852 at 861 and *Re Watts* [1931] 2 Ch 302 at 305.
40 *Clayton v Clayton* [2015] NZCA 30, [2015] 3 NZLR 293 at [113].

'valuation question',[41] the Supreme Court concluded that treating the powers as having a value equal to that of the assets to which they applied, was appropriate.[42] It said:[43]

> 'if Mr Clayton's powers and entitlements under the [illegible] deed were for sale, it is hard to see why Mr Clayton would not attribute to them precisely the same value as he would attribute to the net assets over which those powers give him virtually absolute control.'

Further, the Court commented that this approach to valuation was consistent with prior authority.[44] This approach is undoubtedly right in the somewhat unusual circumstances of the *Clayton* case.[45] However, where the powers in question cannot be used to directly access trust assets (or where there are proper fiduciary constraints) attributing a value to such powers may be more problematic.[46]

3.2. WHEN TO VALUE

The shifting sands of 'value' attributable to any specific asset and the inevitable (and variable) delays between parties separating and an achievement of a just division of relationship property[47] requires some certainty about the 'date of valuation'.

As a general proposition, where values can be attributed to property with confidence, they are to be contemporary values at the hearing date. In section 2G, the PRA provides the foundation principle that value is presumed to be determined as at the date of hearing but offers some flexibility to settle upon another date 'in its discretion'.[48] A simple, and obvious, example is valuing a car retained by one party after separation, to acknowledge its character as a depreciating asset.[49] The onus is on the party seeking departure from a 'hearing date' valuation to demonstrate why justice would be best served in that fashion.

Post-separation events affecting value may be better addressed separately by a specific provision, such as section 18B which provides for adjustments to post-separation contributions by either party.[50] Adjusting the 'date of valuation'

---

41 *Clayton v Clayton [Vaughan Road Property Trust]*, above n 39 at [101].
42 Ibid, at [104].
43 Ibid, at [105].
44 Ibid, at n 102: *Z v Z* [1989] 3 NZLR 413 (CA) and *Walker v Walker* [2007] NZCA 30, [2007] 2 NZLR 261.
45 J Palmer, 'What to Do about Trusts?', ch 8.
46 J Palmer, 'Controlling the Trust' (2011) 12(3) *Otago Law Review* 473, 492.
47 Notwithstanding s 1N(d) encouraging a speedy resolution.
48 See *Burgess v Beaven* [2012] NZSC 71, [2013] 1 NZLR 129 at [23]–[26].
49 *Wareing v Wareing* FC Christchurch FAM-2003-009-3112, 17 June 2005.
50 *Bullians v Bullians* HC Hamilton CIV-2005-419-1283, 7 December 2005.

for the purpose of delivering broad justice to a party who would otherwise be disappointed by a hearing date valuation is no longer the only route to a just outcome.[51] Yet it does remain a weapon in the court's arsenal in appropriate cases.

4. EVIDENCE OF VALUE – THE EXPERT WITNESS

As the preamble to the United States Declaration of Independence would have it, some truths are self-evident. Some, however, are required to be proved by evidence. Reliance on expert opinion evidence has been described as the process by which the court, as fact-finder, receives sufficient information to enable it to properly perform its role.[52]

In relationship property matters, resort to an expert to establish the value of an asset or some 'property' (as defined in section 2 of the PRA) is commonplace and inevitable. Invariably the value of an unrealised asset will be a matter of opinion and the court will need to obtain, and rely upon, expert testimony in that regard:[53]

> 'No one will deny that the law should in some way effectively use expert knowledge whenever it will aid in settling disputes. The only question is as to how it can do so best.'

Less flatteringly, some say that expert evidence 'occupies a grey area between fact evidence and judicial determination'.[54]

In New Zealand, the evidential foundation for the adducing of expert testimony is to be found in the Evidence Act 2006 (NZ). Section 12A of the Family Courts Act 1980 (NZ) provides that, in proceedings under the Act, the provisions of the Evidence Act 2006 (NZ) apply but with the proviso that the court hearing the proceeding may receive any evidence, whether or not admissible under the Evidence Act 2006 (NZ), that the court considers may assist it to determine the proceeding.

The starting point is section 23 of the Evidence Act 2006 (NZ), which provides:

> **23 Opinion rule**
>
> A statement of an opinion is not admissible in a proceeding, except as provided by section 24 or 25.

---

51 *Walker v Walker*, above n 44.

52 *RA v R* [2010] NZCA 57, (2010) 25 CRNZ 138.

53 L Hand, 'Historical and Practical Considerations regarding Expert Testimony' (1901) 15(1) *Harvard Law Review* 40, 40.

54 E Arnold and E Soriano, *The Recent Evolution of Expert Evidence in Selected Common Law Jurisdictions Around the World: A Commissioned Study for the Canadian Institute of Chartered Business Valuators*, 23 January 2013, 1.

Following from that, section 25(1) of the Evidence Act 2006 (NZ) provides:

> **25 Admissibility of expert opinion evidence**
>
> (1) An opinion by an expert that is part of expert evidence offered in a proceeding is admissible if the fact-finder is likely to obtain substantial help from the opinion in understanding other evidence in the proceeding or in ascertaining any fact that is of consequence to the determination of the proceeding.

Expert opinion is the most significant, and frequently utilised, exception to the exclusionary rule against admitting opinion evidence. The role of the expert witness has been the subject of exhaustive analysis by the courts both in New Zealand and elsewhere. A full review of that material is not called for here. Highlighting key issues will suffice: experts are an expensive commodity and are also not easy to identify; their enquiries can be time consuming and may not favour a speedy resolution of matters; in addition, expert testimony (like all other evidence) must be given only appropriate weight. As Evan Bell notes, 'It must be as influential in the overall decision-making process as it deserves: no more, no less.'[55]

Two fundamental points immediately arise. First, the value of expert testimony is a function, both of the capability of the expert and of the capability of the court to assess (make sense of) and synthesise the testimony in the context of its overall decision-making role. Secondly, it is well understood that it is the duty of experts to assist the court, such duty overriding any obligation to a party.[56]

4.1. THE CAPABILITY OF THE EXPERT

Expert witnesses must be properly qualified, as is made clear by the definition of both 'expert' and 'expert evidence' in the Evidence Act 2004 (NZ). 'Expert' is defined as 'a person who has specialised knowledge or skill based on training, study, or experience' and 'expert evidence' is defined as 'the evidence of an expert based on the specialised knowledge or skill of that expert and includes evidence given in the form of an opinion'.[57]

Experts with special skills or knowledge beyond what is commonly known in the community are often able to draw inferences and reach conclusions from the

---

55 E Bell, 'Judicial Assessment of Expert Evidence' (2010) 2 *Judicial Studies Institute Journal* 55, 55.

56 See Schedule 4, High Court Rules 2016 (NZ) ('HCR'), Code of Conduct for Expert Witnesses.

57 Evidence Act 2006, s 4.

available evidence that may not otherwise be apparent to the court. Put simply, the function of an expert witness is to:[58]

> 'educate or inform the court about the relevant aspects of the witness's speciality to enable the court itself to assess the evidence which, without that tuition, the court would be unable to do.'

Expert evidence presented to the court should at all times 'be, and should be seen to be, the independent product of the expert, uninfluenced as to form or content by the exigencies of litigation'.[59] Pure independence, however, is difficult to attain and maintain.[60]

There is also the need, particularly in a relatively small community such as New Zealand, to avoid the potential for 'reputation' or 'experience' to be seen as a substitute for genuine 'expertise'. They are different things. A lawyer, although no doubt better versed in matters legal than the average citizen, is not ipso facto a legal expert. An accountant familiar with the well-known and widely disseminated principles of business valuation is not, automatically, an expert in such matters.[61] Identifying an expert who is indeed a real expert can thus be a challenge. Many professional bodies around the world have now established qualifications and credentials to identify members who hold expertise in particular fields.[62]

However, the court must at all times guard against being in thrall to the siren song of expertise. The integrity of the mathematics and the methodology is key. The fact that 'valuation' is an ever-evolving area in terms of methodology and understanding should not be overlooked. The salutary experience in the United Kingdom of Professor Roy Meadow, once lauded for his work in the area of infant mortality, having his evidence discredited (and subsequently being subjected to severe professional disciplinary sanction) is testament to the need to ensure that expert evidence is, indeed, reliable and trustworthy.[63]

---

58 RN Chesterman, 'The Accountant as Expert Witness', speech delivered to the Institute of Chartered Accountants, Sydney, 12 March 2000, 2 <http://archive.sclqld.org.au/judgepub/2001/CH_Dealing%20with%20Expert%20Witnesses.pdf> accessed 31.05.2017.

59 *Whitehouse v Jordan* [1981] 1 WLR 246 (HL) at 256–57.

60 Nor is lack of independence, of itself, a basis for excluding evidence: *Lisiate v R* [2013] NZCA 129, (2013) 26 CRNZ 292. A lack of independence is a matter which goes to the weight to be placed on the evidence rather than a basis for exclusion: *Commissioner of Inland Revenue v BNZ Investments Ltd* [2009] NZCA 47, (2009) 19 PRNZ 553.

61 Many disciplines have their own standards or codes of conduct with which those purporting to exercise expertise are required to comply (eg New Zealand chartered accountants are required to comply with Advisory Engagement Standard Number 2: Independent Business Valuation Engagements (AES-2)).

62 Chartered Accountants Australia and New Zealand, the governing body for chartered accountants in Australasia, now certifies those members demonstrating competence in valuation as being 'Business Valuation Specialists'.

63 *General Medical Council v Meadow* [2006] EWCA Civ 1390, [2007] QB 462.

Opinions outside the strict boundaries of the witness's acknowledged expertise (sometimes little more than the expert's own inference from the facts) may be invested with 'a spurious appearance of authority'.[64] It is not unknown for experts to embellish their evidence with impermissible opinions[65] or, indeed, to cover outright advocacy with a cloak of expertise.

4.2. THE COURT'S ASSESSMENT OF THE EXPERT EVIDENCE

The touchstone is the test of substantial helpfulness. Expert opinion evidence is admissible if the court is likely to obtain substantial help from the opinion in understanding other evidence in the proceeding or in ascertaining any fact that is of consequence to the determination of the proceeding.[66] In the relationship property context, valuation evidence will readily come under that rubric.

It is not just the question of admissibility of expert evidence to which the court must turn its mind but also the question of weight. And the weight to be given any evidence (expert or otherwise) is necessarily to be calculated in the context of the entire issue for determination, the assessment of a 'just division'. At no point does the court subjugate its role to adjudicate on an issue to the expert. Expert evidence unchallenged either by cross-examination or counter-opinion will inevitably carry considerable weight but need not necessarily be accepted by the court. Where challenges are mounted, it is the court's function to carefully scrutinise such matters as the qualifications and credibility of the expert(s), the reasons for the expert opinion expressed, and the facts upon which such opinions are based.[67] The question, however, is to what extent a judge (particularly a Family Court judge frequently over-burdened by the sheer volume of the caseload of a primary court of jurisdiction) is equipped to undertake that task.

Difficulties inherent in expert evidence called by one party or the other (and there is no reason why court-appointed experts would not be susceptible to the same difficulties) are well known.[68] In an extra-judicial paper by Sperling JA,

---

64 *HG v R* [1999] HCA 2, (1999) 197 CLR 414 at [44].

65 In *Creighton v Creighton* HC Auckland, CIV-2003-404-6892, 10 September 2004, an accountant was chastised for expressing the view that an asset under consideration was not relationship property.

66 NZ courts dealing with the admissibility of expert evidence have endorsed the non-exhaustive guidelines for assessing the reliability of such evidence contained in the US Supreme Court case of *Daubert v Merrell Dow Pharmaceuticals* 509 US 579 (1993), although it is to be noted that these guidelines are primarily related to the reliability of scientific evidence and do not readily translate to an assessment of valuation evidence.

67 *Crichton v Crichton* [1991] NZFLR 529 (HC).

68 For example, the phenomenon of unconscious bias – see *Muller v Steamship Co Pty Ltd v Overseas Tankship (UK) Ltd* [1963] NSWR 737.

'Expert Evidence: The Problem of Bias and Other Things', he commented, amongst other things, that:[69]

> 'An appearance of objectivity is a marketable attribute. Cross-examination or contrary evidence may unmask dissemblance or may not. A judge is ill-equipped to diagnose bias in an expert witness.'

And further:

> 'Judges are interested in valid fact-finding. So long as the adversarial system continues unremittingly, however, the interests of litigants in presenting expert evidence that may win the case will prevail over the interests of judges in obtaining objective assistance on technical issues as a basis for valid fact-finding.'

Bell illuminates the difficulties faced by courts in discharging their responsibility to weigh expert evidence and determine its probative value.[70] Noting that '[t]he evidence of experts has proliferated in modern litigation' and that it 'is often determinative of one or more central issues in a case',[71] Bell highlights (under 13 headings) the hazards of dealing with expert testimony. These include the need to consider expert evidence in the context of all other evidence; and the need (and ability) to assess the quality of the expert's reasoning, and the objectivity and expertise of the expert. To this litany should, perhaps, be added the need to remain alive and alert to the evolution of economic theory which could render traditional valuation approaches open to re-consideration. In the context of this chapter (and the question it is addressing), warning bells sound. Prescriptive rules may smooth out some of the bumps in the litigation road but possibly at the cost of overlooking the inherent difficulties which can, and frequently do, attach to the presentation of expert testimony.

The role of the expert witness has been the subject of some evaluation in both Australia and the United Kingdom with the intention of greasing the wheels of justice or, more precisely, improving access to justice and reducing the cost of litigation. These reviews identified several common issues. First, there is the potential for partisanship and lack of objectivity (illuminating the well-recognised tension between the objective, informative role of the expert and the adversarial nature of litigation). Secondly, experts can exceed their area of expertise. Thirdly, evidence may serve to confound, rather than to clarify. And fourthly, expert evidence is often costly and causes delay.

---

69 HD Sperling, 'Expert Evidence: The Problem of Bias and Other Things' (2000) 4 *Judicial Review* 429, 432.

70 E Bell, above n 55.

71 Ibid, at 55.

In the United Kingdom, the 1996 Woolf Report led to the implementation of new rules of civil procedure which, in simple terms, provide as follows:[72]

- The court has a duty to restrict expert evidence to what is 'reasonably required' to resolve proceedings.
- Experts have a duty to assist the court, which overrides any duty to the person/party from whom instructions are received.
- No party may call an expert or use expert evidence without permission from the court.
- The court can direct that evidence is given by a single expert, or by an expert jointly selected and instructed by the parties, or by the court and instructed jointly by both parties. Directions for single experts precludes the parties from calling their own expert witnesses.
- The court may direct a private discussion between experts to identify issues and to reach agreement where possible.
- An assessor may be appointed to assist the court in any matter in which they have skill or experience.
- Expert evidence must be provided in written form, unless otherwise directed by the court.
- An expert's report must acknowledge the duty owed to the court and note all instructions provided to him/her (instructions are not privileged but limits apply to disclosure).
- A party may put written questions to the single expert or expert instructed by the other party, but only for the purposes of clarification (unless the court or other party agrees to other questions).
- An expert may ask the court for directions to assist them in their function.
- The court can direct that a party must provide information not reasonably available to the other party.
- Where a party has disclosed an expert's report, any party may use that report as evidence.
- A party who fails to disclose an expert's report may not use that report at trial.

The new rules were supplemented by a specific Practice Direction in relation to expert evidence.[73] A discussion paper generated by the Family Court of Australia in 2002 addressed the same issues and made 24 recommendations more or less along the same lines. In New Zealand, the Code of Conduct for Expert Witnesses contained in Schedule 4 of the High Court Rules 2016 (NZ) has been universally adopted in the Family Court although (somewhat surprisingly) it is neither part

---

72 H Woolf, 'Access to Justice: Final Report to the Lord Chancellor on the Civil Justice System in England and Wales', HMSO, London 1996.

73 United Kingdom Ministry of Justice, Practice Direction 35 – Experts and Assessors.

of the District Court Rules 2014 (NZ) nor the Family Court Rules 2002 (NZ). All expert witnesses are expected to comply with that Code and to certify that they have done so.

4.3. PRACTICE AND PROCEDURE

In New Zealand, both the High Court Rules 2016 (NZ) and the District Court Rules 2014 (NZ) give procedural guidance to the calling and management of expert evidence.[74] Of particular note is the ability of the court to appoint, on its own initiative, an independent expert to inquire into and report on any question of fact or opinion (not involving questions of law or construction).[75]

Of some practical import is the court's authority to direct a conference of expert witnesses[76] and even to appoint, with the consent of the parties, an independent expert to convene and conduct such a conference.[77] Such conferences are protected as being without prejudice unless otherwise agreed by the parties.[78] It may be that this provision (essentially a form of mediation between experts) could be given more teeth to greater assist the court.

These court rules, in practice, provide experts with a wide role in the court process. The requirement for valuation evidence to be provided to the court (and exchanged by the parties) in written form ensures the abolition of any vestige of 'trial by ambush'. Case management provides for timely exchange of this information and can (and should) prescribe a process on a case-by-case basis by which valuers endeavour to refine their differences to ensure that the court is troubled only by those matters on which there is genuine controversy. For example, experts are routinely encouraged to confer and provide a joint statement outlining areas of agreement and disagreement (and the reasons).[79] Case management is an aid to effectiveness and not an end in itself (a servant, not a master). Unduly prescriptive rules may in fact impede rather than enhance the process of achieving a just result.

One, rather inelegantly described, method dealing with differing experts which has evolved is the process of 'hot tubbing'.[80] In essence, this involves experts giving evidence at the same time and in each other's presence. The experts are sworn in together, and sit in front of the judge, who puts the same questions and challenges to each expert in turn, effectively acting as 'chair' of a debate between the experts, with the experts also, if permitted by the judge, able to put questions

74 High Court Rules ('HCR') rr 9.36–9.46; District Court Rules 2014 ('DCR'), rr 9.27–9.37.
75 HCR, r 9.36; DCR, r 9.27.
76 HCR, r 9.44; DCR, r 9.35.
77 HCR, r 9.44(3); DCR, r 9.35(3).
78 HCR, r 9.44(6); DCR, r 9.35(6).
79 HCR, r 9.44; DCR, r 3.68.2.
80 This process is available under HCR, r 9.46.

to each other.[81] The objective of a 'hot tub' is to put the two experts on an equal footing and to allow the court to concentrate on the real issues between them, with the experts discussing their differences in professional opinion in real time. This is said to result in a significant reduction in court time by avoiding separate cross-examination of each expert, and an increased likelihood that weak or flawed expert evidence will be revealed.

However, the process has its weaknesses. Experts who are more confident and assertive can dominate the exchange and have a greater impact than would otherwise be the case based on their expert evidence. In addition, hot tubbing requires that the judge has the time to prepare for, and accept, a more involved role in the proceedings.

Section 38 of the PRA permits the court to appoint someone 'to make an inquiry into the matters of fact in issue between the parties, and to report thereon to the court'. Generally this provision is viewed in the context of obtaining relevant financial information and, in that regard, is one weapon in a veritable arsenal[82] to be turned against a reluctant or recalcitrant non-disclosing litigant. But it need not be limited to a mechanism for mere disclosure. In practice (and without doing undue violence to the strict wording of the section) this, arguably underused, provision provides a means of regulating and managing the process of obtaining valuation evidence.[83] There are several cases in which section 38 of the PRA has been utilised to address valuation issues.[84] Moreover, suggestion that resort to this provision is a 'last resort' was well and truly debunked in a recent High Court decision.[85]

Restrictions on the filing of expert evidence are in place in some jurisdictions. Under Part 35 of the Civil Procedure Rules 1998 (UK), there is a prohibition on the calling of an expert or the filing of an expert's report without the court's permission. Seeking permission requires identification of the expert and, more especially, the field in which the expert evidence is required and the issues the expert will be seeking to address. Given the fundamental importance of valuation to the division of relationship property, it is doubtful that such a restriction is of

---

81 For a full description of the process, see *Commerce Commission v Cards NZ Ltd (No 2)* (2009) 19 PRNZ 748 (HC).

82 Including orders for discovery (Family Court Rules 2002, rr 140–55).

83 See *Lavas v Taliano* HC Auckland CIV-2008-404-5609, 31 March 2009; *Cleland v Dixon* [2013] NZHC 2700; *JCB v RFM* [2012] NZFC 7767; *DSA v JRT* [2012] NZFC 7836, (2012) 29 FRNZ 241.

84 *Churcher v Churcher* (1977) 1 MPC 40 (SC) (valuation of land and a partially completed building); *McHardy v McHardy* (1980) 3 MPC 109 (HC) (valuation of shares in a private company); *Marriott v Marriott* (1981) 4 MPC 144 (HC) (valuation of land); *Moyle v Moyle* (1981) 4 MPC 149 (HC) (valuation of an interest in an accounting practice); *Paton v Paton* (1981) 4 MPC 163 (HC) (valuation of household chattels); *Lepper v Lepper* (1977) 1 MPC 118 (SC); *Field v Field* (1977) 1 MPC 75 (SC).

85 *Brainich v Ward* [2016] NZHC 2481.

any utility. Indeed, it is more often than not the lament of judges in this field that they are being asked to adjudicate in the absence of reliable and expert evidence.

It is also doubtful if restrictions on questioning experts (that is, limiting questions to those posed in writing prior to trial or placing time restrictions on cross-examination) will effectively serve the purposes of justice. In New Zealand, the court's ability to regulate its own procedure is well established.[86] Nothing more is needed.

4.4. JOINT SINGLE EXPERTS

In some jurisdictions,[87] explicit provision is made in the rules of civil procedure for the appointment of a 'joint single expert'.[88] The perceived advantages are to overcome prohibitive delays and costs, and to ensure 'independence'. Whilst the specific rules may vary, the overall aim is the same. Unfortunately, the practice seems, on occasion, to fall far short of the perception.

Perhaps the first point to note is that the existence of differing opinions is not, of itself, a bad thing. It is inherent in the concept of an 'opinion' that there may be differing views for valid reasons. By permitting ventilation of differing views the court may, in fact, be better informed and able to fulfil its function. Secondly (and inevitably) parties will frequently retain 'shadow experts' to assist in understanding and, perhaps, challenging any report from the 'joint expert'. Accordingly, the envisaged cost saving disappears. Thirdly, the value of a report for a joint single expert may be dependent on the quality of the agreed brief (itself likely to be a product of discussion between the commissioning lawyers and, on occasion, compromise). Simple issues, such as whether the valuation is to be based on 'market value' or 'fair value' can have a significant impact on outcomes. Judicial oversight of the terms of the brief may, in fact, add to (not diminish) delays.

The solution may lie in a more accurate assessment of situations in which a joint single expert is likely to achieve the stated goals. There are situations where the required expertise is in a substantially established area of knowledge and where it is not necessary for a court to sample a range of opinions.[89] The appointment of a joint single expert is more likely to be useful in what might loosely be called 'low stakes' litigation. Identifying or classifying such cases is a matter of case management.

---

86 See *McMenamin v Attorney-General* [1985] 2 NZLR 274 (CA).

87 The UK and Australia are examples – in Queensland joint experts are mandatory.

88 See, for example, United Kingdom Ministry of Justice, above n 73 at [7]. Section 38 of the PRA could effectively be used to the same end.

89 H Woolf, above n 72.

4.5. ABSENCE OF EVIDENCE

Notwithstanding assertions that the concept of a 'burden of proof' sits uneasily in a relationship property context[90] the production of evidence (and challenges to evidence relied upon by the other party) must remain a key ingredient. There is clear authority for the proposition that where the information to enable a valuation to be arrived at before the court is scant, the court may be prepared to make assumptions to fill the gap.[91] Moreover, where a party peculiarly placed to provide evidence as to value fails to do so, that party must expect assumptions to be made against that party's interests.[92]

Applying such principles can, however, leave a court in very deep water. In *Johnson v Johnson*, Winkelmann J declined to apply the principles to the detriment of the recalcitrant husband but, instead, used section 38 of the PRA to appoint an accountant to provide an expert opinion as to the value of the company.[93] To have done otherwise, Winkelmann J concluded, might have produced an unjust outcome.

5. IS ESTABLISHING A VALUE AN EXERCISE OF DISCRETION?

The nature of the appellate jurisdiction in the family law context has been the subject of much discussion and debate. It is relevant in this context because it sheds light on the nature of a valuation in the relationship property context.

It is well established that an appeal against the exercise of statutory discretion is governed by the principles laid down in *May v May*.[94] To succeed, the 'appellant must show that the Judge acted on a wrong principle; or that [the Judge] failed to take into account some relevant matter or … took account of some irrelevant matter or that [the Judge] was plainly wrong'.[95] The fact that another judge faced with the same evidence may have arrived at a different conclusion will not be sufficient to successfully mount an appeal. A general appeal, as opposed to an appeal from a statutory discretion, entitles the appellant to a rehearing and a judgment in accordance with the opinion of the appellate court even where the decision is one which entails an assessment of fact and degree, and entails a value judgement or evaluation.[96]

---

90 *M v B*, above n 26.

91 *Bell v Bell* (1981) 4 MPC 7 (HC).

92 *Armory v Delamirie* (1722) 93 ER 664 (KB).

93 *Johnson v Johnson* HC Auckland CIV-2003-404-7204, 29 September 2004.

94 *May v May* (1982) 1 NZFLR 165 (CA), endorsed in *Blackstone v Blackstone* [2008] NZCA 312, (2008) 19 PRNZ 40.

95 *May v May*, above n 94 at 170.

96 *Austin, Nichols & Co Inc v Stitching Lodestar* [2007] NZSC 103, [2008] 2 NZLR 141.

So what, precisely, is the nature of a finding attributing a value to a particular asset? Following *Reid v Reid*, the answer seems to be that such a finding is largely one of an exercise of discretion:[97]

> 'Accordingly this Court will not readily interfere with findings made in the Court below in the broad area of the valuation of property involving, as those findings must do, an element of discretion in deciding whether one rather than another method of valuation should be adopted.'

Put another way, the value of property (such as the value of a partnership interest or shares in a private company) will always be a 'jury issue' and not a rigid arithmetic calculation. The approach adopted must be tailored not only to the size and nature of the asset in question (valuing an interest in a 'Big Five' law partnership may require a different approach to the valuation of a provincial two-person law partnership) but also, crucially, to the need to arrive at a figure that is fair and reasonable for both parties. If the flexibility which the New Zealand statute appears to encourage in areas of valuation (considered in light of the overriding principles of the PRA) is to be retained and maintained, then this approach must surely be correct.

In the absence of cogent evidence, a robust approach to the valuation of assets may be required. Will that approach be enhanced by imposing 'rules of valuation'? We suspect not.

6. VALUATION FACTORS

6.1. SALE AS THE ULTIMATE ARBITER

In *Scott v Williams* the parties were at loggerheads about (inter alia) two adjoining properties in an expensive suburb (one containing the former family home; the other a bare section).[98] The husband sought sale and division of the proceeds; the wife sought to retain the properties. In the Family Court, competing valuations were produced, with Judge McHardy preferring one particular valuation[99] and vesting the properties in the wife at that preferred valuation.[100] In the High Court, Faire J (on appeal) disagreed.[101] He framed the appeal as one against a discretion not to order sale of the property. In his view, the best way to value the properties was to order sale (noting that all of the experts concurred that it was best to test

97 *Reid v Reid*, above n 13 at 272. See also *Clark v Clark*, above n 5.
98 *Scott v Williams*, above n 24.
99 *Williams v Scott* [2014] NZFC 7616 at [289].
100 Ibid, at [481].
101 *Williams v Scott* [2014] NZHC 2547, [2015] NZFLR 355.

the market rather than to rely on what were essentially estimates of value).[102] This was in the context of a rapidly 'rising Auckland property market'.[103] The wife took the issue to the Court of Appeal but failed to persuade that Court to revisit the High Court's approach.[104]

In *Carter v Carter*, Hammond J was confronted with an actual market transaction as well as a hypothetical valuation exercise in respect of some company shares in a used car business.[105] It was contended, by the husband, that the sale (to a business colleague) was 'aberrant' and made for '"internal" reasons'.[106] The sale price, he said, did not thus reflect the true value and was artificially high. Despite 'a real sense of unease'[107] at the sale price (and noting that '[a] Court does not leave behind its common sense' when reviewing such evidence)[108] Hammond J could not ignore that it reflected 'a market transaction by men well versed in the industry'[109] and concluded (without entirely excluding the possibility) that it would be a very unusual case in which 'an actual market transaction' would be supplanted by a 'hypothetical exercise' providing a different outcome.[110]

6.2. STATUTORY ADJUSTMENTS TO EQUAL DIVISION

As foreshadowed earlier in this chapter, the New Zealand statute also provides for adjustments for what might loosely (in this context) be called post-separation events.

6.2.1. Sections 18B and 18C – Compensation for Post-Separation Contribution

Compensation is available for a party who has made a post-separation contribution[111] or for a party whose entitlements have been diminished by the post-separation dissipation of relationship property.[112] Such compensation is discretionary ('if [the Court] considers it just' is the wording in section 18B of the

102 Ibid, at [192].
103 Ibid, at [194], quoting *GFM v JAM*, above n 24 at [117].
104 *Scott v Williams*, above n 24.
105 *Carter v Carter* [2001] NZFLR 180 (HC). Resolution of the differences between the valuers on their hypothetical calculations was readily achievable and indeed, by way of judicial postscript, the Court completed that exercise at [69].
106 Ibid, at [44].
107 Ibid, at [66].
108 Ibid, at [62].
109 Ibid, at [66].
110 Ibid, at [65].
111 PRA, s 18B.
112 PRA, s 18C.

PRA) and the court is clearly not constrained by valuation principles in making the necessary adjustment. This is particularly illustrated by the provisions of section 18B; the term 'contribution' is directly related to the definition to be found in section 18(2) which firmly states that '[t]here is no presumption that a contribution of a monetary nature ... is of greater *value* than a contribution of a non-monetary nature' (emphasis added). The word 'value' is placed squarely in this section. But the provision, in rejecting the presumption that a monetary contribution is of greater value than a non-monetary contribution, begs the question of just how one does value a non-monetary contribution (let alone how that is to be weighed in the balance). Evidence of the *fact* of contribution or dissipation, as the case may be, is for the parties to adduce. It is to the measure of any compensation that the court will then turn its mind. The true measure, of course, is the justness of the outcome. There needs to be a weighing of the respective benefits enjoyed, and the burdens assumed, by the parties in the post-separation environment. There will be limits on the assistance that can be provided by valuation evidence in this area.

A classic claim for compensation for a post-separation contribution will arise where one party has, in the post-separation period, reduced the loan secured against the family home by way of a mortgage. The reduction of the loan can be readily measured and the payer can generally expect to be recompensed in full (although such repayment is not prescribed by the PRA, which only speaks of compensation in broad, discretionary terms). Claims to be compensated for 'occupation rent' (where one party continues to occupy the home to the exclusion of the other who thus loses not only the benefit of the accommodation but also access to their share of the capital) are also common. Where such claims are accepted, a standard formula along the following lines is generally adopted (multiplied by the weeks of occupation).[113]

A	–	B	=	C DIVIDED BY 2
(MARKET RENTAL)		(OUTGOINGS PAID)		(ADJUSTMENT)

But the mere fact of the making of such a contribution will not, of itself, justify an award under section 18B. The court must also be satisfied that it is just in all the circumstances that such an order be made.[114] Thus in some cases, an allowance for a 'settling down' period is made.[115] Alternatively, a calculation based on an award of interest on the non-occupying party's capital can be employed.[116]

113 See *Butcher v Haack* [2012] NZHC 2991.
114 See *E v G* HC Wellington CIV-2005-485-1895, 18 May 2006.
115 See *Dyas v Elliott* (2010) 11 NZCPR 252 (HC).
116 *Griffiths v Griffiths* [2012] NZFLR 327 (HC).

Another example is the calculation of compensation for providing the care of a child or an aged/infirm relative (plainly within the realms of a compensable contribution).[117] At first blush, this may seem difficult, but a suitably qualified valuer could indeed base calculations upon (say) the cost of providing a nanny in lieu of unrelenting one-parent care.

The simple point, in the context of this chapter, is that it is entirely feasible to calculate a compensation figure by resort to perfectly valid and respectable methodology. Such calculations cannot, however, transcend the court's discretionary powers, which must bring into account factors other than those capable of calculation. The results in apparently similar cases can be very different and the course to be adopted is essentially a matter of judicial discretion.[118]

6.2.2. *Section 15 – Compensation for Economic Disparity*

Parliament's clumsy attempt to remedy the inequities of an equal division of assets by the introduction of section 15 (compensation for economic disparity) has created its own valuation Frankenstein. Provided the requisite statutory thresholds are met (significantly higher income/standard of living; disparity caused by the effects of the division of functions in a marriage), the court is entitled, if it considers it just, to compensate the economically disadvantaged partner by, inter alia, payment of a sum of money from the relationship property pool. This has spawned a veritable industry of valuers endeavouring to calculate the value of economic disparity whether on a 'but for' basis or on an 'enhancement' basis (or, not infrequently, a combination of the two).

In *Hodgson v Hodgson*, it was blithely pointed out that there were many ways of assessing quantum and that the courts should not be shy to use particular methods to meet the particular circumstances of the case.[119] To some, this may have the ring of 'valuation roulette' about it.

Jack v Jack was primarily concerned with an 'enhancement claim'.[120] As O'Reagan J noted in *X v X*, the object of an award in such cases is 'to provide the disadvantaged partner with a share of the enhancement of the advantaged partner's future income or living standards resulting from the division of roles in the relationship.'[121] However, as Goddard J noted in *Jack v Jack*: 'Past judgments have adopted a prescriptive approach and calculated awards with a degree of mathematical certainty … the words of the section do not require any particular

---

117 See *Stapleton v Stapleton* [2005] NZFLR 218 (FC).

118 *Griffiths v Griffiths*, above n 116.

119 *Hodgson v Hodgson* [2016] NZHC 311.

120 *Jack v Jack* [2014] NZHC 1495. An 'enhancement claim' occurs where a party has supported the other to obtain qualifications and experience that provide that person with an enhanced future earning capacity.

121 *X v X [Economic Disparity]* [2009] NZCA 399, [2010] 1 NZLR 601 at [170].

approach.'[122] This echoed the approach advocated by the wife's lawyer in the Family Court (where the decision was reported as *Carpenter v Carpenter*) who had boldly eschewed 'a prescriptive/accountant's approach as has been primarily the case in the past' but advocated for 'a broad brush approach' (whatever that may mean).[123] The boldness of this approach was reinforced by a decision to place no actuarial evidence before the Court.

Robertson J in *X v X* was emphatic. In a case 'noteworthy for the volume of evidence called from specialists',[124] he noted that the Family Court judge had observed the difficulties in calculating an award: establishing the claimant's 'but for' income was 'enormously speculative' and, in the circumstances, 'probably an unfair task to pose'.[125] His Honour called it 'an unrealistic expectation'.[126] That, however, should not deter the court. Precision was not the point. Awards should not be locked into any particular presumption because parties' circumstances will vary considerably. Such awards (he opined) are 'necessarily a matter of impression and rote applications of formula will not be appropriate'.[127]

The difficulty, of course, is that such an approach creates inherent uncertainty and Robertson J's Panglossian view that 'a sensible and realistic assessment of relevant factors is not beyond the reach of skilled practitioners' offers little comfort.[128] He then went on to elaborate his thinking:[129]

> 'At all levels, the Courts in this case have been inundated with accounting material and asked to slot figures into formulae to produce end figures. I consider that this is a misconceived approach to s 15. The section does not engage the courts in a simple accounting exercise, but in a sensible jury assessment role. Precise analysis of each party's projected financial situation is not possible (although informed estimates can be made as they were here) …
>
> In determining quantum, what is important is the overall circumstances that gave rise to the disparity between the parties and what will be "just between them" going into the future. A court should be transparent in its assessment of the factors that contribute to its decision to make an award and it must be robust in responding to the evidence that is available. However, in the final analysis under s 15(3) there is limited assistance to be garnered from expert's projections. No rote formulae can reliably throw up award sums that are just. The court must determine the justice of an award on the basis of its assessments of the parties' overall financial circumstances, the value of the loss sustained by the claimant party, and the future earning potential of each party.'

122 *Jack v Jack*, above n 120 at [63].
123 *Carpenter v Carpenter* [2013] NZFC 8396, [2014] NZFLR 9 at [135].
124 *X v X [Economic Disparity]*, above n 121 at [127].
125 Ibid, at [66], citing *X v X [Quantum]* [2008] NZFLR 512 (FC) at [34]–[35].
126 *X v X [Economic Disparity]*, above n 121 at [127].
127 Ibid, at [125], citing *M v B*, above n 26 at [147].
128 *X v X [Economic Disparity]*, above n 121 at [126].
129 Ibid, at [128]–[129].

Having outlined a methodology for calculating the compensation award, Robertson J said:[130]

> 'This particular s 15 quantification process is not a universal or precise accounting exercise. The basis on which an award is calculated should always be tailored to the facts of a particular case. An award should be … fair compensation for the consequences arising from the division of functions in the relationship. Because detailed accounting assessments were available, I have utilised them but reject any suggestion that this is the only way to reach a proper figure for s 15 compensation.'

Notably, the majority in *X v X* wrote a separate decision on quantum, but their differences contest the mathematics, not the general approach. In short, prescription was not called for and there was a clear and unequivocal reservation of the decision as a 'sensible jury assessment role'.[131] The Court did not endorse the methodology served up in that case as 'a complete answer for every case of this type'.[132] None of this, however, is contrary to the proposition that some evidential foundation is required.

In *Carpenter v Carpenter*, Judge Grace set out some options for determining the appropriate measure of compensation in that case:[133]

> '(i) Calculating a figure which represents the value of the cumulative difference between the incomes of the respondent which he is projected to earn and the income he could expect to earn in the absence of the applicant's support.
> (ii) Assess in the round a lump sum based on a reasonable percentage of the high income earner's income for a reasonable period of years for enhancement as a result of the division of functions within the marriage (that is, 20 per cent of income for five years); [or]
> (iii) Award the respondent a sum equivalent to one year's tax income on the basis that at the date of separation, the respondent had approximately 11 years to go before age 65.'

Judge Grace settled on an award that (coincidentally?) reflected both a 70:30 division of relationship property (of a relatively modest pool of between $1.6 and $1.8 million) and approximately 30 per cent of the husband's annual income. It was argued on behalf of the husband, in the High Court (where the decision was reported as *Jack v Jack*), that the award was 'obscure', 'impressionistic' and (indeed) 'capricious'.[134] The wife's counsel argued that the award was 'very modest … compared to [the husband's] income'.[135] Goddard J did not consider

130 Ibid, at [135].
131 Ibid, at [128].
132 Ibid, at [175].
133 *Carpenter v Carpenter*, above n 123 at [138].
134 *Jack v Jack*, above n 120 at [71].
135 Ibid, at [74].

that the absence of expert valuation evidence was an impediment to the making of a 'sensible' decision.[136] Rather, her Honour had regard to the overall picture: the position of the parties upon entering the relationship, the length of the marriage, the size of the economic disparity, and the marked inequality of income earning capacity. On such an analysis it might be argued that the benefit of expert evidence, let alone rules on valuation, would seem to be of restricted utility. Conversely, we suggest the integrity of the award may well have been reinforced by reference to a more rigorous approach.

Yet even where there is evidence, the position is far from simple. So far in *Scott v Williams*,[137] three Courts dealing with the same evidence have concluded that the wife's claim for compensation under section 15 was worth $850,000 (in the Family Court),[138] $280,000 (in the High Court),[139] and $470,000 (in the Court of Appeal).[140] In a recent Family Court case, *Underhill v Underhill*,[141] based on a 'but for' claim, the parties each retained experts described in the judgment as 'well respected'[142] and 'experienced and reliable'.[143] The only issue was quantum. The valuers conferred pre-trial, and narrowed their (initial) differences. The husband contended for a figure of $55,000; the wife for a figure of $77,000. The same formula was used with each expert halving the disparity figure to reach the final figure. Neither expert was called for cross-examination. Noting that '[t]here is no legal requirement to halve the amount' and emphasising the need to calculate a 'just outcome',[144] Judge Pidwell settled on a figure of $154,617.[145] In so doing, she did not expressly eschew the valuers' calculations but, instead, injected a broader consideration which (by way of cross-check) she noted resulted in a 60:40 division of relationship property overall.

With such varying analyses, it is difficult to see that the insertion of 'rules on valuation' would address the problems of cost and delay.

7. CONCLUSION

Whilst central to the operation of a property sharing regime, issues of valuation are only an aid to the achievement of a just division of relationship property.

---

136 Ibid, at [81].
137 The matter appears destined to be considered by the Supreme Court, leave having been sought for that purpose.
138 *Williams v Scott*, above n 99.
139 *Williams v Scott*, above n 101.
140 *Scott v Williams*, above n 24.
141 *Underhill v Underhill* [2015] NZFC 10432: the decision is under appeal.
142 Ibid, at [99].
143 Ibid, at [100].
144 Ibid, at [102].
145 Ibid, at [105].

The fact-specific nature of each matter calls for judicial flexibility. The mathematics may be best left to the experts but the equities clearly lie with the court. The rules of the court and the statutory provisions should be sufficiently flexible to provide the court with appropriate tools to achieve the prescribed outcome, as they are in New Zealand. Some cases may suggest that matters in this area are far from settled.[146] They are, however, rare cases and do not, of themselves, bespeak a need to introduce rules of valuation.

146 *M v B*, above n 26; *Scott v Williams*, above n 24.

PART III

HOW SHOULD PROPERTY BE SHARED AT THE END OF A RELATIONSHIP?*

The chapters in Part III of this book address the concept of sharing property following the breakdown of a marriage, civil partnership, or de facto relationship. As in the preceding two parts, the focus in this part is on common law jurisdictions, with New Zealand's sharing regime featuring prominently. But this part of the book also includes a chapter on the matrimonial property regimes in the civil law jurisdictions to provide a comparative perspective on property division. In most common law jurisdictions, the property sharing system applicable on relationship breakdown does not apply when a relationship ends on death of a spouse or partner. New Zealand is unusual in that regard. The application of its sharing regime on death is addressed in Chapter 5 in this book.

The idea of marriage as a partnership to which both spouses contribute equally, albeit in different ways, became part of the common law system only in the latter half of the twentieth century. The Married Women's Property Acts adopted by the common law jurisdictions in the 1880s enabled married women to acquire and deal with property in their own right. It liberated women from their husband's coverture. But the separate property system that replaced coverture treated spouses virtually as strangers for property purposes. Rights to property acquired during the marriage were determined by the general rules of common law and equity, normally to the benefit of the husband. There was no appreciation then that his wife's domestic work and child care had economic value and freed him to accumulate assets for the benefit of the family as a whole. Social changes following World War II, including the increased participation of women in the workforce, made the courts and, eventually, the legislatures aware that the application of general property rules was leading to unjust outcomes on marital breakdown, particularly for women. Characterising marriage as a partnership to which both spouses contributed in different but equally valuable ways allowed spouses to share in the fruits of their partnership. The legislatures

* Part III Introduction by Nicola Peart.

then had to decide how the property of the partnership should be shared and to what extent it should be a matter of state regulation or left to the parties themselves. The chapters in this part of the book address these questions.

The common law and the civil law jurisdictions have responded differently to these questions. In the common law jurisdictions, formal equality was established by the Married Women's Property Acts. But substantive equality, through sharing of property associated with the relationship, has been a gradual development effected in part by legislative intervention and in part by the courts increasingly appreciating the value of non-financial contributions to the marriage partnership and their effect on the earning capacities of the parties to the relationship. In the civil law jurisdictions, by contrast, sharing of matrimonial property has been a part of their law for a very long time through some form of community property regime, but formal equality between the spouses is a more recent development when the husband's marital power was eventually abolished.

Joanna Miles opens this part of the book by asking whether sharing of property at the end of a relationship should be based on rules that directly dispose of the issue or whether it should be left to the discretion of the court to determine in the particular circumstances of each case how the property should be shared between the parties. Division of matrimonial property in the civil law jurisdictions is governed by rules aimed at equal division of the assets classified as matrimonial property. There is little scope for discretion. However, as Jens Scherpe explains, division of matrimonial property is but one pillar of the property consequences of the end of a marriage. The other pillars, maintenance and compensation for adverse effects resulting from the division of functions during the marriage, are addressed separately and involve the exercise of discretion. In most common law jurisdictions, property division is at the discretion of the court. Miles explains that the exercise of discretion is usually constrained by a list of factors to which the courts must have regard, or guidelines or principles, often developed by the courts, which bring the discretionary systems closer to a rule-based approach. New Zealand's relationship property scheme started as a discretionary system and then moved to a rule-based system of equal division of matrimonial or relationship property, but it is subject to exceptions, such as compensation for economic disparity caused by the division of functions during the relationship, which are at the discretion of the court. None of the sharing systems are therefore entirely rule based or discretionary. To a greater or lesser extent, they are a mixture of the two, which is why Miles has reframed the question as the search for the right mix of rules and discretion.

Miles begins by setting out the arguments for and against rules and discretion. A property sharing regime based on rules has the advantage of certainty, predictability, consistency, and efficiency, but the outcomes may not be perfect or even satisfactory for everyone. This sort of system provides average justice and tolerates imperfections that are minor or too expensive to resolve. A discretionary system provides individualised justice for the litigants and is responsive to changing social conditions and expectations. It is particularly well suited to family law, where facts relevant to decision making are often not known in advance and where individual circumstances may require different responses. Miles points out, however, that it is expensive and that inadequate legal aid is likely to limit access to the wealthy, leaving the less well off to negotiate settlements in circumstances where the gendered nature of bargaining and lack of legal advice puts the party seeking to prise assets from their former spouse or partner at a significant disadvantage. In the absence of a clear right to property, Miles is concerned that the discretionary system creates an imbalance between the parties which is likely to be detrimental to the more vulnerable party, usually the woman. Miles is critical of the rule-hating discretionary system in England and Wales. She sees more merit in Scotland's principled justice system, but her preferred system on the rules-discretion continuum is the Canadian rule-friendly discretionary system and recommends that New Zealand adopt a system along those lines.

Mark Henaghan discusses the issue of substantive equality between the parties and how that should be achieved through sharing of property at the end of a relationship. He focuses primarily on New Zealand, where the statutory sharing of relationship property is under some strain, because the equality principle is struggling to accommodate the effects of the division of functions on the parties' earning capacities. The discretion given to the courts to compensate the disadvantaged party out of relationship property sits uncomfortably with the well-established strong presumption of equal division of relationship property. Henaghan argues for an adjustment to the division of property that compensates for the economic disparity resulting from the division of functions and secures substantive equality between the parties.

The range of relationships to which a property sharing regime applies is now very diverse. Creating a system that would serve everyone's purposes is well-nigh impossible. The question then is whether parties to a relationship should have the right to opt out of whatever default system would otherwise apply to them and make their own arrangements. In the common law jurisdictions, contracting out agreements were seen as inimical to marriage and hence against public policy. That view is no longer current. New Zealand permitted spouses to opt out of its matrimonial property system when it first introduced the presumption of equal sharing in 1976. This was a radical departure from the discretionary system of property adjustment that had applied previously. Parliament appreciated that the new regime would not suit all couples. Provided they made the contract in writing after each party had received independent legal advice about the effects and implications of the agreement, the contract would be binding on the parties on marital breakdown unless it was unjust. In England and Wales the Supreme Court of the United Kingdom recently held that ante-nuptial contracts were not against public policy.[1] While spouses could not oust the court's statutory discretion to make orders affecting title, the existence of a contract entered into freely and with full information is a relevant factor in the exercise of the court's discretion and can in appropriate circumstances be binding.

One of the reasons New Zealanders want to contract out of the Property (Relationships) Act 1976 (NZ) is because it captures assets that are not produced by the relationship. For example, the family home and family chattels are always shared, even if they were acquired before the relationship began and were fully paid for by the party bringing those assets into the relationship. Robert Fisher suggests that confining the sharing regime to the fruits of the partnership would reduce or even obviate the need for contracts opting out of the statutory sharing regime. Most civil law jurisdictions now have a matrimonial property regime that applies only to the fruits of the marriage. However, as Jens Scherpe explains, even in those jurisdictions there may still be good reasons to contract out of the default system, and the legislatures have provided for that possibility.

In the final chapter John Caldwell examines spousal maintenance after a marriage or equivalent relationship has ended. He explains that in New Zealand spousal maintenance and property division are regulated by separate statutes. The two regimes were designed to 'sit alongside' each other and their policies are intended to complement each other. Both are aimed at achieving financial finality between the spouses and assist them to become self-sufficient. Spousal maintenance is intended to rehabilitate the recipient spouse to become financially independent within a reasonable time. A clean break is seen as desirable to allow each spouse to start afresh. In view of that aim, Caldwell questions whether a needs-based maintenance system can be justified alongside the compensation provision for relationship-derived economic disparities in the Property (Relationships) Act 1976 (NZ). The interplay between maintenance and compensation for economic disparity has troubled the courts and an award of compensation inevitably erodes the need for spousal maintenance. Caldwell therefore argues for integration between the two regimes to achieve a principled and coherent system for dealing with the financial consequences of a relationship breakdown. Like other chapters in this book, Caldwell's chapter advocates for an integrated model of regulation, rather than the fragmented approach that currently exists in New Zealand.

---

1 *Granatino v Radmacher* [2010] UKSC 42, [2011] 1 AC 534.

CHAPTER 11

SHOULD THE REGIME BE DISCRETIONARY OR RULES-BASED?

Joanna Miles

'The history of law is many things. But one of them is the story of an unremitting struggle between rules and discretion. The tension between these two approaches to legal problems continues to pervade and perplex the law today. Perhaps nowhere is that tension more pronounced and more troubling than in family law.'[1]

'Most judges who are murdered by dissatisfied customers are killed by irate domestic litigants, not by criminals. The reason is simple: in other litigation, fewer emotional issues are involved; more important, the judge has less discretion.'[2]

---

1 C Schneider, 'The Tension between Rules and Discretion in Family Law: A Report and Reflection' (1993) 27 *Family Law Quarterly* 229, 229.

2 R Neely, *The Divorce Decision: The Legal and Human Consequences of Ending a Marriage*, McGraw-Hill, New York 1984, 32 (Justice Neely, W.Va., USA, writing extra-judicially), quoted by M Glendon, 'Fixed Rules and Discretion in Contemporary Family Law and Succession Law' (1985–86) 60 *Tulane Law Review* 1165, 1169.

1. INTRODUCTION

As the opening quotations suggest, the topic explored in this chapter is neither easy nor, perhaps, for our judges even safe! I first reframe the question and clear some ground.

1.1. REFRAMING THE QUESTION

In reality, we are not confronted by a stark choice: discretion *or* rules. The question is better framed as the (elusive) search for the *right mix* of rules and discretion.[3]

However, even that framing obscures the fact that rules and discretion are not the only juristic tools available, and that both 'rules' and 'discretion' come in varying degrees of 'ruleness' and 'discretionness'.[4] As Cass Sunstein and others have catalogued, we have at our disposal an array of legal resources including untrammeled discretion, rules, rules with excuses, presumptions, factors, standards, guidelines, principles, and analogies.[5] To that list we might add, or highlight, formulae as a particular type of – quantitatively expressed – rule. So there is a continuum of more and less rule-like modes in which a legal proposition might be expressed; and there are weaker and stronger forms of discretion,[6] more or less trammeled by another of the tools in the box.

Lastly, 'the regime' that we are examining (or might wish to create) has (or will probably have) more than one component. The current legal framework for the division of capital assets on relationship breakdown in New Zealand itself comprises more than one mode of legal norm: a rule of equal sharing of defined property, subject to exceptions cabined by jurisdictional limits, at least

3 See C Schneider, 'Discretion and Rules: A Lawyer's View' in K Hawkins (ed), *The Uses of Discretion*, Clarendon, Oxford 1992, 47 at 79.
4 To adopt and adapt Sunstein's neologism: C Sunstein, 'Problems with Rules' (1995) 83 *California Law Review* 953.
5 This is the list in his seminal article: C Sunstein, ibid.
6 See R Dworkin, *Taking Rights Seriously*, Duckworth, London 1994, from 31.

one of which (Property (Relationships) Act 1976 (NZ) ('PRA'), section 15), once triggered, ultimately requires the exercise of judicial discretion to determine the extent of departure from equal shares.[7] So whilst one can contemplate essentially rules-based regimes and essentially discretionary financial remedies, it is equally possible – and probably more attractive – to contemplate a mixed scheme.

The question that I shall seek to answer is therefore: what is the appropriate mix of rule, discretion, and other legal tools on that continuum for a statutory scheme for the division of capital assets[8] on relationship breakdown?[9]

1.2. CLEARING SOME GROUND

Before answering my reframed question, two other considerations that bear on the overall position require comment: spousal maintenance and eligibility for the scheme.

1.2.1. Spousal Support

My task is to discuss property division under a future iteration of New Zealand's PRA, an exercise that excludes periodic spousal support (or 'maintenance'), which others in this volume address. But it is clear – not least to English eyes, accustomed to viewing all financial adjustments (capital and income) as part of one overall package deal – that spousal support is a key component. Even if spousal maintenance orders are relatively rare, many couples preferring to achieve a clean break,[10] the *entitlement* to spousal support (paid periodically from income) should still form part of the context in which bargains around property division are struck.

Spousal (and de facto/civil union) support under New Zealand's Family Proceedings Act 1980 is currently granted under a model that (i) attempts[11] to

---

7 Contrast the exceptions in ss 13 and 14 which demand a contribution-based distribution – but that invites debate about how 'contributions' (defined by s 18) are quantified and appropriately expressed in an award.

8 Defined broadly to include superannuation scheme entitlements etc, as in Property (Relationships) Act 1976 (NZ) ('PRA'), s 8.

9 I leave others to consider what, if any, aspects of such a scheme should apply to a relationship terminated by death.

10 See, for example, English findings by H Woodward and M Sefton, *Pensions on Divorce: An Empirical Study*, University of Cardiff, Cardiff 2014 <http://orca.cf.ac.uk/56700/1/14%2002%2011%20Pensions%20on%20divorce%20final%20report.pdf> accessed 09.03.2017 and forthcoming findings from E Hitchings and J Miles (presented at Society of Legal Scholars Conference, Oxford 2016 and Dublin 2017).

11 Compare with B Atkin and W Parker's well-made criticism of the drafting of these provisions as amended in 2001: *Relationship Property in New Zealand*, Butterworths, Wellington 2001, ch 7 esp at 7.2.4.

set out a rule limiting liability: only where the would-be payee cannot meet all or part of his or her reasonable needs for one or more enumerated reasons;[12] further limited by (ii) the rule that, even then, the would-be payee must assume responsibility for meeting his or her own needs within a reasonable time;[13] before (iii) inviting the court, in its discretion, to set a quantum of maintenance guided by a checklist of factors.[14] This model has more in common with the juristic tools deployed in section 15 of the PRA than with other parts of that Act, but evidently differs importantly by being grounded in need, rather than in compensation for economic disparity. As an ongoing, variable remedy, it avoids the crystal ball gazing associated with capital provision directed at future economic disparity. The possibility of capitalising maintenance claims to achieve a clean break sooner (at a discount to allow for future contingences and time-use) may often be appealing. At this point, maintenance entitlements appear to offer an additional rationale for the distribution of capital assets on relationship breakdown.

Whilst we might wish to keep the remedy of spousal support distinct, it is important not to overlook it, so that we achieve a coherent reform for the whole package of remedies.

1.2.2. Eligibility

Others in this volume will be dealing with the important question of eligibility for remedies under the scheme: to which relationships should it apply? But, as has been noted before,[15] this question is connected to the nature of the rights and remedies for which they would be eligible because of the heterogeneity of contemporary couples. Modern relationships exhibit great diversity in their division of functions, degree of economic interdependence, money management practices, attitudes towards the parties' financial relationship, and so on. Whilst spouses and civil union partners share (at least) the fact that the parties have mutually assented to cloak their relationship with a specific legal status, de facto

12 Section 64: there is immediate difficulty in construing several of the items listed in s 64(2) as 'reasons' for the claimant's inability to be self-supporting.

13 Section 64A.

14 Section 65: with a further rule automatically terminating maintenance on the inception of a new relationship (s 70A), responsibility at that point (implicitly) being assumed by the new partner even though no legal maintenance responsibility arises between de factos as such (cf ss 63 and 79).

15 See, for example, J Miles, 'Unmarried Cohabitants in a European Perspective' in JM Scherpe (ed), *European Family Law*, vol III, Edward Elgar, Cheltenham 2016, 82 at 99–101; F McCarthy, 'Playing the Percentages: New Zealand, Scotland and a Global Solution to the Consequences of Non-Marital Relationships?' (2011) 24 *New Zealand Universities Law Review* 499; M Briggs, 'Rethinking Relationships' (2015) 46 *Victoria University of Wellington Law Review* 649.

partners (as a class) have made no equivalent mutual commitment and are especially diverse.[16]

This has implications for the substantive principles that should apply: for example, is a norm of equal sharing apt for all relationships brought within such a scheme?[17] But it also has implications for the mode of legislation: the more diverse the class to whom the scheme must apply, the stronger the case for remedial flexibility and so for a higher degree of discretion to accommodate that diversity and achieve 'fair' outcomes for more relationships covered by it. Yet as Carol Rogerson has observed, 'Ironically, it is at the very time that family law has come to recognize the diversity of family forms that', for reasons that will be explored below, 'the need for rules and standardization has increased'.[18]

2. RULES 'VERSUS' DISCRETION – THE BASICS

As is evident from the voluminous literature, in both generalist and family law canons, this topic is amongst the oldest of old chestnuts. In the present context, where discretion was the primary mode for law-making in much of the twentieth century, it has been associated with family lawyers' existential angst about the apparently a-legal nature of their discipline.[19] In this section, I canter through some of the key arguments from that literature,[20] before turning next to

16 See, for example, the evidence collated by the Law Commission for England and Wales: Law Commission (Eng&W), *Cohabitation: The Financial Consequences of Relationship Breakdown*, Law Com CP 179, TSO, London 2006, from [5.58]; chapters by C Vogler, and C Burgoyne and S Sonnenburg in J Miles and R Probert (eds), *Sharing Lives, Dividing Assets: An Inter-Disciplinary Study*, Hart Publishing, Oxford 2009, 61 and 89; and the small New Zealand study by V Elizabeth, 'Managing Money, Managing Coupledom: A Critical Examination of Cohabitants' Money Management Practices' (2001) 49 *Sociological Review* 389.

17 The Scottish Law Commission (*Report on Family Law*, Scots Law Com No. 135, HMSO, Edinburgh 1992) and Parliament (Family Law (Scotland) Act 2006, ss 25–29) thought not. See also V Grainer's concerns about the assimilation of de factos with spouses by the 2001 reforms in New Zealand: 'What's Yours is Mine: Reform of the Property Division Regime for Unmarried Couples in New Zealand' (2002) 11 *Pacific Rim Law and Policy Journal* 285.

18 C Rogerson, 'Child Support, Spousal Support and the Turn to Guidelines' in J Eekelaar and R George (eds), *Routledge Handbook of Family Law and Policy*, Routledge, London 2014, 153 at 154.

19 See J Dewar, 'Family Law and its Discontents' (2000) 14 *International Journal of Law, Policy and the Family* 59, 78; C Schneider, above n 3 at 48; R Ormrod, 'Judicial Discretion' (1987) 40 *Current Legal Problems* 123.

20 For fuller discussion of the themes addressed here, see the various sources on which I have drawn, including: C Sunstein, above n 4; C Schneider, above nn 1 and 3; M Glendon, above n 2; N Bala, 'Judicial Discretion and Family Law Reform in Canada' (1986) 5 *Canadian Journal of Family Law* 15; J Dewar, 'Reducing Discretion in Family Law' (1997) 11 *Australian Journal of Family Law* 309, 'The Normal Chaos of Family Law' (1998) 61 *Modern Law Review* 467, and above n 19; I Ellman, 'Inventing Family Law' (1999) 32 *University of California Davis Law Review* 855; R Thompson, 'Rules and Rulelessness in

a more considered exploration of some key determinants for this debate in the contemporary family justice context in order to 'grope toward some satisfactory mix of discretion and rules'.[21]

2.1. THE BASIC PROS AND CONS

I shall begin, simply, by reverting to the notion of a straight dichotomy between the notion of a 'rule' (a legal provision that purports[22] to be directly dispositive of the issue at stake) and the notion of 'discretion' (in which the decision-maker is required to exercise his or her own judgement to resolve the case in light of its particular facts pursuant to some more or less broadly framed objective). Rollie Thompson provides an excellent overview of the pros and cons of rules and discretion, or as he puts it: 'why rules?' and 'why not rules?'.[23] So I adopt and adapt his catalogue of arguments to start the discussion.

2.1.1. Why Rules?

Rules help us to decide large numbers of cases in an efficient, consistent, and so predictable manner. They give us more or less rough justice, providing pretty decent answers for the bulk of cases. To the extent that the answer is sometimes imperfect, that may be tolerable where the issues at stake are relatively minor (in dollar amounts or qualitatively) and/or where the transaction costs of fixing on a more 'accurate' answer, customised to each case's more detailed facts, would be disproportionate for the system and the parties. By ruling out closely individualised decision-making, rules create a more level playing field for those litigants who are unable to meet higher transaction costs. By creating predictable answers – and by conferring rights and imposing corresponding duties – rules can both facilitate planning by individuals before issues arise and aid settlement in case of dispute. They encourage equal treatment of like cases and preclude discriminatory or otherwise biased decision-making. They save judges time by removing the need to revisit first principles, and can help bolster

Family Law: Recent Developments, Judicial and Legislative' (2000) 18 *Canadian Family Law Quarterly* 25; J Behrens, 'The Form and Substance of Australian Legislation on Parenting Orders: A Case for the Principles of Care and Diversity and Presumptions Based on Them' (2002) 24 *Journal of Social Welfare and Family Law* 401. This chapter was written before the author read P Parkinson's article making very similar arguments in an Australian context: 'Constitutional Law and the Limits of Discretion in Family Property Law' (2016) 44 *Federal Law Review* 49.

21 C Schneider, above n 3 at 49.

22 The need for interpretation of the language of the rule and application of the rule so interpreted to the facts, of course, makes rules less automatically dispositive than they might appear: see C Schneider, above n 3; C Sunstein, above n 4.

23 R Thompson, above n 20 at section 1.

the position of judges who find themselves having to take tough or otherwise unpopular decisions pursuant to the rule, leaving the legislator to take the flak from dissatisfied pressure groups or disappointed litigants.

2.1.2. *Why not Rules – or Why Discretion?*

Discretion enables the legislator to make law concerning areas in which decisions are needed but there is no consensus on what the determinative rule should be, or values are changing quickly such that any rule might soon become dated. Discretion enables the sort of individualised decision-making that rules cannot provide. This may be particularly important for family disputes where the costs of getting the answer wrong could be high and so the transaction costs required to reach the 'right' decision are considered proportionate given the issue at stake. Discretion can thus ensure a better 'fit' of decisions to cases, avoid the danger of apparently 'equal' treatment in fact failing to respond appropriately to relevant difference in a given case, and give individuals a sense of procedural fairness through having *their* case properly heard on its merits. Discretion can also avoid the sort of 'evasion' that rules may attract if so drafted that they fail to capture some undesirable behaviours or outcomes that manifest the mischief at which the rule is directed.

2.2. THE CONTINUUM OF JURISTIC TOOLS

As discussed above, however, the lawmaker has available a far broader repertoire of juristic techniques than just 'rules' or 'discretion'. The positioning of a given legal provision on the rules – discretion continuum should ideally be determined by whatever balance between the various pros and cons, set out above, meets the demands of the particular substantive context.

At one extreme end of the spectrum lies Sunstein's 'untrammeled discretion': the decision-maker with a choice apparently unconstrained by any limiting principle, criteria, or practical possibility of review.[24] Herbert Hart rejected the notion that a choice exercisable by reference to mere personal preference could properly be called a 'discretion': the exercise of 'discretion' must be founded on some principle deployed by the decision-maker to justify the choice made.[25]

---

24 C Sunstein, above n 4 at 960–61. Compare here the alarmed reaction of Lord Penzance when confronted with an apparently untrammeled matrimonial discretion in *Morgan v Morgan* (1869) LR 1 P & D 644 at 647 quoted by R Ormrod, above n 19 at 125.

25 HLA Hart, 'Discretion', written in 1956 but published posthumously in (2013) 127 *Harvard Law Review* 652. See also I Ellman, above n 20, comparing various forms of traffic rule: Rule 1 most closely resembles this untrammeled discretion, cf Rule 2, which entails the exercise of judgement by the decision-maker by reference to a prescribed standard. See also C Schneider, above n 3 at 61–62, discussing the case of 'khadi-discretion'.

It is perhaps this distinction between arbitrary decision-making and the exercise of judgement (or true 'discretion') which English judge Holman J was concerned to highlight in making the following remarks in a decision under the broad discretionary financial remedies scheme of the Matrimonial Causes Act 1973 (Eng&W):[26]

> '68. I have reached this decision in the exercise of the judicial discretion which Parliament has imposed upon, and entrusted to, the courts. Of course, on one level the decision could be said to be arbitrary. I could have awarded more, or less, and two judges might (and probably would) have reached conclusions which differed to some degree. To that extent *any* exercise of judicial discretion may be said to be arbitrary …
>
> 69. … I, personally, consider that there is nevertheless a distinction between an award which is arbitrary in the true sense, and one which is the product of judicial discretion. An arbitrary result would be one yielded by sticking in a pin, or tossing a coin, or drawing a lot. Judicial discretion is the product of a weighing of all relevant factors and wise, considered and informed decision making by an experienced adjudicator after hearing argument. My decision is a discretionary one, but it is not an arbitrary one' (emphasis as in original).

Lawyers are hard-wired to insist on non-arbitrary decision-making[27] and so want a judge's decision to be defensible in at least one of two ways set out by Hart: first, in terms of the deliberative conditions in which the decision was made (Hart talks here of the decision being's 'justified'); and secondly, in terms of our ability to discern from the decision some underlying principle(s) or criterion/criteria that the judge deployed to reach his or her decision and that might in future be expected to be taken into account by another judge, taking a similar decision, in order to 'justify' that next decision (Hart talks here of the decision's being 'vindicated' by its outcome).[28]

Where we see this (characteristically common law) process of accretion of principle from individual decisions, we may have an instance of Schneider's 'rule-building discretion'.[29] Discretion of that type may be conferred on judges in order to deal with one of two problems identified by Hart that justify the deployment of discretion as a juristic tool: 'relative ignorance of fact' ('RIF') and 'relative indeterminacy of aim' ('RIA').[30]

RIF is arguably characteristic of many family law contexts that use discretion. RIF is the problem that leaves the legislator unable ex ante (or ever) to catalogue

26 *Robertson v Robertson* [2016] EWHC 613.

27 See R Ormrod, above n 19, for an example of this.

28 HLA Hart, above n 25 at 660.

29 C Schneider, above n 3 from 62, contrasting 'rule-failure', 'rule-building', and 'rule-compromise' discretion.

30 HLA Hart, above n 25 at 661–62.

the full range of diverse factual circumstances – including, in family law, predictions regarding future facts[31] – in relation to which a decision may have to be taken.[32] RIA, by contrast, is a growing problem for family law policy given the diversity of contemporary family forms and the abandonment of fault-based matrimonial law with no obvious substitute as a founding principle. RIA is the legislator's more profound (actual or perceived) problem that it may be difficult (practically or politically) to articulate – and achieve consensus upon – the policy that a new law should implement, either at all or in a way thought likely to stand the test of time (a relevant consideration for a legislator intervening in an area in flux).[33] In such circumstances, promulgation of a more or less broadly framed standard or objective by reference to which decisions should be made may be as much as the legislator feels able to do: for example, to advance the 'best interests' of the child in making orders for her living arrangements, or to achieve 'fairness' between parties in financial orders made on divorce. The promulgated standard is likely to be a compromise position, meaning what the various individuals within the legislature want it to mean, and conferring a 'rule-compromise' discretion on the judges. But where it is thought that the judges, with their gradually accumulating experience of the issue, might be (better) able to identify appropriate principles for future decision-making, we have also the makings – *if* the judges are prepared to take the bait[34] – of a rule-building discretion.

Hart talks about a discretion conferred with a general aim (such as 'fairness')[35] creating a 'general matrix susceptible of different types of filling'.[36] So the next question for the legislator, moving further along the continuum, is whether it wishes – and is able – to limit the judges' deliberative freedom and, if so, how far to take that exercise.

---

31 N Bala, above n 20 at 28; J Dewar 'Reducing Discretion in Family Law', above n 20 at 320.

32 So we may alternatively witness here the conferral of 'rule-failure' discretion: where it is thought that it will be impossible to cast any more concrete legal norm to govern such cases, a judge's decision can only be criticised on the basis of clear irrationality and little useful precedent can be accrued: see I Ellman, above n 20 at 867 and 870. See also C Sunstein, above n 4 at 958 on the problem of 'bounded rationality'.

33 See also C Sunstein, above n 4, on the problem of diversity and plurality of values.

34 This is not guaranteed: see concerns expressed about fettering discretion conferred by Parliament by the development of judge-made principles: eg *Mallet v Mallet* (1984) 156 CLR 605, cf *Norbis v Norbis* (1986) 161 CLR 513 (and see remarks in *Hoffman v Hoffman* [2014] FamCAFC 92 at [59]); *White v White* [2001] 1 AC 596 (HL) at 606 (per Lord Nicholls), cf 615 (per Lord Cooke). Such judicial reticence may simply stymie the legislator's intention where the discretion was supposed to be operated in a rule-building manner.

35 He actually uses the example of a 'successful dinner party': HLA Hart, above n 25 at 659–60.

36 HLA Hart, above n 27 at 659. As J Behrens notes, it will inevitably be filled with something by the judge, which we may or may not like: above n 20 at 407.

At a bare minimum, the legislator may wish to provide a checklist of factors to which the judges must have regard (or must ignore).[37] But as Hart notes, whilst it may be possible to identify 'distinguishable constituent values or elements' inherent in the relevant decision-making process, in the case of a discretion there are 'no clear principles or rules determining the relative importance of these constituent values or, where they conflict, how compromise should be made between them'.[38] So the stipulation of a checklist does not get us very far along the spectrum: to use Rollie Thompson's suitably domestic metaphor, a judge ticking off checklist items in order to appeal-proof a decision is engaging not in '[spousal] support analysis' but 'laundry-listing'.[39] And as the American Law Institute commentary puts it (in the context of recommending a formula for quantification of spousal support):[40]

> 'The fact that reasonable judges may differ on a policy choice does not make it beneficial that they should. There is no utility and considerable cost in accommodating varying judicial preferences concerning the minimum tolerable income disparity, or the minimum marital duration at which an award should normally be required. Such variation will uncover no adjudicative principle to guide later decisions, but will impose a considerable cost in inconsistency, unpredictability and the perception of adjudicative unfairness as neighboring cases yield different results because of different judges rather than different facts.'

So the legislator (or judges, exercising a rule-building discretion) may feel that it wants (or that they want) not merely to 'appeal to the judgment of a plurality of impartial spectators' but rather to endeavour to identify 'more determinate principles at work'.[41] And so we gradually move further along the continuum away from discretion, deploying more concrete or particularised guidelines, standards, principles, and presumptions by reference to which the judges must

---

37 For an example of the latter, see UK rules governing discretionary departures from the child support formula: Child Support Maintenance Calculation Regulations 2012, SI 2012/2677, reg 60.

38 HLA Hart, above n 25 at 659.

39 R Thompson, above n 20, main text following n 172 in the source.

40 American Law Institute, *Principles of the Law of Family Dissolution*, Philadelphia 2000, 811; and see J Behrens' objections, above n 20 at 407.

41 HLA Hart, above n 25 at 665. For an illustration of disagreement on the issue of how far the judges may themselves adopt the latter approach through a rule-building exercise of discretion, contrast the attitudes of differently constituted benches of the Court of Appeal for England and Wales in *B v B* [2008] EWCA Civ 543, [2008] 1 WLR 2362 and *Robson v Robson* [2010] EWCA Civ 1171, [2011] 1 WLR 1774 on the one hand, and *Jones v Jones* [2011] EWCA Civ 41, [2012] Fam 1 and *K v L* [2011] EWCA Civ 550, [2012] 1 WLR 306 on the other hand – the former content with a strong discretion relatively uninhibited by only high-level principle, the latter wishing to develop a more comprehensive set of principles by which to structure the exercise of the discretion.

structure their decisions. This process may ultimately result in the creation of rules, including rules subject to prescribed exceptions or rebuttable presumptions, that better signal specific values to the relevant population.[42] Those exceptions or grounds for rebuttal may be capable of relatively concrete expression demanding only an exercise of fact-finding by the judge: for example, is this relationship less than three years in duration? If so, divide the property by reference to the parties' 'contributions' instead.[43] Or they may instead be expressed in a more open-textured way, such as a standard, leaving scope for the exercise of some discretion in the process of interpretation and implementation: for example, divide the property equally unless there are 'extraordinary circumstances', or divide the property in accordance with the parties' agreement unless doing so would cause 'serious injustice'.

But the legislator's (and judges') ability to move further towards the rules end of the spectrum depends upon the extent to which the problems of RIF and RIA can be eliminated or their significance minimised. This depends, in the first instance, on how far it is possible to neutralise concerns about RIF by regarding the finer factual detail of individual cases as insufficiently pressing to impact on the required decision: a willingness to accept a greater degree of 'average' rather than 'individualised' justice[44] in that *factual* sense. And in the second instance, upon the extent to which it is possible for consensus to be achieved regarding the aims of the law in question, to whatever degree of specification is attainable in order to eliminate the problem of RIA: a willingness to accept a more tightly specified, homogenously applicable, legal norm, and so, perhaps, to adopt a more average (but uniform) rather than individualised *substantive* sense of justice.

3. SOME KEY CONTEMPORARY CONCERNS FOR THE RULES/DISCRETION DEBATE

Here, I examine three inter-linked core concerns regarding the rules versus discretion debate. These have all featured in the literature to a greater or lesser extent over the last 30 years at least.[45] But they seem to me to have particular

---

42 See generally J Dewar, 'Can the Centre Hold? Reflections on Two Decades of Family Law Reform in Australia' (2010) 24 *Australian Journal of Family Law* 139 on the 'regulatory' rather than 'adjudicatory' function of family law; and related discussion by J Behrens, above n 20.

43 Note here the inevitability of some exercise of (implied) discretion in the interpretation and implementation of such 'rules': C Schneider, above n 3; C Sunstein, above n 4.

44 C Rogerson, *Developing Spousal Support Guidelines in Canada: Beginning the Discussion*, Department of Justice, Ontario 2002, 6.

45 For example, N Bala, above n 20; M Glendon, above n 2; C Schneider, above n 3; C Sunstein, above n 4; J Dewar, above n 20; I Ellman, above n 20, all of which I have drawn upon in writing this section of the chapter.

force now and so should be uppermost in the policy-maker's mind in choosing between more or less rule-like tools for a scheme of property division on relationship breakdown. I naturally write from a specifically English standpoint, but expect that these concerns resonate with similar force elsewhere.

3.1 ON WHOM SHOULD THE BURDENS OF LAW-MAKING BE ALLOCATED?

As earlier commentators have noted, rules and discretion (and intervening points on the continuum to their varying extents) place different burdens on different agents within the system. This is a debate about where to place burdens created by RIF and RIA if those problems cannot be minimised or eliminated.

Wherever the lawmaker legislates in discretion mode, costs shift to courts and litigants. If the legislator cannot, factually or politically, say that facts a, b, and c alone are relevant (even determinative), then litigants face the burden of proving an array of facts – 'all of the circumstances of the case' – to try to persuade the judge of the rightness of their cause: that their vision of the child's future is that which best promotes the child's welfare, or that their account of the parties' economic positions points the way to a 'fair' division of assets. Judges face the burden of managing all of that information and going back to first principles in order to devise a bespoke solution, one that they feel fits the spirit of whatever loose norm the legislator has prescribed. As Sunstein puts it, this effectively involves 'law-making at the point of application'.[46] Put another way, it involves a considerable amount of economically, intellectually, and emotionally demanding improvisation, by the judges, lawyers, and parties. And of course, no one improv' routine is quite like any other, which may leave some litigants wondering if their case has been dealt with fairly at all, while other would-be litigants think it may be worth performing before a judge to see if they can procure a favourable outcome.

Alternatively, the legislator may feel able to cut through the thicket of infinitely variable facts and to identify and articulate a clear (and relatively prescriptive) principle to govern decision-making, and so produce a more rule-like provision. That exercise is likely to be costly (in terms of economic and political resource) and so is more burdensome on the legislator than propounding a less rule-like provision. It is likely to demand more in-depth, upfront scrutiny of social scientific evidence bearing on the subject matter of the proposed law and careful weighing of the merits and demerits of the varied responses which the legislator could make to it. The end product, however, will burden courts and litigants less: their role will call for much less improvisation – they will have a clearer script

[46] C Sunstein, above n 4 at 956.

to follow. But in another sense, some litigants (and individuals settling their cases privately by reference to the rules) may feel additional burdens where they consider that the rule jars badly for them but have no apparent scope to modify its application. So while the transaction costs may be less, outcome costs may sometimes be higher.

It is here that a choice is required between 'average' justice and 'individualised' justice.[47] To change the metaphor, how much cost should the legislator bear up front in crafting a fairly close-fitting rule in order to reduce transaction costs for its customers, even if some of them are left feeling that the sizing doesn't quite work for their case's shape? Alternatively, is the risk of too many customers being left with badly ill-fitting outcomes such that they, and the courts, should be freed to craft more carefully tailored solutions, albeit at greater cost at the point of tailoring? Is off-the-peg preferable to haute couture? Is the promise of individualised justice for everyone worth the price if some of the would-be customers can only press their noses to the shop window?

3.2. FAMILY JUSTICE IN A COLD CLIMATE

That leads to my next, very pressing, contemporary concern: how realistic is achievement of bespoke solutions via judicial discretion (or the professional judgement of lawyers) given the state of family justice in an age of austerity? Writing in 1993, Carl Schneider remarked that: '"Efficiency" is not a goal family law has historically valued. It is cold virtue for so warm a subject.'[48] But while the motivations of family law and family lawyers may be warm, underpinned by ethics of care and welfare-promotion,[49] the context in which family law and lawyers now ply their craft is increasingly chilly.

Cuts to legal aid put even out-of-court legal advice, never mind in-court representation, beyond the reach of many. Yet the pursuit of individualised justice presupposes and demands access to specialist advisors, negotiators, and, in the last resort, judges. If significant numbers cannot access those services, then the aspiration to achieve any sort of justice *under law* becomes futile. Litigants who, for want of access to professional assistance, attempt to prosecute their cases in person may struggle to navigate the arcane demands of a discretionary system, where the relevance and significance of various facts and arguments may be unclear. The governing norm may, deceptively simply, be one of 'fairness' or 'best interests', yet without access to the 'Talmudic body of knowledge'[50] that

---

47 C Rogerson, above n 44 at 6.

48 C Schneider, above n 1 at 237.

49 S Parker, 'Rights and Utility in Anglo-Australian Family Law' (1992) 55 *Modern Law Review* 311; J Behrens, above n 20.

50 R Bird, 'The Reform of Section 25' (2002) 32 *Family Law* 428, 429.

has accreted around those open-textured norms, the unsupported litigant will struggle to comprehend what is required. Cuts within the court service itself also make bespoke outcomes less deliverable: expert judges may lack the time to deal adequately with the disordered cases presented by many unrepresented litigants. Non-specialist judges who often handle these cases (particularly at the 'everyday' end of the asset-value scale) may lack the expertise and experience to deliver the types of bespoke outcomes that are expected.[51]

Add to this the frequency of family breakdown compared with much of the twentieth century (including that period in which our contemporary welfare-oriented, no-fault discretions were created), and the efficient disposal of cases by more rule-like provisions becomes less unattractive. Family breakdown is, sadly, a common experience, not the sort of rare incident into which the extensive resources of the family justice intensive care team can be devoted to secure optimal outcomes for each patient at whatever cost. Efficiency may not be a warm ambition – but it may be the best we can hope to achieve.

3.3. THE PERCEIVED FAILURES OF DISCRETION AND THE DYNAMICS OF SETTLEMENT

Given the practical inaccessibility and so impossibility of achieving individualised justice in all cases, the reality is that family law is very largely implemented privately (if at all) through settlement activity that may or may not be lawyer-led. It is here that the law's capacity to communicate more directly with its subjects becomes critical.[52] And it is once the resolution of cases moves from the public space of the court room to the hidden space of private ordering that the deficiencies and dangers of discretion become particularly apparent.

Discretion arrived in family law to replace the old, status-based system of rules that flowed from patriarchal and fault-based assumptions of an earlier time – clearly, not all rules are 'good' rules.[53] Discretion has noble, welfare-oriented ambitions to create bespoke outcomes that respond to the lived realities of the individuals concerned. But there is longstanding discontent in many

---

51 See E Hess and J Miles, 'The Recognition of Money Work as a Specialty in the Family Courts by the Creation of a National Network of Financial Remedies Units' (2016) 46 *Family Law* 1335 on the issue of lack of judicial specialty in dealing with money cases in England and Wales. The President of the Family Division has enthusiastically embraced the proposal: see (2017) 47 *Family Law* 575 and 625.

52 See J Dewar, above n 42 and J Behrens, above n 20.

53 See S Parker, above n 49 and many of the authors listed above n 45.

quarters[54] with how discretion operates: its failure to give judges and lawyers (never mind unrepresented parties) clear road-maps for decision-making and its inability to confer concrete *entitlements* on more vulnerable individuals, particularly – in this context – on women whose economic opportunities are constrained by caring responsibilities. Without clear rights to assert, those attempting to negotiate settlement may perceive the economic and emotional transaction costs of achieving a satisfactory outcome to be too high. Writing in the Canadian context, Carol Rogerson and Rollie Thompson have more than once drawn attention to concerns that:[55]

> 'for those without legal representation or in weak bargaining positions, [discretionary] support claims were simply not pursued. Despite a very broad basis for entitlement under the existing law, many spouses did not claim spousal support, being unwilling to engage in the difficult and costly process required.'

But does that mean that more rule-like norms are better for achieving settlement? The core literature is divided, and it is difficult to test the point empirically.[56] Schneider, for example, has suggested that:[57]

> 'the less certain the result a court would reach, the greater the practical scope for bargaining. ... We might, for all the usual reasons given for freedom of contract (yet keeping in mind the usual reasons for being cautious about the consequences of that kind of freedom), prefer a discretionary standard which accorded parties that greater freedom while still giving a court the authority to resolve their dispute if they could not do so themselves.'

Conversely, a rule, rather than removing scope for disagreement, may simply divert disagreement to issues made newly critical by the rule: for example, on the existence or otherwise of some fact necessary to trigger a particular outcome (eg the date on which, or purpose for which, an asset was acquired), or on the valuation of key assets that stand to be shared.

However, it is the parenthetical words in Schneider's remark that prompt careful study before we comfort ourselves that discretion can facilitate fair

---

54 But not all, as responses to a recent consultation exercise for the Law Commission for England and Wales on the law relating to financial needs on divorce reveal, discussed below at 4.1.

55 C Rogerson and R Thompson, *Spousal Support Advisory Guidelines*, Department of Justice, Ontario 2008, 10. See also empirical evidence discussed by C Martin, 'Unequal Shadows: Negotiation Theory and Spousal Support Under Canadian Divorce Law' (1998) 56 *University of Toronto Faculty Law Review* 135, from 155.

56 Cf the attempt made by M Harvey, M Karras and S Parker in *Negotiating by the Light of the Law: A Report on the Effect of Law on the Negotiation of Disputes*, Themis Press, Sydney 2012.

57 C Schneider, above n 3 at 77.

settlements. Mnookin and Kornhauser identified five factors that they considered to be important determinants of the outcomes of bargaining:[58]

> '(1) the preferences of the [parties]; (2) the bargaining endowments created by legal rules that indicate the particular allocation a court will impose if the parties fail to reach agreement; (3) the degree of uncertainty concerning the legal outcomes if the parties go to court, which is linked to the parties' attitudes towards risk; (4) transaction costs and the parties' respective abilities to bear them; and (5) strategic behavior.'

Ambiguity surrounding (2) will exacerbate uncertainty at (3) – in particular where one or both parties cannot afford legal advice which might otherwise have reduced the uncertainty – and that, in turn, will implicate (4), where the parties' abilities to deal with the costs of uncertainty are unequal.

Part of the difficulty in achieving fair settlements in such circumstances is the gendered nature of negotiation. Wilkinson-Ryan and Small, in reviewing empirical studies of men's and women's bargaining behaviours, note that: 'Since gender differences are typically larger when situations are ambiguous, indeterminate legal standards may provide a context in which gender is more likely to matter.'[59] As if in direct response to Schneider's point, they observe:[60]

> 'We might assume, for example, that indeterminate rules leave the parties less constrained in their private negotiations and thus better able to maximize their joint welfare. But if the empirical data suggests that the parties are not maximizing joint welfare or that there is a systematic imbalance between them (and it does), we might question the value of indeterminate rules and their utility for the normative model.'

If, as the research reviewed by these authors suggests, women tend (inter alia) to prioritise relational issues and inter-personal goals rather than individual goals and to behave less competitively in order to maintain a stereotypically acceptable female image, then (perversely) the very discretionary laws that were designed better to protect women's interests will have the opposite effect.[61]

But the problems that may undermine negotiations' propensity to produce fair settlements extend beyond gender. Craig Martin has applied gender-neutral negotiation theory to suggest that the claimant who seeks, in a discretionary context, to prise resources from the respondent-owner's grasp through negotiation is necessarily disadvantaged because of the different ways in which

---

58 R Mnookin and L Kornhauser, 'Bargaining in the Shadow of the Law: The Case of Divorce' (1979) 88 *Yale Law Journal* 950, 966.

59 T Wilkinson-Ryan and D Small, 'Negotiating Divorce: Gender and the Behavioral Economics of Divorce Bargaining' (2008) 26 *Law and Inequality* 109, 111–12.

60 Ibid, at 132. See also J Behrens, above n 20 at 411.

61 Ibid, at 125. See also M Glendon, above n 2 at 1170 and 1180.

parties respond to the prospects of gains foregone and of losses.[62] Contrary to rational choice theory, it is argued, individuals do not view the chance of missing out on a possible gain of (say) $10 and of sustaining a loss of $10 in the same light. Prospect theory instead suggests that the prospect of a loss will be more robustly fought against than the prospect of an equivalent gain will be fought for. So the claimant of financial remedies (who is likely to have fewer resources to press a claim than the respondent will have to defend it) will be satisfied with a smaller gain than might otherwise have been achievable (in order to avoid incurring further transaction costs in the uncertain pursuit of a larger gain). And the respondent will fight harder to avoid a larger loss.

What matters, then, is whether the individual risks incurring a loss (from a position of entitlement) or merely foregoing a potential gain. Applying this in the context of the then state of Canadian discretionary spousal support law,[63] Martin argues that, given the infrequent grant of spousal support, its uncertain legal basis, and its perception as 'money "given" to a woman (or the spouse in need) and "taken" from a man (or the spouse with the greater income)',[64] claimants effectively start at zero. With no clear *entitlement* to any identifiable sum, they can only gain (or forgo a gain), and will accept whatever they can get. Wherever a discretionary system requires claimants to seek provision from what are (by way of starting point) the respondent's resources, their negotiation will be imbalanced in that way.[65] Only the grant of clearer legal rights to a given share in the resources can level the playing field for private settlement.

So the debate comes full circle: away from the bad old rules, through mid–late twentieth-century discretion, and out the other side in search of 'good' new rules and more principled outcomes that endow individuals with rights, better equipping them to protect their interests in settling family disputes, in court or – far more likely – out.[66] Such a process requires confrontation of Hart's RIF and RIA problems: we must identify which facts are truly pertinent

62 C Martin, above n 55 from 149, applying Kahneman and Tversky's prospect theory. For a survey of this and other pertinent literature, see M Gordon, 'Spousal Support Guidelines and the American Experience: Moving Beyond Discretion' (2002) 19 *Canadian Journal of Family Law* 247.

63 Writing before the Spousal Support Advisory Guidelines, discussed below at 4.3, were developed.

64 C Martin, above n 55 at 154.

65 Section 15 of the PRA is arguably such a scheme. Empirical research demonstrating the difficulty of prosecuting such claims seems to support Martin's thesis: F Garland, 'Section 15 Property (Relationships) Act 1976: Compensation, Substantive Equality and Empirical Realities' [2014] *New Zealand Law Review* 355 and M Henaghan et al, *Property (Relationships) Amendment Act 2001 and Retirement: Are Separated Women More Disadvantaged Than Men?*, Commission for Financial Literacy and Retirement Income, 2012, [3.46]–[3.48] <www.cffc.org.nz> accessed 15.03.2017, reporting tentative research findings by Claire Green, PhD candidate at Otago.

66 See also P Parkinson, above n 20 on this theme.

and seek political agreement on more concrete (and substantively acceptable) legal norms. This process is unavoidable: family law, as a branch of *law*, needs underpinning principles that secure equal and so consistent treatment under that law for those subject to it. As John Eekelaar wrote over 30 years ago (in the context of child custody):[67]

> 'Family law has too long suffered from the myth that, as every case is different, their resolution must be left to the discretion of individual judges. Matters of principle are confronted at every turn. It is time we faced up to them.'

4. DIFFERENT JURISDICTIONS, DIFFERENT JOURNEYS

Yet our willingness to address these issues of principle necessarily underlying family law seems to vary depending on where we come from and what our experience has been. In this penultimate section, I chart the course of three jurisdictions that have had markedly different experiences with rules and discretion and, whilst arguably all moving away from open-ended discretion,[68] are at very different points along that trend-line, deploying quite different legal techniques in this field.

4.1. ENGLAND & WALES – THE RULE-HATING DISCRETION-PHILES?

The primary, even sole, determinant of the typical English family lawyer's response to this debate can be summarised in two words: child support.

Whilst the inception of very broad matrimonial discretion in the nineteenth century initially caused judicial alarm, the judges quickly identified their own limits to fetter the discretion and make its operation a task more suited to a legal mind.[69] By the arrival of the Matrimonial Causes Act 1973 (Eng&W), in which the current substantive law governing financial remedies on divorce is found,[70] they were, in the view of one senior family law judge,[71] more acclimatised to

---

67 J Eekelaar, 'Trust the Judges: How Far Should Family Law Go?' (1984) 47 *Modern Law Review* 593, 597.

68 A trend forecast in 1986 by N Bala above n 20.

69 See R Ormrod, above n 19.

70 As amended by the Matrimonial and Family Proceedings Act 1984 (Eng&W), discussed below.

71 See R Ormrod, above n 19. See also the clear preference for discretion on divorce taken by the Law Commission (Eng&W) in *Family Law: First Report on Family Property: A New Approach*, Law Com No. 52, HMSO, London 1973 and *Third Report on Family Property: The Matrimonial Home (Co-ownership and Occupation Rights) and Household Goods*, Law Com No. 86, HMSO, London 1978.

their task and comforted in it (rightly or wrongly)[72] by Parliament's provision of a checklist of factors to which they should have regard. However, it is worth pausing to note changes made in 1984: these repealed the – admittedly impossible – 'minimal loss' objective, and introduced new provisions prioritising the welfare of any minor children of the family and requiring judges to consider whether a clean break could be achieved.[73] This left the legislation without any express overarching objective, a prospect that had divided judicial opinion. The more senior judges (of the Family Division of the High Court, who deal with complex or high value cases and hear occasional appeals from more everyday cases) 'considered that any satisfactory solution ... necessarily involved the court retaining a wide discretion so as to be able to take account of the factual circumstances which present themselves'. Meanwhile, the Registrars (who dealt with the vast bulk of first instance cases) 'pointed out that it was difficult to find a just solution if there were no guiding principle, and urged that "to remove the guiding light is to allow flexibility to go mad"'.[74]

For years, the judges operated the jurisdiction largely as a vehicle for making needs-only provision for the supplicant-claimant from the resources of the owner-spouse. But the House of Lords in *White v White*[75] famously changed the law's direction (at least for higher value cases) by introducing the germ of the sharing principle that took root in *Miller; McFarlane*[76] alongside the principles of need and compensation as the constituent principles of the (implicit) overarching objective of 'fairness'. And so English financial remedy law now operates a discretionary system structured (to a greater or lesser extent)[77] by judge-made (rather than legislated) principle, which is nevertheless experienced by the vast majority of parties (whose combined resources do not exceed their joint needs) as a needs-based discretionary system. It has not escaped continuing criticism: for failing adequately to address key points of principle (for example, about the nature and extent of needs-based obligation and the relationship between the three judge-made principles), for its relative lack of transparency, and concern about the production of inconsistent results on what appears to be a postcode lottery (or even judge-by-judge) basis.[78]

---

72 See R Thompson's 'laundry-listing' critique, above n 20.

73 Effected by the Matrimonial and Family Proceedings Act 1984 (Eng&W): see ss 25(1) and 25(2)(g) as amended, and s 25A and associated provisions in the Matrimonial Causes Act 1973 (Eng&W).

74 See Law Commission (Eng&W), *The Financial Consequences of Divorce*, Law Com No. 112, HMSO, London 1981, [20].

75 [2001] 1 AC 596.

76 *Miller v Miller; McFarlane v McFarlane* [2006] UKHL 24, [2006] 2 AC 618.

77 Different compositions of the Court of Appeal have different views of how far it is proper or desirable to cabin the discretion with those principles: see above n 41.

78 See Law Commission (Eng&W), *Marital Property Agreements*, Law Com CP 198, TSO, London 2010, pts 2 and 3.

Meanwhile, English law had a diabolical experience with the inception of an administratively, rather than judicially, operated system of Byzantine child support rules in the original Child Support Act 1991 (UK). The scheme has long since been heavily modified to remove the worst of the complexity and streamline the system, not least by now discouraging parents from using the system at all and directing them to the simple online calculator (which requires very few inputs) to produce the statutorily mandated sum. However, the horrifying experience of the original child support scheme (exacerbated by IT disasters) completely tarnished the reputation of rules in English family law, such that any suggestion that financial remedies law on divorce might be subjected to a more rule-based system elicits dissent from most quarters. This opposition is based on an assumption, given the local child support experience, that rules and formulae are necessarily 'rigid', and so the antithesis of the system of individualised justice that many professional actors within the court-based system imagine that they currently dispense.

Thus was the recent experience of the Law Commission for England and Wales when it tentatively suggested a more formulaic approach to spousal support.[79] It is interesting to survey the responses received by the Commission to its consultation questions:[80]

> 'Do consultees agree with our central argument that the current law requires reform to ensure that the payment of spousal support is founded on a principled basis that explains what has to be paid by way of spousal support, and for how long?
>
> If consultees favour a principled reform of spousal support, should it take the form of:
>
> 1) a reformed discretionary approach; or
> 2) a formulaic calculation?'

The Commission reported that consultees' views on the latter question were split almost entirely along professional lines: between judges and practitioners (who largely favoured discretion, some defending the current law) and academics and others (who largely favoured exploration of the formulaic option).[81]

The most robust defence of discretion – in its current manifestation – was again made by 12 judges of the Family Division.[82] They entirely rejected the

---

[79] In the course of its project *Matrimonial Property, Needs and Agreements*, Law Com CP 208, TSO, London 2012, and Law Com No. 343, TSO, London 2014.

[80] Law Commission (Eng&W), *Matrimonial Property, Needs and Agreements Consultation (2): Supplementary Consultation*, Law Com CP 208, TSO, London 2012, [4.113] and [4.116].

[81] Law Commission (Eng&W), No. 343, above n 79 from [3.135].

[82] The full set of responses can be accessed online at: Law Commission (Eng&W), *Matrimonial Property, Needs and Agreements Consultation (2): Supplementary Consultation Reponses* <www.lawcom.gov.uk/project/matrimonial-property-needs-and-agreements/> accessed 16.03.2017, the response of the Family Division judges starts at 232; seven of the then current Family

Commission's view that the current law is 'based … upon a mix of mutually inconsistent principles' and that there are currently 'multiple justifications, which generate inconsistent results'. Rather, these judges felt that the law 'is principled and is adequately certain', whilst enabling individualised justice to be done.[83] They drew support for their view that the law is 'sufficiently certain and properly understood' from the fact that about 95 per cent of financial remedy cases brought to court are in fact settled, either prior to proceedings being launched or during the course of contested proceedings, such parties seeking a consent order reflecting the terms of their agreement to make it fully binding.[84] But, given the discussion above, we should not be comforted by the mere *fact* of settlement without knowing in rather more detail how those settlements are being reached and what parties are settling for and why.[85] With respect, the High Court is not the best vantage point from which to evaluate the operation of the law on the ground, not least for the roughly two thirds of divorces in England & Wales in relation to which *no* financial remedy order, by consent or otherwise, is obtained at all.[86] The majority of divorcing couples are operating entirely off radar: we simply do not know what settlements, if any, they are reaching, and how far they reflect the loose 'entitlements' conferred by this discretionary scheme.[87]

The response of the Family Law Bar Association[88] seemed similarly affected by the best vantage point of its members, who get nowhere near most cases. But once we reach the responses of the solicitors, who see rather more of the terrain and are closer to the clients' perspective, we are given a rather different view. Whilst discretion is clearly preferred to formulae (which, it is said, 'could create arbitrary and harsh outcomes' and remove room for manoeuvre in negotiations),[89] there is a feeling that 'the current law on spousal support is not a sustainable policy choice for the future' and that the lack of principle (as they see it, contra the judges' view) 'can increase legal costs and the unnecessary

---

Division judges did not participate in the response, having different views or preferring to express no view. It is interesting to note a nuanced contrast in the opinions of these senior judges and the *slightly* less robust view of the Association of District Judges, the successors of the Registrars, from 270: they seem no longer as concerned about the absence of legislated overarching principle, but saw a need for additional guidance to ensure consistency of approach whilst still permitting uninhibited pursuit of individualised justice.

83 Ibid, at 234.

84 Ibid.

85 Cf E Hitchings, J Miles and H Woodward, *Assembling the Jigsaw Puzzle: Understanding Financial Settlement on Divorce*, University of Bristol, Bristol 2013 <www.bristol.ac.uk/media-library/sites/law/migrated/documents/assemblingthejigsawpuzzle.pdf> accessed 16.03.2017; H Woodward and M Sefton, above n 10.

86 See Family Court Statistics Quarterly, available at <https://www.gov.uk/government/collections/family-court-statistics-quarterly> accessed 30.08.2017.

87 Cf S Arthur et al, *Settling Up: Making Financial Arrangements After Divorce or Separation*, National Centre for Social Research, London 2002.

88 Law Commission (Eng&W), Family Law Bar Association, above n 82 from 387.

89 Ibid, Resolution, the specialist family law solicitors' organisation, at 476.

use of limited court resources' and encourage domestic forum-shopping,[90] 'can create unrealistic expectations for divorcing couples and can render the law inaccessible and uncertain, particularly for self-represented parties'.[91] The latter, in particular, may be disadvantaged by the absence of expectation management by lawyers, who – equipped with the requisite 'Talmudic knowledge' – can often provide the client with some indication of the range of reasonable outcomes for their case.[92] And, arguably most crucially, in the view of one local law society, 'judicial discretion (whether reformed or not) is only available to the privileged few'.[93]

The Law Commission was not dissuaded by these mixed responses from its diagnosis of the problems in the current law.[94] For the immediate future, it recommended that the operation of the existing discretion be rendered more transparent and any inconsistency in its exercise by judges be alleviated by the provision by an authoritative body of (non-binding) guidance to litigants in person and judges/lawyers respectively.[95] As to formulae, the Commission was encouraged by more positive responses from those who had attended events late in the consultation period at which the Canadian system, discussed below, was examined. That exercise made clear to those consultees that the English child support experience is *not* representative of all formula-based systems, and that the problems of rigidity and harsh outcomes can be avoided by intelligent and flexible system design.[96]

However, prospects of any such scheme being devised for England and Wales seem remote, so for the time being we persist with our familiar discretionary scheme which – depending on judicial preferences – may become increasingly structured by further development of judicial principles. To that extent, English law might be thought to be moving – by judicial activity – closer to Scots law, to which I turn next.

---

90 Ibid, at 473.

91 Ibid, The Law Society, at 527.

92 See E Hitchings, J Miles and H Woodward, above n 85, and other empirical studies. Though striking evidence from Australia suggests that practitioners' confidence that they know 'the range' within which outcomes will be reached may be misplaced: J Wade, 'Arbitral Decision-Making in Family Property Disputes – Lotteries, Crystal Balls and Wild Guesses' (2003) 17 *Australian Journal of Family Law* 224.

93 Law Commission (Eng&W), The City of Westminster and Holborn Law Society, above n 82 at 681.

94 See Law Commission (Eng&W) No. 343, above n 79 from [2.44].

95 Ibid, from [3.59]. This has now been done by the Family Justice Council: see Advicenow <www.advicenow.org.uk/guides/survival-guide-sorting-out-your-finances-when-you-get-divorced> accessed 16.03.2017 and Family Justice Council <www.judiciary.gov.uk/wp-content/uploads/2016/04/fjc-financial-needs-april-16-final.pdf> accessed 16.03.2017.

96 Ibid, from [3.121].

4.2. SCOTLAND – THE ROUGH AND READY BUT PRINCIPLED JUSTICE BRIGADE?

North of the border, despite sharing the UK-wide child support horror story, the overall picture – and attitude towards the rules/discretion discussion – is completely different, as is evident from the distinctive Scottish statutes that govern financial remedies on divorce and on breakdown of cohabiting relationships. These create not a broad discretion but expressly legislated frameworks of principles within which the judge must grant any remedy.

Scots law governing financial provision on divorce knew a fully discretionary regime only between the mid-1960s and mid-1980s. Legislation in 1964 had moved the law away from gendered, capital-only provision made (as if the guilty spouse had died!) in accordance with the fixed rights of Scots succession law, instead allowing both income and capital provision on a broad discretionary basis.[97] From 1976, 'guilty' spouses were permitted to seek relief, a minimal reform to recognise the new no-fault basis of divorce law.[98] But in that same year, the Scottish Law Commission was already consulting on further reform, concerned about the lack of any stated objective for, or principles underlying, the exercise of the discretion.[99] This, it considered, entailed the 'abdication of all collective responsibility in favour of the conscience of the single judge',[100] and the resulting lack of transparency and consistency in awards would make it more difficult for lawyers to advise and for parties to settle cases amicably; instead, it was said, a discretionary scheme 'is calculated to increase animosity and bitterness'.[101]

And so, in the same year that the English Law Commission was making the recommendations[102] that from 1984 rendered English law arguably even *more strongly* discretionary, their Scottish counterparts were advocating the reforms enacted in the Family Law (Scotland) Act 1985 ('1985 Act'), which remains in force today. The principled model of this Act in turn formed the basis from which the Scottish Law Commission later made recommendations for more limited financial provision between cohabitants,[103] enacted in the Family Law (Scotland) Act 2006.[104]

---

97 Succession (Scotland) Act 1964, s 26.

98 Divorce (Scotland) Act 1976.

99 Scottish Law Commission, *Aliment and Financial Provision*, Memorandum No. 22, HMSO, Edinburgh 1976.

100 Scottish Law Commission, *Family Law: Aliment and Financial Provision*, Scot Law Com No. 67, HMSO, Edinburgh 1981, [3.37].

101 Ibid.

102 Law Commission (Eng&W), above n 74.

103 Scottish Law Commission, above n 17.

104 See F Wasoff, J Miles and E Mordaunt, *Legal Practitioners' Perspectives on the Cohabitation Provisions of the Family Law (Scotland) Act 2006*, CRFR, Edinburgh 2010 <www.crfr.ac.uk/assets/Cohabitation-final-report.pdf> accessed 17.03.2017.

The 1985 Act commands the judge to make 'such order, if any, as is (a) justified by the principles set out in section 9 of this Act; and (b) reasonable having regard to the resources of the parties'.[105] Those principles, each supported by its own supplementary rules/checklists, require: (1) the 'fair' sharing of the net value of matrimonial property, ordinarily equal sharing unless prescribed special circumstances obtain; (2) 'fair account' of 'any economic advantage derived by either party from contributions by the other' and of 'any economic disadvantage suffered by either party in the interests of the other party or of the family'; (3) 'fair' sharing of the economic burden of child care post-divorce; (4) reasonable transitional support (up to three years) to facilitate adjustment where substantial financial dependency has arisen during marriage; and (5) provision relieving hardship for a reasonable period (with no prescribed maximum) where one party 'seems likely to suffer serious financial hardship as a result of the divorce'.[106]

A team of empirical researchers recently concluded that the 1985 Act was 'built to last'.[107] Their 'overwhelming finding'[108] was one of satisfaction with the current law, with no desire for substantial reform and caution even about tinkering with it. Both legal practitioners *and* judges felt that the law works well, offering the right balance between certainty and flexibility – by contrast with the broad discretion of English law, invoked by several respondents as an example of how not to regulate this aspect of family law.[109] While the principles were felt to provide a clear substantive framework within which the decision must be taken, the varied tools for effecting the required asset transfers provide considerable flexibility and scope for creativity.[110] In the view of one judge interviewed by the researchers, the five principles strike the right balance because they are:[111]

> 'nice and high level … not micro-managed … but at the same time it's not palm tree justice where the judge can do what he sees fit in all the circumstances … People have pegs to hang their arguments on … and therefore people generally will know where they are.'

---

105 Family Law (Scotland) Act 1985, s 8(2).

106 Ibid, ss 9–11.

107 J Mair, E Mordaunt and F Wasoff, *Built to Last: The Family Law (Scotland) Act 1985 – 30 Years of Financial Provision on Divorce*, Nuffield Foundation, Glasgow 2016 <http://eprints.gla.ac.uk/117617/1/117617.pdf> accessed 17.03.2017.

108 See key findings summary, available at <http://eprints.gla.ac.uk/117617/> accessed 01.08.2017.

109 Ibid, from 155.

110 Ibid, from 96, though the Act only allows periodical payments to be used to give effect to the last three principles: see Family Law (Scotland) Act 1985, ss 13–14, unhelpfully depriving the Scots of a tool that could usefully help mitigate concerns about the difficulties of predicting the future for the purposes of economic disadvantage claims.

111 Ibid, at 120.

The point about micro-management is an interesting one for the New Zealand perspective, particularly in relation to its economic disparity provision in section 15 of the PRA. Where the New Zealand case law, responding to the various jurisdictional limits drafted into section 15, has adopted a rather pernickety, quasi-formulaic approach, Scots case law and legal practice – in so far as it deploys the economic advantage/disadvantage principle at all – deploys a broad brush, doubtless aided by less prescriptive statutory drafting.

However, as in New Zealand, it seems that the economic advantage/disadvantage principle has been somewhat under-used on divorce.[112] There is a perception that it is hard to obtain a departure from equal sharing on that basis (the 'fair' sharing of property under that principle adequately addressing the disadvantage),[113] that it is complex to argue, not easy to prove and quantify given its crystal ball gazing aspect (save in the case of forgone professional careers with clear pay-scale progression), and inhibited by a conservative professional and judicial approach.

But the economic advantage/disadvantage principle may be undergoing a small renaissance thanks to its centrality to the scheme applicable between cohabitants on separation.[114] Cohabitants' financial settlements are governed only by a version of that and the economic burden of the child care principle, and so the applicant starts not with a half-share of relationship property but only with what he or she owns. This has necessarily required legal professionals and judges to give the principle rather closer attention than it has received in the matrimonial context, and the Supreme Court decision in *Gow v Grant*[115] has clearly signalled that a broad approach should be taken both to interpretation of the jurisdictional limits inherent in the principle's drafting and to the quantification of awards under it.[116]

So, Scotland, a small jurisdiction with a close-knit legal community and continuing availability of legal aid, seems very largely content with its lot.

---

112 Ibid, from 64.

113 Respondents were critical of the decision in *Coyle v Coyle* 2004 Fam LR 2 for foreclosing arguments under this principle. But the judge declined to make an award under it because the substantial recent increase in value of the assets allocated to the wife under the first principle (for which purpose matrimonial property is ordinarily valued at the date of separation) meant that, viewed in the round, the wife was enjoying a significantly more valuable award than the first principle alone would have allowed her. Lady Smith's judgment is otherwise notable for its broad-brush approach to quantification of economic disadvantage, in preference to use of actuarial tables of the sort used for personal injury awards in tort law.

114 Ibid, from 72, discussing the Family Law (Scotland) Act 2006.

115 *Gow v Grant* [2012] UKSC 29, 2012 Fam LR 80.

116 An encouragement perhaps taken rather too far in *Whigham v Owen* [2013] CSOH 29, where the judge paints not so much with a broad brush as with a roller! Cf suggestions by some research respondents that the more technical (clumsy?) drafting of the economic advantage/disadvantage principle in the 2006 Act encourages a more forensic approach: J Mair, E Mordaunt and F Wasoff, above n 107 at 73.

But it is questionable whether the Scots have embraced the full potential of their legislative scheme, particularly as a means of achieving greater substantive economic equality in cases of economic advantage and disadvantage. There seems to be a reluctance to move out of the equal sharing harbour into the choppier waters of economic disparity, perhaps rightly conscious of the loss of certainty that that will entail. The question is how, if at all, that important substantive issue can be dealt with, particularly when – as in the Scottish legislation – the option of using periodical payments to deal with that head of claim is not available and broader discretion is considered alien.

4.3. CANADA – THE RULE-FRIENDLY DISCRETION-PHOBES?

Lastly, I come to Canada, whose financial remedy laws share some features with New Zealand but diverge in other respects. The first thing to note is Canada's unusually happy experience with child support rules, which have from the outset been administered by judges rather than by faceless bureaucrats.[117] Unlike England & Wales, Canada is not suffering from national post-traumatic stress disorder brought on by a rules-based maelstrom, leaving it better able to take a measured view about the potential of more rule-like systems to help achieve a balance of certainty and fairness on divorce – and to conclude that 'average' rather than 'individualised' justice may be at least tolerable and practical.[118] Rather, Canada's pointedly *unhappy* experience has been with discretion and perhaps crucially – unlike in England & Wales – academics, practitioners, and judges alike were united in their protest against it.[119]

Canadian law, like New Zealand law, treats property division (governed by the relevant provincial or territorial statute)[120] separately from spousal support on divorce (governed by federal legislation).[121] Like other common law jurisdictions, Canada's first forays into property distribution on divorce entailed discretionary systems of equitable distribution. But typical concerns about the operation of judicial discretion in this arena[122] led each of the provinces and territories from the late 1980s onwards to legislate more explicitly for equal sharing of matrimonial property, permitting departure from equal sharing on more or less tightly circumscribed grounds. Meanwhile, spousal support under the federal legislation remains a matter for judicial discretion, framed by four

[117] Noted by C Rogerson, above n 44 at 6.
[118] Ibid.
[119] Ibid, at 4.
[120] For example, Ontario: Family Law Act RSO 1990 c F3 (Ont).
[121] Divorce Act RSC 1985 c 3 (2nd Supp) (Can), s 15.2. Cf provincial and territorial statutes dealing with spousal support on separation.
[122] See generally N Bala, above n 20.

familiar objectives set out in section 15(6) of the 1985 Act: to recognise any economic advantages or disadvantages to the spouses arising from the marriage or its breakdown; to apportion between the spouses any financial consequences of child care going beyond any obligation for child support; to relieve any economic hardship arising from the breakdown of the marriage; and, as far as possible, to promote economic self-sufficiency within a reasonable period.

This was a considerable advance on the much more broadly framed precursor Divorce Act 1968 (Canada), which – typically of many of the first no-fault divorce era statutes – contained no principles or even a checklist to guide the judge's decision.[123] But matters took an unhappy turn thanks to the cumulative impact of three Supreme Court of Canada decisions: *Pelech v Pelech*,[124] *Moge v Moge*,[125] and – most problematically – *Bracklow v Bracklow*.[126] These decisions between them introduced a plethora of mutually inconsistent theories of spousal support – clean break, compensatory, and non-compensatory – which left the law floundering in a state of abject 'rulelessness'.[127] It was impossible to identify precisely whether, when and why spousal support liability would arise in any given case and – in particular, the Supreme Court providing scant guidance on this issue – how to quantify awards and determine their duration.

The resulting experience of spousal support cases created a perception that the law was 'excessively discretionary, creating an unacceptable degree of uncertainty and unpredictability', with the result that individual judges' 'subjective perceptions of fair outcomes play[ed] a large role in determining the spousal support ultimately ordered', and lawyers struggled to predict case outcomes which, in turn, impeded efficient settlement of cases. And parties who lacked access to legal advice or who were in weak bargaining positions were not pursuing support claims at all. All in all, 'the uncertainty and unpredictability … cast doubt upon the fairness of the outcomes, thus undermining the legitimacy of the spousal support obligation'.[128]

The response was the monumental project led by Professors Carol Rogerson and Rollie Thompson,[129] under the aegis of the Department of Justice, to create the (non-binding) Canadian Spousal Support Advisory Guidelines ('SSAG')

---

123 Ibid, from 24.

124 *Pelech v Pelech* [1987] 1 SCR 801: actually a decision under the 1968 Act but one which in practice guided decisions under the new Act – see C Rogerson, 'The Canadian Law of Spousal Support' (2004) 38 *Family Law Quarterly* 69, 78.

125 *Moge v Moge* [1992] 3 SCR 813.

126 *Bracklow v Bracklow* [1999] 1 SCR 420.

127 R Thompson, above n 20.

128 C Rogerson, above n 44 at 5.

129 For an accessible overview of the background to the Guidelines, their development, and the scheme itself, see C Rogerson and R Thompson, 'The Canadian Experiment with Spousal Support Guidelines' (2011) 45 *Family Law Quarterly* 241.

designed to facilitate decision-making about the appropriate quantum and duration of support payments. The SSAG presuppose that a positive decision has already been made about the claimant's entitlement to support (and so the respondent's liability to pay). The guidelines are based on extensive research to identify patterns in a range of case types across Canada, converted into a suite of mathematical formulae for both 'with-' and 'without-child support' cases. The basic components of the (more straightforward) without-child support formula are income disparity and duration of marriage; the various with-child support formulae are more complex, incorporating (amongst other things) child support, associated tax deductions, and welfare benefits. The SSAG were first published in 2008, subject to periodic reviews and revision by their architects since,[130] and their use has been approved by several provincial Courts of Appeal.[131]

It is important to appreciate that the guidelines are quite different in their form from typical child support formulae. Where the latter will produce a single number, which the payor is obligated to pay, the former instead operate in a more nuanced and flexible way. They produce a *range* of figures, for both quantum and duration of support payments, from within which the judge (or parties) then settle on an amount appropriate for their case, given its particular features; the resulting liability can also be capitalised ('restructured') to permit a clean break. Their proper (quite sophisticated) operation depends (at least for the more complex with-child-support formulae) on the use of software and the availability of legal advice to pitch the final award amount appropriately. But a free basic calculator is available online and (for CAD$29.95 for six months) individuals can access a more advanced version able to accommodate more types of input (such as self-employed and some other sources of income, and child-related expenses). Parties arguably only need access to the proprietary software if they had other, more sophisticated, circumstances (such as dividend income) that needed to be factored in.

Guidelines avoid the need (beyond the initial decision that *some* support liability exists) to establish precise causation or to measure economic disadvantage or need. Instead, they adopt proxy measures for those often unprovable, immeasurable items and an immediately quantified way of expressing underlying principles (of income-sharing, of unravelling the merger of the parties' lives over time, of differential loss of the marital standard of living, or whatever principle is adopted), avoiding the head-scratching (and costs) that necessarily flow from any endeavour to identify and calculate these de novo on an individualised basis. They may, therefore, be said transparently to provide a quantitatively rather than qualitatively expressed guide to the acceptable range

---

[130] Current guidelines: Department of Justice, Government of Canada <www.justice.gc.ca/eng/fl-df/spousal-epoux/ssag-ldfpae.html>.

[131] See C Rogerson and R Thompson, above n 128 at 259–60.

of 'fair' outcomes for each individual case.[132] This in turn may 'encourage both spouses that the scope for argument is fairly well defined and that fairness can in some way be quantified', aiding settlement.[133] And, bearing in mind the negotiation theory literature discussed above, the guidelines may particularly support claimants: 'Rather than the payor starting from zero (or as close to zero as possible), the payor is now informed of a "range", as is the recipient.'[134]

The Canadian guidelines unashamedly deliver 'average' rather than 'individualised' justice. But as Ira Ellman, who was to become principal architect of the American Law Institute's spousal support formula in the *Principles of the Law of Family Dissolution*,[135] argued in his seminal article on alimony: 'Even crude approximations of theoretically defensible criteria are probably better than intuitive estimates of what is "fair" under a system lacking established principles of "fairness" in the first place.'[136] While acknowledging various problems being encountered in the use of the guidelines – not least their relative inaccessibility to unrepresented parties – Carol Rogerson concludes in her recent review that 'in this highly-contested area of family law, the greater consistency and predictability of outcomes ultimately leads to greater fairness and legitimacy for the substantive remedy itself'.[137]

5. WHERE NEXT FOR NEW ZEALAND – 'O, CANADA!'?

And so my argument reaches its natural conclusion: that the best future for New Zealand might lie in something akin to the Canadian scheme.

Like Canada, New Zealand started its no-fault life with a fairly broad discretion in the Matrimonial Property Act 1963 (NZ) but was unhappy with the conservative way in which judges exercised their discretion,[138] and so moved away from discretion in its Matrimonial Property Act 1976 (NZ). Properly recognising the inadequacy of equal sharing of capital under the original

132 While English and Scots lawyers can generally convert their qualitatively expressed laws into a range of numbers, that process is self-evidently less transparent than in the Canadian scheme.

133 Response of solicitor and mediator Julia Thackray to the English Law Commission's recent consultation: Law Commission (Eng&W), above n 82 at 587.

134 C Rogerson and R Thompson, above n 128 at 261.

135 American Law Institute, above n 40 at ch 5.

136 I Ellman, 'The Theory of Alimony' (1989) 77 *California Law Review* 1, 79.

137 C Rogerson and R Thompson, above n 128 at 269.

138 See, for example, C Bridge, 'Reallocating of Property after Marriage Breakdown' in M Henaghan and B Atkin (eds), *Family Law and Policy in New Zealand*, OUP, Auckland 1992; K Gray, *Reallocation of Property on Divorce*, Professional Books, Abingdon 1977, 119–24 discussing the position pre-*Haldane v Haldane* [1976] 2 NZLR 715, [1977] AC 673 (PC).

1976 Act, it sought to provide a means of securing greater substantive economic equality by enacting section 15 in 2001, but has been discomfited by the experience of operating that section's inherent discretion.

It is not part of my brief to identify the substantive basis on which economic resources should be distributed on divorce,[139] merely to identify the vehicle(s) that should be used to give effect to whatever rationales are selected. But the Principles set out in section 1N(a) to (c) of the PRA seem to me to express the right essential ideas: a basic principle of equal sharing modified by a recognition that true equality requires a form of *substantive* economic equality that shares the economic burdens created by the relationship and its demise, as well as its capital gains. The Principle enshrined in section 1N(d) rightly acknowledges that the virtue of justice needs to be counterbalanced with the virtues of speed, simplicity, and low cost. But the current law is failing to achieve that balance: substantive economic equality is proving too difficult to operationalise by way of judicial discretion.[140] Some new mechanism is needed.

Inevitably, the nettle of average, rather than individualised, justice must be grasped. In my view, the current problems are best resolved in the New Zealand context with a continuing rule of equal sharing of relationship property (subject perhaps to its other current exceptions), combined with a rule-like, but flexible, scheme (as exemplified by the Canadian guidelines) to achieve *some version* of substantive economic equality, the basis of which would need to be articulated to the extent felt adequate to identify, broadly, the types of case in which equal sharing should be departed from on that ground.[141] The latter element would replace section 15 of the PRA *and* bring what is now the Family Proceedings Act 1980 (NZ) jurisdiction within one overall statutory scheme for economic adjustment (capital and income). The numbers produced

---

139 See J Miles, 'Financial Provision and Property Division on Relationship Breakdown: A Theoretical Analysis of the New Zealand Legislation' (2004) 21 *New Zealand Universities Law Review* 268, for a critique of the mixed principles being pursued by the two NZ statutes; and J Miles, 'Principle or Pragmatism in Ancillary Relief: The Virtues of Flirting with Academic Theories and Other Jurisdictions' (2005) 19 *International Journal of Law, Policy and the Family* 242.

140 The minority report of the Parliamentary Select Committee on the then Matrimonial Property Amendment Bill and Supplementary Order Paper no 25, 109–3 (commentary) at 44 seems to have been prescient as regards s 15: 'The Government has got it wrong because letting judges decide property division on a case-by-case basis means there will be no certainty any more. Different judges will make different assessments giving different results.'

141 That is, the equivalent of the prior, 'liability' stage which the Canadian SSAG do not deal with. Note that the American Law Institute's recommended formulae explicitly operate simply in response to the fact of the relationship (and its duration/presence of children) pragmatically *without* requiring proof of any specific loss or causation of loss: for an overview, see J Miles, 'Dealing with Economic Disparity: An Analysis of Section 15 Property (Relationships) Act 1976' [2003] *New Zealand Law Review* 535, from 542.

via the equal sharing rule and the guidelines for substantive economic equality would then be implemented using a remedially flexible response, that is to say, a comprehensive toolkit of court orders for the transfer (and temporary use)[142] of capital and income resources. Judges and parties could then devise whatever practical divvying of resources to transfer the required quantum best suited the circumstances. Flexibility in that practical arena is more important, desirable, and far more tolerable than flexibility (to the point of inconsistency and/or unworkability) in establishing and quantifying liability.

Devising a guidelines scheme analogous to the SSAG for New Zealand would be no small task, particularly in the absence of a similarly large pool of practice, especially reported decisions, on which to draw in undertaking that exercise. It would require a determination to eliminate Hart's problems of RIF and RIA that drive the law maker towards discretion, by accepting a far narrower range of relevant facts and settling on an agreed formula through which those facts would then point towards a clearly quantifiable answer (or rather, range of answers). But if they can devise a scheme for the nearly 10 million square kilometres and over 36 million people of Canada, conducting a similar exercise across the 268,000 square kilometres and 4.7 million Kiwis must be feasible.

142 In particular, by granting occupation rights over the former family home which may defer sale and division of proceeds to a later date, eg for the benefit of children of the family.

CHAPTER 12

SHARING FAMILY FINANCES AT THE END OF A RELATIONSHIP

Mark HENAGHAN*

* Thank you to Ruth Ballantyne BA (Hons) LLB, University of Otago Faculty of Law's Professional Practice Fellow for her invaluable research and editorial assistance with this chapter.

1. INTRODUCTION

When marriages, civil partnerships (known as 'civil unions' in New Zealand), and de facto relationships end, the division of family finances is inevitable. Family finances consist of all of the parties' assets in existence at that time. The expectation is that the law will provide a fair method for dividing the parties' finances. What is fair or not differs between societies and across generations. Lord Nicholls summed up the subjective nature of fairness well in *Miller v Miller; McFarlane v McFarlane* when he said:[1]

> 'Fairness is an elusive concept. It is an instinctive response to a given set of facts. Ultimately it is grounded in social and moral values. These values, or attitudes, can be stated. But they cannot be justified, or refuted, by any objective process of logical reasoning. Moreover, they change from one generation to the next. It is not surprising therefore that in the present context there can be different views on the requirements of fairness in any particular case.'

After an examination of the underlying purposes of dividing family finances, this chapter focuses on how best to divide family finances, drawing primarily on legislative and judicial analysis from New Zealand and England and Wales. This chapter argues that all the 'fruits' of a qualifying relationship, in terms of both capital assets and human capital (income earning capacity), should be shared equally between the parties upon the conclusion of a qualifying marriage, civil union, or de facto relationship (a 'qualifying relationship').

The chapter ultimately provides a case study of general international application as to how politicians and judges see their society, and what counts most in determining a share in family finances at the end of a qualifying relationship. It provides two possible formulas for ensuring that both parties receive their fair share going into the future.

2. THE PURPOSES OF DIVIDING FAMILY FINANCES

Law is a means of resolving disputes in a society. In order to effectively resolve disputes, the law must be clear in wording and purpose, it must be fair, and it needs to be accessible to all members of society, without the need for expensive litigation. Whilst it is impossible to avoid what HLA Hart famously described as the 'penumbra of uncertainty' surrounding law, as a result of the limitations of language and the possibility of differing interpretations, such uncertainty should

1 *Miller v Miller; McFarlane v McFarlane* [2006] UKHL 24, [2006] 2 AC 618 at [4].

be minimised as much as possible.[2] The best antidote to uncertainty is clear simple language directed towards what the law was designed to achieve. This works best when the underlying purposes of the law in question are entirely transparent. However, as discussed later in this chapter, even when legislation provides clear rules for the division of family finances that are underpinned by stated purposes and principles, judges do not always get it right.[3]

The 'ultimate objective' of dividing family finances at the end of a qualifying relationship is, as Lady Hale said in *Miller v Miller; McFarlane v McFarlane*, 'to give each party an equal start on the road to independent living'.[4] This is consistent with New Zealand law on the division of family finances (known as 'relationship property') which is encapsulated in the Property (Relationships) Act 1976 (NZ) ('PRA') and the Family Proceedings Act 1980 (NZ) ('FPA'). The stated purposes of the PRA are as follows:[5]

> **'1M Purpose of this Act**
>
> The purpose of this Act is –
>
> (a) to reform the law relating to the property of married couples and civil union couples, and of couples who live together in a de facto relationship:
> (b) to recognise the equal contribution of both spouses to the marriage partnership, of civil union partners to the civil union, and of de facto partners to the de facto relationship partnership:
> (c) to provide for a just division of the relationship property between the spouses or partners when their relationship ends by separation or death, and in certain other circumstances, while taking account of the interests of any children of the marriage or children of the civil union or children of the de facto relationship.'

The PRA emphasises that both partners contribute equally to qualifying relationships and that there 'is no presumption that a contribution of a monetary nature ... is of greater value than a contribution of a non-monetary nature'.[6] These provisions were included in the PRA as a direct response to the historic undervaluing of domestic contributions as opposed to financial ones. This issue is discussed in more detail in section 3 below.

In order to ensure a 'just division of relationship property',[7] the PRA prescribes that qualifying spouses and partners are 'entitled to share equally'

---

2 HLA Hart, 'Positivism and the Separation of Law and Morals' (1958) 71(4) *Harvard Law Review* 593, 607.
3 See 3 and 5 below.
4 *Miller v Miller; McFarlane v McFarlane*, above n 1 at [144].
5 Property (Relationships) Act 1976 (NZ) ('PRA'), s 1M.
6 PRA, s 18(2).
7 PRA, s 1M(c).

in all relationship property subject to limited exceptions.[8] However, the PRA recognises that an equal share of all relationship property will not always equate to a 'just division'.[9] This is because the PRA is premised on substantive equality, or equality of outcome.[10] Indeed, one of the guiding principles of the PRA is that:[11]

> 'a just division of relationship property has regard to the economic advantages or disadvantages to the spouses or partners arising from their marriage, civil union, or de facto relationship or from the ending of their marriage, civil union, or de facto relationship.'

This allows for situations where, even after an equal division of relationship property, there will still be a significant economic disparity between the parties in terms of their incomes and living standards.[12] As the latter parts of this chapter demonstrate, this provision (and its stated purpose) has been interpreted narrowly by the courts who find it hard to reconcile with the notion of equal sharing.[13]

The final purpose of the division of family finances in New Zealand is to ensure that, at the end of a qualifying relationship, the 'reasonable needs' of both parties are being met.[14] An individual's 'reasonable needs' are generally based on the parties' standard of living while they were together.[15] In determining whether a party is liable to pay spousal support (known as 'maintenance') under the FPA, the court has discretion to consider whether the party applying for maintenance is unable to meet their own 'reasonable needs' because of the ability of the parties to become self-supporting (which takes into account the effects of the division of functions within the relationship, the parties' earning capacities, and other relevant circumstances), the parties' child care responsibilities, and the parties' standard of living while they were living together.[16] In line with the clean break principle, there is an assumption that parties must resume responsibility for meeting their own reasonable needs within a reasonable time.[17] What is considered to be a reasonable period of time depends on the age of the parties, the duration of the qualifying relationship, and the ability of the parties to

---

8 PRA, s 11. The exceptions to the presumption of equal sharing of relationship property are discussed in 5 below.

9 PRA, s 1M(c).

10 This is analogous to Ronald Dworkin's concept of the equality of resources. See generally, R Dworkin, *Law's Empire*, Fontana, London 1986.

11 PRA, s 1N(c).

12 PRA, s 15. See 5.3 below for a detailed discussion of this issue.

13 See 5.3 below for a more detailed examination of this issue.

14 Family Proceedings Act 1980 (NZ) ('FPA'), s 64.

15 FPA, s 65(5).

16 FPA, ss 64(1) and 64(2).

17 FPA, s 64A.

become self-supporting in all the particular circumstances of the case.[18] The FPA provides for the payment of maintenance via a lump sum or periodic payment.[19]

The PRA requires a court to have regard to any maintenance orders made under the FPA, as well as orders for child support made under the Child Support Act 1991 (NZ).[20] If considered just, the PRA also empowers the court to make an order for maintenance under the FPA, and to discharge, vary, extend, or suspend an order already in existence.[21] It may also make or vary orders involving child support in the context of relationship property proceedings.[22] These powers provide the court with a further mechanism to ensure that individuals' reasonable needs are met at the end of a qualifying relationship.

3. A HISTORICAL ANALYSIS OF THE DIVISION OF FAMILY FINANCES

The history of the division of family finances has always hinged on the different ways contributions to the property in question and/or the qualifying relationship generally have been seen by the courts and policymakers. Historically, the primary vehicle for the division of relationship property was the contribution to the marriage partnership made by the parties. However, as demonstrated below, in quantifying each party's contribution in order to determine a 'fair' division, the courts strongly favoured monetary contributions over domestic ones.

3.1. MARRIAGE AS A PARTNERSHIP

The notion of marriage as a partnership, where both parties make different but equally important contributions, first emerged in the United Kingdom in the 1950s. The 1956 Report of the Royal Commission on Marriage and Divorce said that:[23]

> 'marriage should be regarded as a partnership in which husband and wife work together as equals, and that the wife's contribution to the joint undertaking, in running the home and looking after the children, is just as valuable as that of the husband in providing the home and supporting the family.'

---

18 FPA, s 64A(3).

19 See further on spousal maintenance, J Caldwell, 'Maintenance – Time for a Clean Break?', ch 15.

20 PRA, s 32(1).

21 PRA, s 32(2).

22 PRA, s 32(2).

23 Royal Commission on Marriage and Divorce, *Report of the Royal Commission on Marriage and Divorce*, Cmd 9678, HMSO, London 1956, [644].

Otto Kahn-Freund notes that the concept of marriage as a partnership was connected to the 'universally recognised principle of equality of the sexes'.[24]

In 1965, the notion of partnership was first mentioned in New Zealand relationship property jurisprudence in *Hofman v Hofman*, where Woodhouse J said:[25]

> 'marriage is really a partnership of equals … Marriage is a partnership of a very special nature and, with respect, I think this Act puts a proper emphasis upon that fact. In my opinion it enables the Court to consider the true spirit of transactions involving matrimonial property by giving due emphasis not only to the part played by the husband, but also to the important contributions which a skilful housewife can make to the general family welfare by the assumption of domestic responsibility, and by freeing her husband to win the money income they both need for the furtherance of their joint enterprise. Each is in a unique position to support or to undermine the constructive efforts of the other.'

Woodhouse J held that both parties had contributed in different but equal ways to their marriage:[26]

> 'I am satisfied that in their respective ways the parties have contributed equally to the acquisition of the property in dispute; I think that any common intention which they may have expressed was that their resources should be pooled and that they would then share equally in the assets which they might acquire; and I am clearly of the opinion that the justice and common sense of the case require that upon a sale of the property they should share equally in the proceeds.'

At the core of Woodhouse J's analysis of marriage as a partnership is the concept of spouses making different but equal contributions to a marriage. While the contributions may be different in type, they are at the heart of the moral basis for allocating property equally at the end of a marriage or other relationship where the functions of the relationship are similar.[27]

The main point of contention is whether or not all contributions to the partnership should indeed be counted as equal. For example, an individual who earns a large income may claim that their efforts in doing this should count for more than the support their partner gives them for performing domestic duties. Or when both parties are in the workforce and both perform domestic duties the partner who earns the larger income may well feel their contribution is greater.

---

24 O Kahn-Freund, 'Matrimonial Property – Some Recent Developments' (1959) 22(3) *Modern Law Review* 241, 248.

25 *Hofman v Hofman* [1965] NZLR 795 (SC) at 800.

26 Ibid, at 802.

27 M Briggs, 'Which Relationships Should be Included in a Property Sharing Scheme?', ch 3.

However, once we begin to closely examine each spouse's contribution to this degree, we create a system open to endless dispute. Coleridge J demonstrated the futility of such an approach when he said:[28]

> 'First, they call for a detailed retrospective at the end of a broken marriage just at a time when parties should be looking forward, not back ... But then, the facts having been established, they each call for a value judgment of the worth of each side's behaviour and translation of that worth into actual money. But by what measure and using what criteria? ... Is there such a concept as an exceptional/special domestic contribution or can only the wealth creator earn the bonus? ... It is much the same as comparing apples with pears and the debate is about as sterile or useful.'

It is much more cost effective to accept that while each spouse's contribution may be different, all contributions are to be counted as equal, apart from in the extreme circumstances where one party makes no or very little contribution at all,[29] or where the relationship is so short there has not been time for the contributions to balance out between the parties.[30] However, as the sections that follow demonstrate, New Zealand's judiciary has not always taken this approach.

3.2. THE MATRIMONIAL PROPERTY ACT 1963 (NZ) – NOT ALL CONTRIBUTIONS ARE EQUAL

The Matrimonial Property Act 1963 (NZ) (which only applied to marriages) had regard 'to the respective contributions of the husband and wife to the property in dispute (whether in the form of money payments, services, prudent management, or otherwise howsoever)'.[31] Some judges, such as Woodhouse J above, recognised the intrinsic value of domestic work and the positive contribution such work makes to a marriage.[32] However, not all of the judiciary shared Woodhouse J's progressive views. In *E v E* the majority of the Court of Appeal gave the Matrimonial Property Act 1963 (NZ) a very narrow reading.[33] It is clear from the judgments of North P and Turner J that they had very little respect for a wife of over 20 years who had committed adultery

---

28 *G v G (Financial Provision: Equal Division)* [2002] EWHC 1339 (Fam), [2002] 2 FLR 1143 at 1155.

29 PRA, s 13. For more detailed information about this exception, please see 5.2 below.

30 PRA, ss 14, 14AA, and 14A. For more detailed information about this exception, please see 5.1 below.

31 Matrimonial Property Act 1963 (NZ), s 6.

32 *Hofman v Hofman*, above n 25 at 800.

33 *E v E* [1971] NZLR 859 (CA).

against her husband. North P described Mrs E as having a 'waspish streak'.[34] Turner J said:[35]

> 'It seems that even the basest disregard of wifely obligations is not to serve to diminish, at the end of the day, the share in some property to which her "contributions" would have entitled her had she behaved towards her husband as a wife ought.'

Given this context, it is not surprising that North P concluded:[36]

> 'The mere fact that a wife has been a good wife and looked after her husband well domestically, cannot possibly, in my opinion, justify an order being made in her favour in respect of a business owned by the husband in the running of which the wife had no share.'

In *Haldane v Haldane*, a wife of 26 years, who had five children, claimed that her contribution to a farm, that had been gifted to her husband, retained or increased the value of the farm.[37] However, McCarthy P said 'what she did was relatively unimportant, and certainly insufficient to support a claim under the Matrimonial Property Act'.[38] The courts were clearly extremely reluctant to make any connection between domestic work, such as caring for children and managing the home, and the acquisition and improvement of business assets.

It was the Privy Council in 1976 that finally revived Woodhouse J's concept of marriage as a partnership to which both the husband and wife contribute equally.[39] It said in *Haldane v Haldane*:[40]

> 'By performing her function of home-minder, the wife releases her husband to perform his function as breadwinner. So long as private property is regarded by society as an institution of social value (constituting a sphere within which the individual can make direct choices affecting his or her own life), a law that enabled a husband to claim as his exclusive property all the bread left over from immediate consumption, while vouchsafing to the wife only whatever crumbs she managed to scrape together by her own fortuitous and rare economic activity supervening on her domestic duties, was denying pro tanto the concept of marriage as a partnership of free equals in which the partners performed complementary functions.'

---

34 Ibid, at 867.

35 Ibid, at 888.

36 Ibid, at 885. Mrs E was ultimately awarded half of the value of the equity in the parties' family home, but none of Mr E's business assets.

37 *Haldane v Haldane* [1975] 1 NZLR 672 (CA).

38 Ibid, at 676. Mrs Haldane was awarded a payment of $5,000 out of a total asset pool of $118,500 by the Court of Appeal.

39 *Hofman v Hofman*, above n 25 at 800.

40 *Haldane v Haldane* [1976] 2 NZLR 715, [1977] AC 673 (PC) at 721. Mrs Haldane was ultimately awarded one quarter of one of four farm blocks and $4,000, altogether totalling $19,000 out of a total asset pool of $118,500.

By this time, however, Parliament had intervened by passing new legislation, the Matrimonial Property Act 1976 (NZ).

3.3. THE MATRIMONIAL PROPERTY ACT 1976 (NZ) – THE PULL OF MONEY

The Matrimonial Property Act 1976 (NZ) (which also only applied to marriages) was seen as radical and ahead of its time. The primary shift in emphasis was from the concept of contributions to the property in question, to contributions to the marriage partnership, which were presumed to be equal. The home and family chattels were to be divided equally, no matter when they were acquired, unless extraordinary circumstances made equal sharing repugnant to justice,[41] or the marriage was for less than three years.[42] Other assets acquired during the marriage were also to be divided equally, unless the contributions of one spouse were clearly greater than the other.[43] The key addition introduced by the Matrimonial Property Act 1976 (NZ) was an exhaustive list of the different possible contributions to a marriage encompassing both financial and non-financial contributions.[44] These contributions were:[45]

> '(a) The care of any child of the marriage or of any aged or infirm relative or dependant of the husband or the wife:
> (b) The management of the household and the performance of household duties:
> (c) The provision of money, including the earning of income, for the purposes of the marriage partnership:
> (d) The acquisition or creation of matrimonial property, including the payment of money for those purposes:
> (e) The payment of money to maintain or increase the value of –
> (i) The matrimonial property or any part thereof; or
> (ii) The separate property of the other spouse or any part thereof:
> (f) The performance of work or services in respect of –
> (i) The matrimonial property or any part thereof; or
> (ii) The separate property of the other spouse or any part thereof:
> (g) The forgoing of a higher standard of living than would otherwise have been available:
> (h) The giving of assistance or support to the other spouse (whether or not of a material kind), including the giving of assistance or support which –
> (i) Enables the other spouse to acquire qualifications; or
> (ii) Aids the other spouse in the carrying on of his or her occupation or business.'

41 Matrimonial Property Act 1976 (NZ), s 14.
42 Matrimonial Property Act 1976 (NZ), s 13.
43 Matrimonial Property Act 1976 (NZ), s 15.
44 Matrimonial Property Act 1976 (NZ), s 18(1).
45 Matrimonial Property Act 1976 (NZ), s 18(1). This list of contributions has been retained (with some minor modifications) and is currently located at s 18(1) of the PRA.

It is particularly important to emphasise that section 18(2) of the Matrimonial Property Act 1976 (NZ) also stated that there 'shall be no presumption that a contribution of a monetary nature … is of greater value than a contribution of a non-monetary nature.'[46]

However, this statement of clear legislative intent had little effect on the majority of judges, who did not agree with the philosophy underpinning the legislation, as evidenced by their judgments at the time. This is best summed up in the words of Mahon J in *Baddeley*, where he states:[47]

> 'a wife may leave her husband for just cause or for no cause. She may leave him, bored and discontented after years of marriage, for the sole purpose of starting a new life with another man, but her right to claim one half of the business assets of her husband remains unaffected. She is able to bring to the new marriage a handsome dowry representing half the business assets of her previous husband. While she is basking in the affluent warmth of a last romantic spring-time, her deserted ex-husband is back on the farm struggling with the lawful demands of his mortgagee, his stock company, and his bank.'

Similarly, the next year in *Reid v Reid*, Cooke J said:[48]

> 'however sympathetic the Judge is to the spirit of the Act, comparison of non-monetary and monetary contributions must remain difficult in some cases, for while excluding any presumption in favour of the latter Parliament has left the assessment to judicial discretion rather than attempting fixed rules.'

Some judges did adopt the spirit of the Matrimonial Property Act 1976 (NZ). For example, Woodhouse J said in *Reid v Reid*:[49]

> 'Although the Act operates upon "property" as a subject-matter the law it lays down is not a part of the law of property in any traditional sense. Instead it is social legislation aimed at supporting the ethical and moral undertakings exchanged by men and women who marry by providing a fair and practical formula for resolving the obligations that will be due from one to the other in respect of their "worldly goods" should the marriage come to an end. In that respect it can be regarded as one facet of the wider legislative purpose of ensuring the equal status of women in society.'

---

46 Matrimonial Property Act 1976 (NZ), s 18(2). This rule has been retained in s 18(2) of the PRA.

47 *Baddeley v Baddeley* (1978) 1 MPC 10 (SC) at 12.

48 *Reid v Reid* [1979] 1 NZLR 572 (CA) at 600.

49 Ibid, at 580.

Likewise, Richardson J adopted the underlying purpose of the legislation, finding in *Reid v Reid* that it is not an:[50]

> 'unreasonable premise that the efforts of one spouse in looking after the house and bearing the major domestic responsibilities are intended by both spouses to free the other to concentrate on work outside the home for the benefit of the marriage partnership.'

Richardson J also recognised that over time 'roles and contributions' to a marriage may change.[51] For example, one spouse may do more than the other at certain times, either at home or in the paid workforce, for a whole variety of reasons. However, these contributions will all even out over time.[52] Richardson J concluded:[53]

> 'it is not difficult to see why the legislation presumes that in the ordinary circumstances of marriage the respective contributions of the spouses, whatever form they have taken, will be in balance at the end of the day.'

Apart from the matrimonial home and chattels, other matrimonial property was subject to discretion – if one spouse could show they had made a clearly greater contribution, they would be given a larger share of the property.[54] For example, in *Reid v Reid*, where Mr Reid argued that his business acumen was a greater contribution than Mrs Reid's domestic duties, Woodhouse and Richardson JJ gave him a 60 per cent share of the matrimonial property. However, Cooke J would have given him a 75 per cent share. The court still gave greater weight to farming and business contributions than they did to domestic work.

This view persisted into the future, as evidenced by *Walsh v Walsh*.[55] This case concerned a farming couple whose marriage lasted 10 years and produced two children.[56] The husband had acquired the farm from his father. Half of the farm was transferred to the husband before the parties got married and was therefore his separate property under the Act.[57] The other half was transferred during the marriage and was matrimonial property.[58] During the marriage,

---

50 Ibid, at 611.
51 Ibid, at 611.
52 Ibid, at 611.
53 Ibid, at 611.
54 Matrimonial Property Act 1976 (NZ), s 15.
55 *Walsh v Walsh* (1984) 3 NZFLR 23 (CA). This case was used by the Australian Law Reform Commission as a reason not to adopt New Zealand's Matrimonial Property Act 1976. See Australian Law Reform Commission, *Matrimonial Property*, ALRC 39, 1987.
56 *Walsh v Walsh*, above n 55 at 25.
57 Matrimonial Property Act 1976 (NZ), s 9.
58 Matrimonial Property Act 1976 (NZ), s 8.

the wife played a full part in the farming operations and running the home, doing strenuous physical work on the farm, especially in the early years. She argued that the increase in the farm's value was attributable, to some degree, to her actions, or alternatively, to the application of matrimonial property and hence the increase in value should be classified as relationship property under section 9 of the Act.[59]

However, this provision was interpreted very narrowly, requiring a direct contribution to the increase in value. The wife's exertions were not seen as contributing in a clear and appreciable manner to the increase in value of the land and her 'indirect contributions' to the marriage in terms of caring for children and performing household duties were given little weight. The Court recognised that the wife had made a 'very substantial contribution of fulfilling, and fulfilling well, her role as wife and mother' and working on the farm.[60] However, the Court held that the husband had carried the greater burden of the farm work and had provided the major part of the assets and the means of earning income.[61] The parties' contributions to the marriage partnership were assessed as 75 per cent to the husband, and 25 per cent to the wife.[62]

The stated purpose of the Matrimonial Property Act 1976 (NZ) was to recognise marriage as a partnership of equals. Yet, the presumption of equality of contributions was clearly not being delivered in outcomes under the legislation.

3.4. PROPERTY (RELATIONSHIPS) AMENDMENT ACT 2001 (NZ) – REDUCING THE DISCRETION

In 2001 the Matrimonial Property Act 1976 (NZ) was significantly amended by the Property (Relationships) Amendment Act 2001 (NZ). The 1976 Act was renamed the Property (Relationships) Act 1976 (NZ), because relationships outside of marriage of both opposite and same sexes were now included.[63] All relationship property was now to be divided equally (not just the family home and the family chattels), which took away judicial discretion to weigh up each parties' contribution to the relationship when dividing non-domestic assets and once again stated that all contributions were to be considered equal.

An economic disparity provision was also introduced, which allowed for spouses who had undertaken the bulk of the domestic duties in the relationship

59 Matrimonial Property Act 1976 (NZ), s 9.

60 *Walsh v Walsh*, above n 55 at 32.

61 Ibid, at 32. The wife ultimately received a payment of $152,000 from a total pool (consisting of both separate and matrimonial property) of $1 million.

62 Ibid, at 32.

63 For a closer examination of the types of relationships that are and could by covered by the PRA, see M Briggs, above n 27.

to obtain more than 50 per cent of the relationship property in particular circumstances.[64] This amendment was specifically designed to make the division of family finances fairer in New Zealand, especially for those who had made the greatest domestic contribution in terms of caring for children and running their households, often at the expense of their own careers. As the then Minister of Justice said at the third reading of the Bill introducing the amendments:[65]

> 'This long-overdue legislation is fundamentally about fairness. It is intended to provide fair property division upon the breakdown of a relationship, which is something the current legislation has failed to achieve for many New Zealanders. The Matrimonial Property Act led to many unfair outcomes, because equal division of matrimonial property does not always mean that the partners each get a fair deal. As we all know, partners contribute to a relationship in many different ways. Some develop business interests with lucrative financial outcomes, while others contribute in less tangible, non-material, but nevertheless important ways, such as raising children, domestic duties, and building homes. It is only fair that all contributions, whether financial or domestic, are recognised as valuable contributions to a relationship. Undoubtedly, the care and upbringing of children is one of the most important and valuable roles within our society. It is a sad indictment on our family law that, historically, such an important role has remained largely unrecognised, leading to systemic unfairness under the current legislation.'

However, not all politicians agreed with the introduction of this provision. One opposition MP said that the provision was unfair because it legitimised 'fortune-telling' and allowed 'the court to look into the future and speculate on how much the partners will earn or not earn'.[66] Another argued that economic disparity provisions would create great uncertainty, saying:[67]

> 'There will be no certainty any more. Different judges will make different assessments, giving different results, and the certainty that we have seen for 30 years under the previous legislation will be completely dissipated.'

However, given the wide discretion under both the Matrimonial Property Act 1963 (NZ) and the Matrimonial Property Act 1976 (NZ), and the uncertainty such discretion historically created, such political rhetoric was entirely hollow.

---

64 For a more detailed examination of the economic disparity provision, see 5.3 below.

65 M Wilson, *New Zealand Parliamentary Debates*, 29 March 2001, vol 591, 8625.

66 A Tolley, *New Zealand Parliamentary Debates*, 29 March 2001, vol 591, 8439.

67 T Ryall, *New Zealand Parliamentary Debates*, 29 March 2001, vol 591, 8626.

4. THE CURRENT NEW ZEALAND POSITION

The PRA is still the statute that governs the division of family finances at the end of a qualifying relationship in New Zealand. It distinguishes between what is called relationship property and separate property. Relationship property in general includes the family home and family chattels, whenever they were acquired, as well as all property acquired during the qualifying relationship, or in contemplation of the qualifying relationship.[68] Property acquired by gift,

---

[68] Section 8 of the PRA states as follows:

'8 Relationship property defined

(1) Relationship property shall consist of –
  - (a) the family home whenever acquired; and
  - (b) the family chattels whenever acquired; and
  - (c) all property owned jointly or in common in equal shares by the married couple or by the partners; and
  - (d) all property owned by either spouse or partner immediately before their marriage, civil union, or de facto relationship began, if –
    - (i) the property was acquired in contemplation of the marriage, civil union, or de facto relationship; and
    - (ii) the property was intended for the common use or common benefit of both spouses or partners; and
  - (e) subject to sections 9(2) to (6), 9A, and 10, all property acquired by either spouse or partner after their marriage, civil union, or de facto relationship began; and
  - (ee) subject to sections 9(3) to (6), 9A, and 10, all property acquired, after the marriage, civil union, or de facto relationship began, for the common use or common benefit of both spouses or partners, if –
    - (i) the property was acquired out of property owned by either spouse or partner or by both of them before the marriage, civil union, or de facto relationship began; or
    - (ii) the property was acquired out of the proceeds of any disposition of any property owned by either spouse or partner or by both of them before the marriage, civil union, or de facto relationship began; and
  - (f) *[Repealed]*
  - (g) the proportion of the value of any life insurance policy (as defined in section 2), or of the proceeds of such a policy, that is attributable to the marriage, civil union, or de facto relationship; and
  - (h) any policy of insurance in respect of any property described in paragraphs (a) to (ee); and
  - (i) the proportion of the value of any superannuation scheme entitlements (as defined in section 2) that is attributable to the marriage, civil union, or de facto relationship; and
  - (j) all other property that is relationship property under an agreement made under Part 6; and
  - (k) any other property that is relationship property by virtue of any other provision of this Act or by virtue of any other Act; and
  - (l) any income and gains derived from, the proceeds of any disposition of, and any increase in the value of, any property described in paragraphs (a) to (k).

(2) In proceedings commenced after the death of one of the spouses or partners, this section is modified by section 83.'

inheritance, or as a beneficiary of a trust during a qualifying relationship is separate property, unless it is intermingled with other relationship property.[69]

Any increase in the value of separate property that occurs during the course of a qualifying relationship becomes relationship property if that increase in value is attributable (either wholly or in part) to the application of relationship property, or to the actions of the other partner (whether directly or indirectly).[70] The provision contains an important distinction depending on whether the increase in value was a result of the application of relationship property or the actions of the other spouse. If the increase in value of separate property is due wholly or in part to the application of relationship property, then the entire increase in value becomes relationship property and is divided in the usual way.[71] If the increase in value of separate property is due wholly or in part to the actions of the other partner (whether directly or indirectly), the increase in value also becomes relationship property, but it is shared on the basis of each party's contribution to the increase in value.[72]

While there is a strong presumption in the PRA that all relationship property will be divided equally between the parties at the end of a qualifying relationship,[73] there are three exceptions.[74] They are: marriages, civil unions, or de facto relationships of less than three years;[75] extraordinary circumstances

---

69 PRA, s 10.

70 PRA, ss 9A(1) and 9A(2).

71 PRA, s 9A(1).

72 PRA, s 9A(2). See also *Rose v Rose* [2009] NZSC 46, [2009] 3 NZLR 1. For a more detailed analysis of this issue see M BRIGGS and N PEART, 'Sharing the Increase in Value of Separate Property under the Property (Relationships) Act 1976: A Conceptual Conundrum' (2010) 24(1) *New Zealand Universities Law Review* 1.

73 PRA, s 11.

74 Misconduct is not a ground for departing from equal division: PRA, s 18A. However, it may be taken into account when division is determined by contributions to the relationship, as, for example, in relationships of short duration, or when making orders in respect of children: s 18A(2). Misconduct is relevant then only if it was 'gross and palpable' and 'significantly affected the extent or value of the relationship property': s 18A(3). Both elements must be met and the test is described as 'stringent': *Maxfield v Maxfield* HC Hamilton AP106/02, 22 June 2004 at [131], where it was found that a wife's conduct in removing the parties' household chattels and diminishing the parties' joint bank accounts was 'gross and palpable'. However, there was no evidence that the wife's conduct had 'significantly affected the extent or value of relationship property'. Therefore the criteria in s 18A of the PRA was not made out. As Frater J said at [133]–[134]:

> 'Where the Judge erred, was in failing to address whether Mrs Maxfield's behaviour "significantly affected the extent or value of relationship property". He said that Mrs Maxfield dissembled and concealed and, by way of example, cited various bonus bond transactions. However, there is no evidence whatsoever to establish that any loss resulted.
>
> ... I find that the Judge was wrong to take conduct into account.'

75 PRA, ss 14, 14AA, and 14A.

making equal sharing repugnant to justice;[76] and where there is a significant difference in income and living standards between the parties going into the future.[77] These exceptions are discussed in turn below.

5. EXCEPTIONS TO THE PARTNERSHIP PRINCIPLE OF EQUAL SHARING

5.1. RELATIONSHIPS OF SHORT DURATION

The partnership principle is based on the idea that contributions to a qualifying relationship are equal and balance out over time. Therefore, any property acquired during the relationship should be shared equally. In relationships of short duration, the parties' contributions have generally not had time to balance out, which is why relationships of short duration are excluded from the strong presumption of equal sharing.

A qualifying relationship of short duration is defined as one for a period of less than three years,[78] or for a period of more than three years if, having regard to all the circumstances, it is 'just' for the relationship to be treated as one of short duration.[79] A distinction is made between marriages and civil unions of short duration, and de facto relationships of short duration. De facto relationships of less than three years (or de facto relationships of more than three years that are just to treat as being less than three years in duration) fall outside the scope of the PRA.[80] No order can be made under the PRA unless the relationship fits

---

76 PRA, s 13.

77 PRA, s 15.

78 In terms of marriages of short duration, see s 14 of the PRA. For civil unions of short duration, see s 14AA of the PRA. Regarding de facto relationships of less than three years (unless there is a child of the de facto relationship), see s 14A of the PRA.

79 PRA, s 2E. See, for example, *Pepene v Pepene* [2001] NZFLR 1061 (FC), where Judge Adams found that a marriage of nearly five years should be treated as one of short duration because the couple only cohabitated for 18 months as a result of the husband working in Papua New Guinea and their relationship had deteriorated over time. As Judge Adams said at [32]:

> 'In my assessment of this particular marriage, despite some degree of commitment between the parties (as evidenced by several well-planned holidays, some financial support and some continuing telephone contact), the fact that they cohabited for no more than an aggregate of 18 months, and the reduced quality of the marriage (particularly after April 1995), leads me to the view that this should be treated as a marriage of short duration.'

See also *Martin v Martin* [1979] 1 NZLR 97 (CA) where Woodhouse J stated at 101:

> 'the question in every case will be whether the marriage has been so restricted in point of time and unduly limited in terms of quality that it may justly be described as a marriage of short duration.'

80 PRA, ss 2E and 14A.

within one of two possible exceptions.[81] One exception is where there is a child of the de facto relationship.[82] The other is where the partner applying for the order has made a substantial contribution to the de facto relationship.[83] In both situations the court must be satisfied that failure to make the order would result in 'serious injustice'.[84] If these exceptions are established, then the relationship property is divided according to the contribution each party made to the de facto relationship.[85]

For marriages and civil unions of short duration, the PRA still applies.[86] However, the presumption of equal sharing is weakened, particularly in relation to the family home and family chattels. Equal sharing of the family home and/or the family chattels does not apply in short duration marriages and civil unions if they were owned wholly or substantially by one of the partners when the marriage or civil union began.[87] The same applies if the family home and/or family chattels were acquired by one of the partners during the relationship through succession, survivorship, as a beneficiary under a trust, or by gift from a third person.[88] The family home and/or family chattels are also not shared equally where one party to the marriage or civil union has made a contribution which 'has clearly been disproportionately greater than the contribution of the other'.[89] In regard to any other relationship property, property is shared equally unless one party's contribution to the relationship has been clearly greater than that of the other party.[90] If one of these exceptions applies, each party's share of relationship property is determined by the contribution each party made to the marriage or civil union.[91]

---

81 The court still retains some residual discretion to make an order for division of relationship property where the parties have been in a de facto relationship for less than three years. See, for example, s 14A(4) of the PRA.

82 PRA, s14A(2)(a)(i).

83 PRA, s14A(2)(a)(ii). See, for example, *PH v GH* [2013] NZHC 443, [2013] NZFLR 387, where Katz J held at [69] that the appellant's 'contributions did not go beyond those contributions to a common household that are adequately compensated by the benefit conferred by the relationship itself'.

84 PRA, s 14A(2)(b). See, for example, *Gibbons v Vowles* (2003) 22 FRNZ 946 (FC), where Judge Inglis QC said at [17] that:

> 'An obvious question here is whether the assets with which the applicant was left at the end of the relationship are of a value so significantly less than the value of her financial and non-financial contributions to the relationship so that, having regard to all the other relevant circumstances including the potential availability of *Lankow v Rose* remedies, it can confidently be said that to close off for her the remedy under s 14A(3) would create "serious injustice".'

85 PRA, s 14A(3).

86 PRA, ss 14 and 14AA.

87 PRA, ss 14(2)(a) and 14AA(2)(a).

88 PRA, ss 14(2)(b) and 14AA(2)(b).

89 PRA, ss 14(2)(c) and 14AA(2)(c).

90 PRA, ss 14(4) and 14AA(4).

91 PRA, ss 14(3)(a), 14(5), 14AA(3)(a), and 14AA(5).

5.2. EXTRAORDINARY CIRCUMSTANCES MAKING EQUAL SHARING REPUGNANT TO JUSTICE

The court may refuse to order equal sharing of relationship property where it 'considers that there are extraordinary circumstances that make equal sharing of property or money ... repugnant to justice'.[92] The application of this exception is narrow due to the strict wording involved. The requirement for the circumstances to be 'extraordinary' necessarily requires something very out of the ordinary. 'Repugnant to justice' is also an extremely high threshold. Examples of where this exception has been applied fall into two broad categories. The first is where one party has made no or very little contribution to the qualifying relationship.[93] The second is where one party to the qualifying relationship receives an unexpected windfall (especially near the end of such a relationship) that is not part of the 'fruits' of the relationship.[94]

The longer the qualifying relationship lasts, the more difficult it is to claim 'extraordinary circumstances' because, as discussed above, contributions to a relationship generally balance out over time.[95] Likewise, the shorter a qualifying

---

92 PRA, s 13.

93 See, for example, *D v D* [1997] NZFLR 424 (FC), where the husband who, as a result of the wife's mental illness, maintained the parties' property single-handedly for 80 per cent of the parties' marriage satisfied the extraordinary circumstances criteria. See also, *Sydney v Sydney* [2012] NZFC 2685, where Judge Coyle determined that a relationship of three and a half years in which the husband was a prominent New Zealand artist who contributed the vast majority of the parties' relationship property, and where the parties made equal non-financial contributions, met the criteria of extraordinary circumstances making equal sharing repugnant to justice. As Judge Coyle said at [101]:

> 'Mr Sydney's art collection, which is worth around $350,000 excluding "Southern Crossing", was not an asset purchased over time, but rather an asset by and large created by Mr Sydney, both through his own endeavours, and through his relationships with other artists. It is the combination of this fact, coupled with the disproportionate contributions made by Mr Sydney to the assets of the relationship, which in my view lead to a finding that there are extraordinary circumstances which make the equal sharing repugnant to justice. It is wrong that Mrs Sydney, in a marriage of three and half year's duration, should share equally in a half share of the assets of Mr Sydney, when the bulk of those assets have been created through the artistic endeavours and associations of Mr Sydney over so many years. Mrs Sydney's contribution to the parties' relationship cannot be said to have assisted Mr Sydney in the creation of his earlier wealth.'

94 See, for example, *DWM v LMM* FC New Plymouth FAM-2003-043-198, 14 February 2006, where the wife contributed an inheritance to the parties' marriage just before separation occurred. In this case, Judge Murfitt held at [47] that s 13 of the PRA was satisfied and ordered a 65/35 split of relationship property in the wife's favour.

95 See, for example, *Dalton v Dalton* [1979] 1 NZLR 113 (CA), where Richardson J said at 120:

> 'It is difficult enough in a marriage of only a few years' duration to weigh monetary and nonmonetary contributions and balance the contributions of each spouse to the marriage partnership. In a marriage of this length it is that much harder to conclude that differences

relationship, the easier it will be to establish extraordinary circumstances. This is consistent with Lady Hale's observation that 'the duration of the marriage may justify a departure from the yardstick of equality of division'.[96]

5.3. ECONOMIC DISPARITY

The economic disparity provision contained in section 15 of the PRA is aimed at disparity of income and living standards between the two parties once the relationship property is divided. It is not about whether or not a party has sufficient resources to live on, or how well, in the eyes of the judge, the party has done in the amount of relationship property they have received.

It is based on substantive equality, or equality of outcome: the idea that a 50 per cent share of relationship property for each party is unfair upon the breakdown of a qualifying relationship if one party has been able to develop their career and increase their income and future earning capacity, while the other party scarified their own career to provide support and domestic assistance such as caring for the parties' children and running the parties' household.

In order to obtain an economic disparity order under the PRA, the court must be satisfied that there is a significant disparity between the incomes of each party, a significant disparity in their living standards, and that there is a causal link between the disparity and the divisions of functions in the relationship.[97] The causal link can be because of loss of opportunity and/or enhancement of the other party's earning capacity.

There is no onus of proof on the applicant. The Court of Appeal explained the reason in *M v B*:[98]

> 'Frequently in this area of the law, claims are advanced by the non-titled partner (who more often than not is a woman). The imposition of an onus of proof would be a further impediment to the obtaining of just entitlements under the statutory regime given that, in many respects, the relevant evidence is more than likely in the possession of the titled partner (who more often than not is a man) …
>
> Notions of onus of proof fit uncomfortably within this legislative regime.'

Once the court is satisfied that there is evidence of significant disparity caused by the division of functions within the qualifying relationship, and that it is 'just'

---

in financial contributions, when set against the years of mutual assistance and support, the sharing in the upbringing of children and the services about the home, render repugnant to justice the equal sharing of the focus of the marriage partnership over the years, the matrimonial home.'

96 *Miller v Miller; McFarlane v McFarlane*, above n 1 at [152].

97 PRA, s 15(1).

98 *M v B* [2006] 3 NZLR 660 (CA) at [38]–[39].

to make an award, the court may then order compensation from the relationship property pool, resulting in unequal division of the relationship property.[99] The legislation does not currently provide any guidance as to how such compensation is to be calculated.

5.3.1. *Disparity of Income*

The PRA does not provide a definition of income. This makes it difficult to ascertain what should count as income for the purposes of this provision. The payment of future spousal maintenance under the FPA is income and can be counted as income. However, past spousal maintenance payments would not count, as the focus of section 15 is the future disparity.

Whether super profits are counted as income or not is more complex. In *Williams v Scott*, Faire J in the High Court counted the wife's share of super profits from the husband's legal practice as income, saying, 'While super profits are relationship property, and the division of relationship property is considered before the disparity between income and living standards, super profits are properly considered as income.'[100] The Court of Appeal rightly overruled Faire J on this point,[101] citing its earlier decision in *X v X*,[102] where it held that income is 'limited to income earned from working rather than return on invested relationship property.'[103] As Robertson J said in *X v X*:[104]

> 'Under the Act's equal sharing regime, relationship property is divided equally. Parties have an equal ability to derive income from its investment. At the time of a s 15 award it is not always possible to predict how much actual income each party will derive from investments, given the inherently unpredictable nature of investment returns. Further, the actual income each party derives from investment of relationship property will depend on whether and how various items of property or capital are invested.'

The Court of Appeal concluded in *Scott v Williams* that 'the distribution of super profits did not alter the disparity in income-earning capacity post separation of the two parties. Rather, its effect was neutral.'[105]

---

99 PRA, s 15(3).

100 *Williams v Scott* [2014] NZHC 2547, [2015] NZFLR 355 at [160]. Super profits in this context are defined as 'earnings on capital constituting relationship property less the amount attributable to the earner as an employee in the usual way': *Scott v Williams* [2016] NZCA 356, [2016] NZFLR 499 at [9(c)], n 3. In simple terms, this means a lawyer working for themselves might earn, for example, $200,000 per annum, but if they were a partner in a large law firm they might earn $400,000 per annum because of the advantages of being in partnership. The additional $200,000 would be seen as super profits.

101 *Scott v Williams*, above n 100.

102 *X v X [Economic Disparity]* [2009] NZCA 399, [2010] 1 NZLR 601.

103 *Scott v Williams*, above n 100 at [89], describing the approach taken in *X v X*, above n 102.

104 *X v X [Economic Disparity]*, above n 102 at [87].

105 *Scott v Williams*, above n 100 at [90].

In terms of the calculation of future income, New Zealand cases involving a significant disparity of income between the parties examine the parties' potential incomes, rather than their actual incomes.[106] This is to prevent individuals from reducing their incomes to avoid having to make an economic disparity adjustment.

Case examples show that the calculation of future income is not an exact science. In *X v X*, Mr X earned $7.7 million in gross income in the five years prior to separation.[107] However, he had since given up his high-powered job in favour of work that was less stressful and paid much less. As a result, Mr X argued in the Family Court that his likely future income was between $100,000 to $200,000 per annum.[108] The Family Court held that $180,000 was a 'reasonable assessment of Mr X's likely future income'.[109] This was to be contrasted with Mrs X's likely future income of $65,000 per annum.[110] In the High Court,[111] Rodney Hansen J was doubtful about the Family Court's findings about Mr X's future income and said:[112]

> 'I have a concern that the Judge may not have weighed evidence which tended to suggest that Mr X's intentions, however genuine, were unrealistic. It has to be questioned whether a man as capable, energetic and ambitious as Mr X, whose financial objectives remained unfulfilled, would remain satisfied with the limited goals he had set for himself. The Judge gave no apparent weight to evidence from witnesses who knew him and people like him that cast doubt on the likelihood of his confining himself to such modest personal and financial objectives.'

Parties' earning capacities can change rapidly. For example, in *A v A* a tax partner in an accounting firm earning $900,000 per annum during his marriage fell ill with hepatitis C, which led to depression and alcohol addiction.[113] Mr A retired from the firm and set up his own tax consultancy business.[114] It was in its infancy at the time the dispute came to court and was earning very little. At the time of the hearing Mr A had no income. However, he conceded that he could potentially earn over $100,000 per annum.[115] This was the figure used in the case.

---

106 See V Crawshaw, 'Section 15 Refined', paper presented to the New Zealand Law Society Continuing Legal Education Family Law Conference, Dunedin, October 2015, 465–85. See also *X v X [Economic Disparity]*, above n 102 at [88].
107 *X v X [Economic Disparity]* [2006] NZFLR 361 (FC) at [20].
108 Ibid, at [121].
109 Ibid, at [121].
110 Ibid, at [119].
111 *X v X [Economic Disparity]* [2007] NZFLR 502 (HC).
112 Ibid, at [101].
113 *A v A* FC North Shore FAM-2007-044-1462, 21 June 2010 at [7].
114 Ibid, at [8]–[9].
115 Ibid, at [59].

Once the parties' incomes have been established, it remains for the court to determine the level of income disparity between the parties. In *A v A* (discussed above) Mr A could potentially earn $100,000 per annum from his newly fledged tax consultancy business. This was enough to show his income would be significantly higher than Mrs A's income. Mrs A was a former plasterer retraining to become a teacher and had an expected future income of less than $50,000 per annum.[116] In *T v C*, on the other hand, a husband earning around $98,000 as an economist,[117] and a wife earning $85,000 as an accountant (with scope for additional income from performance bonuses),[118] were held not to have a significant disparity in income.[119]

Any income disparity must be considered in the particular context of the parties and the individual circumstances of their case.[120] An assessment of whether or not there is an income disparity must be made at the date of separation, but the calculation of the quantum of any order is made 'once it is known what each party is going to take from the relationship property pool under the Act's other provisions'.[121]

5.3.2. *Disparity in Living Standards*

In addition to a significant disparity in income, there must also be a significant disparity in living standards. When determining economic disparity, parties' incomes and living standards cannot be looked at entirely in isolation. As the Court of Appeal said in *X v X*, income and living standards are 'discrete elements of the significant disparity test' and both must be met for an economic disparity award to be made.[122] The Court then went on to say that:[123]

> 'In many cases, however, there will be a connection between a party's level of income and their standard (or potential standard) of living, such that it might be artificial to consider each element in complete isolation.'

The Court of Appeal defined a person's standard of living in *X v X* as including:[124]

> 'the amount and quality of their possessions, the facilities and services available to them, the social, travel and daily lifestyle opportunities to which they have access, and their net leisure time.'

---

116 Ibid, at [59].
117 *T v C* FC Wellington FAM-2007-032-453, 9 June 2009 at [4] and [19].
118 Ibid, at [17].
119 Ibid, at [57].
120 *X v X [Economic Disparity]*, above n 102 at [115].
121 Ibid, at [75].
122 Ibid, at [78].
123 Ibid, at [79].
124 Ibid, at [94].

Another way of looking at disparity of living standards is to assess the range of choices each party has going into the future. For example, in *K v K* Mr K attempted 'to provide a false picture of impoverishment' by selectively presenting the consequences of his choices, such as his decision to take on bridging finance, and argued that he 'had insufficient funds from time to time'.[125] Judge Adams said that Mr K had 'options unavailable to Mrs K'.[126] Mr K was earning a reasonable income and was not constrained by child care responsibilities. He had also purchased an expensive new home.[127] The learned judge went on to say that Mrs K did not have 'a range of choice above her current modest living standards'.[128] She was unable to earn an income while she had the primary responsibility for the children and was not in a position to purchase a home.

The key issue is not whether a claimant has a sufficiently high standard of living, but the disparity in living standards between the parties. As the Court of Appeal said in *X v X*:[129]

> 'Both parties may have high standards of living, but ... the comparative test under s 15 is between the parties themselves, not between one (or both) of the parties and the community at large.'

The subjectivity of assessing an individual's living standards is demonstrated by *PEL v FFB*,[130] where the parties' choices affected the analysis of disparity. The Family Court found that there was no significant disparity in living standards between the parties, even though Mr L had a significantly higher income than his former wife Ms B.[131] In making this decision, Judge Burns took into account Mr L's ongoing payments of spousal maintenance to his former wife, ongoing responsibilities for his new wife and child, and the fact that he was unable to house himself because of the division of relationship property.[132] However, it seems unfair that Ms B should be penalised for Mr L's financial and life choices. This may encourage individuals with higher incomes to take on other responsibilities to reduce their living standards.

5.3.3. *Causal Link*

Section 15 was predominantly set up to protect the economic vulnerability of a partner in a qualifying relationship who steps aside from the paid workforce to

125 *K v K* FC Papakura FAM-2003-055-406, 3 July 2007 at [135].
126 Ibid, at [135].
127 Ibid, at [135].
128 Ibid, at [135].
129 *X v X [Economic Disparity]*, above n 102 at [94].
130 *PEL v FFB* [2012] NZFC 9534.
131 Ibid, at [68].
132 Ibid, at [68].

care for children and undertake domestic duties. In such a situation, the courts have determined that the division of functions within the relationship does not need to be the sole or even principal cause of the economic disparity between the parties, but rather one cause of it. The courts also presume that both parties have agreed to the division of functions. Otherwise it would be too easy at the end of a qualifying relationship for one partner to argue that they did not agree to the particular division of functions in their relationship, which would result in drawn-out litigation.

In some cases, parties have tried to argue that the non-earning partner has spent more time undertaking domestic duties than was necessary. However, Hansen J put this argument to rest in *X v X*, saying that:[133]

> 'It was never necessary for Mrs X to devote herself fully to a caregiving and supportive domestic role in the marriage; other options were always available. But it is not for the Court to suggest that at some point in the marriage a different choice could or should have been made, even if greater opportunities then existed. That is … to substitute a retrospective judgment of when it is reasonable for a person to re-enter the workforce for the joint decision of the parties.'

The lack of an established career at the start of a relationship does not disqualify a causal argument. In *RMAFH v LTS*, Principal Family Court Judge Ryan held:[134]

> 'that had she not devoted herself fully to the children, the household and the support of the respondent (apart from a few part-time positions) she could well have pursued and obtained professional qualifications in New Zealand in order to gain registration here as a teacher.'

Some jobs are assumed to be easy to resume with no loss of earning capacity after a period out of the paid workforce. For example, in *A v A*, Mrs A had previously worked as a plasterer, but had taken time out of the paid workforce to raise the parties' children.[135] Judge Murfitt found that Mrs A was able to resume her work as a plasterer after this time without significant disadvantage in terms of her earning capacity:[136]

> 'It may take a little time for her to get back some of the expertise that she had built up as a plasterer but in overall terms, her absence from the workforce has had little if any impact on her ability to earn an income.'

---

133 *X v X [Economic Disparity]*, above n 111 at [116].

134 *RMAFH v LTS* [2012] NZFC 7543 at [64].

135 *A v A* FC North Shore FAM-2007-044-1462, 21 June 2010.

136 Ibid, at [63].

What this fails to account for is that the time out of the paid workforce has negatively affected Mrs A's ability to build up additional expertise within her plastering career and therefore earn additional income. Time is required to rebuild expertise, and this will impact upon Mrs A's income earning capacity, just as in any other career.

Douglas v Douglas demonstrates a particularly unfair rejection of the causal link.[137] Mrs Douglas, who already had five children from a previous marriage when she married Mr Douglas, cared for the parties' foster child throughout the parties' marriage.[138] Mrs Douglas also worked throughout the marriage in lower-paid, usually part-time, jobs.[139] The Family Court found the necessary causal link and awarded Mrs Douglas $63,000 in compensation for economic disparity.[140] On appeal, the High Court set aside the disparity award for lack of causation.[141] Katz J held:[142]

> 'If she had not met Mr Douglas it seems likely that Mrs Douglas would have continued on the path she was on, pursuing part-time work opportunities which fitted in around school hours while her children were young. This would have likely progressed to full-time work as her children grew older.'

This led Katz J to conclude that the division of functions within the parties' marriage had not 'materially adversely impacted on Mrs Douglas's income earning potential following the end of her marriage'.[143] However, this outcome ignores the reality of looking after the parties' foster child and the fact that Mr Douglas knew about and accepted Mrs Douglas's children from a previous relationship. Mrs Douglas's domestic duties were a jointly agreed division of functions, just like any other. The fact Mrs Douglas cared for her children and the parties' foster child was a cause of her income and living standards being much less that those of Mr Douglas. Mrs Douglas's domestic duties also enabled Mr Douglas to continue to advance his career unburdened by domestic responsibilities.

5.3.4. *Enhancement*

Enhancement is premised on the claim that one party, through their domestic support, has enhanced the other party's career, enabling that party to earn a

---

137 *Douglas v Douglas* [2013] NZHC 3022, [2014] NZFLR 235. This case was referred to as *JMA v SCA* by the Family Court and later as *Douglas v Douglas* in the High Court. Both judicially assigned case names are fictional. This section refers to the parties as Mr and Mrs Douglas.

138 Ibid, at [1]–[2].

139 Ibid, at [3].

140 *JMA v SCA* [2012] NZFC 10192 at [67].

141 *Douglas v Douglas*, above n 137.

142 Ibid, at [16].

143 Ibid, at [19].

higher income than they otherwise might have earned.[144] While the qualifying relationship was intact, there was an assumption that both parties would benefit from and share in the higher income generated as a result of both parties' contributions. It would therefore be unjust for the higher paid partner to retain all the benefits of that additional income at the end of the parties' relationship.

In enhancement cases, the court has usually required that the division of functions are *the* cause of the economic disparity (rather than one of the causes). This is not within the spirit of the PRA, the purpose of which is to recognise the advantages and disadvantages of the relationship.[145] The higher earner gains an advantage as a result of the division of functions within the relationship, and the supporting partner suffers a disadvantage.

There have not been a great number of successful enhancement cases.[146] The primary argument against an enhancement claim is that the higher earner generates their income solely as a result of their own ability and skills, and that they would have been just as successful with or without the support of a partner, and they could have just hired professionals to raise their children and/or perform all necessary household tasks. Goddard J gave the best riposte to this argument, stating in *Jack v Jack*:[147]

> 'It is also too simplistic to postulate that the hiring of a nanny or other assistance in the home and in his workplace in the early years of establishing his practice would have inevitably led to the same result. This contention underestimates both the value of Mrs Jack's contribution as well as the undisputed 24/7 nature of Mr Jack's private practice. Furthermore, as I have noted, the focus is not properly on what the parties could have done; it is on what they chose to do. The purposes and principles of the Act, and the wording of s 18 (which sets out the types of contributions to a relationship) are clear. To effect a just division of relationship property the Court must take into account the contributions of both parties to the relationship and the economic advantages arising from that relationship. In this case, what the parties chose to do and how they organised their joint lives conferred an actual economic advantage on Mr Jack through the indirect contributions of Mrs Jack.'

144 Joanna Miles has classified these claims as restitutionary in nature. See J Miles, 'Should the Regime be Discretionary or Rules-Based?', ch 11.

145 Section 1N(c) of the PRA states that:

> 'the principle that a just division of relationship property has regard to the economic advantages or disadvantages to the spouses or partners arising from their marriage, civil union, or de facto relationship or from the ending of their marriage, civil union, or de facto relationship.'

146 In *Jack v Jack* [2014] NZHC 1495 at [34], n 37, Goddard J provided a list of cases when claimants were successful in establishing causation in terms of enhancement. See *Sainsbury v Sainsbury* [2013] NZFC 867, [2013] NZFLR 1056 at [28]; *RMAFH v LTS*, above n 134 at [45] and [65]–[66]; *Smith v Smith* [2007] NZFLR 33 (FC) at [65]–[67] and [89]; *K v K* FC Papakura FAM-2003-055-406, 3 July 2007 at [138]; and *PNK v JMB* FC Wellington FAM-2009-032-92, 5 October 2010 at [136].

147 *Jack v Jack*, above n 146 at [51].

On the facts of *Jack v Jack*, in which Mrs Jack helped Mr Jack establish a medical consultancy practice, cared for the parties' three children, and ran the parties' household, Goddard J found that:[148]

> 'It is not axiomatic that Mr Jack would have achieved the degree of success that he has without the support Mrs Jack has given him while he built his career and throughout the lengthy period of their 28 year marriage.
>
> I find her role in the home, while he was studying for his Part II examination, her support of him while he worked overseas, her role as home-maker and primary caregiver for the children while he established his practice, and her assistance with his networking and at times with his practice, all provide a foundation for concluding that she supported him to obtain what he needed to become successful.'

Disappointingly, Goddard J's reasoning has not been followed in other decisions. For example, in *Williams v Scott* a wife gave up her accounting career to raise the parties' two children and support her husband in his law practice. However the enhancement award granted to her by the Family Court[149] was taken away by the High Court. Faire J held there was insufficient evidence to show a causal connection between the husband's enhanced income and the division of functions in the parties' marriage, despite the fact the wife did real estate work, hosted business functions for the husband, and also provided accounting services for the husband's law firm.[150] Faire J also considered that the wife had already benefitted from her contributions by obtaining a share of the super profits of the husband's practice, and felt it 'would be to double count' her contribution if she were to get an enhancement award as well.[151] The Court of Appeal agreed with Faire J's reasoning that the wife 'cannot have further credit for enhancement of the practice value given she is to receive an equal share of that as part of the division of relationship property'.[152] However, this is not double-dipping at all. The super profits generated by Mr Williams' legal practice are relationship property and should therefore be shared equally. Whereas economic disparity focuses on the ways in which Ms Scott's domestic contribution has enhanced Mr Williams' earning capacity and career. Both parties get an equal share of the relationship property, but then Mr Williams continues to have a much higher salary ($200,000 per annum) in the future than Ms Scott (who earns just $84,000). Ms Scott's domestic contribution has enhanced Mr Williams' earning capacity and diminished her own.

---

148 Ibid, at [45]–[46].
149 *Williams v Scott* [2014] NZFC 7616.
150 *Williams v Scott*, above n 100 at [167].
151 Ibid, at [167].
152 *Scott v Williams*, above n 100 at [107].

5.3.5. *Calculation of Quantum*

Calculating a compensation award under section 15 of the PRA is 'highly speculative'.[153] The PRA does not provide any guidance for judges to follow when exercising their discretion and there is no prescribed formula. In *Scott v Williams* the Court of Appeal said: 'Each case will depend on its own facts, and no rule of thumb can be offered.'[154] In *Hodgson v Hodgson* Moore J said there are many ways of assessing quantum and the courts should not be shy to use particular methods to meet the particular circumstances of the case.[155]

The most common approach used for determining quantum is the method used in *X v X*.[156] In simple terms, as set out by the Family Court, the starting point is what Mrs X would have earned if she had remained in the paid workforce.[157] This is her 'but for' income. A series of calculations are then applied that take into account future contingencies such as non-collection of future income, a contingency discount for the uncertainty of the 'but for' income, as well as when Mrs X will be able to resume full-time employment.[158] Mrs X's 'but for' income was estimated to be $220,000.[159] Mrs X was awarded a lump sum disparity award of $240,000 by the Family Court.[160] This outcome does not fairly reflect an equal share of the combined earning capacity of the marriage, especially considering both parties started their relationship as prize-winning accounting students, but Mrs X gave up her career to raise the parties' children.

The other approach is to use what a senior New Zealand barrister describes as a '"jury" assessment approach'.[161] This was the approach adopted in *Carpenter v Carpenter* (the case was later renamed *Jack v Jack* by the High Court).[162]

---

153 B Atkin, 'Economic Disparity – How Did We End Up With it? Has it Been Worth it?' (2007) 5 *New Zealand Family Law Journal* 299, 302.

154 *Scott v Williams*, above n 100 at [112].

155 *Hodgson v Hodgson* [2016] NZHC 311 at [109], see also [101]–[116].

156 *X v X [Quantum]* [2008] NZFLR 512 (FC). This was largely accepted by the Court of Appeal: see *X v X [Economic Disparity]*, above n 102 at [132] per Robertson J and at [178] per O'Regan and Ellen France JJ.

157 *X v X [Quantum]*, above n 156 at [62].

158 Ibid, at [62].

159 Ibid, at [63].

160 Ibid, at [68]. The quantum of the award was upheld by the Court of Appeal. See *X v X [Economic Disparity]*, above n 102 at [243].

161 V Crawshaw, above n 106 at 482.

162 *Carpenter v Carpenter* [2013] NZFC 8396, [2014] NZFLR 9. This case was referred to as *Carpenter v Carpenter* by the Family Court and later as *Jack v Jack*, above n 146, by the High Court. Both judicially assigned case names are fictional. This section refers to the case as *Carpenter v Carpenter*.

In the Family Court, Judge Grace said the figure could be calculated in a number of ways, including:[163]

> '(i) Calculating a figure which represents the value of the cumulative difference between the incomes of the respondent which he is projected to earn and the income he could expect to earn in the absence of the applicant's support.
> (ii) Assess in the round a lump sum based on a reasonable percentage of the high income earner's income for a reasonable period of years for enhancement as a result of the division of functions within the marriage (that is, 20 per cent of income for five years).
> (iii) Award the respondent a sum equivalent to one year's tax income on the basis that at the date of separation, the respondent had approximately 11 years to go before age 65.'

It is not clear which calculation Judge Grace used in reaching his result, in which Mrs Carpenter was awarded 70 per cent of the parties' relationship property, with Mr Carpenter receiving the remaining 30 per cent.[164] In the High Court, Goddard J upheld the result, commenting that:[165]

> 'I am satisfied that the Judge carefully considered the overall circumstances of the parties that gave rise to the disparity as well as what would be just between the two of them in the future. The justice of the situation is influenced by the position of the parties upon entering the relationship, the length of the marriage, the size of economic disparity and the marked inequality of income earning capacity. All of these factors were taken into account by the Judge in his assessment.'

In *Williams v Scott*, the Family Court awarded Ms Scott a disparity award of $850,000, 10 per cent more than she would have received from an equal sharing of the parties' relationship property.[166] This meant that from the relationship property pool of approximately $8.5 million, rather than each of the parties receiving a $4.25 million share, Ms Scott received $5.1 million while Mr Williams received $3.4 million. The disparity award was reduced to $280,000 by the High Court,[167] and then increased again to $470,000 by the Court of Appeal to recognise Ms Scott's loss of income.[168] The Court of Appeal took into account the likelihood Ms Scott would work longer than Mr Williams, the substantial asset pool, and the income that may be generated from the interest on the award.[169]

---

163 Ibid, at [138].
164 Ibid, at [141]. The total relationship property pool was between $1.6 and $1.8 million.
165 *Jack v Jack*, above n 146 at [83].
166 *Williams v Scott*, above n 149 at [351] and [366].
167 *Williams v Scott*, above n 100 at [169].
168 *Scott v Williams*, above n 100 at [94] and [129(d)].
169 Ibid, at [92] and [93].

The purpose of section 15 is to address the economic disparity between the parties. The fact that income can be generated from the relationship property is not relevant to calculating compensation for economic disparity as both parties can generate income from their share of the relationship property and the economic disparity between the parties remains the same. Economic disparity is about the difference in income and living standards between the parties going into the future. While the court has discretion to do what is 'just', such discretion should be exercised within the spirit of the legislative context.

Overall the amounts awarded by the appeal courts have not been high. For example, in *X v X* the Court of Appeal upheld Mrs X's award of 3 per cent more than what she would have received if the relationship property was shared equally;[170] and in *Scott v Williams* the Court of Appeal awarded Ms Scott 5 per cent more of the relationship property than her equal sharing entitlement.[171]

A simpler method of calculating the quantum of an economic disparity award without the need for valuations or the application of a complex formula would be to first consider the degree of disparity between the parties, and then to award compensation on a percentage basis increasing in 5 per cent increments depending on the degree of disparity. This was the approach used in the Family Court in *Williams v Scott* in determining to award Ms Scott $850,000 more than would have resulted under an equal sharing of the parties' relationship property.[172] The Court of Appeal declined to comment as to whether awarding compensation on a percentage basis depending on the degree of economic disparity between the parties was an appropriate method.[173] This case is currently on appeal to the Supreme Court, the first time that New Zealand's highest court has had an opportunity to consider the economic disparity provision.

6. THE CONSEQUENCES OF THE DISPARITY PROVISION

The lack of clarity in the wording of the disparity provision and the different possible ways of calculating quantum have created a divergence of judicial decision-making in determining and resolving economic disparity between couples upon the termination of their qualifying relationship. There is no doubt that section 15 of the PRA has also led to uncertainty amongst the legal profession. This is demonstrated by Claire Green's work surveying legal

170 *X v X [Economic Disparity]*, above n 102 at [240] and [243].

171 *Scott v Williams*, above n 100 at [7], [94] and [129(d)].

172 *Williams v Scott*, above n 149 at [349]–[351] and [364]–[366].

173 *Scott v Williams*, above n 100 at [112]–[113].

practitioners around New Zealand about their views of the economic disparity provision.[174]

The legal practitioners surveyed were all given the same factual scenario. Their responses revealed a wide range of views on whether the disparity was of significance and whether it was the result of the division of functions in the relationship. The vast majority of those who thought there was disparity agreed that it was 'just' to make some sort of compensatory payment,[175] but their views on quantum ranged enormously.[176] The results of this survey clearly demonstrate the uncertainty created by section 15 of the PRA.

7. WHERE TO FROM HERE?

Most of the rules governing division of property on the breakdown of a marriage or equivalent relationship work tolerably well. There is a strong presumption of equal sharing of relationship property, subject to well-established exceptions for short duration relationships and extraordinary circumstances. However, the operation of the Act does not fully achieve the goal of giving 'each party an equal start on the road to independent living'.[177] Two significant changes would go further towards addressing these inequalities.

7.1. EARNING CAPACITY AS RELATIONSHIP PROPERTY

The current division of capital at the end of a qualifying relationship does not sufficiently take the parties' future earning capacities into account. Section 15 of the PRA was introduced to address this issue. However, in a jurisdiction with a strong presumption of equal sharing, akin to a community property regime, judges in New Zealand are understandably reluctant to depart too far from equal sharing of relationship property. Therefore, in practice, section 15 has failed to deal adequately with parties' disparate earning capacities and has caused great confusion (as discussed above).

The simplest and fairest solution would be to include earning capacity as relationship property in its own right, which would then be divided equally

---

174 C Green, 'The Impact of Section 15 of the Property (Relationships) Act 1976 on the Vexing Problem of Economic Disparity', PhD thesis, Faculty of Law, University of Otago 2014. Dr Green's PhD was co-supervised by Professor Henaghan and Professor Briggs.

175 Ibid, at 113. What was considered to be an appropriate quantum for any such award ranged from less than $150,000, to over $600,000 (from a total asset pool of $3 million).

176 Ibid, at 134.

177 *Miller v Miller; McFarlane v McFarlane*, above n 1 at [144]. The PRA is currently under review by the New Zealand Law Commission. It is hoped that this process will result in recommendations that become the basis for legislative changes in this area.

alongside the parties' other relationship property. This acknowledges that in some cases the most important asset is the economically stronger party's future earning capacity,[178] which they have been able to build up, due, in part, to the efforts and support of the party who has fulfilled the domestic duties in the relationship. Compensation for disparity of future earning capacity is not solely to recompense the parties for the advantages and disadvantages they have each enjoyed or suffered as a result of their relationship. It is also to compensate the parties for the loss of their combined income (and associated standard of living) that they built as a couple and experienced while they lived together, especially in relationships of long duration.

Such an approach would be consistent with the purpose behind section 15 of the PRA, which is to compensate the party who has been most negatively affected in financial terms as a result of 'the effects of the division of functions within the marriage, civil union, or de facto relationship while the parties were living together'.[179] It would also be in accord with the broader purposes and principles of the PRA which are 'to recognise the equal contribution of both spouses to the marriage partnership',[180] and to 'provide for a just division',[181] which has:[182]

> 'regard to the economic advantages or disadvantages to the spouses or partners arising from their marriage, civil union, or de facto relationship or from the ending of their marriage, civil union, or de facto relationship'.

It also avoids the partner who has undertaken the bulk of the domestic duties from suffering a 'double loss'.[183] As Lord Nicholls said:[184]

> 'the parties may have arranged their affairs in a way which has greatly advantaged the husband in terms of his earning capacity but left the wife severely handicapped so far as her own earning capacity is concerned. Then the wife suffers a double loss: a diminution in her earning capacity and the loss of a share in her husband's enhanced income. This is often the case. Although less marked than in the past, women may still suffer a disproportionate financial loss on the breakdown of a marriage because of their traditional role as home-maker and child-carer.'

---

178 See *Miller v Miller; McFarlane v McFarlane*, above n 1 at [142] where Lady Hale describes the 'breadwinner's unimpaired and unimpeded earning capacity' as a 'powerful resource which can frequently repair any loss of capital after an unequal distribution'.

179 PRA, s 15(1).

180 PRA, s 1M(b).

181 PRA, s 1M(c).

182 PRA, s 1N(c).

183 *Miller v Miller; McFarlane v McFarlane*, above n 1 at [13].

184 Ibid, at [13].

In order to avoid lengthy and expensive litigation, a simple and cost-effective calculation is needed to ascertain the amount of earning capacity to be counted as relationship property. Section 5.3.5 above suggested increasing the amount of relationship property to be paid to the disadvantaged party in 5 per cent increments until the economic disparity between the parties has been equalised. Such an approach makes allowances for the fact that one party has a greater income earning capacity than the other. The advantage of such an approach is that a lump sum payment to compensate the disadvantaged party for the disparity in the parties' earning capacity can be made out of relationship property. However, the disadvantage is that there may not always be sufficient relationship property for such a payment to be made and the courts have already shown they have difficulty moving away from equal sharing of relationship property.[185]

A better way of achieving a fair outcome would be via the implementation of a combined income equalisation payment approach. This involves determining the parties' respective future incomes for the 12-month period after their relationship ended and then adding these two figures together to determine the parties' total combined annual income. The parties' total combined annual income should then be divided equally between them in a similar way as any other relationship property is divided. In practical terms, this means the economically stronger party will need to top up the other partner's income until it reaches half of the parties' total combined annual income figure. This is known as the annual combined income equalisation payment. This annual income equalisation payment should then be multiplied by half the number of years the parties have been together (up to a maximum of 10 years). The maximum period of 10 years reflects the fact that, after longer relationships, the economically stronger party is likely to be close to retirement, which will reduce their future earning capacity and thus how much they could afford to pay to the disadvantaged party. Once the annual income equalisation payment has been established, the court must use its discretion to make allowances for relevant contingencies (which will differ across individual cases) such as the parties' respective ages, lengths of time before retirement, health, and stability of employment.

If a lump sum payment is not possible alongside the division of the parties' other relationship property, an ongoing periodic payment (as discussed below) will have to be paid to the disadvantaged party out of the economically stronger party's future earnings.

The adoption of such an approach would eliminate the complexities and costs of obtaining expert valuations and actuaries. It would also provide the opportunity for the courts to establish guidelines to ensure a consistent application of contingencies across different types of cases depending on the

---

185 See, for example, M Henaghan, 'Dealing to Disparity' (2008) 6 *New Zealand Family Law Journal* 51.

length of the relationship, the age of the parties, and the length of time until retirement. The bottom line is to keep things simple, cost effective, and fair.

7.2. PERIODIC PAYMENTS

When an economic disparity award under section 15 of the PRA is considered 'just', the court can currently order a sum of money be paid to compensate the disadvantaged partner (party A) by the partner with the higher income and living standard (party B) out of party B's share of the relationship property, or order the transfer of property to party A out of party B's relationship property.[186] This is, in effect, a one-off lump sum payment to compensate party A for the fact that party B's income and living standards are likely to be significantly higher than their own 'because of the effects of the division of functions within the marriage, civil union, or de facto relationship while the parties were living together'.[187]

However, in some cases there will not be enough relationship property to do this fairly, especially if the above combined income equalisation payment approach is adopted. Periodic payments out of party B's future income, such as those ordered in *Miller v Miller; McFarlane v McFarlane* seem to be a fairer approach, especially in terms of economic disparity awards. As Lord Nicholls said:[188]

> 'If one party's earning capacity has been advantaged at the expense of the other party during the marriage it would be extraordinary if, where necessary, the court could not order the advantaged party to pay compensation to the other out of his enhanced earnings when he receives them. It would be most unfair if absence of capital assets were regarded as cancelling his obligation to pay compensation in respect of a continuing economic advantage he has obtained from the marriage.'

Periodic payments do go against the clean break principle, which is based on the idea that parties should be able to move on with their lives into the future unimpeded by any financial ties to the other party.[189] However, the application of the clean break principle in family finance disputes has meant that overall fairness, in terms of each party receiving an equal share of all of the 'fruits' of their partnership, is compromised.[190]

---

186 PRA, s 15(3).

187 PRA, s 15(1).

188 *Miller v Miller; McFarlane v McFarlane*, above n 1 at [32].

189 The principle is not legislated for and does not apply when children are involved and a financial obligation continues.

190 Section 33(4) of the PRA gives the court discretion, where a sum of money is to be awarded, to direct that it can be paid in one sum or in installments.

Periodic payments are not particularly difficult to calculate once the combined income equalisation payment figure has been determined. The length of the periodic payments will differ depending on the parties' respective incomes, the amount of the award, and the parties' respective obligations.

8. CONCLUSION

For the division of family finances to be fair, all of the 'fruits' of the qualifying partnership, including not just the parties' capital assets, but also their human capital (capacity to earn income) need to be divided equally between the parties. This chapter demonstrates that while courts in recent times have been happy to divide capital assets equally, they have been much more reluctant to equally divide human capital. This chapter provides two possible formulas for doing this in a fair and transparent manner to ensure that both parties receive their fair share going into the future.

CHAPTER 13

SHOULD A PROPERTY SHARING REGIME BE MANDATORY OR OPTIONAL?

Robert Fisher

1. INTRODUCTION

The subject of contracting out of a statutory relationship property regime begins with the regime that would otherwise apply. Only with a proper understanding of that regime can one decide whether the grass in another paddock might be greener. The default regime applicable to marriages, civil unions, and de facto relationships in New Zealand is currently the Property (Relationships) Act 1976 (NZ) ('PRA'). The PRA was an inspired social ideal compromised by its inept execution. The inept execution is the principal reason that so many couples presently have to contract out.

The New Zealand Law Commission commenced a review of the PRA in 2016. There is now an opportunity to substitute a statutory regime which is not merely enlightened in its social goals, but goes on to achieve them on a sound technical footing. That will require a reform which is courageous, imaginative, and fundamental. The downside is that we will be jettisoning our investment in a very large body of authorities. However, they are authorities encrusted onto a flawed framework. The reward of a new regime is that if we go about it in the right way it will be more simple and logical to apply. It will also remove the need to contract out.

2. RATIONALES FOR REDISTRIBUTING ASSETS ON SEPARATION

Relationship property law is mainly about the way in which a couple's assets are redistributed on separation. For the reformer, many other important issues need to be resolved along the way. These include the kind of regime (unitary, separate, full, or deferred community), the way in which the regime is applied (rule-based or discretionary), the relationship between the regime and spousal support (integrated or distinct), and the couple's relationship with creditors (enforcement against either, or both, and on what basis). But the topic of real interest to most couples is simply how much each will get if they separate. As that is what drives contracting out, it is the focus of this chapter.

The inquiry into how much each will get begins with the rationales for redistributing assets on separation. Knowing why assets should be redistributed is important for law reformers and parties alike. If reformers can predict what the majority of couples want, they should be able to put it into the legislation to begin with. Contracting out is the result of a mismatch between a couple's expectations and what they find in the legislation.

What do most couples want? Individuals within a relationship may want different things. But contracting out, as well as democratically determined social policy, must be built on consensus. Most New Zealanders share instinctive expectations over the fate of a couple's assets if they separate. The expectations stem from the underlying rationales for dividing property. Despite the flood of relationship property decisions and commentary, surprisingly little has been said about the underlying reasons for dividing property in the way we do.

Underneath it all there appear to be three contemporary rationales for redistributing assets on separation:

- to give each party a share in those assets which each, in his or her own way, helped to create during the relationship ('causation-based property division');
- to compensate a party for a disparity in earning capacity caused by the division of functions within the relationship ('relationship-caused disparity in earning capacity'); and
- to meet one party's obligation to provide the other with spousal support ('spousal support obligations').

These will be considered in turn.

3. CAUSATION-BASED PROPERTY DIVISION

Whatever views might have been held in New Zealand in the past, it is now generally accepted that the assets which each party takes away from a relationship should reflect the fact that during the relationship each had played a vital role in their acquisition. For this purpose the relationship can be viewed as a form of partnership. During the term of the partnership the various earnings and efforts of the parties normally cause a growth in the partnership capital. The growth is achieved through creating, acquiring or improving assets, or reducing partnership debt. This partnership-created capital, sometimes referred to as the fruits of the relationship ('FOR'), owes its existence to the joint and several efforts of both.[1] The concept has its roots in causation. While the homemaker's contribution is more indirect, it frees the breadwinner from those domestic burdens which the breadwinner would otherwise have to perform in person. In that way both cause the accumulation of capital.

1 New Zealand lawyers are used to the expressions 'relationship property' and 'separate property' to distinguish between divisible and non-divisible property under the Property Relationships Act 1976 (NZ) ('PRA'). Given the PRA's confusion over the reasons for the distinction, it was thought better to start again with 'fruits of the relationship' ('FOR') and 'externally sourced assets' ('ESA') in this chapter.

Once that causative principle is recognised, the second step is to quantify the value of each party's contribution. It is also now generally accepted that in the acquisition of capital, the homemaker's contribution is inherently equal to that of the breadwinner. In many cases both were breadwinners for all or part of the time they were together. Even there, however, the party with the higher earnings tends to finish up with legal title to a greater proportion of their assets. Again, the higher earnings would have been possible only because of the other's domestic contribution. Many regimes, including the PRA, are therefore built on the premise that as each party plays an equal part in accumulating FOR, each should receive an equal share in it when the relationship ends.

In principle, it would be possible for a regime to permit one party to rebut the presumption of equal contribution by proving that, in the particular case, his or her contribution to the relationship – whether financial or domestic – was greater than that of the other.[2] However the simplicity and certainty offered by strict equal sharing might be thought to outweigh the potential justice of comparing the value of contributions made in the individual case. Strict equality also avoids an invidious inquiry into the history of each party's conduct during the relationship. The majority of modern regimes therefore support the principle that FOR should be divided equally.[3]

The division of FOR is to be distinguished from the treatment of assets which a partner already owned when the relationship began, or which were subsequently acquired through third party gift or inheritance. In this chapter it will be convenient to refer to these assets as 'externally sourced assets' ('ESA').

The expectation of most people is that on separation FOR will be shared equally and ESA retained by its recipient. Although Western matrimonial property regimes vary greatly in form, the majority give full or partial effect to those principles and, in particular, to the distinction between FOR and ESA.[4] Even in discretionary regimes such as England and Wales, the same binary distinction is now favoured.[5]

---

2 As was the case in New Zealand during the 25 years between the enactment of the PRA in 1976 and reform of that aspect by the PRA Amendment Act 2001 (NZ).

3 For an excellent comparative survey of contracting out agreements see JM Scherpe, 'Marital Agreements and Private Autonomy in Comparative Perspective' in JM Scherpe (ed), *Marital Agreements and Private Autonomy in Comparative Perspective*, Hart Publishing, Oxford 2012, 443. For a European perspective on the various regimes themselves see JM Scherpe, 'The Financial Consequences of Divorce in a European Perspective' in JM Scherpe (ed), *European Family Law*, vol III, Edward Elgar, Cheltenham 2016, 146.

4 JM Scherpe, 'Marital Agreements and Private Autonomy in Comparative Perspective', above n 3 at 478.

5 A Chandler, '"The Law is Now Reasonably Clear": The Courts' Approach to Non-Matrimonial Assets' (2012) 42 *Family Law* 163; JM Scherpe, 'A Comparative Overview of the Treatment of Non-Matrimonial Assets, Indexation and Value Increases' (2013) 25 *Child and Family Law Quarterly* 61.

Once effect is given to the FOR/ESA distinction, arbitrary periods before invoking automatic equal sharing become redundant. In principle, a party is entitled to an equal share in those assets which he or she helped to create whether the couple has been together for a week or 50 years. 'Marriages of short duration'[6] were invented solely to mitigate the arbitrariness of taking one party's ESA and giving it to the other. The anomaly became even more stark if the couple had been together for only a short time.

4. COMPENSATION FOR DISPARITY IN EARNING CAPACITY

The second potential reason for redistributing assets on separation is to compensate for a relationship-caused disparity in earning capacity.[7] During the relationship the trajectory of the breadwinner's career may have been upward while the homemaker's trended down due to a lengthy period of child-raising and household management. Or one party may have tolerated a relatively modest income as a shop attendant so that the other could acquire high-paying qualifications as a surgeon. In cases of this kind, the result is likely to be a growing disparity in earning capacity.

The existence and extent of such a disparity is measured at the end of the relationship. The disparity may take the form of an enhancement in one party's earning capacity, a diminution in the other's, or both. In capital terms the extent of the disparity can be measured by comparing the estimated present value of one partner's future earnings stream with the present value of the other's after making appropriate allowance for contingencies.

If a disparity of that kind is demonstrated, the final step is to establish its cause. There can be no logical basis for compensation if the disparity was due to different levels of skill, or qualification attained before the relationship began, or to the personal attributes of the parties. However if all or part of the disparity is attributable to the division of functions during the relationship, the disadvantaged party can justifiably look to the other for compensation. The compensation can take various forms, including the award of additional property on separation.[8]

---

6 PRA, s 14.

7 PRA, s 15. Although this is commonly referred to in New Zealand as an 'economic disparity' claim that expression is misleading: the concept is confined to relationship-caused disparity in earning capacity. See also M Henaghan, 'Sharing Family Finances at the End of a Relationship', ch 13.

8 PRA, s 15(3).

5. SPOUSAL SUPPORT OBLIGATIONS

The third potential reason for redistributing assets on separation is spousal support. An award of property ownership or occupation may prove to be the best method of meeting one party's need for personal support in circumstances where the other has an obligation to provide it. Need implies that the claimant lacks the resources or earning capacity to meet his or her reasonable living requirements.[9] However, need alone is normally insufficient.[10] Under most modern regimes, one separated party has an obligation to support the other only where:[11]

- the claimant's need is due to the ongoing daily care of dependent children of the relationship; or
- a limited transition period is required for the claimant to retrain or otherwise adjust to the new circumstances; or
- a longer period is justified due to a permanent reduction in earning capacity attributable to the division of functions during the relationship.

Those three possibilities require further discussion given their potential impact on the division of property.

5.1. ONGOING CARE OF CHILDREN

One party's need for maintenance may stem from the care of dependent children of the relationship. Although a non-custodial parent normally makes a direct financial contribution to the living expenses of the children themselves, that may not be enough. In addition, the custodial parent may suffer a suspension or reduction in the opportunity to earn due to the diversion of time and effort into the day-to-day care of the children. The rationale for maintenance under this heading is that the care of the children is the equal and continuing responsibility of both parents. If the custodial parent discharges that responsibility on behalf of the non-custodial parent, the latter should compensate the caregiver accordingly.[12]

---

9 For example, in New Zealand see Family Proceedings Act 1980 (NZ) ('FPA'), s 64(1).
10 FPA, ss 64(4) and 64A.
11 FPA, s 64(2).
12 PRA, s 15(2)(b); FPA, s 64(2)(b).

5.2. SUPPORT DURING ADJUSTMENT PERIOD

The second rationale for imposing a support obligation is that the claimant may require time to adjust to separation because of the way in which the parties had organised their affairs during the relationship. Typically the breadwinner has acquiesced in, or positively encouraged, an expectation on the part of the homemaker that he or she will be permanently provided for. If that expectation is unexpectedly withdrawn, the homemaker will need time to retrain or adjust. As the responsibility for creating the need to adjust was a shared one, there is good reason for sharing the cost of the retraining and adjustment period.[13]

5.3. SUPPORT DUE TO REDUCTION IN EARNING CAPACITY

As noted earlier, a relationship-produced disparity in earning capacity provides a rationale for redistributing assets accordingly. It can equally be viewed as a rationale for imposing an ongoing obligation to provide spousal support.[14] If viewed as an ongoing support obligation, the remedy can take one of three different forms: periodical maintenance; capital maintenance; or the exclusive possession of the family home or other relationship asset. Each warrants explanation.

5.3.1. *Periodical Maintenance*

The majority of orders for spousal support in New Zealand have tended to be interim orders for periodical maintenance.[15] One of the special reasons for support just discussed must be established before there will be an award of long-term periodical maintenance.

5.3.2. *Capital Maintenance*

Where there are grounds for long-term spousal support, and it is financially practicable, maintenance in the form of immediate capital has the advantage of promoting a clean break.[16] Current New Zealand legislation permits maintenance to be paid in the form of a lump sum.[17] We currently lack statutory authority

13 FPA, s 64(2)(d)
14 FPA, s 64(2)(a)(ii).
15 For jurisdiction see FPA, s 69.
16 In New Zealand the principle is that separated partners must assume responsibility for meeting their own needs as soon as is reasonable: FPA, s 64A.
17 Section 69 of the FPA permits both periodical and lump sum maintenance orders.

for redistributing specific items of property in complete or partial satisfaction of a spousal support obligation. This may not matter a great deal in practice, however, given that an order to maintain by lump sum provides a measure of value which the parties can readily convert into specific assets if so agreed.

5.3.3. *Possession of Relationship Property*

A temporary right to occupy may be a complete or partial alternative to maintenance. The clean break principle suggests a preference for a full and final division of relationship property where practicable. But in some cases the combined value of the parties' assets may be insufficient to provide for the needs of a partner who has an established right to support, especially where the principal asset is the home and it is needed for children of the relationship. In those circumstances support from the absent partner may need to take the form of a right to occupy the home for the custodial parent and children during their dependency.

In New Zealand, support in the form of possession or occupation of relationship property is currently provided for in the PRA,[18] rather than in the legislation where other support matters are to be found.[19] This should not obscure the fact that what is being provided is not a causation-based division of property but a form of maintenance. As a matter of drafting, the jurisdiction for occupation orders could have been included with the maintenance provisions in the Family Proceedings Act 1980 (NZ) and the Child Support Act 1991 (NZ). That might have promoted a clearer understanding of the distinction between causation-based property division, on the one hand, and the right to support, on the other. But so long as that distinction is clearly maintained, little turns on the legislative vehicle chosen to deliver it.[20]

6. RELATIONSHIP BETWEEN THE THREE RATIONALES FOR REDISTRIBUTING ASSETS ON SEPARATION

The three rationales for redistributing assets on separation follow a logical order. The first and primary rationale is that each party has earned half the FOR through his or her direct and indirect contributions during the relationship. Application of that rationale will normally result in each party leaving the relationship with

18 PRA, ss 27, 28, 28A, 28B, and 33 and, for children, s 26.

19 FPA, Part 6.

20 Note also that as presently drafted, s 32 of the PRA permits the review of maintenance in the context of proceedings under that Act.

half the FOR, whether in money or in specific assets. This causation-based division forms the basis for the primary property regime.

Depending on the circumstances, the other two rationales may or may not warrant modification to the equal sharing that would otherwise result. The second rationale was the need to compensate for any relationship-caused disparity in earning capacity. Such an entitlement would require an increment to that party's half share.

The third rationale was that in some circumstances one party will be entitled to spousal support from the other. Putting aside interim arrangements, this cannot be determined until the result of causation-based property division and any earnings compensation claim is known. Only then will it be apparent whether the claimant has been left with a residual need for support. Leaving this determination to last also avoids the duplication that could otherwise result in relation to any relationship-caused reduction in earning capacity.[21]

7. THE NORMAL LIMITS OF PROPERTY SHARING

The principal rationale for a modern property regime is the causal nexus between the joint and several efforts of the parties during the relationship, on the one hand, and the creation of FOR, on the other. That rationale for sharing FOR could have no application to assets which had come to the parties from sources external to the operations of the partnership. For that reason one would expect ESA to be excluded from the process of redistributing assets on separation. The ESA normally comprises pre-relationship property, third party gifts, and inheritances. For understandable reasons, other jurisdictions sometimes extend it to damages for pain and suffering. As the partnership had nothing to do with the acquisition of capital from those sources, there is no rationale for dividing it on separation.

8. IS THE FAMILY HOME A SPECIAL CASE?

The PRA divides the family home in equal shares regardless of source.[22] In the majority of cases no harm is done because the home would be FOR in any event. But a causation rationale for division does not explain how an ESA home could also fall for division.[23] The very fact that the home had come from a source that

---

21 Particular care will be necessary to avoid double-counting under the FPA, s 64(2)(a)(ii).

22 PRA, ss 8(1)(a) and 11.

23 In the interests of simplicity, family chattels have been ignored but the same reasoning must apply, cf PRA, s 8(1)(b). *Sydney v Sydney* [2012] NZFC 2685 provides a striking example of this point in relation to ESA chattels.

was external to the operations of the partnership removes the opportunity for a causal nexus between actions of the parties and the acquisition of the home.

Might there be some other rationale for including an ESA family home in the property division? None was ever articulated by those responsible for the PRA.[24] One is left to speculate. One possibility is that the special treatment of family homes was subconsciously associated with spousal support. The non-owner party will understandably wish to stay on in the home to which he or she has grown accustomed, especially if children are involved. For that reason there will often be good reasons for using the family home in full or part satisfaction of the owner's spousal support obligation, if such obligation exists. But the vesting of a half interest in an ESA home, or the grant of a right to occupy it for that purpose, could be remedial only; the substantive basis for the spousal support right would still need to be independently justified on the support principles discussed earlier. The ESA home would not form part of the basket of properties to which the primary regime applied. It could not explain the PRA approach.

Another possibility is that the special treatment of family homes was subconsciously associated with a form of equitable estoppel. Perhaps it was thought that by allowing the non-owner to live in an ESA family home during the relationship, its owner has fostered an expectation in the non-owner that the latter will acquire a half interest in it or be permitted to live there permanently; in reliance on that expectation the non-owner has acted to his or her detriment by diverting elsewhere the funds which would otherwise have been channelled into a home; by acting in that way the non-owner has foregone the opportunity to save for, and jointly invest in, a home and its subsequent increase in value; to allow the owner to retain sole ownership of the home in those circumstances would be unconscionable; and an immediate right to a half interest is the only way of avoiding an unconscionable outcome.[25]

If that had been the reasoning, it would be unconvincing. To begin with, it is difficult to see how the free use of another's dwelling could ever justify the expectation that it would result in an immediate half interest. What reasonable person would think that? And even if that had been a reasonable expectation for a person left in the dark, the PRA divides the home regardless of discussions and warnings between the parties. Nor would the theory give any credit for the gratuitous nature of the shared use. A calculating owner would have used the ESA capital as an investment and insisted on some other arrangement for the family home. The fact that the owner has generously permitted its use as the home instead is surely not a reason for appropriating half its value. A favour

24 The only recognisable rationales for property sharing identified in ss 1M and 1N of the PRA are causation-based division and earning capacity compensation. No rationale is offered for sharing based on use during the relationship.

25 Assuming, of course, that the relationship has lasted for three years – see PRA, ss 14–14A.

twice extended does not confer a right. And if diversion of earnings elsewhere in reliance on the availability of the home were truly the rationale, why would the quantum of the non-owner's share be unaffected by the duration of the diversion? Surely there would have to be a sliding scale proportionate to time?

Neither of those speculative theories could satisfactorily explain why the PRA singles out the family home for special treatment. The real explanation is undoubtedly historical. The home was the battleground on which women's property rights were first developed. In New Zealand, as in other common law countries, there was growing concern that the law failed to give adequate recognition to the domestic role of women. The earliest inroads into that problem were made through the home.

The courts developed a range of equitable concepts which strove to give the wife some form of proprietary interest. In that exercise there were several reasons for starting with the home. Intentions imputed to the parties more readily related to the asset with which both were most closely associated.[26] As the home was the property where the wife spent most of her time, it was simplistically assumed that that must be the destination for her indirect contributions to property.[27] If any asset required protection from the husband's creditors, the home was the obvious candidate. In New Zealand these notions received early recognition in the Joint Family Homes Act 1950 (NZ) and part VIII of the Matrimonial Proceedings Act 1963 (NZ). At that time, half a loaf was better than none.

All of that lies in the past. The home was no more than a Trojan horse into male-dominated property ownership. As soon as the relationship property net was extended to *all* property acquired by the joint and several operations of the partnership, the reason for singling out the home in particular disappeared. There is no longer any need to rationalise a homemaker's interest in property by imputing fictional intentions to the parties. Nor is there any justification for confining the reach of the homemaker's contribution to the home. The causal connection applies to all assets acquired during the relationship. And for protection against creditors, a notice of claim can now be registered against the title to all assets, not merely the home.

The PRA displays a lamentable confusion between two incompatible concepts. One is a forward-looking recognition of the inherently equal contribution of both parties to wealth-creation during the relationship. The other is a backward-looking retention of jurisdiction based on the home (to which were added other assets that happened to be used by both parties). Certainly the home continues to have special significance when it comes to support for former spouses

---

26 *Rimmer v Rimmer* [1952] 2 All ER 863 (CA); *Bendall v McWhirter* [1952] 1 All ER 1307 (CA); *Masters v Masters* [1954] NZLR 82 (SC); *Reeves v Reeves* [1958] NZLR 317 (SC); *Gissing v Gissing* [1971] AC 886 (HL); *Cowcher v Cowcher* [1972] 1 All ER 943 (Fam).

27 *Hendry v Hendry* [1960] NZLR 48 (SC); *Efstratiou v Glantschnig* [1972] NZLR 594 (CA).

and children. But support rights must be established on their own discrete principles. If the primary property regime is to be founded upon the causes of wealth-creation, homes are no different from any other kind of property. Of all the anomalies in the PRA, this is the greatest. It has also proved to be the most popular reason for contracting out.

9. THE PHILOSOPHICAL APPROACH TO PROPERTY ACQUIRED FOR COMMON USE OR BENEFIT

Similar reasoning applies to other classes of property acquired for the common use or common benefit of both parties.[28] Of course in most cases, property acquired for common use or common benefit will qualify as FOR and therefore be subject to equal division on that basis. But in cases where the asset in question is ESA, it is difficult to find any rational basis for treating it as divisible relationship property. By definition, one of the parties must have owned the ESA before the relationship, or acquired it subsequently by third party gift or inheritance. It can be taken, therefore, that it does not owe its existence to any relevant act, direct or indirect, of the parties.

As with homes, the owner of the ESA capital in question could have invested it, thereby placing it beyond the reach of the other party. The fact that the owner has instead chosen to share its use by acquiring an asset such as a holiday home is no reason for taking half and handing it to the other party. Yet that is the effect of the PRA as it presently stands.[29] That is the second major reason for contracting out.

10. THE PHILOSOPHICAL APPROACH TO TRACING CAPITAL

Capital is fungible in the sense that it is freely exchangeable between cash, bank account credits, investments, and other forms of property, without changing its essential character. So in a commercial partnership it is taken for granted that, as between the partners, earned or contributed funds retain their original character regardless of the various forms through which they might pass. The income earned by partnership operations (the equivalent of FOR) does not cease to be credited in the books as partnership income merely because it is banked, used to buy office furniture, or paid out to one partner as drawings. The same

28 PRA, s 8(d) and (ee).
29 PRA, s 8(d) and (ee).

is true of equity contributions by the partners derived from sources personal to that partner (the equivalent of ESA).

There is no discernible reason for treating family relationships differently. Funds accumulated from earnings and other forms of personal effort are FOR. Funds owned before the relationship began, or received by third party gifts or inheritance during the relationship, are ESA. The capital they represent does not relevantly change its character merely because it passes through the purchase and resale of a succession of properties, is used as the working capital of a business, or is mixed in a common fund. Nor does the fact that funds from both sources have been intermingled prevent an estimation of the relative proportions of FOR and ESA. Tracing is scarcely a novel legal concept even where robust estimations are called for in place of precise calculation.

A tracing technique can be readily applied to increases in value for relationship property purposes. Without more, one would expect an increase in the value of an asset to attract the same FOR/ESA classification as the original asset. Thus an increase in the value of a FOR house, due to a spontaneous rise in real estate values, will attract the same FOR classification. The same can be illustrated by inherited shares (ESA). If the share value rises during the relationship, one would expect the increase to be classified as ESA unless there were special reasons for thinking otherwise.

There are special reasons for thinking otherwise where an increase in the value of an ESA is attributable to partnership efforts or the injection of FOR. If a couple have used their FOR earnings to add a haybarn to the husband's ESA inherited farm, one would expect a corresponding proportion of the farm's increase in value to be treated as FOR. One would expect the same to be true if the increase in the value of the ESA farm were due to the labour of either or both of the parties.[30] Anything created by labour during the relationship must be FOR, because it owes its existence to the operations of the partnership. Of course, this does not extend to spontaneous increases in value attributable to inflation or rises in the value of property of that type. So if an increase is partly spontaneous and partly due to the injection of FOR, an appropriate apportionment is required between the two causes of the increase in value.

The same reasoning applies in reverse where ESA (such as a legacy) has been used to pay for an improvement to a FOR asset (such as a jointly purchased house). In those circumstances one would expect the original owner of the ESA (the party who had inherited the funds) to have a claim on an appropriate proportion of the house, including a proportion of any increase in its value, before equal division of the balance.

---

30 Note the further anomaly that under s 9A(2) of the PRA only actions of the *non-owner* qualify as a relevant contribution to the increase in value of the separate property. Why not actions of the owner as well?

Perhaps those responsible for the PRA thought that tracing capital in this way would be impractical. Certainly one would not expect a couple to retain sufficient records to permit apportionment between two streams of capital on any precise or calculated basis. But the law has never shrunk from broad and robust estimates. Estimates are based on such evidence as may be available, however slender. The assessment of damages at common law is a good example. So is the extent to which spousal efforts during a relationship have contributed to an increase in value.

When it comes to tracing FOR and ESA capital, it is a mistake to try to prescribe detailed rules, such as the present conversion of the whole of an increase in the value of an ESA asset if any part of the increase had been attributable to the injection of FOR capital,[31] or the conversion of inherited property (but not pre-relationship property!) to relationship property if inextricably intermingled.[32] The PRA's bungled attempt to prescribe detailed rules on topics like this has proved a hindrance rather than a help. Far better to return to the concept that underlies the regime as a whole: FOR is to be divided and ESA retained. Where FOR and ESA funds have been channelled into the same asset, the extent to which each contributed to the ultimate value of the asset can be estimated and the total apportioned accordingly. Valuers routinely undertake assessments of that kind.

All of this illustrates something which is conceptually simple: for relationship property purposes FOR and ESA capital should retain its essential character regardless of the various forms through which it might pass. No reason has been identified for any other approach.

Although some attempt was made to implement that principle in the PRA, it failed in critical areas. Probably the most serious is the way in which the whole of an increase in the value of an ESA property is converted to divisible relationship property if any part of the increase was attributable to the application of relationship property.[33] This might sound a technical detail, but in practice has had a huge impact on the treatment of farms and other long-term ESA assets. Over a long period inflation inevitably multiplies the value of such assets many times over. At some point FOR is likely to find its way into an improvement to the original property. A barn or delivery van is paid for from the couple's earnings. By that means the entire increase in the value of an ESA farm or business is converted to divisible relationship property. This has been the third major reason for contracting out.

---

31 PRA, s 9A(1).
32 PRA, s 10(1).
33 PRA, s 9A(1).

11. WHAT WENT WRONG IN NEW ZEALAND?

11.1. HISTORICAL BACKGROUND

In earlier years New Zealand's matrimonial property laws evolved in tandem with other Commonwealth countries. Broadly speaking, English matrimonial property law moved from a unitary regime to one of separate property onto which a series of equitable remedies were then engrafted.[34]

The Matrimonial Property Act 1963 (NZ) ('1963 Act')[35] ushered in a new regime. It permitted New Zealand courts to redistribute assets on a discretionary basis akin to the discretions which continue to operate in England and Australia today. Under the 1963 Act a judge could 'make such order as he thinks fit with respect to the property in dispute'.[36] In doing so the judge was to have regard to 'the respective contributions of the husband and wife to the property in dispute (whether in the form of money payments, services, prudent management, or otherwise howsoever)'.[37]

In 1969 the New Zealand Law Society asked the Minister of Justice to consider the impact of insolvency on matrimonial property rights. The Minister added other issues to consider. The resultant committee of two legal practitioners and two officers from the Department of Justice produced a 26-page report in 1972.[38] The report modestly eschewed any attempt to examine comparative law on the subject,[39] but pointed out that awards for wives were inadequate. The inadequacy was due to an unfortunate Court of Appeal perception at that time that claimants had to be able to trace specific contributions to specific items of property.[40]

The Committee rightly pointed out that contributions to the marriage partnership needed to be applied globally to the assets of the marriage as a whole. However, without attempting to explain why, they went on to recommend that the matrimonial home, property acquired in contemplation of marriage, and accretions to the value of pre-relationship assets should all be treated as 'assets of the marriage' regardless of origin. The Committee's report was handed to the Department of Justice for review.

34 For a more detailed history see *Fisher on Matrimonial and Relationship Property* (looseleaf ed, LexisNexis) at [1]–[1.18].
35 And similar powers in Part VIII of the Matrimonial Proceedings Act 1963 (NZ).
36 Matrimonial Property Act 1963 (NZ), s 5(2).
37 Matrimonial Property Act 1963 (NZ), s 6(2).
38 *Matrimonial Property: Report of a Special Committee*, Wellington, June 1972.
39 Ibid, at [4].
40 *E v E* [1971] NZLR 859 (CA).

After three years of unpublished work by the Department, the government of the day introduced the Matrimonial Property Bill 1975.[41] The accompanying White Paper identified five problems with the 1963 Act:[42]

- The applicant, usually the wife, had the onus of proving specific contributions to property.
- The breadth of the judicial discretion led to uncertainty.
- Awards to wives tended to be less than generous, with wives sometimes receiving no more than a one-quarter or one-third share in the matrimonial home after many years of hard work.
- Contributions had to be traced to specific items of property.
- There was an unsatisfactory overlap between the Matrimonial Property Act 1963 (NZ) and the Matrimonial Proceedings Act 1963 (NZ).

Ironically, many of these difficulties were remedied by the Privy Council decision in *Haldane*.[43] The Privy Council restored a global approach to the tracing of contributions to FOR capital. However, by this stage, the Bill had gained momentum. The White Paper went on to say:[44]

> 'The definition of matrimonial property has proved complex, but its concept is simple. It comprises broadly the matrimonial home, the family chattels (including such amenities as a car or a boat), and all other property acquired by husband or wife after the marriage except by inheritance or gift.'

Nowhere was the rationale for that approach explained. Nor was any reason offered for the ways in which the Bill now converted ESA to divisible matrimonial property. After minor adjustments the Bill was enacted as the Matrimonial Property Act 1976 (NZ) ('MPA'), renamed the PRA in 2001 when de facto relationships were included.[45]

11.2. THE PROPERTY (RELATIONSHIPS) ACT

For understandable reasons those responsible for the PRA preferred a rule-based regime to a discretionary one; conventional separate property principles unless, and until, a couple separated; and strict or presumptive equal division of

41 Matrimonial Property Bill 1975 (125-1).

42 AM Finlay, 'Matrimonial Property – Comparable Sharing: An Explanation of the Matrimonial Property Bill 1975' [1975] *Appendix to the Journals of the House of Representatives* E6, 5.

43 *Haldane v Haldane* [1976] 2 NZLR 715, [1977] AC 673 (PC).

44 AM Finlay, above n 42 at 6.

45 Property (Relationships) Amendment Act 2001 (NZ), s 3.

matrimonial property if they did. These choices appeared to point New Zealand in the direction of one of the many forms of community of surplus regimes which could have been adopted, with or without modification. Instead, the PRA went off in a new and startling direction. In place of the broad principles required to distinguish between FOR and ESA, it attempted to identify particular types of asset or liability to which prescriptive rules would apply. Thus the matrimonial home, household articles, household ornaments (including artworks no matter how valuable), tools, motor vehicles, caravans, and boats were all singled out for strict equal division.[46]

A second collection of asset-types were bundled together for division which was to be equal unless either party could show unequal contributions to the marriage partnership.[47] This category included not only wealth accumulated by the efforts of either or both parties during the marriage – as one would expect – but much other property besides.[48] It captured property acquired before or during the marriage for common use and benefit[49] and (originally) the whole of a life insurance policy or superannuation benefit unless fully paid up before marriage.[50] Also captured in the second category was capital acquired by gift, inheritance, or trust if inextricably intermingled with other matrimonial property, and, in certain circumstances, inflationary increases in value. As originally enacted, if any part of an increase in the value of separate property could be attributed to the actions of the non-owner, or to the application of matrimonial property, the whole of the increase in value was to be treated as matrimonial property.[51] The fact that by far the greater part of the increase was usually due to inflation was ignored.

In a third category were those residual ESA that remained after application of the rules that appropriated property for the first and second categories.[52] Assets in the third category remained the separate property of the owner.

The result was a prescriptive regime of great intricacy. Unfortunately, it had the effect of scooping into the divisible matrimonial property pool much capital which had nothing to do with the efforts of the marriage partnership. Although some of the anomalies have since been addressed,[53] the great majority remain. Much of the PRA still ignores the distinction between FOR and ESA.

46 Matrimonial Property Act 1976 (NZ) ('MPA'), ss 8(a) and (b) and 11(1)(a) and (b); PRA, ss 8(1)(a) and (b) and 11.

47 MPA, s 15, replaced by strict equal division in 2001.

48 MPA, s 8(e).

49 MPA, s 8(d) and (e), amended in 2001 to include pre-relationship property acquired for common use *or* common benefit: PRA, s 8(1)(d) and (ee).

50 MPA, s 8(g) and (i), also amended later in 2001.

51 MPA, s 9(3).

52 MPA, s 9(1).

53 Notably the Property (Relationships) Amendment Act 2001 (NZ), which removed the increase in value anomaly where based on contributory actions of the non-owner but,

11.3. THE FLIGHT TO ALTERNATIVES

Many were unhappy with the new regime. A couple usually expected to share the wealth they created during their relationship; they did not expect to share the property which they already had before the relationship began, or which they acquired subsequently from their parents by gift or inheritance. Their parents were even less impressed. They were happy to give or bequeath property to their own child, and for that child to share its use with his or her partner while they remained together. They resisted the idea that if the couple were to separate, half their child's gift or inheritance would go with the departing spouse.

The essential anomaly was the unwarranted conversion of separate property into relationship property. Those affected sought to escape by one of three means. One was to deliberately keep ESA capital away from the shared life of the couple. One party to a relationship may choose to separately invest ESA funds in his or her own name rather than employ them in a shared amenity such as a holiday home. In that way the funds remain uncontaminated by joint use or benefit. But a choice of that kind presupposes either legal advice or a sophisticated understanding of the PRA. It is also an unwelcome intrusion into what ought to be a relationship of cooperation and pooling of resources.

Secondly one party, or more usually that party's parents, may settle the ESA on a family trust of which the child is merely a discretionary beneficiary. New Zealand trust practitioners always cite this as one of the principal reasons for settling a trust. It goes a long way towards explaining the abnormally high number of family trusts in this country.[54] Attempts to use trusts as a shield behind which FOR can be hidden are usually ineffective.[55] However, even for ESA, they are not fool-proof. There may or may not be other reasons for settling family trusts, but those presently prompted by the PRA would be unnecessary if the primary regime drew a proper distinction between FOR and ESA.

Thirdly, couples have taken refuge in contracting out agreements. Contracting out agreements are particularly common where one party starts out with a major asset (usually a home, farm, or business) or where the relationship

---

inexplicably, retained the anomaly for contributory applications of relationship property (see now PRA, s 9A). Under the same amending Act, life insurance policies and superannuation entitlements became subject to apportionment in accordance with pre-relationship and post-relationship contributions: PRA, s 8(1)(g) and (h).

54 In the 2009–2010 tax year the number of tax returns filed by trusts, including income-earning charitable trusts, was 253,800 compared with a total population of about 4.5 million: Law Commission (NZ), *Review of the Law of Trusts: Preferred Approach*, IP31, Wellington 2012, [1.3] citing Inland Revenue 'Returns Filed 2001 to 2010'. After a slight dip the number of tax returns filed by trusts has risen again to 256,100 for the year 2013–2014 and 261,600 for 2014–2015: Inland Revenue 'Returns Filed 2006–2015' <www.ird.govt.nz/aboutir/external-stats/tax-returns/returns-filed/> accessed 03.04.2017.

55 J Palmer, 'What to Do about Trusts?', ch 8.

in contemplation is a second marriage (where the parties usually combine an inequality of assets with a wariness derived from experience). In either case a regime which respected the distinction between FOR and ESA would make such agreements unnecessary.

11.4. JUDICIAL RECOGNITION OF THE FRUITS OF THE RELATIONSHIP/EXTERNALLY SOURCED ASSETS DISTINCTION

The PRA's anomalous approach to FOR and ESA has not passed unnoticed by the judiciary. The jurisdiction to uphold or set aside contracting out agreements provided judges with an unintended opportunity to demonstrate where their sympathies lay. The courts can set aside contracting out agreements which would result in serious injustice.[56] While many factors can affect the possibility of serious injustice, the significant one for present purposes is the approach taken to FOR and ESA.

As one would expect, judges tend to set aside contracting out agreements as unreasonable if they purport to preserve all or part of the FOR for one spouse alone. Typical was the setting aside of an agreement which would have given the wife only $30,000 in return for forfeiting the right to share in future increases in the value of her husband's substantial businesses.[57] The rejected agreement would have flouted the modern philosophy that the homemaker's indirect contribution is inherently equal to that of the breadwinner. The agreement was struck down because it did not share FOR.

Conversely, judges have normally upheld agreements if their effect is no more than to preserve a party's ESA. They have not been deterred by the use to which the ESA may have been put. So it is considered acceptable to contractually preserve the ESA nature of a house owned before marriage, whether or not it is subsequently used as the family home. This runs directly counter to the PRA's preoccupation with the *use* of property rather than its *source*.

Accordingly, agreements have been upheld where they preserved a pre-marriage ESA dwelling for its owner despite its subsequent use as the family home;[58] or which preserved for the wife alone an ESA house purchased with funds gifted by her parents even though put into the names of both spouses;[59] or which preserved for the husband alone an ESA home which he had owned before the relationship began;[60] or which preserved for the husband alone all

---

56 PRA, s 21J.
57 *Clayton v Clayton* [2013] NZHC 301, [2013] 3 NZLR 236.
58 *Lowry v Lowry* [1994] NZFLR 529 (HC).
59 *Meng v Song* [2012] NZHC 3167.
60 *DMF v GRH [Division of Property]* [2008] NZFLR 425 (FC).

his externally sourced pre-marriage assets, including the proposed family home, while sharing assisted increases in value and giving credit for the sustenance of separate property;[61] or which preserved for each party their unequal externally sourced pre-relationship assets with ability to trace the equivalent ESA capital into replacement purchases and provision for compensation if intermingled with relationship property;[62] or which protected existing ESA while retaining the statutory regime for future acquired matrimonial property.[63] These were all cases in which, left to its own devices, the PRA would have converted all or part of the relevant ESA into divisible relationship property.

Consciously or otherwise, there is an instinctive respect for the distinction between FOR and ESA. Judges rightly shrink from agreements which purport to deny one party, usually the wife, the right to share in wealth created by the activities of either or both during their relationship. But they have been entirely ready to uphold agreements which do no more than preserve the ownership of pre-relationship assets, third party gifts, and inheritances, even where the PRA would have converted them into divisible relationship property. What these decisions show is the lack of any intuitive sympathy for the PRA's propensity for sharing ESA as if it were FOR. The parties should not have had to contract out in order to achieve something which ought to have been built into the statutory regime to begin with.

12. A SUGGESTED REGIME FOR NEW ZEALAND

All of this suggests that the PRA is failing to deliver what people want. Other anomalies are addressed elsewhere in this book. It is sufficient to focus on its propensity for converting ESA into divisible relationship property. That mischief was an inevitable consequence of the ill-advised attempt to divide property by reference to asset-type rather than concept.

Any reform now should start with an understanding of the FOR/ESA distinction and the rationale for sharing the former. The kind of regime that most closely reflects New Zealand norms and expectations is one which divides the FOR in equal shares if and when a couple separates.[64] The finer details vary but there is ample precedent in community of surplus and community of acquest regimes overseas.[65] Regimes of that kind reflect the concept that because

---

61 *Wood v Wood* [1998] 3 NZLR 234 (HC).

62 *Harrison v Harrison* [2005] 2 NZLR 349 (CA).

63 *Hartley v Hartley* [1986] 2 NZLR 64 (CA) at 69 line 37, 74 line 15, and 78 line 44.

64 Whether such a regime should also apply when a relationship ends on death is addressed by N Peart, 'Family Finances on Death of a Spouse or Partner', ch 5.

65 See further JM Scherpe, 'Contracting Out of the Default Relationship Property Regime – Comparative Observations', ch 14.

contributions to wealth-creation by the breadwinner and the homemaker are inherently equal, the couple share equally in the result of their joint and several efforts. Conversely, they do not share assets sourced from outside the operations of the partnership. Pre-relationship assets, inheritances, and third party gifts remain with the original recipients.

If a community of surplus of that kind were adopted in principle, the answer to many secondary issues would follow. These include the way in which FOR and ESA capital would be traced or compensated for; the treatment of partnership efforts which enhance the value of ESA; the treatment of debts as between the two parties; sustenance of ESA; the relationship between the regime and family trusts; the deliberate destruction of property; the treatment of compensation for personal injury; and the apportionment of superannuation or pension rights.

Resolving details of that kind would be relatively easy if built on a clear and consistent rationale for the regime as a whole. The earlier discussion of intermingling illustrates the point. FOR and ESA are often intermingled due to purchases funded from both sources, their mixture in a common fund, or the injection of one into improvements to the other. Once the evidence established that both FOR and ESA had been channelled into the same asset, it is conceptually easy to estimate the extent to which each class of property contributed to its ultimate value. It is often argued that in practice this is impossibly complicated. But that is due to the misconception that the exercise is one of precise calculation. Very broad estimates are more than sufficient for family law purposes, just as they are for the purpose of common law damages, and equitable discretions and remedies.

Complementary sources of jurisdiction founded upon distinct rationales need to be addressed in their own code or sub-code. One is compensation for relationship-caused disparities in earning capacity. A claim under this heading should be the subject of a distinct and additional award after the primary property regime had been applied. Whether this source of jurisdiction is dealt with in the relationship property legislation or distinct legislation aimed at spousal support is immaterial, so long as it is not confused with the rationale for the primary property regime.

Consideration would also need to be given to the relationship between the primary property regime, on the one hand, and post-separation spousal and child support, on the other. The latter are currently catered for in existing legislation.[66] Whether there is any need for change in either of those areas is beyond the scope of this chapter.[67] What does seem worth noting is that the right to occupy the family home should be seen for what it is, an aspect of spousal or child support

66 FPA and Child Support Act 1991 (NZ).

67 Spousal maintenance is addressed by J Caldwell 'Maintenance – Time for a Clean Break?', ch 15.

rather than an aspect of the primary property regime. Putting possession and occupation powers into the Family Proceedings Act 1980 (NZ), rather than the relationship property legislation, would bring together all matters relating to support and remove any room for confusion when applying the primary regime. But regardless of the legislative vehicle, the existing opportunity to review maintenance arrangements when applying the primary regime[68] would need to be preserved.

13. WOULD AN ENLIGHTENED STATUTORY REGIME MAKE CONTRACTING OUT REDUNDANT?

The right to contract out is presently necessary to counter anomalies in the PRA. The final question is whether there would remain any residual justification for contracting out if the anomalies were removed. Five aspects affect the answer:

- the false analogy of normal contracts;
- society's responsibility to protect the vulnerable;
- personal, family, and social pressures;
- drafting challenges; and
- could one size fit all?

13.1. THE FALSE ANALOGY OF ORDINARY CONTRACTS

In most spheres, freedom of choice and freedom of contract are like motherhood and apple pie. They are rallying cries in areas as diverse as alternative dispute resolution and abortion. One can confidently predict that any attempt to whittle down the right to contract out from any new relationship property regime would be vigorously opposed in some quarters on philosophical grounds. It will be pointed out that those who choose to enter into other relationships – partnerships, joint ventures, leases, franchise agreements, and others – are free to choose the terms on which they will do so. The same unfettered approach will be sought for contracting out agreements, particularly by wealthy men.

The analogy with most kinds of contract is inapt. A couple's marital relationship is more personal and emotional than commercial. It is likely to last for a very long time. During that time the relationship will pass through many unforeseen changes of circumstance. Nor are a couple's property rights solely a matter for them. The outcome affects the children of the relationship and the

68 PRA, s 32.

State. The State will need to step in with a welfare benefit if one party is left penniless. A closer analogy might be a residential tenancy, the terms of which are tightly controlled under the Residential Tenancies Act 1986 (NZ). The case for freedom of contract on purely philosophical grounds is weak.

13.2. SOCIETY'S RESPONSIBILITY TO PROTECT THE VULNERABLE

Until the mid-twentieth century, Parliament was content to leave it to couples to determine for themselves how they would organise title to their own property. But the growing pressure for legislation such as the Joint Family Homes Act 1950 (NZ), the Matrimonial Property Act 1963 (NZ), Part VIII of the Matrimonial Proceedings Act 1963 (NZ), the Matrimonial Property Act 1976 (NZ), and its extension to de facto relationships in 2001[69] were all driven by developing social policy. The principal policy goal was to remove gender inequality in the disposition of property between husbands and wives. To a lesser extent it was also to protect children of the union. Leaving it to couples to make their own voluntary arrangements had not worked. Society as a whole had to step in and impose the solution which couples could have adopted voluntarily if they had been so minded.

To encourage contracting out now would be to return to laissez-faire. It would leave it to individual couples to decide. But it is questionable whether they have the will, and the equality of bargaining power, to come up with a formula that would be fair to both. We do not permit couples to contract out of laws created for the protection of the vulnerable – the Crimes Act 1961 (NZ), the Domestic Violence Act 1995 (NZ), the maintenance provisions of the Family Proceedings Act 1980 (NZ), the Care of Children Act 2004 (NZ), the Child Support Act 1991 (NZ), or the Family Protection Act 1955 (NZ). The values which those Acts support were considered too important to allow the parties to contract out.

This suggests that at the very least there should be no right to contract out from those aspects of property redistribution closely associated with a party's personal needs. The two aspects identified earlier were compensation for a relationship-caused disparity in earning capacity and the right to spousal support. They, at least, should be beyond the reach of contracting out. As to the primary property regime itself, we should be slow to allow individuals to contract away spousal property rights that took over 100 years of nurturing to develop.

---

69 Property (Relationships) Amendment Act 2001 (NZ), s 9.

13.3. PERSONAL, FAMILY, AND SOCIAL PRESSURES

Contracting out agreements are not negotiated at arm's length, literally or metaphorically. Modern marriages are normally the consequence of a period of such extreme affection that the couple commit to spending the rest of their lives together. There is a jarring incongruity between that happy state of affairs and the cold commercialism of a contracting out agreement. People should not be required to say, 'I will love you as no man has ever loved a woman before, greater than the mountains, deeper than the oceans, more enduring than the pyramids, and down through the aeons of time. And by the way please sign this document that says if we break up you will have no claim on my pre-marriage assets.' It is unrealistic to model the law on the assumption that if one party wishes to modify the default regime it is easy for him or her to ask the other to do so or, if such a request is made, that it is easy for the other to decline.[70]

In addition to that incongruity at a personal level, the potential for contracting out provides an opportunity for strong family and social pressures to impact on the parties. Parents sometimes let it be known that they want a contracting out agreement for their child to protect property that had emanated from, or is intended to emanate from, the family of origin. There can also be a strong public relations pressure where one party says 'no contracting out agreement, no wedding' at a time when the invitations have already gone out, the dress has been bought, the photographer hired, the florist engaged, and the marquee company booked.[71]

To a limited extent those pressures can be mitigated through legislation. An obvious step is to require independent advice and signing formalities before separate solicitors, as is presently the case.[72] Consideration might also be given to requiring execution of the agreement a minimum period before the marriage.[73] But as the Law Commission for England and Wales has recently pointed out, the time limit would need to be inordinately long if it is to precede the lead time required for modern weddings. The Commission also comments that such a time limit would simply divert the pressure from the eve of the wedding to an earlier date.[74] There is no ultimate antidote to the pressures placed on parties contemplating contracting out.

---

70 *MacLeod v MacLeod* [2008] UKPC 64, [2010] 1 AC 298 at [36] and *Wood v Wood*, above n 61 illustrate the problem.

71 As in *Wood v Wood*, ibid.

72 PRA, s 21F.

73 For example, under Catalan law a pre-nuptial agreement must be concluded at least one month before the wedding – see further J Ferrer-Riba, 'Spain' in JM Scherpe (ed), *Marital Agreements and Private Autonomy in Comparative Perspective*, Hart Publishing, Oxford 2012, 350 at 363.

74 Ibid, at 499.

13.4. DRAFTING CHALLENGES

It is questionable whether many couples can access the expertise and farsightedness required to create a satisfactory alternative to a statutory regime. A couple will obviously have the benefit of advice from their respective solicitors. But contracting out is not for the faint-hearted. In effect it calls for the creation of an ad hoc property regime tailored to the unforeseen future lives of a particular couple.

Creating property regimes is challenging enough for experts and law reformers. Experience over many years suggests that the parties are expecting too much of their regular family solicitors when they ask them to draft agreements that are tailored to their peculiar wishes, compatible with the rest of the PRA, unambiguous, workable, fair, and future-proof. The failure rate has been high. Litigation has frequently followed because the parties and their advisers cannot resort to existing authority to interpret their ad hoc creations.[75]

Drafting expertise may be greater in Europe. The execution of marriage contracts before notaries has been a feature of Continental systems for several centuries. The acceptability of contracts there may have stemmed from the development of narrow conventions and standard forms over many years. Religious and social norms are also very different from those encountered in modern New Zealand.

The European experience might encourage Parliament to annex acceptable contracting out forms to the new statute. But what would be regarded as an acceptable alternative to the new regime? Obvious candidates at the moment are agreements to prevent the unwarranted conversion of ESA to divisible relationship property.[76] But the place to put terms which couples routinely want is in the statutory regime itself. Once that is done, it is difficult to see what place there would be for sanctioned alternatives.

13.5. COULD ONE SIZE FIT ALL?

It will undoubtedly be argued that no single relationship property regime could be expected to cater for all couples and all situations. Every couple, and every relationship, is unquestionably different. But the infinite differences between individuals has never deterred Parliament from enacting laws of general application. As noted earlier, there is little or no opportunity to contract out

---

[75] For two out of innumerable examples, see *Harrison v Harrison* [1996] NZFLR 699 (HC) and *Moor v Marston* [2015] NZCA 421.

[76] For possible precedents see *Fisher on Matrimonial and Relationship Property*, above n 34 at 40,101–40,206.

of other family law legislation, no matter how idiosyncratic the family or its circumstances.

The courageous course would be to abolish contracting out altogether. But it is difficult for reformers to foresee every eventuality. The more craven, but probably more realistic, course would be to retain the right but couple it with an onus on the party seeking to uphold the agreement. On that approach the onus on the proponent of a contracting out agreement could be the deliberately high one of persuading the court that (i) application of the statutory regime would have been unjust, and (ii) application of the agreement would be just in all the circumstances. If the proponent failed to discharge the onus, the agreement would be void.

14. CONCLUSIONS

The following conclusions can be drawn:

- The PRA was an inspired social ideal compromised by its inept execution. The greatest anomalies have resulted from its confusion between (i) capital created by a couple's joint and several efforts during the relationship (FOR), and (ii) assets owned before the relationship began or subsequently acquired by third party gift or inheritance (ESA).
- Contracting out is presently the principal way in which couples preserve their own ESA. The courts will normally uphold agreements entered into for that purpose while setting aside agreements calculated to prevent equal division of FOR. In doing so, the courts are instinctively endorsing the fundamental distinction between FOR and ESA overlooked in the PRA.
- Whether and to what extent we should permit contracting out depends on the statutory regime we adopt to replace the PRA.
- The new regime should be founded upon equal sharing of FOR and non-sharing of ESA.
- If that foundation were adopted, the concept on which it rested would govern secondary topics such as tracing, intermingling, and increases in value. All these matters could be dealt with at a conceptual level. It would be a mistake to descend into detailed rules based on asset-type, common use, common benefit, and other matters better left to valuers. Prescriptive rules dealing with family homes, family chattels, life insurance, superannuation, compensation for lack of family homes, homesteads, family homes owned by both spouses at the outset, and 'marriages of short duration' would all be redundant.
- For clarity of reasoning, it should be recognised that compensation for earning disparity and spousal support have distinct rationales and require distinct assessments. Those jurisdictions should be exercised after application of the primary statutory regime.

- One party should be entitled to earnings disparity compensation from the other amounting to half the present value of any relationship-caused disparity in earning capacity after allowance for contingencies. The compensation should be a matter of entitlement rather than the exercise of a judicial discretion.
- As is presently the law, one party should also be entitled to post-separation spousal support in appropriate circumstances. Possession and occupation of relationship property should be seen as an aspect of support for spouses and children. There should also be a power to discharge support obligations by the transfer of property as an alternative to payment in the form of a lump sum or periodical payments.
- The loss of a right to share in a breadwinner's ESA could reduce the overall value of awards made in favour of homemakers and carer parents if compensating steps were not taken in relation to family support and earning disparity compensation. Reforming the basic property regime must therefore be accompanied by a greater readiness to discharge family support and earning disparity obligations in a capital form, that is to say, by making a substantial property award over and above equal division of the FOR (as is broadly the approach in England and Australia).
- It should not be possible to contract out from earnings disparity compensation or the right to spousal support.
- If the primary statutory regime is carefully drafted there should be little or no need for contracting out.
- Even with an enlightened statutory regime, the safer course is probably to retain a power to contract out but with a heavy onus on the party seeking to uphold the agreement. The onus on the proponent of an agreement should be the high one of showing that (i) application of the statutory regime would have been unjust, and (ii) application of the agreement would be just in all the circumstances.

CHAPTER 14

CONTRACTING OUT OF THE DEFAULT RELATIONSHIP PROPERTY REGIME – COMPARATIVE OBSERVATIONS

Jens M Scherpe*

* All figures in this chapter were produced by the author.

1. INTRODUCTION – THE CORE OF RELATIONSHIP RECOGNITION LAW

The question at the heart of this paper is whether the parties of a legally recognised relationship should be permitted to opt/contract out of the default legal regime governing their property relations by entering into marital agreements (often also referred to as nuptial agreements). Unsurprisingly, the answer to that question depends very much on what legal consequences the underlying default system would bring with it – and what exact policies the jurisdiction in question pursues (or intends to pursue) with the default rules. As the purpose of this chapter is to offer some comparative observations on what is often simply referred to as 'contracting out' (or opting out) of the default regime, it is therefore imperative to be aware of what the default rules are, taking into account the legal, social, historical, and political context of the jurisdiction in question. The rules on contracting out can only be understood against that background and, more importantly, the *limitations* that the jurisdictions have placed on this contracting out can only be understood against that background. These limitations reflect what, in that particular jurisdiction, is the absolute core of the law governing the relationship – the core which is so essential to the regulation of the relationship that it is not at the disposition of the parties and therefore cannot be opted out of.

2. TERMINOLOGY AND FOCUS OF THIS CHAPTER

Before describing the systems and explaining the rules on contracting out, it is necessary to say a few words on terminology. The title of this chapter speaks of 'relationship' rather than 'marital' property. In the twenty-first century, this increasingly will be the better term to use, with more and more relationships other than marriage being recognised by the law, including property consequences and/or regimes, in an increasing number of jurisdictions. Arguably, New Zealand has gone the furthest here: with regard to a central element of this chapter, namely the division of relationship property, only very few differences are now made between marriages, civil unions, and qualifying de facto relationships in New Zealand,[1] all of which are open to couples irrespective of legal gender. This is certainly not the case in many of the jurisdictions that will be discussed in this chapter. These jurisdictions have different relationship recognition patterns, which may or may not include same-sex marriages, registered partnerships, or de facto/cohabitation relationships. The recognised relationships in these jurisdictions also often have very distinct consequences with regard to the property of the couples; while some are equated to marriage, others are deliberately designed to be different from marriage.

However, all the jurisdictions canvassed have settled laws in place with regard to marriage, and those rules are the most intense and far-reaching ones with regard to the property consequences. Therefore, the focus of this comparative chapter will be on the laws governing marriage. But it is important to point out that what is being described and discussed in the following is not necessarily restricted to marriages but may (and in many cases does) apply equally to other forms of recognised relationships. In particular, this is true for the conditions of 'contracting out' as, in many cases, what applies to the law of marriage applies (or should apply) to opting out of the default regimes for other recognised relationships.

Finally, it is necessary to briefly explain the terminology with regard to 'contracting out'. This contribution will use the term 'marital agreements' as an umbrella term for all agreements which seek to change/opt out of the default rules that would otherwise apply. Of these, matrimonial property agreements (as the name makes rather clear!) are those that merely deal with the division (or the absences of a division, as the case may be) of the couple's property – and it is these agreements that this contribution will focus on.

A distinction between agreements is also made based on the time the agreement is entered into. 'Pre-nuptial agreements'[2] is the term used for agreements concluded before the marriage, and 'post-nuptial agreements' is used for agreements concluded during the marriage, but before the time of separation or divorce. For agreements concluded at the point in time when the couple have decided to divorce and want to regulate the financial side of this process themselves (with or without the help of lawyers) the term 'separation agreement' is used.[3] The crucial difference between pre- and post-nuptial agreements, on

---

1 On this see, for example, M Briggs, 'Marital Agreements and Private Autonomy in New Zealand' in JM Scherpe (ed), *Marital Agreements and Private Autonomy in Comparative Perspective*, Hart Publishing, Oxford 2012, 256.

2 Sometimes also referred to as 'ante-nuptial agreements'.

3 In several jurisdictions there is the possibility of some form of judicial separation as a precursor or an alternative to divorce, which may or may not be accompanied by an agreement on the terms of the separation. But in this chapter the term 'separation agreement' is used as indicated above and should not be confused with issues about judicial separation

the one hand, and separation agreements, on the other, is that in the former the parties are contracting about a (more or less) uncertain future, whereas in the latter they know (or at least are in a position to know) what the financial consequences of their marriage have been.

3. PROBLEMS WHEN COMPARING MATRIMONIAL PROPERTY REGIMES AND THE FULL FINANCIAL CONSEQUENCES OF DIVORCE/RELATIONSHIP DISSOLUTION

While the contribution in the following will primarily focus on the property consequences of divorce, it is absolutely essential to keep in mind that this – the division of the matrimonial property – is only a part of the financial consequences of divorce. In all the jurisdictions canvassed, there are additional financial and property consequences of divorce ranging from lump sum and periodical (maintenance) payments and orders regarding pensions, to allocations of specific items for use (particularly the matrimonial/family home). Where these additional remedies are, in principle, considered separately from matrimonial property, one could say that the full financial consequences of divorce rest on several 'pillars' – of which matrimonial property division often (but not always) is the central one. By contrast, where matrimonial property division is considered alongside other remedies as part of an integrated whole (as, for example, in England and Wales, Australia, and Ireland) the process could be described as a 'holistic approach'.[4] However, it is crucial to keep in mind that irrespective of whether a 'pillar' or 'holistic' approach is taken, all the matrimonial property regimes looked at here were created in the full knowledge that remedies other than division of property *would* be available to the spouses and, indeed, often would be relied upon to create fair outcomes, which in some cases the rigid and static regimes by themselves would be unable to do. Furthermore, it is, as always in comparative law, not possible to understand and explain each of the regimes without looking at their full legal, social, and societal context. So, for

---

other than divorce. It is also interesting to note that in New Zealand a separation agreement is generally referred to as a 'compromise agreement' or 'settlement agreement', terms which imply that the couple has negotiated the terms of the agreement and found a compromise or settled their differences. This certainly reflects the ideal, but not necessarily the reality of some of these agreements. It may also explain the peculiar (and internationally fairly unique) legal evaluation of these agreements in New Zealand (on which see 5.1 below).

4 On this (and for a broader comparison of matrimonial property regimes and marital agreements) see JM Scherpe, 'Marital Agreements and Private Autonomy in Comparative Perspective' in JM Scherpe (ed), *Marital Agreements and Private Autonomy in Comparative Perspective*, Hart Publishing, Oxford 2012, 443, esp at 476 ff.

example, female labour market participation, property structures and whether there is a functioning rental market, availability of state-supported child care, the general level of social welfare, and the general understanding of the meaning and function of marriage do matter greatly, and are necessary to fully grasp the practicalities of the default regime, and indeed the limitations on opting out.

4. DEFAULT MATRIMONIAL PROPERTY REGIMES/ FINANCIAL CONSEQUENCES OF DIVORCE – IN A NUTSHELL

Having stated above that a full exposition is needed in order to present and explain the approaches in the various jurisdictions properly, it needs to be said that space precludes such a full exposition here.[5] The focus therefore will be on the general structures rather than the details.

As a basic starting point, there are only two possibilities for matrimonial property regimes/the financial consequences of divorce: either the fact of marriage has an immediate impact on the property relations and some kind of community of property is created (on which see 4.1 below), or it does not and there is essentially a separation of property during the marriage (on which see 4.2 and 4.3 below).

4.1. COMMUNITY OF PROPERTY JURISDICTIONS

It is important to state at the outset that because marriage has an immediate proprietary effect in jurisdictions operating with a default matrimonial property regime that involves some form of community of property, the effect of pre- and post-nuptial agreements is also immediate. This is a marked difference from jurisdictions where the default regime is based on a separation of property. The agreements therefore cannot be legally and morally dismissed as 'divorce agreements', or politically dismissed as being about marriages 'planning to fail', as they apply not only in the case of divorce but also *during* the marriage. Hence the reasons for entering into these agreements may not necessarily be (although they, of course, often are) rooted in the wish to mitigate/control the effects of a potential divorce. On the contrary, they may have been entered into specifically to ensure that certain or all property is held separately during the marriage, which may simply be for tax or estate planning purposes, or to protect from

---

5 But see, for example, the national reports in JM Scherpe (ed), *Marital Agreements and Private Autonomy in Comparative Perspective*, Hart Publishing, Oxford 2012, with further references.

claims by third parties. So, for example, if one of the spouses is exposed to grave financial risks or potential liability, it may be prudent to enter into a separation of property agreement to protect the other spouse from the risk of losing assets they have contributed to the communal property. Therefore, in jurisdictions which have a default regime of some form of community of property, arguably the possibility to contract out of the default regime is essential in order to meet the needs of spouses – and, in some cases, to protect the financially weaker spouse.

4.1.1. Universal Community of Property

The most extreme form of community of property is the 'universal community of property' – which applies eg in the Netherlands for marriages entered into before 1 January 2018. Essentially, from the day of marriage all property that the spouses bring in or acquire during the marriage becomes communal property, including inheritances and gifts.[6]

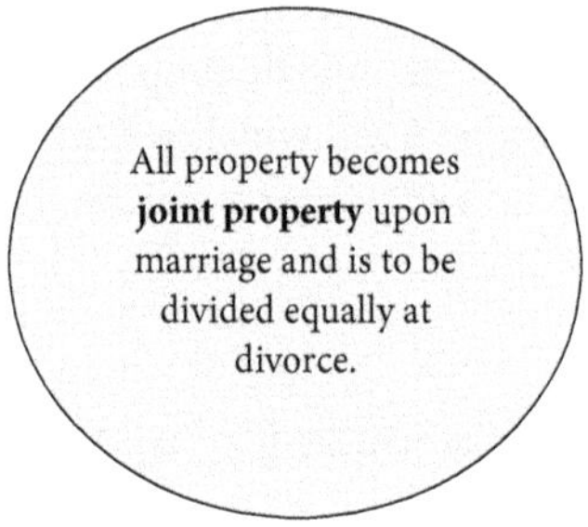

Unsurprisingly, very few legal systems operate with such a matrimonial property regime. It reflects an outdated view of marriage where the couple 'become one' and financially lose their individuality.

On divorce, the community property is divided equally and, where required, additional remedies, such as maintenance payments, can be awarded. This appears to make universal community of property jurisdictions the perfect jurisdictions to 'marry into money'. Also, in an age where a large number of marriages do not last for life, where there are many second and third marriages, and where there will often be children from previous relationships, it is apparent

---

6 On this see K Boele-Woelki and B Braat, 'Marital Agreements and Private Autonomy in the Netherlands' in JM Scherpe (ed), *Marital Agreements and Private Autonomy in Comparative Perspective*, Hart Publishing, Oxford 2012, 229. See also F Swennen, 'The Changing Concept of "Family" and Challenges for Family Law in the Benelux Countries' in JM Scherpe (ed), *European Family Law Vol II: The Changing Concept of 'Family' and Challenges for Domestic Family Law*, Edward Elgar, Cheltenham 2016, 5.

that this matrimonial property regime is simply not adequate for the needs of the spouses (and their families). Therefore, rather predictably, in these jurisdictions marital agreements creating a different property framework for the marriage are very common.[7]

4.1.2. Community of Acquest

By contrast, the community of acquest (sometimes also referred to as a community of acquisitions) is a *limited* community of property system. As the name indicates, the community is limited to the marital acquest, ie those assets acquired during the marriage. However, inheritances and gifts received during the marriage are excluded and are treated in the same way as pre-marital property, because they are not regarded as the 'fruits of joint labour' and therefore should not be shared.[8] The community of acquest is the most common form of default matrimonial property regime in Europe and South America.[9]

The community of acquest operates with three groups of property: the communal property (acquest) and the two separate properties of the spouses.

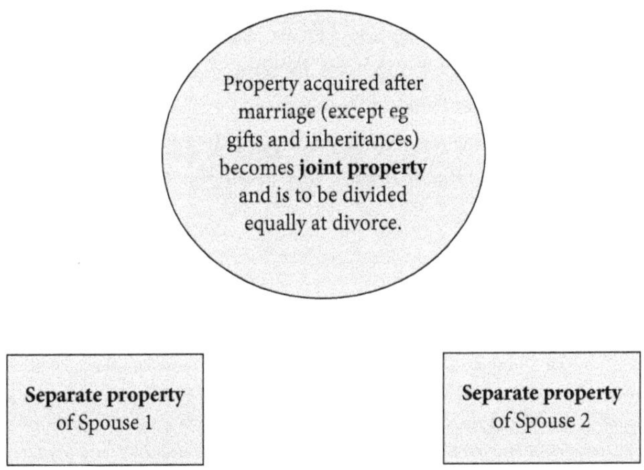

---

7 K Boele-Woelki and B Braat, above n 6 esp at 248 ff.

8 It needs to be noted that amongst the jurisdictions that have the community of acquest as the default matrimonial property regime, there are differences as to how income derived from separate property (such as rents, dividends, interest etc) is classified. In some, for example Belgium, France, the federal law of Spain, and Portugal, such income becomes communal; in others, for example Slovenia, Serbia, and Croatia, income from separate property remains separate property.

9 Compare W Pintens, 'Matrimonial Property Law in Europe' in K Boele-Woelki, J Miles and JM Scherpe (eds), *The Future of Family Property in Europe*, Intersentia, Antwerp/Cambridge 2011, 19, esp at 21 ff.

In case of divorce, the approach at first glance appears simple: each spouse retains their separate property and is entitled to half of the communal property. In most jurisdictions there is no room for discretion with regard to the division of assets, and even in those jurisdictions where there theoretically is discretion, it is hardly ever exercised.[10] However, in reality the three groups of property will not be fully separated from each other. For example, if the wife inherited a house during the marriage, and its roof was in need of repair, this may have been paid for by the communal property. Therefore, it is necessary to trace all the payments/contributions made from one group of property to another and – in the abstract – 'reverse' them, that is to make deductions or additions to the groups of property. So in the example, the money spent on repairing the roof would have to be deducted from the separate property of the wife and added to the communal property.[11] Needless to say, this can often be difficult, as families tend not to keep detailed accounts on all financial transactions within the family. So this will usually only be invoked for larger (and easy to prove) transactions. Furthermore, the courts may allocate specific assets from the communal property to one of the parties (such as the former matrimonial home or property required by one of the spouses for their work). This does not affect the equal division of the communal assets. It is merely a preferential allocation, meaning what is received is deducted from the overall claim.[12]

As mentioned above, it should not be forgotten that even after the division of the matrimonial property the other pillars remain available. For example, in France, Catalonia, and the federal law of Spain, lump sum payments in the form of a *prestation compensatoire/prestación compensatria/pension compensatoria*

[10] For example in Poland and Serbia, compare W Pintens, above n 9 at 26 with further references. By contrast, in some of the US jurisdictions this discretion seems to be exercised more often; see IM Ellman, 'Marital Agreements and Private Autonomy in the United States' in JM Scherpe (ed), *Marital Agreements and Private Autonomy in Comparative Perspective*, Hart Publishing, Oxford 2012, 403, esp at 405.

[11] It further needs to be noted that the nature of the contribution to the other groups of property is viewed differently in the community of acquest jurisdictions. Some see it as a contribution made at the time, and thus the sum to be 'reversed' is exactly the original contribution. In others, including France and Belgium, the money paid is seen as an 'investment' in the sense that any increase (or decrease) in the value generated needs to be taken into account in the 'reversal' (on this see, for example, W Pintens, 'Marital Agreements and Private Autonomy in France and Belgium' in JM Scherpe (ed), *Marital Agreements and Private Autonomy in Comparative Perspective*, Hart Publishing, Oxford 2012, 68, esp at 74 ff). For example, if the husband buys a house for $500,000 and uses $400,000 of his own separate property and the communal asset contributes $100,000, but at the time of the divorce the house has increased in value to $600,000, the sum 'reversed' proportionally would include the value increase, and therefore would be $120,000.

[12] If the value of the asset allocated in this way is greater than the spouse's share of the communal property, then the recipient must compensate the other spouse for the difference.

are available,[13] while in other jurisdictions significant maintenance payments as well as the allocation of the *use* of specific assets may be ordered. Unlike the division of the matrimonial property, these remedies are usually subject to the court's discretion.

4.2. SEPARATION OF PROPERTY JURISDICTIONS

Unlike in the community of property jurisdictions, in the separation of property jurisdictions marriage has no major immediate impact on the couple's property relations. The spouses are still seen as individuals and can administer their own property freely – although in almost all jurisdictions there are restrictions on the disposition of certain items (such as the family home), and each spouse is protected against actions of the other spouse intended to deprive them of what they might otherwise receive in the event of divorce (or death).

Of course, all of the separation of property systems have some default legal mechanisms in place so that when a marriage is terminated through divorce or death, the spouses participate in each other's assets. Even though no community of property is created through marriage, marriage is seen as a union of equals,[14] which extends to their financial relations. But this participation in the other spouse's wealth is deferred until the marriage ends, rather than being immediate through prescribing a communal property. Some scholars therefore refer to the separation of property jurisdictions as having 'participation systems'.[15] As the participation is deferred, this means that while marital agreements can have some influence on the property relations during the marriage (for example, with regard to the restrictions just mentioned) the main purpose of such agreements in separation of property jurisdictions is to regulate the financial (and other) relations of the spouses in case of divorce or death of one of the spouses.

---

13 For an in-depth analysis of the *prestación compensatoria/pension compensatoria* in Spain and Catalonia see L Allueva Aznar, *Prestación Compensatoria y Autonomía Privada Familiar*, Tirant lo Blanch, Valencia 2016; on Spain and Catalonia also see J Ferrer-Riba, 'Marital Agreements and Private Autonomy in Spain' in JM Scherpe (ed), *Marital Agreements and Private Autonomy in Comparative Perspective*, Hart Publishing, Oxford 2012, 350, esp at 356 f and A Lamarca Marqués, 'The Changing Concept of "Family" and Challenges for Family Law in Spain and Catalonia' in JM Scherpe (ed), *European Family Law Vol II: The Changing Concept of 'Family' and Challenges for Domestic Family Law*, Edward Elgar, Cheltenham 2016, 289. On France see W Pintens, above n 11.

14 Although to a lesser degree in Greece – see below.

15 Compare W Pintens, 'Ehegüterstände in Europa' (2009) *Zeitschrift für Europäisches Privatrecht* 268 ff; W Pintens, 'Ehegüterrecht' in J Basedow, KJ Hopt and R Zimmermann (eds), *Handwörterbuch des Europäischen Privatrechts*, vol I, Mohr Siebeck, Tübingen 2009, 350 ff; W Pintens, above n 9 at 19 ff; see also K Boele-Woelki and M Jänterä-Jareborg, 'Initial Results of the Work of the CEFL in the Field of Property Relations Between Spouses' in K Boele-Woelki, J Miles and JM Scherpe (eds), *The Future of Family Property in Europe*, Intersentia, Cambridge 2011, 47.

4.2.1. *Deferred Community of Property*

The deferred community of property is the default matrimonial property regime in the Nordic Countries.[16] In principle it does what the name says: the universal community of property is deferred, that is, it comes into existence only when the marriage comes to an end. Hence the Nordic Countries seek to combine the ideal of the independent spouse during the marriage with the ultimate protection in case of divorce or death, by making the community of property a universal one which, in principle, is to be shared equally.[17]

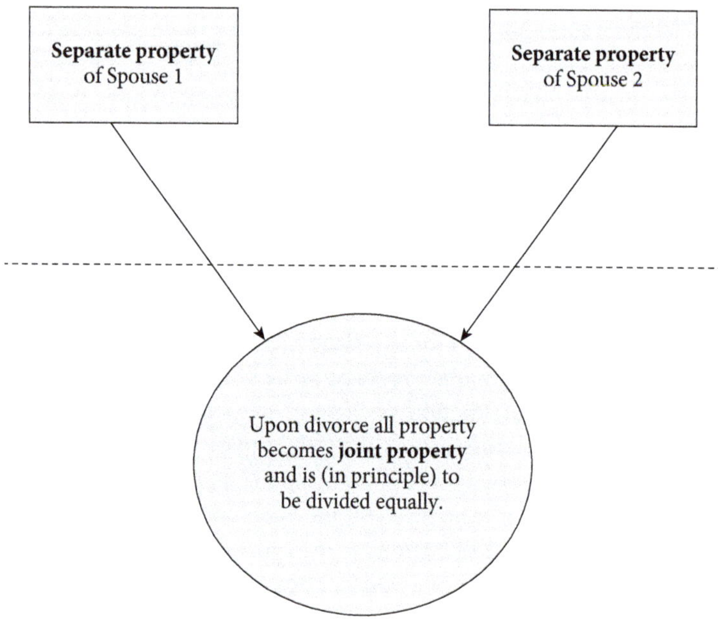

---

[16] See, for example, for Sweden M Jänterä-Jareborg, 'Marital Agreements and Private Autonomy in Sweden' in JM Scherpe (ed), *Marital Agreements and Private Autonomy in Comparative Perspective*, Hart Publishing, Oxford 2012, 370, and on all Nordic Countries, T Sverdrup, 'The Changing Concept of "Family" and Challenges for Family Law in the Nordic Countries' in JM Scherpe (ed), *European Family Law Vol II: The Changing Concept of 'Family' and Challenges for Domestic Family Law*, Edward Elgar, Cheltenham 2016, 186 and JM Scherpe, 'Privatautonomie im Familienrecht der nordischen Länder' in S Hofer, D Schwab and D Henrich (eds), *From Status to Contract? – Die Bedeutung des Vertrages im europäischen Familienrecht: Beiträge zum europäischen Familienrecht*, Gieseking, Bielefeld 2005, 209.

[17] Unlike, for example, New Zealand and Singapore which have defined categories of relationship/matrimonial property, and therefore operate with a deferred community of relationship/matrimonial property rather than a deferred community of property, see 4.2.2 below.

But, importantly, in all the Nordic jurisdictions the court has the discretion to deviate from the equal sharing of the communal property when doing otherwise would be inequitable. The exact criteria for this differ between the jurisdictions, but generally apply in marriages of short duration (meaning five years or less) or where the majority of the assets were pre-marital or received by one of the parties as a gift or inheritance during the marriage. That said, this discretion generally appears to be used sparingly.[18]

Norway reformed its law in 1993, to reflect more modern views of marriage, by introducing a provision that allowed one of the parties to exclude pre-marital, inherited, or gifted assets from the sharing pool, provided that the spouse can prove their non-matrimonial origin. However, the other spouse may then offer evidence that excluding these assets from the property division would be inequitable. This effectively reverses the burden of proof: what could be termed 'non-marital property' will not be shared unless the court is convinced that it would be unfair to exclude it.[19]

It ought to be mentioned here briefly (as this is a major social, legal, and cultural difference from many other jurisdictions) that the additional remedies (or 'pillars') available on divorce, in particular maintenance, are less important in the Nordic jurisdictions. The reason for this is the different understanding not only of marriage but also of the role of the state. There is general consensus in the Nordic Countries that the state should provide for citizens in need, irrespective of the reason for their need. So, where one of the spouses has maintenance needs after the marriage comes to an end, the state is generally expected to provide financial support rather than the former spouse. This, of course, has to be judged against the background of the deferred (universal) community of property as the default matrimonial property regime, on the one hand, and the comparatively generous provision of the welfare state, on the other. Not only is there ample provision for child care and so forth, but the monetary and practical support for citizens who cannot support themselves (such as offering occupational retraining and providing housing) is set up to enable most persons to reach the level of self-sufficiency relatively quickly. Where such a level cannot be reached, there is ongoing support for rent and household expenses. Hence, covering post-marital 'need' is not necessarily the responsibility of the former spouse.

---

18 See the references in n 16 above.

19 This approach therefore is closer to the division of relationship property in New Zealand and matrimonial property in Singapore than the other Nordic jurisdictions, as this effectively limits the communal property but, crucially, the courts in Norway retain discretion to decide otherwise and redistribute all property if, in their view, the case requires it.

4.2.2. *Deferred Community of Relationship Property*

Some jurisdictions, including New Zealand and Singapore, have a default regime that is a variation of the deferred community of property.[20] The starting point is similar: the property relations of the parties do not change on marriage. They both retain their separate properties. However, on divorce the community that then comes into existence (and is shared equally, subject to some discretion)[21] is not a universal one but rather a limited one. That is why referring to these regimes as a 'deferred community of property' system is not entirely correct, although this is common practice in both New Zealand and Singapore.[22] In Singapore, the 'matrimonial assets' which are subject to division are defined in section 112(10) of the Women's Charter as follows:

> '(a) any asset acquired before the marriage by one party or both parties to the marriage –
>
> (i) ordinarily used or enjoyed by both parties or one or more of their children while the parties are residing together for shelter or transportation or for household, education, recreational, social or aesthetic purposes; or
>
> (ii) which has been substantially improved during the marriage by the other party or by both parties to the marriage; and
>
> (b) any other asset of any nature acquired during the marriage by one party or both parties to the marriage, but does not include any asset (not being a matrimonial home) that has been acquired by one party at any time by gift or inheritance and that has not been substantially improved during the marriage by the other party or by both parties to the marriage.'

In New Zealand, the Property (Relationships) Act 1976 (NZ) ('PRA') defines 'relationship property' in section 8(1):

> 'Relationship property shall consist of –
>
> (a) the family home whenever acquired; and

---

20 On those jurisdictions see, for example, M Briggs, above n 1, and WK Leong, 'Marital Agreements and Private Autonomy in Singapore' in JM Scherpe (ed), *Marital Agreements and Private Autonomy in Comparative Perspective*, Hart Publishing, Oxford 2012, 311.

21 The discretion of the courts is, at least in theory, significantly greater in Singapore than it is in New Zealand (compare s 112, Women's Charter (Singapore) and pt 4, Property (Relationships) Act 1976 (NZ) ('PRA')), but it does not seem to exercised excessively and in the vast majority of cases the property is split equally; see WK Leong, above n 20 at 314–16 and WK Leong, *Elements of Family Law in Singapore*, LexisNexis, Singapore 2007, 697–98.

22 See, for example, on Singapore WK Leong, 'Division of Matrimonial Assets: Recent Cases and Thoughts for Reform' [1993] *Singapore Journal of Legal Studies* 351, 353; and see the judicial approval of this classification in the Singapore Court of Appeal in *Lock Yeng Fun v Chua Hock Chye* [2007] 3 SLR(R) 520 per Phang JA at [40] and *Lau Siew Kim v Yeo Guan Chye Terence* [2008] 2 SLR(R) 108 per Rajah JA at [80].

(b) the family chattels whenever acquired; and
(c) all property owned jointly or in common in equal shares by the married couple or by the partners; and
(d) all property owned by either spouse or partner immediately before their marriage, civil union, or de facto relationship began, if –
  (i) the property was acquired in contemplation of the marriage, civil union, or de facto relationship; and
  (ii) the property was intended for the common use or common benefit of both spouses or partners; and
(e) subject to sections 9(2) to (6), 9A, and 10, all property acquired by either spouse or partner after their marriage, civil union, or de facto relationship began; and
(ee) subject to sections 9(3) to (6), 9A, and 10, all property acquired, after the marriage, civil union, or de facto relationship began, for the common use or common benefit of both spouses or partners, if –
  (i) the property was acquired out of property owned by either spouse or partner or by both of them before the marriage, civil union, or de facto relationship began; or
  (ii) the property was acquired out of the proceeds of any disposition of any property owned by either spouse or partner or by both of them before the marriage, civil union, or de facto relationship began; and
(f) *[Repealed]*
(g) the proportion of the value of any life insurance policy (as defined in section 2), or of the proceeds of such a policy, that is attributable to the marriage, civil union, or de facto relationship; and
(h) any policy of insurance in respect of any property described in paragraphs (a) to (ee); and
(i) the proportion of the value of any superannuation scheme entitlements (as defined in section 2) that is attributable to the marriage, civil union, or de facto relationship; and
(j) all other property that is relationship property under an agreement made under Part 6; and
(k) any other property that is relationship property by virtue of any other provision of this Act or by virtue of any other Act; and
(l) any income and gains derived from, the proceeds of any disposition of, and any increase in the value of, any property described in paragraphs (a) to (k).'

Separate property is then defined in section 9:

'(1) All property of either spouse or partner that is not relationship property is separate property.
(2) Subject to sections 8(1)(ee), 9A(3), and 10, all property acquired out of separate property, and the proceeds of any disposition of separate property, are separate property.
(3) Subject to section 9A, any increase in the value of separate property, and any income or gains derived from separate property, are separate property.

(4) The following property is separate property, unless the court considers that it is just in the circumstances to treat the property or any part of the property as relationship property:

(a) all property acquired by either spouse or partner while they are not living together as a married couple or as civil union partners or as de facto partners:

(b) all property acquired, after the death of one spouse or partner, by the surviving spouse or partner, as provided in section 84.

(5) …'

Hence both jurisdictions operate with a limited community of property, with the limits defined (more or less) clearly by statute. Pre-marital property (and post-marital property) as well as gifts and inheritances are generally not part of the 'sharing pool'. This system therefore differs from the deferred community of property described in 4.2.1 above, because there is separate property as well as communal property on divorce:

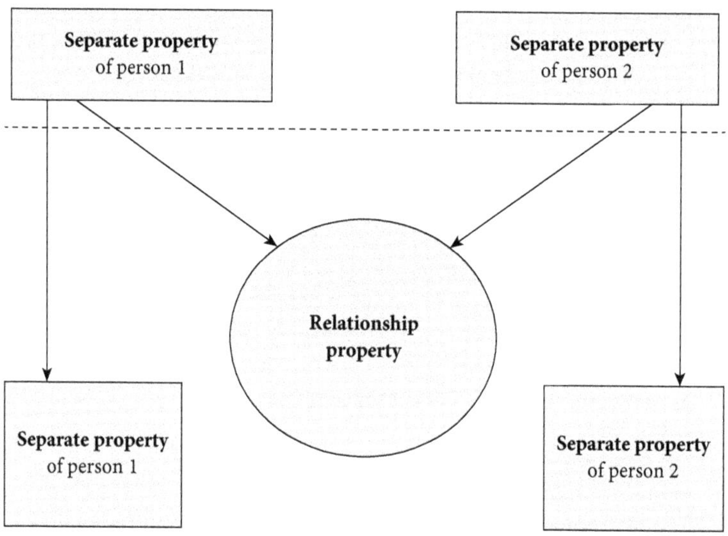

Both jurisdictions expressly provide for what might be called a 'familiarisation' of property: property that would ordinarily remain separate property (for example because it was acquired before the relationship) can become part of the sharing pool of relationship property if used for (or intended to be used for) the family. This often concerns the family home, but can also apply to chattels and any other property.[23] The reason for this is that the property has become part of the life

23 For some problematic cases see *Hyde v Hyde* [2009] NZCA 125, [2010] 1 NZLR 224 and *HES v GCS* (also known as *Sydney v Sydney*) [2012] NZFC 2685; *Rose v Rose* [2009] NZSC 46, [2009] 3 NZLR 1.

of the family – hence familiarised. Interestingly, similar rationales for sharing such assets can be discerned in the reasoning for discretionary decisions by the courts, for example, in England and Wales (on which see 4.3 below).

A criticism that can be levelled at this process of familiarisation of property is that anyone who has sufficient legal knowledge, or takes legal advice, could avoid this familiarisation, for example by renting out the property they own rather than living in it with their family. Thus, a rational and economically driven actor would be encouraged to keep their separate property fully separate rather than have the family benefit from it. It is highly questionable whether this is desirable and whether the law is setting the right incentives here. Furthermore, most people will not have, or acquire, sufficient legal knowledge and thus are often rather surprised, particularly when their second marriage/relationship comes to an end, that the property they firmly regarded as 'theirs' is suddenly subject to division.[24]

4.2.3. *Statutory Compensation Jurisdictions*

Unlike in deferred community of property and deferred community of relationship property systems, in statutory compensation jurisdictions the separation of property remains intact even on divorce or death. However, there are statutory rules regulating participation by one spouse in the other's assets. Hence, while the separation is maintained, there nevertheless is recognition of the marriage as a union of equals (except in Greece, see below 4.2.3.2) and that the fruits of joint labour should be shared.

4.2.3.1. Community of Accrued Gains

The German community of accrued gains (*Zugewinngemeinschaft*) is somewhat unfortunately named as at no point in time is there actually a community of property in any form.[25] The system is based on an assessment of the property

---

24 See, for example, *HES v GCS*, above n 23. Interestingly, the New Zealand courts have generally refused to set aside agreements as unjust if they merely exclude pre-relationship property from division (see eg *Lowry v Lowry* [1994] NZFLR 529 (HC) and *DMF v GRH [Division of Property]* [2008] NZFLR 425 (FC)). As noted by R Fisher, this goes to show that there is an 'intuitive sympathy' with the intention of keeping this type of property separate: 'Should a Property Sharing Regime be Mandatory or Optional?', ch 13. This view presumably also reflects the general expectation of most persons (and indeed, as this chapter shows, most jurisdictions) about sharing – and certainly that of the husband in *HES v GCS*, above n 23.

25 On this see, for example, A Dutta, 'Marital Agreements and Private Autonomy in Germany' in JM Scherpe (ed), *Marital Agreements and Private Autonomy in Comparative Perspective*, Hart Publishing, Oxford 2012, 158; D Martiny, 'The Changing Concept of "Family" and Challenges for Family Law in Germany' in JM Scherpe (ed), *European Family Law Vol II: The Changing Concept of 'Family' and Challenges for Domestic Family Law*, Edward Elgar, Cheltenham 2016, 65.

(including debts) of each spouse at two points in time: on the day of marriage (so-called initial assets) and on the day a spouse receives the other's petition for divorce. Gifts and inheritances are counted as parts of the initial assets, even if acquired during the marriage. For each spouse, the initial assets are subtracted from the final assets.[26] The result is the 'accrued gain' for each spouse.[27] The regime stipulates that each spouse should participate equally in the accrued gain acquired by both spouses during the marriage. Hence, the sums of accrued gains are added and then divided in half: this is the accrued gain that each spouse should have. If the accrued gain of one spouse is greater, then that spouse owes the other an 'equalisation payment' so that both spouses leave the marriage with the same accrued gain. So, while there is no actual community of property, there is an entitlement to half of the accrued gain.

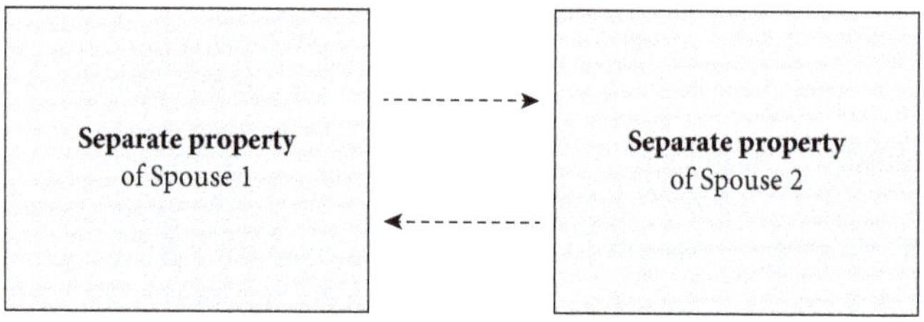

If at the time of divorce the accrued gain of one Spouse is greater than the other Spouse, the latter can bring a claim against the former as the accrued gain of the Spouses is to be divided equally.

Only in very extreme cases is it possible to deviate from equal sharing of the accrued gain (§ 1381 German Civil Code) – for example if one spouse tried to kill the other.[28] Mere hardship, or even extreme hardship, is insufficient to trigger unequal sharing. The German approach for dealing with needs is not via the division of property, but rather through the other 'pillars', especially maintenance and pension sharing/splitting.

As the German approach is a purely mathematical one, it can create what many see as potential unfairness, particularly if the accrued gain includes damages for pain and suffering, or severance payments, or is simply the result

---

[26] The actual sum is adjusted for inflation according to an index. See JM Scherpe, 'A Comparative Overview of the Treatment of Non-Matrimonial Assets, Indexation and Value Increases' (2013) 25 *Child and Family Law Quarterly* 61.

[27] If the result is negative, ie there was a loss, the 'accrued gain' is deemed to be 0.

[28] Compare D Schwab, *Familienrecht*, 24th ed, CH Beck, Munich 2016, 129 f, with further references.

of inflation of pre-marital assets. The German system[29] is blind to the source of, or reason for, the accrued gain. Changing the system was discussed, for example by making such payments or value increases part of the initial gains, like gifts or inheritances, which would avoid having to share them, but proposed changes were rejected during the latest reforms.[30] Retaining the current approach is therefore a conscious decision and apparently represents the German understanding of marital financial solidarity.

4.2.3.2. Participation in Acquests

The problems of the German approach mentioned in the previous paragraph are, to a certain extent, addressed in the participation in acquests regime, which is the default regime in Switzerland and Greece.[31] This regime is essentially a combination of the accrued gains and the community of acquests systems. But unlike the latter, there is never a community of property of any sort. Instead, this regime operates with four groups of property: the separate property of each spouse and the *separate* acquests of each spouse. The separate property remains separate even on divorce (hence there are no issues with regard to value increases and so forth), and the spouse is merely entitled to participate equally in the acquest of the other spouse on divorce.

While in many ways this appears to be an appealing approach, there are significant practical difficulties.[32] As in a community of acquests, before the actual calculation and participation can be effected, it is necessary to trace the

29 Unlike the optional Franco-German matrimonial property regime, see *Abkommen zwischen der Bundesrepublik Deutschland und der Französischen Republik über den Güterstand der Wahl-Zugewinngemeinschaft* (BGBl. 2012 II, 178); German and French text available at <www.bundesgerichtshof.de/DE/Bibliothek/GesMat/WP17/W/WahlZugewinngem.html> accessed 18.05.2017. Explanatory notes in German can be found at <www.bundesgerichtshof.de/SharedDocs/Downloads/DE/Bibliothek/Gesetzesmaterialien/17_wp/WahlZugewingem/erlaeuterungen.pdf;jsessionid=2C6E2580105943DCC684B0243144477E.1_cid368?__blob=publicationFile> accessed 18.05.2017. An English explanatory summary by the EU Directorate-General for Internal Policies (PE 425.658) can be found at <www.europarl.europa.eu/RegData/etudes/IDAN/2010/425658/IPOL-JURI_NT(2010)425658_EN.pdf> accessed 18.05.2017. On the agreement see also MG Cubeddu Wiedemann (ed), *The Optional Matrimonial Property Regime*, Intersentia, Cambridge 2014, with English, Italian, and Spanish translations of the agreement and the explanatory notes.

30 See references in n 25 above.

31 On Switzerland and Greece see, for example, I Schwenzer and T Keller, 'The Changing Concept of "Family" and Challenges for Family Law in Switzerland' in JM Scherpe (ed), *European Family Law Vol II: The Changing Concept of 'Family' and Challenges for Domestic Family Law*, Edward Elgar, Cheltenham 2016, 309; and E Zervogianni, 'The Changing Concept of "Family" and Challenges for Family Law in Greece' in JM Scherpe (ed), *European Family Law Vol II: The Changing Concept of 'Family' and Challenges for Domestic Family Law*, Edward Elgar, Cheltenham 2016, 86.

32 Compare I Schwenzer and T Keller, above n 31 at 316.

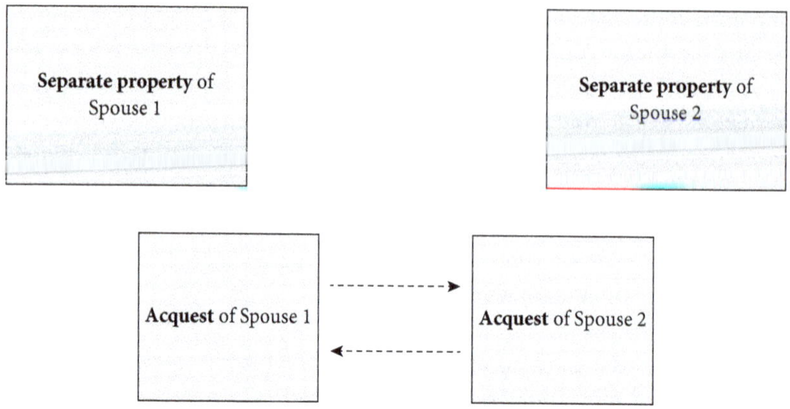

All of the property of the Spouses remains separate at all times. But upon divorce each Spouse participates in the acquest of the other.

payments made between the four groups of assets. However, it is very unlikely that the spouses would have actually kept their finances entirely separate, or their financial transactions carefully documented.

In stark contrast to all other jurisdictions in Europe, Greece is the only jurisdiction in which there is no assumption of equality between the spouses. Instead, there is a rebuttable presumption that each spouse contributed one third to the acquest of the other spouse. In practice this presumption leads to homemaker spouses receiving less than the half share they would receive in other European jurisdictions. Moreover, Greek law has rather strict and ungenerous rules regarding the family home, household goods, and maintenance, which further disadvantages the homemaker spouse.[33]

4.3. ENGLAND AND WALES – A JURISDICTION WITHOUT A MATRIMONIAL PROPERTY REGIME

England and Wales is one of the common law jurisdictions without a matrimonial property regime, and will be looked at as an example for this kind of approach.[34] The absence of an express regime has been interpreted by some to mean that

---

33 Compare E Zervogianni, above n 31 at 90 ff.

34 Other jurisdictions include Australia, Ireland, and Northern Ireland. On Australia see, for example, O Jessep, 'Marital Agreements and Private Autonomy in Australia' in JM Scherpe (ed), *Marital Agreements and Private Autonomy in Comparative Perspective*, Hart Publishing, Oxford 2012, 17; on Ireland see L Crowley, 'Marital Agreements and Private Autonomy in Ireland' in JM Scherpe (ed), *Marital Agreements and Private Autonomy in Comparative*

England and Wales operate a separation of property *regime* – which is incorrect. While there is indeed a separation of property and no community of property is ever created by or during marriage, this does not mean that there is a *regime* in place. This was confirmed in *Sorrell v Sorrell*,[35] where Bennett J expressly rejected the suggestion by Cretney that a community of property system had been 'imposed by judicial decision'.[36] Similarly, Baroness Hale held in *Miller v Miller; McFarlane v McFarlane* that: 'We do not yet have a system of community of property, whether full or deferred.'[37] In both cases the concept of a regime to describe the English approach was expressly rejected.

Instead of having a regime or rule-based participation approach (like the jurisdictions described in 4.2 above), the English view appears to be that only a fully discretionary system is able to administer 'fairness' in all cases. Hence, the approach is a 'holistic' one, taking into account all the circumstances of the individual case. It eschews not only clear rules and guidance, but arguably also a 'pillar' approach, as the division of assets, pensions, and maintenance are not dealt with separately. Instead, the idea underlying the English approach is to deliver a 'tailor-made' package for each case, which may or may not contain these elements. Lord Denning once described this approach as follows:[38]

> 'The Family Court takes the rights and obligations of the parties all together – and puts the pieces into a mixed bag. Such pieces are the right to occupy the matrimonial home or have a share in it, the obligation to maintain the wife and children, and so forth. The court then takes out the pieces and hands them to the two parties – some to one party and some to the other – so that each can provide for the future with the pieces allotted to him or to her. The court hands them out without paying any too nice a regard to their legal or equitable rights but simply according to what is the fairest provision for the future – for mother and father and the children.'

Still, the guiding principle of achieving a 'fair' outcome is a rather elusive one and inevitably subjective, as Lord Nicholls has pointed out in one of the seminal decisions:[39]

> 'Everyone would accept that the outcome on these matters, whether by agreement or court order, should be fair. More realistically, the outcome ought to be as fair as is

Perspective, Hart Publishing, Oxford 2012, 200, and B Sloan, 'The Changing Concept of "Family" and Challenges for Family Law in Ireland' in JM Scherpe (ed), *European Family Law Vol II: The Changing Concept of 'Family' and Challenges for Domestic Family Law*, Edward Elgar, Cheltenham 2016, 127.

35 *Sorrell v Sorrell* [2005] EWHC 1717 (Fam), [2006] 1 FLR 497 at [96].

36 S Cretney, 'Community of Property Imposed by Judicial Decision' (2003) 119 *Law Quarterly Review* 349, commenting on *Lambert v Lambert* [2002] EWCA Civ 1685, [2003] Fam 103.

37 *Miller v Miller; McFarlane v McFarlane* [2006] UKHL 24, [2006] 2 AC 618 at [151].

38 *Hanlon v Law Society* [1981] AC 124 (HL) at 147.

39 *White v White* [2001] 1 AC 596 (HL) at 599.

possible in all the circumstances. But everyone's life is different. Features which are important when assessing fairness differ in each case. And, sometimes, different minds can reach different conclusions on what fairness requires. Then fairness, like beauty, lies in the eye of the beholder.'

Indeed, the notion of what is 'fair' regarding the financial consequences of divorce changed dramatically in England and Wales at the beginning of this century.

The statutory provisions contain rather limited guidance, merely listing in section 25(2) of the Matrimonial Causes Act 1973 (Eng&W) many factors to which the court 'shall … have regard to'. But, as the mandate in section 25(1) makes clear, this list is non-exhaustive as the court is to have regard to 'all the circumstances'. The only prioritised consideration is the welfare of the children of the family,[40] which must be the 'first consideration'.[41]

The statute therefore does not give firm (or even 'unfirm'!) guidance on how a judge is to exercise discretion. In the last century, it was generally accepted that the homemaker spouse's claims could be confined to his or her (but usually her) 'reasonable requirements'. In so-called 'big-money cases' this led to the breadwinner spouse being entitled to keep a larger share of the property. There was no concept of participation in the wealth of the other spouse. This changed radically and dramatically in *White v White*.[42] The House of Lords interpreted fairness to mean that the spouses' contributions were to be valued equally:[43]

> 'there is one principle of universal application which can be stated with confidence. In seeking to achieve a fair outcome, there is no place for discrimination between husband and wife and their respective roles … There should be no bias in favour of the money-earner and against the home-maker and the child-carer.'

The firmness with which this was pronounced surprised many, even though at the time the equality of spouses was already a principle of universal application in most jurisdictions.[44] England and Wales were rather late in 'joining the club'.

40 Matrimonial Causes Act 1973 (Eng&W), s 25(1). It is important to note that 'child of the family' includes a child treated by the couple as a child of their family, s 52(1)(b) Matrimonial Causes Act 1973 (Eng&W), and thus can include children who are not the joint children of the couple or even of either spouse.

41 Matrimonial Causes Act 1973 (Eng&W), s 25(1). However, it is worth noting that the term used is not 'paramount', unlike, for example, in the Children Act 1989 (UK). Hence the welfare of the children of the family does not necessarily trump all other considerations – although in practice it does carry great weight.

42 *White v White*, above n 39.

43 Ibid, at 605.

44 Apart from Greece, see above at 4.2.3.2.

In subsequent cases the modern approach to fairness was developed further, culminating in *Miller v Miller; McFarlane v McFarlane.*[45] In this case the House of Lords identified three 'strands' or 'rationales' of fairness: needs, equal sharing, and compensation (for relationship-generated disadvantages).[46] The work of Joanna Miles on this topic was clearly known to the judges, as it was referred to in proceedings.[47] She later rightly pointed out that these 'strands' are difficult to reconcile, as each represents a different (and sometimes contradictory) view of the function of marriage. Moreover, the concepts overlap, so applying them consistently and clearly in practice is difficult, if not impossible.[48]

Nevertheless, this case (and subsequent practice) has offered much needed guidance to the exercise of discretion. In particular, it is now clear that for the majority of cases, the rationale of needs[49] is the dominant one,[50] and that considerations of compensation[51] and equal sharing really only apply in cases where there is a surplus, once the needs of the parties and their children are covered.

Interestingly, the two leading opinions in *Miller v Miller; McFarlane v McFarlane* agreed on the rationales in principle, but appeared to differ on how to approach equal sharing. While both Lord Nicholls and Baroness Hale (as she then was) distinguished between two groups of property for the sharing exercise, Lord Nicholls referred to them as 'matrimonial' and 'non-matrimonial'[52] assets, while Baroness Hale called them 'family assets' and 'other assets'.[53] Nevertheless, both judges agreed on the policy underlying the distinction: between them, there are nine references to the 'fruits' of the marriage/matrimonial partnership/

---

45 *Miller v Miller; McFarlane v McFarlane*, above n 37.

46 Ibid, at [11]–[16] per Lord Nicholls and [138]–[141] per Baroness Hale.

47 Especially J Miles, 'Principle or Pragmatism in Ancillary Relief: The Virtues of Flirting with Academic Theories and Other Jurisdictions' (2005) 19 *International Journal of Law, Policy and the Family* 242.

48 J Miles, 'Marital Agreements and Private Autonomy in England and Wales' in JM Scherpe (ed), *Marital Agreements and Private Autonomy in Comparative Perspective*, Hart Publishing, Oxford 2012, 89, esp at 93 ff; J Miles, '*Charman v Charman (No 4)* – Making Sense of Need, Compensation and Equal Sharing after *Miller/McFarlane*' (2008) 20 *Child and Family Law Quarterly* 378.

49 To be seen particularly in conjunction with the 'first consideration' of the welfare of the children in s 25(1) Matrimonial Causes Act 1973.

50 Notwithstanding the practical difficulties of quantifying needs. On this see Law Commission (Eng&W), *Matrimonial Property, Needs and Agreements*, Law Com CP 208, TSO, London 2012, and Law Com No. 343, TSO, London 2014, available at <http://lawcommission.justice.gov.uk/areas/marital-property-agreements.htm> accessed 11.05.2017.

51 Which tend to be subsumed into 'needs ... generously interpreted' anyway: see eg *Lauder v Lauder* [2007] EWHC 1227 (Fam), [2007] 2 FLR 802; *VB v JP* [2008] EWHC 112 (Fam), [2008] 1 FLR 742; *McFarlane v McFarlane (No 2)* [2009] EWHC 891 (Fam), [2009] 2 FLR 1322. See also J Miles, 'Marital Agreements', above n 48 at 95.

52 *Miller v Miller; McFarlane v McFarlane*, above n 37 at [21]–[25].

53 Ibid, at [149], building on a distinction developed by Lord Denning in *Wachtel v Wachtel* [1973] Fam 72 (CA) at 90.

the couple's labours[54] and three to the 'joint'/'common endeavours'[55] of the spouses when describing the marital/family assets. From this it follows that only what may be termed the 'marital acquest' should, in principle, be subject to equal sharing. Pre- (and post-)marital assets as well as gifts and inheritances received during or after the marriage do not fall within this definition.[56] Given the special status of real estate and the property prices in England and Wales, both judges also agreed that the family home should always be in the sharing pool, irrespective of how and when it was acquired.[57] So while the statute in England and Wales does not prescribe any definition of 'matrimonial property', case law seems to have established that in exercising its discretion, the courts ought to treat matrimonial and non-matrimonial property differently when the equal sharing principle applies. As Wilson LJ (as he then was) pointed out in *K v L*, at the time of the hearing there did not seem to be a single:[58]

> 'reported decision in which the assets were entirely non-matrimonial and in which, by reference to the sharing principle, the applicant secured an award in excess of her or his needs.'

As argued elsewhere,[59] in practice, this appears to lead to the following approach regarding the division of property on divorce:

- *Matrimonial property* is to be shared upon divorce unless considerations of fairness demand otherwise. Such considerations can include the (short) duration of the marriage and, very exceptionally, 'stellar' contributions, but primarily will be the aspects of needs and compensation.

---

54 *Miller v Miller; McFarlane v McFarlane*, above n 37 at [17], [19], [20], [21], [85], [141], [149] and [154] (twice).

55 Ibid, at [22], [91] and [143].

56 For an example of the practical application, see *S v AG (Financial Remedy: Lottery Prize)* [2011] EWHC 2637 (Fam), [2011] 3 FCR 523, where a recent lottery win was held to be non-matrimonial property rather than result of a joint endeavour – an interesting contrast to the decision by the German Federal Court of Justice (*Bundesgerichtshof*) (16.10.2013) XII ZB 277/12, *Neue Juristische Wochenschrift (NJW)* 2013, 3645, where the Court held – somewhat formulaically – that a lottery gain even after separation but before the actual divorce constituted an accrued gain that needed to be shared in case of divorce.

57 Compare J Miles and JM Scherpe, 'The Future of Family Property in Europe' in K Boele-Woelki, J Miles and JM Scherpe (eds), *The Future of Family Property in Europe*, Intersentia, Cambridge 2011, 423.

58 *K v L* [2011] EWCA Civ 550, [2012] 1 WLR 306 at [22].

59 JM Scherpe, 'Towards a Matrimonial Property Regime for England and Wales?' in R Probert and C Barton (eds), *Fifty Years in Family Law: Essays for Stephen Cretney*, Intersentia, Cambridge 2012, 133; JM Scherpe, above n 4 at 481 ff; JM Scherpe, above n 26; JM Scherpe, 'The Financial Consequences of Divorce in a European Perspective' in JM Scherpe (ed), *European Family Law Vol III: Family Law in a European Perspective*, Edward Elgar, Cheltenham 2016, 146, esp at 167 ff.

- *Non-matrimonial property* is not to be shared unless considerations of fairness demand otherwise. Again, such considerations can include the duration of the marriage, but also the contributions made to the overall welfare of the family, particularly past and future child care and related sacrifices, as well as other relationship-generated advantages and disadvantages and, of course, the needs of the spouses.

So, while arguably we see elements of a matrimonial property regime, it is crucial to repeat that: (a) the approach to the division of assets is still subject to the full discretion of the courts; and (b) in exercising this discretion the courts are still undertaking a holistic exercise, meaning they are not merely looking at the division of assets but at the available financial remedies as a whole. Thus the law of England and Wales is still far from having a matrimonial property 'regime' in the actual sense.

4.4. A BRIEF COMPARISON

4.4.1. Community vs Separation

The overview above has shown that the default approaches to matrimonial property or division of property on divorce differ fundamentally between jurisdictions. Where community of property is the default matrimonial property regime, an 'immediate solidarity' between the spouses is created. The sharing technically begins as soon as the marriage is solemnised. By contrast, where there is a separation of property during the marriage, the different ways of sharing are deferred until divorce (or death). Curiously, proponents of both basic approaches claim that their approach promotes equality of the spouses. The argument for this in community of property jurisdictions is that particularly for more 'traditional' marriages – where only one of the spouses is generating an income or enjoys a significantly higher income – the approach secures an immediate and equal participation.[60] By contrast, systems that are based on a separation of property postpone such participation, but since during the marriage no mandatory sharing takes place, they arguably better promote the independence of the spouses.[61]

The claim that both systems promote equality can be explained by differing views on what equality means. Certainly, the policy behind both approaches

60 A Röthel, 'Die Zugewinngemeinschaft als europäisches Modell?' in V Lipp, E Schumann and B Veit (eds), *Die Zugewinngemeinschaft – ein europäisches Modell?*, Göttinger Juristische Schriften, Universitätsverlag Göttingen 2009, 57; W Pintens, above n 9 at 42; W Pintens, 'Ehegüterstände in Europa', above n 15 at 279 ff.

61 W Pintens, above n 9 at 43; W Pintens, 'Ehegüterstände in Europa', above n 15 at 279 ff.

is rather different. A separation of property promotes a model of financially independent spouses with a safety net in case of divorce; a community of property system arguably promotes a model that better enables the spouses to choose to forgo financial independence to focus on the family, should they so wish.[62]

4.4.2. *Certainty vs Discretion*

Discretion with regard to the division of matrimonial property really only plays a minor role in the civil law jurisdictions canvassed (essentially only in the Nordic Countries and Austria).[63] One of the main aims of the rules regarding the division of property is certainty; in that, the rules on matrimonial property do not differ from the general law of property. This is markedly different in England and Wales where certainty was deliberately eschewed and the overarching aim is to allow for fairness in each individual case. Whether this can actually be achieved is debatable, particularly since going to court and availing oneself of the so-called 'Rolls Royce legal system'[64] is financially impossible for the vast majority of divorcing couples. In addition, there seems to be an assumption that systems based on fixed matrimonial property regimes are incapable of producing fair outcomes – which is a misconception. Where there are fixed rules on the division of property, overall fairness is meant to be achieved through the other 'pillars' of the financial consequences of divorce (admittedly, it is debatable whether that can always be achieved). In any event, the legal uncertainty which is a necessary consequence of a broad discretion may be a high price to pay (and in many cases actually create unfairness). Therefore it is not unreasonable for couples to look for ways to instil more certainty through marital agreements (on which see 5 below).

4.4.3. *Common Perceptions of Fairness*

Despite the differences between the jurisdictions canvassed, certain common themes can be observed.[65]

---

62 Compare JM Scherpe, 'The Financial Consequences of Divorce in a European Perspective', above n 59 at 187 ff.

63 On Austria see S Ferrari, 'Marital Agreements and Private Autonomy in Austria' in JM Scherpe (ed), *Marital Agreements and Private Autonomy in Comparative Perspective*, Hart Publishing, Oxford 2012, 51.

64 The irony of boasting of having a 'Rolls Royce legal system' seems to be lost on those who use the term; after all, what percentage of the population can afford a Rolls Royce? Staying within the somewhat unfortunate realm of car metaphors, perhaps one should aim to have a Toyota/Volkswagen/Skoda legal system instead?

65 On these see also JM Scherpe, 'The Financial Consequences of Divorce in a European Perspective', above n 59 at 186 ff; JM Scherpe, *European Family Law Vol IV: The Present and Future of European Family Law*, Edward Elgar, Cheltenham 2016, 56 ff; and JM Scherpe, above n 4 esp at 478 ff.

First, in all jurisdictions (except Greece, see above 4.2.3.2) the spouses are considered to be equals, and therefore in principle are to participate equally when property is divided.

Second, the property that is to be divided generally does not include pre-marital property, or gifts or inheritances received during the marriage. These are not the 'fruits of joint labour', and therefore not necessarily subject to sharing should the marriage come to an end.

Third, there appears to be general agreement that 'needs' of a spouse ought to be covered, although the approaches to this differ greatly – ranging from needs being covered by the state in the Nordic Countries to the expectation that they are fully covered by the former spouse (as, for example, in England). However, a trend towards time-limiting needs-based claims can be observed.[66] And, needless to say, the perception of what qualifies as 'need' differs greatly from jurisdiction to jurisdiction.

Finally, it is generally acknowledged that one of the spouses may have incurred a disadvantage (for example by sacrificing their career to take care of the children) and that there ought to be some form of compensation for this disadvantage that persists after the marriage comes to an end. However, this is often subsumed into 'needs, generously interpreted' as, for example, expressly in England and Wales.[67]

5. CONTRACTING OUT – MARITAL AGREEMENTS

The default rules on the financial relations of the spouses (as indeed family law as a whole) were introduced with particular policy objectives in mind. At the heart of these rules is the desire to offer protection to certain family members, a protection which the general law did not offer. Hence family law is created specifically to supersede the general law. The real question therefore, is to what extent spouses should be allowed to contract out of the protective system that was created. This will of course depend on what a society's view of marriage (or of the recognised relationship) is, and what therefore the inalienable, irreducible core of the marriage or relationship commitment is deemed to be.

---

66 See JM Scherpe, 'The Financial Consequences of Divorce in a European Perspective', above n 59 at 192 f, with further references.

67 Compare J Miles, 'Marital Agreements and Private Autonomy in England and Wales', above n 48 at 95. For an application of this in practice see *Lauder v Lauder*, above n 51; *VB v JP*, above n 51; *McFarlane v McFarlane (No 2)*, above n 51.

5.1. THE BASIC FUNCTIONS OF MARITAL AGREEMENTS

5.1.1. *Are Separation Agreements Different from Other Marital Agreements?*

There is no uncertainty about the function of marital agreements: to replace the default rules with those the parties have agreed on. This by necessity, means that one of the spouses will benefit from the existence of the agreement while the other will be in a worse position than they would have been if the default regime had applied. Hence, it would be rather absurd to focus solely on 'how much worse off' a spouse is because of the marital agreement when assessing its fairness and validity, given that creating that difference is probably the very reason for the agreement being made in the first place.

It is here that New Zealand takes a rather unique position with regard to separation agreements in contrast to contracting out agreements. The current interpretation of section 21A of the PRA[68] according to *Harrison v Harrison* is that agreements must more or less reflect what the outcome under the default regime would have been – which basically means an equal division of relationship property:[69]

> 'In most compromise cases, the parties will presumably set out to provide for a division of property which accords, at least broadly, to what would be ordered under the statutory regime. So where there is a significant discrepancy between what the agreement provides and the way in which the relevant statutory regime would have operated, this in itself may well suggest that the agreement is unfair or unreasonable and, as well, may well require explanation. In the case of a contracting-out agreement, of course, the very purpose of the parties is to make provision which differs from the statutory regime.'

The Court of Appeal, therefore, makes the outcome under the default rules the yardstick against which separation agreements are to be measured. But somewhat unexpectedly, this decision also established that for separation agreements, the limitations of contracting out are much tighter than they are for other marital agreements. This is rather surprising, and indeed to a certain extent counter-intuitive, given that in separation agreements the couple know exactly (or at least could know exactly) what they are contracting about, whereas all other marital agreements are essentially agreements about an uncertain future. Therefore,

---

68 The section is entitled 'Spouses or partners may settle differences by agreement', but it actually only deals with separation agreements – which in New Zealand are generally referred to as 'compromise agreements'.

69 *Harrison v Harrison* [2005] 2 NZLR 349 (CA) at [81]. On this see M Briggs, above n 1 at 278 and JM Scherpe, above n 4 at 505.

other jurisdictions generally give greater protection and engage in more intense scrutiny in cases involving pre-nuptial and post-nuptial agreements, and greater contractual freedom in those concerning separation agreements. This approach is based on the fact that in the general law, we allow people to enter into all sorts of disadvantageous agreements and will, as a general rule, hold them to these agreements unless particular circumstances apply, provided they knew what they were doing. Therefore a yardstick of what the spouse would have received without the agreement is not applied, and the autonomy of the parties (on which see below) is given greater weight.[70] The most likely explanation for the view of the New Zealand Court of Appeal is that the spouse has built up an 'entitlement' in the relationship and that they should not be deprived of this. While this may be seen as the desire to give effect to the protection the PRA is meant to afford, it is not convincing when at the same time the Court accepts (and indeed expressly states) that such a deprivation in advance would be *more* acceptable if the agreement was entered into a longer time ago – when the couple actually did not yet know how their lives (and finances) were going to develop. Admittedly, the obvious difference is that at that point in time no entitlement had built up yet. But given the overall aims of family law in general, and of relationship property law in particular, it seems very odd that signing away your statutory protection *unknowingly* (that is without knowledge of what the potential entitlement under the default regime will be) is deemed more acceptable than *knowingly* waiving your protection. As said, it appears that no other jurisdiction takes this position, and if any difference in the scrutiny of agreements is being made, it is separation agreements that are subject to a lesser degree of judicial control because the couple was agreeing on the basis of known facts rather than speculation about the future.[71]

5.1.2. The Intention of the Parties – More than just Divorce Agreements?

The general nature and function of marital agreements greatly depends on the rules that would apply in the absence of an agreement, that is, the default rules. As already mentioned above (at 4.1),[72] in community of property-based regimes such agreements can, and often do, fulfil important functions *during*

---

70 See, for example, for England *Edgar v Edgar* [1980] 1 WLR 1410 (CA) at 1417: 'formal agreements, properly and fairly arrived at with competent legal advice, should not be displaced unless there are good and substantial grounds for concluding that an injustice will be done by holding the parties to the terms of their agreement'; and *X v X (Y and Z intervening)* [2002] 1 FLR 508 (Fam) at [103]: 'The fact that the parties have made their own agreement is a very important factor in considering what is the just and fair outcome.'

71 On this see JM Scherpe, above n 4 esp at 511–14.

72 See also JM Scherpe, above n 4 at 484 ff.

the marriage and are not necessarily entered into merely with the possibility of divorce in mind. Also, as Lord Wilson put it:[73]

> 'a marital agreement which – as in a civil law country – replaces one defined outcome with another defined outcome is very different from one which – as in a common law country – replaces an undefined outcome, dependent on the future exercise of a court's discretion, with a defined outcome.'

It is therefore essential to understand and evaluate the rules of any jurisdiction in the specific context in which they are meant to apply. This will often require a thorough examination of the facts and the circumstances under which these agreements were entered into. If, for example, the spouses agreed on a separation of property to protect one of them from potential claims of creditors of the other spouse, we would be dealing with an agreement of a very different nature compared to one where a very rich spouse insisted on the agreement because they wanted to make sure they were not merely 'married for the money'.[74] The former agreement was entered into to regulate the consequences of the *marriage*, and the consequences for divorce may have been incidental, whereas the latter agreement was concluded specifically with divorce in mind to minimise the financial risk of the relationship failing. Another reason a spouse may agree on a separation of property is when they want to 'ring-fence' their property to ensure that when they die it will pass to their children from a previous relationship and not be claimed in full, or in part, by the spouse in case of a divorce (or death). Here the agreement is not aimed at effects during the marriage or on divorce, but rather to protect third parties.

However, the outcome is the same: a separation of property is always a separation of property. Different factual backgrounds and motivations do not necessarily mean that the evaluation of the validity of the terms of the agreement *must* be different – but they may well be, and therefore must be explored properly when passing judgement (and judgment) on marital agreements. This is of particular importance in cross-border cases, where the agreement was entered into in one jurisdiction but is subject to court proceedings (and potentially the lex fori) in another.[75]

---

73 The Lord Wilson of Culworth, 'Foreword' in JM Scherpe (ed), *Marital Agreements and Private Autonomy in Comparative Perspective*, Hart Publishing, Oxford 2012, vii.

74 For a recent Australian example on this, see *Kennedy v Thorne* [2016] FamCAFC 189, [2016] FLC 93-737 (26 September 2016) and [2015] FCCA 484 (4 March 2015).

75 Compare JM Scherpe, 'Foreign Marital Agreements: The Approach of the English Courts' [2010] *Private Client Business* 181; JM Scherpe, 'Ehegüterrecht und Eheverträge im Common Law – Beratungshinweise' (2016) *Deutsche Notar-Zeitschrift (DNotZ)* 644; JM Scherpe, 'Ehegüterrecht und Eheverträge im Rechtsvergleich – oder: Wer hat Angst vorm Common Law?' in A Röthel and K Schmidt (eds), *Internationale Familienunternehmen*, Bucerius Law School Press, Hamburg 2016, 59; JM Scherpe, 'Rapporti patrimoniali tra

Ultimately, the evaluation of a marital agreement not only depends on the facts of each individual case, but also more broadly on what the jurisdiction in question sees as the core values of their relationship laws.

5.2. THE LIMITS OF CONTRACTING OUT

When looking at 'contracting out', it is first worth noting that in many jurisdictions an agreement on a full separation of property is expressly provided for in the civil codes/statutes and is therefore not seen as objectionable per se.[76] Rather, the ability to choose a different regime for the relationship is seen as a necessity because it is accepted that the default matrimonial property regime may be unsuitable for the life situation of some couples. But when considering this for comparative purposes, it is crucial once again to remember that in those jurisdictions the division of marital property is only one of the pillars of the financial consequences of divorce, and that different rules apply to contracting out of the other pillars (if that is possible at all, see below).

The spectrum of what couples are permitted to contract out of and what is beyond their contractual control is wide. Some jurisdictions prohibit *any* form of contract about the financial consequences of divorce (for example, Slovenia),[77] while others allow the spouses to opt out of the default rules completely (for example, Scotland).[78] But these extreme positions are outliers, and the vast majority of jurisdictions allow the spouses to opt out of some, but not all, obligations arising from marriage.[79]

This, practically speaking, is now true even in England and Wales with its system of fully discretionary remedies. However, because Parliament in that jurisdiction has given the courts very broad discretion to determine the financial consequences of divorce, the starting point is that spouses cannot oust

---

coniugi e convenzioni prematrimoniali nel common law – alcuni suggerimenti pratici', *Rivista di diritto civile* 4/2017, 920–938.

76 For example, in Germany and France.

77 See B Novak, 'The Changing Concept of "Family" and Challenges for Family Law in Slovenia' in JM Scherpe (ed), *European Family Law Vol II: The Changing Concept of 'Family' and Challenges for Domestic Family Law*, Edward Elgar, Cheltenham 2016, 272, esp at 276.

78 K McK Norrie, 'Marital Agreements and Private Autonomy in Scotland' in JM Scherpe (ed), *Marital Agreements and Private Autonomy in Comparative Perspective*, Hart Publishing, Oxford 2012, 289, esp at 301 ff.

79 For the Francophone jurisdictions, for example, it is not possible to opt out of the rules which fall under the *régime primaire*; since the focus of this contribution is on the financial consequences of divorce which do not fall under this, this will not be discussed here but see, for example, W Pintens, above n 11. For a European comparative view on marital agreements see N Dethloff, 'Contracting in Family Law: A European Perspective' in K Boele-Woelki, J Miles and JM Scherpe (eds), *The Future of Family Property in Europe*, Intersentia, Antwerp 2011, 65.

the court's jurisdiction by contract.[80] Nonetheless, in *Radmacher v Granatino* the majority of the Supreme Court held that the general approach to marital agreements should be that:[81]

> 'The court should give effect to a nuptial agreement that is freely entered into by each party with a full appreciation of its implications unless in the circumstances prevailing it would not be fair to hold the parties to their agreement.'

So while marital agreements cannot *bind* the courts or prevent a spouse from seeking a judicial decision on the financial consequences of the divorce,[82] the courts 'will give effect' to them – which effectively achieves the same as a prima facie binding marital agreement on which there is litigation.

Certain structural commonalities in the assessment of the limits of contracting out can be identified in the jurisdictions canvassed, namely that an assessment of the agreement essentially focuses on two points in time: first, when the agreement is entered into, and second, when the agreement is relied upon by one of the spouses. This two-stage inquiry can be identified expressly in the dictum of the United Kingdom Supreme Court cited above,[83] but also in the jurisprudence of the German Federal Court of Justice.[84] The inquiry has a very different focus at each of the stages. At the first stage, the aim is to establish whether the parties did actually make a fully informed and autonomous decision, and the actual substance of the agreement is not really scrutinised. The enquiry into the substance of the agreement takes place at the second stage, and if the agreement between the parties (which was found to be based on their autonomous decision at the first stage) transgresses certain boundaries the courts will not enforce it, but rather replace it with a different outcome. Therefore it is apt to call the two stages of inquiry 'protection of autonomy' (on which see 5.2.1 below) and 'protection from autonomy' (on which see 5.2.2 below).[85]

---

80 *Hyman v Hyman* [1929] AC 601 (HL), confirmed in *Radmacher v Granatino* [2010] UKSC 42, [2011] 1 AC 534 at [127].

81 *Radmacher v Granatino*, above n 80 at [75].

82 On the possible impact of such agreements on third parties see J Miles, 'Marriage and Divorce in the Supreme Court and the Law Commission: For Love or Money?' (2011) 74 *Modern Law Review* 430.

83 *Radmacher v Granatino*, above n 80.

84 Bundesgerichtshof (BGH) 11 February 2004, *BGHZ* 158, 81 = *FamRZ* 2004, 601, 604. On this decision and subsequent case law see A Dutta, above n 25.

85 See JM Scherpe, 'Fairness, Freedom and Foreign Elements – Marital Agreements in England and Wales after *Radmacher v Granatino*' (2011) 23 *Child and Family Law Quarterly* 513; JM Scherpe, above n 4 esp at 514 ff; JM Scherpe, *The Present and Future of European Family Law*, above n 65 at 61 ff; JM Scherpe, 'The Financial Consequences of Divorce in a European Perspective', above n 59 at 194 ff.

5.2.1. *Protection of Autonomy*

In many ways, the enquiry at this first stage is of a formal and procedural nature, aiming to ensure that the spouses were fully aware of the consequences of their decision and that no undue pressure was put on them to enter into the agreement. It is generally acknowledged that marital agreements are fundamentally different from other contracts and that therefore heightened standards of scrutiny must apply. As in many areas of law (for example, consumer law, labour law, or insurance law) when the two parties may not be negotiating 'at arm's length' and there is a power imbalance, additional protective mechanisms are needed. For marital agreements, this was expressed succinctly by the American Law Institute in their Principles of the Law of Family Dissolution:[86]

> 'While there are good reasons to respect contracts relating to the consequences of family dissolution, the family context requires some departure from the rules that govern the commercial arena. First, the relationship between contracting parties who are married, or about to marry, is different than the usual commercial relationship in ways that matter to the law's treatment of their agreements. Persons planning to marry usually assume that they share with their intended spouse a mutual and deep concern for one another's welfare. Business people negotiating a commercial agreement do not usually have that expectation of one another ... These distinctive expectations that persons planning to marry usually have about one another can disarm their capacity for self-protective judgment, or their inclination to exercise it, as compared to parties negotiating commercial agreements. This difference justifies legal rules designed to strengthen the parties' ability and inclination to consider how a proposed agreement affects their own interest ...'

Moreover, in this (but certainly not only this) context it is important to acknowledge that merely nominal autonomy does not mean actual autonomy – the very particular social situation needs to be taken into account. So in addition to the 'normal' rules of the laws of contract, special protective mechanisms apply. These include, for example:

- either separate and independent legal advice or the advice of a notary (who is neutral and under a legal duty to fully advise both parties);[87]

---

86 American Law Institute, *Principles of the Law of Family Dissolution: Analysis and Recommendations*, American Law Institute Publishers, St Paul (MN) 2002, comment c on § 7.02, 1063 ff. See also IM Ellman, above n 10 esp at 426 ff and N Dethloff, above n 79 at 86 f with further references.

87 On the difficulty of notarial advice in cross-border cases in particular, see JM Scherpe, 'Ehegüterrecht und Eheverträge im Common Law', above n 75; and JM Scherpe, 'Ehegüterrecht und Eheverträge im Rechtsvergleich', above n 75. In any event, it is doubtful whether legal advice is actually capable of offering protection against even extremely disadvantageous agreements; compare JM Scherpe, above n 4 at 491–95 and JM Scherpe, above n 85 at 519 f.

- full and frank disclosure (although in jurisdictions where certain property is excluded by law from the division on divorce, no such disclosure is necessary);[88] and
- time requirements, meaning that the agreement must be entered into a certain period of time before the wedding (but whether such requirements actually offer a sensible protection is debatable).[89]

The actual substance of the agreement is not the focal point of the scrutiny at this first stage. Rather, the purpose of the inquiry is to ensure that the parties entered into the agreement willingly, consciously, and with sufficient information about its consequences (or, as the United Kingdom Supreme Court put it, 'freely' and 'with a full appreciation of its implications').[90]

5.2.2. *Protection from Autonomy*

By contrast, the substance of the agreement – that is, the outcome if it were to apply – is at the centre of the inquiry at the second stage, and it is the more important one with regard to assessing the actual limits on opting out of the protective mechanisms that the default regimes provide. This second stage will only be necessary if it has been established that the agreement was reached in a proper way and that the parties did make an autonomous decision to enter into it. Therefore this second stage clearly demarcates the substantive limits of marital agreements. If agreements fall short of the requirements each jurisdiction sets for them with regard to substance, they will be set aside notwithstanding that the parties freely entered into them. Hence this second stage ensures that the parties are protected *from* their autonomous decisions and the criteria applied reveal the inalienable core of the marital obligations – those that the parties cannot contract out of.

As mentioned in 2 above, one of the key issues of marital agreements is that they are essentially contracts about an uncertain future. The lives of the spouses may well have developed very differently from the way they anticipated when signing the agreement, and even very fundamental assumptions with regard to the basis of their relationship may have been incorrect. As spouses are very unlikely to revisit and renegotiate their marital agreements when their life circumstances change, the agreement may now have become inappropriate for their marital relationship. In addition, of course, there are agreements

---

88 For the usefulness of disclosure requirement see JM Scherpe, above n 4 at 495–98 and JM Scherpe, above n 85 at 520 f.

89 For a broader discussion of time requirements in this context see JM Scherpe, above n 4 at 498 f and JM Scherpe, above n 85 at 518 f.

90 *Radmacher v Granatino*, above n 80 at [75].

which were inappropriate from the outset. Therefore, in almost all jurisdictions limitations on marital agreements exist which relate to the potential outcomes if an agreement were to apply and be enforced.

A comparison of the different approaches to limiting marital agreements reveals certain common features.[91] While English law requires 'fairness' to prevail,[92] Irish law insists on a minimum of 'proper provision';[93] in Austria agreements can be set aside if they are 'inequitable',[94] in Sweden if they are 'unreasonable',[95] in Spain if they are 'seriously detrimental' to the other spouse,[96] and in New Zealand if enforcing the agreement would cause 'serious injustice'.[97] The Netherlands[98] and Germany[99] utilise the basic concept of an agreement being against 'good faith' if it oversteps certain boundaries. So essentially, in some shape or form all of the jurisdictions canvassed operate with a – rather vague – notion of fairness. What is 'fair' of course not only depends on the specific values and policies of the jurisdiction in question, but also on the circumstances of the case.

That said, certain common themes can be identified when comparing the approaches to substantive fairness in the various jurisdictions. To highlight these themes, it is useful to focus on examples from two very different jurisdictions. In Germany the Federal Court of Justice has developed what is called the 'core theory doctrine' (*Kernbereichslehre*).[100] This doctrine 'ranks' the various remedies available to spouses in case of divorce according to their closeness to the core of the protective scope of divorce law. The closer to that core the remedy is that the spouses agreed to contract out of or modify, the less likely the courts are to allow that deviation from the default rules to stand. Given that agreeing on a complete separation of property (that is, opting out of sharing) is expressly regulated and thus permitted in the German Civil Code (§ 1414 BGB), it is not surprising that such agreements are deemed to be furthest away from the 'core'

91 See JM Scherpe, above n 4 at 484 ff; JM Scherpe, 'The Financial Consequences of Divorce in a European Perspective', above n 59 at 201 ff.
92 *Radmacher v Granatino*, above n 80 esp at [75]; see also J Miles, 'Marital Agreements', above n 48 at 104 ff.
93 L Crowley, above n 34 at 217.
94 S Ferrari, above n 63 at 64 f.
95 M Jänterä-Jareborg, above n 16 esp at 391 ff; JM Scherpe, above n 16 esp at 228 ff.
96 J Ferrer-Riba, above n 13 esp at 363 f.
97 Section 21J(1) PRA. This wording was chosen to create a heightened standard compared to the previous one of 'injustice'. Nevertheless, it seems odd that this means that the courts have to give effect to agreements that lead to injustice when the injustice is not 'serious', given that the layperson would assume that the role of the courts is to do justice, not 'acceptable injustice'. On this see also JM Scherpe, above n 4 at 506 f with further references.
98 K Boele-Woelki and B Braat, above n 6 at 250 ff.
99 A Dutta, above n 25 at 174 ff.
100 On this see A Dutta, above n 25 esp at 174 ff, and JM Scherpe, 'A Comparative View of Pre-Nuptial Agreements' [2007] *International Family Law Journal* 18.

of the marital obligation. But maintenance obligations because of needs arising from ongoing child care, or old age and infirmity are deemed to be closest to the core and thus, in practice, are almost impossible to contract out of. These payments are also intended to contain compensatory elements.[101]

In England and Wales, the United Kingdom Supreme Court in the seminal decision of *Radmacher v Granatino*[102] developed a similar approach, building upon the three 'strands' of fairness that guide the courts' discretion when considering financial remedies at the point of divorce in the absence of an agreement (developed in the cases of *White v White* and *Miller v Miller; McFarlane v McFarlane*)[103] namely 'needs', 'compensation', and 'equal sharing':[104]

> 'Of the three strands identified in *White v White* and *Miller v Miller*, it is the first two, needs and compensation, which can most readily render it unfair to hold the parties to an ante-nuptial agreement. The parties are unlikely to have intended that their ante-nuptial agreement should result, in the event of the marriage breaking up, in one partner being left in a predicament of real need, while the other enjoys a sufficiency or more, and such a result is likely to render it unfair to hold the parties to their agreement. Equally if the devotion of one partner to looking after the family and the home has left the other free to accumulate wealth, it is likely to be unfair to hold the parties to an agreement that entitles the latter to retain all that he or she has earned.
>
> Where, however, these considerations do not apply and each party is in a position to meet his or her needs, fairness may well not require a departure from their agreement as to the regulation of their financial affairs in the circumstances that have come to pass. Thus it is in relation to the third strand, sharing, that the court will be most likely to make an order in the terms of the nuptial agreement in place of the order that it would otherwise have made.'

These approaches can be found in similar ways in many other jurisdictions: the spouses cannot contract out of providing for needs and compensation.[105] Where a matrimonial property regime is in place, this means that sharing assets can be contracted out of by agreeing on a full separation of property. But the other

---

101 But see the criticism by B Dauner-Lieb, 'Gütertrennung zwischen Privatautonomie und Inhaltskontrolle' (2010) 210 *Archiv für die civilistische Praxis* 580, esp at 602 ff and N Dethloff, above n 79 esp at 90 ff.

102 *Radmacher v Granatino*, above n 80 esp at [75] ff.

103 *White v White*, above n 39. *Miller v Miller; McFarlane v McFarlane*, above n 37. On this see 4.3 above.

104 *Radmacher v Granatino*, above n 80 at [81]–[82].

105 If that is deemed to be part of the general marital obligations – which, for example, it is not in the Nordic Countries, see above 4.2.1.

remedies ('pillars') which are (also) meant to cover needs and compensation[106] cannot be contracted out of.[107] Thus the law wants to ensure that the needs of the spouses are met and that certain, usually relationship-generated, disadvantages are in some form compensated for. So from a comparative view, these two policy aims (which of course differ in substance between jurisdictions) appear to represent the absolute core of the marital obligation that is not at the disposition of the spouses.

6. CONCLUSION – MATRIMONIAL PROPERTY, MARITAL AGREEMENTS, AND THE CORE OF MARRIAGE LAW

Despite the fact that the underlying default regimes are very different, there seem to be some common core policy objectives that the jurisdictions canvassed in this chapter share, albeit to varying degrees.

With regard to the default regime, the common theme is an understanding of marriage as a relationship of equals, resulting in the basic approach that the fruits of joint labour should be shared equally.[108] Thus pre-marital property as well as gifts and inheritances received during the marriage are generally not part of the sharing pool, although they can become 'familiarised' by the way they have been used during the marriage.[109] That said, all jurisdictions recognise that there is more to marriage than just a pooling (and then division) of assets. All jurisdictions therefore have remedies in place which can cover the needs of the former spouse after the marriage comes to an end, and also compensate for relationship-generated disadvantages beyond that.[110]

When it comes to contracting out of the default regime, the common theme appears to be that the parties are (more or less) free to decide that their relationship is one in which they do *not* share everything, that they are free to maintain separate property and retain it when the relationship ends. However, another common theme is that nevertheless the marital relationship (and others, where applicable) brings with it responsibilities which cannot be contracted out of. Entering into the relationship, and living in it, brings with

106 However, these additional remedies may be insufficient or unsuited for this, depending on the case at hand; see the references in n 101 above and JM Scherpe, above n 4 at 517 f.

107 So, for example, the spouses cannot agree to both not make any claims for the *prestation compensatoire* in France or the *pension compensatoria/prestación compensatoria in Spain/ Catalonia*, see the references in n 13 above.

108 Except in Greece, see 4.2.3.2 above.

109 See 4.2.2 above.

110 However, the nature and range of the available remedies differ greatly, compare the contributions in JM Scherpe (ed), *Marital Agreements and Private Autonomy in Comparative Perspective*, Hart Publishing, Oxford 2012.

it certain responsibilities for the spouse or partner that continue even after the relationship ends. Mostly, these responsibilities relate to what are often called 'relationship-generated' disadvantages, and the remedies are of a compensatory nature and/or intended to cover a former spouse's needs, at least for a certain period.[111] This appears to be what most jurisdictions deem to be the inalienable core of their relationship law which is not at the disposition of the parties.

[111] If one took a cynical view, maintaining these duties after the relationship ends does not have to be seen as a necessary expression of the commitment that was made but rather as the result of cold fiscal considerations – as otherwise the state would have to pick up the bill. As mentioned above (4.2.1), in the Nordic Countries there are hardly any maintenance obligations etc. In these jurisdictions the basic view is that a spouse is not the insurer of the other, and that any citizen in need (even as the result of a relationship breakdown), is entitled to state support.

CHAPTER 15

MAINTENANCE – TIME FOR A CLEAN BREAK?

John CALDWELL

In New Zealand, the relationship property and adult maintenance regimes on the breakdown of a marriage, civil union, or de facto relationship have long been dealt with under two discrete legislative regimes. Relationship property assets of the parties are divided pursuant to the detailed provisions of the Property (Relationships) Act 1976 (NZ) ('PRA'), whereas the adult maintenance and future income needs of any one party are governed by the essentially discretionary provisions found in Part 6 of the Family Proceedings Act 1980 (NZ) ('FPA'). While the two regimes are clearly distinct, there is nevertheless an acknowledged complementarity in their policies.[1] After all, both share the common goal of facilitating a fair resolution of financial problems ensuing from a failed relationship, and the legislative amendments in 2001 to both the PRA and the FPA were designed to 'sit alongside' each other.[2]

---

1 As pointed out in *PN v PN* (1984) 3 NZFLR 277 (HC) at 280.

2 See the comments of Hammond J in *M v B* [2006] 3 NZLR 600 (CA) at [220]. (The potential for a provision in the Family Proceedings Act 1980 (NZ) ('FPA') to cover relationship

In 2016 the New Zealand Law Commission commenced a review of the PRA. This review provides an ideal opportunity to reflect on whether there could now be further integration of the two regimes and, indeed, whether the concept of separate adult maintenance even remains justifiable in principle at all. In particular, given the regime for property division in New Zealand encompasses compensation for relationship-derived economic disparities (though admittedly a little incongruously),[3] it may be timely to reconsider the purpose and future of our so-called rehabilitative, needs-based maintenance. It may be time to think about fortifying the 'clean break' principle.

The clean break principle is premised on the notion that the parties will use their respective shares of the relationship property to start afresh.[4] Its purpose is to achieve financial finality and to assist the parties to self-determine and become self-sufficient.[5] While no overt or implicit reference to this principle can be found in any of the specific provisions of the PRA, including in sections 1M and 1N which set out the purposes and principles of the PRA, there can be no doubt that the statutory regime as a whole is firmly grounded on the philosophy that 'there should be a clean break between the parties as soon as practicable, with each able to take up their future life independently of the other'.[6]

The FPA, dealing with adult maintenance, does not actually contain any statement of statutory purposes or principles at all, and the authorisation of continuing income support for one party under sections 63 and 64 of the FPA[7] might well be regarded as innately antithetical to the clean break principle. Nonetheless, the clean break is in fact promoted in provisions such as sections 64(4) and 64A of the FPA which provide directions, albeit ambiguously, on the limits of the duration of maintenance liability.[8] The Court of Appeal

---

property issues was highlighted, in a quite different context, in the Supreme Court judgment on trusts in *Clayton v Clayton [Claymark Trust]* [2016] NZSC 30, [2016] 1 NZLR 590.)

3 See M Henaghan, 'Sharing Family Finances at the End of a Relationship', ch 12.

4 *Clayton v Clayton [Maintenance]* [2015] NZHC 765, [2015] NZFLR 501 at [6] per Courtney J.

5 J Eekalaar, 'Post-Divorce Financial Obligations' in SN Katz, J Eekelaar and M Maclean (eds), *Cross Currents: Family Law and Policy in the United States and England*, OUP, Oxford 2000, 405 at 413.

6 See Casey J's analysis of the provisions of the Matrimonial Property Act 1976 (NZ) in *Turner v Doak* (1982) 1 NZFLR 250 (HC) at 253.

7 Section 63 essentially governs the period between separation and dissolution of a marriage or civil union; s 64 governs the period following dissolution of a marriage or civil union, or the end of a de facto relationship.

8 As Winkelman J said in *NGC v HAH [Maintenance]* [2010] NZFLR 677 (HC) at [32], s 64(4) emphasises the policy that 'dissolution should in the ordinary course provide a clean break of financial ties'. Courtney J also cited s 64A as a reflection of the clean break principle: *Clayton v Clayton [Maintenance]*, above n 4 at [6].

in *Scott v Williams* recently described the essence of the present maintenance scheme thus:[9]

> 'after dissolution of marriage [the respondent] is liable to pay maintenance to meet the reasonable needs of [the applicant] that she cannot practically meet because of the division of functions within the marriage and [the applicant's] likely earning capacity … [but the applicant] must, however, assume responsibility for meeting her needs within a reasonable time.'

Such a statement is deceptively simple, for the maintenance provisions of the FPA are notable for their extensive reliance on judicial discretionary judgments and their strikingly indeterminate boundaries. Uncertainty, for example, resides at the very heart of section 64A(1)(a), the key threshold provision for the continuation of maintenance, with its elusive reference to a period of time that is deemed 'reasonable in all the circumstances of the … case'. Similarly, there is considerable elasticity linked to the pivotal concept of 'reasonable needs' in sections 63(1), 64(1), 64A(2), and 65(2)(b) of the FPA, and to the concept of 'practicably' in sections 63(1) and 64(1). As well, a 'significant discretion'[10] has been conferred on the courts whenever they undertake the task of determining quantum under section 65 of the FPA. All this means that current social thinking on the value of the clean break principle and the philosophical justification, if any, for adult maintenance can become highly relevant when any assessment is to be made of the generic or specific need for this form of relief.

Certainly, in an early judgment dealing with the spousal maintenance provisions contained in the previous Domestic Proceedings Act 1968 (NZ), Richardson J, delivering the judgment of the Court of Appeal, openly accepted the philosophy of the clean break principle declaring that:[11]

> 'The social policies underlying the Matrimonial Property Act, the increasing recognition in all spheres of the equality of the spouses, and the developing philosophy that the parties to a marriage which has broken down should go their own ways in so far as they reasonably can, free of continuing claims on one another, sit uneasily with any notion that, come what may, a woman on marriage obtains an entitlement to maintenance for life.'

The Matrimonial Property Act 1976 (NZ), referred to by Richardson J, was replaced in 2001 by the PRA,[12] included in which was a radically new provision

9 *Scott v Williams* [2016] NZCA 356, [2016] NZFLR 499 at [115].

10 See the observation of the Court of Appeal in *Z v Z* [1997] NZFLR 241 (CA) at 277.

11 *Bunce v Bunce* [1980] 2 NZLR 247 (CA) at 255–56.

12 The Property (Relationships) Act 1976 (NZ) was renamed in 2001 because de facto relationships were brought into the Act: Property (Relationships) Amendment Act 2001 (NZ), s 3.

that aimed to address issues of economic disparity. Section 15 thus allowed the court to make an order to depart from the normal regime of equal sharing of relationship property where such a departure would be 'just' in order to compensate a party for an income shortfall occasioned by the divisions of functions during the relationship.[13] At the stroke of the legislative pen, the compensatory rationale advanced in a number of overseas jurisdictions[14] for a separate regime of continuing adult maintenance had been supplanted and rendered far less potent in New Zealand. For just as the French system of *prestation compensatoire* (which allows a lump sum to compensate the financially weaker party for the financial consequences of dissolution of marriage)[15] reportedly replaced the post-divorce maintenance obligation in France,[16] it became correspondingly arguable that the PRA (containing not only section 15 itself but other provisions, detailed below, that recognise the accommodation and other needs of the carer of dependent children) should, at least where there is sufficient relationship property, be considered generally exhaustive of one party's financial claim against the other. A troubling question arose: was there any rational basis for needs-based adult maintenance once compensation for the financial consequences of the relationship had been addressed?

In view of the fact that virtually all claimants for adult maintenance to date have been females seeking financial provision from their former male partners,[17] any discussion of such a question might be perceived to require an analysis of gender equity issues. To some extent, however, the argument around maintenance can be fairly explored in a gender-neutral way, in that it is no longer unrealistic or utopian to postulate examples where a female is in a superior financial position to her 'house-husband' male partner. Statistics from the United States, for instance, suggest that between 25 and 33 per cent of women earn more

---

13 There is also the power under s 15 to make an award to recognise the enhanced position of the other party.

14 For a leading academic exposition, see I Ellman, 'The Theory of Alimony' (1989) 77 *California Law Review* 1; see also the analyses of B Fehlberg, 'Spousal Maintenance in Australia' (2004) 18 *International Journal of Law Policy and the Family* 1, 4–6, and P Parkinson, *Family Law and the Indissolubility of Parenthood*, Cambridge University Press, Cambridge 2011, 250–54. Compensation was also an important strand of the judgments of the Supreme Court of Canada in *Moge v Moge* (1993) 99 DLR (4th) 456 and the House of Lords in *Miller v Miller; McFarlane v McFarlane* [2006] UKHL 24, [2006] 2 AC 618.

15 See the useful discussion of this system by P Parkinson, above n 14 at 31.

16 W Longrigg, 'Financial Relief on Divorce: A Civil Law and Common Law Perspective from England with an Eye to France and Germany' [2013] *International Family Law* 194, 195.

17 See the study of M Henaghan et al, *Property (Relationships) Amendment Act 2001 and Retirement: Are Separated Women More Disadvantaged Than Men?*, Commission for Financial Literacy and Retirement Income, Dunedin 2012, 38.

than their male partners.[18] Thus, when debating the continuing rationale and justification for needs-based maintenance, it would be perfectly reasonable to frame the issue in terms of whether any sound reason can be identified as to why an economically stronger female partner, say a corporate chief executive, should bear any moral or legal responsibility for the financial well-being and needs of her former male partner, say a cleaner, once the couple's property rights, including any compensatory adjustments under section 15, have been properly determined? Should not the woman, and any new partner, be entitled to a break, a 'clean' break?

1. CLEAN BREAK UNDER THE FAMILY PROCEEDINGS ACT?

1.1. THE BROAD DISCRETIONARY COMPONENTS OF THE MAINTENANCE PROVISIONS

When the 2001 amendments to the FPA, and extensions to the relationship property regime, were debated in the House of Representatives, an Opposition Member of Parliament, Stephen Franks, correctly discerned that 'the clean break principle is superseded by provisions encouraging the award of maintenance'.[19] After all, not only did the various amended provisions of the FPA extend the possibility of continuing income support, ensuring that the parties could thereby potentially remain even more tethered to each other, but the provisions continued to apply on a discretionary basis, meaning the hopeful litigant might well feel encouraged and incentivised to bring a claim against his or her former partner. Even the very lodging of such a claim would inevitably mean the two parties thereupon became interlocked in renewed conflict.

Certainly, as noted above, a 'statutory steer'[20] to the clean break principle can be discovered in sections 64(4) and 64A(1) of the FPA. Thus, section 64(4) states that, except as is provided for, neither party following a dissolution of marriage

18 A Amundsen 'Removing the Parachute: Recent Trends in Alimony Modification: Part I of II' (2015) 29 *American Journal of Family Law* 61, 62, suggesting almost a third of American women earn more than their spouses, and P Parkinson, above n 14 at 256, who points to a 2004 study that suggests 25.5% of American women in marriages earned more than their husbands. Overall in New Zealand, however, in 2015 an 11.8% gender pay gap was shown to exist between men and women for median hourly earnings: Ministry for Women 'Gender Pay Gap' <www.women.govt.nz/work-skills/income/gender-pay-gap> accessed 11.04.2017.

19 *New Zealand Parliamentary Debates*, 1 June 2000, vol 584, 2755.

20 The phrase comes from English jurisprudence: see, for example, *Matthews v Matthews* [2013] EWCA Civ 1874, [2014] 2 FLR 1259 at [13].

or civil union or the ending of a de facto relationship is liable to maintain the other. Section 64A(1) further provides:

> 'If a marriage or civil union is dissolved or, in the case of a de facto relationship, the de facto partners cease to live together, –
>
> (a) each spouse, civil union partner, or de facto partner must assume responsibility within a period of time that is reasonable in all the circumstances of the particular case, for meeting his or her own needs; and
> (b) on the expiry of that period of time, neither spouse, civil union partner, or de facto partner is liable to maintain the other ...'

The steer in that provision was, however, far from unwavering. The apparent presumptive policy in favour of a clean break was subject to the discretionary qualification contained within section 64A(1) that financial self-sufficiency needed only to be assumed in a period of time that was 'reasonable in all the circumstances of the particular case'. That same wording in the same predecessor provision enabled the Court of Appeal, in the leading case of *Z v Z*, to hold that there was nothing 'to preclude a lengthy period of time, or even an indefinite period' as '[t]he determination of what is reasonable in the particular case is not informed by any general principle.'[21] The Court of Appeal continued to aver that while such provisions were 'undoubtedly' intended to give effect to the clean break principle, there was nothing which required the self-sufficiency objective of the FPA to be carried through to the point where the provisions operated unfairly and harshly on one of the spouses.[22] Then, in concluding its landmark judgment, the Court of Appeal commended the possibility of legislative review whereby Parliament could re-examine, inter alia, 'the merit of the clean break principle and the desirability of resolving the parties' financial affairs by way of a property adjustment rather than periodic maintenance support'.[23]

1.2. THE 2001 CHANGE TO EXTENDED DURATION OF MAINTENANCE

The governmental review envisaged by the Court of Appeal did result in significant legislative changes in 2001 to both the matrimonial property and adult maintenance regimes, and the enactment of section 15 in the relationship property statute could reasonably have been anticipated to have encouraged the favoured shift away from periodic payment support in favour of property adjustment

---

21 *Z v Z*, above n 10 at 276.
22 Ibid.
23 Ibid, at 278.

alone. However, whereas the previous section 64(3) of the FPA had provided the court with the discretion to extend the period of adult maintenance only in circumstances where, having regard to the ages of the parties and duration of the marriage, it was unreasonable to require one party to do without maintenance and reasonable to require the other to pay, the newly introduced section 64A(3)(c) significantly extended the circumstances in which maintenance could potentially be prolonged. Thus, liability was extended out to a situation where a party remained liable to meet the reasonable needs of the other because of:[24]

> '(c) The ability of the spouses, civil union partners or de facto partners to become self-supporting, having regard to –
> (i) the effects of the division of functions within the marriage, civil union or de facto relationship …
> (ii) the likely earning capacity of each …
> (iii) the responsibilities of each … for the ongoing daily care of any minor or dependent children …
> (iv) any other relevant circumstances.'

As Atkin observed, that amendment seemingly allowed continuing obligations in 'virtually any situation'.[25] For instance, no apparent constraints could be identified as to what circumstances might be deemed 'relevant' under section 64A(3)(c)(iv), and the clean break policy, already rather cloudy as a consequence of the qualifying proviso requiring self-sufficiency only in a period of time that was 'reasonable in all the circumstances of the particular case',[26] proved to have been weakened rather than strengthened.

1.3. SOME JUDICIAL DECISIONS ON DURATION

The real debate over maintenance is around its duration. Needless to say, judges will still continue to pay due homage to the clean break principle,[27] and continue to invoke the spirit of section 64A.[28] Early dicta of the Court of Appeal in *Slater v Slater*, endorsing the view that maintenance should be seen as only a temporary bridge to assist a party who was 'consciously moving towards self-sufficiency',[29] are still considered by the current judges to possess

24 FPA, s 64A(3)(c).
25 B Atkin, 'Financial Support – Who Supports Whom' in M Henaghan and B Atkin (eds), *Family Law Policy in New Zealand*, 4th ed, LexisNexis, Wellington 2013, 163 at 201.
26 FPA, s 64A(1).
27 See, for example, *CAM v JMP* [2013] NZHC 592 at [81] per Andrews J.
28 See, for example, *Clayton v Clayton [Maintenance]*, above n 4 at [6] per Courtney J.
29 *Slater v Slater* [1983] NZLR 166 (CA) at 176.

'considerable authority'[30] (despite the Court of Appeal in *Z v Z* having expressed concern that the *Slater* dicta might have been 'either misconstrued or applied with undue rigidity in practice').[31] As Miller J put it, the clean break principle, whilst rather attenuated, does remain as 'an important consideration in what remains a no-fault dissolution regime'.[32] To take one example, Judge Walsh was openly unimpressed by the perceived failure of a 53-year-old woman, with a special needs adult child, to take reasonable steps towards self-sufficiency, and by her apparent 'mindset' that the husband had an ongoing duty to maintain her, on the basis that marriage was forever.[33]

Generally, the requirement of reasonableness within section 64A is taken to necessitate a maintenance period that is defined and limited in time; and while the extent of a 'reasonable' period of time is left unspecified, some judges seem to adhere to the view that the expected length of time would ordinarily be in the realm of three to four years following separation.[34] One Family Court judge said that from his search of the case law, the longest period he had been able to find for continuation of spousal maintenance was for a period of five years from the date of separation.[35] And in *M v B*, Robertson J held that after five years of separation, with the children having grown up and the property division having been finalised, it was indeed 'time for a clean break'.[36]

On the other hand, it is not exactly exceptional to discover judges who are sympathetic to the award of quite lengthy periods of maintenance. Even in *M v B* itself, Hammond J, though expressing his general agreement with Robertson J's judgment, did feel that the five-year limit may have been 'on the light side'.[37] In *B v B*, Rodney Hansen J upheld an award of maintenance of $1,900 per month for a total period of eight years following dissolution.[38] The judge reasoned that the challenges faced by a woman in her mid-50s re-establishing

30 See the comment of Judge Callinicos in *TJO v GGO* [2012] NZFC 857 at [7]. The *Slater* dicta were also accepted by the Court of Appeal in *C v G [Maintenance of Former Partner: Period of Liability]* [2010] NZCA 128, [2010] NZFLR 497 at [31].

31 *Z v Z*, above n 10 at 276.

32 *JES v JBC* [2007] NZFLR 472 (HC) at [51].

33 *BJR v VMR [Economic Disparity]* [2007] NZFLR 177 (FC) at [92].

34 See, for example, the comment of Judge McHardy in *Kininmonth v Kininmonth* FC Auckland FAM-2004-004-509, 27 August 2008 at [94], upheld on appeal: *KK v HK* HC Auckland CIV-2008-404-6161, 31 July 2009. In the study of M Henaghan et al, above n 17, the average duration of maintenance was for a period of 24 months, at [5.11].

35 *PEL v FFB* [2012] NZFC 9534 at [77] per Judge Burns (the five-year period, in the case of a marriage of 13 years duration and with two children, was upheld by Gilbert J on appeal *Lawrence v Baker* [2013] NZHC 2378 at [35]). A period of maintenance for five years post-separation was also considered reasonable by Judge O'Dwyer in the circumstances of *Waldorf v Hugglesitch* [2015] NZFC 3413, [2015] NZFLR 909 at [121].

36 *M v B*, above n 2 at [157].

37 Ibid at [265] (it is interesting to compare the seemingly less generous approach of Hammond J in a much earlier judgment of *Mackie v Mackie* [1993] NZFLR 213 (HC)).

38 *B v B* HC Dunedin CIV-2011-412-000328, 26 September 2011 at [30]–[31].

herself after 25 years of being engaged predominantly in child-rearing activities should not be understated, and that the mother in this particular case had care of a child with special needs who was about to commence intermediate school. In one case concerning a 67-year-old superannuitant in part-time work after a marriage of 23 years' duration, Keane J indicated, in obiter, that post-dissolution maintenance could potentially be considered beyond a three-year time span.[39] Citing an earlier judgment of Panckhurst J in *D v D*,[40] Keane J pointed out that awards for even an indefinite period were not unknown.[41]

It is true that many of the maintenance awards of a more extended duration have tended to involve quite lengthy relationships. Nevertheless, Andrews J opined in a case where the relationship had lasted only two years and two months, but where there were two children of the relationship and the applicant was undertaking study, that she:[42]

> 'would not be willing to hold that, as a matter of principle, a maintenance liability for three-and-a-half, or even five-and-a-half, years after a relationship of short duration is, by reason of its duration alone, reasonable, or unreasonable'.

There are, of course, limits. Unsurprisingly, the possibility that a spousal maintenance order could continue for 42, or even 20, years was seen as completely contrary to the spirit of the FPA.[43] Moreover, in *NGC v HAH [Maintenance]*, Winkelmann J attested to some difficulty with the notion of indefinite orders in the absence of clear justificatory reasons.[44] And it should be pointed out that the circumstances of a case such as *D v D* (where, in the course of a 25-year marriage, the wife had left the television industry to manage the home and care for the children) would now fall neatly within the purview of a claim under section 15 of the PRA.[45]

2. RELATIONSHIP PROPERTY AND MAINTENANCE CONNECTION

The crucial inter-relationship of economic disparity awards under section 15 and maintenance awards under the FPA is specifically examined in the section

39 *Beran v Beran* [2005] NZFLR 204 (HC) at [93].
40 *D v D* [2001] NZFLR 613 (HC).
41 *Beran v Beran*, above n 39 at [93].
42 *CAM v JMP*, above n 27 at [32]. The Family Court award was upheld, but the quantum was reduced from $2,000 to $1,680 per week as from the time of the High Court judgment.
43 *IRD v ALH* [2013] NZFC 2115, [2013] NZFLR 1022 at [9].
44 *NGC v HAH [Maintenance]*, above n 8 at [65].
45 *D v D*, above n 40.

below, but the more general symbiotic relationship between maintenance and relationship property is also worth exploring. Any agreements negotiated between the separated parties, for instance, are likely to involve bargaining property against income support;[46] and thus, for example, a less generous provision for property may well be offered if there is to be an extended maintenance obligation.[47]

Likewise, where court proceedings are involved, the inter-relationship of property and maintenance issues is recognised by section 32 of the PRA. This section, to facilitate a degree of cogency, allows the court in relationship property proceedings to make a maintenance order for a spouse or partner (section 32(2)), and equally provides that the court must have regard to any maintenance order that has been previously made (section 32(1)). Furthermore, as discussed below, certain child support orders can also be made pursuant to section 32. The close inter-relationship between the two remedies of maintenance and relationship property is also recognised in section 65(2)(a)(ii) of the FPA, which provides that if a maintenance order is to be made then the court in fixing the quantum of the order is required to have regard, inter alia, to the 'means derived from any division of property'.[48]

Where the parties have yet to resolve the division of relationship property, they can, of course, be placed in a highly unsettling transitional period that may, as discussed below, require maintenance support.[49] In *Clayton v Clayton [Maintenance]*, Courtney J ruled that the wife's inability to meet her reasonable needs arose because she had been unable to access her share of relationship property.[50] In fact, as Robertson J stated in *M v B*, 'reasonable needs' cannot even be accurately assessed while issues relating to the division of relationship property remain extant.[51] In the circumstances of *Clayton* itself, final maintenance was ordered under section 64 of the FPA, but many successful maintenance awards these days will be in the form of interim orders under section 82 of the FPA;[52] and, again as argued more fully below, interim orders can be more readily supported

46 As observed by Holland J in *PN v PN*, above n 1 at 279.

47 As commented on by the Court of Appeal in *C v G [Maintenance of Former Partner: Period of Liability]*, above n 30 at [43].

48 As recently noted by the Court of Appeal, this will include an income shortfall award: *Scott v Williams*, above n 9 at [123].

49 *KBP v PK* FC North Shore FAM-2007-044-001783, 21 August 2009 at [11]. Robertson J observed in *M v B*, above n 2, that it was not uncommon for maintenance to be dealt with as a separate proceeding to ensure that a partner was able to survive financially, while legal proceedings were completed, at [126]. In *Cavanagh v Cavanagh* [1994] NZFLR 365 (DC), maintenance was ordered to be terminated at the date when matrimonial property issues were determined; see also *McGregor v McGregor (No 2)* [2003] NZFLR 596 (DC) at [71].

50 *Clayton v Clayton [Maintenance]*, above n 4 at [48] and [73] (this was held to fall under 'other relevant circumstances' in FPA s 64(2)(a)(iii)).

51 *M v B*, above n 2 at [129].

52 See the case sample of M Henaghan et al, above n 17 at [5.37].

as a temporary solution to protect the financially disadvantaged party's position pending the final outcome of relationship property proceedings.

Overall, the need for any general maintenance might be thought to be inversely proportional to the benefits of a relationship property division.[53] Given that the two remedies currently subsist in tandem, it would certainly be preferable if the issue of the need, if any, for maintenance was to be decided either contemporaneously or subsequent to an order for property division. Equally though, under current statutory regimes it is by no means mandatory, as Winkelmann J has intimated, for property issues to be resolved before final maintenance.[54]

Once the division of the relationship property has been finally ordered, then the parties are expected to plan on becoming self-supporting,[55] and the High Court has consistently declared that when relationship property is divided it becomes incumbent upon the parties to organise their capital so as to become self-sufficient.[56] In other words, the clean break principle only truly comes into full play once the property has been divided. At that point the parties are expected to begin their lives anew, and it is at that point that the payment of periodic maintenance truly does become ideologically anomalous.

3. ECONOMIC DISPARITY AWARDS AND MAINTENANCE

While Robertson J, delivering his judgment in *M v B*, held that section 32 of the PRA did not signify that section 15 should be linked with the maintenance inquiry,[57] or that an economic disparity award should be treated as capitalised maintenance,[58] the two remedies have elsewhere been judicially described as 'inextricably linked'.[59] In *M v B* itself, Hammond J was content to describe

53 As noted in *Fisher on Matrimonial and Relationship Property* (online looseleaf ed, LexisNexis) at [18.86].

54 *NGC v HAH [Maintenance]*, above n 8 at [64] (her Honour said it was easy to envisage circumstances where there would be a lengthy delay between dissolution and resolution of property issues). See also the observation of Judge Malosi in *Youngman v Austin* [2015] NZFC 5081 at [25].

55 See, for example, the comment of Judge Burns in an application for interim maintenance in *AMG v S(S)G* FC Auckland FAM-2011-004-002021, 16 December 2011 at [43].

56 See, for example, *Bratten v Bratten* [2013] NZFC 2171, [2013] NZFLR 941 at [101]–[104] and *Clayton v Clayton [Maintenance]*, above n 4 at [6] per Courtney J.

57 *M v B*, above n 2 at [126].

58 Ibid, at [122]–[124]. Young P also stated that he would not treat the s 15 claim on the basis it was intended to provide for capitalised maintenance, at [191]; but cf Hammond J, at [272].

59 See the observation of Priestley J in *FH v LH* [2013] NZHC 1044 at [48]. Extra-judicially, J Doogue has noted the trend for cases to identify a nexus between economic disparity

economic disparity compensation as 'the functional equivalent of a lump sum for future maintenance'.[60]

As Robertson J also conceded, the actual subject matters of both section 15 of the PRA and sections 63 and 64 of the FPA are indeed 'remarkably similar'.[61] The Court of Appeal in *Scott v Williams* also pointed out recently that a section 15 income shortfall award may be justified on the same basis as a spousal maintenance award.[62] Both sets of provisions are essentially concerned with the same issue of the 'income differential between parties on the breakdown of a relationship';[63] and, while there are certainly different governing rules for the two remedies, the division of functions during a relationship will potentially be important in both maintenance and economic disparity proceedings, and the evidence led by the parties might well relate to both claims.[64] Hence in *JES v JBC*, Miller J noted the close link between the applicant's case for an economic disparity award resting on the loss of a relatively modest earning capacity, and the maintenance award resting on an inability to meet reasonable needs.[65]

At present, the close linkage between the two remedies does mean one remedy will inevitably be offset against the other.[66] As the Court of Appeal recently ruled: 'It cannot be the case that the s 15 award does not affect the extent of entitlement to spousal maintenance'.[67] A section 15 entitlement will fundamentally affect the extent to which it is 'necessary' for some maintenance provision, past or future, to be made. Nevertheless, the order in which the respective claims should be decided is quite indeterminate,[68] and it has been observed that there is presently an 'uneasy tension'[69] between the two remedies. In short, and as had been predicted by the Family Law Section of the New Zealand Law Society at the time

---

and spousal maintenance claims: 'Sections 15 and 15A of the Property (Relationships) Act 1976 – Six Years On: Certainty or Uncertainty?' (2007) 5 *New Zealand Family Law Journal* 282, 283.

60 *M v B*, above n 2 at [272].

61 Ibid, at [122].

62 *Scott v Williams*, above n 9 at [26].

63 As identified by B Atkin, 'Harmonising Family Law' (2006) 37 *Victoria University of Wellington Law Review* 465, 473.

64 As had happened in the High Court in *Hodgson v Hodgson* [2015] NZHC 602, as noted by Williams J, delivering the judgment of the Court of Appeal: *Hodgson v Hodgson* [2015] NZCA 404, [2015] NZFLR 979 at [21].

65 *JES v JBC*, above n 32 at [47].

66 See the early discussion of Judge Adams in *V v V* [2002] NZFLR 1105 (FC) at [62]–[64].

67 *Scott v Williams*, above n 9 at [126].

68 See the differences between Robertson, Hammond, and Young JJ in *M v B*, above n 2 at [125], [266], and [207] respectively.

69 As noted by C Green, 'The Impact of s 15 of the Property (Relationships) Act 1976 on the Vexing Problem of Economic Disparity', PhD thesis, Faculty of Law, University of Otago 2014, 147.

of the Bill's passing,[70] the inter-relationship of the two remedies has been the cause of great confusion and uncertainty.[71]

The question, then, is whether these two remedies should continue to co-exist side-by-side into the future. In the past, a number of judges and academics have proffered a preference for maintenance over a section 15 award as the more appropriate remedy to assist the financially disadvantaged party.[72] In *Hammond v Hardy*, for example, Priestley J speculated that if the circumstances of the case had justified some additional capital entitlement, a lump sum maintenance award would have provided a much easier and less expensive route than a section 15 order.[73] The argument of this chapter, however, is that it might be timely to consider, at least where there is sufficient relationship property, whether a section 15 compensatory award should not be considered the more acceptable of the two remedies.

Certainly, as identified above, the circumstances of some cases, such as *D v D* decided before the 2001 amendments,[74] seem to fall squarely within the parameters of a section 15 claim. There have been cases subsequent to the amendments where judges have indicated that an economic disparity award did subsume some of the factors raised in a maintenance claim.[75] The remedy overlap also emerged in the judgment of Hammond J in *M v B*, when his Honour hinted that the purposes of the FPA were relevant in the Court's holistic evaluation of whether a section 15 award was 'just'.[76]

The section 15 determination is, of course, grounded on discretion; and, in a relationship property statute dedicated to the codification of 'clear and inflexible' rules,[77] the reliance on discretion has been the subject of some disquiet. Other difficulties surround the scope and application of section 15 (including most notably, for our immediate purpose, the restrictive requirement that awards

70 See M Henaghan, 'More Maintenance Claims Likely' (2001) 3 *Butterworths Family Law Journal* 286, 287.

71 As noted by B Atkin and W Parker, *Relationship Property in New Zealand*, 2nd ed, LexisNexis, Wellington 2009, 166.

72 See, for example, the comments of Judge Ellis in *G v G* [2003] NZFLR 289 (FC) at [132] and Priestley J in *De Malmanche v De Malmanche* [2002] 2 NZLR 838 (HC) at [191]. B Atkin has also consistently argued in favour of maintenance awards: for example, 'Financial Support – Who Supports Whom', above n 25 at 202; 'The Disparity in Economic Disparity: The Need for a Full-Scale Overhaul of ss 15 and 15A and Maintenance', paper presented to the New Zealand Law Society Family Law Conference, Wellington 2005, 226; and 'Harmonising Family Law' above n 63 at 474.

73 *Hammond v Hardy* [2007] NZFLR 910 (HC) at [97].

74 *D v D*, above n 40.

75 See the comments of Allan J in *B v M* [2005] NZFLR 730 (HC) at [187]–[188]; the judgment of Allan J was upheld on appeal by the Court of Appeal in *M v B*, above n 2.

76 *M v B*, above n 2 at [227].

77 *Hammond v Hardy*, above n 73 at [40] per Priestley J.

may be sourced from relationship property alone). Section 15 is one of the specific matters to be scrutinised by the New Zealand Law Commission. Some recommendations for future reform seem entirely possible. However, the moral foundations of the provision have never been particularly contentious, and the fundamentals of the clean break principle can be seen to be served, rather than thwarted, by the award of a compensatory lump sum founded on the role division of a failed past relationship. The same embrace of the clean break ideal obviously cannot be claimed, though, for an award of periodic maintenance designed to help meet a party's income needs into the future.

4. A POTENTIAL DIFFICULTY WITH A CLEAN BREAK – CHILDREN

The familiar mantra that 'parenthood is forever' captures the belief that the severance of the intimate relationship with an adult partner will not result in the termination of responsibilities to minor children; and many applicants who seek maintenance orders will ground their argument on their professed inability to meet their reasonable needs as a result of their child care responsibilities. Obviously enough, the possibilities for work, including available hours, are affected by the need to care for children.[78] In the case of pre-school children, for example, the costs of child care may well absorb any income from the likely range of employment options available to the applicant.[79] Even in the case of school-age children, economic choices are inevitably reduced when there is a need for a parent to confine her or his work to school hours, and to be available on 'stand-by' if, for example, the child should be ill or have some special needs.[80]

At first sight, a clean break without continuing maintenance might therefore appear to conflict with the needs of children. Any courts working in the family jurisdiction are hardly likely to eschew child welfare considerations or to deny the quotidian practicalities confronting the adult carers of young children. Nor will they be indifferent to the possible benefits flowing to young children if the parent has additional time to be physically available to provide care.[81] Hence, Judge Burns ruled in a case concerning the mother of a 10-month-old child that: 'it would be wrong for the Court to adopt a policy requiring parents of

---

78 See, for example, *Douglas v Douglas* [2013] NZHC 3022, [2014] NZFLR 235 at [44]–[47]; also *A v A* FC North Shore FAM-2007-044-1462, 21 June 2010 at [68].

79 See the comment of Judge Burns in *EID v AD* FC Manukau FAM-2010-092-002080, 1 September 2011 at [24]. The judge proceeded to have regard to the principles of ss 4 and 5 of the Care of Children Act 2004 (NZ) and the importance of strengthening a child's relationship with his or her parents.

80 See the observation of Rodney Hansen J in *B v B*, above n 38 at [31].

81 See, for example, *Bratten v Bratten*, above n 56 at [98].

young children to go into paid employment when they do not choose to do so.'[82] Likewise, Allan J referred to the need to ensure the after-school welfare of a then nine-year-old child in *B v M*.[83] In the circumstances of that latter case, however, his Honour did rule that maintenance should end five years after separation, when the child had reached the age of 10, saying it would be appropriate for alternative arrangements to be made for after-school care and for the mother to undertake full-time work.[84] On appeal, the Court of Appeal agreed the clean break should take place at that point.[85]

Thus, even on the current approach to maintenance, the courts might anticipate that parents caring for children will take on some part-time work.[86] Cases can be found where judges have been unimpressed that an applicant with children has not made greater efforts to seek out work or retrain.[87] The courts have also warned against any glib assumptions or stereotypes about 'caregivers',[88] especially in this era of increased shared care of children where men are much more likely than in previous times to be involved in the care and upbringing of children.[89]

What is also clear from a number of judgments is that an application for adult maintenance, including interim maintenance, is not to be used as a backdoor method for recovering child maintenance.[90] Until the child reaches the age of 18, the child's needs are plainly to be met through the provisions of the Child Support Act 1991 (NZ). Accordingly, the courts have insisted that an adult maintenance claim must be for the purpose of meeting the expenses for the needs of the adult party alone, rather than the expenses for the needs of any child of the applicant's household. As Judge Burns put it: 'It seems obvious that spousal maintenance is for the spouse and children receive their support via child support.'[91] Thus, in any judicial consideration of applications for interim adult maintenance, the courts will examine the household budget (required to meet the financial expenses of the applicant and children), assess its reasonableness, and then deduct the quantum that would be payable by child support.[92]

---

82 *EID v AD*, above n 79 at [25].

83 *B v M*, above n 75 at [200].

84 Ibid, at [206].

85 *M v B*, above n 2.

86 For example, *Waldorf v Hugglesitch*, above n 35 at [114].

87 For example, *BJR v VMR [Economic Disparity]*, above n 33.

88 See the warning issued by Hammond J in *Mackie v Mackie*, above n 37 at 219.

89 For example, the circumstances identified in *Youngman v Austin*, above n 54 at [72].

90 For example, *Youngman v Austin*, ibid, at [46] and *Copley v Wing* [2013] NZFC 4632, [2014] NZFLR 388 at [14].

91 *AMG v S(S)G*, above n 55 at [18].

92 See the comments of Judge Burns in *AMG v S(S)G*, above n 55 at [23], which were accepted and followed by Moore J in *Collins v Collins* [2014] NZHC 2121 at [31]. The same approach had been adopted by Winkelman J in *Day v Weldon Day* HC Hamilton CIV 2007-419-1291, 3 December 2007 at [10]. Similarly, see the comments of Judge Callaghan in *MHL v DJRL [Spousal Maintenance]* [2006] NZFLR 174 (DC) at [12]–[14].

Even under the present maintenance provisions, therefore, there is theoretically no extra child care allowance to be granted under the FPA. The purpose of adult maintenance is not to boost the children's financial well-being.

That is not to say the New Zealand statutes dealing with the financial welfare of adult parties post separation are indifferent to the plight of children. The PRA envisages that certain types of child support orders can be made alongside property orders. Lump sum child support orders, for example, can be made, and capitalisation might be authorised if it enables a party to acquire a family home from the other party where this would otherwise not be possible.[93]

Moreover, the needs of children are recognised in various other provisions of the PRA.[94] Section 1M(c) provides the purpose of the Act is to provide a just division of relationship property 'while taking account of the interests of any children', and section 26 of the PRA mandates the court to have regard to the interests of minor or dependent children. There is also the power under section 26 for the court, if it considers it 'just', to settle property on children.[95] Additionally, while the clean break principle may lie at the heart of the PRA, there is specific provision in section 28A for the court to make an occupation order and to delay the sale of the home having 'particular regard to the need to provide a home for any minor or dependent child[ren]'.[96] There is even a wider power under section 26A of the PRA to postpone the vesting of a share in the relationship property if the court is satisfied that immediate vesting would cause undue hardship for a person who is the 'principal provider of ongoing daily care for 1 or more minor or dependent children'.[97] All such provisions are sensitive to the needs of children and family life. Should the courts be prepared to take a child-centric approach,[98] there is a further ability to compensate for post-separation child care contributions under section 18B of the PRA.

In short, any shift away from the adult maintenance regime in the FPA in favour of reliance on the PRA regime should not be viewed as intrinsically hostile to the needs of children. There is, in fact, a more distinct and overt focus on the needs of children discoverable in the relationship property statute than

---

93 See the comment of Judge Ryan in *HEG v IRG* FC North Shore FAM-2007-044-001982, 17 June 2010 at [41].

94 N Peart has suggested the provisions have only had a limited effect: 'Protecting Children's Interests in Relationship Property Proceedings' (2013) 11 *Otago Law Review* 27. See also N Peart and M Henaghan, 'Children's Interests in Division of Property on Relationship Breakdown', ch 4.

95 While only used in exceptional circumstances, see, for example, *Hader v Hader* [2015] NZFC 4376, [2016] NZFLR 107.

96 Not many occupation orders are made, but see the discussion in *W v W* [1997] NZFLR 543 (HC) at 547–48 and *R v R [Occupation Orders: Trusts]* [2010] NZFLR 555 (FC) at [64].

97 There is a high threshold for this: see *Hammond v Hardy*, above n 73 at [114].

98 See the discussion in *DPC v PMB [Relationship Property]* [2013] NZFC 1105, [2014] NZFLR 277 at [240] and *Roocker v Delgado* [2015] NZFC 9450, [2016] NZFLR 37.

in the rather mishmash provisions of the adult maintenance legislation. If the rights and liabilities of the adult parties were to be confined to the relationship property and child support statutes alone, there would be no need to fear that the interests of minor children would be overlooked.

5. INTERIM MAINTENANCE

In the immediate aftermath of a relationship breakdown, with all the concomitant turmoil and tension, there could well be unmet economic needs which must be addressed as a matter of urgency if hardship, either absolute or relative in nature, is not to be visited upon one of the parties.[99] It would seem somewhat heartless to expect an instant reordering of financial lives while the parties are still coming to terms with the emotional and financial fallout of their separation. Some buffer zone does seem desirable. Section 82 of the FPA accordingly provides judges with the jurisdiction to make an order of interim maintenance, and it is intended to allow judges to act swiftly in the aftermath of a relationship breakdown if that should be necessary to ameliorate immediate ensuing hardship.[100] Such orders presently last for a period of only six months, and ensure that in the period immediately following separation an affected party can fund the normal and recurring expenses of living and accommodation, and temporarily maintain the previous lifestyle.[101] Independence, as the Law Commission for England and Wales recently pointed out, cannot be expected to be sudden.[102]

Maintenance of this purely interim kind under section 82 can perhaps be more easily accepted than final maintenance, given its purpose is merely to provide stopgap protection of a party's position pending the determination of substantive proceedings and property division.[103] The clean break principle can only really arise once relationship property has been allocated, and it might seem undesirable for parties to be forced to diminish their capital assets in order to maintain themselves until the division of the relationship property has actually taken place.[104] Thus, provided short-term maintenance is achieving

---

99 As identified, for example, by Brewer J in *RMA v JB* [2013] NZHC 2984, [2014] NZFLR 169 at [15].

100 Ibid, at [38].

101 If a significant period of time has in fact elapsed since the separation, but before the application, then the court will need to determine if the party's current reasonable needs can be properly equated with what they were during the relationship: *Owen v Thomas* [2014] NZHC 2200 at [45] per Duffy J.

102 Law Commission (Eng&W), *Matrimonial Property, Needs and Agreements*, Law Com No. 343, TSO, London 2014, 2.

103 See *B v B [Maintenance]* [2008] NZFLR 789 (HC) at [33] and *Cornell v Cornell* [2016] NZFC 1795 at [5].

104 *B v B [Maintenance]*, above n 103 at [33] and *FH v LH*, above n 59 at [11].

more than simply a 'therapeutic interlude',[105] it might be thought reasonable for a respondent to make some contribution to the applicant's costs for a defined period of time pending division of the property.

Thus, if final maintenance obligations and orders were to be reviewed and rolled back, as is being provisionally argued for here, the interim maintenance order could still have a role to play as a temporary holding measure. Some review, though, would still be necessary. For instance, the present discretion under section 82 has consistently been held to be broad and 'unfettered',[106] presumably because of the stopgap nature of the interim orders, but whether under a new revised legislative regime such an order should be entirely discretionary is perhaps a more open question.

Likewise, if a new legislative approach to interim orders were to be taken, this would raise the question of whether the order should continue to expire automatically at the end of six months. A global settlement or determination is, of course, always the desired goal, and in practical terms a six-month period will normally be insufficient to enable this.[107] While successive applications may be discouraged by the appellate courts,[108] most High Court and Family Court authorities recognise practical realities and do allow for the possibility of multiple interim maintenance orders[109] with fresh evidence being required on each occasion.[110] In light of the uncertainty, specific consideration on the question of duration of section 82 orders or some equivalent[111] may be warranted – as indeed may some exploration into the alternative of making interim distributions of relationship property under section 25(3) of the PRA.

6. FUTURE DIRECTIONS

The maintenance provisions originally contained in the Family Proceedings Bill 1978 were previously characterised by Atkin as 'very messy'.[112] Over 30 years later the same author continued to lament that the maintenance rules were still

---

105 *FH v LH*, above n 59 at [18].

106 The judgment of the Court of Appeal in *Ropiha v Ropiha* [1979] 2 NZLR 245 (CA) at 247 and 250 is almost invariably cited in interim maintenance applications.

107 As noted by Judge Moss in *Head v Wyman* [2014] NZFC 5787 at [19].

108 As stated by A Logan, 'Interim Maintenance and Costs', paper presented to the New Zealand Law Society Family Law Conference, Dunedin, October 2015, 59.

109 For example, *T v H [Spousal Maintenance]* [2006] NZFLR 560 (HC) at [22]; *Horsfall v Potter* HC Wellington CIV-2009-485-2358, 25 May 2010 – leave to appeal was declined: *H v P* [2010] NZCA 584; and *Zola v Abel* [2015] NZFC 9058, [2016] NZFLR 81. Compare though *Cooper v Pinney* [2016] NZFC 511, [2016] NZFLR 439.

110 *Zola v Abel*, above n 109 at [23].

111 Perhaps a modified version of s 63 awards.

112 WR Atkin, 'Custard Pies and the Family Proceedings Bill 1978' [1979] *New Zealand Law Journal* 66, 66.

'complex and not entirely a model of clarity'.[113] Even from the perspective of necessary tidying up, therefore, some reconsideration of the maintenance rules would seem opportune so that, as a bare minimum, a greater degree of internal coherence could be achieved. To take but one example, the distinctions made in sections 63 and 64 between the periods after separation and dissolution of the marriage (two years later) are, as Atkin has argued, 'somewhat vaporous', and the differences could very happily be done away with.[114]

Thus the Law Commission's review of the PRA does provide a golden opportunity to consider the parallel question of whether a needs-based adult maintenance regime remains fit for purpose and, indeed, whether adult maintenance could be safely folded into the relationship property regime. While Parliament in 2001 may well have intended that the FPA amendments would provide the courts with greater flexibility, and would address economic disparities where a relationship property settlement did not,[115] the full ramifications of the newly introduced compensatory orders under section 15 of the PRA may not have been properly appreciated at that time. Seemingly, the possibility of integrating the separate maintenance and relationship property regimes was neither considered nor addressed, and the relationship of maintenance and economic disparity has consequently become one of 'confusion'.[116] In 2006, the need to overhaul the law on the inter-relationship of capital and income was described as 'urgent'[117] and, today, that need clearly still persists.

Assuming the clean break principle does remain a desirable societal aspiration (and while Hammond J in *M v B* counselled against pressing the clean break principle too far,[118] most would presumably wish for former partners to be emotionally and financially free of each other),[119] then the ambiguities of the FPA adult maintenance provisions are unfortunate. As discussed above, the notions of 'reasonable' and 'necessary' in the key statutory provisions of the FPA do allow for the infusion of public policy considerations and value judgments, as do the frequent statutory references to 'other relevant circumstances'[120] and the ability of the court to do 'as [it] thinks fit'.[121] Correspondingly, the

---

113 B Atkin, *Family Law Policy in New Zealand*, above n 25 at 198.
114 B Atkin, 'The Disparity in Economic Disparity', above n 72 at 224.
115 See the Supplementary Order Paper 2000 (25) Matrimonial Property Amendment Bill 2000 (109-3), cited by Hammond J in *M v B*, above n 2 at [256].
116 As suggested by B Atkin, 'Harmonising Family Law', above n 63 at 473.
117 Ibid, at 474. See also the call of B Atkin and W Parker for a refashioned ordering of the law, above n 71 at 166.
118 *M v B*, above n 2 at [262].
119 P Parkinson identifies reasons why, from a woman's perspective, a clean break in terms of property settlement might be better than maintenance: 'Family Law and the Indissolubility of Parenthood', above n 14 at 260.
120 See, for example, ss 63(2)(iii), 64(2)(a)(iii), and 64A(3)(iv) of the FPA.
121 Section 70(2)(a) of the FPA.

clean break principle could comfortably inform judicial thinking under all the key provisions. Nonetheless, as also pointed out above, insoluble internal contradictions unfortunately exist under the current statute, and it may be time for the legislature to become more definitive with the clean break principle, and to examine anew the question of whether there is any need for maintenance to meet recurring living expenses at all (at least beyond a temporary interim maintenance period). Certainly, similar questions over the ambit and need for final maintenance are being addressed in overseas jurisdictions, with greater restrictions on alimony now evident in a number of American states[122] and with the possibility of guidelines being floated by the English Law Commission.[123]

The heart of the maintenance problem is that the fundamental moral question of exactly *why* one party should be liable to provide income support to an ex-partner has never been properly addressed or answered.[124] Perhaps the need for relationship-derived compensation does offer some explanatory rationale for maintenance in overseas jurisdictions. However, as has been frequently reiterated above, this particular justification has been rendered otiose in New Zealand (at least where there is sufficient relationship property from which to make a compensatory section 15 award). The statutory provisions of the FPA are simply not designed to cover the issue of economic disparity specifically.[125] And while the FPA does expressly provide that the means, earning capacity, responsibilities, and needs of the respondent may affect the quantum of any maintenance,[126] it regrettably fails to shed any light on why maintenance liability to meet the applicant's living expenses should fall on the respondent in the first place.

A sharing of gains and losses attributable to a past relationship might seem morally justifiable, but the question remains unanswered as to why there is any additional moral duty imposed on one individual of a failed sexual and emotional relationship to financially support the other. Indeed, yet another question can be usefully interposed at this point. If we should believe it is fitting for one individual to have a legal entitlement to continuing income support

---

122 See A Amundsen, above n 18 and M Ryznar, 'Alimony's Job Lock' (2015) 49 *Akron Law Review* 91.

123 Law Commission (Eng&W), above n 102. In Canada, where a more generous approach is taken to spousal maintenance, Spousal Support Advisory Guidelines were released in July 2008: C Rogerson and R Thomson, 'The Canadian Experiment with Spousal Support Guidelines' (2011) 45 *Family Law Quarterly* 241.

124 As noted by Mostyn J in *SS v NS [Spousal Maintenance]* [2014] EWHC 4183 (Fam), [2015] 2 FLR 1124 at [25]. C Starnes likewise expresses surprise that family law offers no answer to this fundamental question: 'Alimony Theory' (2011) 45 *Family Law Quarterly* 271.

125 A point made by J Miles in 'Dealing with Economic Disparity: An Analysis of Section 15 Property (Relationships) Act 1976' [2003] *New Zealand Law Review* 535, 551 and in 'Financial Provision and Property Division on Relationship Breakdown: A Theoretical Analysis of New Zealand Legislation' (2004) 21 *New Zealand Universities Law Review* 268, 305–08.

126 FPA, s 65(2).

against another individual, why should that claim not lie just as naturally against a person biologically related, such as a parent or a sibling?[127]

In truth, as Miles concluded in 2004, income support and needs, in so far as they cannot be met through property entitlements and compensation, surely need to be met by the wider community and not by the former partner.[128] When the cause of financial difficulty is attributable in the main to considerations such as prevailing socio-economic circumstances, societal values, or an individual's personal skill set, it is indeed hard to determine why, once the compensatory obligation has been discharged, a former partner bears any responsibility at all to meet the other's reasonable needs.

Certainly there is no available evidence to suggest that community thinking would favour anything other than a clean financial and psychological break taking place between former lovers and partners. In the early 1980s, Richardson J suggested community attitudes concerning the end of relationships had been affected by social changes whereby women remained in, or returned to, the workforce in pursuit of economic independence and personal fulfilment.[129] Today, the so-called 'working woman' is not a phenomenon but a routine reality. Moreover, since the mid-1980s the neoliberal social and economic policies of successive New Zealand governments have, for better or for worse, fostered an individualist culture. It seems entirely likely that, as in the USA,[130] the ordinary citizen in New Zealand would not feel particularly enthusiastic over the notion of continuing streams of income for a former partner when, once compensation has been eliminated from the reckoning, an income shortfall cannot be attributed to anything the respondent has personally done.

McMullen recently argued that people now seek marriage relationships less for any possible economic benefits and more for their provision of love and emotional fulfilment, and that the sharing of earning and parenting responsibilities by ever-growing numbers of couples has changed social expectations about what is regarded as fair upon divorce.[131] A clean break may

---

127 It has been noted that under the Destitute Persons Act 1910 (NZ) relatives could be the subject of a maintenance order, with the focus of the orders being heavily on parents and husbands: M Henaghan et al (eds), *Family Law in New Zealand*, 17th ed, LexisNexis, Wellington 2015, 886–87. In an influential article, I Ellman also specifically queried why a former spouse should provide support rather than the spouse's parents, children, or society as a whole: above n 14 at 5.

128 J Miles, 'Financial Provision and Property Division on Relationship Breakdown: A Theoretical Analysis of New Zealand Legislation', above n 125 at 308.

129 *Slater v Slater*, above n 29 at 173.

130 See J McMullen, 'Spousal Support in the 21st Century' (2014) 29 *Wisconsin Journal of Law, Gender and Society* 1, 18.

131 J McMullen, 'Alimony: What Social Science and Popular Culture Tell Us About Women, Guilt, and Spousal Support After Divorce' (2011) 19 *Duke Journal of Gender Law and Policy* 41, 51.

be seen as expected and entirely realistic, and even 20 years ago this author was arguing that most women would not regard marriage as an anchor for their economic security and that any concept of maintenance liability might be viewed as a disincentive to couples then contemplating marriage.[132]

That, of course, is not to deny that many persons entering into marriages 30 years ago may well have had different expectations. In the 1980s, Ellman argued that maintenance was based upon a desire to encourage sharing behaviour in a marriage relationship, or at least not to penalise it.[133] On the other hand, numerous scholars, including feminist scholars, have long recognised that the fact that maintenance has traditionally been awarded to the female partner serves to create an unfortunate dependence of female upon male, and they have argued for changes to both social thinking and structures in order to allow for the desired clean break.[134] Women in a relationship need to continue working; and men need to do more child care.

Some of those desired social changes may be under way and, as noted, female participation in the workforce and shared parenting, for example, are hardly remarkable. These days relatively few maintenance orders under the FPA are in fact made. But maintenance awards may need to become even more exceptional than they presently are, as the fact of their very existence does seem questionable in light of New Zealand's relationship property regime with its enlightened, though admittedly conceptually awkward, compensatory regime. 'Interim' orders, in a modified form, could undoubtedly have some value as a form of emergency relief until the relationship property issues are resolved, and legislative changes to render section 15 more flexible (perhaps, for example, allowing awards out of separate property, as with section 15A) may well be warranted. Nevertheless, it does seem time to consider whether the break between the parties might not be made somewhat cleaner than it currently is.

---

132 See J Caldwell, 'The Case of *Z v Z*: Future Earnings, Matrimonial Property and Spousal Maintenance' [1996] *New Zealand Law Review* 505, 515–16.

133 I Ellman, above n 14 at 61.

134 See, for example, A Diduck and H Orton, 'Equality and Support for Spouses' (1994) 57 *Modern Law Review* 681, 686 and B Fehlberg, above n 14 at 6–7.

INDEX

www.ingramcontent.com/pod-product-compliance
Ingram Content Group UK Ltd.
Pitfield, Milton Keynes, MK11 3LW, UK
UKHW051846100926
8556IPUK00005B/477

9 781780 684642